D1212383

THE

SUPREME

COURT

AND

LEGAL

CHANGE

THE THORNTON H. BROOKS SERIES IN AMERICAN LAW AND SOCIETY

LEE EPSTEIN

JOSEPH F. KOBYLKA

THE

SUPREME

COURT

AND

LEGAL

CHANGE

ABORTION AND THE DEATH PENALTY

The University of North Carolina Press

Chapel Hill and London

The paper in this book meets the guidelines for permanence
and durability of the Committee on Production Guidelines for
Book Longevity of the Council on Library Resources.

96   95   94   93   92   5   4   3   2   1

Library of Congress Cataloging-in-Publication Data
Epstein, Lee, 1958–
    The Supreme Court and legal change : abortion and the death
penalty / by Lee Epstein and Joseph F. Kobylka.
        p.   cm. — (The Thornton H. Brooks series in American law and
society)
    Includes bibliographical references (p.   ) and index.
    ISBN 0-8078-2051-2 (cloth : alk. paper). — ISBN 0-8078-4384-9
(pbk. : alk. paper)
    1. United States. Supreme Court.   2. Abortion—Law and
legislation—United States.   3. Capital punishment—United States.
4. Political questions and judicial power—United States.
I. Kobylka, Joseph Fiske.   II. Title.   III. Series.
KF8742.E67   1992
344.73'0546'0269—dc20
[347.3045460269]   92-53618
                                                              CIP

To four extraordinary teachers
LYDIA ESSLINGER
HARVEY KLEHR
LINDA MOLM AND
THOMAS WALKER
— L. E.

To my parents
JOE AND
FAITH
(for usually saying yes
and occasionally saying no)
— J. F. K.

CONTENTS

TABLES AND FIGURES

PREFACE

. . . .

The life of the law has not been logic: it has been experience. The felt necessities of the time, the prevalent moral and political theories [and] intuitions of public policy . . . have had a good deal more to do than the syllogism in determining the rules by which men should be governed. —Oliver Wendell Holmes, *The Common Law*

With those words, Oliver Wendell Holmes suggested that the predominant mode of legal decision making—reasoning by example—was not necessarily the way judges do or even should reach decisions. And he planted the seeds for a jurisprudential movement—legal realism—that would forever change the way we think about the law.

Still, Holmes's denunciation of brute legalism was subtle. He was not urging judges to abandon, as Roscoe Pound put it, "law in books"; rather, he was pressing them to integrate into their jurisprudence "law in action." It was the adapters of Holmes's philosophy, the legal realists of the 1930s, who loudly asserted their belief that "the law" had little or no place in judicial decision making. Precedents and the like, they argued, were mere smoke screens judges used to mask the attitudes and values that actually framed their decisions. When political scientists in the 1940s through the 1960s demonstrated the plausibility of this perspective, the behavioral revolution was set into motion. Since then, with few exceptions, there has been no turning back. We, as political scientists, were schooled in this tradition. We were taught to see jurists as single-minded seekers of legal policy, as political actors who use "the law" to justify—not to reach— their conclusions.

This, if anything, was the bias we brought to our study of legal xiv

. . . .

PREFACE

change. We sought to address a single question—why does the law, as articulated by the U.S. Supreme Court, experience abrupt change—and we hypothesized three possible answers—because of changes in the Court, in the political environment, or in the involved legal actors (for example, attorneys and interest groups). Given our training as political scientists we suspected that it would be the first possibility—changes in the Court— that largely accounted for doctrinal alteration.

We were wrong. Or, at the very least, we were not fully correct. The Court's composition—its ideological makeup—can set the stage for legal change, but it does not always provide the best explanation for it. Rather, we found that "the law," as legal actors frame it, matters, and it matters dearly. Justices may be seeking to maximize their policy positions, but many—particularly the moderates, the ones whose votes often make a difference—do so in response to the legal stimuli presented to them in the judicial context that engulfs them.

So, is the life of the law not logic but experience? Was Holmes wrong? Not really. It is those analysts who took his views to an extreme who are off track. The life of the law may not be fully the stuff of logic, but it is not wholly experience either. It is, as we shall argue, both.

The Supreme Court and Legal Change is the product of a six-year-long discussion between two people who share a common interest in things legal but who approach the research enterprise from somewhat different angles. We sought to merge the empirical and the theoretical to find some middle but, hopefully, higher ground.

It is partly the product of those who taught us to do the things we do. Kobylka thanks the government faculty at Beloit College—Harvey Davis, Milt Feder, and Paul Pollock—who introduced him to the joys of thinking about and exploring the political, and Frank Sorauf, Sam Krislov, Hal Chase, Susan Olson, and Paul Murphy at the University of Minnesota, who taught him the discipline of good, balanced, and close scholarship. Epstein dedicates the book to four teachers who took the time to make a difference, each in a distinct way: Lydia Esslinger taught her to think analytically; Harvey Klehr instilled in her an interest in thinking analytically about political problems; Linda Molm gave her the tools to animate her interest; and Thomas Walker showed her how to put it all together.

It is partly the product of our common experience at Southern Methodist University, where Epstein worked for five years and where Kobylka currently teaches. The Department of Political Science provided everything we needed to do our work—both tangible and intangible. We owe special thanks to June Manton for typing portions of the manuscript and to Dennis Ippolito for helping to create an atmosphere conducive to collaborative endeavors. Our students at

SMU kept us attuned to issues and controversies that are often submerged in the discipline. Several who passed through our classrooms and offices deserve specific mention: Leslie Moss, Tracey George, Peter Huff, Shannon Smithey, Rod Miller, and Tom Vincent. Epstein also thanks her colleagues at her new home institution, Washington University. As the manuscript neared completion, they provided her with invaluable support and suggestions.

It is partly the product of the profession of which we are a part. Our colleagues in the subfield of law, courts, and judicial processes, in particular, are an extraordinary bunch. Many were willing to listen, relisten, read, and reread, when they had long since tired. We are especially indebted to John Brigham, Micheal Giles, Neal Milner, Susan Olson, Gerald Rosenberg, Jeffrey Segal, Harold Spaeth, and Thomas Walker. Robert Salisbury, Frank Sorauf, and James Stimson also tendered extremely useful advice at a critical stage of this project—its earliest.

It is partly the product of our interaction with the University of North Carolina Press. To Paul Betz we owe a debt of gratitude that will forever remain. He is the finest editor with whom either of us have ever worked. Paul read every word of this book, not once, but three times, and made significant comments. He also lined up two excellent reviewers, Tony Mauro and Gregory Caldeira, whose comments made this work much stronger. Our managing editor, Ron Maner, considerably smoothed the publication process, making it as painless as can be. Paula Wald is the ideal copyeditor for two academics. She preserved the scholarly character of our effort, while revising wording that was beyond the range of but a small circle of experts. She also has a splendid eye for detail, which saved us from many an inconsistency and error. Of course, tradition and good sense require us to take responsibility for any errors that remain.

Finally, this work is partly the product of our lives away from our offices. Epstein thanks her parents, Ann and Kenneth Spole, for being pillars of support, professionally and personally. And her husband, Jay Epstein, for pulling her share when she didn't have the time or energy to do so. Kobylka owes, as always, deep thanks to his wife, Janet, and his children, Keith, Jeff, and Kevin, for their tolerance, support, and love. He dedicates this book to his parents, Joe and Faith, whose love, guidance, and encouragement will stay with him forever.

L. E.
St. Louis

J. F. K.
Dallas

THE

SUPREME

COURT

AND

LEGAL

CHANGE

ONE

. . . .

INTRODUCTION

*[W]e want to know what principles you would apply, what
philosophies you would employ as you exercise the awesome,* and I
emphasize awesome, *power you will hold if you are confirmed as a
Justice, an Associate Justice, to the Supreme Court of the United
States.*—Senator Joseph R. Biden, Jr., Opening Statement,
Senate Judiciary Committee hearings on the nomination of
Judge David Souter to the U.S. Supreme Court, 13
September 1990

Hyperbole? Perhaps. But surely, over the past half century or so, it is
incontestable that the U.S. Supreme Court has spoken authoritatively
on an increasing number of significant issues of public policy and, in the
opinion of many, has entered decisively the political fray once largely
reserved for the elected branches of government. Its decisions on
school prayer, reapportionment, racial discrimination, abortion, and the
like have generated a great deal of substantive debate and set political
agendas for years to come. They also have raised anew questions about
its institutional function. Should the Court be directing public policy on
the most salient issues of the day? Why don't legislatures, which presumably are closer to the citizenry, perform this function? In short, why
do we, as Americans, allow what is purported to be an essentially legal
body to assert itself as a political one?

Addressing these questions is a challenging task well beyond the
scope of our inquiry. What we are concerned with is why such questions
arise in the first place. Why is it that citizens, political actors, and legal
scholars so often call into question the institutional powers of the
Court? We suspect the answer to this is embedded in the tension that
exists between Americans' vision of the proper role of the judiciary in
society and its actual function, a "tension" that is not at all new. Indeed,
it may be the case that many, in the 1990s, envision the ideal role of the

Court in much the same terms as did the founders of our nation in the 1780s. Yet, the Court never has fully met that expectation.

The framers of the Constitution took great pains in creating and empowering the U.S. Supreme Court. They desired it to be a significant part of the new system and thus bestowed it with potential jurisdiction over a wide range of disputes.[1] Still, many proponents of a robust judiciary argued that the Court required the power of judicial review—the "duty" to "declare all acts contrary to the manifest tenor of the Constitution void" (*Federalist Papers*, no. 78)—to be a coequal branch of the national government.[2] To give effect to this duty, the Court would need to be far different in character than the other institutions; if tied to the same constituencies as the other branches, it might be hesitant to strike down the improper acts of Congress and the president.

The constitutional solution to this puzzle is found in the unique selection and retention system of the federal judiciary: presidential nomination, Senate confirmation, and life tenure.[3] By releasing judges from the control of the electorate, the framers felt they had accomplished the all-important end: the judiciary's constituency was now very different from that of the other institutions of the government. Congress and the president would reflect the popular will, responding to the ebb and flow of ordinary politics. The Court, on the other hand, would confine its attention to the law. It would stand above the political fray and enforce the law free from overt political forces and influence. It would be a force for legal stability; politics would be neither its guide nor measure. It would decide cases brought to it according to the *law*: the Constitution, statutes, and precedent. Navigating by these stars, the justices would enforce the limitations on governmental power and "guard the constitution and the rights of individuals from the effects of those ill humours which the arts of designing men, or the influence of particular conjunctures, sometimes disseminate among the people themselves" (*Federalist Papers*, no. 78).

Thus, at least according to the author of essay number 78 of the *Federalist Papers*, Alexander Hamilton, the constitutional authority of the Court stems largely from its peculiar function as a governmental branch removed from common political pressures—the Court was to "declare the sense of the law" through "inflexible and uniform adherence to the rights of the constitution and of individuals" (*Federalist Papers*, no. 78). Independent of political influence, the law—as decided and announced by the Court—would be relatively fixed and stable over time. It also would accommodate majoritarian preferences within constitutional limitations.

Herein, though, lies the tension: however ingenious this plan, it no longer fully describes the operation of the courts. A long line of scholarship demonstrates that political influences are now abundantly present in the judiciary, and that the effect of this politicization has touched virtually all aspects of the Court. Studies of judicial decision making (Schubert 1965, 1974; Rohde and Spaeth 1976) have shown that judges frequently act as if their political attitudes dominate their decisions, leading them to stray occasionally from rigid adherence to the law. Students of the courts also have demonstrated that the political environment— encompassing factors such as party control of the government, public opinion, and political setting (Cook 1973, 1977; Marshall 1989)—is at least sometimes associated with judicial outcomes. We also know that interest groups and other political actors regularly try to influence its decisions, often with substantial success (Cortner 1968; Vose 1959). Clearly, the judiciary is different from the other departments of the national government, but its history and opinions show that it is not as different as Madison and Hamilton suggested: political forces and influences do seep into its decisions, especially when it considers politically sensitive topics.

The results of this politicization are many, but surely among the most significant is the susceptibility of judicially framed "law" to profound change and even reversal. If the Court and its members are not free from overt political forces and influences, then how can they be the stabilizing force the framers envisioned? It is this concept of *legal change* that we suspect Americans find so troubling. If they perceive the Court in terms similar to those of our founders, then questions undoubtedly arise: Why are abortion rights expansive at one point but subject to severe restrictions at another? Why is capital punishment permitted in 1992 when it was held to be unconstitutional in 1972? Other examples—such as the Court's vacillation on the rights of the criminally accused—are similarly easy to summon. In short, the question is why the Court's treatment of some issues frequently takes on the appearance of a roller-coaster ride when its design purports to remove such bumps and loops from its track?

This is an important question, the answer to which probably lies, in some sense, in the increasingly political nature of the Court and its environment. But in what facet of that politicization? The most obvious answer is that of personnel changes and the concomitant attitudinal alterations they often occasion. Such an effect has been manifest since the earliest period of the Republic when, in the dying days of his administration—the last Federalist administration America was to see—President John Adams installed his secretary of state, John Marshall, as chief justice of the Supreme Court. Through the Court, Marshall kept the Federalist agenda alive for over thirty years. To no one's real surprise, when finally afforded the opportunity to replace Marshall, President Jackson chose his erstwhile supporter, Roger Taney, and the Court shifted its interpretative direction away from Marshall's determined nationalism.

The more recent controversy surrounding the retirement of Justice Lewis

Powell and his proposed replacement with Judge Robert Bork also was, in part, a result of the aspirations and fears about legal change harbored by many of the Supreme Court's constituencies. Some elements had hoped that this personnel change would propel a rightward judicial drift that originated in the winds blowing out of the Nixon White House. Others feared that this drift would curtail or reverse law developed by the Burger Court as well as that which traced its lineage to earlier judicial times. The debate over Bork's nomination—and, to a lesser degree, that of David Souter and Clarence Thomas—was a conversation between these various constituencies about the likelihood and legitimacy of judicially crafted legal change.

In a sense, these debates assumed their conclusions: changes in Court personnel yield changes in constitutional interpretation. This, of course, can happen. Franklin Roosevelt finalized his victory over Court-based opponents of his New Deal when he replaced the "Conservative Four Horsemen" with justices committed to his vision of federal-state relations (Jackson 1941). Richard Nixon had similar success in matters of criminal law when he appointed four new justices to the Court during his first term as president (Levy 1974). This said, however, it is important to note that the Court does not always chart new and immediately predictable directions as the result of the appointment process. Nixon did not get the legal answers he wanted on the questions of abortion and executive privilege, for example. Neither did President Reagan completely redraw the legal map by elevating his choices to the Supreme Court. Yet legal change, prompted from the bench of the Supreme Court, *did* occur during their presidencies—some of it not to their liking. Such change cannot, at least in total, be attributed to personnel changes.

What this suggests is that shifts in the composition of the Supreme Court, though they can bring about legal change, do not necessarily produce it. Even so, students of the courts have tended to fix on personnel changes as *the* explanatory factor accounting for judicially driven doctrinal change. This conclusion is a natural outgrowth of research guided by behavioral assumptions and conceptualization: much of what has been written on the courts in the recent past has fixed on the behavior of individual justices and judges, who, it is assumed, act as ideologically motivated goal maximizers. In some cases, they are; but in others, their decisions seem to be influenced by factors other than personal ideological preferences.

Insofar as this is the case, change in legal doctrine can result from the interplay of a broad range of factors. Although it may result from personnel changes, it also can be understood, for example, as the product of evolving doctrine, the climate of the times in which cases are decided, the issues thrust upon the Court, and the configuration of actors framing arguments and pressing claims through the courts. Thus, to understand the dynamics of legal change, it is necessary to contemplate the variety of legal and political forces at work, to identify the relationship of these factors to the emerging law articulated by the Supreme Court, and to examine their operation over an extended period of time in settings where we can most readily identify and assess their impact.

ANALYZING LEGAL CHANGE: A RESEARCH STRATEGY

The phenomenon of legal change is hydra-headed, comprehending formal judicial actions, executive and legislative behavior, and the behavior of relevant publics. As a result, the concept is subject to definition and observation from a wide variety of perspectives. It could be profitably viewed as an alteration in grass-roots legal and political activities, customs, and attitudes, and studied accordingly. Such an approach would take account of formal governmental institutions but would concentrate primarily on noninstitutional relationships and activities. An alternative, and the one that we have chosen to employ, defines legal change as a Court-created shift in (or a reversal of) a particular prevailing legal doctrine. This approach emphasizes the importance of processes and constitutional doctrine in setting the parameters of subsequent political and policy choices.

Although these different approaches to legal change vary in their animating perspectives, according to the questions they ask and the data they assess, both seek to come to grips with the forces that make up the complex matrix of law-governed relationships constituting the American polity. Our approach does not deny the utility of other, more sociological frameworks; they tell us much about important linkages between law and society. Rather, for purposes of analytical clarity and depth, and because we think that "law" as articulated by the Supreme Court sets the general legal and political context for the resolution of any given contentious issue, we confine our study to an assessment of three factors that work to promote or retard doctrinal shifts in the decisions of the Supreme Court: the Court itself, the political environment, and the organized pressure groups lobbying the Court.

A variety of strategies exist to study the role these factors play in promoting legal change. We have decided to invoke a comparative case-study approach. This design, like all case studies, has its inherent flaws; for example, some may argue that it does not permit the development of the sort of systematic general-izations that often accompany statistical or formal modeling. What it does allow, however, is an in-depth analysis of the legal, contextual, and environmental factors contributing to interpretational dynamism. As such, this design will permit us to generate hypotheses, which in turn facilitate the development of richer explanations for the process of legal change.

Moreover, the case-study approach we employ differs from those undertaken in the past. Rather than focusing exclusively on one legal area, we selected two groupings of cases for comparative analysis. In each grouping, the initial case established a clear doctrinal change or innovation; the later case(s) represented a doctrinal and decisional shift away from the earlier holding. In this way, the Court created within each specific issue area two distinct, temporally spaced sets of legal change. The subjects we consider are the Court's treatment of death penalty and abortion litigation:

CAPITAL PUNISHMENT	ABORTION
Furman v. Georgia (1972)	*Roe v. Wade* (1973)
Gregg v. Georgia (1976)	*Webster v. Reproductive Health Services* (1989)
McCleskey v. Kemp (1987)	

We based our selection of these cases on a number of considerations. We thought it important, for example, to examine two areas of the law that raised different legal issues (albeit equally salient and controversial ones) to overcome some of the inherent limitations of the case-study approach in developing generalizable propositions. The cases we chose for inclusion, thus, tap a spectrum of issues, arguments, and constitutional provisions, from criminal law and procedure through doctrines of privacy and liberty.

Yet, as we detail in appendixes 1 and 2, the cases contained in the two groupings are remarkably similar on several dimensions. For one, the cases in each group presented virtually identical questions to the Court. *Furman*, *Gregg*, and *McCleskey* all raised queries about Georgia's procedures for implementing the death penalty; *Roe* and *Webster* treated the constitutional status of the abortion choice. As we shall describe in the next chapter, they also generated a great deal of interest among organized pressure groups and other institutional actors; they were, in short, highly salient cases. Because of this, we will be able to assess the respective roles of the political environment and of legal actors as catalysts of the doctrinal changes that occurred in these areas.

More important, however, is that both case groupings are characterized by the judicial adoption of a clear policy stance followed by a sudden shift in legal result. Consider *Furman* and *Gregg*. Throughout our nation's history, the death penalty was a legitimate form of punishment. Suddenly, in 1972, the Court struck down as unconstitutional the procedure used by most states for imposing capital punishment; but, four years later (in *Gregg*) it reasserted the constitutionality of the death penalty, upholding a newly devised schema for its execution. *Roe* and *Webster* also represent stark alterations in legal policy. Since the 1860s, many states had proscribed abortion except when necessary to save the life of the mother. Then, in 1973, the Court shocked the country when it ruled that abortions performed during the first trimester of pregnancy were not subject to state regulation and that those before viability could be restricted only in ways reasonably related to the mother's health. Two decades later, in *Webster*, the Court gave the states substantially more leeway for constraining the right to choose an abortion. This decision cut severely into the basic underpinnings of the *Roe* decision, effectively undermining the "fundamental right" articulated only sixteen years before.

In both instances, one set of interests "won" their cases at time A only to see this victory, in part or in total, reversed at time B. As such, the groupings raise two pointed questions. First, what forces generated the dramatic legal changes witnessed in *Furman* and *Roe*? Second, why did the turnabouts in *Gregg* and *Webster* occur so rapidly?[4] Close examination of these cases yields insight into the factors that initiated and conditioned the interpretational shifts they manifest.

PLAN OF THE BOOK

In what follows, we strive to provide some answers to the questions posed above, exploring intensively the phenomenon of legal change. Before we turn to each of our substantive pairs, in chapter 2 we provide a more focused discussion of potential explanations for why the law occasionally experiences dramatic alterations. In particular, we consider three potential agents of legal change: the Court itself, the political environment, and organized pressure groups.

In chapters 3 and 4, we focus on capital punishment; in 5 and 6, on abortion. In particular, we analyze empirically and contextually the events preceding and antedating the particular legal alterations in question, with a good deal of emphasis on the substance of the issues. We do so mindful, however, of our greater interest in generating broad-based propositions about the causes of legal change.

In chapter 7, we summarize our findings and, more important, reach some conclusions about why legal change occurs. In brief, we conclude that legal change, at least in the doctrine generated by the Supreme Court, is not solely a function of alterations in the internal makeup of the Court. Nor is it simply a product of the climate of the times in which the relevant cases are decided; while that environment sets the context in which decisions are tendered, it does not decide them itself. Finally, legal change is not neatly prompted by the type of litigants who press claims on the Court; they help to set and structure the Court's agenda, but they do not decide its cases. All of these factors, while clearly relevant to the dynamics of doctrinal change, are insufficient to account for the observed shifts in the law. Rather, it is *the law and legal arguments as framed by legal actors* that most clearly influence the content and direction of legal change.

TWO

· ·

THE

AGENTS

OF

LEGAL

CHANGE

Why does the law, as interpreted by the Supreme Court, occasionally experience abrupt changes? Based on the wide-ranging research on the Court and the factors conditioning its decisions,[1] we offer three possible agents of change: the Court itself, the political environment, and organized pressure groups lobbying the Court.

Before we review these explanations, two notes of clarification are in order. First, our concern is with legal, doctrinal change produced by the U.S. Supreme Court. This does not mean, however, that we believe *all* legal change occurs solely as a result of Court decisions. After all, the relationship between law and society is interactive: legal doctrine does affect society, but social forces condition both the law and the context within which judicial decision makers operate. This interrelationship, undoubtedly, can produce legal change even in the absence of an explicit Court ruling. Conversely, simply because the Court hands down a decision, however important, does not mean behavioral alterations will necessarily occur; rulings are not self-implementing but rely on a slew of other actors—some governmental, others not—to give them effect (Johnson and Canon 1984). Our focus neither denies nor deprecates these potential sources of legal change—our concern is simply more Court centered.

Second, it is virtually impossible, in the absence of formal empirical analysis (and the contextual costs such an approach entails), to separate the agents of legal change into discrete, mutually exclusive categories. Inevitably, overlaps exist; for example, interest groups are both architects and elements of the political environment—they help set institutional agendas (Caldeira and Wright 1988; Cobb and Elder 1983) and their fate is often tied to the ebb and flow of the "mood" of the bodies they seek to influence (Stimson 1991). Thus, any attempt to sever "interest groups" from the "political environment" in which they operate will result in some conceptual ambiguity.

This noted, we think that groups *do* merit separate analytic treatment, and we treat them accordingly. Unlike other components of the Court's general environment, groups present arguments directly to the Court through formal legal channels; they are an institutionalized part of the process of legal argumentation. Because of this, they act as framers of governmental agendas as well as agents who react to the agendas and actions of others. The uniqueness of this dual role—part active and defining agent, part reactive agent—suggests the utility of an analysis that treats groups as qualitatively distinct from the web of elements that constitutes the Court's political environment. This distinction occasions some conceptual ambiguity; yet, in our view, it is tolerable ambiguity.

To put it simply, we treat the three agents of change separately more as heuristic devices than as absolute categorizations. They are inevitably dynamic and interactive, not static constructs or mutually exclusive prompters of legal change.

THE COURT

The most obvious explanations of legal change, as noted in the introductory chapter, lie within the Court itself. Here, we locate two possibilities: one is found in the traditional understanding of judicial decision making, the other is more behaviorally defined.

A TRADITIONAL APPROACH TO DOCTRINAL CHANGE: THE LEGAL MODEL

It is possible that doctrinal evolution accounts for the differential outcomes we observe—that is, "the law," in some sense, drives itself. This is the explanation suggested by the traditional "legal model" of judicial decision making. In its

II

. . . .

THE AGENTS OF LEGAL CHANGE

starkest form, legalism centers on a simple assumption about judicial decision making: jurists derive rules from precedential cases, statutes, and the Constitution and then apply them to specific cases to reach decisions. It views judges as constrained decision makers who "will base their opinions on precedent and will adhere to the doctrine of *stare decisis*" (Wasby 1988, 210). Some scholars label this "mechanical jurisprudence" because the process by which judges reach decisions is highly structured.[2] Others call it a "robes on" theory: that is, once jurists don their black robes, they immunize themselves from all influences other than "the law" itself.

Legalism primarily concerns itself with exploring the Court's decisions *qua* decisions, yet it yields several propositions about the nature of legal change, the most stalwart of which is this: because judges merely apply existing law to disputes, the law itself never alters, only the questions and facts within cases do. Segal's work (1984) on search-and-seizure cases provides an ample illustration. Although many characterize law governing the Fourth Amendment as a "mess," he found that this was not necessarily the case. Underlying the so-called "hodge-podge" of legal doctrine was "a coherent set of decisions," largely explicable by the facts present in extant disputes. For example, the Court was far more likely to find unconstitutional a search inside of a home than outside of it, a seizure conducted without a warrant than with one, and so forth.

At first blush, such a perspective could certainly explain the "change" observed in the pairs we have selected for analysis. Consider the death penalty grouping. In *Furman*, attorneys asked the Court whether a state's death penalty procedure, which gave jurors full discretion over sentencing, violated constitutional principles. The Court held that it did. In *Gregg*, one of the questions was subtly different: Did death penalty procedures, providing jurors with sentencing guidelines, violate the Constitution? The justices ruled that it did not. Surely, this seeming "change of heart" may not have been a change at all but only the appearance of an alteration made possible by variation in questions and facts.

While the legal model continues to dominate educational processes within the nation's law schools, few subscribe to it in the stark form set out above. Most legalists would now argue that changes in the "law" are possible through a case-by-case modification of governing doctrine. Consider, for example, the Court's decisions leading up to *Brown v. Board of Education* (1954). As Kluger (1976) and Greenberg (1977) have chronicled, *Brown* did not happen overnight. Rather, beginning about four decades after *Plessy v. Ferguson* (1896), in which the Court promulgated the infamous "separate but equal doctrine," it began to modify that decision as it applied to graduate schools and then to undergraduate institutions.[3] Finally, in 1954, a unanimous Supreme Court overturned *Plessy* and the prevailing doctrine controlling this area of the law *sub silento*. A variety of explanations exist for the 1954 ruling—many of which suggest that factors other than "the law" came into play. Yet, we could reasonably ascribe this "change" to a case-by-case modification—that is, the logic and the holdings of the Court's post-*Plessy* decisions incrementally ate away at its core, culminating in *Brown*.

This understanding of the process of legal change also could explain, at least in part, the changes we observe in some of our pairings. The decision in *Roe v. Wade*, for example, may have been the result of an incremental reexamination of the right to privacy, which began in earnest in *Griswold v. Connecticut* (1965) when the Court fully explicated the right. Virtually from the day *Griswold* was decided until 1973, the justices altered and revised its parameters.[4] Hence, the enunciation of legalized abortion in *Roe* may have been nothing more or less than the logical outgrowth of those interstitial modifications rather than an abrupt transformation.

In short, any serious analysis of legal change must, at a minimum, consider such jurisprudentially framed forces. Despite the ardor with which some scholars fight this approach, arguing that a whole host of other factors unrelated to the state of the law determine judicial outcomes, we must not forget that the Court is constituted as a legal body and that its members conceive of it as such.[5]

In so writing, however, we want to be clear about what we are and are not saying. We have no interest, for example, in resurrecting the long-discredited view of Justice Owen Roberts in *United States v. Butler* (1936, 62) that "the judicial branch of the government has only one duty; to lay the article of the Constitution which is invoked beside the statute which is challenged and to decide whether the latter squares with the former." Nor are we suggesting that "the law" (for example, the Constitution, statutes, precedents, and doctrine) is a unidimensional straitjacket binding the interpretational limbs of jurists. Interpretation, the giving of meaning to disembodied rules, is clearly colored by the perspective of the interpreter; rules are not self-defining. However, judges are attorneys and attorneys are schooled in the law, therefore—while individual jurists may interpret its commands differently—to the extent that they take it seriously, the law shapes their decisions. As such, it can guide or constrain legal change and its policy manifestations and implications. This is not to suggest anything as formal as the relationship asserted by Roberts, but it counsels the need for sensitivity to the ways in which the law is defined and used by the parties to legal proceedings—both litigants and judges. They act as if it matters; we should remain open to the possibility that it does as well.

What we are suggesting, then, is that the language of law—precedents and so forth—arguably channels and constrains judicial choices (Brigham 1978; O'Neill 1981). As Shapiro (1972) put it, we cannot ignore "the fact that appellate courts and the lawyers that serve them spend an overwhelming proportion of their energies communicating with one another, and that the judicial opinion, itself conforming to the style of *stare decisis*, is the principal mode of communication."

BEHAVIORAL PERSPECTIVES ON LEGAL CHANGE: COURT MEMBERSHIP

Though doctrinal perspectives continue to dominate legal education, scholars working from a behaviorally defined framework have shown that the law does not explain all aspects of the judicial process. Empirical political science has demonstrated that other forces affect legal decision making and thus can bring about doctrinal change. At its core, this body of literature holds that jurists bring to the bench a set of well-developed attributes, attitudes, and values. These factors, not the law per se, frame their understanding of the issues before them and determine the votes they cast to resolve them.[6] In shorthand terms, justices, above all else, are persons, a status that does not magically change when they don their black robes.

Some basic propositions about the nature and sources of legal change spin off from this perspective, the most important of which is that periodic turnovers in the membership of the Court can give way to major doctrinal alterations (Baum 1985, 142). This appointment-change dynamic occurs when presidents succeed in replacing justices of one philosophical stripe with those committed to another. In some instances, that change need only involve the replacement of one justice, as when a liberal replaces a conservative or vice versa. In other instances, when the Court is composed primarily of conservatives or liberals, it might require wholesale personnel changes. Further, even when replacements are of similar ilk to the justices they replace, shifts in the overall balance of the Court can occur.

Presidents and Senates clearly understand the importance of Court personnel and the consequences of alterations in its membership. A vast body of literature (Abraham 1985; Goldman 1989; Scigliano 1971; Segal 1987) reveals that most presidents, even some of our earliest (for example, John Adams) and most renowned (for example, Franklin Roosevelt), sought to stack the federal judiciary with partisan political supporters. The most recent attempts at such "Court packing" came during the Nixon, Reagan, and Bush presidencies as these men sought to leave their imprints, appointing so-called "right-thinking" justices to the bench (H. Schwartz 1988; Tribe 1985). Because of the relationship between these latest attempts and the specific legal changes with which this book is concerned, we consider the appointments made by Presidents Nixon and Reagan in some detail.

TABLE 2-1. Profile of the Justices of the U.S. Supreme Court, 1967–1990

Support for Liberal Position
in Nonunanimous Cases[a]

	Civil Liberties		Economics		Baum
	%	N	%	N	Ranking[b]

WARREN COURT IN 1967–69[c]

Warren (1953–69)	77.6	576	79.2	457	8/26
Black (1937–71)	74.7	582	83.6	450	9/26
Brennan (1956–90)	76.0	509	71.5	382	5/26
Douglas (1939–75)	96.1	583	86.4	455	1/26
Fortas (1965–69)	81.1	159	51.1	90	7/26
Harlan (1955–71)	22.1	555	20.9	402	15/26
Marshall (1967–91)	83.5	79	56.0	25	3/26
Stewart (1958–81)	39.6	424	33.8	299	11/26
White (1962–)	44.2	278	62.9	175	14/26

BURGER COURT IN 1980[d]

Burger (1969–86)	17.6	1,099	25.0	328	21/26
Blackmun (1970–)	39.5	1,056	46.5	310	13/26
Brennan (1956–90)	85.5	1,086	74.2	329	5/26
Marshall (1967–91)	88.5	1,078	68.2	321	3/26
Powell (1971–87)	31.2	940	29.7	256	16/26
Rehnquist (1971–)	5.6	959	22.8	285	25/26
Stevens (1975–)	61.4	676	52.6	211	10/26
Stewart (1958–81)	43.6	782	32.1	234	11/26
White (1962–)	33.7	1,103	50.6	328	14/26

The Nixon Appointees

Richard Nixon did little to veil his hostility to the decisions of the Warren Court. During his 1968 campaign and the early days of his presidency, he emphasized the theme of "law and order," claimed that the Supreme Court had gone too far in protecting the rights of the criminally accused, and pledged to appoint conservative, "strict constructionists" to rebalance constitutional priorities. He remarked in his August 1968 acceptance speech that "tonight it's time for some honest talk about the problem of order in the United States. Let us always respect, as I do, our courts and those who serve on them, but let us also recognize that some of our courts in their decisions have gone too far in weakening the peace forces as against the criminal forces in this country." Although some

TABLE 2-1 *(continued)*

	Civil Liberties		Economics		Baum
	%	N	%	N	Ranking[b]
REHNQUIST COURT IN 1990[e]					
Rehnquist (1971–)	20.7	58	50.0	30	25/26
Blackmun (1970–)	77.6	58	60.0	30	13/26
Kennedy (1988–)	36.2	58	50.0	30	Not ranked
Marshall (1967–91)	86.2	58	70.0	30	3/26
O'Connor (1981–)	39.7	58	43.3	30	20/26
Scalia (1986–)	29.3	58	46.7	30	Not ranked
Souter (1990–)	32.1	53	44.4	27	Not ranked
Stevens (1975–)	81.0	58	70.0	30	10/26
White (1962–)	43.1	58	53.3	30	14/26

[a]Source for Warren and Burger Court data is Segal and Spaeth 1989; data for Rehnquist Court collected by Jeffrey A. Segal.

[b]Source for ranking is Baum 1989a. Baum devised a technique (see Baum 1988) for comparing the ideological behavior of justices across Courts. These rankings represent the "adjusted scores" of 26 justices' pro–civil liberties voting in cases decided between the 1946 and 1985 terms. So, for example, Douglas's ranking of 1/26 asserts that he was the most liberal member of the Court during the period under analysis.

[c]Data are for nonunanimous cases decided between 1953 and 1969.

[d]Data are for nonunanimous cases decided between 1969 and 1986.

[e]Data are for nonunanimous cases decided during the 1990 term.

suggest that Nixon purposively exaggerated the liberalism of the Warren Court as a campaign device (Kamisar 1983, 63), it is hard to deny that his accusations were grounded, at least in part, in fact: the Warren Court of the mid-1960s, in particular, was far more open to such criticism than its predecessors or successors (Epstein, Walker, and Dixon 1989).

Why this Court embarked on a path of expanding the rights of defendants and of other disadvantaged interests is not difficult to discern. As shown in table 2-1, the justices comprising its majority were among the most liberal in the Court's history. Chief Justice Warren and Associate Justices Black, Douglas, Brennan, Fortas, and Marshall forged the way, supporting the "have-not" position in an unusually large percentage of cases. Although, as table 2-1 also indicates, the Warren Court was not monolithically left of center, these six liberals energized the Court (Heck 1986, 76) and raised the ire of Nixon.

Nixon soon got the chance to effectuate his promise to restore law and order to American communities by appointing four justices to the Court. One of his earliest presidential acts was the nomination of Warren Burger to fill the chief justiceship vacated by Earl Warren.[7] In Nixon's eyes, Burger was an ideal choice to lead a counterrevolution against the Warren Court's liberal jurisprudence. Prior to his ascension to the Supreme Court, Burger had been a judge on the "famously liberal" U.S. Court of Appeals for the District of Columbia, where he was a "vocal dissenter whose law and order opinions made headlines" (Woodward and Armstrong 1979, 11). When Burger was confirmed by a 74 to 3 margin just eighteen days after he was nominated, the beginnings of a radically different Court era seemed imminent.

Still, the Court remained shorthanded after Burger's confirmation, and finding a replacement for resigning Justice Abe Fortas proved difficult.[8] After the Senate rejected Nixon's first two nominees (Clement F. Haynsworth and G. Harrold Carswell), he finally secured the confirmation of Harry A. Blackmun. Although not the "southerner" Nixon had promised to appoint, Blackmun's jurisprudence reflected values important to the president. His appellate record was moderate on civil rights issues and conservative—opposed to judicial protection—on criminal process and civil liberties. His restraintism and moral conservatism made Blackmun appear to be Richard Nixon's kind of justice (Kobylka 1989).

The September 1971 resignations of Justices Black and Harlan left two more holes on the Court. To replace Harlan, Nixon chose William H. Rehnquist. Though he had no prior judicial experience, Rehnquist's intelligence, conservatism, and Republican party loyalty were firmly established. He had been clerk to Justice Robert Jackson, urging him to take a segregationist stance in *Brown*;[9] he worked for Barry Goldwater in 1964; and he served as an assistant attorney general in Nixon's Justice Department, where he categorically denounced liberal Warren Court decisions. He was, in short, a force with which liberal interests, however unhappily, would have to reckon.

Nixon's other nominee, Lewis Powell, was a lesser-known quantity. Hailing from Virginia, which he left only to attend Harvard Law School, Powell also had no prior judicial experience, but, unlike Rehnquist, he had not made known his ideological predilections. Powell's legal career "blended political conservatism with conciliation" (Simon 1973, 243). While chair of the Richmond School Board (1953–61), Powell kept schools open in the wake of integration, despite demands from the white populace to close them down. His stint as president of the American Bar Association was marked by similar moderation. Yet, his "go slow" approach did little to endear him to civil rights leaders. Nonetheless (and despite controversy over Rehnquist),[10] the Senate confirmed both Nixon appointees in early December of 1971.

The additions of Rehnquist and Powell, as shown in table 2-1, increased the overall "conservatism" of the Court. But the results of that ideological shift were not felt across all issues. The "new" Court was far less supportive of criminal rights than was Warren's, but it was the Burger Court that, among other innovations, legalized abortion, legitimated school busing, and provided women with heightened protection under the Fourteenth Amendment. As Wasby (1976, 7–8) astutely observed:

> Perhaps because of the fanfare President Nixon made over his desire to change the Court's direction, the tendency of many commentators has been to *expect*—and from that to *see*—much change. . . . Starting from a presumption of discontinuity, they have tended to emphasize discontinuities with the Warren Court rulings. . . .
>
> A close look at what occurred through the 1973 Term does *not* produce such a picture. There has indeed been change. However, the importance of maintaining earlier rulings has been under-estimated, areas of noticeable continuity have been missed, and areas where the Burger Court has advanced along the paths first marked by Earl Warren and his brethren have been set aside. Growth has been ignored, while the amount of erosion has been played up.

The Burger Court's relatively supportive attitude toward many disadvantaged interests (aside from the criminally accused) was not substantially interrupted by the 12 November 1975 resignation of the Court's most stalwart liberal, William Douglas. Though it was highly unlikely that Ford would appoint a justice with an ideological approach akin to that of Douglas, his agenda was not Nixon's either. This became apparent, just sixteen days later, when he nominated John Paul Stevens.

That the Ford administration was able to agree on a candidate so quickly was, in part, a testament to Stevens's impressive credentials.[11] He graduated first in his class at the University of Chicago, going on to co-edit the law review at Northwestern University. From there, he served as a clerk to Supreme Court Justice Wiley B. Rutledge, "one of the most liberal Justices ever to sit on the Court" (Sickels 1988, ix), and later joined a Chicago law firm where he became an expert on antitrust matters. He also taught part-time at the University of Chicago and Northwestern law schools until Nixon nominated him to the U.S. Court of Appeals for the Seventh Circuit, where he served until his appointment to the Supreme Court. Stevens maintained his reputation as a "judge's judge" on the Supreme Court and provided the Warren Court holdovers with important votes in many cases. His support for abortion, separation of church and state, and even the occasional criminal defendant kept the conservative agenda from becoming fully realized (Sickels 1988).

The Reagan-Bush Court

Ronald Reagan picked up where Richard Nixon left off. Where Nixon highlighted one issue on the Republican agenda—law and order—Reagan stressed the entire range of issues. He had no trepidation about criticizing the Burger Court's "activist" stances on abortion, affirmative action, and other issues. Neither did he make any bones about his strategy of judicial appointment: he would nominate jurists who shared his values (H. Schwartz 1988). His first chance to act on this pledge came in July of 1981, when he named Sandra Day O'Connor to replace Potter Stewart.

A state court judge, O'Connor was a relative unknown to most in the legal world; she had taken few public stances on the salient issues of the day. Still, her credentials were quite good: a Stanford law degree (where she had been a classmate of Rehnquist's), a law review editorship, and a stint as a state assistant attorney general. Even more important from Reagan's perspective was her support of and by the Republican party. She had served as an Arizona state legislator for six years, two as Republican majority leader. Moreover, she was apparently brought to Reagan's attention by one of the nation's foremost conservatives, Barry Goldwater. She was, in short order and without much organized opposition, unanimously confirmed.

Table 2-1 reveals that Presidents Reagan and later Bush had more opportunities to shape the bench. The 1986 retirement of Chief Justice Burger and the elevation of Rehnquist to that position gave way to the appointment of Antonin Scalia, a favorite of "ultraconservatives" in the Republican party (H. Schwartz 1988). As a judge on the U.S. Court of Appeals for the District of Columbia, Scalia consistently voted with his more conservative brethren (including Judge Robert Bork), leading many to conclude that "his jurisprudence was similar to Rehnquist's" (McGuigan and O'Connell 1987). "Nevertheless," as H. Schwartz (1988) wrote, "Scalia was unanimously approved. Potential Democratic opponents were preoccupied with the simultaneous Rehnquist nomination, and it was felt that no major changes would result from Scalia's election—he was simply replacing an almost equally conservative Burger."

This was not at all the case when the next vacancy arose. Almost immediately after Lewis Powell announced his resignation in June of 1987, concern mounted over his replacement. In large measure, this was due to the perception of liberals and conservatives alike that Powell had been a swing vote in many significant cases. Though this may not have been so in the aggregate (Blasecki 1990) or across his entire tenure (George 1989), Powell did cast key votes in some highly salient cases, including *Regents of the University of California v. Bakke* (1978), in which the Court struck down quota systems but paved the way for affirmative action plans, and *Bowers v. Hardwick* (1986), in which the Court upheld sodomy laws aimed at homosexuals. Most significant, though, was that many viewed Powell as the swing on abortion; just the term before his resignation, in *Thornburgh v. American College of Obstetricians and Gynecologists* (1986), he voted with a slim majority of five to uphold the basic tenets of *Roe*.

Reagan's nomination of Judge Bork, therefore, added fuel to an already raging fire. While conservatives cheered the president's choice, liberals were outraged. As a law professor and a court of appeals judge, Bork offered a "jurisprudence of original intent" that left little room for the right to privacy, equality for women, speech that was not "explicitly political," or just about anything else that he could not divine directly from the text of the Constitution, its "history," or the intentions of those who framed it.[12]

Virtually every left-of-center interest sought to block the nomination. The intensity of their lobbying efforts, coupled with Bork's rigid approach to the Constitution (despite what some have called a "confirmation conversion"), led to his rejection (Bork 1990; Bronner 1989a). Shortly thereafter, Reagan nominated another federal appellate court judge, Douglas Ginsburg. Just nine days later, however, Ginsburg was forced to withdraw amid allegations that he had smoked marijuana with students, among other questionable activities. The administration then nominated Anthony Kennedy, an appellate court judge who exhibited no particularly stringent approach to constitutional interpretation nor any controversial views on salient issues. He was, to be sure, no liberal, but, at least on the surface, he bore no resemblance to Bork. The Senate unanimously confirmed him in early 1988.

President Bush continued the transformation of the Court's personnel. In fact, because he replaced staunch liberals (and Warren Court holdovers) Brennan and Marshall, it is tempting to say that he closed the book on the Warren era. The replacement of Brennan with David Souter, a New Hampshire Supreme Court justice, was especially significant. Though Bush nominated him largely on the basis of recommendations from White House Chief-of-Staff John Sununu and Senator Warren Rudman, Souter's comportment before the Senate apparently allayed concerns that he possessed some hidden agenda, and he was confirmed by a margin of 90 to 9. The ascension of Clarence Thomas has, in effect, exchanged the Court's last strong "liberal" for a justice who, all concede, is substantially to Marshall's political and jurisprudential right.[13] The net result of these appointments, coupled with the Nixon-Reagan holdovers, is substantial. As table 2-2 demonstrates, they have driven the Court further to the right. The Warren Court legacy has come to a close: of its current members, only Justice White served under Warren, and he represents little of what that Court has come to symbolize.

TABLE 2-2. From the Warren Court to the Rehnquist Court: Support for Civil Liberties Claims

Warren Court	Burger Court: Nixon Appointees	Rehnquist Court: Reagan/Bush Appointees
Warren (.808)	Burger (.278)	Rehnquist (.190)
Black (.733)	Rehnquist (.190)	Scalia (.293)[a]
Douglas (.901)	Stevens (.575)	
Harlan (.440)	Powell (.348)	Kennedy (.362)[a]
Brennan (.787)		Souter (.321)[a]
Stewart (.521)		O'Connor (.284)
White (.442)		
Fortas (.790)	Blackmun (.432)	
Marshall (.803)		Thomas

Source: Baum 1989a.
Note: Unless otherwise indicated, scores in parentheses represent justices' support of civil liberties positions from 1946 through 1985. Also, justices' names are aligned across columns so that the succession for a given seat can be seen by reading from left to right.
[a]Represents support for civil liberties during the 1990 term.

It goes without saying that the personnel changes that have occurred over the past three decades could have substantial bearing on the direction of legal change. Indeed, the carefully thought-out appointments to the Court made by the three Republican presidents could have fomented the profound legal change manifest in our case groupings. Compare, for example, the Court's composition at the time *Roe v. Wade* (1973) was decided with that of *Webster v. Reproductive Health Services* (1989); between the two, it experienced a turnover in four-ninths of its membership. Similarly, between its decisions in *Furman* and *Gregg*, Stevens replaced Douglas, who had voted with the slim (5–4) majority to overturn Georgia's death penalty law.

THE POLITICAL ENVIRONMENT

With the demise of the myth that the Court is an apolitical body composed of neutral, nonpartisan decision makers, analysts have explored a range of environmental, extralegal factors that may affect judicial decisions. Two emerge as particularly significant: the public and its elected representatives.

PUBLIC OPINION

Does the Court consider or mirror the views of the public in rendering its judgments?[14] The Republican theory of the framers would suggest a negative response: federal judges are to be accountable only to the Constitution, not to any public constituency. From this perspective, Mr. Dooley's quip was mistaken—the Supreme Court does not follow the election returns.

Although the institutional relationship between justices and the public is not the "electoral connection" that links elected officials and their constituencies, this does not necessarily mean that the Court is immune from the ebb and flow of public opinion. The Court-public relationship simply may be different from that which characterizes other branches. As Marshall (1989, 97) asserts: "Most modern Court decisions reflect public opinion. When a clear cut poll majority or plurality exists, over three-fifths of the Court's decisions reflect the polls. By all arguable evidence the modern Supreme Court appears to reflect public opinion as accurately as other policy makers."

Research supporting the view that in some sense the Court "follows the election returns" (Barnum 1985; Caldeira 1991) inevitably raises the question of why justices *do* consider the views of the public in reaching judicial determinations when their jobs *do not* depend upon winning public approval. Scholars posit a number of reasons. First, since they are political appointees, nominated and approved by popularly elected officials, it is logical that the justices will reflect, however subtly, the views of the majority. It is probably true, for example, that an individual radically out of sync with either the president or the Senate would not be nominated, much less confirmed (Dahl 1956). A second reason relates to the institutional setting of the Court; put simply, the justices lack any real mechanism for enforcing their decisions. In this way, they depend not only on other political actors to support their positions but also on general public compliance.

This is particularly true for highly controversial Court opinions, which often have ramifications well beyond the particular concerns of the parties to the suit. Finally, the Court, at least occasionally, views public opinion as a legitimate guide for decisions. It has even gone so far as to incorporate that dimension into some of its jurisprudential standards. For example, in evaluating whether certain kinds of punishments violate the Eighth Amendment's cruel and unusual clause, the Court proclaimed that it would look toward "evolving standards of decency," as defined by public morals (George and Epstein 1992).

Accordingly, we must consider public opinion as a potentially significant factor conditioning Court-driven legal change. This is particularly true given the nature of our cases, which are highly salient and controversial. For example, not only has the Court viewed public opinion as relevant in deciding death penalty cases (Vidmar and Ellsworth 1974), but, according to research by Weissberg (1976), its opinions in this area closely track the public's views. Franklin and Kosaki (1989) suggest the same for abortion: the Court's decision in *Roe* affected the citizenry's attitudes toward abortion, "polarizing" opinions to one side or the other. This, in turn, may have had some impact on subsequent rulings in the area.

INSTITUTIONAL ACTORS

A second environmental factor is the posture of other political actors, particularly the president and members of Congress. As Casper (1972, 293) has written, we cannot underestimate "the importance of the political context in which the Court does its work. . . . [T]he statement [that the Court follows the election returns] recognizes that the choices the Court makes are related to developments in the broader political system." If this is correct and the other governmental institutions have some influence on judicial behavior (despite the fact that the justices have no electoral connection or mandate of responsiveness), then it follows that they could help foster legal change as well.

Presidents may have the greatest opportunity to prod the Court, largely because direct links exist between them and it, including the power to nominate justices and, thereby, to shape the Court (Abraham 1985; Danelski 1964); the relationships many presidents have enjoyed with sitting justices (for example, Franklin Roosevelt's with James Byrnes, Lyndon Johnson's with Abe Fortas, and Richard Nixon's with Warren Burger); and the notion that, having been elected within the previous four years, the president may carry a popular mandate, reflecting the preferences of the people, which would affect the environment within which the Court operates (Barnum 1985).

It is also true that presidents, through the executive branch operating under their direction, have other means of influencing the Court. The bureaucracy, for instance, "can aid the Court in obtaining implementation of its policies or refuse to help" (Baum 1985, 134), a fact of which the justices are well aware. The Supreme Court cannot implement or execute its own decisions. Without such authority, it often must depend on the executive branch to give its decisions effect (Canon 1991; Johnson and Canon 1984). Perhaps more important is the role a presidential appointee, the solicitor general, and the solicitor general's office play in two aspects of Supreme Court decision making. The Court relies on the office to act as a preconference screening device, filtering out insignificant petitions. To the extent that solicitors general help the Court set its agenda, they are able to ensure that the justices consider the administration's political goals and priorities (Provine 1980). In addition, the justices expect that the solicitor general will lend expertise to them, through written briefs and oral argument, thereby becoming the Court's "tenth justice" (Caplan 1987). Not surprisingly, numerous analyses have indicated that the solicitor general is a most successful player in Supreme Court litigation, regardless of the particular individual holding that post (Puro 1971; Scigliano 1971; Segal 1984, 1991).

That the president and the executive branch are in a position to affect Supreme Court decision making is undoubtedly true. What also seems to be the case is that the particular party affiliation of the president has a great deal to do with the ideological direction of that influence. It is no secret that presidents want to see their partisan views translated into law. This informs the sort of justices they nominate and is reflected in an unbroken pattern of judicial selection politics beginning with Washington's packing the Court with Federalists and extending through Bush's appointment strategy (Tribe 1985; Witt 1986). It also is demonstrated in the kinds of arguments their solicitors general bring into the Court. As O'Connor (1983) has shown, solicitors general representing Democratic administrations tend to present more pro-rights positions; those from the ranks of the Republican party, more restrictive arguments. Hence, not only do we know that presidents can and do influence Court decision making, but that the direction of that influence occurs in fairly predictable patterns, corresponding to partisan lines.

Like the president, Congress possesses a vast "array" of powers "over matters important to the Court" with which the justices can hardly afford to be unconcerned (Baum 1985). Some of these resemble those of the president (such as the Senate's role in confirmation proceedings and the implementation of judicial decisions); but others exist as well. Congress can restrict the Court's jurisdiction to hear cases, enact legislation or propose constitutional amendments to undo Court decisions, and hold judicial salaries constant (Choper 1980; Murphy 1962; Wasby 1988). Therefore, "the Court's policies may be affected by a desire to deter Congress" from taking these steps (Baum 1985, 132). Often-cited illustrations include the Court's willingness to defer to the Radical Republican Congress after the Civil War and the New Deal "switch in time that saved nine." In addition, as these examples suggest, relations between the Court and Congress are hardly random. The political composition of the legislature vis-à-vis that of the Court plays a major role in determining the course of those relations, be they antagonistic or amiable (Pritchett 1961).

Changes in political institutions can, thus, affect the resolution of judicial cases, which can in turn usher in doctrinal changes. Indeed, in the areas under study here, institutional backlash to Supreme Court decisions—from the proposal of pro-life amendments in the wake of *Roe* to the reactions of legislatures to *Furman* to the persistent efforts of Nixon, Reagan, and Bush to frustrate abortion and promote capital punishment—is manifest and pronounced. No study of legal change can afford to ignore the political environment as a factor explaining those alterations.[15]

INTEREST GROUP PRESSURE

Contrary to the expectations of the constitutional founders, litigation has become increasingly political over time. Manifestations of this can be seen in our discussion of the Court- and environment-based factors associated with legal change, but they are present elsewhere as well. A striking example of this politicization is the increasing incursion of groups into the judicial process. The arguments they make to the courts can shape the way the courts resolve the issues their cases present and thus establish a part of the interpretational context in which jurists do their work. Further, their mere presence before the bench forms an important part of the political environment in which the judiciary works, one unforeseen by the framers of the institution.

The systematic study of group litigation is of relatively recent scholarly interest. Traditional legal models find the subject incomprehensible and cannot provide an analytical framework for its examination. Individuals bring cases to courts, which decide the cases through applications of law. Early behavioral approaches, in focusing on the political preferences and characteristics of the justices deciding cases, left little room for consideration of the effect of external factors on the resolution of judicial questions. Accordingly, both traditional and behavioral approaches to legal study long neglected group pressure, as exerted through the courts, for want of adequate focus and conceptual categorization. With the advent of the pluralist paradigm, however, it was only a matter of time before the judicial activity of groups was unearthed and investigated.

Because it focuses on groups as the unit of analysis, the pluralist perspective invites close examination of organizational involvement in the courts. Arthur Bentley contended in *The Process of Government* that there were "numerous instances of the same group pressures which operate through executives and legislatures, operating through supreme courts" (1908, 338). This insight suffered through an extended period of scholarly dormancy until it was resurrected by David Truman in *The Governmental Process* (1951). Although he did not examine it empirically, Truman held that the group activity which animated American politics extended into the judiciary:

> Relations between interest groups and judges are not identical with those between groups and legislators or executive officials, but the difference is rather one of degree than of kind. For various reasons organized groups are not so continuously concerned with courts and court decisions as they are with the functions of the other branches of government, but the impact of diverse interests upon judicial behavior is no less marked. (1971, 479)

Gradually, students of the judiciary heeded Truman's call to investigate the linkages between groups and the courts. Those explorations have led to an accumulation of information about the present state of the pressure group environment in the Court (Caldeira and Wright 1990; Epstein 1991; Lawrence 1990), the most fundamental finding of which is this: group involvement has grown substantially over the years so that the vast majority of today's Supreme Court cases attract the participation of interest groups as direct sponsors (that is, when groups provide attorneys and resources to bring suit) or as amici curiae (when groups file third-party, "friend-of-the-court" briefs). As we detail in appendixes 1 and 2, the cases contained in our pairings reflect this overall trend, with those involving abortion providing the more attenuated example. In *Roe*, organized interests and governments filed 12 amicus curiae briefs; *Webster* generated 78 friend-of-the-court briefs, breaking the previous record of 57 set in the affirmative action case of *Regents of the University of California v. Bakke* (1978).

To say that interest groups are now regular players in Court litigation is one thing. For our purposes, the more important issue is whether they can prompt legal change of the magnitude observed in the capital punishment and abortion cases. Literature on group litigation speaks to this, albeit indirectly, to the extent that we know groups attempt to use the judiciary to reach specific ends. In their quest to do so, then, legal change may be a goal in and of itself or it may occur as a by-product. In either case, a consideration of those objectives leads us to conclude that groups, just as the other agents we have explored, can condition dramatic alterations in doctrine.

MOTIVATIONS AND GOALS OF INTEREST GROUP LITIGATORS: "WINNING" CASES

Why do interest groups turn to the Court? The most widely accepted reason is that they seek to etch their policy objectives into law—a goal most readily accomplished when the Court rules in their favor. This objective requires little explication. When an organization spends hundreds of thousands of dollars and other organizational resources to get a case to the Supreme Court, it is only common sense to conclude that it would like to achieve legal victory. A positive ruling from the justices can mean the fulfillment of years of dreams and struggles, as was the case when the National Association for the Advancement of Colored People Legal Defense and Educational Fund won *Brown v. Board of Education* (1954); an adverse holding can spell disaster for an organization, as occurred when the National Consumers' League failed to convince the Court to uphold minimum wage laws and virtually closed up shop (Vose 1972).

The relevant question, then, is not necessarily whether groups want to achieve legal victories. Obviously they do. Rather, we need to discover how groups maximize their quests to win cases and whether even the most successful litigation campaign can produce significant doctrinal change.

Maximizing Test-Case Strategies

The first question has been the subject of a great deal of scholarly analysis, with works coalescing around a deceptively simple vision of the ideal litigation campaign—the NAACP LDF's use of the legal system to integrate school systems and to end restrictive covenants. This model posits that the most assured way groups can achieve legal success is to bring test cases to chip gradually away at existing, adverse precedent and forge new principles for future litigation. Hence, when the NAACP LDF sought to eradicate *Plessy*'s "separate but equal" doctrine, it did not race into the nation's courtrooms, asking judges to overrule it. Rather, it brought a series of cases, each designed to erase incrementally the vestiges of *Plessy* until it no longer existed.

The gradual erosion and replacement of precedent plays to the Court's natural inclination to avoid radical departures from any given policy. Significantly (and somewhat paradoxically), use of this strategy presupposes a traditionally "legal" approach to decision making in which law changes slowly, not overnight. Yet, a test-case strategy of this sort can involve a good deal more than merely sponsoring "ideal" suits. In fact, scholars have suggested that groups using such a strategy can maximize it even further by engaging in some of the following tactics:

• Becoming repeat players by continuously and repeatedly turning to the judicial process to achieve policy ends (Galanter 1974; Greenberg 1977; Kluger 1976; Kobylka 1987, 1991; O'Connor 1980; Vose 1972).
• Hiring expert staff attorneys committed to organizational goals and well versed in areas of interest to the group (Epstein 1985; Greenberg 1974b; Manwaring 1962; Meltsner 1973; Sorauf 1976).
• Developing a sharp issue focus by concentrating on a small number of legal issues (Cowan 1976; O'Connor 1980; Wasby 1983).
• Obtaining and retaining the financial resources necessary to carry out litigation strategy (Belton 1978; Sorauf 1976).
• Amassing social scientific proofs of legal arguments (O'Connor 1980; Vose 1957, 1972).
• Generating legal publicity by writing (or commissioning) law review articles supportive of arguments (Greenberg 1977; Vose 1959).
• Coordinating with other organizations for help with legal strategy, supplemental funds, and amicus curiae briefs (Sorauf 1976; Kluger 1976; Handler 1978; Baker and Asperger 1982; O'Connor and Epstein 1983).
• Attaining assistance from the solicitor general in the form of supporting amicus curiae briefs (Krislov 1963; Scigliano 1971; Puro 1971; Vose 1972).

Winning Cases and Generating Legal Change

If organizations pursue a test-case strategy using these and other tactics, are they on their way to legal victory? Can they, in the context of our study, eventually generate major legal change? Conventional wisdom suggests affirmative answers to these queries; groups using these tactics are inordinately successful players in the litigation game.

The roots of this wisdom lie in a number of sources, but foremost are case studies. Clement Vose's *Caucasians Only* (1959), an exploration of the restrictive covenant suits, was the first in a long series of treatments of successful litigation campaigns waged by interest groups. His painstaking study of the NAACP's successful quest to end racially based housing discrimination stirred our imaginations and set the tone for later analyses. Though the scope of such inquiries has broadened considerably, most begin and end with Vose's basic proposition: group-sponsored litigation is more successful than nongroup litigation. In short, group litigants are winners whose efforts prompt significant legal change (Cortner 1968, 1970, 1988; Cowan 1976; Kluger 1976; Lawrence 1990; Manwaring 1962).[16]

Though the conventional wisdom about group activity in Court is well entrenched—and, to some extent, well justified—many challenges, resulting from the disquieting fact that what we think we know and what we observe occasionally fail to correspond, have emerged. Epstein and Rowland (1991) tested the group success assumption by pairing cases presenting similar legal stimuli to the same judge during the same year, with the only difference being that one was sponsored by an organization, the other brought by private counsel. They found no significant differences between the group-sponsored suits and those brought by nongroup attorneys. A similar phenomenon may occur at the level of the Supreme Court. Consider the unsuccessful challenge to the Adolescent Family Life Act brought by the American Civil Liberties Union (ACLU) in *Bowen v. Kendrick* (1988). In this instance we observed a known repeat player, an organization with great expertise in religious establishment clause litigation (Morgan 1968; Sorauf 1976) and with substantial resources, lose a significant case. The same year also saw the NAACP LDF go down in defeat in *City of St. Louis v. Praprotnik* (1988), a case involving a constitutional challenge to the racial consequences of a city's layoff plan. Are these isolated instances? Perhaps. But we cannot be certain without systematic investigation.

Another question arises from the judicial environment in which groups litigate. As we know, most groups that regularly resort to litigation characterize themselves as "liberal" (O'Connor and Epstein 1989). Yet, the Burger and Rehnquist Courts, at a minimum, sought to contain the expansion of rights and liberties (Blasi 1983; Schwartz 1987). If those Courts were capping rights, as many have suggested, how can groups such as the ACLU and NAACP LDF contemporaneously be achieving their objectives?

This leaves us with one last question: How does group litigation—in light of changes in Court personnel and doctrine and the larger sociopolitical environment in which cases are brought and arguments made—relate to changes in the substance of the law pronounced by the judiciary? Put another way, how does group litigation factor into the larger process of doctrinal change? Past studies have largely assumed their conclusion—that group litigation leads to legal change in the direction sought by the group. Yet, given that groups form an important set of litigators and at least occasionally lose the cases they bring to court, the full dimensions of group litigation, and its relationship to legal change, are at best incompletely understood.

Despite these questions, we do recognize that when groups enter the litigation fray—by sponsoring cases—they assume the responsibility (by selecting issues, goals, cases, and argumentational strategies) for providing courts with the stimuli that can prompt legal change. Sometimes organizations emerge as legal winners, successful in their efforts to secure favorable rulings and doctrine, sometimes as legal losers, unable to convince the Court to adopt their policies. In either event, assuming that group efforts are relevant to judicial outcomes, the groups themselves can condition the process of legal change. Operating under this supposition, then, we conclude that those factors (for example, a group's focus, personnel, or resources) that enhance prospects for group success in litigation might inhibit them as well.[17] Thus, in examining the forces working on legal change, we will pay particular attention to these characteristics as they pertain to the groups litigating capital punishment and abortion cases.

OTHER MOTIVATIONS AND GOALS OF INTEREST GROUP LITIGATORS:
AGENDA SETTING AND BALANCING

In the days when Vose (1959) published his account of the NAACP's quest to end restrictive covenants, many scholars of interest group processes conceptualized the goals of organizations, as did Vose, in essentially monolithic terms.[18] They suggested that the goal of most groups was to see their policy objectives etched into law. This was, undoubtedly, adequate and accurate during that time: the few groups that litigated prior to the 1960s generally went to court to win favorable policy (Vose 1972). However, with ever increasing numbers of groups entering the judicial fray, the motivations for litigation have broadened. The primary concern of most groups remains "winning" their cases, but they also use the judiciary to achieve other, more subtle ends. These include setting institutional agendas and providing a balance to competing interests (Gates and McIntosh 1989). Though the acquisition of these ends may be less monumental than that of concrete legal victory, they nevertheless may affect legal change, however indirectly or inadvertently.

Setting Institutional Agendas

"Where do policy issues come from?" How are "issues created and why do some controversies . . . come to command the attention and concern of the formal centers of decision-making, while others fail?"[19] Scholars give a variety of answers to these questions, with one of the more predominant being that issues "arise from group conflict" (Cobb and Elder 1983, 160; Dahl 1956). According to this view, it is organizations that expand the "scope, intensity, and visibility" of a particular issue so that they can attract the attention of policy makers, who will in turn elevate it to the governmental agenda. Why groups wish to do this is plain: they desire to change the status quo (Truman 1971). If they favored the existing state of public policy, there would be little reason for them to disturb it. It is those organizations dissatisfied with present conditions and eager for change who seek out the attention of policy makers.

How groups accomplish this varies from institution to institution. As previous research indicates, each branch of government possesses unique rules and norms governing access to its corridors. The Supreme Court is no different. Gaining admission into the Court, helping to set its agenda, depends substantially on getting the justices to take a case. Yet, this represents a monumental task since the justices receive nearly 5,000 petitions each term, granting review to only 130 or so. Organizations seeking to influence this process have several avenues available to them. They can file amicus curiae briefs at the review stage. Because such briefs act as "cues," alerting the justices to the importance of a particular dispute, they significantly increase the likelihood that the Court will hear it, or in legal parlance, grant certiorari (Caldeira and Wright 1988). Groups also can use the Court's own rules to their advantage. In particular, Supreme Court Rule 19 specifies that it is important to consider for review those cases "[w]here a court of appeals has rendered a decision in conflict with the decision of another court of appeals in the same matter; or has decided an important state . . . question in a way in conflict with applicable state . . . law." Savvy groups, then, can manipulate the review process, by generating conflict among the circuits. Relatedly, they can bombard federal (and state) courts with litigation of a similar ilk. In pursuing such an "impact" strategy, groups may be less concerned with forcing splits among various judicial entities than they are with generating so many like cases that they inevitably garner the attention of the Court.

Through these and other tactics, groups can help the Court set its agenda. The more fundamental question for us, though, is whether agenda setting per se can generate legal change. The answer, we think, is obvious. Doctrinal alteration cannot occur unless the Court confronts existing doctrine. If groups actively seek to place an issue on the institution's agenda, then they become agents of that change since, without their intervention, change could not occur in the first place. Whether legal alteration will occur in the direction desired by groups is another matter altogether; suffice it to say for now that, minimally, agenda setting can foster it.

Balancing

As noted earlier, the pressure group environment surrounding the judiciary has changed markedly over the past decades, with the most prominent alteration being the ever increasing numbers of organizations turning to the courts. Another major change involves the types of groups that use litigation. Scholars once assumed that only a very specific set of groups, those representing liberal and/or underrepresented interests, lobbied the judiciary. They based this presumption largely on the so-called disadvantaged thesis, best articulated by Cortner (1968, 287):

> [Politically disadvantaged groups] are highly dependent upon the judicial process as a means of pursuing their policy interests usually because they are temporarily or, even permanently, disadvantaged in terms of their ability to attain successfully their goals in the electoral process, within the elected institutions of government or in the bureaucracy. If they are to succeed at all in the pursuit of their goals they are almost compelled to resort to litigation.

This is no longer, if it ever was (Vose 1972), the case. As Caldeira and Wright (1990) and Epstein (1991) report, a wide range of organizations, from corporations to charitable and community groups to professional associations, regularly use litigation to achieve policy ends. Perhaps more important is that conservative groups—both single-issue ones and those with more broadly defined agendas—have followed the lead of their liberal counterparts and now regularly resort to the courts (Epstein 1985; O'Connor and Epstein 1983).

Why are businesses, trade associations, corporations, and other presumably "advantaged" interests turning to litigation? A number of explanations exist, with one of the more plausible being the desire to balance their own concerns with those of groups that were making greater use of the courts. Beginning in the 1970s, many so-called "upperdogs" not only were in adversarial relationships with "underdogs" but found themselves outgunned and outmatched as well. By this time disadvantaged interests had developed years of expertise in litigation and flooded the courts with the products of that learning process. Advantaged interests, who had experienced only political battles in legislative and executive arenas, found themselves overpowered. Hence, they went into courts to win cases but also to assert their arguments and counter their opponents' claims. In short, at least initially, they viewed the balancing of countervailing interests as a goal in and of itself.

Our case pairings make evident that these groups have succeeded in broadening the organizational horizon presented to the Court. As we can see in appendixes 1 and 2, in *Furman* the ratio of amicus curiae briefs opposing and supporting Georgia's position was 8:1; fifteen years later, in *McCleskey*, it was 2:1. In *Roe*, only 5 amicus curiae briefs supported the pro-life position; by *Webster*, that figure rose to 46.

Sheer numbers, however, need not prompt legal change. The Court is operating in an increasingly pluralistic environment, but the question is whether this reconfiguration of group forces substantially affects the dynamics of legal change. Traditional pluralist theory, with its "doctrine of countervailing interests," suggests that such mobilization would alter the content of public policy decisions. Does this effect hold for Court-based group politics? We suspect so. Traditional group litigators (for example, the ACLU and the NAACP LDF) now know that they will face skilled opponents who have just as much legal expertise in particular issue areas as they do. Consequently, they will have to develop arguments to counter their organized opposition and not simply to advocate their particular causes. Surely this hinders their object of generating change; no longer do they have a clear and largely obstacle-free path to the Court. Further, newly introduced competing groups might even succeed in blocking them completely, thus generating legal change favorable to their cause. The data presented in appendixes 1 and 2 speak to the plausibility of this for both areas of the law. Is it merely happenstance that Court turnabouts in capital punishment and abortion occurred as the number of groups favoring those changes increased? Or, did their mounting presence and countering legal arguments affect the development of law?

CONCLUSION

Legal change, conceptualized as doctrinal alteration established by the Supreme Court, is a significant phenomenon deserving of extended analytical treatment. Traditional models of judicial decision making suggest that if such change occurs at all, it does so as the result of a gradual application of past doctrine to new holdings incrementally tendered. Sometimes this may be the case. Often it is not. Our concern is with coming to grips with the forces, legal or extralegal, that condition and foster such change. In selecting areas of the law that experienced rapid doctrinal reversals, we have set an experimental stage that we think will help us to identify more precisely the forces that, in some configuration, work to bring about legal alteration.

This chapter reviewed the factors the literature considers relevant to doctrinal shifts. These—the Court, the political environment, and interest group presence—form the independent variables that we suspect conditioned the Court's change of heart on the legal and political issues represented in our case groupings. By intensely examining the warp and woof of death penalty and abortion litigation, we seek to capture and explain the specific configuration and interrelationship of factors that prompted the Court, after a short period, to reverse its doctrinal ground.

One final note. Our approach to the question of what fosters legal change is an eminently political one. We accept as guiding assumptions the findings of those before us, from the legal realists to the behavioralists. The Supreme Court is a political institution that deals with political issues framed as legal controversies.

Its justices, although trained in legal reasoning and approach, are drawn from a pool of the politically active and are appointed by presidents with an understanding of the political significance of judicial decisions. This being said, however, it is important to recognize that the Court is not a purely political institution. To a degree uncommon to other governmental institutions, it is bound to an established set of value judgments that guide and often constrain its holdings. These are neither absolute nor unyielding, but clearly they are present. An explication of legal change that ignores them ignores much of that which makes the judiciary a unique branch of the government.

Hamilton may have been wrong in ascribing to the Court complete autonomy from political influences, but he was correct in noting that its peculiar characteristics provide it an insulation not present for the other institutions. Too often social scientists neglect the legal nature of the Court in stressing its political side. This tells only part of the story and, perhaps, in some instances, the less important part. The "myth of the robe" *is* a myth, but the robe is a reality. In explicating the phenomenon of legal change, our goal is to use the insights of social science while at the same time paying heed to the peculiarly legal and rule-guided nature of the judicial process.

THREE

· ·

CAPITAL

PUNISHMENT I:

THE ROAD

TO *FURMAN*

In the early morning hours of 11 August 1967, a young white couple, the Mickes, awoke to a noise in their Savannah, Georgia, home. Thinking that it might be their eleven-year-old son sleepwalking, William Micke arose to put him back to bed. A few seconds later, his wife heard a "real loud sound and [her husband] scream." Fearing the worst, she gathered together her five children, locked them and herself into a bedroom, and shouted for help. A neighbor heard her screams, and upon his arrival, Mrs. Micke called the police.

Sergeant Spivey, who was only a few blocks away, responded to the call. Because he was unsure of whether the intruder was still in the house, he first checked the front door; it was locked. He went around to the back. Finding the door open, Spivey entered and immediately spotted Micke's body, shot through the chest with one bullet. The sergeant then called for assistance. When two other officers arrived, they scanned the surrounding area, hoping to find the intruder. Within minutes, one of the officers spotted a twenty-five-year-old black man, later identified as William Henry Furman, emerge from a wooded area near the Micke house. Upon seeing the officer, Furman started to run. After a pursuit, police finally caught up with him at his uncle's house. A search incident to arrest yielded a .22 caliber pistol, the weapon that killed Micke.

Furman confessed to shooting Micke, but he gave two different versions of the crime. At the time of his arrest, he told a detective "that he was in the kitchen; the man came in the kitchen, saw him in there and attempted to grab him as he went out the door; . . . the man hit the door instead of catching him, he hit the door, the door slammed between them, he turned around and fired one shot and ran" (*Furman*, Brief for Petitioner, no. 69-5003, 5). At his trial, held on 20 September 1968, however, he denied making this statement. There he claimed, "I admit going to these folks' home and they did caught me in there and I was coming back out, backing up and there was a wire on the floor. I was coming out backwards and fell back and I didn't intend to kill nobody. I didn't know they was behind the door. The gun went off and I didn't know nothing about no murder until they arrested me, and when the gun went off I was down on the floor and I got up and ran. That's all to it" (*Furman*, Brief for Petitioner, no. 69-5003, 5–6).

The all-white jury, though, had no difficulty sorting through these stories. In less than two hours it found Furman guilty of murder and sentenced him to death. An open-and-shut case, so it seemed.

On 13 May 1978, Warren McCleskey and three other black men entered an Atlanta furniture store with the intent of committing an armed robbery. As they were holding up the store—forcing customers to lie face down and tying up some employees—a white police officer, Frank Schlatt, responded to a silent alarm. When he walked through the front door, "two shots rang out"; one, hitting him in the head, proved fatal.

After the bullets were fired, the robbers fled the scene. Several weeks later, when police arrested McCleskey in connection with another theft, he confessed to participating in the furniture store robbery but denied that he shot Schlatt. The state thought otherwise[1] and brought him up on murder charges as well as two counts of armed robbery. An Atlanta jury, consisting of eleven whites and one black, found him guilty, sentencing him to death.

Although the circumstances of Furman's and McCleskey's cases differ, many dimensions are strikingly similar: black men allegedly murdering white men in Georgia, for which they received sentences of death. And, as it turned out, both cases reached the U.S. Supreme Court, where their respective attorneys made very similar arguments about the fate of their clients. Furman's team of lawyers, all working under the auspices of the National Association for the Advancement of Colored People Legal Defense Fund (NAACP LDF), urged the justices to reverse his sentence on the grounds that punishments of death are "rare, random, and arbitrarily" inflicted (*Furman*, Brief for Petitioner, no. 69-5003, 11), and all too often they are imposed on blacks. When Justice Douglas queried, "Is there anything in the Georgia record on what kind of people Georgia executes?," Furman's attorney responded, "It is that Georgia executes black people." Mc-Cleskey's counsel, also from the LDF,[2] made an even more pointed argument; they based their case on a statistical study, indicating clear racial discrimination in the imposition of sentences of death.

Similar cases with similar arguments, yet they resulted in wholly divergent outcomes—in 1972, the Supreme Court of the United States reversed Willie Furman's death sentence; in 1991, the state of Georgia executed Warren Mc-Cleskey. In this chapter, we examine the road that led the Court to its decision in *Furman*. In the next, we explore the path forged between *Furman* and *McCleskey* and identify the factors that seem to explain the discrepancies between the outcomes of these two cases.

THE SETTING: AMERICANS AND THE DEATH PENALTY THROUGH THE 1950S

In the course of our discussions with a range of people on the death penalty, one statement stood out because of its simplicity and accuracy: "That issue has been kicking around for a long time." Indeed, for more than two hundred years, Americans have debated the viability, morality, and efficacy of punishment by death (Davis 1957; Filler 1952; Mackey 1973; Sellin 1980; Spear 1844).

That the death penalty has generated so much interest in the United States is hardly surprising. Virtually every society, country, and culture imposing capital punishment has witnessed equally heated arguments over similar issues: Does the death penalty deter crime? Can it be imposed in a fair manner? Is it just for a society to seek retribution through capital punishment? Is the death penalty compatible with various religious and moral tenets?[3] Addressing these questions has spurred something of a cottage industry, with capital punishment now the subject of voluminous philosophical, legal, empirical, scientific, and penological analyses. Many of these focus on the use of the death penalty within particular countries or in specific historical eras. Still others have something of a global perspective, identifying trends and patterns in the usage of legal executions dating back to ancient times. What they suggest is that virtually all civilized societies codify and adopt death penalties at the time of their formation. As countries evolve, however, they evince trends toward reform and, eventually, abolition of capital punishment.[4]

At least through the mid-1970s, the United States gave some indication of following this worldwide historical pattern. Quite clearly, death penalties were very much a part of the traditional norms of criminal law and procedure in the colonial era.[5] And they remained intact during the founding period; it is in-controvertible that the framers of the Constitution had no intention of eradicating capital punishment for either federal or state crimes. Though they included a provision in the Eighth Amendment that prohibits "cruel and unusual punishments," they did not consider the death penalty to breach that guarantee.[6] By the same token, the Fifth Amendment's due process clause ("No person shall be . . . deprived of life, liberty, or property, without due process of law") actually provides for the taking of life.[7]

TRENDS TOWARD REFORM AND ABOLITION:
LOBBYING THE STATE LEGISLATURES

That the framers supported the death penalty does not mean that it has been universally uncontroversial. As early as the 1780s, rumblings for reform began what would be a long-term, albeit slow-paced, call to abolish capital punishment. Between that period and the 1920s, in fact, at least three distinct abolitionist movements surfaced, all of which sought to eradicate death penalties through legislative lobbying.[8] Taken together, these movements had a significant cumulative impact on the status of capital punishment; by the 1950s the number of people legally put to death had declined precipitously.[9] Though data prior to 1930 is somewhat suspect,[10] we can estimate that states executed many thousands before that time, but only 2,892 through the 1950s. The 1940s, in particular, witnessed the onset of a dramatic drop in executions.

Seen in this way, it appeared that the United States was reflecting the historical, worldwide trend toward reform mentioned earlier. Nonetheless, aggregated data on execution rates mask several important phenomena. The first was a nonrandom trend in state usage of capital punishment. As Zimring and Hawkins (1986, 30) point out, the United States was increasingly a divided nation. While most regions steadily reduced the number of executions, the South, with a deeply rooted tradition of capital punishment, continued to impose death at a rather steady, if somewhat declining, rate. By the 1950s, southern states were responsible for well over 50 percent of all executions occurring in the United States, with no end or even reform in sight. Hence, because of their "dominant role in use of the death penalty, they largely determined that national pattern in executions" (Zimring and Hawkins 1986, 32).

The second phenomenon is a bit more obvious. The trend toward reform did not necessarily translate into abolition, as it did in other parts of the world. Table 3-1 suggests something of an erratic picture of abolition of the death penalty through 1969 in the United States. Early interpretations would place the United States at the vanguard of a movement that eventually would spread throughout

TABLE 3-1. Status of the Death Penalty, 1840s–1960s

Decade	States Abolishing Death Penalty	States Restoring Death Penalty	European Countries Abolishing Death Penalty
1840s	Michigan (1848)[a]		
1850s	Rhode Island (1852),[b] Wisconsin (1853)		
1860s			Portugal (1867)
1870s	Iowa (1872), Maine (1876)	Iowa (1878)	Netherlands (1870), Switzerland (1874)
1880s	Maine (1887)	Maine (1883)	
1890s	Colorado (1897)		
1900s	Kansas (1907)	Colorado (1901)	Norway (1905)
1910s	Minnesota (1911), Washington (1913), Oregon (1914), North Dakota (1915), South Dakota (1915), Tennessee (1915), Arizona (1916), Missouri (1917)	Tennessee (1917), Arizona (1918), Missouri (1919), Washington (1919)	
1920s		Oregon (1920)	Sweden (1921)
1930s		Kansas (1935), South Dakota (1939)	Denmark (1930)
1940s			Iceland (1940), Italy (1944), Finland (1949), West Germany (1949)

the world.[11] Later scholarship, though, would suggest that the movements to abolish capital punishment through state legislative action were ultimately a failure. Of the fifteen states abolishing before the 1920s, nine restored the death penalty within the next two decades; some actually abolished and reinstated within a two-year period. Further, by the end of the 1950s, only six states imposed no death penalties.

Why states failed to abolish, despite the efforts of various reform movements, is not so mysterious. Americans, at least through the 1950s, widely and uni-

TABLE 3-1 *(continued)*

Decade	States Abolishing Death Penalty	States Restoring Death Penalty	European Countries Abolishing Death Penalty
1950s	Alaska (1957), Hawaii (1957), Delaware (1958)		
1960s	Oregon (1964), Iowa (1965), Vermont (1965),[c] West Virginia (1965),[c] New York (1966),[c] New Mexico (1969)[c]	Delaware (1961)	New Zealand (1961), United Kingdom (1965–66)

Source: Adapted from Zimring and Hawkins 1986, 29, 31.
[a]Retained for treason until 1963.
[b]Restored in 1882 for a life term convict who commits murder.
[c]Retained for certain extraordinary civil offenses.

formly supported capital punishment. On 4 April 1936, when the Gallup organization took its first survey of public opinion on the subject, 62 percent responded that they were in favor of the death penalty for murder; by 30 November 1953, that figure increased to 68 percent (Erskine 1970).[12] As a result, legislators faced very little pressure from constituents to eliminate death penalties. If anything, the citizenry attempted to persuade representatives to reinstate or retain it.[13]

A TURNING TIDE: THE DEATH PENALTY IN THE EARLY 1960s

As discussed above, through the 1950s hope for total abolition of the death penalty through legislative action was limited. Attempts to create major changes through legislation fared quite poorly; states in the South did not even contemplate reform, much less abolition; those elsewhere reformed their laws but did not abolish capital punishment permanently. Neither Americans nor their representatives, it seemed, wanted to take that ultimate plunge.

Yet by the early 1960s capital punishment again found its way onto the public agenda. Indeed, while state legislators—under virtually no pressure from reformist elements—were relatively inactive, key ingredients for change were in the wind. For the first time in decades, the legal community started to consider the issue seriously; the Supreme Court began refining its approach to the cruel and unusual punishment clause; and two major organizations, the NAACP LDF and the American Civil Liberties Union (ACLU), entered the fray, an entry that started somewhat tentatively but soon turned into a major mission.

INVOLVEMENT OF THE LEGAL AND SCHOLARLY COMMUNITIES

Although the movement to reform and, more pointedly, abolish the death penalty seemed hopelessly stagnated through the 1950s, the issue was attaining increased levels of interest from the legal and scholarly communities. The first sign of this came in the late 1950s with the involvement of the American Law Institute (ALI). For several years, some highly visible members, including Justice Robert Jackson, urged the ALI to recommend abolition on the grounds that death penalty cases bog down the criminal justice system. Countering this was a proposal by Columbia Law School Professor Herbert Wechsler that sought to reform two procedures used in most state capital cases. The first involved the trial itself. At the time, most such cases used unitary proceedings in which triers (jurors or judges) reached verdicts of guilt or innocence and sentences of life or death simultaneously. Wechsler's proposal called for a "bifurcated trial" of the sort used in California. There, defendants were tried in two stages: a guilt phase and then, if necessary, a penalty phase to determine whether they "should be sentenced to life or death" (ALI 1959, sec. 201.6). The second section of the Wechsler proposal involved the penalty phase of the trial. At the time, most states had no particular standards for juries to follow in determining whether to sentence a defendant to life or death; in essence, they exercised virtually unlimited discretion. The ALI proposed that their decisions should be guided by consideration of "aggravating" (those supporting a sentence of death) and "mitigating" (those supporting a sentence of life) circumstances and further suggested that triers should find at least one factor in aggravation[14] and none in mitigation[15] before they imposed death.[16] Although an ALI advisory committee supported abolition, its council voted against taking any policy position, believing that the institute "cannot be influential on [the issue's] resolution . . . either way" (ALI 1959, 65). Instead, it adopted a model code incorporating both proposals (Bedau 1974).

The ALI was not the only interested member of the legal community. In the early 1960s, several legal scholars began to "question seriously for the first time the constitutionality" of the death penalty and/or its procedures (Loh 1984, 198). Among the most influential works on the topic from this period was a piece written by Gerald Gottlieb, a volunteer attorney for the ACLU in southern California. In its first incarnation, his "essay" was actually a memo to the ACLU affiliate, raising a "novel" suggestion: that a potential legal challenge, based on the cruel and unusual clause, could be mounted to capital punishment (reproduced in Schwed 1983). This memo was later published in the *Southern California Law Review* (Gottlieb 1961) where it received widespread attention.

Around the same time, Walter Oberer, a University of Texas law professor, published an article in the *Texas Law Review*, explicating another potential legal avenue by which to challenge death penalties: opposing death-qualified jury laws. In general, these laws permitted state prosecutors to challenge for cause members of the venire who expressed any "conscientious objections" to or "scruples" against capital punishment. Dating back to the nineteenth century, such laws were enacted by many states after they eliminated mandatory sentencing to ensure that the death penalty would not be in essence abolished. Oberer suggested that the exclusion of such jurors might constitute a denial of fair trial guarantees because a death-qualified jury not only would be biased in favor of the death penalty but of guilt as well.

THE SUPREME COURT

Reformist elements received additional support from the U.S. Supreme Court. Prior to the 1960s, the Court was in no way inclined to find capital punishment contrary to constitutional guarantees, even though it had many opportunities to review cases in which death had been imposed. Some were minor cases of criminal law and procedure, long forgotten in the annals of legal history. Others were quite celebrated. Consider the fate of the "Scottsboro boys," seven black youths who allegedly raped two white women on a train heading toward Alabama. When the "boys" alighted in the town of Scottsboro, they were met by a lynch mob, a town judge who appointed the entire bar of the city to represent them so that no one lawyer would take responsibility, and a white jury ready to execute any black, regardless of the evidence (Carter 1979). Another example was the case of Ethel and Julius Rosenberg, whom the government accused of spying for the Communist party at the height of the cold war.

The "Scottsboro boys" and the Rosenbergs received sentences of death, but the Supreme Court decided their cases on issues quite apart from the constitutionality of capital punishment.[17] To be sure, in the opinion of most legal scholars of the day it would have been ludicrous to argue that the death penalty per se violated the Constitution when it apparently did not. In fact, the closest the Supreme Court came even to hearing arguments, much less ruling, on the constitutionality of the death penalty was in several cases involving modes of execution or punishment.[18] In *Wilkerson v. Utah* (1879), a unanimous Court upheld the use of public execution (by a firing squad) for premeditated murder.[19]

Eleven years later, in *In re Kemmler* (1890), the Court addressed the question of whether electrocution constituted cruel and unusual punishment. Writing for the majority, Chief Justice Fuller defined such punishments as those involving "torture or lingering death," a category into which electrocution did not fall.

In the late 1950s, however, the justices reconsidered their approach to the Eighth Amendment. In *Trop v. Dulles* (1958), the Court addressed whether the government could strip Albert Trop of his citizenship for deserting the U.S. Army, a crime for which he was court-martialed. Writing for a five-member majority,[20] Chief Justice Warren held that "denationalization" constituted cruel and unusual punishment in violation of the Eighth Amendment. Based on past Court decisions,[21] Warren reasoned that "the words of the Amendment are not precise . . . [but] their scope [is] not static." Thus, "the Amendment must draw its meaning from the *evolving standards of decency that mark the progress of a maturing society*" (*Trop* 1958, 101; emphasis added).

The meaning behind Warren's words was not altogether clear: he declared that "the basic concept underlying the Eighth Amendment is nothing less than the dignity of man" (100), but he provided no examples, beyond denationalization, of what would constitute cruel and unusual punishment. Scholarly analyses of this case, however, suggested that the "evolving standards" and "dignity of man" approaches held new hope for abolitionists. Even though the opinion explicitly denied that the death penalty fell under that rubric,[22] it showed a tempering of the Court's previous position; if the day was to come when the public rejected capital punishment, so too might the Court. What the scholars perhaps did not anticipate was that for one justice, Arthur Goldberg, that day would come sooner than later. Though he was known for his liberal positions, particularly in the area of criminal rights,[23] no one, especially the majority of his colleagues, was prepared for his actions in the 1963 case of *Rudolph v. Alabama*.[24]

At first blush, *Rudolph* was not an exceptional case; it involved an interracial southern rape for which the defendant received death. And, like the other six cases the Court received for review in 1963 that in some way touched on the subject of capital punishment, it did not raise what many thought a foregone conclusion—the constitutionality of the death penalty. Rather, it and the others hinged on procedural questions. *Rudolph*, for example, involved the voluntariness of the defendant's confession and not his sentence per se. Despite this, prior to the conference at which the Court would decide whether to hear the case, Goldberg circulated a memo informing the justices that he would raise this question: "Whether and under what circumstances, the imposition of the death penalty is proscribed by the Eighth and Fourteenth Amendments to the U.S. Constitution?" He recognized that none of the attorneys briefed this issue;

nonetheless, he felt the Court should consider the question because he was convinced that "'the evolving standards of decency that mark the progress of [our] maturing society' now condemn as barbaric and inhumane the deliberate institutionalized taking of human life by the state."[25] Goldberg reinforced this view with reports on the status of capital punishment in other countries, public opinion polls, statistical evidence, legal and scholarly analyses, and precedents.[26]

Many of the justices were shocked by Goldberg's memo,[27] complaining that it went well beyond the Court's authority—that to implement his plan, they would have to proceed *sua sponte*.[28] Not surprisingly, then, the Court not only rejected the memo's suggestion but refused to hear the case as well. To this denial of certiorari, Goldberg—joined by Douglas and Brennan—took the unusual step of writing a dissent in which he urged the Court to address three questions (*Rudolph* 1963, 889–91).

1. In light of the trend in this country and throughout the world against punishing rape by death, does the imposition of the death penalty by those states which retain it for rape violate "evolving standards of decency that mark the progress of [a] maturing society," or standards of decency more or less universally accepted?

2. Is the taking of human life to protect a value other than human life consistent with the constitutional proscription against "punishments which by their excessive . . . severity are greatly disproportioned to the offenses charged"?

3. Can the permissible aims of punishment (e.g., deterrence, isolation, rehabilitation) be achieved as effectively by punishing rape less severely than by death—e.g., by life imprisonment; if so, does the imposition of the death penalty for rape constitute "unnecessary cruelty"?

THE MAKING OF A MOVEMENT: ORGANIZED INTEREST GROUPS AND THE POLITICAL ENVIRONMENT OF THE 1960S

Under normal circumstances, a dissent from a denial of certiorari would have no real legal import. But the *Rudolph* dissent was rather unusual: it sent a signal to the legal community that at least some of the justices were interested in the unthinkable, challenging the constitutionality of the death penalty—a signal delivered loud and clear when Goldberg's law clerk, Alan Dershowitz, sent copies of the opinion "to every lawyer in America who [he] knew" (Gray and Stanley 1989, 331). Given the composition of the Court and its rulings in other areas involving criminal rights and procedure, this was not a message the legal community could afford to take lightly.[29] And it did not; in fact, among those apparently receiving Goldberg's message were the NAACP LDF and the ACLU. While their initial entrance into the fray was a cautious one, by the end of the 1960s, they were the major players in advancing the abolitionist cause.

Though both organizations eventually worked together to eradicate capital punishment, they were drawn into the debate for somewhat different reasons. Prior to 1960, one LDF attorney suggests that "capital punishment was not on the Fund's agenda" (Meltsner 1973) because it "simply had too much else to do." As a group dedicated to creating legal change through litigation on behalf of the black community, it found itself in the middle of the civil rights movement, a movement it helped spearhead through its litigation campaigns and in which it stood in the vanguard.[30] Keeping up with the demands placed on the organization during the drive for equality proved a difficult task, making any all-out attack on other issues, such as the death penalty, unfeasible.

Yet sometime in the mid-1960s the LDF did begin to contemplate and eventually undertake a full-blown litigation campaign against capital punishment. The reasons it made this decision remain murky. LDF attorneys themselves disagree over the exact genesis of this campaign. In *Cruel and Unusual: The Supreme Court and Capital Punishment* (1973), Michael Meltsner, an LDF consultant and staff attorney, tells this story:

> One afternoon, several months after announcement of the Goldberg dissent, [two other LDF attorneys] . . . and I . . . bought sandwiches . . . and sprawled out on the thin Central Park grass to discuss the implications of the opinion for the Fund. We tossed . . . problems around for an hour until [one attorney] reminded us that the Fund received several requests each month to represent black defendants under sentence of death. . . . "If we aren't able to turn these cases away, we might as well focus on the real issue—capital punishment. . . ."
>
> A week later, we persuaded [legal director Jack] Greenberg that a staff attorney should be assigned to investigate the possibility of proving the existence of racial sentencing in rape cases. (31)

The LDF's legal director at the time, Jack Greenberg, has called Meltsner's account "total nonsense" (Muller 1985, 164). Rather, as he tells it, the LDF had "debated the possibility of attacking the constitutionality of the death penalty" fifteen years prior to Meltsner's lunch because, in the minds of its attorneys, race was a major, if not the primary, determinant of capital punishment; many studies,[31] as well as intuition and previous litigation experience, indicated that blacks faced discrimination in sentencing. As Greenberg and another LDF attorney wrote in 1969:

Early cases in criminal law involving Negroes, such as the Scottsboro case, posed issues of the right to counsel, jury discrimination, forced confessions, among others. But lurking in the background of each case was the awareness that what was at stake was not merely justice, not just the legal standards that evolve out of new situations, not simply the number of individuals affected, but the irreversible fact of death. (Greenberg and Himmelstein 1969)

Among the most important of these cases, according to Greenberg, was *Hamilton v. Alabama* (1961), in which the LDF defended a black man who was sentenced to death for burglary with intent to commit rape. Given the severity of the sentence in proportion to the crime, LDF attorneys planned to take a risk: at his new trial (the Supreme Court had set aside his original conviction on other grounds), they were to argue that his death sentence constituted cruel and unusual punishment because it was disproportionate to the offense. Because Hamilton received a life sentence, they never had the opportunity to make this claim. Nonetheless, Greenberg and others insist that it was this case that crystallized the need for serious litigation in this area.

Based on our information, it is virtually impossible to say with certainty which version is correct.[32] What Meltsner and Greenberg agree on, however, is more significant: both underscore the importance of the Goldberg dissent. It indicated to them "that the arguments which they would have advanced on retrial in *Hamilton v. Alabama* were arguments worth making" (Muller 1985, 166). Furthermore, even though Goldberg was silent on the subject of race,[33] his memo seemed to imply that the Court would be open to that line of argument. Not only had the justices afforded sensitive treatment to blacks in other legal areas, but Rudolph was a black man accused of raping a white woman, a profile fitting 90 percent of those executed for rape since 1930 (Greenberg 1977, 431).[34]

Around the same time the LDF made a commitment to a capital punishment campaign, the ACLU was contemplating a similar course. Prior to the 1960s, it had no formal policy statement on the subject.[35] It seemed that some of its attorneys agreed with previous doctrine that the death penalty per se was constitutional; others did not consider it to present a civil liberties issue (Dorsen 1968).[36] This changed in 1963 when, apparently at the prodding of some of its affiliated chapters,[37] it undertook what would become a "study of the highly emotional, morally complex issue" of capital punishment (ACLU 1964–65, 59). The organization asked one of its attorneys, Norman Dorsen, to prepare a memorandum "presenting both sides of the argument, along with a recommendation to the Union on the question of abolition." In the final analysis, Dorsen concluded that the death penalty may not "impair" individual liberty "in the constitutional sense," but it "dehumanizes the society which employs it." To wit, he suggested that the ACLU adopt a pro-abolitionist policy statement and implement that policy through legal action, raising "any substantial constitutional issue that could save the convicted person from execution," and through legislative repeals of capital punishment law (Dorsen 1968, 269, 277).

After what Dorsen (1968, 278) described as "much internal debate," the ACLU's board adopted his recommendation. It cited a range of arguments as contributing to its decision: the death penalty violated norms of fairness (due process), discriminated against blacks (equal protection), and constituted cruel and unusual punishment (Eighth Amendment).[38] In announcing the policy change, ACLU officials noted that they would seek, "as a matter of civil liberties concern, the commutation of death sentences, until such time as the death penalty is eliminated as part of law and practice of the United States" (*New York Times* 1965).

The campaign for abolition thus took shape within a rather short period of time. Prior to 1963, the issue of capital punishment had virtually no place on the public agenda; by 1965, an abolitionist movement of sorts, spearheaded by the LDF and the ACLU, was in the making. And these groups could not have picked a more auspicious time to enter the debate over capital punishment: the political environment had rarely been so favorable to the abolitionist view. Though no state had abolished the death penalty since 1958 (when Delaware did so, only to restore it three years later), by the early to mid-1960s, the political horizons had begun to change. In 1964 Oregon voters decisively abolished the death penalty, although such a referendum had failed in 1958. This was soon followed by legislative abolition in five other states (see table 3-1), which meant that more states had abolished capital punishment in three years than over the past forty years combined.[39]

These developments, of course, did not occur in a vacuum. Rather, they echoed public opinion, which for the first time suggested that a majority of people favored eradication of the death penalty. As we can see in figure 3-1, a radical alteration occurred in Americans' views of capital punishment. Between October of 1953 and July of 1966, public support for the death penalty plummeted 26 points.[40]

Not all indicators, however, pointed toward an abolitionist trend. In 1966 two states with the biggest death row populations, Florida and California, replaced governors sympathetic to abolition with avid proponents of capital punishment.[41] Ronald Reagan (California) and Claude Kirk (Florida) fully intended to live up to campaign promises to sign death warrants in their respective states. Even before he took his oath of office, Reagan had appointed a pro–death penalty

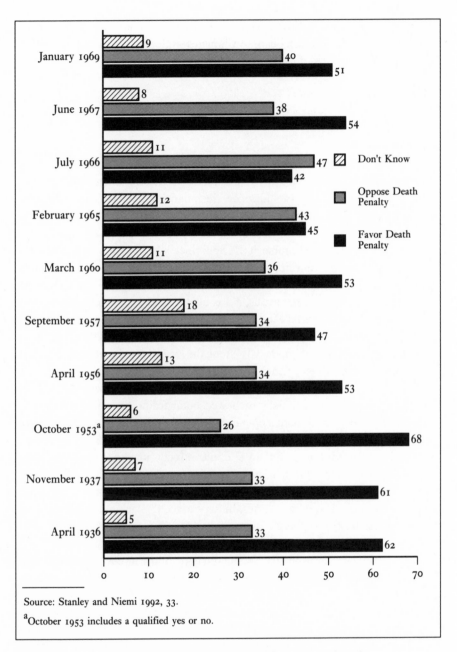

FIGURE 3-1. Public Opinion on Capital Punishment, 1936–1969

"clemency secretary"—Edwin Meese III (Turner 1966b). On the campaign trail, Kirk shook hands with death row inmates while telling them that he would see to their executions, if elected (Waldron 1967).

THE FIRST ROUND: DISCRIMINATION AND THE DEATH PENALTY

Despite the elections of Reagan and Kirk, the entry of the LDF and the ACLU into the capital punishment fray could not have been better timed. The question was whether they could capitalize on the relatively hospitable environment. Their initial strategy was simple; various accounts indicate that the two organizations divvied up the primary lobbying arenas. The ACLU was to take on the state legislatures, a reasonable course at the time since it lacked the resources necessary to undertake a major litigation effort; it was already occupied with, among other things, defending conscientious objectors to the Vietnam War. Conversely, given the LDF's tax-exempt status, it was unable to engage in legislative lobbying. Even if it could, it (unlike the ACLU) lacked the state affiliates or grass-roots lobbying apparatus so crucial to successful legislative campaigns (Schwed 1983).

From the beginning, then, the LDF took the lead in developing and executing a litigation strategy (Neier 1982). Overall, the plan of this campaign was reasonably clear; it had one goal: to eradicate the death penalty. To accomplish this, organizational attorneys initially eschewed bombarding the courts with cases; this was not their usual modus operandi. What they did have to determine was the line of legal arguments that the group would employ. After all, by 1965 many alternatives existed: they could, for example, directly attack the constitutionality of capital punishment through *Trop*'s "evolving standards of decency" approach. Alternatively, they could have mounted challenges to the procedures used in capital cases: death-qualified juries, unitary trials, the lack of sentencing standards, and so forth. Goldberg's dissent in *Rudolph*, an emerging body of scholarly literature, and the ALI's proposals made all these realistic possibilities.

In the end, LDF attorneys settled on the issue of the utmost concern to them and the one with which they had the greatest expertise: southern racism in the capital sentencing of black men accused of raping white women. To defend such individuals, LDF attorneys felt they could bring two arguments into court. First, that death for rape constituted cruel and unusual punishment because it was disproportionate to kill a man when he took no life. Second, that racially biased jurors and judges in the South were far more likely to impose death on blacks than whites, thus creating unconstitutional discrimination.

Though these arguments appeared reasonable, Greenberg and other group attorneys were not blind to their possible flaws: they knew it would be difficult to convince courts of the presence of racially biased sentencing. They learned this lesson in the case of *Maxwell v. Bishop* (1970), which involved a twenty-two-year-old black man, Maxwell, living in Hot Springs, Arkansas, who was convicted for a 1961 rape of a white woman (*Maxwell* 1968).[42] In the Arkansas courts, Maxwell's first attorney alleged that juries in the state engaged in racially biased sentencing. To support this, he presented some "bare" statistical evidence of racial discrimination: testimony from a prison superintendent on the racial composition of those executed.[43] The Arkansas court, however, rejected this argument on the grounds that the "statute for rape applies to all citizens of all races. . . . [W]e find no basis whatever to declare [it] unconstitutional in . . . verbiage or application" (*Maxwell* 1963, 118). After that ruling, a state NAACP leader contacted LDF lawyer Frank Heffron, who, in turn, applied for a writ of habeas corpus to a U.S. District Court. There he made a Fourteenth Amendment equal protection claim: that Maxwell had been the subject of discrimination. Heffron also tried to reinforce this with statistical proof gleaned from interrogations of court clerks about rape cases in other Arkansas counties. As Meltsner (1973) reports, though, the judge was "not impressed" and rejected Maxwell's case in 1964. Heffron refused to give up and appealed to the U.S. Court of Appeals for the Eighth Circuit.[44]

The lesson of the still-pending *Maxwell* case seemed clear: while LDF attorneys believed that racial discrimination was evident in capital sentencing, they also discovered that judges would not accept anecdotal evidence of the sort presented in *Maxwell* to prove it. What they needed was a full-blown, comprehensive statistical study definitively indicating the presence of racial discrimination in sentencing, around which they could build legal arguments.

As virtually all accounts reveal, this research became a reality because of the "willingness of two men to join" hands with the LDF on the issue of capital punishment: Anthony Amsterdam and Marvin Wolfgang (Bedau 1977; Greenberg 1976; Meltsner 1971, 1973). Amsterdam, a University of Pennsylvania law professor at the time, was not an unknown quantity to the LDF: he had served as a "consultant" since 1963, participating in several of its conferences, and he had prepared materials on the First Amendment for its Civil Rights Law Institutes lectures. LDF attorneys had been extremely impressed with him then. And with good reason. As a summa cum laude graduate of Haverford College, an editor in chief of the *University of Pennsylvania Law Review*, a law clerk to Felix Frankfurter, and an assistant U.S. attorney ("to learn something from the inside"), Amsterdam had impressive credentials (Mann 1973). But perhaps more significant was that he possessed keen lawyering skills and a work ethic to match. Over the years, stories of his legal expertise have taken on mythical proportions. An article entitled "Anthony Amsterdam: Renaissance Man or Twentieth Century Computer?" reported this story:

> Once, while prosecuting a case before the D.C. Circuit Court of Appeals in Washington, Amsterdam responded to a question from the bench by citing a case, complete with the volume and page number of the law book in which it could be found.
>
> The judge immediately called for the book, could not find the case in question, and informed the confident young attorney that his citation was incorrect. Amsterdam broke the hushed silence in the courtroom by quickly replying, "Your honor, your volume must be mis-bound." It was. (Mann 1973, 34)

His drive, too, was the stuff of legend. He apparently required little sleep, existing mainly on coffee so strong that most people would consider it undrinkable. Meltsner even claimed that over the course of the 1965–72 period Amsterdam devoted "no less than forty hours a week" to representing the criminally accused (Meltsner 1973, 86).

Amsterdam's earliest contribution, though, was his recruitment of Marvin Wolfgang. As chair of the Department of Sociology at the University of Pennsylvania, Wolfgang was widely reputed to be among the country's leading scholars of criminal justice systems. By the spring of 1965, when Amsterdam (on behalf of the LDF) contacted him, he already had conducted a major inquiry into the death penalty (Wolfgang, Kelly, and Nolde 1962).

Together, these men designed the sort of study the LDF thought it required. With the help of student volunteers, they collected data on rape cases occurring in twelve southern states between 1945 and 1965. To mitigate some of the objections raised by jurists in the then-pending *Maxwell* case, race became just one of twenty-nine variables the study would examine. Others included the offender's characteristics (for example, age, marital status, previous record), the victim's characteristics (age, dependent children), and the circumstances of the offense (Wolfang and Reidel 1973).[45]

While Wolfgang and others began to code and analyze the data in the fall of 1965, LDF attorneys sought postponements in as many rape trials as possible, hoping that they could incorporate the findings into their briefs and arguments. As it turned out, the waiting paid off. The results of Wolfgang's study seemed to confirm the suspicion of LDF lawyers: racially biased sentencing was rampant in southern rape cases. Of the 119 individuals receiving sentences of death, 110 were black (for other results, see Wolfgang and Reidel 1973). Wolfgang's conclusion was clear: "Negro defendants convicted of rape of white victims were . . . disproportionately frequently sentenced to death. . . . In less than one time in a

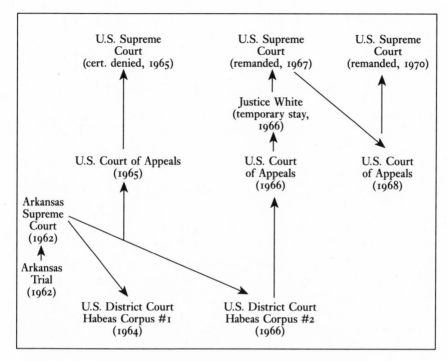

FIGURE 3-2. Litigation History of *Maxwell v. Bishop*, 1962–1970

thousand could these associations have occurred by the operation of chance factors alone" (U.S. Congress 1972).[46]

With these results in hand, the LDF thought it had the ammunition it needed to launch a full-blown litigation campaign. It could now incorporate Wolfgang's data into its arguments, beginning with the *Maxwell* case. By this time, as we illustrate in figure 3-2, *Maxwell* had worked its way up the federal ladder once, with the U.S. Supreme Court denying certiorari in 1965. Shortly thereafter, the state scheduled Maxwell's execution date for early September 1966. This swung LDF attorneys into action. In April 1966, they publicly announced the results of the Wolfgang study (Johnson 1966); two months later, they filed a second habeas corpus petition, incorporating "every legal argument" they could find, including those raised by the ALI challenge of standardless jury sentencing and unitary trials. The brief, however, placed special and primary emphasis on racial discrimination. Indeed, at the new proceeding, which began in August 1966, Wolfgang served as their chief expert witness, explaining the design and results of his study. The state's attorneys, "rather cavalierly," did not challenge the "soundness of the data or analysis" (Loh 1984).

All of this, however, failed to prevent U.S. District Court (Chief) Judge

Henley from ruling against *Maxwell*. Not only did he question specific aspects of the study (for example, missing or unknown variables, sample size), but he took issue with this sort of analysis more generally, writing that "[s]tatistics are elusive things at best and it is a truism that almost anything can be proven by them" (*Maxwell* 1966, 720). In short, this newly fashioned, sophisticated study fared no better than did Heffron's simplistic nonrandom sample of court clerks conducted for the first habeas corpus proceeding; neither district court judges nor Arkansas triers accepted the statistical evidence.

This rejection did not deter LDF lawyers from appealing to the U.S. Court of Appeals for the Eighth Circuit; after all, they had lost many cases at trial only to win, and win big, in federal appellate courts. But such was not to be the fate of *Maxwell*. After the Eighth Circuit refused to stay the execution, the LDF tried to convince Justice Byron White, who was in charge of the circuit, to grant one. He did so, ordering postponement of the execution until all the justices could hear oral arguments. This small victory, however, was short-lived as the full Court remanded the case back to the Eighth Circuit (see figure 3-2), where it would sit for more than a year.[47]

A BROADER PLAN OF ATTACK

In 1967, as a result of the Supreme Court's inaction in *Maxwell*, LDF attorneys began to reconsider their emphasis on sentencing disparities in southern interracial rape cases. They remained committed to advancing *Maxwell* and other cases in which they had raised similar claims,[48] but they had become aware of three problems with this approach. First and foremost was that statistical demonstrations of racial discrimination were having virtually no impact on judges;[49] the group had gone to considerable expense and effort with the Wolfgang study, only to have its results dismissed by every court that reviewed it.[50] As a result, LDF attorneys universally concluded that they "could never win unless the fact that a high proportion of blacks were subject to execution emerged as but one distasteful aspect of a far greater evil" (*Time* 1973). A second problem created by *Maxwell* was one the LDF (and most other public interest law firms, for that matter) had faced repeatedly: determining whether the organization owed its allegiance more to the client or to the cause. In some areas of the law, the answer was obviously the cause; for example, because it is often true in abortion litigation that the mother has already had the procedure or has given birth to the child well before the case reaches the Supreme Court, concerns about the client are negligible compared with the greater goal. Death penalty cases, though, are far more complex. As the LDF recognized, by building legal arguments solely around racial discrimination in southern rape cases, they necessarily excluded other arguments that might have been more beneficial to their client, whose life was at stake (in fact, while the LDF poured its energies into racially biased rape cases, three men were executed in the United States). As Greenberg noted (1976, 56), "[W]e could not have in good conscience attacked capital punishment for rape on ground of race discrimination, without raising other issues which also might strike down the conviction or sentence" of other death row inmates.[51] Finally, and somewhat tangentially, LDF attorneys were taking stock of the political environment. Though they thought it conducive to a death penalty campaign, they knew that the issue lacked momentum; it was just one of many social problems with which the country was grappling in the 1960s. As such, it needed "a symbol, a threat of crisis."

All of these concerns led the LDF's "war council of capital case lawyers" (for example, Greenberg, Amsterdam, and Meltsner) to change their strategy dramatically in 1967. Rather than exclusively defending southern black rapists on racial discrimination grounds, they would now provide counsel to *all* death row inmates and raise the spectrum of legal arguments: those against standardless sentencing, unitary proceedings, and death-qualified juries.[52] They thought that this revised approach would address each of their concerns, not the least of which would be providing a jolt to the political environment. The logic was simple: if the LDF could provide legal assistance to all prisoners sentenced to death, their cases would be tied up in courts for years, and as a result, no executions would occur. Then, as Meltsner (1973, 106) explains, "for each year the United States went without executions the more hollow would ring claims that the American people could not do without them; the longer death-row inmates waited, the greater their numbers, the more difficult it would be for courts to permit the first execution." This strategy, later called "moratorium," was litigation laced with psychological warfare. If the LDF could cause a pileup on death row, it was betting that no governor, judge, or court would want responsibility for executing hundreds of people with a single decision.[53]

MORATORIUM IN ACTION

Once the LDF made this decision, the question became one of implementation: to carry out the proposed moratorium, the organization needed funding, attorneys, a coordinating unit, and so forth.[54] Defending every death row inmate— that is, involvement in hundreds of cases across the United States—was an undertaking of massive proportions.

Luck and careful planning fortuitously combined in 1967 to make moratorium a reality. The funding came through when the Ford Foundation, a regular patron of public interest law, gave the LDF $1 million to create a National Office for the Rights of Indigents (NORI). The foundation thought the group would spend this money on providing legal care for the poor (and, thus, "probably did not have capital punishment in mind") (Meltsner 1973, 109); nevertheless, Green-berg approved its use for the death penalty campaign. The LDF also hired Jack Himmelstein, a twenty-six-year-old Harvard Law School graduate, to serve as managing attorney for the drive. While his responsibilities included coordinating the effort, Amsterdam would remain as the key litigating force.

One of the first steps Himmelstein and Amsterdam took was to put together what LDF lawyers would later call a "Last Aid Kit," a package of materials (drafts of habeas corpus petitions, applications for *in forma pauperis* motions and stays of execution, and papers for appeal) that would assist LDF-cooperating attorneys in defending death row inmates (Greenberg 1977, 444). Once they assembled these materials, they wrote to sympathetic lawyers, scholars, and other groups to enlist their services for the campaign.

By the spring of 1967, moratorium was slowly coming together; over fifty inmates had LDF-supported counsel. As impressive as it was, LDF attorneys surely foresaw problems with the campaign. Would it ever be possible to provide legal representation to all death row prisoners? Should the organization sacrifice control over the suits—the detailed planning and timing of every case—for the sake of coverage—providing or finding attorneys for every inmate? An ACLU attorney suggested some possible answers.

Up to this point, the ACLU had not been overwhelmingly successful on the legislative front.[55] Although its annual reports claimed that its affiliates were "actively lobbying state legislators" and "testifying against the death penalty" (ACLU 1965–67, 45), some suggest that the ACLU's concerns were elsewhere (such as with civil liberties issues arising from the Vietnam War effort), and thus it was not pursuing this avenue with any vigor. Aryeh Neier, executive director of the New York Civil Liberties Union during this period, commented on those early years:

> If the ACLU . . . which possessed the nationwide structure to undertake a lobbying campaign, had taken the lead in 1965 in efforts to oppose capital punishment, the campaign might well have been as heavily legislative as litigative. And, if resources comparable to those the LDF invested in litigation had been made available for a state legislative campaign, a good many states might have been persuaded to repeal their death sentence laws. (Neier 1982, 198)[56]

What the ACLU failed to contribute by way of legislative action, the head of its Florida affiliate, Tobias Simon, perhaps made up for in litigation strategy.

Florida, which had one of the largest death row populations in the United States, in 1965 had elected a governor bent on restoring capital punishment. When this threat became a reality,[57] Simon was up in arms at the "prospect of keeping tabs" on every death row inmate's status—more than fifty in Florida, which was as many as the LDF had taken on throughout the country. The small LDF staff, with which Simon was cooperating, also came to the conclusion that obtaining stays of execution for all was simply "unworkable" (Schwed 1983, 111). In desperation, Simon devised a "novel" plan: Why not file a multiparty (that is, class action) habeas corpus petition on behalf of all state death row inmates? After all, he reasoned, if Florida's capital law denied constitutional rights to one prisoner, did it not deny them to all?

One of Simon's ACLU associates apparently contacted the LDF to discuss this approach. The staff there was skeptical, with good reason—a class action suit never had been successfully invoked in a criminal case—and rejected the proposal on several grounds.[58] Undeterred, Simon filed his petition (*Adderly v. Wainwright*), and in April 1967 U.S. District Court Judge McRae issued a temporary stay of all executions while he contemplated the writ. After a "full factual inquiry," he certified the prisoners as a class. With this decision, a moratorium, however temporary, was achieved in Florida.

As word of the class action strategy spread, attorneys inundated the LDF with requests to file multiparty suits in their respective states. For various reasons, however, Greenberg and Amsterdam discouraged their use elsewhere. In a July 1967 letter, Greenberg urged Melvin Wulf, an ACLU attorney, to "avoid, if possible, setting up the Florida and California [where abolitionists had also launched a class action][59] victories, as tenuous as they are, as targets to shoot down. It may be premature . . . to do anything in other jurisdictions before the California and Florida cases jell" (Schwed 1983, 119). Amsterdam echoed the sentiment when he wrote to a Louisiana attorney that "the legal problems [with multiparty habeas corpus petitions] . . . are staggering. . . . Take it from me. I have spent the past couple of months on virtually nothing else." He added that "some third lawsuit" might create a "backwash," particularly if it was heard by "some unsympathetic district court judge." Amsterdam concluded by noting that "death cases are not occasions for venturesomeness in litigation" (Meltsner 1973, 134–35).

Over the course of the entire death penalty campaign, this was a key decision, but was it strategically correct? Naturally, it is easier to second guess a litigation strategy with the benefit of a twenty-year perspective than it is to formulate one in the midst of a campaign. Perhaps as the *Harvard Law Review* concluded, "It should be possible to structure the group and formulate the corresponding issues in a manner suitable to multiparty adjudication" (1968, 1510). Perhaps not. In any event, the LDF successfully convinced attorneys elsewhere to forego the class action in favor of individual defense.

THE SUPREME COURT AND MORATORIUM

Despite the controversy over the class action approach, the victory in Florida (which temporarily stayed the executions of fifty-four inmates) did give the LDF/ACLU "consortium" some breathing room in 1967 to plot its next course of action.[60] But the grace period was cut short: in December 1967, the U.S. Supreme Court announced its intention to hear arguments on several death penalty–related cases, the most important of which was *Witherspoon v. Illinois*,[61] involving the constitutionality of death-qualified juries, the subject of Oberer's article six years earlier. An Illinois law, like laws in other states, permitted prosecutors to remove for cause members of the venire who opposed or had any qualms or scruples against the death penalty (Burt 1987, 1746). The resulting jury was death qualified in the sense that it "consists of jurors who survive elimination based on their attitudes toward capital punishment" (Loh 1984, 271). Such a jury convicted William Witherspoon of murdering a police officer. Before *voir dire* commenced, the judge commented, "Let's get these conscientious objectors out of the way without wasting any time on them." The prosecutor proceeded to do just that, eliminating almost half the venire, only five of whom said they were unequivocally opposed to capital punishment (*Witherspoon* 1968, 514). The impaneled jury convicted Witherspoon, placing him on death row, where he sat for eight years and through fifteen postponed executions, while his attorney, Albert Jenner, carried his appeal to the U.S. Supreme Court.

In his briefs and at orals, Jenner made a claim that could be rephrased into the following syllogism: "The Sixth Amendment right to an impartial jury means an unbiased jury; a death-qualified jury is biased because it is *more likely to convict*; therefore, death qualification violates the Sixth Amendment Right" (Loh 1984, 214; emphasis added). What this amounts to is a "prosecution-proneness" plea: that a death-qualified jury is slanted toward the state's position, both in verdict and in sentencing. In his petition for certiorari, Jenner reinforced this claim with two unpublished studies, examining "the attitudes of college students, rather than potential jurors" (Meltsner 1973, 120). In his primary brief, he added a third study, which was based on interviews with 1,248 jurors (see *Witherspoon* 1968).

Though *Witherspoon* was not an LDF case, the organization's counsel viewed it with more than a passing interest. Since virtually every death row inmate had been sentenced by a death-qualified jury, the LDF saw *Witherspoon*, in particular, as raising a highly significant issue.[62] If the U.S. Supreme Court could see its way to striking these laws (a real possibility given the Court's composition), then LDF attorneys reasoned that massive resentencing would necessarily follow. The problem, in their view, was that Jenner's prosecution-proneness argument rested on shaky ground. Would the Court adopt a position that was reinforced by two "tentative" and unpublished studies?

That the LDF even raised this issue is somewhat ironic. After all, this was the same organization that introduced the results of a similarly tenuous study— Kenneth Clark's "Doll Test"[63]—in *Brown v. Board of Education* (Loh 1984, 215). Why it had qualms about the prosecution-proneness research is difficult to determine, but it did—so much so that Amsterdam "rushed into" Court with a ninety-four-page amicus curiae brief supporting Witherspoon's position, but on different grounds—a concurrence of sorts.

In part, Amsterdam asked the Court to avoid ruling on the prosecution-proneness argument (or to remand it back to the lower court) because it had yet to be factually developed in published, systematic research. He explained that the LDF had "arranged to have Louis Harris and Associates . . . conduct" a full-blown study, which would determine whether in fact it was a valid argument,[64] and further implied that the Court should "wait" for these results (*Witherspoon*, Brief for the LDF and NORI, no. 1015, 56).[65] In the meantime, Amsterdam suggested that the justices could strike death-qualified juries based on the following argument: "The Sixth Amendment right to an impartial jury requires that jurors represent cross-sections of the population with respect to death penalty attitudes; a death-qualified jury *does not represent cross sections because of the exclusion of those opposed to the death penalty*; therefore the death qualified jury violated the Sixth Amendment" (Loh 1984, 215). Amsterdam supported this with Harris and Gallup poll data indicating quite clearly that half the public had some doubts about capital punishment.

After orals, LDF attorneys continued their defense of death row inmates, while also holding a May 1968 National Conference on the Death Penalty, to which they invited over a hundred abolitionist scholars and lawyers. They had planned this conference after the Florida "moratorium," viewing it as a crucial step. Since they were simultaneously discouraging class actions and encouraging pileups and moratoriums, it was inevitable that the LDF was "forced to delegate responsibility whenever possible." As a result, it thought a conference would give the movement "a cohesion that it had lacked" (Meltsner 1973, 114).

In their addresses to the assembly, LDF attorneys outlined legal strategies, which, if followed, would "restrain uninformed or careless attorneys from going into court to save a client with ill-conceived frontal attacks on the constitutionality of the death penalty" (Schwed 1983, 112), and continued to stress some basic aspects of their game plan. They stated in no uncertain terms that lawyers should avoid Eighth Amendment arguments since such an approach was still too risky, with precedent, history, and even the Constitution militating against its success. Rather, as they had thought for more than a year, the Court might be "receptive" to arguments constructed around the due process clause (for example, those involving death-qualified juries, single-verdict trials, and standardless sentencing) and even to Fourteenth Amendment equal protection arguments (Schwed 1983, 114–15). Indeed, though the LDF had almost no hope for success with discrimination claims, it continued to stress the racial inequity in capital sentencing, a fact on which the press actively reported (see *New York Times* 1968). LDF staffers also emphasized that they would exclusively use litigation to achieve abolition, further reinforcing the ACLU's role as the legislative lobbying agent on this issue (Schwed 1983, 113).

That the LDF and other abolitionists seemed to be on the right track was confirmed a month after the conference, in June 1968. In a 6–3 decision, the Warren Court ruled that Illinois's death-qualified jury procedure violated Witherspoon's rights. Writing for the majority, Justice Stewart declared that the "state crossed the line of neutrality. In its quest for a jury capable of imposing the death penalty, the state produced a jury uncommonly willing to condemn a man to die." Stewart's opinion, which one observer called "vintage Warren Court" (Burt 1987, 1749), adopted the LDF's rationale while dismissing the prosecution-proneness argument, saying that it could only "speculate" on the "validity" of its generalizations because the evidence was too "tentative" and "fragmentary" (*Witherspoon* 1968, 517). Whether it would have dismissed the claim had the LDF not called attention to this is questionable; it is true that Stewart specifically pointed out that the LDF had raised this point. At the time, though, it did not matter since the Court felt Illinois had "stacked the deck against the petitioner."[66]

Undoubtedly, LDF attorneys viewed *Witherspoon* as their biggest victory to date; they assumed that it would lead to the resentencing of nearly every death row inmate and thus a virtual abolition of capital punishment. As it turned out, state courts and legislatures found ways of "circumventing the Court's decision."[67] Still, *Witherspoon* demonstrated a continued sensitivity on the part of the Warren Court to the abolitionist cause.

After *Witherspoon*, what was left of 1968 generally boded well for abolition. One month after the case, Attorney General Ramsey Clark, on behalf of the Johnson administration, formally asked Congress to abolish capital punishment. The legislature, which was about to take its Fourth of July recess, took no immediate action. Even so, Clark's request represented a milestone in executive action on abolition: it was the first time that the executive branch had called for

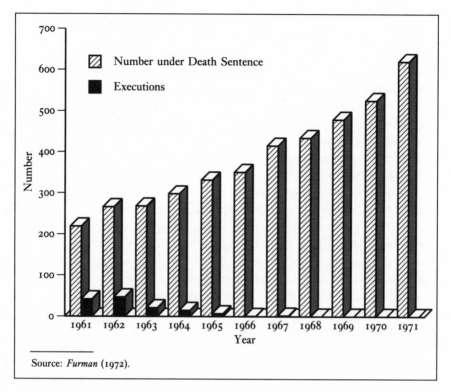

FIGURE 3-3. Status of Death Row Inmates, 1961–1971

the abolition of the penalty of death for some fourteen federal crimes[68] that carried such a penalty.[69]

Likewise the LDF/ACLU moratorium strategy could not have been going any better. As noted in figure 3-3, 1968 was the first year in American history in which no executions occurred. An article in the *New York Times* on the last day of that year credited the phenomenon to the "national courtroom campaigns against the death penalty" waged by the LDF and ACLU. It also contained several quotes from group directors Greenberg and Wulf testifying to the success of the moratorium strategy. Greenberg declared it had resulted in the "de facto national abolition of the death penalty." After explaining how difficult it was for the ACLU to achieve success in the legislatures, Wulf agreed: "[Y]ou might say that capital punishment has been de facto abolished—by court stays" (Graham 1968b).

Not only had moratorium worked in the most literal sense—no one had been executed—but it also primed the subtle, psychological effects for which abolitionist attorneys had hoped. Prisoners on death row numbered over four hundred, prompting Greenberg to remark, "The longer this de facto abolition lasts the tougher it is going to be to just open the gas chambers again some day and march a thousand guys in there" (Graham 1968b). In addition, Americans were being shown that they could live without capital punishment, and the public grew more divided than ever on the issue of death. Gallup polls taken in 1960 revealed that 53 percent of the public favored the death penalty for murder; by 1966, that figure fell to 42 percent, the first time since the advent of polling that more Americans were against capital punishment than were for it (see figure 3-1).[70]

For a brief moment, it looked as if abolition would become a reality. However, despite the victories abolitionists had won, in retrospect the year probably marked a political turning point for the worse—at least from the LDF/ACLU perspective. The trouble started in the summer of 1968 with a series of political events, some anticipated, some not. On 4 June, Sirhan-Sirhan assassinated presidential hopeful Robert Kennedy. From the abolitionist perspective, this presented two problems: in the short run, murders of visible figures always serve to ignite public views in favor of capital punishment, and this murder was no exception; and in the long run, it virtually eliminated whatever hopes the Democrats had of retaining the presidency.

Given the aims of the next president, Richard Nixon, the LDF had good reason to be alarmed. Though he did not speak directly to the issue of capital punishment during his campaign, his message to the American public was of "restoring law and order." Nixon, along with the "silent majority" of Americans, thought the Vietnam War protests, the Warren Court, and Attorney General Clark had all gone too far—that we had become a society run by criminals who had the upper hand on the streets and in courts of law. It is easy to dismiss "law and order" as campaign rhetoric; yet it cannot be denied that it touched the public. Not only did they embrace it on a national level, but on a state one as well. The message helped elect and reelect many pro–death penalty governors, including Ronald Reagan in California.

More bad news came from the federal judiciary. In July 1968, the Eighth Circuit finally resolved the *Maxwell* dispute, the first in which the LDF introduced the results of Wolfgang's study. If LDF attorneys were harboring any doubts about their decision to expand the death penalty campaign to include all inmates, such misgivings vanished with this decision. Writing for the circuit jurists, Judge Harry Blackmun completely dismissed the statistically based argument. As he stated:

> We . . . reject the statistical argument in its attempted application to Maxwell's case. Whatever value that argument may have as an instrument

of social concern, whatever suspicion it may arouse with respect to southern interracial rape trials as a group over a long period of time, and whatever it may disclose with respect to other localities, we feel the statistical argument does nothing to destroy the integrity of Maxwell's trial. Although the investigation and study made by Professor Wolfgang . . . is interesting and provocative, we do not, on the basis of that study, upset Maxwell's conviction and, as a necessary consequence, cast serious doubt on every other rape conviction in state courts in Arkansas. (*Maxwell* 1968, 147–48)

With these words, Blackmun drove the final nail into the Wolfgang study's coffin; no court would ever accept it as a foundation for legal arguments.

1969: A TRANSITION

The inauguration of Richard Nixon in January 1969 would prove to be an ominous event for abolitionists. At the time, though, the damage seemed minimal: about the only major change ushered in by the new administration was a reversion to a pro–death penalty stance. Nixon himself refrained from commenting on the issue, but his new attorney general, John Mitchell, proclaimed that he was "not opposed to capital punishment" (Graham 1969a). From the LDF/ACLU perspective, though, its target of pressure activity—the Supreme Court—remained unscathed for the time being. Warren had resigned but remained as chief justice. What's more, the six members of the *Witherspoon* majority (Schwartz 1983, 738) voted to hear oral arguments in two more death penalty cases: *Maxwell v. Bishop* and *Boykin v. Alabama*.

The LDF was delighted with the Court's selections. *Maxwell* had been up and down the legal system, culminating with Judge Blackmun's unfavorable opinion (see figure 3-2). The Supreme Court had agreed to review it (a good sign since the Court usually takes cases to reverse them), but on issues apart from racial discrimination. It specifically asked attorneys to address two aspects of capital cases: standardless sentencing and unitary trials. Why it chose to confront these issues, and not the results of Wolfgang's study, puzzled some attorneys. Yet the Court action did not trouble the LDF; all signs pointed to a favorable outcome. And the effect of such a ruling would be enormous: all but 5 of the 476 death row inmates could have their sentences vacated on the standards issue; 250 on the single-verdict question (Bigart 1969).

Boykin was another promising case, or so the LDF thought. An Alabama jury sentenced the defendant to death for a robbery during which no murder occurred. Boykin's attorney raised two narrow points: the defendant was sentenced by a jury lacking any standards, and he pled guilty to the offense unaware that his plea could subject him to execution (Greenberg 1977, 456). Additionally, because this was a seemingly disproportionate punishment (even in the South, more than 95 percent of those given death committed a murder or rape), he also made an Eighth Amendment argument: that death for robbery constituted cruel and unusual punishment. *Boykin*, thus, constituted the first case challenging capital punishment under the Eighth Amendment, a line of argument the LDF had wanted to avoid. But LDF counsel felt that this case was well suited to such a claim and, in fact, viewed it as a "golden opportunity to narrow the scope of the death penalty" (Meltsner 1973, 170).

Accordingly, Amsterdam filed an amicus curiae brief, which adapted many of the points raised by Goldberg's dissent in *Rudolph*. Like the justice, Amsterdam relied heavily on *Trop*'s evolving standards approach, using public opinion polls and falling execution rates to show that there is a "distinction between what public conscience will allow the law to say and what it will allow the law to do—between what public decency will permit a penal statute to threaten and what it will allow the law to carry out" (*Boykin*, Brief of the NAACP LDF and NORI, no. 642, 38).

It was a prepared Amsterdam who went before the U.S. Supreme Court on 4 March 1969, the day the justices heard arguments in both *Boykin* and *Maxwell*. After four years and more than $300,000 invested in the death penalty campaign, LDF attorneys recognized that this moment presented a "critical plateau" (Zion 1969) and they were ready. When Amsterdam stepped up to the podium to present the LDF's position in *Maxwell*, everything seemed to proceed as planned. The justices' questions were not unfamiliar or surprising; however, a point of potential trouble was raised by a highly unlikely source. In litigation of paramount importance, the Court sometimes allows, or even requests, third parties to present oral arguments as amici. Here they extended that opportunity to the state of California, whose attorney suggested that the Court remand the case on the basis of *Witherspoon* (Maxwell had been tried by a death-qualified jury) and avoid altogether the questions of jury standards and verdict procedures. Amsterdam was taken aback at this suggestion: the LDF's brief had not contemplated this tack since it wrote its petition for certiorari, on which its main arguments rested, two years prior to *Witherspoon* (Meltsner 1973, 163). To compound matters, Justice Stewart, a possible swing vote, "seized" upon this point, asking the California attorney how the Court could adopt the *Witherspoon* rationale.

Fortunately for the LDF, not only had Amsterdam left some time for rebuttal, but he was exceedingly fast on his feet. He would have to be: he must deal with *Witherspoon* in such a way as to avoid damaging the LDF's arguments, while also acting in the best interests of his client. This was a dilemma of some magnitude: the LDF wanted the case decided on the widest possible grounds, yet the

California attorney, however unwittingly, possibly provided them with a way to save Maxwell's life. Once again, and in the middle of oral arguments before the Supreme Court no less, the LDF would have to confront that basic ethical issue: What happens when "obligations to individual clients clash with the interest of the whole class of condemned men" (Meltsner 1973, 166)? Amsterdam's solution was to "welcome" the Court to consider the *Witherspoon* claim but to "emphasize" that an unconstitutional exclusion of jurors in *Maxwell* "did not justify the Court's avoidance of the standards and single verdict issues" (Meltsner 1973, 166). In short, he astutely tried to protect both his client's and the LDF's interests simultaneously.

After arguments, the LDF was less confident of complete victory, viewing the *Witherspoon* question as a tricky one. What it could not have known, however, was that at the Court's conference, just two days after orals, the justices tentatively voted in favor of both LDF arguments—that unitary trials and standardless sentencing were unconstitutional. What was more, the division was a wide 8–1, with only Justice Black siding with the state.[71] However, the justices expressed some disagreement over the issues and rationale. In a memo written after the first conference, Justice Douglas, in fact, labeled the "discussions of the case" as not "very conclusive or illuminating" (Schwartz 1985, 397). In his recollection, there were never "more than four votes to hold that standards for the impositions of the death penalty were constitutionally necessary. There was finally, however, a majority vote holding that a bifurcated trial was constitutionally required. But those who made up the majority included perhaps one who felt standards were not" (Urofsky 1987, 191).

The day after conference, coalitions unraveled even further. Justice Harlan wrote a letter to Warren, noting that he was "not at rest" with his vote yesterday "to reverse [*Maxwell*] on the basis of the 'split trial issue'" (Schwartz 1983, 739; Brennan 1986). He asked the chief to call for more discussion. Warren acceded, holding another conference some weeks later. The vote remained 8–1, but the justices' views had crystallized a bit more. Warren, Brennan, and Douglas agreed the Court should reverse *Maxwell* on both grounds. Fortas and Marshall tentatively concurred yet thought the unitary trial issue more persuasive. It was then that Stewart raised the pesky *Witherspoon* question, suggesting that the Court could dispose of the case solely on those grounds. Harlan continued to vacillate on the standards issue but voted with the others on the unitary trial procedure.

Since Warren assigned the majority opinion to him, Douglas would have to navigate among these views. In his original draft, however, he took the uncompromising position that *Maxwell* ought to be reversed on both grounds and proceeded to combine the claims. In an accompanying memo, Douglas justified his position: "As I got deeper into the two problems, they became inseparable to me" (Schwartz 1985, 397). Justice Brennan quickly persuaded Douglas to divide up the issues, addressing them as distinct questions.

The response to Justice Douglas's revised, two-part opinion was less than enthusiastic. Fortas wrote that he could not go along with the standards section because "if they are legislated, the results will be substantially to increase the number of cases of imposition of death penalties." His logic was simple: if standards exist, juries might feel more confident and comfortable about sentencing defendants to death. Marshall concurred with this view. Harlan stated that he could not join the standards argument and, in fact, had doubts as to whether he could sign the unitary trial section either. Stewart (and White) circulated a separate opinion, prepared as a concurrence, disposing of the case on *Witherspoon* grounds.

Hoping to salvage at least part of his opinion, Douglas omitted the standards issue, focusing exclusively on unitary trials for which he knew he had five votes. Warren and Brennan were less than delighted with this tack; they wanted some discussion of standards and, thus, proceeded to write a concurrence, which Douglas planned to join. But for a separate concurrence by Harlan, *Maxwell* was ready to go; the LDF had won a solid, if incomplete, victory.

As the Court was fighting over the *Maxwell* case, another battle, of far greater consequence, was brewing. Political and journalistic forces were putting Justice Fortas through the wringer. Pressure soon mounted and, as a result, Fortas tendered his resignation from the Court on 14 May 1969. The implications of this were enormous for abolitionists. In terms of its long-range plans, the LDF knew that Nixon would have the opportunity to appoint a chief justice (to replace Warren) and an associate justice (to replace Fortas). It would be a safe bet that neither would be as supportive of abolition as were Fortas and Warren.[72]

The short term, namely *Maxwell* and *Boykin*, also looked bleak. After Fortas resigned, Douglas had only four votes to support his *Maxwell* opinion. Harlan refused to "provide the fifth vote in such a crucial case"; indeed, he had only recently assigned one of his law clerks the task of drafting what would have been an inconsequential concurrence (Schwartz 1983, 748). Hence, Harlan "now decided that the best course of action would be to have the case reargued. Justice Stewart agreed, and having seen his majority disappear, Justice Douglas also finally pushed" to have the case rescheduled. The Court would hear rearguments on 26 May 1969 (Brennan 1986, 317).

One week later, the Court announced its decision in *Boykin*. By a 6 to 2 vote, the justices struck down Boykin's death sentence on the narrowest of grounds—the guilty plea had been involuntary. Justices Harlan and Black dissented, claiming that the issue had not been raised in his appeal to the Alabama Supreme

Court and that it contravened established precedent. The Eighth Amendment issue went completely unaddressed.

Reactions to *Boykin* were mixed. Many abolitionists were relieved that they won the case, albeit on a technicality. Some commentators, including former Justice Goldberg and his clerk Alan Dershowitz (Goldberg and Dershowitz 1970, 1798), lambasted the Court, writing that its "failure to decide the constitutionality of the death penalty is not accidental" and that *Boykin* "is illustrative of a more general theme in the Court's treatment of capital punishment cases—and of criminal cases generally. It had been deeply concerned with the area of criminal law. But for the most part that concern has related largely to matters of fair procedure."

With all of this, the 1968 term went out with a whimper, not with the bang for which the LDF had hoped. The Court ignored its Eighth Amendment plea in *Boykin*. And as for *Maxwell*, what began as an "absolutely critical case" (Bigart 1969) turned into a 1968 term "criminal landmark *manque*" (Schwartz 1983, 742). Only years later would the LDF learn how close it had come to winning on all points.

THE RETURN OF "LAW AND ORDER"

The justices called for rearguments in *Maxwell* on 13 October 1969, but these were postponed because the Court was not at full strength by the start of the 1969 term. It did have a new chief justice—Warren E. Burger—whom Nixon nominated specifically to restore a "law and order" posture to the Court, but it lacked an eighth associate justice; finding a replacement for Fortas proved difficult. After two failed nominations, Harry A. Blackmun received quick Senate confirmation on 12 May 1970.

Neither Burger nor Blackmun was, apparently, sympathetic to the abolitionist position. As a circuit court judge, Burger had rejected claims against unitary trials. And this was the same Harry Blackmun who, as an appellate court judge, not two years earlier had dismissed the Wolfgang study in *Maxwell*; the same Harry Blackmun who claimed prior to his confirmation that he had personal disdain for the death penalty but told the Senate that he would support it if legislatures so desired. For the time being, though, the LDF would not have to worry about Blackmun. A few days after he was nominated and confirmation looked assured, attorneys received word that the Court would hear rearguments on *Maxwell* on 31 April 1970. No reason existed to delay the proceedings since Blackmun had decided the case as a court of appeals judge and would be unable to participate anyway.

The LDF was exceedingly apprehensive going into the 1970 orals. With

Fortas and Warren gone, chances of a favorable outcome had dwindled considerably, even under the best of circumstances. However, the political environment had changed dramatically over the course of the year. When the LDF first argued *Maxwell*, public opinion favored abolition (albeit by a small margin), and the Johnson administration supported the same end. The context had changed by 1970. The latest Gallup polls showed that public opinion again had shifted from 42 percent in favor of the death penalty (47 percent opposed) in 1966 to 51 percent in favor (40 percent opposed) in late 1969. March 1970 brought another setback as Nixon asked Congress to reinstate federal death penalties for bombings if fatalities occurred (Naughton 1970). Nearly the only thing the LDF had going in its favor was moratorium. Since 1968, no one had been executed in the United States; as a result, death row populations swelled to five hundred. The LDF hoped that this would weigh heavily on the minds of the justices, since in essence their decisions could result in mass executions. As it stood, eighty-four death penalty appeals to the U.S. Supreme Court were awaiting the outcome of *Maxwell*.

LDF attorneys expected orals to be difficult; they were not disappointed. The justices "contained themselves" through Amsterdam's opening remarks but then had at him. The new chief justice was particularly unimpressed, questioning the compatibility of the LDF's arguments with the Constitution, the practicality of creating standards for sentencing, and the use of statistics. Justice White also grilled Amsterdam with questions about the reasonableness of mandating standards for capital cases but not for other kinds of cases (Meltsner 1973, 202–11).

On 1 June 1970—fifteen months after the Court had first heard arguments— the justices issued a short *per curiam* opinion. Despite the fact that Harlan, at conference following reargument, stated that he could "not imagine a more flagrant violation of due process than the unitary trial" (Brennan 1986, 317), Stewart and White apparently convinced him otherwise. In a 7 to 1 vote, the Court remanded *Maxwell* in light of *Witherspoon*.[73] The ruling was a great disappointment for the LDF; it had pursued the case, in all its incarnations, since 1964, only to see it create no precedent—favorable or not. The "absolutely critical" case was not to be.[74] This, however, was not the worst news of 1 June.

After dispatching *Maxwell*, the Court granted certiorari in two new death penalty cases, *McGautha v. California* and *Crampton v. Ohio*, with the hope of resolving the issues of standards and unitary trials, on which the fate of more than five hundred death row inmates now rested. Even in the heyday of the Warren Court era, the LDF might have been less than "overjoyed" with the selection of this pair (Schwed 1983, 125); now it was downright nervous. The problem, as attorneys saw it, was that the "facts of the two cases . . . did not augur" well for a positive outcome (Meltsner 1973, 228). Dennis McGautha had committed a "vicious" and "brutal" murder during the course of a robbery in California. After the trial stage, the jury sentenced him to death, an arguably "reasonable" decision given the crime and the fact that he had a long list of prior convictions. What was more, because the state was one of only a handful using the bifurcated trial procedure, the sole question raised was one of sentencing standards. Crampton was an equally unsympathetic character: a drug addict who allegedly murdered his wife while she was on the toilet. Since Ohio used a single trial procedure and provided no sentencing guidelines, *Crampton* allowed the Court to address the twin issues. Counsel for Crampton and McGautha forwarded virtually indistinguishable arguments: that the procedures surrounding their clients' trials were fundamentally unfair, violating norms of due process. Neither raised constitutional claims about the death penalty per se.

The LDF had not been substantially involved in either case, but because of its interest (it was representing two hundred of the over five hundred death row inmates), it filed an amicus curiae brief. In it, attorneys stressed the inherent inequities of the capital procedures, while reiterating the racial discrimination theme (even though Crampton was white). Citing their briefs in *Boykin* and *Maxwell*, they noted that "the long experience of LDF attorneys in handling death cases has convinced us that capital punishment in the United States is administered in a fashion that consistently makes racial minorities, the deprived and downtrodden, the peculiar objects of capital punishment" (*McGautha*, Brief of the LDF, no. 203, 2). They did, however, make clear that their purpose was not "to rehash the argument [they] made recently in *Maxwell*," but to "explore" the differences between Ohio and California sentencing schemes and those at issue in *Maxwell*.

Several groups and individuals also filed amicus curiae briefs on behalf of the defendant,[75] but the states of Ohio and California had a powerful ally of their own: the U.S. government. Given the potential importance of the cases, the Court invited Nixon's solicitor general, Erwin Griswold, to participate as an amicus curiae in oral arguments. Not surprisingly, Griswold took the side of the prosecution, arguing that the "Constitution does not require that . . . legislatures . . . proscribe statutory standards to guide or govern the jury's determination of sentences in capital cases." He pointed out to the justices, as did the state attorneys, that jury discretion is a legitimate part of the criminal justice system and, if it is to be changed, it is "something that should be done by the people." Finally, Griswold could not help but show his disdain for the strategy of the LDF and company, calling their cases "diversionary tactics" (*New York Times* 1970a).

After oral arguments, on 17 November 1970 one LDF counsel (Meltsner 1973, 229) said it had been "a quiet day in court—too quiet." He further noted that it was clear from the justices' questions that "the standards issue was a lost cause." Realistically, that was true even before orals. As previously noted, in the Warren Court conference on *Maxwell*, only Brennan, Warren, and Douglas fully supported standards. With Warren's vote lost, the LDF's prospects looked even bleaker.

A TURNABOUT (AGAIN)

Despite these problems, 1970 ended on a positive note for abolitionists. About a month after orals in *Crampton* and *McGautha*, the U.S. Court of Appeals for the Fourth Circuit became the first in American history to hold that the death penalty constituted cruel and unusual punishment under some circumstances. The case, *Ralph v. Warden*, was a vintage LDF suit involving the conviction of a southern black man accused of raping a white woman who was otherwise physically unharmed. Though the court rejected statistics indicating racial discrimination in sentencing, it ruled that the Eighth Amendment's cruel and unusual punishment clause prohibited Ralph's execution for rape since he did not take or endanger the life of his victim (1970, 793). It justified this conclusion on two grounds: that many states now considered death for rape "excessive" and that the infliction of death for a crime short of murder is "anomalous," random, and infrequent.

Ralph was not the only pleasant surprise at the turn of the new year. In December, the lame duck governor of Arkansas, Winthrop Rockefeller, commuted all fifteen death sentences in his state, with the hope that his action would "have an influence on other Governors" (Bedau 1977, 63). The following month, the attorney general of Pennsylvania ordered the dismantling of all the state's electric chairs (Schwed 1983, 127). Further, in January 1971, after three and a half years of work, the twelve-member Presidential Commission on Reform of Federal Laws recommended, among other things, the total abolition of capital punishment—a recommendation that made front-page headlines (Graham 1971).[76]

These developments heartened abolitionists, but the LDF remained quite concerned about *McGautha* and *Crampton*, which had yet to come down. Rather than wait idly, Amsterdam, Himmelstein, and others met in February to plot their next course of action should the Court rule as they feared in the pending cases. They arrived at several plans: to "focus attention on the plight of death-row inmates," to go back to the states and lobby for executive commutations, and to consider mounting a constitutional challenge to capital punishment in murder cases (Meltsner 1973, 238). They also decided to hold another conference on 15 May 1971 to explore these and other options with cooperating abolitionists.

The advance planning was not in vain: on 3 May 1971 the Court announced its decisions in the Ohio/California pairing. In a 6–3 opinion, which the LDF called "disheartening" but not "surprising" (Schwed 1983, 127; Meltsner 1973, 241), the Court found no constitutional "infirmity" either in unitary trials or standardless sentencing. Writing for the majority, Harlan—who not two years prior had announced that he could not "imagine a more flagrant violation of due process" rights than the unitary trial—suggested that "compassionate" justice would be served no better by a two-stage trial. As for sentencing standards, Harlan was equally clear, holding that it would be virtually impossible for a Court "to attempt to catalog the appropriate factors . . . for no list of circumstances would ever be really complete." In his view, "the infinite variety of cases and facets to each case would make general standards either a meaningless 'boiler-plate' or a statement of the obvious that no jury would need."

Not surprisingly, three of the Warren Court holdovers, Douglas, Brennan, and Marshall, dissented. What startled participating attorneys, though, was a concurrence written by Justice Black. Not only did he agree with Harlan's opinion, but he went one step further, addressing the Eighth Amendment issue that attorneys had worked hard to avoid. He squarely argued that the death penalty did not violate the cruel and unusual provision because it is "inconceivable . . . that the framers intended to end capital punishment by the Amendment" (*McGautha* and *Crampton* 1971, 226). To some, this concurrence, not to mention the majority opinion, was a "severe setback" (Meltsner 1971, 5), perhaps "the end of the road" (Schwed 1983, 129). Even Justice Brennan (1986, 321), in retrospect, was dismayed: "In candor, I must admit that when *McGautha* was decided, I was convinced that it was not just a lost skirmish, but rather the end of any hope that the Court would hold capital punishment to be unconstitutional."

These rulings, however, only strengthened the LDF's resolve "to pledge all of [its] resources to the successful completion of [their effort] . . . to leave no stone unturned" (Montgomery 1971). To this end, the LDF held its conference just two weeks after *McGautha* and *Crampton*. Greenberg and Amsterdam explained to the one hundred who attended that the cases produced an "extraordinary crisis" because 25–125 inmates could be executed immediately under the new precedents. To prevent this, LDF lawyers outlined a three-prong plan: they asked participants to support a congressional bill that would impose a two-year moratorium on executions; to prompt state executives to grant clemencies; and to continue litigating the more than 120 outstanding cases. The LDF promised to "give the lawyers the legal equipment to prepare writs and briefs . . . and if necessary, to give them financial backing" (Montgomery 1971).

ATTACKING THE DEATH PENALTY HEAD ON:
FURMAN V. GEORGIA ET AL.

What the LDF could not have known as it was formulating emergency plans and "hassl[ing] over last-ditch strategy" (Meltsner 1973, 246) was that the U.S. Supreme Court had ideas of its own. In a note to his clerks one month after the California/Ohio cases came down, Douglas had summed up the capital punishment situation at the time, noting that Burger, Blackmun, Stewart, Brennan, Marshall, and he were disposing "of all capital cases" by "merely denying review."[77] But now there was "a drive inside the Court to reach [an end] so that, to use the words of Justice Black, 'it may be disposed of once and for all,' as if that were possible."[78] By way of compromise, the Court, Douglas explained, "decided to name a committee composed of Brennan and White to go through the some 185 capital [petitions] . . . and to pick cases from each of the three groups [rape, robberies, and "run of the mill murders"] with the view of recommending that they be argued October 1971" (Urofsky 1987, 193–95).[79]

On 28 June 1971, the Court said it would review four capital cases: *Aikens v. California, Furman v. Georgia, Jackson v. Georgia*, and *Branch v. Texas*. Astonishingly, the order limited arguments and briefs in each case to a single question: "Does the imposition and carrying out of the death penalty in this case constitute cruel and unusual punishment in violation of the Eighth and Fourteenth Amendments?"[80] LDF attorneys could waste no time puzzling over this. Since three of the four cases (all but *Branch*) were "theirs" (indeed, they had raised the Eighth Amendment issue in their petition for certiorari),[81] they had only four short months to prepare arguments for orals, scheduled on 21 October 1971. Given the cases chosen by the Court, this would be no easy task; their facts varied wildly, ranging from the most egregious of murders—that committed by Aikens[82]—to perhaps an accidental killing—that involving Furman—to the interracial rapes committed by Jackson and Branch.

As if all of this was not bad enough, the current Court looked no more promising. By 1971, the Court had ruled on six capital cases, with, as we depict in table 3-2, certain patterns emerging. Clearly, the LDF could rely on the votes of Douglas, Brennan, and Marshall. Though none had ever declared capital punishment unconstitutional per se, they had supported the LDF's position in all six cases. Conversely, the chances of capturing Black, Burger, Blackmun, and even Harlan looked next to nil.

The LDF had to pin its hopes on Stewart and White. Judging from the votes he had cast (see table 3-2), Stewart was the most likely fourth vote in their camp. With the exception of the 1970 cases, he had opposed the death penalty, writing the Court's opinion in the all-important *Witherspoon* case. Assuming his support,

TABLE 3-2. Justices' Voting in Six Capital Punishment Cases, 1968–1970

	Blackmun	Burger	White	Stewart	Marshall	Douglas	Brennan
Jackson (1968)			S	D	NP	D	D
Witherspoon (1968)			S	D	D	D	D
Boykin (1969)			D	D	D	D	D
Maxwell (1970)		D	D	D	NP	D	D
Crampton (1971)	S	S	S	S	D	D	D
McGautha (1971)	S	S	S	S	D	D	D

Note: D = Pro–Defendant; S = Pro–State; and NP = No Participation.

that left White as the "swing," the justice who would break the 4–4 tie. Based on the data, it would be easy to discount White—only twice had he voted with the liberals in a capital punishment case. Also, his overall behavior in cases involving criminal law did not bode well. Over the previous term (1970), the newly emerging Burger Court supported the defendant in only six (35.3 percent) of the seventeen cases involving criminal justice issues. And, as the continuum displayed in figure 3-4 shows, White was clearly a vote on which the conservative wing of the Court could count. The only possible point of optimism, from the LDF's vantage point, was that White usually voted with Stewart, agreeing in sixteen (94 percent) of the seventeen cases. If Stewart decided to strike down the state laws, perhaps White would as well.

PREPARING FOR ORAL ARGUMENTS

Given this unpromising, perhaps bleak, context, the LDF started to prepare its briefs and arguments. On 23 July 1971, Amsterdam, who was coordinating the effort, issued a progress report, excerpted in table 3-3. He was taking a no-holds-barred approach, attempting to marshal evidence from all corners to support his position. In essence, though, his briefs would stress the two arguments emphasized in his memo. First and foremost was that the Eighth Amendment now prohibited capital punishment because it "affronts basic standards of decency," an argument based directly on Warren's opinion in *Trop* and the LDF brief in *Boykin*. To support this view, attorneys gathered various sorts of evidence: death penalties are not widely accepted or invoked nation- or worldwide (as falling execution rates indicate); they are infrequently imposed even in states that have not abolished them; victims tend to be black, "poor and powerless, personally ugly, and socially unacceptable"; and Americans find the death penalty repugnant, making executions private, not public, affairs. Attorneys rein-

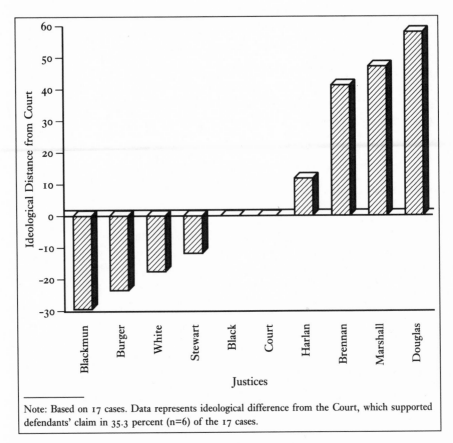

Note: Based on 17 cases. Data represents ideological difference from the Court, which supported defendants' claim in 35.3 percent (n=6) of the 17 cases.

FIGURE 3-4. Support for Defendants in Criminal Cases, 1970 Term

forced each of these points with citations to myriad studies and legal precedent, and mounds of statistical data. Second, the brief emphasized one view of the Court's institutional function: that it is a protector of minority interests and, as such, has a responsibility to strike down laws that impinge on rights. In making this claim, LDF attorneys tried to counter the competing argument that reform in capital punishment should be done by the people, through their legislators, not by the unelected judicial branch.[83]

As the LDF strategy unfolded, a host of other organized interests also began to prepare legal arguments in the form of amicus curiae briefs.[84] In general, amici reiterated and highlighted key points raised by lead counsel. Virtually all stressed the lack of deterrent value (or, at the very least, that studies were inconclusive on this point) and the role of the Court in protecting minority interests. About the only new piece of information concerned the views of

TABLE 3-3. Memo by Amsterdam on Preparations for *Furman* et al., 23 July 1971

(1) Hugo Bedau[a] has agreed to send JH [Himmelstein] within 10 days:
  (a) a 10-page review of the sociological literature on deterrence, with references . . .
  (b) a 10-page memo on the world history of capital punishment, focusing on . . . the progressive abandonment of the death penalty . . . ;
  (c) a brief memo on the role of scientists and learned men in that history, stressing the enlightened character of abolitionists;
  (d) some notes on humanistic literature. . . .

(2) [We must] . . . design an economic cost analysis of the administration of capital punishment.

(3) As per my discussion with Doug Lyons[b] on 7/22, DL is doing
  (a) a memo on published descriptions of executions;
  (b) some notes on humanistic literature to add his reflections to [Bedau's] in point (1) (d) *supra*.

(4) The following memos will be assigned within the LDF office:
  (a) . . . the major conceptual approach to an argument that the Eighth Amendment is concerned with the psychiatric state of the man who undergoes a punishment . . .
  (b) . . . recent Eighth Amendment developments in non-capital cases in the lower courts . . .
  (c) . . . An exhaustive review of [Supreme Court] Eighth Amendment decisions, involving two parts: (A) analyses of each case, including the issues; the holding; the language used to define the Eighth Amendment test, standard or approach employed to judge the constitutionality of penalties challenged as cruel and unusual; and any references made by the Court to interpretative aids (constitutional history, English history, world history, etc.); and (B) analyses of the support which the cases lend to [the following theories:] (1) the Eighth Amendment standard is dynamic, not static; it evolves, and may condemn in 1971 what it permitted in 1791; (2) rarity of application of a penalty is a major (or at least a relevant) consideration in branding it cruel and unusual; (3) enlightened conceptions of "decency" and "human dignity" are the measure of the Amendment; (4) judges look to enlightened contemporary moral standards, with some independence of legislative judgment, in applying the Eighth Amendment to test legislation; (5) punishment which is disproportionately severe is unconstitutional under the Eighth Amendment, so that a penalty which might be constitutional for crime A may be cruel and unusual for crime B; and, in particular, death is disproportionately severe for rape; (6) punishment which is "unnecessarily" harsh violates the Eighth Amendment, so that courts must consider whether lesser penalties would not equally serve the end supposed to justify a harsher one; (7) the psychiatric state of the person upon whom a

TABLE 3-3 *(continued)*

punishment is imposed is relevant . . . ; and (8) mental suffering, as well as physical suffering, is relevant . . .

(d) . . . A history of the punishments in common use in the Colonies, England and other "civilized" nations in 1791, to show that banishment, dismemberment, flogging, stocking, branding, etc. were widespread, for the purpose of demonstrating that the death penalty cannot be sustained in 1971 upon the theory that it was commonly used at the time adoption of the Eighth Amendment without also asserting that these horrors are all equally constitutional.

Source: Meltsner 1973.
[a]Professor of Philosophy, Tufts University.
[b]President of Citizens against Legalized Murder.

various religions. Briefs by the Synagogue Council, the West Virginia Council of Churches, and the National Council of Churches pointed out to the justices that virtually all religious sects and denominations opposed legal executions.

No organized interest groups aligned to challenge the abolitionist position. Rather, the legal opposition consisted of attorneys representing California, Georgia, and Texas. Briefs from these states made some arguments independent of the LDF's (for example, that a literal reading of the Fourteenth Amendment could not possibly outlaw capital punishment), but, overall, attorneys felt more compelled to refute defendants' claims, particularly that of "evolving standards." Georgia's briefs, in particular, raised two challenges to that view: if death was so offensive, why did the citizenry not pressure their legislators to abolish it and why did public opinion polls indicate support for capital punishment? Likewise, most of the governmental litigators took a crack at the LDF, claiming that reductions in executions occurred, not because juries failed to impose death, but because "the condemned have averted the carrying out of the penalty by pursuing a variety of appeals."[85]

Groups and states were not alone in preparing for orals. Three weeks before the Court entered the order to hear the death penalty cases, Justice Douglas assigned his clerks their "summer research project." In a 7 June 1971 memo, he wrote: "The question of the death penalty has been a hobby of mine for some years. I have always thought it was extremely unwise as public policy to enforce it. That of course is a far cry from saying that it is cruel and unusual punishment under the meaning of the Eighth Amendment." He then dictated how the clerks should proceed: "We need a solid piece of work this summer on the sociological, penological, psychiatric, and legislative aspects of this whole problem," adding the admonition that he was "not interested in a collection of cases to show what judges have decided on the matter because judges by and large are pretty ignorant people" (Urofsky 1987, 194–95). So much for stare decisis.

If the account in Bob Woodward and Scott Armstrong's *The Brethren* (1979) is to be believed, Douglas was not the only justice engaged in advance planning; Justice Marshall was doing some preparation of his own.[86] Privately, Marshall thought the odds of getting five votes to strike capital punishment were slim. But, like LDF attorneys, he viewed the situation as something short of hopeless, primarily because moratorium was still in effect. At that point, 704 men and women sat on death row, leading Marshall to surmise that the other justices, perhaps even the Nixon appointees, would not "want that much blood" on their hands (Woodward and Armstrong 1979, 207). So, like Douglas, he put his clerks to work, gathering whatever they could to show that the death penalty was passé and, as such, should be adjudged unconstitutional under the "evolving standards of decency" rationale. Brennan also had decided that he would vote to strike down capital punishment. Interestingly, though, he thought he was alone on this point. As he later wrote (1986, 322): "Before leaving for the summer vacation, I directed my law clerks to begin research for what I fully expected would be a lone dissent."

THE NIXON COURT?

As preparation of the death penalty cases was well under way, the composition of the Court was altered. On 17 September 1971, after thirty-four years on the Court, Justice Black announced his resignation, owing to poor health. His colleague of sixteen years, Justice Harlan, did the same just six days later. The nation prepared itself for new confirmation battles; abolitionist attorneys took stock of these developments. One thing was clear: the Court would postpone orals in *Aikens* et al. until it was back at full strength; the justices would not decide cases of such importance without nine members. They also recognized that while neither Harlan nor Black were votes in their camp, Nixon nominees could only be worse.

On this score, given Nixon's nomination of William Rehnquist, LDF attorneys were at least partially correct. His other nominee, Lewis Powell, was less predictable. He lacked previous judicial experience and, unlike Rehnquist, had not revealed his ideological leanings. Still, in Powell many saw a Justice John Harlan incarnate—not a hopeful sign for abolitionists. Nonetheless, the LDF and company would have to prepare themselves: the Senate confirmed both nominees in early December. A few weeks later, they were initiated into the roller-coaster ride of capital punishment when a full Court heard four hours of oral arguments in *Aikens* et al.

The LDF could not have anticipated the changing tide on the Court. Brennan left for the summer recess thinking he would be the sole vote to strike. But when he returned in the fall, "there were signs that [he] might not be alone. Justice White remarked to [him] that he was not sure how he would come down," an astonishing statement in Brennan's view, given his colleague's previous record. Even more startling, right before arguments, Justice Marshall handed Brennan "a typed draft of an opinion concluding that the death penalty was unconstitutional" (Brennan 1986, 322). He gave a copy to Stewart as well.

These developments did not make orals any easier, however. With the exceptions of Brennan and Powell, who "seemed merely content to listen hour after hour" (Bedau 1977, 80), the justices incessantly interrupted counsel. Especially active questioners were Douglas, who continuously asked all counsel about the racial composition of those receiving death sentences, and Stewart, who obviously was concerned about the authority of the Court to rule in this area. Given the wildly divergent views of counsel, it is also not surprising that the justices focused their inquiries on the language and history of the "cruel and unusual" provision and on the deterrent value of capital punishment. Overall, as Brennan recalled, the transcript "reveals a somewhat unfocused discussion between bar and bench," with the "difficult issue for everyone [being] how the Court could responsibly interpret the broadly-worded prohibition against cruel and unusual punishment" (1986, 322–23).

Although few unexpected questions arose, it undoubtedly was a rough day— an "uphill battle"—for Amsterdam (Brennan 1986, 322). Not only did he argue two of the cases, but, as transcripts of orals reveal, his positions were the ones most targeted for questioning by the justices. They gave him some room to begin and complete his argument; otherwise they were unrelenting. State attorneys also tried to poke holes in his claims, albeit in a generally decorous fashion. The proceedings did, however, take at least one nasty turn when a California attorney accused Amsterdam of "regarding himself as some self-appointed guardian of evolving standards of decency" (Bedau 1977, 80).

AWAITING THE DECISION

On the day after the Court heard arguments on the most significant capital cases in American history, one might have expected front-page news coverage. Yet the *New York Times* carried only a short synopsis of the proceedings on page 15, reporting that from the questions asked, Marshall and Douglas appeared most sympathetic, Burger and Blackmun least sympathetic, and Stewart and White "most troubled" and perplexed (Halloran 1972, 15). This paucity of coverage can be explained by the fact that on the same day, the New Jersey Supreme Court struck down that state's death penalty as being incompatible with a previous U.S. Supreme Court decision (*United States v. Jackson* 1968), the position urged by Amsterdam and the public defender who had argued the case (Sullivan 1972, 1). The state court also took the opportunity to criticize the federal bench, stating that the justices' "handling of this important subject is not [its] idea of effective judicial administration" (*State v. Funicello* 1972, 66).

If the action of the New Jersey court was a pleasant surprise for abolitionists, the ruling of the Supreme Court of California a month later was almost a cause célèbre. In *People v. Anderson* (1972), one of the early LDF/ACLU cases staged in California, the court struck down the death penalty as a violation of the state constitution's cruel *or* unusual punishment provision. The court wrote that the death penalty "degrades and dehumanizes all who participate in its processes. It is unnecessary to any legitimate goals of the state and it is incompatible with the dignity of man and the judicial process" (*People v. Anderson* 1972, 899). In penning these words, the state justices automatically commuted all death sentences to life imprisonment.

The reactions were predictable. Governor Ronald Reagan, whose death row population (107) was the largest in the country and contained criminals of some notoriety (for example, Sirhan-Sirhan and Charles Manson), was "deeply disappointed" (Caldwell 1972). He called it a "case of the courts setting themselves above the people and the legislature" and vowed revenge (Schwed 1983, 132).[87] LDF/ACLU attorneys were ecstatic, not simply because a state court had struck down the death penalty, but because it was the California Supreme Court. Largely regarded as the most important and innovative state judicial body in the country—Amsterdam once said that it is to courts what "UCLA is to basketball" (Meltsner 1973, 266)—it had set "an example, which was not easily ignored," particularly "in the face of a country increasingly inclined to social conservatism" (Schwed 1983, 132). More significant, as one LDF attorney put it, it was an example that "the Justices of the United States Supreme Court could not fail to be influenced by" (Meltsner 1973, 285).

Apparently, however, the federal justices had made up their minds before *Anderson* came down;[88] it was probably true that most knew how they would vote prior to conference discussions on 21 January. Burger started the proceedings, noting that if he were a legislator he would vote to abolish, but that since he was a justice, he would have to accede to the wishes of the states. The other three Nixon appointees followed suit. Douglas, Marshall, and Brennan voted to strike, leaving White and Stewart.

Stewart was apparently tormented by the issue; Woodward and Armstrong in

The Brethren (1979, 209) claim that "he had been staying up nights thinking about the issue, and particularly about those 700 individuals on death row." His questions at orals, though, suggested that he found compelling neither the discrimination argument nor the evolving standards of decency claim. Still, he acknowledged that parts of Amsterdam's presentation had been "seductive," especially those about the randomness and arbitrariness of the imposition of death. When it came time for him to cast his "tentative" vote, Stewart was anything but hesitant: he voted to strike. This left the Court deadlocked, with White breaking the tie. Somewhat surprisingly, he also was inclined to strike the laws, but on different grounds. Because of the infrequency of its use and the lack of empirical data proving otherwise, White thought the death penalty was not serving any deterrent function.

Given the importance of the cases, coupled with the divergence of their views, the justices decided to write their own separate opinions and then circulate drafts. Though some of the conservatives tried, through their drafts, to dissuade Stewart and White from voting with liberals, they had no success. Inside the Court, it was apparent that state death penalty laws would be struck by the slimmest of margins.[89] On 29 June 1972, the Supreme Court made it official, announcing its decision, or more aptly its decisions, on the series of death penalty cases that would now be known as *Furman v. Georgia.*

The majority's joint opinion had to be one of the shortest yet most significant in American history. Framed as a *per curiam* opinion (but written by Justice Brennan, according to Woodward and Armstrong [1979, 220]), it said: "The Court holds that the imposition and carrying out of the death penalty in these cases constitute cruel and unusual punishment in violation of the Eighth and Fourteenth Amendments" (*Furman* 1972, 329–30). Following this terse statement, however, were nine separate opinions (five "for" the LDF; four "against"), comprising 243 pages and 50,000 words—the longest in Court history (Brennan 1986).

THE *FURMAN* SPLIT DECISIONS

The views presented in the opinions of the five-member majority varied considerably, with the bottom line being that three (White, Stewart, and Douglas) thought capital punishment, as currently imposed, violated the Constitution, while two (Brennan and Marshall) adopted the position that it is unconstitutional under all circumstances. Beyond these general groupings, the five justices agreed on one major point of jurisprudence: that those states using capital punishment do so in an arbitrary manner (Bowers 1984). However, even this was framed in divergent terms. To Douglas, arbitrariness led to discriminatory sentencing and thus constituted a denial of equal protection. Brennan used arbitrariness as part of a four-prong test to measure against the *Trop* standard. Marshall adopted a similar approach and explained that arbitrariness was only one reason why capital punishment was unusual and "morally unacceptable." To Stewart arbitrariness in sentencing meant that the death penalty was imposed in a "wanton" and "freak[ish] manner," akin to being struck by lightning. Finally, for White, arbitrariness led to the infrequency of imposition, which in turn made death an unlikely deterrent.

Moving away from a strictly legal perspective, two other points of commonality exist. First, all made some use of "empirical data," explicitly or not, to support their views (White 1976). Given that most centered their arguments on the arbitrariness and infrequency of the imposition of death, this is hardly surprising. Second, arguments raised by the LDF and some amici found their way into all of the justices' opinions. In the case of Douglas, Marshall, and Brennan, this is probably a coincidence since they had already decided and perhaps drafted their opinions before briefs were filed. Yet, as shown in table 3-4, organized interests appear to have played a leading role in convincing White and Stewart, the "pivotal" bloc, to vote to strike. Both adopted parts of the LDF's arguments, as briefed and as argued; indeed, Justice White later remarked that Amsterdam's arguments had been the best he had ever heard (Mann 1973).

The dissenters, the four Nixon appointees, were more uniform in their critiques. To a lesser or greater extent, all expressed the view that the Court was encroaching on legislative turf and that Americans had not "repudiated" the death penalty. Blackmun, in particular, lambasted the majority for expressing views wholly inconsistent with *McGautha* and *Crampton*, even though they raised due process, not Eighth Amendment, claims. He pointed out that in the 1970 cases Stewart and White had agreed with Harlan's majority opinion that it would be virtually impossible to create sentencing standards, but now they were striking laws in part because of the absence of such standards. Also, Brennan and Marshall had dissented in *Crampton*, arguing for standards, but now suggested that these would be virtually worthless since "arbitrary" sentencing would occur anyway (see Burt 1987 for more on this point). In general, Blackmun's point was that "*McGautha* sought . . . to require that juries . . . be given standards. . . . In *Furman*, however, it is precisely this 'untrammeled' discretion . . . that . . . is offensive" (Junker 1972, 101).[90]

Chief Justice Burger's opinion was similar in tone, yet it did raise a unique issue: he noted that the plurality (Douglas, Stewart, and White) had not ruled that capital punishment under all circumstances was unconstitutional and that it may be possible for states to rewrite their legislation to meet their objections. As he asserted: "[I]t is clear that if state legislatures and the Congress wish to

TABLE 3-4. Reactions of Justices Stewart and White to LDF Arguments in
Furman et al.

	Stewart	White
LDF ARGUMENTS (BRIEFS)		
Evolving standards of decency		
National/international trends	No	No
Decreasing usage (execution rate)	Yes	No
Infrequency of imposition	Yes	Yes
Concealment of executions from		
public view	No	No
Discrimination in sentencing	—[a]	No
Rare usage "deprives" it of any		
penological value (e.g., deterrence)	Yes	Yes
Responsibility of Court to protect rights	Yes	Yes
Mental illness (*Furman*)	No	No
LDF ARGUMENTS (ORALS)		
Eighth Amendment guarantee as		
a protection of individual rights	—[b]	Yes
Pile-up on death rows	No	No
Discrimination on the part of juries	No	No

[a]He seemed to concur with Douglas and Marshall on this point but put "it to one side" for now
(*Furman* 1972, 310).
[b]Stewart did not explicitly agree but seemed to concur with others.

maintain the availability of capital punishment, significant statutory changes will
have to be made. . . . [L]egislative bodies may seek to bring their laws into
compliance with the Court's ruling by providing standards for juries and judges
to follow . . . or by more narrowly defining crimes for which the penalty is
imposed" (*Furman* 1972, 400). Privately, though, Burger thought his suggestion
futile, lamenting later that "[t]here will never be another execution in this
country" (Woodward and Armstrong 1979, 219).[91]

This view was echoed in many quarters. One University of Washington
professor of law (Junker 1972, 109) wrote, "My hunch is that *Furman* spells the
complete end of capital punishment in this country." Abolitionist attorneys were,
predictably, ecstatic. Amsterdam called it "the biggest step forward criminal
justice has taken in 1,000 years" (Mann 1973, 31–32). Meltsner (1973, 289)
simply wrote that "fantasy had become reality."

Such reactions hardly seemed misplaced; after all it appeared as if the Court's decisions in *McGautha* and in *Furman* left virtually no room for state legislation, despite Burger's recommendation. In 1970, the justices declared that it would be virtually impossible to impose sentencing standards on triers of capital cases; in 1972, the plurality held that unbridled jury discretion led to the "freakish" imposition of death. The tension between the two rulings seemingly left legislators with little recourse. The other option—mandatory death penalties for certain crimes—some thought would comply with both *McGautha* and *Furman*. Yet several of the justices, implicitly or explicitly, had expressed their disdain for such automatic sentencing.

The future of the campaign to abolish the death penalty seemed rather secure. *Furman* was an immense win for which LDF attorneys unabashedly took credit. Some years later, when an interviewer asked Greenberg to name the LDF's most important victories, his first response was *Furman v. Georgia* (*Civil Liberties Review* 1975, 118). LDF attorney Meltsner undoubtedly agrees; in the preface to *Cruel and Unusual*, he wrote: "This book tells much about the operation of the Court and the law of capital punishment, but its primary purpose it to convey the craft and cunning of the lawyers who orchestrated a stunning legal victory" (1973, xi).

There is some truth to these views. Unquestionably, without the LDF's intervention, capital punishment would not have seen its way to the Court's docket so quickly. By bringing so many appeals, the LDF acted as an "agenda setter" (Caldeira and Wright 1988), pressing the Court to resolve an issue its attorneys had largely created. By the same token, it seems that the group's arguments profoundly influenced the two pivotal justices—White and Stewart—to come over to its side. Neither had been especially committed to an abolitionist perspective or to promoting the rights of the accused. Yet their opinions reflect, at least in part, important LDF themes. The eight-year campaign, false starts and all, somehow had worked; as Greenberg noted (1982, 915), "*Furman* and pre-*Furman* anti–death penalty litigation resulted in vacated sentences for about 860 defendants, including all 629 persons on death row at the time of *Furman*." At least for the time being, the LDF emerged from its litigation campaign as a "winner"—virtual abolition had occurred in the United States.

Undeniably, the abolitionist victory in *Furman* was impressive. Despite the fact that they were fighting against a form of punishment that had existed in the United States since colonial times, despite the many losses they had suffered in the lower courts, despite their mid-stream shift in litigation strategy, despite a public that was not necessarily opposed to, but certainly less than enthusiastic about, their goals, and despite existing legal precedent, the LDF and its allies convinced the justices to strike down all existing death penalties. Further, this was accomplished after less than a decade of concerted effort.

Nonetheless, was the victory as complete and thorough as some observers of the day presumed? Writing in 1991, we know that it was not, for just beneath the surface of *Furman* lay significant problems. Most important was the potential development of a political backlash. Surely *Furman* did not require much in the way of implementation—the Court had simply prohibited states from using current capital procedures. No money needed to be spent; no enabling legislation needed to be passed; no specific judicial body needed to interpret the ruling to assure compliance. But the difficulty lay in the question, Would state legislators allow the eradication of their statutes? Given the long-standing and previously unquestioned tradition of capital punishment, within the southern states in particular, such a nonresponse seemed highly unlikely. And, in the probable event that states wanted to revise their laws, they needed to look no further than the Court's opinions; Burger, in particular, informed them of how they might maneuver around *Furman*. He noted that seven members of the Court had not found capital punishment per se repugnant to the Constitution; what offended the plurality was the manner in which states currently sentenced capital defendants.

It was only a matter of time, then, before those states determined to return capital punishment to their justice systems would pick up on Burger's lead and enact legislation designed to circumvent the Court's ruling. What form those new laws would take, the litigation strategy death penalty reformers would invoke to combat them, and the Court's reaction to both constitute a whole new set of concerns, as the battle to abolish capital punishment continued in the wake of *Furman*.

FOUR

. . . .

CAPITAL

PUNISHMENT II:

FROM *FURMAN*

TO *MCCLESKEY*

THE REPERCUSSIONS OF *FURMAN*

While the U.S. Supreme Court was contemplating the 1972 capital
cases, the National Association for the Advancement of Colored People
Legal Defense Fund (NAACP LDF) was formulating emergency plans
should the justices reach an adverse decision. The LDF contacted Marvin Wolfgang about the possibility of a new study, and it considered
launching a line of due process arguments arising from *Witherspoon*
(Meltsner 1973, 288). Apparently the LDF never considered what
would happen if it won the case; as such, it failed to anticipate the tremendous backlash that would greet the *Furman* decision (Muller 1985).

Perhaps the group was caught off guard because during moratorium
most Americans were not very concerned about capital punishment. To
be sure, they had opinions on the subject—mostly they approved of it.
So many other items occupied the political agenda, however, that the
death penalty hardly had a place of eminence. What the Court's opinion
and the attendant press coverage did was to focus the issue and to move
it up on the agenda of the day. Before 1972, it was just one of many
concerns; after, it frequently arose in discussions among legislators,
lawyers, scholars, and even average citizens. From available information, they were indeed discussions and not debates: virtually every
political indicator pointed to massive disdain for *Furman v. Georgia*.

THE FEDERAL GOVERNMENT

The first political response came, not surprisingly, from the Nixon administration. On the day after the Court handed down *Furman*, the president held a press conference, during the course of which he addressed the issue of capital punishment. Although he said that he had not gotten "through all nine opinions," he had read the chief justice's dissent. Based on Burger's opinion, he found "the holding of the Court must not be taken . . . to rule out capital punishment" (*New York Times* 1972c). Nixon provided no details on the sorts of laws states and the federal government could pass to circumvent the Court's ruling, but his comments were important: they were the first major public statement that *Furman* did not abolish capital punishment. Moreover, Nixon did follow through and eventually introduced a law that reflected the proposal offered by the American Law Institute (ALI) in the late 1950s. It specified several federal crimes (such as treason, kidnapping, and hijacking) carrying penalties of death. Defendants accused by the government of committing one of these crimes would face a bifurcated proceeding: a regular trial phase followed by a sentencing phase. The law also defined and prescribed guidelines (standards) for sentencers: if they found no mitigating circumstances and one aggravating factor, the defendant automatically received death; if one circumstance in mitigation existed, the defendant would be spared. All in all, the Justice Department reasoned that the law would garner the support of at least six members of the Court because it removed the "arbitrariness" to which some had objected (Weaver 1973b).

After the package was formally introduced into Congress, some observers predicted that it was "liable to have a long and stormy course" (Weaver 1973a). This expectation, however, misjudged the extent to which members of Congress supported capital punishment. Less than a year after Nixon sent the bill to Capitol Hill, it received a favorable recommendation from the Senate's Judiciary Committee, which found that capital punishment was a "valid and necessary social remedy against dangerous types of criminal offenders." The committee's report suggests that the members gave serious consideration to the Court's opinions in *Furman*, particularly to those of Stewart and White. Based on that reading, it concluded that two sorts of laws would meet their objections: the modified ALI proposal of the Nixon administration and strictly mandatory laws. Finding the latter "inhumane," it approved the president's version. Shortly thereafter, the full Senate held eight hours of "emotional" but generally pointless debate on the bill: "Most members had made up their minds long ago." The chamber easily approved what was hailed as a bipartisan reinstatement of capital punishment by a vote of 54–33 (Weaver 1974a).[1]

THE STATE LEGISLATURES

Some suggest Nixon's staunch support of the death penalty was quite real, that he genuinely believed it to be a deterrent; others argue that the president had ulterior motives. As one commentator (Shawcross 1973) wrote, Nixon knew "very well" that few federal crimes would be punishable by death. "What he presumably hopes is the legislation will encourage states to go further and reimpose the death penalty." If that was his intent, he was too late. Months before he formally submitted new death penalty legislation, the states were on the move. Indeed, prior to the Senate's vote, almost half the states had restored capital punishment.

As indicated in table 4-1, the return of death penalties came earlier in some states and its course varied. California was the site of the first public battle.[2] After that state's high court struck down capital punishment (months before *Furman*), Governor Reagan vowed revenge. He lived up to that threat by proposing a public initiative—Proposition 17—that would restore capital punishment, thereby overriding the state court's decision. Just four months after *Furman*, in November 1972, California voters passed the proposal by a 2–1 margin. In September of the following year, Reagan signed a bill of formal reinstatement.

Florida was the first state to restore by legislation. Immediately after the Court handed down *Furman*, Governor Reubin Askew created a Committee to Study Capital Punishment to address the following question: Would a capital punishment statute be acceptable in light of the 1972 decision? After making a careful inquiry into all the alternatives, including the state attorney general's suggestion of a mandatory law, the committee concluded that Florida should not attempt to reinstate capital punishment until a comprehensive study could be undertaken. In its final report of 20 October 1972, in fact, it suggested that no law—whether like that proposed by the ALI or mandatory—would pass constitutional muster; it also asserted that the margin on the Court against such legislation would be even wider because some of the dissenters would change their votes "out of respect" for *Furman* (Ehrhardt et al. 1973).

The state legislature, however, chose to ignore the committee's recommendation. In a four-day special session called by Governor Askew, the House (by a 116–2 vote) and the Senate (by a 36–1 margin) reinstated capital punishment on 8 December 1972. The law itself resembled what would be Nixon's variation on the ALI code. It called for a bifurcated trial for defendants charged with committing certain crimes (such as premeditated murder and rape of a child). If the jury reached a determination of guilt, it would issue an advisory sentence of life or death based on a consideration of codified mitigating (for example, no history of criminal activity, emotional duress) and aggravating (for example,

TABLE 4-1. State Legislation on the Death Penalty, Pre- and Post-*Furman*

Pre-*Furman*	Post-*Furman*	
	No Death Penalty	Death Penalty
NO DEATH PENALTY BY LAW		
Alaska, Hawaii, Iowa, Maine, Minnesota, Oregon, West Virginia, Wisconsin	Alaska, Hawaii, Iowa, Maine, Minnesota, Oregon, West Virginia, Wisconsin	Oregon (1978)
NO DEATH PENALTY BY JUDICIARY		
California, New Jersey		California (1974), New Jersey (1982)
RESTRICTIVE USE OF DEATH PENALTY		
New Mexico, New York, North Dakota, Rhode Island, Vermont	New York (inv. 1977), North Dakota, Vermont	New Mexico (1973), Rhode Island (1973)

crime is committed along with another felony, crime is especially heinous, motive is pecuniary gain) factors. The judge would then review the jury's sentence of death, and if he or she agreed, the defendant would have an automatic appeal to the state's highest court.

Members of the governor's committee harshly criticized the new law, calling it "seriously defective" and "an expedient response to election-time politics rather than a sound response to the constitutional and penological needs of the state" (Ehrhardt and Levinson 1973, 21). Likewise, an article in the *Florida State University Law Review* (1974, 150) called it "constitutionally deficient" because it did not "effectively eliminate . . . excessive discretion" and it was "regressive in view of the eighth amendment."[3]

Nonetheless, many states followed Florida's example and enacted new capital punishment statutes between 1973 and 1976 (see table 4-1). Some provided for "guided discretion" for sentencers with the power to impose death. Most mandated a bifurcated trial and specified aggravating and (sometimes) mitigating circumstances. In passing such laws, some states did seem concerned over constitutional questions, particularly the compatibility of their new statutes with

TABLE 4-1 *(continued)*

Pre-*Furman*	Post-*Furman*	
	No Death Penalty	Death Penalty

DEATH PENALTY

Alabama, Arizona, Arkansas, Colorado, Connecticut, Delaware, Florida, Georgia, Idaho, Illinois, Indiana, Kansas, Kentucky, Louisiana, Maryland, Massachusetts, Mississippi, Missouri, Montana, Nebraska, Nevada, New Hampshire, North Carolina, Ohio, Oklahoma, Pennsylvania, South Carolina, South Dakota, Tennessee, Texas, Utah, Virginia, Washington, Washington, D.C., Wyoming	Kansas, Massachusetts (inv. 1975), Washington, D.C.	Alabama (1976), Arizona (1973), Arkansas (1973), Colorado (1975), Connecticut (1973), *Delaware* (1974), Florida (1972), Georgia (1973), Idaho (1973), Illinois (1974), Indiana (1973), Kentucky (1975), Louisiana (1973), Maryland (1975), Mississippi (1974), Missouri (1975), Montana (1974), Nebraska (1973), *Nevada* (1973), *New Hampshire* (1974), *North Carolina* (1974), Ohio (1974), *Oklahoma* (1973), Pennsylvania (1974), South Carolina (1974), South Dakota (1979), Tennessee (1974), Texas (1973), Utah (1973), Virginia (1973), Washington (1973), Wyoming (1973)

Sources: Zimring and Hawkins 1986, 43; Bowers 1984, 525–31.

Note: inv. = invalidated by federal or state court. States in italics had some form of mandatory capital punishment; the balance enacted "guided discretion"–type laws.

Furman and *McGautha*. Yet the voting margins were generally quite lopsided. In Georgia, for example, the Senate followed the House's lead, enacting death penalties by a vote of 47–7. Though Governor Jimmy Carter had "some questions of its constitutionality," he signed the bill into law (Flint 1973). Other states instituted mandatory sentencing, making the imposition of death automatic for certain crimes (see table 4-1). That they believed these laws compatible with *Furman* seems to stem from several sources,[4] the most important of which was a 1973 Supreme Court of North Carolina ruling.

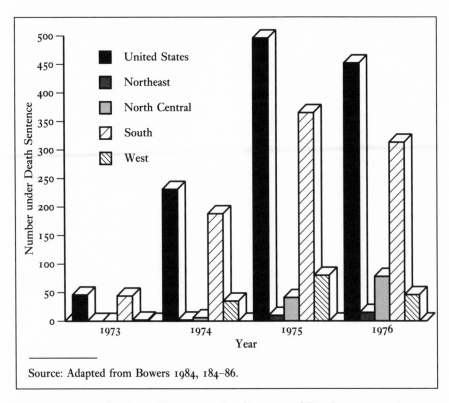

FIGURE 4-1. Number of Persons under Sentence of Death, 1973–1976

After *Furman*, state courts (and U.S. courts of appeal) generally struck down existing legislation as incompatible with the new precedent. Such opinions were what sent legislators back to the drawing board in Florida, Georgia, and elsewhere. In 1973, however, the North Carolina Supreme Court took something of a unique position. In *State v. Waddell*, it held that *Furman* made it unconstitutional for juries to play any discretionary role in capital cases; thus, a jury could no longer recommend a life sentence (that is, "show mercy") rather than execution. However, it did not strike down the state's law in toto—just the mercy provision; the statute itself "survived" as a mandatory one. The legislature formalized *Waddell* in 1974, enacting automatic imposition of capital punishment for specified crimes.

Hence, by the time Nixon formally proposed federal death penalty legislation, many states had already acted. Six months prior to the U.S. Senate's approval, thirteen had restored the death penalty, two were awaiting gubernatorial action, and sixteen were debating the issue. Figure 4-1 reveals that by the end of 1974,

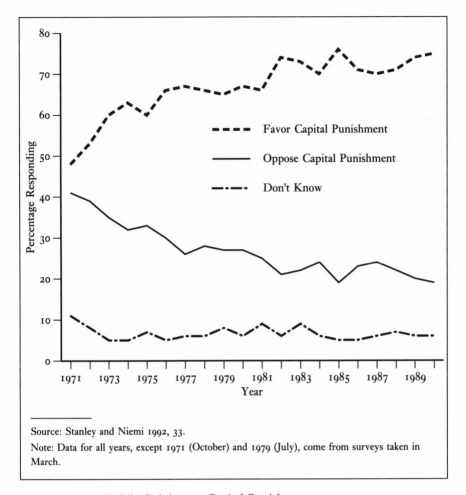

FIGURE 4-2. Public Opinion on Capital Punishment, 1971–1990

231 people had been sentenced to death under these new laws. This occurred despite the fact that nobody even knew if they were constitutional.

That politicians responded negatively to *Furman* is an understatement. With very few exceptions,[5] the push to reinstate was intense (Schwed 1983, 144–45). The reasons for this reaction remain open to speculation. As the previous description of early abolitionist efforts revealed, it is often difficult to gauge the behavior of state legislatures. One thing we do recognize, though, is that they often succumb to the will of the people: this was true in the 1900s; it remained so in the 1970s. Note that in figure 4-2, around the time of the *Furman* decision, Americans were relatively divided on the issue, though generally supportive. By

November 1972, those in favor jumped by 7 percentage points; by 1974, roughly two-thirds of all Americans supported execution.

Undoubtedly, legislators knew the views of their constituents and, in turn, pressured executives to introduce legislation or hold special sessions to address the issue. While Nevada's governor read his state of the state address to the legislature in 1973, he "was interrupted by applause just once," when he called for a return to capital punishment. New York's Governor Rockefeller received "thunderous" applause when he made the same suggestion at a labor conference (Flint 1973). The message from the constituents was apparently delivered loud and clear.

It was also true (as it has been throughout American history) that pro-abolitionist views were not well represented in the states. The LDF, because of its tax-exempt status, could not engage in legislative lobbying. Other legal groups, such as the American Bar Association, delayed taking any position because of the "unsettled" state of the law. In fact, the American Civil Liberties Union (ACLU) and its affiliates appear to be the only anti–capital punishment forces that attempted to pressure state legislators. After *Furman*, the ACLU noted that it was working to stop "efforts [that] quickly got underway in several state legislatures to pass new death penalty measures." It was highly optimistic of victory: "While strenuous efforts may still be necessary to preserve the victory, it seems likely that these efforts will succeed" (ACLU 1971–72, 23). ACLU official Aryeh Neier, however, claims that the group did not enter the legislative arenas "in a significant way" until 1974, when it appointed a coordinator of state efforts. In retrospect, this was too little, too late; by then, "nearly a decade after public antipathy to the death penalty peaked in the 1960s, it was extremely difficult to prevail in state legislative battles" (Neier 1982, 206).[6]

THE ABOLITIONIST RESPONSE

In the heady days immediately following *Furman*, abolitionists were confident that they had won a decisive victory (Schwed 1983). Most felt that the legislative attempts to circumvent *Furman*—with mandatory or discretionary guidelines—would not pass constitutional muster.[7] What they did not anticipate was the magnitude of the backlash against the Court's decision. In a 1985 interview, LDF attorney Jack Greenberg "asserted quite straightforwardly that the LDF did not worry about this backlash effect" (Muller 1985). Another LDF attorney agreed: "We were surprised at the explosion. . . . [S]tates returned so quickly and enthusiastically" (Gray and Stanley 1989, 344). Legal scholars had much the same reaction. One noted that "*Furman* was not greeted with surprise, but no one expected the legislative response to the decision" (Reidinger 1987, 50).

It is clear, though, that the LDF recognized the decisions did not firmly and finally abolish capital punishment in the United States. Prior to *Furman*, Anthony Amsterdam had planned a meeting of California abolitionists for 7 July 1972 with the intent of mounting a campaign against Proposition 17. After *Furman*, many participants called Amsterdam to see if the conference would be canceled; to some it looked as if the Court's ruling nullified the referendum. Acknowledging that *Furman* left open the possibility, however small, for new legislation, Amsterdam was definitive: the conference would be held as scheduled. In fact, despite the magnitude of the victory in *Furman*, the atmosphere at that meeting was one of pervasive pessimism; many participants expressed the view that Proposition 17 would pass. The conference was so downcast that Amsterdam quipped, "This group has me seriously wondering whether winning *Furman* was a good thing after all" (Meltsner 1973, 307).

"NEW" STRATEGIES: THE SCHOLARLY COMMUNITY

While the victory in *Furman* began to look less than complete (particularly with passage of Proposition 17 a certainty), abolitionists at this point showed "no signs of panic," still "calmly and flatly" predicting that America "will never have another execution" (Caswell 1974). They did recognize, however, that the war might not be over, that they would have to contemplate counterattacks. To this end, the LDF held a conference of "two dozen leading researchers and scholars" at Columbia University in October 1972. At this meeting, Amsterdam unveiled a three-part post-*Furman* strategy. First, he explained that the ACLU would undertake a lobbying campaign to stop restoration efforts. Second, he promised that the LDF would continue to litigate, challenging any new laws. Finally, and concomitantly, he told the gathering that attorneys would need ammunition for new cases, in the form of social science evidence, which they then could incorporate into their legal briefs (Caswell 1974).[8]

By all accounts (for example, Bedau 1977; Caswell 1974; Pierce 1975), philosophy professor Hugo Adam Bedau took the lead in developing this research enterprise. In February 1973, he obtained a $32,000 grant from the Russell Sage Foundation, "to identify and stimulate research that might be usable in future court cases." Bedau took his mission quite seriously, organizing conferences of academics and lawyers at universities throughout the United States to explain to researchers the sorts of issues requiring investigation and to encourage research.[9] Table 4-2 depicts the major scholarly efforts undertaken

TABLE 4-2. Post-*Furman* Research, 1972–1976

Author	Study	Findings
PUBLIC OPINION		
Ellsworth and Ross (1976)	Examination of public views based on surveys administered in California in 1974.	Public opinion in favor of the death penalty reflects views at odds with the Court's opinion, that is, citizens want "selective application . . . on the basis of the criminal rather than the crime."
Sarat and Vidmar (1976)	Examination of public views based on interviews of citizens in Massachusetts.	Confirms Justice Marshall's theory that if people were informed about capital punishment, they would reject it.
Thomas and Foster (1975)	Examination of public views based on surveys administered in Florida in 1973.	Support for the death penalty is based largely on a fear of crime, and capital punishment is a means of reducing that fear.
Vidmar and Ellsworth (1974)	Examination of public views based on 1973 Harris survey data.	Public opinion polls are normally too simplistic to capture. Need detailed, comprehensive studies.
DETERRENCE[a]		
Bailey (1975)	Examination of homicide rates based on data obtained from state bureaus of corrections.	Homicide rates are higher in states restoring capital punishment. Rejects deterrent theory.
Bailey (1976)	Examination of rape rates based on Uniform Crime Reports and Teeters and Zibulka inventory.	Rape rates are higher in death states. Rejects deterrence theory for rape.
Baldus and Cole (1975)	Evaluation of Ehrlich.	Finds flaws in Ehrlich's analysis. Rejects his conclusions.

TABLE 4-2 *(continued)*

Author	Study	Findings
Bedau (1972–73)	Response to Nixon's claim that capital punishment has a deterrent effect on crime.	Demonstrates that this may be a premature conclusion.
Bowers and Pierce (1975)	Evaluation of Ehrlich.	Finds flaws in Ehrlich's analysis. Rejects his conclusions.
Ehrlich (1975)	Econometric study of deterrence, using Uniform Crime Reports.	Finds that death penalties deter murders.
Gibbs and Erickson (1976)	Review of literature and previous results.	Advocates of capital punishment must demonstrate deterrent effect because it is virtually impossible to provide evidence to controvert.
Passell (1975)	Cross-sectional analysis of deterrence.	Finds no deterrent effect.
Passell and Taylor (1976)	Evaluation of Ehrlich.	Finds flaws in Ehrlich's data/time period. Rejects his conclusions.

RACIAL DISCRIMINATION[b]

Reidel (1976)	Racial composition of death row, 1971–75.	87% of death sentences were given to those who killed white victims.
Wolfgang and Reidel (1976)	Reexamination of Wolfgang data, using multivariate analyses.	Same results.
Zimring et al. (1976)	Study of 204 homicides in Philadelphia.	65% of blacks who killed whites received death; 25% of whites who killed blacks received death.

[a]For reviews of some of these studies, see Barnett 1981 and Wilson 1983.
[b]For a review of some of these studies, see Kleck 1981.

between 1972 and 1976 and their major findings. As we can see, most of the work clustered around public opinion, deterrence, and, to a lesser extent, race.

Why the first—public opinion—attracted the balance of scholarly interest is rather easy to discern. The LDF's primary argument in *Furman* had been that evolving standards of decency now made capital punishment an outmoded form of sentencing. By 1974, flaws in this argument were evident; the reaction of state legislatures, expressed public opinion, and continued prosecutions building up death row populations all undermined its thrust. What the new wave of research tried to demonstrate was that aggregated public opinion polls may be masking nuances in public views toward the death penalty (Caswell 1974). If so, the "evolving standards" argument may be more apt than it seemed.

The issue of deterrence attracted scholarly interest for similar reasons. Justice White's opinion rested heavily on the infrequent use of capital punishment and questioned whether it could serve as a credible deterrent when it was so rarely invoked. This was a reasonable claim to make at the time, since the evidence was so inconclusive (Shin 1978). After *Furman*, however, one analyst—Isaac Ehrlich—argued that White was wrong, that "contrary to all previous investigation—each execution saved seven or eight innocent lives by deterring murders that would otherwise occur" (Ehrlich 1975, 414; see also Bowers 1984, 280–81). Ehrlich's investigation was important: it was the first econometric study of deterrence, it received significant media attention (for example, *Time* 1974), and it eventually was published in a visible journal. It also prompted a wave of critiques and research on deterrence. Indeed, much of the research identified in table 4-2 lambasted his study, concluding that he found only the "illusion of deterrence" not an actual effect.

Other analyses focused on racial discrimination and general arbitrariness in the application of capital punishment. Virtually all of this new work confirmed the basic finding of the Wolfgang study: black defendants accused of murdering or raping white victims were far more likely to receive death sentences than whites. As Riedel (1976, 282) concluded, "[T]here is no evidence to suggest that post-*Furman* statutes have been successful in reducing the discretion which leads to a disproportionate number of nonwhite offenders being sentenced to death."[10]

BACK TO THE COURTS

With the scholarly community in high gear, LDF attorneys focused their attention elsewhere. For one thing, they were watching the situation as it unfolded in the states, compiling vast amounts of data on legislation, sentencing, and death row populations (Gross and Mauro 1989). This information surely assisted the organization—it would need it to launch later appeals. It also helped it externally: virtually every newspaper account of capital punishment between 1972 and 1976 contained data obtained from LDF sources. The result was the establishment of a convenient, symbiotic relationship between some newspapers (particularly the *New York Times*) and the LDF. For example, on Christmas Eve (Wicker 1973) and on New Year's Eve (King 1973) of 1973, the *Times* ran two highly sympathetic stories on death row inmates, with a specific focus on North Carolina. Both were full of statistics (many of which came from LDF sources) about the numbers of inmates and their racial composition. One was so pro-abolitionist that it elicited a response (in the form of a letter to the editor) from Greenberg (1974a), who called it "moving and informative."

In addition to compiling data and publicizing the cause, the LDF began to pursue the second prong of Amsterdam's plan, moving back into legal arenas and renewing a "judicial assault on the death penalty" (Bowers 1984, 176). Because of the widespread reinstatement of death penalty laws, however, the organization could not handle all the new cases involved. In fact, the LDF's situation in 1974–75 was less than optimal. It had a budget of around $3.6 million, but given other areas of interest (such as employment discrimination and school desegregation), it devoted only 10 percent to capital punishment. Moreover, it could only afford to allow two of its twenty-four staff attorneys to work full-time on death penalty cases (Bedau 1987).

Still, many of the veterans of *Furman*, including Amsterdam (now a professor at Stanford), were more than eager to toil. As one attorney noted, Amsterdam was involved "in every case, planning, advising, identifying issues and trying to shape the way new statutes were interpreted by the state courts" (Gray and Stanley 1989, 345). Also, other groups (such as Team Defense and the Southern Poverty Law Center) and sympathetic attorneys pitched in, particularly at the state level. The LDF would often "assist" them there and then bring appeals into the federal arena.

In essence, then, the organization's post-*Furman* strategy was not wholly different from moratorium: it attempted to provide legal representation to all prisoners sentenced under the new laws (Gray and Stanley 1989, 345; Meltsner 1974, 39), with a great deal of litigation occurring in North Carolina, Georgia, and, to a lesser extent, Florida. The reason for more litigation in these states had to do with the numbers. Of the 147 inmates on death row nationwide (as of 1974), 49 were in North Carolina, 29 in Georgia, and 18 in Florida, thereby accounting for 65 percent of the total.[11] Abolitionists were also concerned with the varying sentencing schemes used by these states.

North Carolina's mandatory death penalty had garnered a great deal of public attention, in part because of the numbers sentenced under it, in part because it was unusual—few states had mandatory penalties. North Carolina asserted that its scheme was constitutional because it removed capriciousness and arbitrariness; the LDF maintained that it did no such thing. To bolster this contention, its attorneys argued that the state should have given every burglar (forty thousand in 1973), for example, the death penalty, but that only one received it. Why? Because of prosecutorial discretion: district attorneys plea-bargained cases, reducing offenses to noncapital crimes. What this proved, in the group's view, was that "discretion has not been eliminated, it has merely become less visible." Moreover, it argued that the North Carolina system was still discriminatory: thirty-three of its forty-seven death row inmates were black (Meltsner 1974, 39).

Attorneys looked to Georgia (and Florida) for another reason: its guided discretion law was quite typical. Although the state (and the thirty-odd others that had passed similar laws) claimed that the law was compatible with *Furman*, abolitionists suggested that "the new law works much like the old one. . . . [A]ggravation is vaguely defined and mitigation isn't defined [in the Georgia code], [so] that [it] still doesn't help jurors decide who should be executed" (Meltsner 1974, 39). In briefs filed in Georgia cases, attorneys sought to demonstrate this by the numbers: only eighteen individuals sat on death row, while twenty-three thousand had committed capital offenses during the same time period (Weaver 1974c).

THE SUPREME COURT

As the states continued to pass death penalty laws and the scholars published articles, abolitionists were appealing cases up to the Supreme Court. By the start of the October 1974 term, the justices had at least nine cases (two from Georgia, seven from North Carolina) among which they could select for full review. LDF attorneys were optimistic that the Court would grant certiorari in at least one; after all, executions would simply be delayed until they reviewed the new laws. They were almost as optimistic that the Court would strike down the laws in all their incarnations. They had reason to be: the statutes seemed incompatible with the catch-22 situation created by the gap between *Furman* and *McGautha*; the composition of the Court had not changed since the 1972 opinions; a wealth of scholarly and legal data seemed to confirm the continued arbitrariness and lack of deterrent value of capital punishment; and another moratorium of sorts was in effect—no one had been executed since 1967. As the death row population continued to mount, the LDF felt confident that the Court would not order mass executions.

As it turned out, attorneys were correct on the first score: in October 1974, the justices agreed to hear arguments in one of the LDF's North Carolina cases,

Fowler v. North Carolina, but denied certiorari to the cases from Georgia. Organizational attorneys remained unperturbed; they thought the North Carolina "law" was the weakest of all and, thus, the least likely to pass constitutional muster. The mandatory scheme under which the defendant had been sentenced seemed so out of line with the underpinnings of *Furman* that the LDF thought the case would surely succeed. Although *Fowler's* positive resolution probably would not have much impact (few states possessed mandatory laws), it could provide some indication of the Court's post-*Furman* approach to capital punishment and further buttress the group's 1972 victory.

Again it was Amsterdam who led the LDF into the legal battle, writing its brief and later arguing the case. In general, he saw *Fowler* as an opportunity to "consolidate and widen *Furman*" (Bedau 1977). To that extent, his legal arguments encompassed those made in 1972—especially that capital punishment was incompatible with evolving standards of decency. They also were geared toward the mandatory law at issue. In particular, he claimed that the North Carolina system was essentially the same as pre-*Furman* schemes, that it allowed and even encouraged the same "arbitrary" and "selective" imposition because prosecutors exercised discretion in trying defendants. For example, had Fowler's prosecutor decided to offer a plea bargain or reduce the charge to second-degree murder, he would not have received death.[12]

As LDF attorneys prepared for *Fowler*, they received some disturbing news: in early March 1975, U.S. Solicitor General Robert Bork filed a seventy-eight-page amicus curiae brief in support of capital punishment. This was troublesome to the extent that the solicitor general's voice often carries great weight with the justices (Segal 1991), but it was perhaps most disturbing because it was rather bizarre. For starters, the federal government had stayed out of the 1972 cases, probably viewing them as matters of state concern only.[13] Now, under Bork, it was asserting a "federal" interest in the matter. Doing so certainly reflected the Justice Department's more adamant views on the subject. Just two months before Bork filed the brief, attorney general designate Edward Levi announced that the death penalty can only be a deterrent to crime if it is "quickly enforced and acceptable to the community" (Charlton 1975). The decision to file the brief also represented the personal wishes of Bork (Bronner 1989a, 82). To his way of thinking, state legislatures had acted, and it was "inappropriate for [the] Court to substitute its judgment for [theirs]." Bork firmly believed that the death penalty had deterrent value. Indeed, in his brief he relied quite heavily on Ehrlich's as of yet unpublished study.[14]

The other unusual aspect of the brief was that it did not address the core issue of the case: North Carolina's mandatory law. Rather, Bork sought to address the larger issue of whether death penalties constituted cruel and unusual punishment (Weaver 1975b). In making his plea for judicial restraint (and, concomitantly, for reconsideration of *Furman*), he wrote that the government was far more favorable to Georgia's type of laws than to North Carolina's mandatory scheme because it had been devised in essence by a court, not a legislature. In an odd twist, then, Bork's brief supported capital punishment, but it did not really condone North Carolina's practice.

Bork's presence in *Fowler* complicated the LDF's task. In the past, its death penalty litigation had been difficult enough, what with constitutional history and public opinion working against it, but at least it faced adversaries—state attorneys—with largely parochial interests (that is, upholding their states' laws), varied legal skills, and little experience before the Supreme Court. Now, Bork had upped the ante. The LDF would face a skilled opponent, who approached litigation in much the same way it did—as a means to bring about broad policy change. LDF attorneys did, however, have time to prepare a response to Bork. The justices did not schedule *Fowler* for argument until 30 March, ordering orals for 21 April 1975, apparently awaiting the return of Justice Douglas, who had been hospitalized with a stroke since New Year's Eve (Weaver 1975b).

With Douglas back, LDF staffers could breathe a sigh of relief; their fifth vote appeared intact. Still they had to respond to Bork's brief, in particular, to his claim that the "empirical judgment" about deterrence on which some of the *Furman* opinions rested should be reevaluated in light of Ehrlich's study. Recognizing that they could not afford to lose a single vote, five days before orals Amsterdam submitted a reply brief containing Pasell and Taylor's (1976) study, which seriously questioned the data, methods, and assumptions of Ehrlich's research.

On 21 April, the day of orals in *Fowler*, the scene in the courtroom was nothing short of dramatic. As three attorneys—Amsterdam, North Carolina Deputy Attorney General Jean Benoy, and Bork as an amicus—waited to make their presentations, Justice Douglas, "who had left the hospital to be there," entered in a wheelchair (Oelsner 1975). The stakes were high: at this point thirty-one states had restored capital punishment and 253 people sat on death row. Though North Carolina's mandatory sentencing scheme was unique, it was clear that the Court's decision would have a major, if symbolic, impact on the future of the death penalty.

The drama of the setting was apparently unmatched by content of the orals. One observer wrote that "the argument was not quite so emotional as the issue." Perhaps this was because Justice Douglas, an active participant in past cases, asked no questions during the ninety-minute session; perhaps the justices had heard it all before and had already staked out their positions. Indeed, during orals, Stewart appeared unpersuaded that mandatory laws wiped out the "freak-ishness" that so concerned him in 1972. Even Bork seemed rather subdued. After enunciating his basic contention that "capital punishment is constitu-tional," he did not once mention the issue of deterrence or the Ehrlich study.[15] All in all, the case looked like another "winner" for the LDF. The lines seemed to be holding.

The morning after orals, Douglas checked into a New York hospital, missing conference discussion on *Fowler*. When the justices deadlocked at 4–4, they decided to reschedule it for argument the next term (Weaver 1975c). The Court's decision, or more aptly nondecision, made front-page news. The effect, though, was not good news from the LDF's perspective: states could continue to sentence to death persons accused of a wide array of offenses. Death row populations would continue to grow.

Because the justices could not decisively rule on *Fowler*, the fate of the death penalty remained uncertain. As a result, during the summer of 1975, petitions for review continued to pour into the Court. The justices did not quite know how to handle these appeals. The four dissenters in *Furman* thought they lacked the votes to make any substantial inroads into the 1972 decisions; the liberals seemed equally distraught in part because one of their own was becoming less and less a functioning member of the Court. From his hospital bed in late July, Douglas asked his clerks to "[t]ell Justice Brennan to pass on to conference that I am unsettled as to what disposition to recommend in the capital cases. On the new capital cases that have come this term I am undecided whether to affirm or deny" (Urofsky 1987, 195). The inference was clear to even his closest allies: Douglas's days on the Court were numbered. On 12 November 1975, this suspicion was confirmed: after thirty-six years of service, Douglas resigned.

The question of his successor was of substantial interest to the LDF; with Douglas gone, the Court was apparently deadlocked 4–4 on capital punishment. But it did not have to wait long: just sixteen days after Douglas retired, John Paul Stevens was nominated to fill the position (Abraham 1985, 323).

A NEW COURT AND NEW CASES:
TO *GREGG V. GEORGIA* ET AL.

LDF attorneys did not know what to make of Stevens. While some women's groups opposed him because of his stance on the Equal Rights Amendment, the LDF had little to go on—the new justice had never ruled on a death penalty case. The LDF did know that his vote, while not a sure thing (as was Douglas's), was necessary to keep *Furman* alive. And it recognized that it would not have to wait long to find out where he stood. When Stevens arrived at the Court, fifty appeals, most of which were brought by the LDF, were pending.

Because some of the justices were anxious to resolve the capital punishment question, Burger called a "special Saturday session" to examine the petitions for certiorari in mid-January 1976. At that time, the justices agreed to try to clarify the Eighth Amendment issue as it applied to the range of new laws. They also agreed that they would take only murder cases. Apparently, though, there was some disagreement over which petitions they should grant. In *The Brethren*, Woodward and Armstrong suggest that Burger "wanted to hear the most brutal" murder cases, but he could not muster three supporting votes. Rather, "a consensus emerged that the Court should take only relatively straightforward cases where the facts were clear and presented no side issues, such as racial prejudice" (Woodward and Armstrong 1979, 431). This squares with what the justices did: on 22 January, Burger issued an order to review five capital murder cases from North Carolina, Louisiana, Texas, Florida, and Georgia, involving six defendants, three of whom were black and three, white. Including *Fowler*, the Court would resolve six disputes.

As table 4-3 indicates, the facts of these cases and the laws under which the defendants received their death sentences varied substantially. Two involved mandatory schemes: *Roberts v. Louisiana* and *Woodson and Waxton v. North Carolina*. The latter was a duplicate of *Fowler* in that the state mandated death for murder and rape. The Louisiana law at issue in *Roberts* was distinct because it contained a mercy provision under which a jury could reach a verdict of guilt on an offense lesser than murder. The Florida, Georgia, and Texas cases (*Profitt v. Florida*, *Gregg v. Georgia*, and *Jurek v. Texas*) involved variations of the ALI code. They mandated bifurcated proceedings and stipulated guided discretion standards for sentencers. Florida's law specified both mitigating and aggravating circumstances; Georgia's only codified factors in aggravation. Texas's was something of a mixed bag, as it required that the jury respond to statutorily defined questions posed by the judge rather than to specified circumstances.

FORMULATION OF ARGUMENTS AGAINST CAPITAL PUNISHMENT

Given the wide array of laws and facts involved in the cases, it seemed that the Court was sending a signal to all concerned that it was intent on dealing with capital punishment in its totality. If this was so, the message was not lost on LDF attorneys, who had sponsored three of the five cases (*Jurek*, *Woodson*, and *Roberts*). Now the ball was back in their court: Could they duplicate the impressive victory in *Furman*?

TABLE 4-3. The 1976 Death Penalty Cases

Case	Facts	State Law
Gregg v. Georgia (428 U.S. 153)	Gregg was convicted of murdering and robbing two men who had picked him up while hitchhiking.	Bifurcated trial after which the jury weighs evidence in mitigation and aggravation. The Georgia law specifies 10 aggravating circumstances; factors in mitigation are not codified. Automatic appeal to state supreme court.
Jurek v. Texas (428 U.S. 262)	Jurek was convicted of murder (by strangulation and drowning), while committing a forcible rape.	Bifurcated trial after which attorneys may introduce any relevant evidence for/against a sentence of death. The judge, then, presents the jury with questions (2–3) that are defined by law. If a unanimous jury responds positively, judge must sentence defendant to death.
Profitt v. Florida (428 U.S. 242)	Profitt was convicted of murder (by stabbing) during the course of a burglary.	Same as Georgia law, except specifies 8 aggravating and 7 mitigating circumstances.
Roberts v. Louisiana (428 U.S. 325)	Roberts was convicted of murder during the course of a robbery.	Mandatory death for first-degree murder. But under a provision for "responsive verdicts," juries are to be instructed on second-degree murder. They can reach a verdict of guilt on a lesser offense.
Woodson and Waxton v. North Carolina (428 U.S. 280)	Woodson and Waxton were convicted of murder while committing armed robbery.	Mandatory death sentence for first-degree murder.

On one level, achieving that goal seemed well within reach. Though they had lost Douglas, the LDF seemed assured of at least four votes: most indicators of judicial voting suggested that White, Stewart, Marshall, and Brennan would stick by *Furman*. Since the stimulus (capital punishment) was the same, constrained microlevel theories of judicial behavior would predict an identical response. Doctrinal analysis also led to the conclusion that the *Furman* plurality would remain intact: an examination of law review articles published between 1972 and 1974 reveals a consensus that Stewart and White would reject new state efforts to restore the death penalty.[16] One article (Butler 1973, 937) stated that "if the Justices concurring in *Furman* hold to their opinions . . . it is likely that at least some . . . sections [of the Georgia law] will be struck as unconstitutional."[17] Some even posited that one or two of the 1972 dissenters "would bend to the precedent of *Furman* and vote against any new imposition of capital punishment" (Irvin and Rose 1974, 189; Ehrhardt et al. 1973). As former Justice Goldberg wrote (1973, 367), "In view of legislative reconsideration of the matter, it is pertinent that a decisive majority of the Court expressed personal abhorrence of the death penalty."

At another level, though, things had changed since *Furman*, and not for the better for the LDF. For starters, its attorneys would have to capture the vote of Stevens, or at least one of the dissenters, while keeping the plurality intact. They also would have to find some way of coping with the hostile post-*Furman* environment while retaining some semblance of the evolving standards argument. Finally, they would have to deal with a skilled and policy-oriented adversary, the solicitor general, while maintaining a focus on the individual components of the state laws.

Navigating this course was the chief responsibility of Amsterdam and the LDF staff. While other attorneys (public defenders) were involved, they were fully prepared to follow Amsterdam's lead. After all, this was the man who had won *Furman* in what was "generally regarded as a masterpiece in advocacy" (Mann 1984, 62). No reason existed to abandon ship now and, it appears, no one did: in the final analysis, all five briefs followed an identical approach. First, they sought to demonstrate that each element of the new laws retained some measure of discretion (and, thus, of arbitrariness), and second, they reiterated claims made in *Furman* that the death penalty constituted cruel and unusual punishment.

Table 4-4 outlines the basic arguments presented by all attorneys. Almost all the briefs devoted far more attention to the first major claim—the discretionary nature of the laws—than to the others. In so doing, they raised the same objection: each stage of the death penalty process is so dependent on discretion that it will inevitably perpetuate the same sort of arbitrariness condemned in *Furman*. All attorneys then went through their respective death procedures (from prosecutorial decision through executive clemency) to demonstrate how discretion crept into the process. Each marshaled different evidence to support this contention, with the briefs filed in *Jurek* and *Profitt* providing the greatest contrast. In the former, LDF attorneys made their most universal, broad-based arguments. Though they cited case- and state-specific examples, the brief itself was full of statistics, citations to law review articles and to social science research, and far-reaching statements about capital punishment. The *Profitt* brief was more narrow. Rather than stressing social science evidence, Profitt's counsel (public defenders) supported their claims with trial testimony, examples of other Florida cases, and the like. The remaining submissions fell somewhere in between, mixing data and social science evidence with case-specific information.

Abolitionist attorneys handled the second part of the argument, that death penalties constituted cruel and unusual punishment, in a similar fashion. The *Jurek* brief set out the claim in its entirety; it was, in essence, an amalgam of everything the LDF had put forth to date on the subject: that the death penalty is "an absolute penological failure"; it is "so abhorrent to contemporary American processes of justice that the discretionary operation of those processes has demonstrated its repudiation in the most eloquent manner, by saving from execution all but a bare sample of the culprits whose conduct . . . [made] them eligible for [it]"; and it is "the source of an always arbitrary and frequently discriminatory infliction of death that can be decently viewed only as an enduring cause of national shame" (*Jurek*, Brief for Petitioner, no. 75-5394). The brief supported each of these assertions with data, citations to law reviews and social scientific studies, and precedents. It was, in short, a tour de force statement of abolition. The other four submissions merely cited the LDF briefs in *Jurek* and *Fowler* and explained that "to avoid burdening this Court with repetitive matters, petitioner adopts and incorporates the argument put forth in [the *Jurek*] brief" (*Gregg*, Brief for Petitioner, no. 74-6257, 35).

As a whole, then, the abolitionist attorneys tried to walk a fine line between different issues. They attempted to demonstrate that Stewart's and White's observations about the arbitrariness of the pre-*Furman* statutes were relevant to and dispositive of those newly enacted. They also sought to meet Burger and Powell's criticism that they lacked sufficient empirical evidence to prove the validity of these arguments. Finally, they tried to avoid, as best they could, grounding their arguments wholly on the "evolving standards" approach, without contradicting the position they took in *Furman*.[18]

TABLE 4-4. Arguments in the 1976 Capital Punishment Cases

	Gregg	Jurek	Profitt	Roberts	Woodson
DEFENDANTS' ARGUMENTS					
1. Discretion inherent in all laws continues to perpetuate the arbitrary infliction of death sentences.					
A. Prosecutorial discretion in charging and plea bargaining					
Law reviews	Yes	Yes		Yes	
Other state capital cases		Yes	Yes	Yes	Yes
Precedent	Yes				
Other attorney briefs		Yes		Yes	Yes
B. Discretion of trier at guilt phase					
Law reviews		Yes			
Other state capital cases				Yes	
Precedent		Yes	Yes		
Trial transcripts			Yes	Yes	Yes
C. Discretion of sentencer[a]					
Law reviews		Yes			
Other state capital cases			Yes		
Trial transcripts			Yes		
Data/social science evidence		Yes			
D. Appellate review					
Other state capital cases	Yes		Yes		
E. Executive clemency					
Law reviews	Yes	Yes			Yes
Other state capital cases			Yes		
Data/social science evidence		Yes			
2. Capital punishment amounts to excessive cruelty					
Law reviews		Yes			
Precedent		Yes			
Data/social science evidence		Yes			
Other attorneys' briefs	Yes		Yes	Yes	Yes

THE PROPONENTS OF CAPITAL PUNISHMENT

As was the case in 1972, the abolitionists' adversaries were not organized interests but state attorneys. Georgia, Texas, and California (as an amicus curiae) again argued for capital punishment and now were joined by lawyers from North Carolina and Florida. The tone and emphasis of their briefs,

TABLE 4-4 *(continued)*

	Gregg	Jurek	Profitt	Roberts	Woodson
STATE ATTORNEYS' ARGUMENTS					
1. Discretion is meaningful, not arbitrary					
A. Limited to only the most abhorrent of crimes	Yes	Yes	Yes	Yes[b]	
B. Appellate review is effective	Yes				
C. Defendants fail to connect discretion to arbitrariness		Yes			
2. Death penalty serves a legitimate purpose	Yes		Yes		
3. Capital Punishment is not cruel and unusual	Yes	Yes	Yes	Yes[c]	Yes
A. Analysis of the Constitution, intent of framers		Yes			Yes
4. Judicial restraint			Yes		Yes
5. Not racially discriminatory			Yes		

[a]Not applicable in mandatory cases.

[b]This was a very short brief because "[t]he State of Louisiana [did] not feel that it should take the time of the Court to again discuss the merits or demerits of capital punishment per se.... This question has been thoroughly briefed and discussed by the United States ... and the State of Louisiana adopts" its arguments.

[c]This argument was implied (*Roberts* 1976, Brief for Respondent, no. 75-5844, 24).

however, were far different than those tendered in *Furman*. In 1972 states mostly refuted LDF arguments. Here they altered their strategy: although they responded to LDF charges of arbitrariness, they presented new claims and approaches. In short, they added an offense to complement their defense.

Unlike their opponents, though, the states took the offense in distinguishable ways, pursuing various avenues of inquiry with very little overlap among them (see table 4-4). Some tried to refute point by point the argument that discretion necessarily leads to arbitrariness. Others returned to constitutionally driven claims about the intent of the framers and the plain words of the document. Still others maintained that the new laws served legitimate governmental purposes and urged the justices to exercise judicial restraint. Yet, aside from detailing their own states' laws, attorneys did articulate one major point of agreement: that the evolving standards prophecy of *Furman* had failed to emerge; to the contrary, the public and their representatives had defined "decency" by their complete support of renewed capital punishment.

California and the U.S. government filed amicus curiae briefs in support of the states. The first largely reiterated the claims brought to light by the parties, adding little new information. However, Solicitor General Bork's brief was a wholly different story. It was unusually long for a governmental brief—134 pages including appendices—and its content was most significant. If *Jurek* was the abolitionists' tour de force, Bork's brief was the proponents' counterpart.

At its core, Bork's argument was, simply put, that "death" is not a constitutionally "different form of punishment and should not be reviewed under a standard more robust than that of any other criminal penalty." To make this claim, Bork embarked on a long discourse, consisting of four interrelated parts. In the first, he canvassed familiar terrain—the intent of the framers, the history of the Eighth Amendment, and precedent—and concluded that all these factors reinforced the view that capital punishment per se is constitutional. The second and third parts served to tie that point to his broader conclusion. He began with the view that "it is inappropriate for this Court to substitute its judgment about the propriety of the death penalty for that of legislatures," particularly when those laws serve a legitimate function and are accepted by the community. Bork's purpose here was surely to urge the exercise of judicial restraint. Recognizing that some already had rejected that broad position, he argued more concretely that "several of the empirical observations by the Justices who concurred in *Furman* require reassessment in light" of the data he had presented. To wit, Bork engaged in a fairly detailed discussion of deterrence, public opinion, and the like. In particular:

• He cited many of the same studies as did the LDF; for example, to substantiate the claim that the public accepts capital punishment, he referred the justices to Vidmar and Ellsworth's (1974) research (see table 4-2), which attempted to demonstrate just the reverse contention.
• He pointed out that in 1972, White and Stewart both claimed that the "legislative will is not frustrated if the [death penalty] is never imposed"; but, in light of massive restoration, Bork argued, "the legislative will is frustrated unless the death penalty is imposed" (*Gregg*, Brief for United States, no. 74-6257, 60–62).
• He met head-on White's concern that capital punishment is an unproven deterrent because it is so seldom invoked. Bork reiterated Ehrlich's findings and included an appendix that described in some detail the scholarly debate over the issue; he implied that while "moratorium" was in effect, homicide rates had skyrocketed.
• He sought to demonstrate that capital sentencing was not racially biased. His review led him to conclude that the data could be read to show that racially biased sentencing was not occurring and that even if it was

appearing in the aggregate, it was the microlevel (that is, the case) on which the justices should focus: "[T]he possibility of racial discrimination in the selection or imposition of a particular punishment depends strictly upon the facts and circumstances of the case."[19]

In the final section of his brief, Bork devoted substantial space to refuting the LDF's basic contention that arbitrariness still exists in the new capital laws. In so doing, he zeroed in on the argument's key weakness by pointing out that discretion does not necessarily lead to arbitrary treatment. In fact, he asserted that "arbitrariness" and "freakishness" are not even apt terms to describe the criminal justice system because it is, inherently, a system based on disparities: "Is it freakish when an individual is sentenced to five years imprisonment rather than three, when the statutory maximum is life imprisonment?" To argue such, in Bork's view, one would have to claim that "death is different," and the only way one could make such an argument was through the Eighth Amendment. However, as he stated at the beginning, the amendment did not support such a conclusion.

Bork had written a tidy brief, with a clean and logical argument, the ingenuity of which did not escape the LDF attorneys. Surely they recognized that this was the strongest argument presented by the pro-death forces. And they wasted no time in filing a reply brief, which largely addressed the middle portion of Bork's argument. They lambasted the solicitor general's (and the state attorneys') interpretation of the scholarly research. In particular, they asserted that "it was plainly irresponsible to suggest [that increases in homicide rates] are attributable to any 'judicial moratorium'"; that the U.S. "government's . . . citation [to Schuessler's (1952) study on deterrence] is disturbing" because it ignored findings to the contrary within the research; that the government was in error when it asserted that Ehrlich had "remedied" the defects of his unpublished study. They sought to convey to the justices that the government had used the social scientific studies selectively, ignoring the balance of their conclusions (*Jurek*, Consolidated Reply Brief, no. 75-5394, 6).

All in all, the briefs had the makings of a hostile confrontation. With Bork calling the abolitionists' arguments "strange," full of "speculation," and "begging of questions," and the LDF responding that his claims were "disturbing," "notably lax," and "baseless," the kid gloves had come off. Whatever sense of decorum had characterized the *Furman* proceedings seemed lost in *Gregg*. The stakes had gotten too high.

ORALS IN *GREGG* ET AL.

The emotion of the briefs crept into oral arguments on 30–31 March 1976. The format itself was a bit unusual: because Amsterdam was arguing the first two cases (*Jurek* and *Roberts*), the Court gave him one hour, with the states replying during the next. That hour may have been the longest in Amsterdam's career. Although the justices gave him some leeway to explain how the laws worked in theory and in practice, they relentlessly attacked the core of his argument—that discretion led to arbitrary treatment. To make matters worse, the most vehement critic appeared to be Justice Stewart, as revealed in the following exchange:[20]

> *Stewart:* Mr. Amsterdam, doesn't your argument prove too much? In other words, in our system of adversary criminal justice, we have prosecutorial discretion; we have jury discretion . . . ; we have the practice of submitting to the jury the option of returning verdicts of lesser included offenses; we have appellate review; and we have the possibility of executive clemency. And that is true throughout our adversary system of justice. And if a person is sentenced to anything as the end product of that system, under your argument, his sentence, be it life imprisonment or five years imprisonment, is cruel and unusual punishment because it is the product of this system. This is your argument, isn't it?
>
> *Amsterdam:* No.
>
> *Stewart:* And why not?
>
> *Amsterdam:* It is not. Our argument is essentially that death is different. If you don't accept the view that for constitutional purposes death is different, we lose that case, let me make that very clear.

Apparently, by the time Amsterdam made that last point—that "death is different"—he was quite vehement, speaking "loudly" to the Court (Oelsner 1976c).

The justices also peppered the state attorneys with questions, but of a much more informational nature. Many, including Stevens, wanted to know how their codes worked and who was being sentenced under them. The one outburst of emotion came from the Texas attorney general when he proclaimed, "This Court is not the keeper, any more than Amsterdam is, of the social values, the conscience, the moral standards of the people" of this country. As one observer summarized, "Some of the questions of the justices indicated the challengers of capital punishment may face a more difficult task" than they did in 1972 (Oelsner 1976c).

If the first day of orals was tough for abolitionists, the second was far worse. On 31 March, the Court heard arguments from California and the United States as amici curiae in all four cases; from Amsterdam and North Carolina in *Woodson*; and, finally from the attorney in *Gregg*.[21] The justices continued to ask many questions, but Bork and Amsterdam were the focus of their attention. The solicitor general was particularly prepared and eloquent and certainly as firm in his views as was Amsterdam. He wanted the justices to see that his opponent's position ("death is different") made little sense under the Constitution and that, in fact, neither did the justices' opinions in *Furman*. In support of this, Bork cited study after study on the Constitution, juries, discretion, deterrence, and so forth.

More interesting, though, was that Bork's presentation "brought unusually blunt questioning" from Burger, Blackmun, and Powell—three *Furman* dissenters—who made no bones about where they stood on the issue. Just as Bork was winding down his presentation (his time was up), Justice Powell said: "Mr. Solicitor General, you haven't had an opportunity to address in your oral argument the issue of deterrence. I recognize, of course, that the statistical data can be construed in various ways, and I would agree that it is perhaps not controlling or conclusive. Yet I would invite your attention to some figures and then ask you a question." At this point, Powell read a series of statistics from a 1973 FBI report, which pointed to a 43 percent increase in murder rates. Powell then suggested: "It is perfectly obvious from these figures that we need some way to deter the slaughter of Americans. . . . Would you care to comment, elaborate, or state your views with respect to the deterrent effect, if any, of the death sentence?" In asking this question, or, more pointedly, making this statement, Powell gave Bork an extra five minutes. Beyond this, it opened the door for a discussion of the deterrence issue from the prosecutorial perspective. Bork (1990, 275) later described the exchange in his autobiography:

> My time expired and I was turning away from the lectern when Justice Powell said he would like to ask me a question. Controlling his emotion over the incidence of murder with some difficulty, he recited the number of killings annually in America and then asked me to comment. It was a deliberately given license to make any additional points I wished in the form of a comment on his statement. I have never heard a question from the bench I liked more.

While the justices handled Bork in a sympathetic way, they accorded Amsterdam precisely the opposite treatment. They attempted to punch holes in every one of his claims, letting nothing slide by. Quips from Burger (for example, "Mr. Amsterdam, would you argue for abolishing the jury system" because of some "irrational acquittals"?), Blackmun, and Powell were not unexpected. More troublesome moments arose when Burger and Powell returned to the point raised by Stewart the previous day:

> *The Court:* Your argument is that death is different. This is where you must end up, as yesterday when Mr. Justice Stewart asked you the question. And your answer has to be that death is different. And if it isn't you lose.

Amsterdam: This is absolutely correct. If death is not different, we lose on every argument we have got.

The Court: If one wanted to argue retribution, one could say that the victims whom you never mention have already lost.

Amsterdam: What did you say?

The Court: I say if one wanted to argue retribution, one could say that the victims whom you never mention have already lost.

Amsterdam: If one wanted to argue that the system of killing [the defendants] was retributive, yes, but there is no rational retributive justification for killing people who killed . . .

The Court: I guess you missed my point. I mentioned victims of the four defendants.

Amsterdam: Yes. Victims are unquestionably—

The Court: Dead.

So, it seemed, were the LDF's arguments.

THE 1976 DECISIONS

Amsterdam, some say, had not been at his best; one account holds that the justices were disturbed by his presentation and demeanor: "Brennan, Stewart, and White were all upset at Amsterdam's self-righteousness. Amsterdam had lectured them, and at one point, had even bordered on being rude to Blackmun" (Woodward and Armstrong 1979, 434). Whether this affected White and Stewart is unknown at present. But we do know is that on 2 April, the LDF lost the overall cause. In a 7–2 conference vote, the justices agreed that capital punishment was not unconstitutional per se. This was not unanticipated; after all, only Justices Brennan and Marshall had taken the opposite position in *Furman*. What was also eminently clear was that the LDF would lose at least three of the other cases: the majority voted to uphold the guided discretion laws of Georgia, Texas, and Florida. Conference discussion on the mandatory schemes was somewhat less focused, with the outcomes uncertain as several justices passed; yet a majority had voted to strike at least North Carolina's.

Evidently, Burger assigned Justice White the task of preparing majority opinions in all five cases, a puzzling choice in as much as he had been in the minority in the North Carolina case; thus Brennan as the senior member of the plurality should have made the assignment.[22] By this time, however, Brennan and Marshall were so "discouraged" that they were paying little attention to vote counts. So Stevens, Stewart, and Powell took it upon themselves to talk to Burger. When

TABLE 4-5. Coalitions among Justices in the 1976 Capital Punishment Cases

Justice	Guided Discretion			Mandatory	
	Tex.	Ga.	Fla.	N.C.	La.
Stewart	MU	MU	MU	MS	MS
Stevens	MU	MU	MU	MS	MS
Powell	MU	MU	MU	MS	MS
Burger	MU	MU	MU	DU	DU
White	MU	MU	MU	DU	DU
Rehnquist	MU	MU	MU	DU	DU
Blackmun	MU	MU	MU	DU	DU
Brennan	DS	DS	DS	MS	MS
Marshall	DS	DS	DS	MS	MS

Note: MU = majority to uphold law; MS = majority to strike law; DU = dissent to uphold; DS = dissent to strike.

he was not "very responsive," Stewart went to White, who in turn "formally submitted all five cases back to conference for reassignment."

On 5 May, Burger called a new conference for that purpose. Votes had by now solidified into the three coalitions shown in table 4-5: one composed of Burger, Blackmun, Rehnquist, and White voting to uphold all the laws; one of Brennan and Marshall voting to strike all five; and a third of Powell, Stewart, and Stevens held the Court at bay, voting to eliminate mandatory death penalties but upholding those with guided discretion. This triumvirate prevailed, and it was decided that they would write for the majority in all five cases; the others would concur and dissent where appropriate. To draft these majority opinions, a somewhat daunting task, the trio divided the work. Stevens would summarize the facts; Powell would use his dissent in *Furman* to demonstrate that the death penalty did not violate the Eighth Amendment; and Stewart would have the difficult task of explaining the Court's decision, in particular, why guided discretion was compatible with *Furman* and *McGautha* but mandatory imposition was not.

THE WAIT

Naturally the LDF could not have known the outcome of conference or of the internal politicking among the justices. As the Court labored, though, its attorneys were undeniably concerned. In fact, it appears as if abolitionists made some attempts to ignite the political environment in the hopes that it would affect the justices' opinions. Four days after orals, the *New York Times* highlighted Reidel's (1976) study (see table 4-2) and its conclusion that "blacks and other nonwhites are now more likely [under the new laws] to receive the death penalty" (*New York Times* 1976a). On the same day, columnist Tom Wicker (1976) commented on the results of Zimring, Eigen, and O'Malley's research (1976) on "murder in Philadelphia," concluding that since the study "showed no clear reason why some murders received mandatory life sentences and others got short prison terms, there probably could be 'no clear indication of special moral turpitude to warrant mandatory death' for some murders but not for others."

The success of these efforts was quite limited. A Gallup poll taken at the end of April 1976 indicated that 65 percent of Americans favored capital punishment for murder; 28 percent were opposed; 7 percent had no opinion (see figure 4-2). This amounted to a near-record level of support (unparalleled since the 1950s) made more dramatic by the fact that just ten years before, most Americans favored abolition. Given such levels of support, it is not surprising that Democratic and Republican presidential front-runners Carter and Ford echoed the sentiment.[23] Hence, if the justices were at all interested in the opinions of the populace, there was no question as to where it stood. Despite the efforts of abolitionist groups and writers to relay information and data, Americans—Democrats and Republicans, young and old, men and women—strongly supported the retention of death penalties.

THE DECISION

On 2 July 1976, in what one reporter (Oelsner 1976d) described as a "somber and dramatic session," the justices announced their opinions in *Gregg* et al. The occasion was anything but dramatic for abolitionists; by this time, some probably recognized that they were going to lose. Now it was a question of degree: How damaging was the defeat? Accounts in the popular press suggested a loss of some magnitude. Virtually all reports started on a similar note: "[T]he Supreme Court ruled by a vote of 7 to 2 that the death penalty is not inherently cruel or unusual" (Oelsner 1976d). For most Americans, this was all they needed or wanted to know; the United States would not be joining the growing list of abolitionist nations. But the over two hundred pages in the *U.S. Reports*, amounting to twenty-four majority, dissenting, and concurring opinions, revealed a far more complex picture.

Let us begin with the plurality of Stevens, Stewart, and Powell, whose votes swung the Court in favor of guided discretion and against mandatory imposition. In essence, their opinions in *Gregg*, *Profitt*, and *Jurek* were virtually identical in that they were composed of two major sections: the first a discourse on why capital punishment per se is not unconstitutional and the second on why the particular law in question was constitutional. The broad Eighth Amendment issue was most fully explored in *Gregg*. Here, the justices borrowed heavily from Powell's dissent in *Furman* and from Bork's brief. They sought to demonstrate that precedent, history, and the intent of the framers all mitigated against Amsterdam's position. Using the solicitor general's arguments (and some from the state attorneys), they also indicated that evolving standards of decency did not support an abolitionist outcome, nor did judicial restraint. Finally, they adopted the rather controversial position that death penalties serve the legitimate governmental functions of retribution and deterrence.

In exploring the validity of the state laws, it was no coincidence that the Court led off with *Gregg*; it was clear that they thought the Georgia law the better of the three because it allowed for the greatest consideration of the particularized circumstances of the case. Yet this was not to the detriment of the others: the guided discretion schemes of Texas and Florida also eliminated the possibility of wanton and freakish discretion inherent in the *Furman* laws and, thus, the possibility of arbitrary treatment. They saw nothing in the LDF's briefs and arguments to convince them otherwise. It all boiled down to a simple matter of logic for Stewart, Stevens, and Powell: the basic "constitutional infirmity" of the 1972 laws was that their "unbridled discretion" led to arbitrariness. Since the new plans called for guided discretion, for a consideration of the particularized circumstances of the case, and for appellate review, chances for arbitrary imposition had dissipated considerably.

Justices White, Burger, Rehnquist, and Blackmun concurred. Writing for Burger and Rehnquist, Justice White again reiterated the hole in Amsterdam's argument: he had "overstated" the view that the new laws necessarily produce arbitrary results. The justice, in fact, called that a "naked assertion," one "untenable" and "absent facts." Given his opinion in *Furman*, White also felt some need to reconcile his position on the deterrent question. In 1972 he had found death penalties to be uncredited deterrents because they were so infrequently imposed. Here, he simply stated that "I cannot conclude at this juncture that the death penalty . . . will be imposed so seldom and arbitrarily as to serve no useful penological function."

Brennan and Marshall filed dissents. Brennan's was quite short, filled with quotes from his opinion in *Furman*. His conclusion was also the same: "I therefore hold . . . that death is today a cruel and unusual punishment prohibited" by the Constitution. Marshall's was a longer discourse focused mainly on the purpose of capital punishment. He challenged the majority's position that it serves legitimate governmental ends and criticized it for relying on the Ehrlich study, which "is of little, if any, assistance in assessing the impact of the death penalty." He concluded that it is an "unnecessary" and "excessive penalty forbidden" by the Constitution.

Brennan's and Marshall's opinions smacked of resignation; they, like the LDF, had lost on the key points. Even in *Roberts* and *Woodson*—cases they "won"—they merely reiterated their view that capital punishment per se is unconstitutional. The plurality writers—Stewart, Powell, and Stevens—though, went to some length to justify their position that mandatory laws were invalid while those calling for guided discretion were not. In short, they approached the task in much the same way as they did in *Gregg*. They began with an examination of history, which revealed that Americans generally regarded mandatory penalties as "unduly harsh and unworkably rigid." They then tried to demonstrate that such penalties were also inconsistent with the spirit and letter of *Furman*: they do not reflect contemporary values, they do not replace "wanton" discretion with "objective standards," and they do not permit for the consideration of case-specific circumstances.

White, Rehnquist, Burger, and Blackmun dissented, with the first two writing at length. In White's view, the mandatory schemes freed capital punishment of the problems he outlined in *Furman*; mandatory penalties would not be seldom imposed, discretionary, or arbitrary. He also felt that judicial restraint called for the Court to uphold the laws. Rehnquist lambasted the plurality's reading of American history, noting that it failed to demonstrate a rejection of mandatory sentencing. Moreover, he found the scheme consistent with *Furman*, in part because it called for appellate review.[24]

REACTIONS TO *GREGG*

On one level, the Court's opinions in *Gregg* et al. were as confusing and varied as they were in *Furman*; there was no definitive majority opinion. The signal sent out, though, was far clearer: five agreed that mandatory laws were "out" and guided discretion was "in." The states knew generally what they could and could not do. This was not so after *Furman*.

It is, thus, interesting to note that the reactions to *Gregg* were somewhat murkier than they were to *Furman*. In 1972, most analysts recognized that the Court's decisions did not outlaw capital punishment but asserted with equal vigor that the justices would strike future attempts to restore. After 1976, there were some who were willing to wager guesses at the effect of *Gregg*. The secretary of state in California said that "in light of the . . . ruling 'we anticipate that the California death penalty statute will be held constitutional.'" Philadelphia's mayor called the decisions "a giant step in favor of the safety of our citizens" (Goldstein 1976). Jimmy Carter supported "the direction in which the Supreme Court has gone." Even some scholars were now terming the decisions "inevitable." As one wrote, between 1972 and 1976 the Court "stepped to the sidelines . . . to observe without comment this new flurry of political activity." In *Gregg*, the justices simply "respected these national trends" (Loh 1984, 266–67).

Others, however, were more uncertain than ever. As one scholar wrote: "The reactions of law review critics, editorial writers, political candidates, and leaders of various interest groups were confused and mixed" (Combs 1980, 14). Another commented that "no seamless web of logic united the Supreme Court's opinion on capital punishment. . . . [T]he decisions create a nightmare for those seeking immutable principles to explain the Court's behavior and predict its future deliberations" (Murchison 1978, 535).

Abolitionist attorneys expressed the most puzzling views of all. One might have expected them to condemn the Court with much the same vigor as they had praised it in 1972. But this did not occur. Their predominant public response was one of achievement and pride. In 1976, Greenberg did not stress the loss (and, thus, the fact that the LDF failed to achieve its original objective) but noted the positive gains of the campaign to date: as a result of LDF cases, thousands of "lives were spared" and the number of crimes for which capital punishment was applicable had been reduced. The next year, he said that while "the prospects . . . of an across the board abolition of the death penalty are exceedingly dim," the campaign had been quite effective. Immediately after the decision, Amsterdam concurred, noting that "[d]eath row seems to be cut in half. Exactly where that half falls is difficult to say." Indeed, only a handful of abolitionists would say, as did the U.S. Catholic Conference, that the decision "can only mean a further erosion of the value of human life and an increased brutalization of our society" (Goldstein 1976). In sum, many abolitionist attorneys tried to portray the 1976 decisions as ushering in a new stage of death penalty litigation, not as slamming the door shut. Greenberg asserted, "We intend to pursue a variety of other approaches to stop executions" (Goldstein 1976), because the decisions had "created a situation which possibly will allow further efforts, possibly over many years, to eliminate capital punishment" (Greenberg 1977, 659).[25]

IN THE AFTERMATH OF *GREGG:*
THE DEATH PENALTY THROUGH 1990

Despite the statements of abolitionist attorneys, it is undeniable that they lost the battle in *Gregg* and did so by a decisive 7–2 margin. The question remains, however, did they lose the war, as well?

On one level, the answer is obvious and affirmative. By upholding certain forms of capital punishment, the Court rejected the view that evolving standards of decency now condemn the death penalty. A majority of justices continue to subscribe to this position. As a result, the United States remains the only "Western industrial nation" still sanctioning legal executions (Zimring and Hawkins 1986, 3).[26] It is also true that the politics of abolition have changed little over the past decade or so. Since 1976, we have not elected a president who has taken a position against capital punishment. Some even suggest that one factor contributing to the overwhelming defeat of Michael Dukakis in 1988 was his support of abolition.[27] The majority of states also continue to sanction death penalties; in many of those affected by *Gregg* et al. (for example, states with mandatory laws), legislators quickly amended them to conform to the decision (Bowers 1984).

Why virtually all candidates—Democrats and Republicans alike—running for state and federal offices continue to support capital punishment seems clear: it is a popular position. Public opinion has never been clearer; today more citizens favor capital punishment than ever (see figure 4-2). This creates a vicious cycle of sorts for the abolitionist cause: "[M]indful of mounting concern about crime, of public opinion polls overwhelmingly supporting execution, and aware of the electoral fate of Governor . . . Dukakis . . . many politicians quickly embrace capital punishment" (Malcolm 1989).

All these indicators lead to the conclusion that the LDF lost not only a battle involving capital punishment but the larger war of abolition as well—all indicators, that is, but one: the number of executions. After *Gregg*, many anticipated massive use of the death penalty. Yet this has not occurred, even though death row populations, as revealed in figure 4-3, have surpassed all previous levels. Between 1977, when Gary Gilmore died before a firing squad (despite the efforts of the LDF and ACLU),[28] and 1990 states have executed over 140 individuals (Stanley and Niemi 1992, 32).[29] Such low numbers, in comparison to the burgeoning death row populations across the country, may reinforce Amsterdam's view that Americans seem to want capital punishment in theory but not in practice. This may be true in part, but it is an oversimplification. Low execution rates may indicate some level of discomfort with legally mandated death; yet they also are a testament to the efforts of abolitionist attorneys across the country, who have labored diligently to prevent massive executions.

PULLING VICTORY FROM THE JAWS OF DEFEAT?

After *Gregg*, attorneys (from the LDF, ACLU, public defenders' offices, and volunteers) tried to keep moratorium alive by continuing to provide representation to as many on death row as possible; they were, by necessity, reverting to a

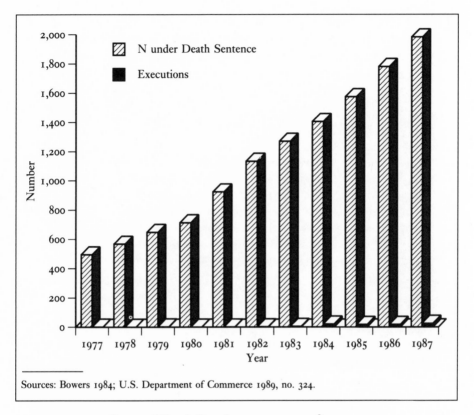

FIGURE 4-3. Status of Death Row Inmates, 1977–1987

pre-*Furman* strategy. In Neier's words: "[T]he major thing [we want] to try and do is block executions. If that means going to court, to the legislature, or making a lot of fuss, we'll do that" (Schwed 1983, 153). Thus, abolitionist attorneys persisted, bringing hundreds of cases after *Gregg*.[30] If they could not keep moratorium alive, at least they could narrow the scope of capital punishment in application.

On what grounds were they appealing? In the fifty-two U.S. Supreme Court cases decided with some opinion through the 1989 term, attorneys were using *Gregg* to challenge procedural practices adopted by states. In fact, as noted in table 4-6, post-1976 cases generally centered on three questions involving the imposition of the death penalty by juries and judges:[31] Upon whom can decision makers confer a sentence of death; who can make the decision between life and death; and what factors should sentencers consider in their deliberations? Despite the increasingly conservative propensity of the Supreme Court in areas of

TABLE 4-6. Capital Punishment Cases, 1976–1989 Terms

S.Ct. Cite	Case Name (Term)	Issue	Outcome
WHO CAN IMPOSE THE DEATH PENALTY?			
100/2382	*Adams v. Texas* (1979)	Scrupled jurors	Defendant
105/844	*Wainwright v. Witt* (1984)	Exclusion of a juror	State
105/2633	*Caldwell v. Mississippi* (1984)	Jury as "final" sentencer	Defendant
106/1758	*Lockhart v. McCree* (1985)	Absolutely opposed jurors	State
106/2464	*Darden v. Wainwright* (1985)	Absolutely opposed jurors	State
107/2045	*Gray v. Mississippi* (1986)	Scrupled/absolute	Defendant
107/2906	*Buchanan v. Kentucky* (1986)	Death-qualified for co-defendant	State
108/2273	*Ross v. Oklahoma* (1987)	Juror challenge/composition	State
109/1211	*Duggar v. Adams* (1988)	Jury as "final" sentencer	State
110/1227	*McKoy v. North Carolina* (1989)	Unanimous jury/mitigation	Defendant
ON WHOM CAN DEATH BE IMPOSED?			
97/2861	*Coker v. Georgia* (1976)	Rapists	Defendant
100/2382	*Beck v. Alabama* (1979)	Lesser included offenses	Defendant
102/2049	*Hopper v. Evans* (1981)	Lesser included offenses	Defendant
102/3368	*Enmund v. Florida* (1981)	Robbers	Defendant
104/3154	*Spaziano v. Florida* (1983)	Lesser included offenses	State
106/689	*Cabana v. Bullock* (1985)	Application of *Enmund*	State
106/2595	*Ford v. Wainwright* (1985)	Insane prisoners	Defendant
107/1676	*Tison v. Arizona* (1986)	Nonkiller with reckless mental state	State
107/2716	*Sumner v. Shuman* (1986)	Prison inmate (mandatory)	Defendant
108/2687	*Thompson v. Oklahoma* (1987)	Under the age of 15	Defendant
109/2934	*Penry v. Lynaugh* (1988)	Mentally impaired/retarded	Mixed
109/2969	*Sanford v. Kentucky* (1988)	Under the age of 16	State
WHAT FACTORS CAN BE CONSIDERED?			
97/1197	*Gardner v. Florida* (1976)	Nonrefuted pre-sentence report	Defendant
98/2954	*Lockett v. Ohio* (1977)	Limit on mitigating factors	Defendant
98/2977	*Bell v. Ohio* (1977)	Limit on mitigating factors	Defendant
100/1759	*Godfrey v. Georgia* (1979)	Overly broad aggravating factor	Defendant
102/869	*Eddings v. Oklahoma* (1981)	Limit on mitigating factors	Defendant
102/1856	*Zant v. Stephens* (1981)	Invalidated aggravating factor	State
103/2733	*Zant v. Stephens* (1982)	Invalidated aggravating factor	State
103/3418	*Barclay v. Florida* (1982)	Aggravating factor	State

TABLE 4-6 *(continued)*

S.Ct. Cite	Case Name (Term)	Issue	Outcome
104/871	*Pulley v. Harris* (1983)	Comparative proportionality review	State
105/2727	*Baldwin v. Alabama* (1984)	Limit on discretion	State
106/1669	*Skipper v. South Carolina* (1985)	Limit on mitigating testimony	Defendant
106/1749	*Poland v. Arizona* (1985)	Aggravating factor	State
107/837	*California v. Brown* (1986)	Jury charge (no "sentiment")	State
107/1821	*Hitchcock v. Dugger* (1986)	Limit on mitigating factors	Defendant
107/2529	*Booth v. Maryland* (1986)	Victim impact statement	Defendant
108/546	*Lowenfield v. Phelps* (1987)	Jury instructions/ aggravating factor	State
108/1853	*Maynard v. Cartwright* (1987)	Overly broad aggravating factor	Defendant
108/1860	*Mills v. Maryland* (1987)	Consideration of mitigating factors	Defendant
108/1981	*Johnson v. Mississippi* (1987)	Invalidated aggravating factor	Defendant
108/2320	*Franklin v. Lynaugh* (1987)	Mitigating factor	State
110/1078	*Blystone v. Pennsylvania* (1989)	Consideration of mitigating factors	State
110/1190	*Boyde v. California* (1989)	Jury instructions/ mitigating factors	State
110/1257	*Saffle v. Parks* (1989)	Jury instructions/ mitigating factors	State
110/3047	*Walton v. Arizona* (1989)	Aggravating factor	State
110/3092	*Lewis v. Jeffers* (1989)	Overly vague aggravating factor	State

OTHER

97/2290	*Dobbert v. Florida* (1976)	Sentencing under old law	State
103/3383	*Barefoot v. Estelle* (1982)	Stays/psychiatric testimony	State
107/1756	*McCleskey v. Kemp* (1986)	Race discrimination	State
109/2207	*South Carolina v. Gathers* (1988)	Prosecutorial statement	Defendant
109/2765	*Murray v. Giarrantano* (1988)	Counsel for indigents	State
110/1441	*Clemmons v. Mississippi* (1989)	Federal Court review	State (in result)
110/1717	*Whitmore v. Arkansas* (1989)	Standing	State
110/1880	*Delo v. Stokes* (1989)	Habeas corpus	State
110/2223	*Demosthenes v. Baal* (1989)	Habeas corpus filed by parents	State
110/2822	*Sawyer v. Smith* (1989)	Retroactivity	State

criminal law generally (Epstein, Walker, and Dixon 1989), at least up until the 1989 term,[32] its answers to these questions had the effect of narrowing the scope of capital punishment and thus its application.

The first question is who is eligible for execution. By 1976, most states had eliminated the death penalty for all but convicted rapists and murders. In a series of cases, the Court limited capital punishment to felony murders only (Murchison 1978). Among the most important was *Coker v. Georgia* (1977), in which it eliminated death for rapists. Given the LDF's long history and involvement with these sorts of cases, *Coker* was particularly satisfying to the group.[33] Likewise, on the issue of who can impose death, the Court has generally clung to its decision in *Witherspoon*. While it limited this ruling (for example, in *Lockhart v. McCree* [1986]), it is still true that "the death penalty may not be imposed if the jury that assesses it was selected so as to exclude anyone who expressed general objections to capital punishment or religious or conscientious scruples against it" (Whitebread and Slobogin 1986, 637). Finally, through 1990, the Court took a very serious look at aggravating and mitigating circumstances, narrowing and broadening the scope of the circumstances in ways suited to abolitionists' preferences. As we already know, the death penalty cannot be made mandatory or applied in a randomized fashion. But, at least through 1988, the Court struck down factors in aggravation that were overly broad or vague and scolded trial court judges for excluding consideration of certain circumstances in mitigation (see table 4-6).

On the whole, then, the Court had been willing to limit the application of *Gregg* to a narrowly defined set of circumstances. We see this at a doctrinal level as well as at a more aggregated one.[34] In table 4-7, we compare how the justices voted in criminal cases (excluding capital punishment) with those involving the death penalty. Over the past decade or so, some justices were far more willing to find for the defendant in capital cases than in general criminal disputes. Brennan and Marshall never voted with the prosecution in death penalty litigation, though they did so on a few occasions in other cases. More important—at least in the context of the day—was the voting of the *Gregg* plurality. Powell, Stewart, and Stevens showed a rather strong propensity to support defendants in capital cases; since 1986, Stevens voted against them only once. Their votes (coupled with Brennan's and Marshall's) led the 1976–80 Court to take a markedly more liberal position in capital cases than in others (88 percent for the defendant versus 43 percent). This gap narrowed during the 1981–85 period largely due to Stewart's resignation (and the ascension of O'Connor) and Blackmun's continued conservatism. By 1986, though, the margin widened again; Blackmun shifted to the left; Stevens, Marshall, and Brennan continued to support defendants. When they were joined by Powell, a slim majority emerged. All in all, the

TABLE 4-7. Comparison of Justices' Voting in Capital and Non-Capital Cases Involving Criminal Justice Issues, 1976–1989: Support for Defendants by Natural Court

Justice	1976–80[a] % Capital	%Non	1981–85[b] %Capital	%Non	1986[c] %Capital	%Non	1987–89[d] %Capital	%Non
Blackmun	88	37	56	40	88	52	87	54
Brennan	100	89	100	79	100	97	100	88
Burger	63	33	11	15	—	—	—	—
Kennedy	—	—	—	—	—	—	16	13
Marshall	100	92	100	83	100	93	100	92
O'Connor	—	—	22	17	25	7	9	28
Powell	88	49	29	22	50	14	—	—
Rehnquist	0	19	11	8	13	0	9	13
Scalia	—	—	—	—	13	10	9	28
Stevens	100	62	61	63	100	59	96	61
Stewart	88	54	—	—	—	—	—	—
White	63	48	17	24	13	7	22	22
Total	88	43	33	25	50	14	26[e]	22

Note: Justices may not have participated in all cases.
[a]N of capital cases = 8; N of non-capital cases = 90.
[b]N of capital cases = 18; N of non-capital cases = 108.
[c]N of capital cases = 8; N of non-capital cases = 29.
[d]N of capital cases = 23; N of non-capital cases = 54.
[e]This percent is a bit deceiving. During the 1987–88 terms, the Court supported defendants in 42 percent of the 12 capital cases; in its 1989 term, it decided 11 capital cases, supporting the defendant in only 1. Its voting in non-capital cases hardly changed (18 percent v. 22 percent).

Court supported defendants in nearly half of the forty-one capital cases compared to only a third of the 265 other criminal cases. Hence, at least through 1990, the majority of the justices adapted, in practice, a watered-down version of Amsterdam's position: death is different, if only somewhat.

THE "DOWNSIDE": *MCCLESKEY V. KEMP*

The discussion above should not be read to suggest that the LDF and its allies won every post-*Gregg* battle. Far from it. The foothold afforded by *Furman* continued to erode. *Gregg* remained authoritative, and its constitutional gloss remained wholly opposed to abolitionists' central concerns. Though capital cases (through the 1988 term) fared better than the average criminal dispute, abolitionists lost about 50 percent of their cases. Some of these involved fairly narrow procedural issues (see table 4-6), but others—particularly those decided in 1987–91—were quite devastating. Perhaps the one with the most far-reaching implications was the LDF-sponsored *McCleskey v. Kemp* (1987).

On the surface, *McCleskey* does not seem very significant; if anything, it appears more akin to *Maxwell v. Bishop* and other, older LDF cases involving claims of racially based discrimination on behalf of southern rapists. In fact, except for the crime (murder, not rape), the parallels are quite striking: the state of Georgia convicted Warren McCleskey, a black man, of murdering a white police officer and sentenced him to death. In defending McCleskey, the LDF argued that he had been the victim of racial discrimination in sentencing and, thus, of "arbitrary" treatment. To bolster this contention, it introduced the results of a study indicating clear sentencing disparities in capital cases when a black was accused of murdering a white. Since this sounds oddly familiar, perhaps even a reversion to an old, unsuccessful strategy, why was the 1987 case of *McCleskey v. Kemp* hailed as the "most important capital case in a decade," a "landmark decision" (Kaplan 1988)? Put in different terms, what differentiated *McCleskey* from the older LDF race-based cases?

One factor was the increasing attention members of the U.S. Supreme Court were giving to the issue around the time of *McCleskey*. In the mid-1980s many justices addressed the question of capital punishment in a variety of public forums. Ironically, it was the "media-shy" Chief Justice Burger who initiated this public dialogue with a 1985 comment, suggesting that the capital appeals process was too protracted, making executions virtually impossible to implement. This statement was followed by refutations from Justice Marshall. In September 1985 and again in March 1986, he chastised his colleagues for their "bizarre willingness to ignore standard procedures as [they] please in order to bring about speedy executions" (Taylor 1985; *New York Times* 1986a). Others complained not about the procedures but about the "strain" of capital litigation. In 1986 addresses, Blackmun and Powell spoke of the "excruciating agony" of last-minute appeals that had "haunted and debilitated the Court" during the previous term; Blackmun actually called the 1985–86 years "perhaps the most difficult" of his tenure (*New York Times* 1986b). Given the sentiment expressed by members of the Court, *McCleskey* arrived at a critical juncture. Some members of the Court's center, in particular, were expressing concern over capital cases; perhaps now they would consider the issue in a different light.

Another factor was the dimension of race per se. After *Gregg*, a spate of sophisticated, multivariate analyses purported to show obvious racial discrimination in sentences imposed under the post-*Furman* statutes. Two years after publication of Reidel's (1976) study, Bowers asserted that blacks were "grossly overrepresented" on death row (King 1978), a conclusion for which he later provided a good deal of statistical evidence (Bowers 1984; Bowers and Pierce 1980). After reviewing seventeen thousand murder cases in eight states, Gross and Mauro (1984) found rather dramatic differences between sentences meted out to those accused of killing whites versus blacks. These and other studies (for example, Radelet 1981; Zeisel 1981) received a good deal of media attention (for example, Joyce 1984; *New York Times* 1978a). One journalist (Greenhouse 1985c), in fact, claimed that "any statistical overview of capital punishment inevitably leads to race."

As important as those analyses were, a study conducted by professors David Baldus, George Woodworth, and Charles Pulaski moved to center stage. Their research started simply enough: in 1979, Baldus "dispatched" students to the state of Georgia to code attributes of all cases in which a "person [had been] convicted of murder at a guilt trial" between 1973 and 1978 (*McCleskey* 1984, 353; White 1987, 128). Like many others, he and his colleagues were interested in the relationship between such aspects as the victim's race, the defendant's race, and the sentencing decision. The LDF "learned [of the project ("The Procedural Reform Study")] and retained him" to conduct a second one. Entitled "Charging and Sentencing Study," it expanded the previous analysis. By the time it was completed, the data base consisted of 2,484 Georgia murder and non-negligent homicide cases from 1973–79 coded for some 230 variables. To analyze this mammoth amount of data, Baldus employed a multivariate technique, which allows researchers to demonstrate the effects of independent variables (such as race of the defendant or victim) on outcomes (such as decision to sentence to death).[35] It was, as one observer noted, "the most exhaustive study of racial discrimination in capital sentencing that has ever been conducted" (White 1987, 126).

Baldus's conclusions were dramatic. Among the most noteworthy were the following:

- The chances of receiving a death sentence were 4.3 times greater for defendants whose victims were white than for defendants whose victims were black.
- Of the 128 cases in which death was imposed, 87 percent (108) involved white victims.
- Prosecutors sought the death penalty in 70 percent of cases involving black defendants and white victims, but in only 32 percent in which both the defendant and victim were white.
- Black defendants were 1.1 times more likely than other defendants to receive death sentences.

Given the sophistication of the study, these findings were not readily accessible to the average person. Yet, as Greenberg wrote (1988, 74), "no matter how one looked at the numbers the unavoidable conclusion emerged that blacks who murder whites are sentenced [to death] significantly more frequently than defendants involved in cases of any other racial combination."

From the LDF's perspective, then, it was the Baldus study that differentiated *McCleskey* from previous cases (for example, *Maxwell*). Here, the LDF had a sophisticated, exhaustive demonstration that the laws condoned in *Gregg* were resulting in discriminatory sentencing.[36] In the abolitionists' view, the Court had struck down the old systems at issue in *Furman* because they were possibly resulting in arbitrary sentencing (Greenberg 1988, 74). Now they possessed evidence that the prophecy of *Furman* had concretely manifested itself in procedures sanctioned by *Gregg*. This was something, they thought, that even the *Furman* dissenters could not ignore.[37]

Thus, the LDF took the plunge: it filed a habeas corpus petition on behalf of McCleskey, based in large measure on the Baldus study.[38] A team of LDF attorneys (including Amsterdam) argued that he had been the subject of racial discrimination, as borne out by the research, and therefore the death penalty was "administered arbitrarily, capriciously, and whimsically in the state of Georgia." In essence, these attorneys asked the Court to strike capital punishment both on Fourteenth and Eighth Amendment grounds.[39]

This risk, albeit a calculated one, transformed *McCleskey* into the capital case of the decade. After *Gregg*, virtually every suit had attacked some procedural aspect of the post-*Furman* laws. Now, the LDF struck at their core, reasserting the big constitutional issues—discrimination and arbitrariness. A favorable decision could upset "the death sentences of all 105 convicted on Georgia's death row, and could affect the 36 other states with death penalty laws" (Moss 1987, 51); if the Court found racial discrimination in the Georgia system, massive resentencing might follow. Even more important, should the Court concur with the LDF, it might find capital punishment an inherently arbitrary form of sentencing, one that could never be imposed fairly.[40] This would, in effect, resurrect and extend *Furman*. On the downside, the possibility of disaster loomed large. As observers noted, this case could present the "last remaining generic" challenge to capital punishment (Greenhouse 1985c). In one blow, the Court could make it "virtually impossible" for defendants to win cases "based on statistical evidence of race discrimination." This would extinguish the remaining faint flame from *Furman*.

Things did not go well for the LDF in the lower courts. In a lengthy and detailed analysis of the methods, data, and assumptions of the Baldus study,[41] the district court firmly rejected all LDF claims emanating from the study, claiming that "the database for the study is substantially flawed, and the method utilized is incapable of showing the result of racial variables in cases similarly situated" (*McCleskey* 1984, 37). The following year, sitting *en banc*, the U.S. Court of Appeals for the Eleventh Circuit also held that the study failed to support the claim of discrimination, but its grounds were somewhat different. For one, it did not completely reject the Baldus study as poor social science; to the contrary, it accepted the findings, albeit in a manner adverse to the LDF's position. As it wrote,

> Viewed broadly, it would seem that the statistical evidence presented here . . . confirms rather than condemns the system. In a state where past discrimination is well documented, the study showed no discrimination as to the race of the defendant. The marginal disparity based on the race of the victim tends to support the state's contention that the system is working far differently from the one which *Furman* condemned. (*McCleskey* 1985, 899)

More significant (and more troublesome for defense attorneys) was its broader interpretation of the utility of statistical evidence. It suggested that even if the data were valid, they were insufficient to "support a conclusion that the race of *McCleskey's victim* in any way motivated the jury to impose the death sentence in *his* case" (1985, 899; emphasis added). Statewide discrimination was irrelevant to the defendant's specific case; discrimination must be found in the record of *his* trial.

Undeterred by these defeats—had they not lost *Furman* in lower courts?— LDF attorneys filed a certiorari petition in May 1985. Over a year later, in July 1986, the Court granted the writ, an indication that the case was "uncommonly troublesome."[42] With oral arguments scheduled for 16 October, the LDF prepared a brief that read like a social science journal article. After a concise review of the facts, attorneys launched into a detailed discussion of the Baldus study and of racial discrimination generally. They attempted to counter the Eleventh Circuit's view of the significance of the statistics, while simultaneously hammering home the extent of discrimination. One tack it took was to compare the use of data in capital cases with cases involving other issues: "Evidence of racial discrimination that would amply suffice if the stakes were a job promotion or the selection of a jury, should not be disregarded when the stakes are life and death" (*McCleskey*, Brief for Petitioner, no. 84-6811).

The state of Georgia devised an interesting counterattack. While it reviewed the district court's findings, it did not criticize the study per se;[43] to the contrary, it suggested that "statistics are a useful tool in many contexts." What it did instead was to reinforce the logic of the Eleventh Circuit, arguing that there "is no evidence to show that Petitioner's sentence in the instant case was arbitrary or capricious and no evidence to show that either the prosecutor or the jury based their decision on race," and "that there are simply too many unique factors relevant to each case to allow statistics to be an effective tool in proving discrimination" (*McCleskey*, Brief for Respondent, no. 84-6811).

Two amicus curiae briefs were filed in support of this position.[44] California suggested that LDF attorneys had "used statistics 'as a drunk man uses a lamp post—for support and not illumination.' " The other, written by the Washington Legal Foundation (WLF), a conservative public interest law firm, constituted one of the first times an organized interest group had opposed abolitionist efforts in a major legal battle. In its brief, WLF attorney Dan Popeo raised two major points. He suggested that if the Court adopted the LDF position, its decision would become the "source of disastrous upheaval for the entire criminal sentencing process." He also stressed that the LDF was "evad[ing]" the facts of the cases (and even some of the study's results) to try to "salvage" it.[45]

Oral arguments reflected these varying themes.[46] LDF attorney Jack Boger placed the greatest emphasis on the Baldus study, asserting that "this is not some kind of statistical aberration. We have a century-old pattern in the state of Georgia." His opponent simply countered that "statistical analysis is not appropriate . . . [because] you cannot come up with two similar cases. . . . [E]ach is unique." One observer (Taylor 1986) noted that the justices expressed varying degrees of skepticism about both arguments. The LDF was pressed hardest by Rehnquist, White, and Powell, all of whom seemed to take the position that racial discrimination could only be proved by looking at "McCleskey's particular jury." Conversely, Stevens, Scalia, and Marshall, in questioning the state attorney, were apparently unconvinced "that it would be virtually impossible to show race discrimination in death sentences through any kind of statistical evidence." O'Connor evidently was perplexed, twice calling the case "curious." She did, however, appear quite concerned with whether a Court holding in favor of the LDF would virtually abolish capital punishment. On the whole, then, the day was an uneven one. Unlike the *Gregg* orals, in which the outcome seemed quite clear, the justices did not give much away.

Neither side had to wait long, though, to find out where the Court stood: on 22 April 1987, it ruled against the LDF position. Writing for a five-member majority that included Rehnquist, O'Connor, White, and Scalia, Justice Powell acknowledged that the Court "has accepted statistics as proof of intent to discriminate," but only "in certain limited contexts" (*McCleskey* 1987, 1767). Capital punishment did not fall into any of those "contexts," at least at an aggregated level. Echoing the reasoning of the Eleventh Circuit, the Court held that it could not "infer" discrimination in a specific case based on statewide data. Pressing the point, Powell addressed the core of the LDF's thesis that the Baldus study provided the evidence to demonstrate the prophecy of *Furman*—freakish and wanton sentencing was now a reality. Powell expanded on his general theme, noting that "[a]t most the Baldus study indicates a discrepancy that appears to correlate with race. Apparent discrepancies are an inevitable part of our criminal justice system. The discrepancy indicated by the Baldus study is a far cry from the major systematic defects identified in *Furman*."

Justices Brennan, Marshall, Stevens, and Blackmun dissented, adopting various parts of the LDF's arguments. That the first three dissented was not at all surprising: Brennan and Marshall were firmly committed to eradicating capital punishment, and Stevens, albeit less extreme in his views, had sided with the two liberals far more often than not (see table 4-7). However, Blackmun was something of a surprise. Undoubtedly he had moved further and further away from the conservative wing of the Court, on capital cases in particular. Yet this was the same jurist who had adamantly rejected the Wolfgang study in *Maxwell*. Here, however, emerged a new Harry Blackmun—one apparently "sensitized to the vagaries of death penalty litigation." His departure from *Maxwell* was indeed dramatic; he asserted in 1987, "The Court sanctions the execution of a man despite his presentation of evidence that establishes a constitutionally intolerable level of racially based discrimination leading to the imposition of his death sentence" (*McCleskey* 1987, 1794).

McCleskey may have been the "biggest" capital case of the decade; surely it was a major loss for abolitionists, reinforcing the futility of pursuing racially based claims.[47] Despite predictions to the contrary, however, it was not the end of line.[48] Attorneys continue to bring capital punishment cases to the Court (see table 4-6), and they remain hopeful. When asked whether she could "offer any optimistic look for the future," one LDF attorney recently responded, "Absolutely, it's hard to do this work without one." An ACLU lawyer echoed the sentiment: "Ultimately, a generation down the pike, we will abolish this lingering throwback, this ghastly reminder of unenlightened times" (Gray and Stanley 1989, 297).[49] The key word here is "generation," thanks to the potent one-two punch in *Gregg* and *McCleskey*. Abolitionists may still fight technical, procedural bouts in court, but it seems that there will be no quick return—especially in light of the Court's most recent rulings—to the glory that was theirs after *Furman*.[50]

ANALYSIS: WHAT HAPPENED?

Abolitionist attorneys, inclined to paint a rosy picture of their movement, might emphasize that, except for the last several terms, the Court has been a hesitant advocate of capital punishment; its willingness to review even the smallest procedural questions has nearly led to a virtual moratorium. Beyond this, however, the picture darkens. Procedural hesitancy is just that—procedural. Without substantive qualms embedded in the law—as they were in *Furman*—the goal of abolition is only a distant hope.

The death penalty remains a legitimate form of sentencing in the United States, and states are making increasing use of it. If the LDF's goal was complete abolition (and its briefs and public statements indicate that it indeed was), the organization has not achieved its objective. One day, the LDF might win the war. Perhaps, as Justice Brennan (1986, 331) wrote, "a majority of the Supreme Court will one day accept that when the state punishes with death, it denies the humanity and dignity of the victim and transgresses the prohibition against cruel and unusual punishment." For now, however, it seems that the course of the battle turned in *Gregg* and the war was lost in *McCleskey*.

Why did abolitionist forces fail to eradicate capital punishment, especially considering their initial victory in *Furman*? Put into the context of our investigation, what happened between *Furman* and *Gregg*? To answer such questions, we consider a number of interrelated explanations.

THE COURT

In our quest to explain the "discrepancy" between *Furman* and *Gregg*, we need to consider the Court itself. Obviously, the Court's decisions did cause the shift in death penalty policy—the change from its recognized arbitrariness to its constitutional permissibility. The relevant question, however, is not whether the Court "explains" the failure of abolitionism—it, in some sense, undoubtedly must—but whether attorneys could have extended their victory in *Furman*, given the composition of the 1976 Court. On the one hand, we know that a personnel change occurred, and that it was not a positive one from the LDF vantage point. In Douglas it had a clear vote for abolition; in Stevens, an unknown who ultimately went against abolition. Hence, it lost a key player in a game in which every participant counted. On the other hand, the personnel change does not completely explain the policy shift. If it were the sole reason, *Gregg* should have been decided by a slim majority of five, with Stevens holding the swing position. As we know, though, seven voted against the LDF, two of whom—White and Stewart—shifted from their *Furman* postures.

Had abolitionists been able to retain the votes of White and Stewart, would they have won *Gregg*? Mathematically speaking, no; the vote would have been 5–4 against their position. Yet, as our discussion has made clear, logic and math seem to have little place in capital litigation. Along the way, for example, we saw an 8–1 anti–death penalty majority suddenly become a 6–3 pro–capital punishment coalition. In short, this seems to have been an area of the law in which some justices were open to persuasion from their colleagues and attorneys.

We emphasize "some" because there were, indeed, a few justices whose views were both more flexible and, in essence, more significant than those of the others. It is clear that Rehnquist and Burger were lost causes for abolitionists, just as Brennan and Marshall were for state attorneys. Conversely, White and, especially, Stewart were key players before and after *Furman*. Not only were their votes critical to any successful litigation campaign, but also their views seemed to carry a great deal of weight with the others. For example, in *Maxwell* eight justices voted to reverse death penalty laws on both grounds of standardless juries and unitary trials. In response to Douglas's strongly worded opinion, however, Stewart and White wrote a concurrence, disposing of the case on *Witherspoon* grounds. Two years later, this "concurring" opinion became the majority's position. The course of *Maxwell* and so many other cases depended on the votes and postures of Stewart and White. Put simply, with them, the LDF won its cases; without them, it failed. Extending that logic to *Gregg*, if abolitionists had been able to hold White and Stewart, as they had in *Furman*, the 1976 cases might have had a very different ending.

In fact, several different scenarios could have led to such an end, with the most likely one involving Stevens. It is almost foolhardy, in retrospect, to believe that Stevens would not have been a possible vote if Stewart and/or White had lured him in that direction. Surely we have reason, given his death penalty votes and opinions since *Gregg*, to suspect that the Ford appointee was (and is) at least somewhat sympathetic to the abolitionist cause. With a little lobbying from his senior colleagues, he might have been a fifth vote to strike the capital laws, not a seventh to uphold.

This is, obviously, conjecture, but it is conjecture based on an analysis of virtually every key legal development occurring before and since *Furman*. Such an examination leads to the following conclusions: based on their positions in *Furman*, White and Stewart were possible (if not probable) votes to strike the capital laws at issue in *Gregg*; if they had been inclined to cast their votes in that direction, they might have been able to persuade Stevens to follow their lead; in a 5–4 vote the Court would have overturned the new capital laws.

Thus, we are still left with the fundamental question of why the discrepancy exists between *Furman* and *Gregg*. But now we can address the question a bit more pointedly by asking why Stewart and White altered their views on capital punishment, and concomitantly, whether their votes were ever potential abolitionist votes in *Gregg*.

THE POLITICAL ENVIRONMENT

The bulk of the LDF's campaign against the death penalty was waged, except for a period in the mid-1960s, in a general climate of political hostility to its goal of ending state-sanctioned executions. Indeed, as its litigation reached the Supreme Court in the late 1960s, many environmental indicators pointed away from favorable—from its perspective—judicial resolution of the issue. Public opinion was dropping away from its abolitionist high point in 1966. Murders of public figures (for example, Martin Luther King, Jr., and John F. Kennedy) reinforced death penalty legislation already on the books and prompted new efforts promoting its extension. The Nixon administration came out, foursquare, in favor of the appropriateness of capital punishment. In fact, the Supreme Court, once a promising port for LDF arguments, was transformed by four early Nixon appointees. It was in this politically inhospitable environment, where myriad factors worked against its goals, that the LDF brought its most important capital cases before the Supreme Court.

Against this tide, however, the LDF continued its campaign. Fortified by its successes in the later Warren years—*United States v. Jackson* (1968), *Witherspoon v. Illinois* (1968), and *Boykin v. Alabama* (1969)—and undeterred by its early Burger period losses—*McGautha v. California* (1971) and *Crampton v. Ohio* (1971)—it continued to press its unpopular position through the federal courts. Then, with its stunning victory in *Furman v. Georgia* (1972), it seemed to have climbed to the top of the judicial mountain: for the first time in its history, the Supreme Court struck death penalty legislation on grounds sufficiently broad to suggest its ultimate legal demise. Again, it is critical to note that the LDF's accomplishment came in spite of a generally unfavorable political environment. The organization, the quintessential underdog working in an area of extreme disadvantage, had used the courts to secure its policy goal. Or so it thought. The Court's dramatic shift in *Gregg v. Georgia* (1976) demonstrated otherwise. Despite the LDF's procedural victories in a host of post-*Gregg* cases, the *McCleskey v. Kemp* (1987) decision made clear that, from a legal perspective, the organization had "lost" the war.[51]

Just as it is tempting to cede responsibility for this turn of events to the change in the Supreme Court's membership wrought by Douglas's departure, so too is it tempting to explain the LDF's loss in terms of the unfavorable political environment in which it brought its cases to the Court. There is no question that this environment was unrelentingly hostile to the organization's goals. Even though conservative groups did not mobilize in an organized way against the decision— as they did in the abortion case examined in the next two chapters—the *Furman* backlash was loud, quick, and broad based. Public opinion, generally supportive of capital punishment before June 1972, became even more so in the immediate aftermath of the decision. State legislatures across the country, and not just in the South, could barely wait to reconvene and pass new laws, which, given the *Furman* majority and informed commentary on it, were of dubious constitutionality.

Even the national government, hardly the primary definer and enforcer of criminal law in America, got into the act. The day after *Furman* came down, President Nixon seized on Burger's dissent in noting that the Court had not completely ruled out capital punishment. He subsequently sent to Congress a bill calling for the death penalty for certain federal crimes, a law modeled on the American Law Institute proposal of the late 1950s. After careful deliberation, the Senate approved the legislation and sent it to the House, where a segment of it was passed in 1974.

More significant, however, was the new aggressiveness shown by the Justice Department. Though Nixon's first solicitor general, Erwin Griswold, argued for the constitutional permissibility of capital punishment in *McGautha* and *Crampton* as an amicus curiae (at the invitation of the Court), the administration was not involved in *Furman*. Robert Bork, Nixon's last solicitor general and the man who held that office during the Ford presidency, took on the abolitionists with a vengeance, delivering a characteristically well-developed and biting critique in *Fowler v. North Carolina* (1976) and *Gregg* et al. Instead of meeting state attorneys general with minimal experience before the Supreme Court, the LDF now had to deal with a crafty and skillful advocate of the position they assailed. Further, there is evidence that the arguments proffered influenced the way some of the justices approached the resolution of *Gregg*.

Nevertheless, to explain the *Gregg* shift as the Court's reaction to a political environment clearly hostile to pushing ahead with the abolitionist implications of *Furman* proves both too much and too little. If environmental factors caused the Court to shift on this point, why did they not cause it to change its approach in other controversial issues of the day (such as abortion, church-state relations, or racial discrimination)? Indeed, why was the environment at the time of *Gregg* perceived to be more relevant than that four years earlier when *Furman* was decided? Politically, the contexts of *Furman* and *Gregg* were not substantially that different. In 1972, as in 1976, public opinion, state legislation, and the national administration clearly supported capital punishment. Yet the Court did strike the imposition of death even in that context. Although it may be argued that the state legislation passed on the heels of *Furman* altered the environment by demonstrating broad-ranging public support for capital punishment and by remedying the defects of pre-*Furman* statutes, LDF attorneys—armed with a battery of studies—made at least as plausible a showing of arbitrariness in their application and enforcement in 1976 as they did in 1972. Thus, what a majority saw as troubling in *Furman* remained present in *Gregg*. Though the "political environment"—especially Bork's efforts—probably contributed to the resolution of *Gregg*, it cannot be treated as determinative of it; it alone cannot explain the Court's about-face on the question of death.

GROUP STRATEGY

If neither the replacement of Douglas with Stevens nor the political environment in which the decision in *Gregg* was rendered can fully explain the LDF's loss in 1976, perhaps the organization itself set the stage for its own defeat. If so, it was not the result of a change in its staff, for Anthony Amsterdam guided the LDF litigation throughout the entire period. Nor was it a function of a transfer of organizational resources away from the capital punishment campaign: although it never received a majority share of the organization's budget, the funding of this litigation did not decrease after the victory in *Furman*. Nor was the *Gregg* defeat the result of insufficient legislative lobbying. Though the ACLU clearly did not, as it had pledged to do, carry the ball in this area, the *Furman* win was not predicated on legislative victories. Something other than these group-specific factors contributed to squelching the promise of *Furman*, namely the arguments and argumentational strategy the LDF used in its efforts to capitalize on its 1972 victory.

The strategic deficiencies start with the LDF attorneys' understanding of the *Furman* majority. Simply put, they overestimated the degree of their victory, treating the majority vote as if it were something of a monolith. It clearly was not. Although Brennan, Marshall, and Douglas (before his resignation) were solid votes to strike any capital law, White and Stewart were not. This fact was not completely lost on Amsterdam and his cohorts. Indeed, the research they commissioned on the application and deterrence of the death penalty was, in part, designed to reinforce the concerns these two justices expressed in their concurring opinions in *Furman*.

LDF attorneys, however, assumed that the presence of White and Stewart in the majority meant that their difficulties with the *Furman* statute—that infrequency of application eliminated its deterrent value and that its application was arbitrary, respectively—were rooted in the same basic concern as that of the more abolitionist justices—that "death was different" and, as a result, statutes imposing it had to be held to a higher than normal standard of review. In this, the LDF attorneys were not alone; the bulk of the scholarly legal community felt this way as well. Indeed, nowhere is this assumption more obvious than in Amsterdam's oral presentation in *Jurek* and *Roberts* when, in response to questioning from Stewart, he said: "Our argument is essentially that death is different. If you don't accept the view that for constitutional purposes death is different, we lose that case, let me make that very clear." The irony is that Amsterdam apparently thought this was exactly what White and Stewart thought; this is how he understood their 1972 opinions.

Amsterdam was, as *Gregg* et al. demonstrated, wrong. White and Stewart were concerned with the procedures and processes used in assessing the death penalty, but their concern was more about due process than cruel and unusual punishment. If their votes were to be won, Amsterdam had to capture them on the former rather than the latter grounds. By blasting the discretion inherent in the sentencing process, and by inextricably linking it to cruel-and-unusual-punishment concerns grounded in the notion that "death is different," he lost the two justices he needed the most. Once he lost on the broadly defined due process argument—and, amazingly, he told the justices that this was precisely the case—the only arrow he had left in his quiver was the "evolving standards of decency" argument. This could get the votes of Brennan and Marshall but not Stewart and White. Statistical data and social scientific studies could be used to address their due process concerns, but they could not be used to convince them that "death is different."

Bork seemed to understand this, or at least his arguments—both oral and written—read as if he understood. His argument was as brilliant as it was simple. First, death is not different, or at least not constitutionally so. It is explicitly and implicitly endorsed in the text of the Constitution and the body of constitutional history and practice. Only an act of supreme judicial activism could make death constitutionally different. Second, he emphasized that public opinion, in the aggregate, supported the death penalty. Even though the social scientific studies claimed that, when disaggregated, the data ultimately told a different story, Bork urged on the justices the "common sense" of the matter, that general public opinion and legislative action gave lie to the conclusions wrought by sophisticated statistical techniques. Finally, Bork leaned on the Ehrlich study to argue that the death penalty did have a deterrent effect or, at a minimum, it could be plausibly understood by legislators to have such an effect. Even if only the latter were true, judicial restraint would counsel deference to the states.

Bork's arguments, and Amsterdam's inability to counter them beyond the assertion that "death is different," drew Stewart and White to support the permissibility of capital punishment. Does this suggest that Amsterdam's position was inherently a losing one? Not necessarily. His mistake seems to have been that he thought *Furman* itself held that "death is different,"[52] and he framed the LDF's post-*Furman* strategy on that assumption. Although Amsterdam did not believe that *Furman* ended the war, he clearly thought he won it. What remained was a legislative and judicial cleanup campaign to stave off the onslaught of new legislation and maintain the moratorium begun in the late 1960s; if successful, such a plan would allow the death penalty to die of its own weight. He announced the LDF's three-fold strategy—lobbying (by the ACLU), litigation, and scholarship on the effect of the death penalty—at the 1972 LDF Conference at Columbia University. What this post-*Furman* approach lacked was a clearly articulated legal strategy beyond challenging new legislation on *Furman*. This begged an important question, though one Amsterdam had apparently resolved in his own mind: What did *Furman* mean?

Had Amsterdam been more critical of the LDF's success in *Furman* and less assured of his optimistic interpretation of that decision's meaning, he might have developed a multileveled litigation strategy more diversified and flexible than the "death is different"/"evolving standards of decency" argument he took to the Supreme Court in 1975. Such a layered judicial strategy, while continuing to employ the "death is different" line of argument, would not have treated it as the sole basis of the organization's legal appeal. Indeed, had more emphasis been placed on the kinds of practical, process-based arguments that characterized the LDF's pre-*Furman* litigation, it is conceivable that Stewart and White would have been less inclined to abandon the abolitionist position in *Gregg* et al. If the underlying principles of moratorium had been maintained as a plausible line of judicial attack, insuring that the number of bodies on death row continued to increase, these justices, and perhaps others like Stevens, Powell, and Blackmun, who time and further litigation showed to be sympathetic to some procedurally defined LDF concerns, would have been less inclined to replug the electric chair that had been unplugged, in reality, since 1967 and by law since *Furman*.

It is possible that the narrowness of the LDF's legal and strategic vision going into *Gregg*—the blind spots revealed and exploited by Bork in briefs and oral argument—was the result of the paucity of organized legal opposition to its abolitionist claims. Virtually no conservative groups mobilized to support, through legal argument and judicial participation, state reimposition of capital punishment after *Furman*. Bork's involvement in this issue came suddenly and late in the day, well after the LDF set its argumentational course. Perhaps if proponents of the death penalty had been more organized, had they mobilized legal arguments defending reimposition well prior to *Gregg* et al., the LDF would have been more self-critical of both the substance and scope of the arguments it was preparing to tender to the justices. We will never know. What we do know is that those arguments it took into the Supreme Court in March 1976 were inadequate to secure the outcome it desired.

A layered litigation strategy, which did not place primary or nearly exclusive emphasis on the absolute and immediate eradication of the death penalty, would have left LDF attorneys with more argumentational room before the Supreme Court. It would have allowed them to offer the justices, especially those committed to the constitutionality of the death penalty but leery of its actual operation, a way to strike laws or their application without confronting their essential acceptance of the punishment per se as constitutional. It would also have given the LDF a way to avoid the problem that all organizations using the courts to advance general policy concerns must face—that is, the tension between the cause and the client. In the realm of the death penalty, this tension—given the nature of the punishment—is especially acute. A litigation strategy that made use of a broadly based constitutional argument (the Eighth Amendment), but which also strongly urged less grand grounds of reversal, has the added utility of protecting, as best it can in the context of group litigation, the interests of both the organization and the client.

Use of such a strategy might extend the time frame required to achieve organizational goals (and, not inconsequentially, increase the costs of the group in pursuit of those goals), but it would provide a more varied palette to offer the justices and minimize the effects of adverse decisions. Given the badly splintered majority in *Furman*, such a strategy—by giving the middle justices something less global than complete abolition on which to grab—might have furthered LDF goals more readily than the "all or nothing" approach that Amsterdam presented the Court in *Gregg* et al. At a minimum, it seems that such a strategy merited discussion among group leaders. Because Amsterdam and his colleagues misinterpreted *Furman*, though, this is a strategy that they did not seem even to ponder. They were trapped by the "tyranny of absolutes," the belief that legal absolutes—here those seemingly secured in *Furman* (such as death is always different)—would enable them to avoid a more incremental path, in this instance away from state-sponsored executions. The tyranny of absolutes led them to go for the knockout punch in *Gregg* rather than continue a series of body blows that would ultimately knock the legal legs out from under the states. This may well have proved a fatal flaw in their effort to end capital punishment once and for all.

There is, of course, no guarantee that a layered argumentational strategy would have won *Gregg* et al. for the LDF. The *Furman* backlash was immense; the *Furman* majority was tenuous; and the Court had undergone an important change in personnel. However, given a political environment supportive of capital punishment at the time *Furman* was handed down, given the fact that Stewart and White were sufficiently leery of the death penalty to oppose it in 1972, and given that Stevens, though no Douglas, was no Rehnquist either, *Gregg* et al. were not lost causes from the start. These were cases that could have been won.

Winning them, however, would have required the LDF to mount an adroit post-*Furman* litigation strategy that made use of carefully constructed and layered arguments that could have spoken to all potential members of a favorable majority. This it did not do. Its loss in *Gregg* et al. paved the way for a further extended litigation campaign, one that time, the resumption of executions, and personnel changes on the federal courts rendered more arduous and problematic. In the end, it led to *McCleskey*, the frustration of the LDF's policy goals, and a revitalization of the death penalty as a constitutionally permissible punishment. Indeed, *McCleskey* cemented the *Gregg* loss; the LDF's moment formally passed. After coming out of *Furman* a doctrinal "winner," it proved unable to maintain the momentum of legal change. In terms of its stated goal—abolition of capital punishment—the LDF, once so close to victory, emerged as a legal "loser."

FIVE

. . . .

ABORTION I:

THE ROAD

TO *ROE*

In the summer of 1969, Norma McCorvey found herself pregnant.[1] As an unwed twenty-one-year-old, with no steady source of income, she wanted to obtain an abortion. She first approached her physician; he declined to help, citing a Texas state law that prohibited abortions not necessary to preserve a mother's life. She then went to a Dallas abortion clinic but "didn't like what [she] saw and decided [she] wasn't going to end up on the slab." Apparently giving up on the idea of attaining an abortion, she consulted with an attorney, Henry McCloskey, who handled adoptions. Upon hearing her story, McCloskey referred her to another attorney, Linda Coffee, who he knew was interested in pursuing a legal challenge to the Texas law.[2]

In December of 1969, McCorvey met with Coffee and her law school classmate, Sarah Weddington. They explained to her their plans to seek judicial nullification of the state's prohibition on abortion services and their need to find a woman who would serve as a plaintiff in a suit. When McCorvey agreed to help them, she became Jane Roe and the two attorneys launched their attack, later known as *Roe v. Wade*.

Seventeen years after Coffee and Weddington embarked on their legal odyssey, in June 1986 the state of Missouri enacted a law to discourage women from obtaining abortions. Though it did so on a number of grounds, the act's preamble best expressed its overall sentiment that "the life of each human being begins at conception" and that "unborn children have protectable interests in life, health, and well-being."

Reproductive Health Services and Planned Parenthood of Missouri, two clinics offering family-planning services, and several "health professionals" affected by the law's provisions immediately brought suit. Represented by Frank Susman, an attorney who had made quite a name for himself challenging some of Missouri's other attempts at limiting the right to choice, they argued that the law was unconstitutional, that its effect was similar to that in *Roe*.

Although the laws at issue in the Texas and Missouri cases differed, commonalities did exist. First, they shared a core concern: it is the business of the state to protect the unborn and, as a result, to regulate the right to obtain an abortion. Second, both were challenged in the Supreme Court of the United States, where attorneys made strikingly similar arguments against them. Roe's lawyers alleged that the Texas prohibitions abridged fundamental rights and liberties. Arguing for the clinics, Susman suggested the same, that Missouri's law amounted to a proscription on freedom of choice.

Similar laws, similar arguments, yet they resulted in wholly divergent outcomes: the Supreme Court struck down the Texas law but upheld Missouri's. Why it legalized abortion in *Roe* represents the core concern of this chapter. In chapter 6, we explore the rather dramatic legal turnabout manifest in *Webster v. Reproductive Health Services*.

THE SETTING: AMERICANS AND ABORTION THROUGH THE 1950S

"Make no mistake, abortion-on-demand is not a right granted by the Constitution. No scholar . . . has argued that the framers of the Constitution intended to create such a right." In making this statement, Ronald Reagan (1984, 16) sought to reiterate one of the pro-life movement's more recent battle cries—that our nation's founders failed to enumerate an affirmative right to an abortion and thus, by omission, sought to ban the practice. Of course, Reagan is right: the Constitution contains no specific reference to abortions. But that does not necessarily mean that the founders wanted to proscribe them. After all, abortions did occur in the 1700s: Americans knew of them[3] and some women even sought to obtain them.[4]

More to the point, research of the last few decades reveals that Reagan is correct to the extent that the framers may not have considered seriously the concept of "abortion on demand," yet they were aware of a thirteenth-century English common law doctrine called "quickening" (Means 1968). Under it, abortions were not considered criminal until the fetus "had manifested some

semblance of a separate existence: the ability to move" (Mohr 1978, 3).[5] Because only the woman herself could make this determination, prosecutions
were quite rare before or even after quickening (between the sixteenth and
eighteenth week).[6] Still, the framers did not repudiate the "quickening doctrine"
in the Constitution. If anything, Americans firmly adopted the pre- and post-
quickening distinction even after Britain abandoned it;[7] for instance, U.S. courts
relied on it during the founding period, with the most oft-cited example being
Commonwealth v. Bangs (1812). In that case, Massachusetts charged Isaiah Bangs
with performing an abortion. The judge dismissed the suit on the grounds that
the woman was not "quick with child at the time."

According to many experts, *Bangs* set the tone for the next four decades of
legal development. As Mohr (1978, 6) wrote, "Prosecutors took the precedent so
much for granted that indictments for abortion were virtually never brought into
American courts. Every time the issue arose prior to 1850, the same conclusion
was sustained: the interruption of a suspected pregnancy prior to quickening was
not a crime itself." Courts were not the only ones to adopt the doctrine. Between
1821 and 1841, ten states codified the pre- and post-quickening distinction,
enacting legislation that made the latter, but not the former, a crime. Exemplary
was Connecticut's 1821 statute, the first of its kind passed in the United States:

> Every person who shall, willfully and maliciously, administer to, or cause to
> be administered to, or taken by, any person or persons, any deadly poison,
> or other noxious and destructive substance, with an intention him, her, or
> them, thereby to murder, or thereby *to cause or procure the miscarriage of any
> woman, then being quick with child,* and shall be thereof duly convicted shall
> suffer imprisonment in newgate prison, during his natural life. (emphasis
> added)

The majority of states enacting legislation between 1821 and 1841 followed
Connecticut's example (Weinberg 1968); the remaining ones relied on the *Bangs*
precedent.[8]

That they did so led to a rather ironic situation in American policy toward
abortion. As Justice Blackmun (*Roe* 1973, 140) observed, it probably was easier
for a woman "to terminate a pregnancy" in the mid-nineteenth century than in
the middle of the twentieth. The home medical journals of the day provided
abortifacient information, with remedies ranging from bathing to "violent exercise; raising great weights; reaching too high . . . ; stroking on the belly; falls"
(Buchan 1816, 400, 403–4). Concomitantly, regular doctors (those who had
some medical training) knew how to perform abortions and faced a great deal of
"pressure" to do so, particularly to fix botched jobs started by women. As a
result, "abortion came out into public view; by the mid-1840s the fact that

Americans practiced abortion was an obvious social reality, constantly visible to the population as a whole" (Mohr 1978, 46). Signs of this were everywhere. Newspapers regularly published abortion advertisements placed by doctors and "irregulars" (those without medical training) offering their services; the market was flooded with "self-help" books; a growing number of "women's clinics" were willing to perform the surgery; and medical school professors began preparing their students "for the numerous abortion requests they would receive" (Sauer 1974, 54). By the mid-1800s, abortion was big business.

This explosion did not go unnoticed. While some applauded it, America's first full-fledged right-to-life movement was fomenting. Like most social movements, this one was composed and driven by diverse elements with equally divergent reasons for wanting to proscribe abortions.[9] By far, though, the "most visible interest group agitating for more restrictive abortion laws was composed of elite or 'regular' physicians" (Luker 1984, 15). They also were among the first to get involved. In 1857, at the urging of pro-life doctor and lawyer Horatio Storer, the American Medical Association (AMA) appointed a committee on criminal abortion to look into the subject. With Storer as its chair, the committee issued its report two years later: "Physicians have now arrived at the unanimous opinion that the fetus in utero is alive from the very moment of conception. . . . The willful killing of a human being, at any stage of its existence, is murder" (Wardle and Wood 1982, 31).

The AMA not only adopted this position but avowed to see it etched into law, mounting a two-prong campaign to do so.[10] On one level, it sought to educate the public about the evils of the procedure. To accomplish this, it enlisted the press, which was only too willing to publish "sensational accounts" of trials involving botched abortions (*Arizona State Law Journal* 1980; Olasky 1988).[11] Astutely, physicians also worked the paths of government. The AMA strenuously lobbied state legislators and sent copies of its resolution to the president of the United States and to all governors. It then enlisted the state medical societies to help lobby their respective legislatures (Wardle and Wood 1982, 31).

Unquestionably, the AMA's campaign succeeded. By 1910 (with a burst of activity in the 1860s–80s) every state followed its directive[12] and abolished the pre- and post-quickening distinction.[13] Though some variation existed among the laws,[14] they uniformly (in forty-two states) curtailed nontherapeutic abortions, generally those not necessary to save the life of the mother.[15] In addition, most enacted legislation to reinforce their pro-life policies. Twenty-nine, for example, prohibited the advertisement of abortion services.

The effects of this first wave of legislation were many. It forced courts to abandon the legally well-entrenched quickening doctrine and begin to uphold

prosecutions (the pace of which increased considerably). Perhaps more important, doctors achieved "a subtle transformation of the grounds of the debate. By
asserting that women had abortions because they were ignorant of scientific
knowledge, doctors shifted the focus of the debate from moral *values* to empirical
facts" (Luker 1984, 26). This preempted most grounds of potential critique:
those without formal medical training lacked the expertise to argue against the
doctors' position. The medical profession had convinced the populace that
abortion was a technical question best left to the experts.

THE SEEDS OF CHANGE (1930S–1960S)

Some have labeled the decades between 1930 and 1960 as a period of "silence"
on the subject of abortion. Among the citizenry, this was largely the case. The
issue was rarely discussed in the popular press,[16] and no public opinion polls
were taken on it. Nonetheless, it was starting to generate interest among some
elites, particularly doctors, lawyers, and other activists. At first, that interest was
located primarily in a "venturesome wing" of the birth control movement[17] of
the early 1900s, the National Committee on Maternal Health.[18] But it soon
branched out to one group within the medical profession: psychiatrists (*Arizona
State Law Journal* 1980, 106; Sloan 1988, 8). While they, of course, did not
perform abortions, increasingly other physicians consulted with them on "therapeutic" abortions, asking them to determine if the "mental" health of the women
would be greatly affected if they carried the fetus to term. Since this was a highly
discretionary issue—a judgment call—psychiatrists began to hold panels on the
subject at their conferences (Rosen [1954] 1967). After about a year of these
discussions, psychiatrist Harold Rosen held a symposium on abortion in 1953,
inviting psychiatrists, obstetricians, gynecologists, and clergy to contribute. Although these proceedings (and the compendium they generated, *Therapeutic
Abortion*) failed to garner significant public attention,[19] they did convince one
of the more prominent participants—Dr. Alan Guttmacher, president of the
Planned Parenthood Federation of America—that the issue would not disappear
so quickly and that his organization would need to contemplate some form of
involvement.

To this end, Planned Parenthood and the New York Academy of Medicine
held a conference in 1954, the proceedings of which it published in 1958
(Calderone 1958). It was by far the most significant event, to that date, on the
subject. Participants hailed from many walks of life (physicians, professors,
government officials, students) and, as such, the topic was covered from all

angles: legal and illegal abortions, death rates, indications for therapeutic abortions, psychiatric issues, and abortion versus contraception.

Based on the data presented—particularly on the number of and circumstances surrounding criminal abortions—participants issued the following statement: "[P]resent laws and mores have not served to control the practice of illegal abortion.... To keep on the books, unchallenged, laws that do not receive public sanction and observance is of questionable service to society" (Calderone 1958, 181). The symposium did not propose legislation to replace the old laws, but it did suggest that the following steps "would contribute to a material reduction of the high incidence of illegal abortions":

• gathering data on the motives of women seeking such abortions,
• establishing "consultation centers" for women seeking abortions,
• distributing more contraceptives,
• instituting sex education, and
• promoting a study of the issue by "authoritative bodies such as . . . the ALI [American Law Institute]."

By the decade's end, virtually all these suggestions were effectuated, including what would prove to be the conference's most important suggestion—that the American Law Institute get involved. Just a year later, at its May 1959 meeting, the ALI recommended liberalization of current abortion legislation. Section 207.11 of the proposed model code stated:

(1) *Unjustified Abortion.* A person who purposely and unjustifiably terminates the pregnancy of another otherwise than by a live birth commits a felony of the third degree or, where the pregnancy has continued beyond the twenty-sixth week, a felony of the second degree.

(2) *Justifiable Abortion.* A licensed physician is justified in terminating pregnancy if:

(a) he believes there is substantial risk that continuance of the pregnancy would gravely impair the physical or mental health of the mother or that the child would be born with grave physical or mental defect, or the pregnancy resulted from rape by force or its equivalent as defined in § 207.4(1) or from incest as defined in § 207.3; and

(b) two physicians, one of whom may be the person performing the abortion, have certified in writing their belief in the justifying circumstances and have filed such certificate prior to the abortion in the licensed hospital where it was to be performed, or in such other place as may be designated by law. (ALI 1959, sec. 207.11)

In its day, this code was radical, indeed. At the time, most states allowed abortions only to save the life of the mother; now, the ALI proposed an entirely new legal framework, significantly broadening the circumstances under which the procedure could be legally performed. The code was so "extreme," in fact, that the ALI did not adopt it until three years later, in May 1962. Yet the mere fact that the prestigious ALI had even contemplated the issue was, in itself, significant (Clark 1969).

THE MOVEMENT FOR CHANGE: THE 1960S

Even though portions of the medical and legal communities had begun to explore the abortion issue as the Eisenhower era ebbed, it had yet to interest the general public. Three independent events of the early 1960s worked to change this picture:

- the Sherri Finkbine saga, involving a television celebrity who had taken thalidomide, which focused attention on whether she had been right to obtain an abortion;[20]
- an outbreak of German measles in which the media squarely confronted the nation with the issue of whether women who contracted German measles early in their pregnancies should be able to have abortions;[21] and
- the beginnings of the modern feminist movement, heralded by publication of Betty Friedan's *The Feminine Mystique* in 1963, which served to "disseminate the idea of group oppression to women across the United States," with control over one's reproductive system as a component of that message. (McGlen and O'Connor 1983, 28)[22]

These events became the pegs on which a new and very public discussion of the issue would hang. In a real sense, they heralded the beginnings of the modern period of abortion politics. Still, despite all the publicity the issue was starting to attract, it remained for the average citizen something "nice" people did not discuss. Evidence of this abounds. A poll taken during the Finkbine episode, for example, indicated that while the public supported her efforts to obtain an abortion, only 8 percent approved of the procedure on demand (that is, for any reason) (Sauer 1974). Also, even though women were obtaining criminal abortions in vast numbers,[23] many were "ashamed" and "humiliated by the memory of their desperation" (Dworkin 1983, 73–75). Publication of *The Feminine Mystique*, though noteworthy, did little to allay these fears. Further, the established medical community remained silent. As late as 1965, the AMA refused to change its position on the subject, despite the urgings of some members that it endorse the ALI code (O'Toole 1965).[24] With women and doctors fearful of talking or taking any position, and the public in no mood to listen, it is not surprising that abortion reform went nowhere in the early 1960s. No state, save California, seriously considered it.[25]

THE FORMATION OF A MOVEMENT

Despite the relative lack of interest and discussion among the general populace, the events of the early 1960s—the adoption of the ALI code, the Finkbines' dilemma, the German measles epidemic, and the publication of *The Feminine Mystique*—all helped to plant the seeds for a social movement aimed at overhauling the nation's laws. Small abortion-oriented organizations were founded on both the West and East coasts, the women's movement began to take shape, and more established groups (the American Civil Liberties Union [ACLU], Planned Parenthood) began to take a serious look at the issue. Gradually, these strains would band together, however loosely, to fight for reform.

As illustrated in table 5-1, initially these forces worked in relative isolation, apparently not fully aware what the others were doing. Moreover, their memberships varied, as did their goals and tactics for achieving them. In New York, members of the medical and legal communities and of Planned Parenthood and the ACLU established the Association for the Study of Abortion (ASA) in the mid-1960s. Some, particularly Planned Parenthood's Guttmacher, wanted a vehicle by which "to promote legalization of abortion without committing the birth control movement as a whole . . . until there was little danger in taking this step" (Grisez 1970, 240). ACLU members also were looking for an outlet since their organization had yet to take a position, and the ASA turned out to be it. Reflecting the interests of its members,[26] ASA approached abortion cautiously: it had no intention of radicalizing the issue but sought to increase public awareness. As a result, it initially viewed itself as something of a clearinghouse on the subject—compiling vast amounts of data, arranging for public speakers, and mobilizing the medical and legal communities.

In marked contrast was the Society for Humane Abortions organized by Patricia Maginnis in California. When that state held public hearings on abortion reform in the early 1960s and many came out in support of legislation against abortion, Maginnis rallied her troops against the law on unique grounds: she thought all abortion laws should be repealed, that the service should be available on demand. To this end, the society engaged in some fairly radical tactics—dispensing abortion information, holding "self-abortion" classes, and crashing

TABLE 5-1. The Early Abortion Reform Movement, 1967: Participants, Goals, and Strategies

Organization or Individual	General Description	Goal/Strategy
Planned Parenthood[a] (Guttmacher since 1954)	Provide services, education, and information on contraceptives and family planning.	Produce change in existing laws through education and information.
Lawrence Lader (since early 1960s)	Writer/leader of abortion movement.	Repeal by showing unenforceability of the existing laws through referrals and the "politics of confrontation."
Association for the Study of Abortion (since 1964–65)	Single-issue focus on abortion.	Disagreement over strategies and tactics, but generally created to collect and disseminate information.
Society for Humane Abortions (since early 1960s)	Single-issue focus on abortion.	Repeal through encouraging civil disobedience and self-help.
National Organization for Women (since 1967)	Promote gender-based equality; eliminate discrimination against women.	Repeal by placing it under the rubric of women's rights; politics of confrontation.
Clergy Consultation Service (since 1967)	"Loose federation of autonomous abortion counseling services."[b]	Prevent botched abortions by referring clients to qualified physicians.
Bill Baird (since 1967)	Birth control advocate/clinic operator.	Repeal by offering services, engaging in civil disobedience.
American Civil Liberties Union (since 1967)	Defense of civil liberties.	Repeal through lobbying and litigation.
American Medical Association (since 1967)	Major representative of physicians in the United States.	ALI reform through education and information.

[a]Planned Parenthood announced its support for repeal in 1970.
[b]From Balides, Danziger, and Spitz 1973, 498.

conferences on the subject. In short, it viewed civil disobedience as the only way to make the " 'unspeakable' speakable" (Luker 1984, 96).

As these single-issue groups embarked on their varied missions, the movement received some much needed reinforcement from more well-established, or at least broader-based, forces. In November 1967, at the second conference of the National Organization for Women (NOW), the group considered a "Bill of Rights" to present to candidates running in 1968 elections. Among them was "[t]he right of women to control their own reproductive lives by removing from the penal codes laws limiting access to contraceptive information and devices and by repealing penal laws governing abortion." Although controversy erupted over this plank, NOW members endorsed it,[27] marking the entrance of the women's movement into the campaign (Freeman 1975, 81). In the same year, the national ACLU also joined the movement (Granfield 1969; Walker 1990). At its June meeting, after a "long debate," it adopted the following blanket statement:

> A. It is a civil right of a woman to seek to terminate a pregnancy, and of a physician to perform or refuse to perform an abortion [prior to viability],[28] without the threat of criminal sanctions.
>
> B. Abortions should be performed only by doctors, governed by the same considerations as other medical practices.

Around the same time, organized religion began to take stances, with some sects coming out in favor of full repeal and others, of reform. Even the AMA decided to reformulate its policy. At its June 1967 meeting, it formally supported laws similar to the ALI code, marking its first official policy change since 1871 (Jackson 1967, 1).

In addition to these various groups, individuals launched virtually one-person campaigns. In New York, Lawrence Lader, although initially involved with the ASA, pursued a more radical strategy than the association. As a scholar of the birth control movement,[29] Lader believed that change in the laws of abortion would come about only through a "politics of confrontation," which would involve civil disobedience.[30] Another vehement birth control advocate was Bill Baird, who ran a contraceptive clinic in Hempstead, New York. In 1967, he expanded his services to include abortions, making it the only "referral service with its own clinic." Baird's contribution to the growing movement was his flamboyance; he was a "master manipulator," unafraid of getting arrested (which he was on many occasions) to draw attention to the cause, and in the opinion of many, himself. Regardless of his motives, Baird's involvement had its benefits for those seeking reform (Lader 1973, 51).

Although Lader called all of this activity part of one interlocking campaign, the picture is far more splintered. Not only did the groups and individuals engage in divergent strategies and tactics, but they had varying goals: some thought the best political course of action would be to lobby for legislation like the code of the ALI; others thought repeal was the answer (see table 5-1). Still, they had a general impact on the direction of abortion policy in the United States on a number of levels. First, as summarized in table 5-2, there was an outpouring of writings on the subject. This was not by coincidence. Many pro-choice advocates thought the "best chance to build a movement was through public relations" (Lader 1973, ix; Olasky 1988). After all, was this not how the AMA started its campaign against abortion? Therefore, many books and articles were generated both by those from within and outside of the movement, and they carried a similar message: myriad problems with the old abortion laws were leading to intolerable public problems, ranging from increasing mortality rates to amorphous definitions of "therapeutic abortions" to a lack of women's control over their bodies. Other emerging arguments focused on discrimination against the poor; as Guttmacher (1967, 8, 9) pointed out, "In the United States abortion is largely carried out clandestinely by physicians, particularly for the well-to-do. . . . The poor are likely to abort themselves or resort to non-medical amateurs."

Unlike past works (for example, Taussig 1936), these efforts did not go unnoticed by the public. As Hall (1967, 224) wrote: "A few years ago 'abortion' was a dirty word. Everyone knew it existed, but almost no one wanted to talk about it. Today it is the most popular of subjects." Undoubtedly, this was in large measure due to the media's interest in the topic and its willingness to publicize the activities and writings of the movement. Figure 5-1 presents the number of articles listed under "abortion" in *The New York Times Index*, the *Readers' Guide to Periodical Literature*, the *Guide to Law Reviews*, and the *Social Science Index*. As we can see, coverage grew precipitously over the decade. This time it was the sort of exposure the pro-choice side desired; one author (Buutap 1979) found that 90 percent of those stories appearing in the *New York Times* between 1965 and 1973 favored the pro-choice position. Again, this was hardly coincidental: abortion advocates sought out "sympathetic editors" (Olasky 1988, 112) and worked to enlist them in the cause.

As a result, this aspect of the movement's strategy—disseminating the message and encouraging citizens to reformulate their views—was having some effect (Tatalovich and Daynes 1981). Note this comparison between the percentage of respondents approving of abortion in various circumstances in a 1965 National Opinion Research Center poll and one taken by Gallup in 1967. The question in both instances was, "Do you approve of abortion if

TABLE 5-2. Books Promoting the Abortion Movement, 1958–1971

Book	Purpose	Relation to the Movement
Abortion in the United States (Calderone 1958)	To open debate and suggest reforms.	Proceedings of a conference sponsored by Planned Parenthood.
The Abortionist (Freeman 1962)	To highlight the horrors associated with botched abortions; to open debate on rights of doctors and women.	Dedicated to women who have been "maimed" or killed by botched abortions.
Criminal Abortion (Bates and Zawadzki 1964)	To demonstrate the extent of criminal abortion activity; to open debate.	Guttmacher wrote the fore-word, suggesting that "nothing will be done about the problem until we force it into the open forum."
Abortion (Lader 1966)	To identify and elucidate the problem in laypersons' terms; to bring it out into the open.	Written by abortion advocate, Lader.
The Case for Legalized Abortion Now (Guttmacher 1967)	To discuss the reform move-ment and delineate variations of opinion within it.	Edited by Guttmacher with contributors representing various forces within the reform movement.
The Right to Abortion (Group for the Advancement of Psychiatry 1970)	To critique ALI reforms and demonstrate why they will be ineffective.	Statement on the need for repeal by the Group for the Advancement of Psychiatry.
Abortion in a Changing World (Hall 1970)	To "expose" knowledge of abortion to public scrutiny.	Proceedings of the ASA's 1968 conference.

	1965	1967
The woman's health is seriously endangered	71	86
She became pregnant as a result of rape	56	72
There is a strong chance of a serious defect in the baby	55	62
The family has a low income and cannot afford the baby	21	25
She is not married and does not want to marry the baby's father	18	28
She is married but does not want any more children	15	21

TABLE 5-2 *(continued)*

Book	Purpose	Relation to the Movement
Abortion Rap (Schulder and Kennedy 1971)	To advocate the woman's position on the issue; to urge repeal.	Description of a New York court case launched by women.
Everything You Need to Know about Abortion (Hendin 1971)	To advocate the woman's position.	Informational.
Everywoman's Guide to Abortion (Ebon 1971)	To "wipe out ignorance" about abortion.	Informational.

Source: Adapted from Sarvis and Rodman 1973.

The second goal of at least some members of the movement—to encourage state legislatures to reform their laws—was also gaining momentum. In 1967, Colorado, North Carolina, and California all adopted some version of the ALI code, marking the first major legislative changes of the century (Grisez 1970; Luker 1984; Merton 1981; Sloan 1988).[31]

THE MOVEMENT COALESCES: THE CALL FOR REPEAL

Despite these successes, various components of the movement perceived problems down the road. The more radical elements—those who sought repeal of all abortion laws—believed that if it continued along this somewhat haphazard and divided path, it would achieve little, with perhaps the exception of more states adopting versions of the ALI code. And, by 1968, leaders of the more moderate organizations recognized that the movement would falter unless they could coalesce around a unified goal. Ultimately, repeal of all existing laws became the thread that would draw them together, and, as such, the agenda of the radicals came to define the movement.

The first real attempt to unify the "forces" came in 1968 when the ASA held an international conference in Hot Springs, Arkansas (Hall 1970). Here, participants from many spheres of the movement[32] were inundated with information on the inability of laws similar to the ALI code to remedy perceived problems.[33] Not surprisingly, by the end of the meeting, the group came to the "almost unanimous" conclusion that "all abortion laws should be abolished" (Clark 1969, 3).[34]

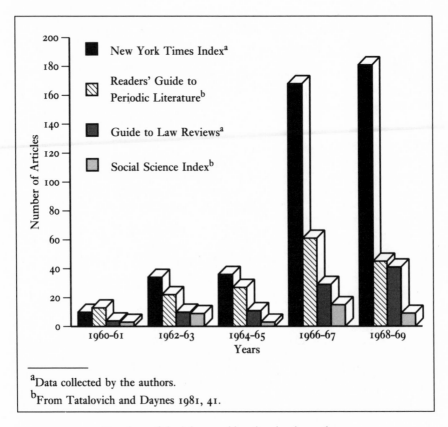

FIGURE 5-1. Number of Articles on Abortion in the 1960s

With this, ASA leaders decided the time had come to bring all the various constituencies under one umbrella organization. They called for another conference to be held in February 1969 in Chicago and invited "prestigious organizations" (such as the American Baptist Convention, the ACLU, and the Physicians Forum) to sponsor the event (Lader 1973, 89). That meeting was a huge success, with more than three hundred delegates, representing forty organizations, attending. Though the three-day session consisted mainly of workshops and informational panels, the conference specifically accomplished two things: it established itself as a new organization, with the name National Association for the Repeal of Abortion Laws (NARAL), and took the position that "the decision for or against abortion should be made without legal incumbrances so that women and physicians may be able to exercise their own best judgment" (*New York Times* 1969, 32).

ABORTION IN THE POLITICAL ARENAS, 1969–1973

Although most of the pro-choice groups of the day were members of NARAL, this common association did not lead to agreement on the strategy necessary to effectuate repeal. The positions taken on this question—the question of how to generate legal change—were as varied as the groups themselves. NARAL sought to establish state-based affiliates that would invoke traditional legislative lobbying strategies: testifying before committees, providing information, and so forth. With its network of state and local affiliates already in place, the ACLU attempted much the same thing (ACLU 1970–71). Some women's organizations engaged in fairly extreme publicity-oriented practices. Radical groups (such as the Women's International Terrorist Conspiracy from Hell and New York Radical Women Redstockings) "now saw abortion as one of the key issues in the women's liberation movement" and pursued repeal with vigor (Rubin 1987, 23). They "stormed" legislative hearings, picketing and parading with coat hangers dipped in red lacquer; they started "abortion rap," "speakouts" in which women would tell politicians about "horrors" of their illegal abortion experiences; and they staged sit-ins at hospitals and AMA conventions (McGlen and O'Connor 1983; Deckard 1975; Schulder and Kennedy 1971).

As more and more groups entered the fray in diverse ways, states holding legislative hearings were bombarded. After listening to testimony from obstetricians, gynecologists, radical feminists, psychiatrists, NOW members, Protestants, church leaders, public health associations, and many others, the Michigan Senate Committee on Abortion Law Reform issued a 461-page report on the subject (Davis 1985). Such involvement was not atypical. By lobbying state legislatures intensely, pro-choice forces pursued their goal of total repeal.

For a while, it appeared as if this "impact strategy" would succeed. Figure 5-2 illustrates changes in state laws occurring over a one hundred–year period. As we can see, in the late 1960s fifteen states adopted versions of the ALI code; in 1970, four allowed some form of "abortion on demand," including New York, which was gaining a reputation as the "abortion capital of the world."[35] Yet by 1970 it became apparent that pro-choice forces had reached an impasse; no other states were willing to repeal their restrictive laws. Indeed, in 1971 thirty-four states considered repeal, but all rejected this option (Wardle and Wood 1982, 43).

It is not easy to explain why this trend toward reform and repeal stalled, but it is clear that pro-choicers hit not one but many obstacles by the end of 1970. First, despite the publicity they had managed to garner for their cause—particularly the vast dissemination of data on the problems of legislation based on the

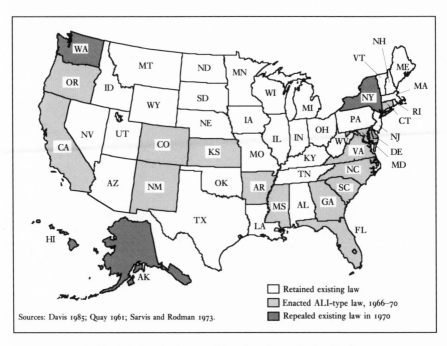

Sources: Davis 1985; Quay 1961; Sarvis and Rodman 1973.

☐ Retained existing law
▨ Enacted ALI-type law, 1966–70
■ Repealed existing law in 1970

FIGURE 5-2. Legislative Action on Abortion through the Early 1970s

ALI code—the public remained skeptical. The data presented in figure 5-3, which depicts responses to survey questions on abortion between 1962 and 1972, well illustrates the problem. The citizenry was willing to go along with abortion under those conditions specified in the ALI code (women's health and fetal defects), but a majority, albeit a decreasing one, was unsupportive of the procedure "on demand" (because of low income). Despite the efforts of NARAL and others, this message apparently found its way to state legislators. While pro-choicers were lobbying for repeal, most politicos, simply reflecting the views of their constituents, would go only as far as "reform." Laws similar to the ALI code, in essence, were viewed as a handy compromise position.

The cause of repeal also lacked the support of a key organizational player, the AMA. It had remained silent on the subject since its 1967 support for reform. Just how important was its voice? Not only did its opposition to abortion lead states toward the adoption of restrictive laws in the 1800s, but many suggest its support of reform in 1967 set the states in action as well. There is some truth to this: although ALI approved the code in 1962, it was not until 1967 that any state adopted it. Whatever the case, it is undeniable that the AMA's silence was not helping the repeal movement.

Finally, and perhaps most important, by 1970 serious organized opposition to

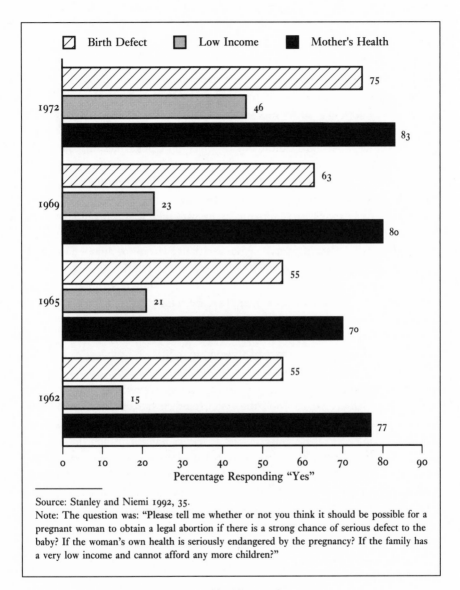

FIGURE 5-3. Public Opinion on Abortion, 1962–1972

pro-choice forces began to emerge. Through the 1960s, it was generally the Catholic church that exerted its influence to stymie the movement. Yet, because its attention was split between fighting abortion and birth control, it was less effective than it might otherwise have been.[36] This changed somewhat in the late 1960s as grass-roots organizations opposed to abortion reform began to spring up across the United States.[37] Still, during the 1960s, the pro-life movement resembled its counterpart in the pre-NARAL days—it was relatively unorganized and fragmented.

By 1970, though, a true right-to-life movement was in the offing when prominent pro-lifers, upset by the repeal victories in New York, Hawaii, Washington, and Alaska, met at Barat College in Illinois. Out of that meeting (and others) came a number of tactics that the movement would use for many years to come: targeting pro-choice candidates for electoral defeat, picketing hospitals that performed abortions, using pictures of aborted fetuses in literature and books,[38] and lobbying state legislatures to reverse their repeal laws. These strategies proved effective—every time a state legislature considered reform or repeal in the early 1970s, pro-lifers turned up with their literature and pictures. Wherever they went, the laws were defeated (Merton 1981).[39]

Pro-life forces also received some assistance from a more-than-likely source—President Richard Nixon. Most members of Congress viewed abortion as a state issue and, thus, generally avoided the fray (Vinovskis 1980b).[40] Likewise, Nixon "had no excuse [to intervene] except in the case of military bases and government territory. [Yet he] used this slim wedge and expanded it into a national assault" (Lader 1973, 176). In 1971, for example, Nixon altered governmental policy on the performance of abortion in military hospitals. Prior to that time, such facilities would abort fetuses, regardless of local/state policy; under the president's new directive, they could only do so where it was legalized. In making this change, Nixon took the opportunity to attack abortion: "From personal and religious beliefs I consider abortion an unacceptable form of population control. Further, unrestricted abortion policies, or abortion on demand, I cannot square with my personal belief in the sanctity of human life— including the life of the yet unborn. For surely, the unborn have rights also, recognized in law, recognized even in principles expounded by the United Nations" (*New York Times* 1971). This statement was merely icing on the cake. By the time Nixon issued it, the pro-life movement, at least in legislative arenas, was a force that pro-choice advocates could not overcome.

THE EARLY LITIGATION CAMPAIGNS

Conventional wisdom of the day, particularly among pro-lifers, held that pro-choice forces took to the courts in the early 1970s after they saw their legislative campaigns repeatedly repelled. As Hilgers and Horan (1972, 99) wrote, since their political efforts had been "stymied . . . there is a feeling among advocates of abortion that relief will be found through the courts. . . . It is likely that the strategy of those groups and individuals . . . will increasingly shift toward attempts to influence the courts." This seems a compelling explanation for why pro-choice forces entered the legal arena; it fits with traditional views of the motivations of group litigation (Cortner 1968) and the context of the day. Nonetheless, it is largely incorrect. Sectors of the movement began contemplating litigation as early as 1964 and, in fact, by the early 1970s were involved in dozens of lawsuits.

THE ONSET OF LITIGATION: THE BIRTH CONTROL CASES

To this point our discussion of abortion has seldom touched upon the courts and law. This is for good reason: as former Justice Clark (1969, 1) wrote, "In my day at the bar all discussion of abortion was taboo. . . . The law [lagged] behind as usual." While this was true of American courts, the situation in England was far different. In fact, a 1939 court ruling generated major change in the status of abortion there. In *Rex v. Bourne*, an obstetric surgeon (Dr. Bourne) sought to test England's restrictive law (the same as those used in most U.S. states) by having himself arrested for performing an abortion. The presiding judge turned out to be quite "sympathetic" to the surgeon's position; in his charge to the jurors, he told them to take a "reasonable" view of the law—that under the circumstances Bourne had operated "for the purpose of preserving the life of the woman." In so doing, the judge gave a far broader meaning to "preserving life" than had previous courts. When the jury acquitted Bourne, it ushered in a "new epoch" in the status of abortion in that country (Shaw 1968, 48–49).

For the better part of two decades, American courts not only failed to follow their English counterparts but avoided the subject of abortion or even contraceptives altogether.[41] That changed somewhat in 1961 when the Supreme Court heard the case of *Poe v. Ullman*, involving the constitutionality of an 1879 Connecticut law prohibiting even married couples from using birth control. A Connecticut physician, Dr. Buxton, challenged the act on behalf of two women who wanted to use contraceptives for health reasons.

When the case reached the Supreme Court, attorneys submitted a variety of arguments in opposition to the statute. Buxton's lawyer, Yale Law School professor Fowler Harper, made the general claim that it was unconstitutional on its "face . . . in that [it] deprives [appellants] of life, liberty, or property without due process of law, contrary to the Fourteenth Amendment" (*Poe*, Brief for Appellant, no. 60). Amicus curiae Planned Parenthood, represented by Harriet Pilpel, pointed to the "anachronistic nature of the law"; "whatever may have been the situation when these laws were initially enacted, they must be tested in light of present knowledge and the practice of the medical profession." And another amicus, the ACLU, tried to take Harper's due process argument one step further, suggesting that the law "arbitrarily invades the privacy of . . . married persons and thereby violates the due process clause of the Fourteenth Amendment." This was, of course, a rather unique argument: while some members of the Court had previously acknowledged the existence of a right to privacy, they did so in the areas of torts and searches and seizures—not sexual relations. Indeed, in raising this claim, ACLU attorneys cited a slew of Fourth Amendment cases.

In conference, after orals, the majority of justices expressed qualms about deciding the case on the merits.[42] Chief Justice Warren, in particular, thought the Connecticut law, for all intents and purposes, dead.[43] Accordingly, the Court dismissed the case, leaving unaddressed the substantive issues it raised.

A minority of four disagreed with this disposition,[44] with the most surprising note of dissent registered by Justice Harlan. Not particularly known as an activist or liberal, he was the law's loudest and most vehement critic, generally adopting—in conference and in his ensuing opinion—Harper's argument that due process could be used to strike the law: it unduly burdened individual liberty and it was an "intolerable and unjustifiable invasion of privacy." In making this claim, he took great pains to demonstrate that these two concepts—liberty and privacy—were inextricably bound.

Harlan's opinion was extraordinary in several regards.[45] Most important, some have asserted that it resurrected the long-dead doctrine of substantive due process under which the Court read the word "liberty" in the Fourteenth Amendment to prevent governments from using their police powers to regulate business practices.[46] During the New Deal period, substantive due process fell into disrepute as the citizenry demanded government involvement to straighten out the economy. Now Harlan wanted to reinject new substance into the word "liberty," but with a twist. Rather than protecting economic rights, in his "formulation due process protects fundamental rights," those the Court believes to be important in the concept of ordered liberty (Neier 1982, 112). One of these "fundamental" liberties—privacy—provides the other novel aspect of Harlan's opinion. Although he was not writing on a clean slate—in the early 1900s, Justice Louis Brandeis had written about a "right to privacy" in the contexts of libel and search and seizure (Prosser 1960)—Harlan's application of it to marital sexual relations, per the ACLU's argument, was bold.

Harlan's opinion generated some measure of debate and interest in a variety of circles, not the least of which was the ASA. Since the ASA's founding several years after *Poe*, its leaders—especially Pilpel, who (as an attorney involved with Planned Parenthood and the ACLU) had a long-standing interest in civil liberties issues—had considered using litigation to push for abortion reform.[47] At that time, though, neither she nor the ASA envisioned litigation as a method of "repealing" existing abortion laws; rather, they contemplated a test case akin to England's *Rex v. Bourne* (1939) that would reinterpret existing laws in such a way as to provide doctors more discretion. As Pilpel said in a March 1964 speech at the Columbia-Presbyterian Medical Center in New York, "Our abortion laws today, like birth control laws in the past, must be interpreted by the courts. We can reasonably assume that a test-case in abortion might give physicians enlarged freedom of judgment in the abortion field just as the *One Package*[48] case did in the birth control field in 1936" (Lader 1966, 154). Two months later, in June 1964, Pilpel reiterated this theme at the ACLU's Biennial Conference. On a panel entitled "Civil Liberties and the War on Crime," she argued that "current laws criminalizing abortion and consensual homosexual conduct were civil liberties issues infringing on privacy" and depriving liberty (Walker 1990, 267, 302).

By providing some legal bases for "doctor suits"—privacy and liberty—Pilpel was attempting to convince the ACLU to enter the fray. But it was not yet ready to be convinced: "[S]ome feared it would offend valuable allies," others thought her "legal foundations" shaky and lacking any basis in civil liberties (Walker 1990, 302). Given the absence of a Supreme Court ruling to the contrary, these concerns certainly had merit: a majority of the justices had yet to strike or even interpret birth control laws, much less abortion. All of this was to change in 1965, when the Court startled even civil libertarians with its decision in *Griswold v. Connecticut*.

A BREAKTHROUGH: *GRISWOLD V. CONNECTICUT*

While the ASA searched in vain for the perfect doctor plaintiff to challenge existing abortion laws, the Supreme Court docketed *Griswold* for arguments in March 1965. At its heart, *Griswold* was a slightly modified version of *Poe*, designed to overcome the shortcomings of the earlier case (Friendly and Elliot 1984; Roraback 1989). Estelle Griswold, the wife of a Yale University professor and executive director of the Planned Parenthood League of Connecticut, and Dr. C. Lee Buxton, a physician associated with the Yale Medical School (and the appellant in *Poe*), opened a birth control clinic in 1961 with the full intent of being arrested for violating the old Connecticut law (at issue in *Poe*). Griswold was arrested just three days later for dispensing contraceptives to a married couple.

Counsel to the state's Planned Parenthood League, Catherine Roraback, and Harriet Pilpel handled the case through the Connecticut judicial ladder. When it was clear that it had potential to reach the Supreme Court, the Planned Parenthood Federation "hired" Professor Harper, who had argued *Poe*, to present the case to the Court. As a scholar of the First Amendment, Harper was initially inclined to use that as the centerpiece of his argument—in particular, that Connecticut's law infringed upon a doctor's right to speak ("give advice") to his patients. After spotting a 1962 law review article written by Norman Redlich, he (and others working on the case) rethought this plan (Roraback 1989).

On the surface, Redlich's piece was a simple exploration of the use of the Fourteenth Amendment's due process clause to incorporate the Bill of Rights. Yet beneath that analysis lay a complex argument about the nature of fundamental rights. Redlich was concerned about those rights which, while not specifically enumerated, were arguably of constitutional dimensions; in particular, would they also apply to the states and if so, how? In his view, such an application could be accomplished through the Ninth Amendment. He claimed that the Court "could start a strong historical argument that [it] was intended to apply in a situation where the asserted right appears as fundamental to a free society, but is, nonetheless, not specified in the Bill of Rights." By way of example, Redlich pointed to the "right to maintain the intimacy of the marital relationship without governmental interference."

This argument, combined with Harlan's dissent in *Poe* and several more recent Court decisions,[49] convinced Harper "that they should use the Ninth Amendment and, more important, base their defense on the idea of a privacy right" (Faux 1988, 70). In essence, this is precisely what the jurisdictional statement argued (*Griswold*, filed in no. 496). It suggested that the Connecticut law violated a right to privacy, a right that was not specifically mentioned in the Constitution but "ought to be" because the Fourth, Ninth, and Fourteenth amendments imply it. To support this unique claim, Harper cited *Poe*, Redlich's article, and histories of the Ninth Amendment. But he did not base all of his arguments on the issue of "privacy." Should the Court be unwilling to accept that claim, he gave it other grounds on which to strike, including the First Amendment and abridgment of personal liberty as discussed in Harlan's *Poe* dissent.

To the surprise of some, the Court agreed to hear the case. Unfortunately, Harper died before the main briefs had been finished, so his Yale colleague Thomas Emerson took over. His submission resembled Harper's in that he gave the Court an array of choices by which to strike the law; his emphasis, however, varied significantly. While Harper stressed a privacy right grounded in the Ninth Amendment, Emerson highlighted the substantive due process argument, and this made the two briefs read quite differently. Emerson did not ignore the issue of privacy; if anything, he bolstered it, arguing that several other amendments (besides the Fourth, Ninth, and Fourteenth) contributed to it: the First Amend-

ment guaranteed freedom of religion and the Third prohibited quartering sol-
diers (*Griswold*, Brief for Appellants, no. 496, 78). Still, the core of his argument
lay with Harlan's notion of substantive due process.

After orals, at their 2 April 1965 conference, the justices voted 7–2 to strike
the law,[50] "but the majority . . . did not articulate a clear theory on which to
base their decision." Douglas suggested that the "simplest rationale" would rest
on First Amendment association grounds, to which Black responded that the
"Right of Association is for me a right of assembly and [the] right of the husband
and wife to assemble in bed is new right of assembly to me." Stewart agreed with
Black, asserting that he could not "find anything in the First, Second, Fourth,
Fifth, Ninth or other Amendments. So [he'd] have to affirm."

Given that Douglas was virtually the only one willing to enunciate a theory, it
was he who wrote an initial draft for the majority.[51] He sent a copy to Brennan,
who in turn made the suggestion that Douglas adopt the Harper/Emerson
approach on privacy—one roughly paralleling Douglas's opinion in *Poe*. Douglas
did so but in an even more stylized fashion. His opinion of the Court (*Griswold*
1965, 484) asserted that "specific guarantees in the Bill of Rights have pen-
umbras, formed by emanations from [First, Third, Fourth, Fifth, and Ninth
Amendment] guarantees that help give them life and substance." In other words,
Douglas claimed that, although the Constitution specifically failed to mention
"privacy," clauses within the document created "zones" that gave rise to the
right.

Six members agreed with Douglas's ultimate resolution of the case but expressed varying degrees of disagreement with his reasoning, particularly with the
specific constitutional locus of privacy. Justice Goldberg, joined by Warren and
Brennan, did not explicitly refute Douglas's "penumbra" theory. What he chose
to emphasize instead was the "relevance" of the Ninth Amendment. In Goldberg's view (*Griswold* 1965, 488–89), that amendment—"The enumeration in
the Constitution, of certain rights, shall not be construed to deny or disparage
others retained by the people"—could be construed to contain a "right to
privacy." His logic was simple: the wording of the amendment, coupled with its
history, suggested that it was "proffered to quiet expressed fears that a bill of
specifically enumerated rights could not be sufficiently broad to cover all essential rights," including one to privacy. Harlan (joined by White) took the opportunity to reiterate his *Poe* stance that the due process clause of the Fourteenth
Amendment prohibits such legislation. In holding to his *Poe* opinion, Harlan
(*Griswold* 1965, 500) explicitly rejected the Douglas penumbra theory, asserting
that "[w]hile the relevant inquiry may be aided by resort to one or more of the
provisions of the Bill of Rights, it is not dependent on them or any of their
radiations."

Thus, despite the centrality of *Griswold* to the right to privacy, the Court's rationale was muddled. Seven agreed, more or less, that a right to privacy existed, but they located it in three different constitutional spheres: the zones of privacy emanating from the First, Third, Fourth, Fifth, and Ninth amendments; from the Ninth Amendment alone; and from the Fourteenth Amendment. Still, *Griswold* was a landmark decision. It created a very generally defined constitutional right to privacy. Moreover, even though the specific issue at hand was birth control, a few thought that its logic could be applied to the abortion issue. Shortly after *Griswold*, Emerson (1965) wrote an important article for the *Michigan Law Review*, in which he speculated on its possible extensions and applications. Among other things,[52] he suggested (1965, 232) that the right to privacy may open the way "for an attack upon significant aspects of the abortion laws." Not surprisingly, Pilpel incorporated *Griswold* into her growing list of arguments to challenge restrictive laws.

Still, for the most part, many "litigators did not seriously contemplate" using *Griswold* as a basis for attacking abortion laws. Some attorneys—including several affiliated with the ACLU—felt that society viewed birth control laws as "anachronistic" but did not place abortion laws into the same category. Public opinion polls bore out this sentiment: less than 13 percent of the public in 1965 thought abortions should be legalized unless they were necessary to save a mother's life; the same year 81 percent responded affirmatively when asked whether birth control information should be available to anyone who wanted it. A general consensus also existed that more "public discussion was necessary before abortion laws could be changed"; abortion remained a taboo subject (Neier 1982, 114).

THE LITIGATION "AVALANCHE"

Although public debate on abortion was still generally taboo in the mid-1960s, such discussions were becoming at least more frequent. Legislative hearings, especially those in New York and California (Neier 1982, 114), went a long way toward making public consideration of abortion less awkward. With this, the earlier ASA musings about the possibility of litigation as a tool of reform resurfaced. The formal beginnings of this strategy can be, perhaps coincidentally, traced to the ACLU's 1967 announcement that anti-abortion laws violate a woman's right to liberty, infringe on rights of privacy, discriminate against poor women, are unconstitutionally vague, and "impair the right of physicians" to practice medicine (ACLU 1976, 231). This triggered a series of "scholarly" debates, framing the issue as an essentially legal one, and created a political context that facilitated an avalanche of abortion litigation.

Initially, relatively disjointed discussions centered on how to challenge such laws. The ASA and the New York ACLU, generally speaking, continued to press for cases similar to *Rex v. Bourne*, predicated on expanding interpretations of existing statutes by way of criminal prosecutions brought against doctors. Their problem was finding such litigants: few "respected" doctors were willing to serve as guinea pigs and even fewer (or so it seemed) prosecutors were willing to bring charges against them (Lader 1973, 12). Others contemplated litigation on behalf of women and/or doctors who had not been prosecuted but who desired to challenge the law on particular grounds—those enunciated in *Griswold* and, perhaps, substantive due process. In other words, they wanted to move toward an offensive strategy rather than merely defend prosecuted doctors.

Interestingly, there was never a particular push among organizational leaders of the ASA and the ACLU to seize on and adopt a single tack. Abortion was unlike other areas of the law—for example, capital punishment—in which leading participants felt a need to rally around one line of argument and work actively to prevent competing views from infiltrating into the court system. At ASA's 1968 Hot Springs conference, for example, Pilpel and several other attorneys participated on a panel entitled "The Means of Assessing and Testing the Constitutionality of Abortion Law in the United States." Transcripts of the discussion (Hall 1970) reveal a free-flowing exchange among the participants, in which ideas were considered, not dismissed. By its end, participants offered an array of arguments against laws restricting abortion: First Amendment association and religious establishment, Eighth Amendment cruel and unusual punishment, women's rights (equal protection), doctors' rights, doctor-patient and husband-wife relations, vagueness, and privacy. A willingness to encourage argumentational experimentation rather than to restrict creativity also was reflected in a prominent article published in the *North Carolina Law Review*. Written by Roy Lucas (1968), an assistant professor of law at the University of Alabama who had been working with the ACLU on this issue, its main point was to encourage litigation. To do so, Lucas suggested that attorneys develop a broad range of arguments and test them out in court.

Why the movement failed to coalesce behind a particular legal strategy remains open to speculation. One contributing factor was the lack of leadership by a single attorney or group organizing litigation efforts or urging others to follow a specific line of argument. The ACLU was interested in the issue, but during the 1960s it had so many other issues on its agenda that abortion was simply not a priority. NOW and other women's rights groups were in much the same boat. That left matters largely to the ASA, which had a preference for suits involving doctors but did not discourage other kinds of litigation. Rather, owing perhaps to the novelty of this legal area, those involved were anxious to test as many different claims as possible. Also, the attorneys involved surely did not envision the U.S. Supreme Court enunciating doctrine on abortion in one fell swoop; thus far it had generally managed to side step the issue. Therefore, they thought their best hope was "impact litigation" designed to raise the consciousness of the public and to test a variety of specific challenges in the courts and not necessarily the presentation of the perfect test case.

This "do your own thing" attitude triggered what was justifiably called an "avalanche" or "flood" of litigation (Rubin 1987). As shown in table 5-3, between 1968 and 1973 almost thirty cases were resolved by or pending before the U.S. Supreme Court alone; dozens more were before lower federal and state courts (Vergata et al. 1972). Not surprisingly, the litigation was far from mono-lithic. Some cases were brought by movement and interest group attorneys, most notably Nancy Stearns, later known for her association with the Center for Constitutional Rights (CCR); Roy Lucas, who was now working for the James Madison Constitutional Law Institute; and Harriet Pilpel and others of the ACLU. Others were sponsored by "private" attorneys, who were working on a "for fee" basis or who were particularly interested in abortion reform. Moreover, the legal challenges varied in kind. Some continued to reflect the initial emphasis on doctors' rights. Others took the offensive, bringing cases on behalf of women who wanted, but could not obtain, abortions.[53]

A final point of distinction among these cases was that their outcomes varied widely: some were total losers, others were big winners. Among the latter was an important "doctor suit" of the sort for which the ASA and some ACLU members had been pushing, involving Milan Vuitch, a Washington, D.C., physician to whom Lader had been referring patients for abortions for years. After his arrest in May 1968, "Vuitch and his lawyers, Joseph L. Nellis and Joseph Sitnick . . . agreed to make a frontal attack by testing the constitutionality of the District law itself" (Lader 1973, 12). Pro-choice advocates were delighted. They viewed the Washington law as vulnerable; it was one of the few that permitted abortions to preserve a woman's life and health. Further, they liked the idea of launching a test case in a city that would naturally provide some visibility for the cause.

In 1969, armed with an amicus curiae brief filed by the ACLU, Vuitch's attorneys challenged the Washington law in a federal district court on "core" constitutional issues: doctors' and women's rights and the right to privacy. Just months later, in November 1969, "before a hushed audience filling every seat" in the court (Lader 1973, 15), Judge Gesell issued his opinion:

> The true crux of the controversy . . . concerns [the phrase] "as is necessary for the preservation of the mother's life or health. . . ." The word "health" is not defined and in fact remains so vague in its interpretation and the

practice under the act that there is no indication whether it includes varying degrees of mental as well as physical health. . . . Its many ambiguities are particularly subject to criticism for the statute unquestionably impinges to an appreciable extent on significant constitutional rights. (*Vuitch* 1969, 1034)

Because the ruling permitted licensed Washington physicians to perform abortions in accordance with their own "medical judgment," *Vuitch* was a monumental decision. Moreover, it was the first time a U.S. federal court had overturned an abortion law.[54]

While *Vuitch* had limited application, Gesell's opinion had a substantial impact on the movement. In general, it demonstrated to litigators that the courts "had quickly become [more] receptive to abortion litigation than organizers of the movement for change had anticipated in 1965 and 1966" (Neier 1982, 116). This encouraged some of the litigation noted in table 5-3; in fact, a *New York Times* article written after the decision came down concluded that *Vuitch* signaled "more than a shift in tactics. Those seeking change are increasingly disenchanted with liberalization of anti-abortion laws, and instead wish to strike them completely from the statute books." Accordingly, some in the movement thought they could use *Vuitch* as a "precedent in test cases designed to bring the issue before the Supreme Court quickly" (Graham 1969b).

As it turned out, the victory in *Vuitch* would not provide as much of a vehicle for future litigation as pro-choice attorneys had hoped. On appeal, the U.S. Supreme Court reversed the lower court's ruling. Writing for the majority, Justice Black disagreed with Gesell's view that the term "health" was unconstitutionally vague. Still, the fact that the decision was ambiguous meant that it did not represent a total and complete defeat for the pro-choice side (Rubin 1987). Black clearly sympathized with the position of the physicians in abortion procedures. Though the law per se was constitutional, in his view it had been misapplied. He wrote,

> It would be highly anomalous for a legislature to authorize abortions necessary for life or health and then to demand a doctor, upon pain of one to ten years' imprisonment, bear the burden of proving that an abortion he performed fell within that category. Placing such a burden of proof on a doctor would be peculiarly inconsistent with society's notions of the responsibilities of the medical profession. . . . We therefore hold that . . . the burden is on the prosecution. (*Vuitch* 1971, 70–71)

Thus, if the government wanted to prosecute a physician, it had to prove that the doctor had performed an abortion unnecessary to preserve the mother's life or

TABLE 5-3. Abortion Litigation through 1972

U.S. SUPREME COURT CASES ON WHICH THE COURT ACTED

Case	Action	Attorney Type
State v. Moretti (244 A.2d 499, 1968)	Denied cert. to New Jersey Supreme Court's rejection of void-for-vagueness argument (doctor conviction).	Private counsel
Cooper v. Beto (447 S.W.2d 179, 1969)	Declined review of a Texas court decision, which would not provide relief from a revocation of a probated sentence for drunken driving after a conviction under a state abortion statute that had been held unconstitutional.	Private counsel
People v. Belous (458 P.2d 194, 1969)	Denied cert. to California Supreme Court decision striking down as vague state's 1850 abortion law (doctor conviction).	ACLU
United States v. Vuitch (305 F.Supp. 1032, 1969)	Washington, D.C., abortion law not unconstitutionally vague if "health" construed broadly (doctor conviction).	ACLU/ movement attorney
Abodeely v. Iowa (179 N.W.2d 347, 1970)	Dismissed appeal of Iowa Supreme Court, upholding state abortion law and defendant's guilty plea under it (doctor conviction).	Private counsel
Bolton v. Doe (319 F.Supp. 1048, 1970)	Dismissed appeal of federal district court ruling, holding parts of Georgia's ALI law unconstitutional (suit on behalf of practitioners, women, and clergy).	ACLU
Hodgson v. Minnesota (see *Doe v. Randall*)	Dismissal of a Minnesota state court decision, denying a constitutional challenge (doctor conviction).	ACLU/ movement attorney
Doe v. Randall (314 F.Supp. 32, 1970)	Affirmed federal court's dismissal of suit challenging constitutionality of Minnesota law (brought by doctor and her patient).	ACLU
Lashley v. Maryland (268 A.2d 502, 1970)	Dismissed appeal of Maryland court decision, affirming conviction (doctor conviction).	Private counsel
McCann v. Babbitz (310 F.Supp. 293, 1970)	Dismissed appeal from federal court decision that Wisconsin's law was unconstitutional on privacy grounds (doctor conviction).	Movement attorney

TABLE 5-3 *(continued)*

Case	Action	Attorney Type
Molinaro v. New Jersey (254 A.2d 792, 1970)	Dismissed appeal of state ruling, upholding conviction of conspiracy to commit abortion (doctor conviction).	Private counsel
Nichol v. Kennan (326 F.Supp. 613, 1971)	Affirmed federal court order temporarily restraining prosecutions under Wisconsin's abortion law.	Movement attorney
Vuitch v. Maryland (271 A.2d 371, 1971)	Declined review on the grounds that no constitutional issues were presented.	Movement attorney

U.S. SUPREME COURT CASES DOCKETED/PENDING (THROUGH 1973)

Case	Lower Court Decision	Attorney
Doe v. Bolton (319 F.Supp. 1048, 1970)	Federal court held Georgia's ALI law unconstitutional, in part (suit on behalf of women, practitioners, and clergy).	ACLU
Roe v. Wade (314 F.Supp. 1217, 1970)	Federal court held Texas's law unconstitutional on privacy and vagueness grounds but did not enjoin enforcement (suit on behalf of women and physicians).	Private counsel
Rosen v. Louisiana State Board of Medical Examiners (318 F.Supp. 1217, 1970)	Federal court upheld state statute permitting license revocation or suspension of doctor who performs abortions (doctor conviction), against constitutional arguments.	James Madison Institute
Rogers v. Danforth (W.D. Missouri)	Federal court dismissed case under abstention doctrine (suit on behalf of doctors, clergy, and married women).	ACLU/ movement attorney
Corkey v. Edwards (322 F.Supp. 1248, 1971)	Federal court upheld North Carolina's ALI law in light of Ninth Amendment arguments (suit on behalf of doctors and nurses).	James Madison Institute
Crossen v. Breckenridge (446 F.2d 833, 1971)	Federal court ruled that physicians, women, and ministers had standing to challenge Kentucky's abortion law.	Movement attorney
Doe v. Rampton (366 F.Supp. 189, 1971)	Federal court denied standing to pregnant women on grounds that law applied to abortionists.	Private counsel

TABLE 5-3 *(continued)*

Case	Lower Court Decision	Attorney
Doe v. Scott (sub noms. *Hanrahan v. Doe* and *Heffernan v. Doe*) (321 F.Supp. 1385, 1971)	Federal court held Illinois law unconstitutional on vagueness and privacy grounds (suit on behalf of doctors and women).	ACLU/Legal Aid Bureau
Thompson v. Texas (493 S.W.2d 913, 1971)	Texas state court upheld conviction of doctor (doctor conviction).	Private counsel
Abele v. Markle (342 F.Supp. 800, 1972)	Federal court struck down Connecticut's law on grounds of privacy and due process.	Law Center for Constitutional Rights
Byrn v. New York City and Hospitals Corporation (286 N.E. 2d 887, 1972)	State court rejected law professor's attempt to be appointed guardian ad litem for fetuses so that he might challenge New York law. Court ruled that fetuses are not persons under the Constitution.	New York/ Law Center for Constitutional Rights
Sasaki v. Kentucky (485 S.W. 2d 897, 1972)	Kentucky court upheld state abortion law (doctor conviction).	Movement attorney
Schulman v. NYC Health and Hospitals Corporation (335 N.Y.S.2d 343, 1972)	State court struck New York City's requirement of patient name and address disclosure (suit on behalf of doctor and patient).	Private counsel
South Dakota v. Munson (201 N.W. 2d 123, 1972)	State court held abortion law unconstitutional (doctor conviction).	James Madison Institute

Sources: This listing is derived in part from Vergata et al. 1972, 50–55 and U.S. Commission on Civil Rights 1975.

Note: Except where no lower court cites are listed, this table does not include cases with unpublished opinions.

health. By the same token and for the same reasons, Black let stand the lower court's interpretation of the word "health," which was a broad one, incorporating the "psychological as well as the physical."

Another promising aspect of *Vuitch* were the views some of the justices expressed in separate opinions. White, for one, wrote that "[n]o one of average intelligence could believe that under this statute abortions not dictated by health considerations are legal." More interesting was the dissent in part filed by Douglas,[55] the only opinion that tackled the abortion issue squarely. Not only did it take issue with the Washington law, asserting that it did not meet "the requirements of procedural due process," but it also spoke prophetically about the controversial nature of the issue: "The subject of abortion . . . is one of the most inflammatory ones to reach the Court. People instantly take sides and the public, from whom juries are drawn, makes up its mind one way or the other before the case is even argued. The interests of the mother and the fetus are opposed. On which side should the state throw its weight? The issue is volatile: and it is resolved by the moral code which the individual has" (*Vuitch* 1971, 79–80).

In the end, then, *Vuitch* sent pro-choice forces mixed signals. Although the justices showed some sympathy for the doctor's position, a five-person majority upheld the law against arguments of vagueness and privacy. It refused to consider any arguments based on *Griswold*, reading the "opinion of the Court below . . . as holding simply that the statute was void for vagueness." And, as such, it gave attorneys little insight, one way or another, into the majority's view on this line of argument. However, the Court was not done with abortion. *Vuitch* was just the beginning of the avalanche. Two more cases were about to engulf it: *Roe v. Wade* and *Doe v. Bolton*.

THE 1973 ABORTION CASES: *ROE* AND *DOE*, ROUND ONE

Roe and *Doe* would eventually become landmarks in legal history, but in their original incarnations, as revealed in table 5-4, they typified the range of cases being brought by the movement at the end of the 1960s. First, concerning the state statutes at issue, *Roe* represented a challenge to the "old" abortion laws (in force in thirty states) enacted in the 1860s at the urging of the AMA, and *Doe* was aimed at reform laws based on the ALI code (in sixteen states).[56] Likewise, the attorneys bringing the cases illustrated the spectrum of private-sector and organizational involvement in abortion litigation. Two young and inexperienced lawyers, Sarah Weddington and Linda Coffee, had brought the Texas challenge.[57] This duo had been involved with NOW and the women's movement, but at the time they initiated their challenge, they had neither group support nor any expertise on the topic.[58] For them, the issue of abortion was an ideological one, not personal or organizational (Faux 1988, 10–35).

In marked contrast were the counsel in *Doe*. Led by Margie Hames, almost all were experienced litigators with ties to the ACLU. Hames, herself, was a board member of the national ACLU and vice president of the Georgia affiliate; and

TABLE 5-4. Profiles of *Roe* and *Doe*

	Roe	*Doe*
Laws at Issue	1866 law (revised in 1879), making it a crime to "procure an abortion" unless it is "procured or attempted by medical advice for the purpose of saving the life of the mother."	1968 ALI-type reform law, making abortion criminal unless performed by a Georgia-licensed physician who determines that "based on his best clinical judgment . . . an abortion is necessary" because: 1) pregnancy would endanger the life of the mother; 2) the fetus would be born with a serious mental or physical defect; or 3) the pregnancy resulted from rape. If one of these three conditions exist, an abortion can be obtained if: 1) the woman is a resident of Georgia; 2) her doctor's written judgment is supported by the "written concurrence" of two other doctors; 3) the abortion is performed in a licensed and accredited hospital; 4) advanced approval is obtained by a hospital abortion committee; and 5) appropriate records are kept and certification made in cases of rape.
Attorneys	Linda Coffee and Sarah Weddington (recent law school graduates, both under 30).	Georgia ACLU attorneys and ACLU board members.
Plaintiffs	Roe (21 years old, unwed): could not obtain abortion in Texas. The Does (childless couple): she has a "neural chemical" disorder and cannot take oral contraceptives or get pregnant. Dr. James Halliford (intervenor): doctor under indictment for violating Texas law.	Doe (22 years old, separated): applied for abortion; was not approved by hospital committee. 23 residents of state: 9 doctors, 7 nurses, 5 clergy, and 2 social workers. 2 state corporations: Planned Parenthood Association of Georgia and Georgia Citizens for Hospital Abortion.
Three-Judge District Court Decision	17 June 1970	21 July 1970

TABLE 5-4 *(continued)*

	Roe	Doe
Standing	Denied for Does.	Denied for all but Doe.
Merits	Law is unconstitutionally vague as applied to Dr. Halliford. Law violates Ninth Amendment and due process guarantees as applied to Roe.	Fourteenth Amendment due process clause "embodies abortion," but that right is not absolute because the "potential" for life exists.
Holding	Declaratory judgment that the law is unconstitutional. No injunction issued.	Judgment that portions of the law are unconstitutional; others are upheld. No injunction issued.

"[t]he ACLU mobilized its top legal talent to work" on the case (Walker 1990, 303). The interests represented in the two cases also compressed all of the various combinations of litigants found in the 1960s "avalanche." Collectively *Roe* and *Doe* were initiated on behalf of pregnant women who could not obtain abortions under their respective state laws; a couple, who for health reasons could not take contraceptives and for whom pregnancy could prove fatal; a physician under indictment for performing abortions; various interested individuals and professional health-care providers; and two organizations (see table 5-4).

Practically the only dimension of *Roe* and *Doe* that did not typify the range of pending lawsuits was their treatment in the lower courts. Decided within a month of each other, both suits were successful to the extent that their three-judge federal courts struck the state laws (or portions thereof) on constitutional grounds. Yet neither granted standing to all involved plaintiffs, nor, more important, did they issue injunctions against enforcement of the laws (see table 5-4); the Georgia and Texas statutes remained as good law. A district attorney in Texas asserted after the lower court ruling, "Apparently, we're still free to try [abortionists], so we'll do just that" (Faux 1988, 165).

Given the nature of these rulings, it was not long before *Roe* and *Doe* joined the half dozen or so cases pending on appeal to the U.S. Supreme Court (see table 5-3). Interestingly, though, in their jurisdictional statements to the Court, the respective teams of attorneys highlighted different dimensions of their cases. Hames and the ACLU lawyers stressed the procedural issue of standing and the lower court's failure to grant injunctive relief; Weddington and Coffee also discussed these points, but they emphasized the importance of abortion as a policy issue as well: for example, they pointed to the divisions among lower courts, the substantial number of pending cases, and the increasing amount of legal scholarship.

Why the attorneys stressed different points is open to speculation. We suspect, however, that the divergence arose from their varying aims. At this point, few scholars or groups suspected that either of these cases would become the vehicles by which the Court would set the constitutional dimensions of the policy; they were just part of the ever-increasing barrage (Sigworth 1971; Rubin 1987). Therefore, the ACLU probably thought it best to get the Court to clarify some of the nagging procedural issues that stood as obstacles to other litigation. If it could get the justices to agree that women, who were pregnant at the time a suit was initiated but no longer so by the time it was in process, still had legal standing to challenge laws against abortion or that the case was still a "live" controversy, then it would have accomplished a significant end. For Weddington and Coffee, though, that would have been insufficient. Even though by the time they filed their appeal, movement attorneys were assisting them, their goal was more substantive: they wanted the justices to strike down the Texas law (not necessarily *all* laws) on constitutional (not procedural) grounds.

COURT PREPARATIONS: THE PRO-CHOICE SIDE

In the end, the distinctions between the jurisdictional statements became trivial. In May 1971, the Supreme Court separated *Roe* and *Doe* from the group, and it docketed the cases for oral arguments to be heard on 13 December 1971. Why the justices chose to hear them over the other cases—or even why they decided the time had come to take a serious look into the abortion problem—has been the subject of some speculation.[59] To pro-choice forces, however, those questions were irrelevant. What mattered now was that a major ruling on abortion probably was in the offing,[60] and they had four months to file their briefs.

Given the ACLU's developing expertise in abortion litigation, *Doe* appeared to be in good hands. This was not necessarily true for *Roe*: neither Weddington nor Coffee had ever prepared a U.S. Supreme Court brief, much less argued a case in the "marble palace." As Milbauer (1983, 52) put it, "Margie Hames had the facilities of the American Civil Liberties Union; Dorothy Beasley [who represented Georgia in *Doe*] had [her] state facilities; and Sarah Weddington and Linda Coffee had a problem." Thus, when the ASA offered its assistance, they were only too happy to accept: Weddington[61] flew to New York, where the ASA obtained an apartment for her (Milbauer 1983) and opened up their files.[62]

In addition to providing Weddington with legal assistance, the ASA "offered to handle the amicus curiae briefs" for both *Roe* and *Doe*.[63] Between the docketing of the cases and August 1971, numerous pressure groups expressed their interest in filing, but ASA leaders "had no intention of leaving the amici curiae briefs entirely to chance. They decided to 'orchestrate' the briefs," which they did on two fronts. First, ASA staffers sought to enlist amici representing the diverse constituencies of the movement: religious, feminist, medical, and professional. Second, they kept careful watch over the language used in the briefs; for example, they substituted "fetus" for "baby." They also coined the phrase "pro-choice" rather than the more value-laden "pro-abortion."

The results of all this preparation and coordination were dramatic. Taken independently, neither Weddington's brief (see table 5-5) nor any of the amicus curiae briefs (see table 5-6), save Planned Parenthood's, were particularly impressive. But together they made quite a case, serving to supplement each other rather than merely reinforce. Weddington's brief, after dealing with the procedural and jurisdictional issues and providing some background material on abortion, launched into its primary claim: unless the state could provide a compelling and narrowly drawn interest, the Texas law violated the First, Fourth, Ninth, and Fourteenth amendments. She also attempted to demonstrate that the law was vague and violated individuals' and doctors' rights. Each of these claims was reasonably well presented, with none taking a back seat to the others.

Nonetheless, much was missing from the Weddington effort, making the amici all the more important. The weakest part of the submission dealt with the "compelling interest" notion because she did not take very seriously state claims concerning the rights of the fetus. Although none of the amici specifically addressed countervailing arguments of fetal rights (see table 5-6), they filled in many gaps in Weddington's presentation. For example, the brief filed by the American College of Obstetricians and Gynecologists (ACOG) fully explicated the vagueness argument presented in the main brief. While Weddington used court cases to illustrate that hospitals, and even doctors within a given hospital, interpreted the law differently, ACOG drew on its vast practical experience, making the argument more effective. More illustrative were briefs filed by New Women Lawyers (NWL) and the American Association of University Women (AAUW). Weddington's brief barely mentioned the interests of women; it spoke in the more general terms of "individual rights." The NWL and AAUW sharpened the point, marshaling a variety of arguments to show how the restrictive laws infringed on women's rights.

It was Harriet Pilpel's brief for the Planned Parenthood Federation, however, that dealt most comprehensively with the topic. Surely this was not unexpected: of all the attorneys involved in *Roe*, Pilpel had been involved in the movement the longest. She saw the issue in all its dimensions—legal, social, and political—and

TABLE 5-5. Comparison of Arguments Made by Appellant and Appellee in *Roe v. Wade* (First Round of Arguments)

Argument	Appellant	Appellee
I. Procedural and Jurisdictional Issues		
Standing	Pregnancy is "capable of repetition." It is an "ongoing problem" (3 pages).	Case is mooted because she is no longer pregnant.
Case/ Controversy	Live case because Texas enforces its laws (thus, it is unlike *Poe*) (5 pages).	Implies that her claim might be hypothetical because only proof is an "alias affidavit" (6 pages).
Lower Court Relief	Injunction should have been issued; no other available state remedy exists (27 pages).	"Historically, there has been a great reluctance by federal courts to interfere in state operations" (7 pages).
II. Background Material on Abortion	History, contemporary medical standards (30 pages).	None.
III. Constitutional Arguments		
Individual Rights	Amendments 1, 4, 9, 14 violated because right to end pregnancy is an "integral part of privacy" with which the state can only interfere with a compelling interest (19 pages).	Constitution gives no right to abort fetus. Abortion does not interfere with "marital intercourse" (4 paragraphs).
Doctors' Rights	Amendments 1, 9, 14 violated because law constitutes arbitrary interference with the practice of medicine (4 pages).	Law does not interfere with doctor-patient relationship (1 paragraph).

her brief reflected such insight. It contained a slew of data indicating the physical and mental health risks associated with the restrictive laws; it also presented the most complete and well-articulated refutation of state claims. In short, with a bit more development on the legal end, the brief could have served as *Roe*'s (and *Doe*'s) best vehicle.

TABLE 5-5 *(continued)*

Argument	Appellant	Appellee
Vagueness	The law is vague: too much variation from hospital to hospital, doctor to doctor; court cases illustrate confusion (15 pages).	"All homicide laws have some degree of vagueness."
IV. Compelling State Interest	None; e.g., no public health risk (2 pages); fetus is not a human being with rights (7 pages).	"Humanness" of fetus (24 pages, 9 photos), as depicted in detailed description of gestational cycle.

THE PRO-LIFE SIDE PREPARES

In the highly charged political environment surrounding abortion in the 1990s, state attorneys cannot ignore the issue. Such was not the case in the early 1970s. From the onset of *Roe*, the Texas attorney general's office looked at the litigation as a waste of time. Besides the fact that district attorneys hardly ever prosecuted anyone under the laws and that the office had other priorities (it was deluged with civil rights suits), state attorneys thought *Roe* an easy case. In their view, the fact that the plaintiff was no longer pregnant made the controversy moot. Even if the Court reached a decision on the merits, surely the state had a legitimate interest in protecting life. The briefs they filed reflected these assumptions. The attorneys devoted about four paragraphs to counter the arguments based on individual rights brought by their opposition (see table 5-5). Their response to the vagueness claim was similarly underdeveloped. It was the issue of fetal rights—which went largely uncountered by the pro-choice side—with which Texas was most concerned. It devoted twenty-four pages, along with nine photographs of fetuses at various stages of development, to depict the "humanness" of the unborn. Its basic argument, though, was the position most frequently favored by pro-life forces: that states possess a compelling interest in protecting human life, and since fetuses, as the photos and text sought to demonstrate, are life, the government can restrict their destruction by abortion (*Roe*, Brief for Appellee, no. 70-18).

The state side, on the whole, lacked the depth possessed by its opponents. Georgia's brief, though somewhat tighter and more legalistic than Texas's, did very little to counter *Doe*'s position. The bulk of it was devoted to procedural and

TABLE 5-6. Comparison of Amicus Curiae Briefs Filed on Behalf of Appellants and Appellees in *Roe* and *Doe* (First Round of Arguments)

For Appellants	For Appellees

PRACTITIONERS/MEDICAL COMMUNITY

American College of Obstetricians and Gynecologists et al.[a]	*Certain Physicians . . . of the American College of Obstetricians and Gynecologists*[b]

1. Unconstitutionally vague because it is inconsistent with the best medical practice.
    A. Infringes on constitutionally protected rights of patients and doctors.
2. Law bears no relationship to a public health interest.
	1. The obstetrician has "two patients: mother *and* child."
	
	2. Medical "hazards" exist in "legally induced abortions."
	    A. It is "deplorable to think discussions of mortality can so easily exclude the child [whose] mortality . . . is nearly 100 percent."

3. Law advances "no legitimate interest in protecting human life."	3. It is a "scientific fact" that the unborn are "autonomous human beings" and thus "persons" under the Constitution.
Planned Parenthood Federation, et al.[c]	*Nurses and Doctors (see Women for the Unborn)*

1. Data on "unwanted births, contraceptives and abortion show the compelling need for action by this court."
    A. Restrictive laws endanger women's lives.
    B. Restrictive laws most hurt poor and adolescents.
2. Laws violate Amendments 9, 14 unless a compelling interest can be shown. But,
    A. no "moral" effect (laws do not reduce illicit sex),
    B. no desire to increase population,
    C. no health interest as it is a safe procedure,
    D. fetal interests can not be given precedence over woman's.	

TABLE 5-6 *(continued)*

For Appellants	For Appellees

WOMEN'S ORGANIZATIONS

New Women Lawyers et al.[d]

1. Violates women's rights under the due process clause of Amendment 14.
    A. "Persons seeking to uphold restrictive laws argue that the state has a compelling interest in protecting life. Amici could not agree more:" the life of the woman.
    B. Pregnancy "severely limits a woman's liberty."
2. Denial of women's rights under the equal protection clause of Amendment 14.
    A. A "woman who has a child is subject a whole range of *de jure* and *de facto* punishment."

3. No compelling state interests.
    A. No scientific evidence that fetus is a person, so ultimately arguments fall on particular religious view. Thus, violation of religious establishment clause of Amendment 1.
4. Restrictive laws violate the cruel and unusual punishment clause of Amendment 8.
    A. Pain and suffering associated with unwanted pregnancy.
    B. Punishing women for sexual activity.

American Association of University Women et al.[f]

1. Women have a right to "reproductive autonomy."
2. Restrictive abortion laws have a serious effect on the "life, dignity, and personal freedom" of women.
    A. Illegal abortions subject women to health problems.
    B. Unwanted pregnancies affect a woman's educational plans, mental health, marital relations, etc.

Women for the Unborn et al.[e]

1. "We realize that pro-abortionists are often acting out of mercy. They want to save the mother. . . . But is that sufficient reason to kill?"

2. "Despite assurances by abortion advocates," many in the "black community seem to suspect that numerous clinics in ghetto areas could end up as the 'white man's' solution to the problems of poverty and race."

3. Protects life of the unborn, which is a "distinct individual."

TABLE 5-6 *(continued)*

For Appellants	For Appellees

GROUPS REPRESENTING THE POOR

State Communities Aid Association

1. The "impact" of restrictive laws "is felt most heavily by the poor and non-white," and thus they constitute discrimination under the equal protection clause of Amendment 14.

National Legal Program on Health Problems of the Poor et al.[g]

1. No health interest of the state is served; "on the contrary, [the law] has created a severe health problem."
2. Laws discriminate against the poor and nonwhite, forcing them to seek illegal abortions.

RELIGIOUS INTERESTS

American Ethical Union et al.[h]

1. Laws constitute an invasion of liberty and privacy.
2. "The religious view that the product of every conception is sacred may not validly be urged by the states as a justification for limiting the exercise of constitutional liberties, for that would be an establishment of religion."

SINGLE-ISSUE (ABORTION) GROUPS

National Abortion Action Coalition (see New Women Lawyers)

Celebrate Life (see Women for the Unborn)

Minnesota Citizens Concerned for Life (see Women for the Unborn)

Americans United for Life

1. "Child in the womb" is a person under the equal protection clause of Amendment 14.

   A. If abortion is legal, it would make the child "the victim of an unreason-

TABLE 5-6 *(continued)*

For Appellants	For Appellees
	able classification and invidious discrimination."
	2. The child's rights are not inferior to the mother's.

National Right to Life Committee

1. Neither Amendment 9 nor 14 prohibits "the state from protecting against the destruction of human life."

    A. It is an "indisputable medical fact that the fetus" is life.

    B. Anglo-Saxon law has "always had a compelling interest in preventing the destruction of the unborn."

2. Hence, "life" must take constitutional precedence over privacy.

League for Infants, Fetuses, and the Elderly

1. "The right to life is the most nearly absolute right."

2. "Abortion is only the opening wedge of a broad based social attack on the right to life."

---

[a]Cosigned by American Psychiatric Association, American Medical Women's Association, New York Academy of Medicine, and 178 Physicians.

[b]Filed on behalf of Certain Physicians and Fellows of the ACOG, not the ACOG itself.

[c]Cosigned by American Association of Planned Parenthood Physicians.

[d]Cosigned by Women's Health and Abortion Project, National Abortion Action Coalition. The brief was authored by CCR attorneys.

[e]Cosigned by Celebrate Life, Women Concerned for the Unborn, Minnesota Citizens for Life, New York State Columbiettes, 87 Nurses, and 55 Doctors.

[f]Cosigned by American Association of University Women, National Board of the YWCA, NOW, National Women's Conference of the American Ethical Union, Professional Women's Caucus, Unitarian Universalist Women's Federation, Women's Alliance of First Unitarian Church of Dallas, and 46 individuals.

[g]Cosigned by National Welfare Rights Organization and American Public Health Association.

[h]Cosigned by American Friends Service Committee, American Humanist Association, American Jewish Congress, Episcopal Diocese of New York, New York State Council of Churches, Union of American Hebrew Congregations, Unitarian Universalist Association, United Church of Christ, and Board of Christian Social Concerns of the United Methodist Church.

jurisdictional issues; the remainder, to supporting the assertion that "Georgia has long maintained a public policy of recognizing that an unborn child has protectable interests" (*Doe*, Brief for Appellee, no. 70-40). Likewise, the amicus curiae briefs filed in their support (see table 5-6) did little to supplement state arguments; rather, they were "me-too" efforts centered on (to a greater or lesser extent) the notion of fetal rights.[64] The fact that many interested parties chose to stay outside of the fray presented another problem for the pro-life side. Not one state wrote a supporting brief, even though forty-six had laws similar to the ones at issue in *Roe* and *Doe*.[65] Perhaps more interesting and certainly more important was that the Nixon administration, despite the president's stated abhorrence of abortion, failed to take any action in the cases.

On balance, then, the legal record of *Roe* and *Doe* reveals much about the relative forces at work on this issue in the early 1970s and the sorts of arguments they made. The competing sides bore little resemblance to one another: the pro-choice movement was broad-based and more diffuse in composition and organization than the narrowly focused pro-life forces (see table 5-6), reflecting the varying manners in which the two were founded and the ways in which they evolved. Further, even though the pro-life side was, qualitatively and quantitatively, overmatched in legal preparation, the pro-choicers were not as strong as they might have been. In fact, neither side paid much attention to the core arguments of the other (see tables 5-5 and 5-6); indeed, this inattention bordered on outright ignorance. How the Court would deal with this argumentational gulf was a question left for orals.

ORAL ARGUMENTS

It is usually the case that attorneys enter oral arguments with a fairly concrete sense of how the Court or, at least, some justices will vote. To an extent, this was true in the abortion battle as well. Based on their votes and opinions in the only two cases of any real relevance—*Griswold* and *Vuitch*—it was reasonably clear that of the seven sitting justices the pro-choice side could count on Brennan and Douglas. Also, given his propensity to ally with Brennan in other areas, Marshall was probably a safe bet. The remaining four justices were largely unknowns on the issue. White and Stewart both participated in *Griswold* and *Vuitch* but had come to different conclusions. Stewart dissented in *Griswold*—expressing the view that the law was obsolete but not unconstitutional per se—but he also dissented in *Vuitch*, writing that he would immunize doctors from prosecution under Washington's law. Although White concurred in *Griswold* on Fourteenth Amendment due process grounds, he also concurred with Black's opinion in *Vuitch*, upholding the Washington abortion law.

Burger and Blackmun, the two Nixon appointees, were equally difficult to predict. Neither had been on the Court very long nor had they participated in any privacy-related case, save *Vuitch*, in which they voted with the majority. Additionally, even though neither could be categorized as a liberal (especially on criminal process questions), *Roe* and *Doe* presented a novel issue, one on which the role of ideology remained unknown. This was perhaps more true for Blackmun than for Burger. As a former counsel to the Mayo Clinic, and as an individual deeply interested in medical issues, the most junior justice may have formed some opinion about abortion; regardless, his position—or even whether he had one—was as yet unknown. Accordingly, both sides entered the courtroom on 13 December 1971 with less information than usual about the Court's predisposition. And if they expected orals to help them clear up some of the unknowns, they were in for a disappointment: it was a disjointed morning.

That the justices and the attorneys were somewhat confused, or at least in disagreement about the primary issues involved, was evident almost as soon as Weddington stepped up to the podium. After a brief exchange with Burger (in which he suggested that *Vuitch* might have "disposed of some of the questions raised" here), she launched into a policy-oriented argument about the inability of "the poor and the disadvantaged"[66] to obtain abortions in Texas.[67] Stewart broke in, suggesting that she could make any constitutional claims she wished, but that "before [she] get[s] to those, there are a good many threshold questions." He turned the discussion to procedural and jurisdictional issues, but Weddington returned the issue to a substantive focus, going on for nearly ten minutes about the problems faced by women who found themselves with unwanted pregnancies. Perhaps because she stressed that issue more in her argument than in the brief, or maybe because she sounded more like a lobbyist staking out a policy position than an attorney making a legal claim, White set a trap. He asked specifically in what provision of the Constitution an abortion right rested. Weddington was ambiguous: she mentioned the Ninth Amendment, then the Fourteenth. Finally, she relented, asserting: "We had originally brought this suit alleging both the due process clause, equal protection clause, and the Ninth Amendment, and a variety of others." To which White responded, "And anything else that might obtain." The justice would not leave it at that. He targeted the weakest element of the pro-choice argument: its failure to address the fetal rights issue. In particular, he wanted Weddington to respond to an issue not briefed: whether abortions should be conducted during all stages of pregnancy or should somehow be limited. The following discussion between Weddington and White ensued:

White: And the statute doesn't make any distinction based upon at what period of pregnancy the abortion is performed?

Weddington: No, Your Honor. There is no time limit or indication of time, whatsoever. So I think—

White: What's your constitutional position there?

Weddington: As to a time limit—

White: What about whatever clause of the Constitution you rest on—Ninth Amendment, due process, the general pattern penumbra—that take you right up to the time of birth?

Weddington: It is our position that the freedom involved is that of a woman to determine whether or not to continue a pregnancy. Obviously I have a much more difficult time saying that the State has no interest in late pregnancy.

White: Why? Why is that?

Weddington: I think that's more the emotional response to a late pregnancy, rather than it is any constitutional—

White: Emotional response by whom?

Weddington: I guess by persons considering the issue outside the legal context, I think, as far as the State—

White: Well, do you or don't you say that the constitutional—

Weddington: I would say the constitutional—

White:—right you insist on reaches up to the time of birth, or—

Weddington: The Constitution, as I read it . . . attaches protection to the person at the time of birth. Those persons born are citizens. The enumeration clause, we count those people who are born, the Constitution, as I see it, gives protection to people after birth.

At this juncture, Douglas helped her out by bringing the discussion back to jurisdictional issues and starting anew the procedural-to-substantive-to-procedural cycle. White's point, however, was clear: he had some concerns about the interests of the state in protecting the fetus. Whether other justices shared those concerns was still unknown.

If Weddington's performance was less than stellar, that of Texas's assistant attorney general, Jay Floyd, was downright awful. His problems began with his opening comment. Referring to the fact that his opponents (Weddington and Hames) were women,[68] he said, "Mr. Chief Justice, may it please the Court: it's an old joke, but when a man argues against two beautiful ladies like this, they are going to have the last word." Apparently, the offensiveness of his quip did not dawn on him until dead silence fell in the courtroom. A bit flustered, he continued with his presentation, but he never got on track. He gave poor, even incorrect, answers to questions involving procedure and jurisdiction. For example, after suggesting that the controversy was moot, the following discussion ensued:

> *The Court:* How do you suggest, if you're right, how do you—what procedure would you suggest for any pregnant female in the State of Texas ever to get any judicial consideration of this constitutional claim?
>
> *Floyd:* Your Honor, let me answer your question with a statement, if I may. I do not believe it can be done. There are situations in which, of course as the Court knows, no remedy is provided. Now I think she makes her choice prior to the time she becomes pregnant. That is the time of the choice. It's like, more or less, the first three or four years of our life we don't remember anything. But, once a child is born, a woman no longer has a choice, and I think pregnancy then terminates that choice. That's when.
>
> *The Court:* Maybe she makes her choice when she decides to live in Texas.
>
> [Laughter]

Perhaps Floyd's gravest problems occurred when Marshall questioned him, from a pro-choice vantage point, about the state's interest in much the same way White had queried Weddington from a pro-life perspective.

> *Marshall:* What is Texas' interest? What is Texas' interest in the statute?
>
> *Floyd:* Mr. Justice . . . the Court of Criminal Appeals did not decide the issue of privacy. It was not before the court; or, the right of choice issue. The State—the State Court, Court of Criminal Appeals, held that the State had a compelling interest because of the protection of fetal life—of fetal life protection. They recognized the humanness of the embryo, or the fetus, and they said we have an interest in protecting fetal life.
>
> Whether or not that was the original intent of the statute, I have no idea.

Floyd later added: "I speak personally, if I would think that even when this statute was first passed, there was some concern for the unborn fetus." And Marshall pursued the issue:

> *Marshall:* Well, in any event, Mr. Floyd, apart from your personal attitude, your court has spoken on the intent of the statute, has it not?
>
> *Floyd:* Yes.
>
> *Marshall:* Well, I can't quite square that most recent pronouncement with the earlier decisions of the Texas Court, that refer to the mother as the victim. Can you?

Floyd: Well, as I say, Your Honor, the—I don't think the courts have come to the conclusion that the unborn has full juristic rights—not yet. Maybe they will. I don't know. I just don't feel like they have, at the present time.

Marshall: In the first few weeks of pregnancy?

Floyd: Sir?

Marshall: In the first few weeks of pregnancy?

Floyd: At any time, Mr. Justice. We make no distinctions in our statute.

Marshall: You make no distinctions whether there's life there or not?

Floyd: We say there is life from the moment of impregnation.

Marshall: And do you have any scientific data to support that?

Floyd: Well we begin, Mr. Justice, in our brief, with the development of the human embryo, carrying it through the development of the fetus from about seven to nine days after conception.

Marshall: Well, what about six days?

Floyd: We don't know.

Marshall: But the statute goes all the way back to one hour?

Floyd: I don't—Mr. Justice, there are unanswerable questions in this field. I—

[Laughter]

Marshall: I appreciate it.

Floyd: This is an artless statement on my part.

Marshall: I withdraw the question.

All in all, then, neither attorney dominated orals. Though Floyd's lack of preparation, incorrect responses, and "artless statements" made his presentation inferior, Weddington acted more like a policy advocate than a constitutional lawyer. This ineptitude was in part a function of the nature of the case: the justices were clearly in disagreement over the primary issues at stake—procedural or substantive—and were also relatively clueless about the entire issue. Orals could have provided them, or at least some of them, with a direction from which to approach the question. Yet, in the opinion of many observers, neither attorney had charted a clear path. The justices returned to their chambers with little more than when they had left.

DECIDING HOW TO DECIDE: DECEMBER 1971–JUNE 1972

THE COURT

The Court's division over the abortion cases, manifest at orals, carried over into its conference of 16 December.[69] About the only point on which all seemed to agree was that procedural issues were essentially irrelevant. As Chief Justice Burger stated in his opening remarks: "Jane Roe is unmarried and pregnant. She doesn't claim health; just doesn't want the baby. [She] has standing. She didn't lose standing through mootness. . . . She's entitled to an injunction if the statute is [unconstitutional]." Beyond that, the justices divided into roughly three camps over *Roe*: one found the law unconstitutional, another felt it was constitutional, and a third was largely ambivalent.

A four-person majority consisting of Douglas, Brennan, Marshall, and, somewhat surprisingly, Stewart thought the Texas law ought to be stricken, though for somewhat different reasons. Douglas expressed a policy-oriented position: abortion is "a medical and psychiatric problem" that should not be restricted by state legislatures. Brennan argued that the "right to an abortion should be given a constitutional basis." Stewart agreed with this, but he believed that "[t]he state can legislate, to the extent of requiring a doctor and that, after a certain period of pregnancy, [she] can't have an abortion." Marshall embraced a bit of everything when he averred: "I go with Bill Douglas, but [the] time problem concerns me." He, like Stewart, thought that the state could not prohibit abortions "in the early stage [of pregnancy] but why can't the state prohibit after a certain stage?" He also agreed with Brennan, suggesting that he found the right to abortion within the Fourteenth Amendment's due process clause.

The remaining three justices were more fragmented. White came down most definitively in favor of the pro-life position. As he put it, "[O]n the merits I am on the other side. They want us to say that women have a choice under the Ninth Amendment." This White could not accept, therefore he voted to uphold the statute—the only certain vote in favor of the statute in 1971. Burger and Blackmun were less decisive, though the chief justice leaned toward the state's position and Blackmun toward the Douglas camp. In his opening comments on the merits, Burger said, "The balance here is between the state's interest in protecting fetal life and the woman's interest in not having children." His initial "balancing" led him to this conclusion: "I can't find the Texas statute unconstitutional, although it's certainly archaic and obsolete." What this meant remained somewhat unclear, but some members thought Burger had allied himself with White. After flatly stating that the "girl has standing," Blackmun asked: "Can a state properly outlaw all abortions? If we accept fetal life, there's a strong argument that it can. But there are opposing interests: the right of the mother to life and mental and physical health, the right of parents in case of rape, the right of the state in case of incest. I don't think there's an absolute right to do what you will with [your] body. [But] this statute is a poor statute that . . . impinges too far on her."

According to B. Schwartz (1988), the discussion of *Doe* "paralleled" that in

Roe, "with only a few minor exceptions." Burger was more definitive, asserting that he would "hold this statute constitutional." His usual ally, Blackmun, was a bit more confident in expressing his views on the Georgia law but was still uncertain. Schwartz (1990, 299) reports Blackmun's comments as follows:

> Once again, Justice Blackmun's position was ambivalent. "Medically," he pointed out, "this statute is perfectly workable," but he emphasized the competing interests at stake. "I would like to see an opinion that recognizes the opposing interests in fetal life and the mother's interest in health and happiness." Blackmun also indicated interest in Douglas's approach. "I would be perfectly willing to paint some standards and remand for findings as to how it operates: does it operate to deny equal protection by discriminating against the poor?"

Thus, although there was disagreement over the logic to be used in resolving these cases, the result was clear: the pro-choice side would win by a vote of 5–2 or 4–3, depending on how Blackmun voted; for example, Douglas expected that Blackmun would vote with Burger. This also assumed that Burger—consistent with his conference comments—would vote to uphold both laws or at least that involved in *Doe*.

Even though Blackmun seemed to be in the minority in both *Roe* and *Doe*, Burger assigned the opinion to him. He probably did this under the assumption that Blackmun, as the weakest link in the Brennan-Douglas-Stewart-Marshall chain (if he was, in fact, part of that chain), would author the narrowest possible opinion. This (mis)assignment triggered a series of events, the first of which was an irate letter from Douglas to Burger. He had two bones to pick: first, as the senior member of the majority, he should have assigned the opinion; second, Blackmun should not have received the assignment in any event because his tally sheets put him in the minority. As he wrote: "I would think, therefore, that to save time and trouble, one of the four [in the majority], rather than one of the three [in the minority], should write the opinion." Burger responded two days later: "At the close of discussion of this case, I remarked to the Conference that there were, literally, not enough columns to mark up an accurate reflection of the voting in either the Georgia or the Texas cases. I therefore marked down no votes and said this was a case that would have to stand or fall on the writing, when it was done." Burger concluded, "That is still my view of how to handle these two . . . sensitive cases, which, I might add, are quite probable candidates for reargument."

On the heels of this dispute, some of the justices began preparing draft opinions. It took Douglas only four days to circulate a "dissent" to Brennan. In it, he essentially adopted the view Marshall expressed at the conference: the right to an abortion could be found in the word "liberty" in the due process clause (B. Schwartz 1988, 93). Brennan responded ten days later with some suggestions for revision and with the admonition that Douglas should hold off sending the draft to Blackmun until he circulated his. Douglas heeded this advice, redrafting the opinion to center on a woman's right to obtain abortion services. By late February, though, he became impatient awaiting Blackmun's opinion and sent his revised opinion to the junior justice.

It was not until mid-May 1972 that Blackmun circulated his draft of the *Roe* opinion.[70] While he stressed in his cover memo that this was a "first and tentative draft," Douglas and Brennan were deeply disappointed. He struck the Texas law on the narrowest possible grounds, those raised by Burger in his first question to Weddington centering on vagueness,[71] and did not deal with the "core constitutional questions"—individual liberty and "freedom from bodily restraint"—that the conference majority had framed.[72]

Several days after both Brennan and Douglas urged him to recast his draft, Blackmun circulated his *Doe* opinion. This one was far more to the liberals' liking because it adopted much of what Douglas's second draft had to say about privacy and women's rights. Where they thought Blackmun went astray was in exploring the state's interest in protecting life. In this version, he stressed the point that somewhere around quickening a woman's right to privacy is no longer "unlimited. It must be balanced against the state. [Thus] we cannot automatically strike down . . . features of the Georgia statute simply because they restrict any right on the part of the woman to have an abortion at will." Despite the qualms Brennan and Douglas had over such a balancing approach (actually suggested by Burger in conference), they planned to sign the opinion;[73] it led Blackmun to the "right" result.

Just when it appeared as if a five-person majority would coalesce around Blackmun's opinion, Burger reinitiated efforts to have the case reargued. Ostensibly, his reason was that "[t]hese cases . . . are not as simple for me as they appear for the others." He also "complained that part of his problem . . . resulted from the poor quality of oral argument." Brennan, Douglas, Stewart, and Marshall felt differently. In their view, Burger pushed for reargument because he was displeased with Blackmun's opinion in *Doe* and thought his side would stand a better chance of victory next term when two more Nixon appointees—Powell and Rehnquist—would participate in orals. Also, Douglas later suggested that Burger believed the *Doe* opinion would prove embarrassing to President Nixon's reelection campaign and sought to minimize the damage. Unfortunately for the pro-choice wing, on the same day, 31 May, Blackmun also suggested that the cases be reargued. In a memo to conference, he wrote: "Although it would prove costly to me personally, in the light of energy and hours expended, I have now concluded, somewhat reluctantly, that reargument in *both* cases at an early date in the next term, would perhaps be advisable."[74] Despite Brennan's and Douglas's attempts to thwart this action, after White and the two new appointees voted with Burger, on the last day of the 1971 term the Court ordered rearguments in both *Roe* and *Doe*.[75]

THE PRO-CHOICE SIDE

As the Court went through its spring 1972 deliberations over abortion, "a veil of lethargy settled over the reform movement" as they were "preoccupied" with waiting (Faux 1988, 255). This may have been true of Weddington, personally, but surely not of movement attorneys generally. Many continued to press their cause, sometimes in rather unconventional ways. After orals in *Roe*, for example, ASA member Professor Cyril Means wrote Burger a letter, asking if he could send the justices a copy of his soon-to-be-published law review article, "The Phoenix of Abortional Freedom." The manuscript, which initially served as a NARAL amicus curiae brief in a state court abortion case (Lader 1973, 163), tried to dispel definitely the argument that fetuses possess constitutional rights. Among other things, Means (1971) indicated that medieval theologians rejected complete humanness until birth, the census has never counted fetuses, and early court decisions never contemplated them as citizens with rights.

Pro-choice forces also continued to "lobby" courtrooms in the more traditional sense—through legal suits. In fact, during the spring of 1972 they won several judicial battles, the most noteworthy being *Eisenstadt v. Baird* (1972) and *Abele v. Markle* (1972). *Eisenstadt* jelled when in 1967 family-planning advocate Bill Baird was arrested in Massachusetts for exhibiting and distributing contraceptives to unmarried people. After several rounds in state and federal courts, the U.S. Supreme Court struck down the Massachusetts law just four months after it had heard arguments in *Roe* and *Doe*. Writing for a six-person majority (with only Burger dissenting), Brennan asserted that it violated the "rights of single people" under the Fourteenth Amendment's equal protection clause. In dicta, he went much further:

> If under *Griswold* the distribution of contraceptives to married persons cannot be prohibited, a ban on distribution to unmarried persons would be equally impermissible. It is true that in *Griswold* the right of privacy in question inhered in the marital relationship. Yet the marital couple is not an independent entity with a mind and heart of its own, but an association of two individuals each with separate intellectual and emotional makeup. If the right of privacy means anything, it is the right of the *individual*, married or single, to be free from unwarranted governmental intrusion into matters so

fundamentally affecting a person as the decision whether to bear or beget a child. (*Eisenstadt* 1972, 453)

Whether he wrote this with *Roe* and *Doe* in mind we do not know for sure. But clearly *Eisenstadt* provided pro-choice forces with more ammunition for their argumentational assault.

Even more on point was a lower federal court's decision in *Abele*, which struck down as unconstitutional a Connecticut law that was a replica of the Texas law at issue in *Roe*. The court's opinion stressed the rights of women, asserting, "The decision to carry and bear a child has extraordinary ramifications for a woman." It also cited *Eisenstadt* to support its opinion that women possess a fundamental right to choose abortion, if they so desire.

THE POLITICAL ENVIRONMENT

As pro-choice forces racked up victories in the nation's judiciary,[76] the outside political environment remained relatively ambiguous. From the pro-choice perspective, the two most encouraging events occurred in February and March 1972. At its mid-year meeting, the American Bar Association's House of Delegates overwhelmingly adopted a proposal calling for "abortion on demand" within "20 weeks of the onset of pregnancy" (Graham 1972). On the heels of this came the March announcement by a Nixon-appointed commission created to study population problems that it too supported abortion on demand.[77] Based on its examination (which indicated that the availability of abortion decreased maternal and infant deaths, illegal abortions, and out-of-wedlock births), the commission recommended "that women should be free to determine their own fertility, that the matter of abortion should be left to the conscience of the individual concerned, in consultation with her physician, and that states should be encouraged to enact affirmative statutes creating a clear and positive framework for the practice of abortion on request" (*New York Times* 1972b).

Still, the political environment remained uncertain on both elite and mass levels. Since 1972 was a presidential election year, one might think abortion would constitute a major source of debate between the parties. This was not the case. Although in the previous year, Nixon had issued a strongly worded statement against abortion, he worked hard to present a neutral image in 1972; more pointedly, as White (1973, 243–44) notes, his staff's "overwhelming advice to him was to be silent." The Democratic party front-runner at that point, George McGovern, probably favored the liberalization of abortion laws, but his official position was "to leave the decision . . . to each state's legislature as it interpreted its state's position" (Tatalovich and Daynes 1981, 197).

Such posturing seems to have reflected the opinions of Americans, which, as

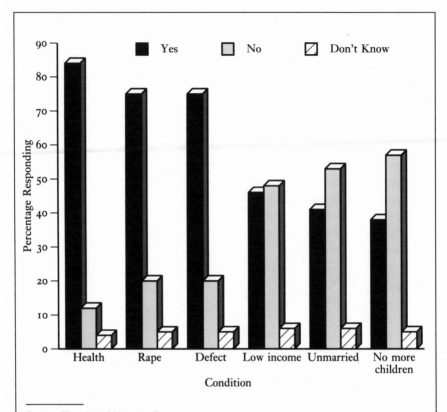

Source: Ebaugh and Haney 1980, 492.

Note: Data are derived from National Opinion Research Center General Survey, 1972. The question was: "Please tell me whether or not you think it should be possible for a pregnant woman to obtain a legal abortion 1) if the woman's health is seriously endangered by the pregnancy; 2) if she is pregnant as a result of a rape; 3) if there is a strong chance of serious defect in the baby; 4) if the family has a very low income and cannot afford any more children; 5) if she is not married and does not want to marry the man; 6) if she is married and does not want any more children."

FIGURE 5-4. Public Opinion on Abortion, 1972

demonstrated in figure 5-4, remained ambiguous. Though only 12 percent of the population totally disapproved of it (that is, under no circumstances should abortions be permitted), only 38 percent approved of it "on demand," under all circumstances. The rest remained somewhere in the middle, with responses highly dependent on the context of choice. As a result, political actors seemed reluctant to take an absolute stance; they were waiting until the public moved significantly one way or the other.

REDUX

PREPARING (AGAIN): SUMMER 1972

In the midst of this politically uncertain environment, the attorneys received word the Court wanted to rehear the cases. While neither side knew precisely what to make of the order, they did have some idea of the Court's motivation. About a week after the request for rehearing came down, the *Washington Post* (4 July 1972) published a reasonably accurate account of the Court's inner workings on the abortion cases, including the facts that Blackmun was writing the majority opinion, that Douglas had protested that assignment, and that there had been a fight over reargument. Under normal circumstances, pro-choice forces should have been delighted: the article revealed that they had the votes to win. But circumstances were far from normal—two new justices (Rehnquist and Powell), and Nixon appointees at that, would now have a say in the outcome.

With the order for a rehearing, Roe's and Doe's attorneys decided to file supplemental briefs, apprising the Court of recent developments, legal and otherwise,[78] as did Planned Parenthood.[79] In addition, two new amicus curiae briefs arrived at the Court. One, submitted by the California Committee to Legalize Abortion on behalf of two other groups,[80] made a relatively unique argument: existing abortion laws violate the Thirteenth Amendment's prohibition against involuntary servitude. The other, written by five state attorneys general, represented the first and only discretionary governmental participation in the case.

While the pro-choice side prepared, their opponents remained idle. Neither state filed additional briefs, because, at least in the case of Texas, governmental attorneys were preoccupied with other matters. The state's attorney general, Crawford Martin, had failed to gain reelection. As a result, the assistant attorney general who would be arguing *Roe*, Robert Flowers, "had too many other things on his mind to spend much time preparing. . . . [He] and most of his staff were about to be unemployed. They were devoting as much time to job hunting as to the still heavy load of cases" (Faux 1988, 281).

As the attorneys, or at least those on the pro-choice side, prepared for rearguments, most of the brethren were probably occupied with other matters over the summer. At this point, there was little for Brennan, Stewart, Marshall, or Douglas to do. By the same token, White had drafted his dissent before the end of the term. Burger was sitting tight, awaiting orals. Only Blackmun, it seemed, spent much of his summer researching the issue. He sought out a quiet spot in the Mayo Clinic's library, where he worked arduously on the abortion opinions, redrafting both.

What he (and the rest of the Court) apparently did not know was that one of the new justices would cast a strong vote for the pro-choice side. Lewis Powell had a clear opinion about restrictive abortion laws, garnered from his father-in-law and brothers-in-law, all of whom were obstetricians: he thought them "atrocious." Hence, he too spent part of the summer contemplating a legal rationale for striking them. He did not have to look far: according to Woodward and Armstrong (1979, 230), he was most impressed with the lower court's opinion in *Abele* and planned to adopt its reasoning.

THE COURT RETURNS TO THE FRAY

By the time of orals (11 October 1972), it was relatively clear that a majority of the Court would vote to strike the laws. This was fortunate for Weddington because her performance was, if anything, worse the second time around. Though she had reviewed the new decisions that had come down and the current crop of statistics, she faltered on two series of questions. One came from Blackmun who, apparently in the course of his summer research, became somewhat concerned over the Hippocratic oath. Presumably he was puzzled over how one of its mandates ("I will not give to a woman a pressary to produce abortion") could be squared with her position. When he queried her about this, it was clear that she had not given much thought to the matter. In the end, she dismissed it as being "old" and "not pertinent" to her argument. This did not seem to satisfy Blackmun, but he let the matter go.[81]

More significant was a series of questions, coming mainly from Stewart, White, and Burger, over fetal rights. At first, she handled them with aplomb:

The Court: Well, is it critical to your case that the fetus not be a person under the due process clause?

Weddington: It seems to me that it is critical, first, that we prove this is a fundamental interest on behalf of the woman, that it is a constitutional right, and second—

The Court: Well, yes. But about the fetus?

Weddington: Okay. And second, that the State has no compelling State interest. And the State is alleging a compelling State interest in—

The Court: Yes. But I'm just asking you, under the Federal Constitution, is the fetus a person, for the protection of due process?

Weddington: All of the cases—the prior history of this statute—the common law history would indicate that it is not. The State has shown no—

The Court: Well, what about—would you lose your case if the fetus was a person?

Weddington: Then you would have a balancing of interests.

The Court: Well, you say you have anyway, don't you?

Weddington: Excuse me?

The Court: You have anyway, don't you? You're going to be balancing the rights of the mother against the rights of the fetus.

Weddington: It seems to me that you do not balance constitutional rights of one person against mere statutory rights of another.

The Court: You think a State interest, if it's only a statutory interest, or a constitutional interest under the State law, can never outweigh a constitutional right?

Weddington: I think—it would seem to me that—

The Court: —so all talk of compelling State interest is beside the point. It can never be compelling enough.

Weddington: If the State could show that the fetus was a person under the Fourteenth Amendment, or under some other Amendment, or part of the Constitution, then you would have a situation of trying—you would have a State compelling interest which, in some instances, can outweigh a fundamental right. This is not the case in this particular situation.

In this way, Weddington avoided the trap of having to argue that the case would be lost if the Court failed to accept her primary argument. What she did not handle as well were repeated inquiries from the justices about cutoff points; she apparently did not pick up on the fact that most of the justices would be unwilling to allow abortions during the entire course of pregnancies. The following exchange demonstrates how she dealt with this set of questions.

The Court: Do you make any distinction between the first month, and ninth month of gestation?

Weddington: Our statute does not.

The Court: Do you, in your position in this case?

Weddington: We are asking, in this case, that the Court declare the statute unconstitutional; the State having proved no compelling interest at all.

There are some states that now have adopted time limits. Those have not yet been challenged. And, perhaps that question will be before this Court. Even those statutes, though, allow exceptions. Well New York, for example, says an abortion is lawful up to 24 weeks. But, even after the 24 weeks it is still lawful where there's rape or incest; where the mother's mental or physical health is involved. In other words, even after that period, it's not a hard and fast cutoff.

The Court: Then it's the weighing process that Mr. Justice White was referring to. Is that your position?

Weddington: The legislature, in that situation, engaged in the weighing process. And it seems to me that it has not yet been determined whether the State has the compelling interest to uphold even that kind of relation. But that's really not before the Court in this particular case.

That last statement underscored her strategic naïveté. Whether the issue was formally "before the Court" was far less significant than the fact that the justices were obviously concerned about it. Indeed, when it came right down to it, this point was one that escaped the entire pro-choice side. Having not dealt at all with gestational cycles or, perhaps, perused the photographs in the pro-life briefs, they simply failed to grasp the impact these considerations were having on even the most liberal members of the Court.

However poor Weddington's performance had been, once again her opponent's was worse. Flowers was unprepared and faltered at almost every turn. At one point, he practically gave away his case:

Flowers: Gentlemen, we feel that the concept of a fetus being within the concept of a person, within the framework of the United States Constitution and the Texas Constitution, is an extremely fundamental thing.

The Court: Of course, if you're right about that, you can sit down, you've won your case.

Flowers: Your Honor—

The Court: Except insofar as, maybe, the Texas abortion law presently goes too far in allowing abortions.

Flowers: Yes, sir. That's exactly right. We feel that this is the only question, really, that this Court has to answer. We have a—

The Court: Do you think the case is over for you? You've lost your case, then, if the fetus or the embryo is not a person? Is that it?

Flowers: Yes, sir, I would say so.

Though the orals in *Roe* and *Doe* were certainly not ideal models of appellate advocacy, it hardly mattered. Conference following them revealed that none of the original majority had changed their votes. Indeed, they were joined by Powell (but not Rehnquist, who said, "I agree with Byron. . . . I'm not going to second-guess state legislatures in striking the balance in favor of abortion laws"). One of the few points of discussion, in fact, concerned whether *Roe* or *Doe* should be the lead case. Blackmun argued for *Doe*, but the others agreed with Powell's sentiment that "Texas should be the lead." With this, the issue was settled.

A month or so later, Blackmun sent around the drafts of *Roe* and *Doe* he had revised over the summer and had apparently fine-tuned after orals. Douglas was the first to respond, writing that Blackmun had "done an excellent job," but that he would file a concurring opinion on some minor points. Brennan, Marshall, and Stewart also commended Blackmun but requested alterations in his draft. Revisions continued to circulate through December. It was not until 22 January 1973 that the Court was ready to announce its opinions.

ROE AND *DOE:* THE DECISIONS

Given the controversial nature of the abortion issue, coupled with the over one-year gap between the time the Court initially heard arguments and announced its opinion, many suspected that the justices would be quite divided over the issue. Indeed, some thought their *Roe* opinion would resemble the decision handed down the previous term in the capital punishment cases, when each member took the opportunity to write separately. This failed to transpire. In the final analysis, seven of the justices coalesced behind Blackmun's majority opinions in *Roe* and *Doe*, with only three writing concurrences. Justices White and Rehnquist filed separate, yet complementary, dissents. Why the Court rallied around the Blackmun opinion has something to do with the way in which he structured the final version, not to mention his willingness to compromise on some key points. Blackmun's arguments are detailed in table 5-7. After a brief introduction, over which Blackmun later said he "agonized,"[82] he gave relatively short shrift to the procedural issues; in fact, he adopted in full pro-choice arguments concerning the mootness question. Where Blackmun devoted the majority of his space, time, and effort was in that section of the opinion which detailed the history of abortion from ancient times to the present. In doing so, he relied quite heavily on the scholarship of pro-choice advocates, particularly of Means and Lader, and on information provided in amicus curiae briefs filed by professional organizations.

Blackmun's analysis of the history of abortion has been the subject of a great deal of criticism, scholarly and otherwise. Some argue that he relied too heavily on the works and writings of those squarely in the pro-choice camp; others suggest that he ignored certain historical periods that did not support his position. Still, Blackmun had his reasons. He wanted to use this history to scrutinize rationales for the current status of restrictive laws, which he identified as three: to discourage "illicit sexual conduct," to ensure the medical well-being of pregnant women, and to protect prenatal life. Invoking arguments supplied by amici and appellants, he rejected completely the first two. Although he had misgivings about the third, which represented the crux of the National Right to Life Committee's claims, he would not firmly commit to rejecting it. On the one hand, he seemed to accept the pro-choice argument that it was not the original purpose of the laws to protect prenatal life; the early pre- and post-quickening

TABLE 5-7. Blackmun's Opinion in *Roe v. Wade*

Section/Argument	Support	Explanation
I. Introduction (2 pages): "We forthwith acknowledge our awareness of the sensitive and emotional nature of the abortion controversy, of the vigorous opposing views, even among physicians, and of the deep and seemingly absolute convictions that the subject inspires."		Blackmun claims later that he "agonized" over this paragraph.
II. Procedural Issues (9 pages)		
A. Roe: Given the brevity of the gestation period, if termination of pregnancy "makes a case moot, pregnancy litigation would seldom survive much beyond the trial stage." It is also "capable of repetition."		
B. Does/Halliford: Dismissed their claims.		
III. History of Abortion (17 pages)		
A. Ancient attitudes: "Greek and Roman law afforded little protection to the unborn."	Scholarship (e.g., Lader, Edelstein).	
B. Hippocratic oath: "The oath originated in a group representing only a small segment of Greek opinion . . . and it was not accepted by all ancient physicians."	Work on the oath by Edelstein.	Blackmun mentions that neither party briefed this issue.
C. Common law: Quickening was used as demarcation point. Unclear whether aborting even a quick fetus was a crime.	Work by Means.	Blackmun relies quite heavily on Means's 1971 law review article.
D. English statutory law: Briefly reviews restrictive laws passed in the early 1800s; discusses in-depth *Rex v. Bourne*.		
E. American law: Describes development of abortion laws, reaching the conclusion that "a woman enjoyed a substantially broader right to terminate a pregnancy [throughout much of the nineteenth century] than she does in most states today."	Scholarship (Lader, Means, Quay).	
F. AMA's position: Reviews early push for restrictive laws, then action taken toward liberalization in 1970.	AMA records.	Blackmun is among the first to recognize the significant role the

TABLE 5-7 *(continued)*

Section/Argument	Support	Explanation
		AMA played in lobbying states to enact nineteenth century laws.
G. Positions of APHA and ABA: Reviews recent actions taken by both toward liberalization.	Organizational records.	
IV. Reasons/Justifications for Laws (4 pages)		
A. Discourage illicit sex: If this were true, then (as amici and appellant argue) law would be overbroad because it applies to single and married.		Notes that Texas did not brief this.
B. Concerns about safety: These are no longer relevant.	Medical evidence and studies discussed in Lader.	
C. Protecting prenatal life.	Cite to amicus National Right to Life Committee.	
1. Pro-choice forces argue that this was not the original purpose of the laws.	"There is some scholarly support for this" (cite to Means) and the use of quickening reinforces this view.	
2. Yet case turns on the issue of that state interest versus the interests of women.	This forms the core of many lower court opinions.	
V. Constitutional Claims (11 pages)		
A. Right to privacy: "Whether found in the 14th Amendment's concept of personal liberty . . . , as we feel it is . . . or in the 9th Amendment . . . [privacy] is broad enough to encompass a woman's decision whether or not to terminate a pregnancy."	Precedent (e.g., *Griswold*, *Baird*).	

TABLE 5-7 *(continued)*

Section/Argument	Support	Explanation
1. Too much harm to a woman if she does not have a choice (mental, physical, psychological, social stigma).		Does not cite any amici, but adopts arguments put forth in the several "women's briefs."
2. Yet "we do not agree" with appellants and some amici that the right is "absolute." At some point in the pregnancy state interests "become sufficiently compelling."	"Balancing approach" used in many lower court cases.	Even though Blackmun casts the right in Fourteenth Amendment terms, he accepts the compelling standard.
B. State interests in protecting fetus: If the fetus is not a person under the Fourteenth Amendment, the state's case "collapses."	Admission of state attorney on reargument.	Blackmun pokes a bit of fun at the attorney, noting that he made this argument but could provide no legal support for it.
1. A review of the use of the word "person" within various portions of the Constitution reveals that "none indicates, with any assurance that it has any possible pre-natal application."		This is Means's argument, but Blackmun does not cite to it.
2. Hence, "the word 'person,' as used in the 14th Amendment, does not include the unborn."		
C. State interests versus woman's: Still, "the pregnant woman . . . carries an embryo, and later, a fetus." Thus, she is not "isolated in her privacy." At some point, state interests come into play. But at what point?	Cites to medical literature.	
1. The state's position of conception is not supported, largely because a consensus does not exist with relevant populations, nor have other areas of the law given credence to the view that life begins before birth.	Cites to brief of American Ethical Union, Lader, medical literature, court cases.	
2. Doctor's position has largely concerned itself with viability of fetus.		

TABLE 5-7 *(continued)*

Section/Argument	Support	Explanation
3. In the end, then, the interests of states and doctors grow "in substantiality as the woman approaches term and, at a point during pregnancy, . . . become compelling."		
VI. The Holding (5 pages)		
A. Stage prior to the end of the first trimester: "The abortion decision and its effectuation must be left to the medical judgment of the pregnant woman's attending physician."		The division of pregnancy into trimesters seems to come from nowhere. That is so because Blackmun originally had divided pregnancy in two. Trimesters, in essence, represented a compromise between "quickening" and viability.
B. Stage subsequent to the end of the first trimester: "The state . . . may regulate the abortion procedure in ways that are reasonably related to maternal health.		
C. Stage subsequent to viability: "The state . . . may . . . regulate, and even proscribe abortion, except where necessary" to preserve the "life or health of the mother."		

distinction supports this. On the other hand, he gave credence to the view that virtually all lower court judges sought to balance the interests of the state against those of the woman.

In what followed, Blackmun explored those opposing positions. He asserted in general, with the sort of ambivalence that characterized Weddington's argument, that the right to privacy, whether located in the Ninth Amendment or, as he felt, in the Fourteenth Amendment, "encompasses" the right to obtain abortion services. Nonetheless, that right is not unlimited; at some point state interests come into play. The final question, and thus perhaps the most significant, was at what point states can become involved in the abortion decision. The frame of reference he used throughout the opinion—pre- and post-quickening—seemed a logical dividing line. Yet Blackmun eschewed it for the so-called trimester scheme (see table 5-7). And he adopted "viability"—not quickening—as the demarcation of the point separating when states may regulate abortions to protect maternal health and when they may proscribe it.

Why viability? Why the trimester scheme? Blackmun's opinion seemed to adduce these determinations from his reading of medical journals, which gave his holding something of an empirical aura, reflective of the current state of scientific-medical knowledge. Memoranda of the justices circulated in the months directly preceding the announcement of the decision, however, reveal a much more complex story (Urofsky 1987; Woodward 1989; Schwartz 1990). In a letter drafted on 21 November 1972, Blackmun informed his colleagues that he would separate choice from proscription at thirteen weeks (roughly the first trimester). He acknowledged that this was "arbitrary . . . but, perhaps any other selected point, such as quickening or viability (of the fetus), is equally arbitrary." Shortly thereafter, three justices registered separate complaints: Marshall wanted the line drawn at viability, Douglas preferred the original first trimester standard, and Stewart was concerned about the desirability of the dicta being so inflexibly "legislative."

In the final analysis, Blackmun mediated among these views to articulate the plan in *Roe*. In doing so, he allowed for the creation of a strong majority, which coalesced around a standard that would give states clear guidelines for subsequent legislation. Indeed, only three majority justices wrote separately. Two—Douglas and Stewart—merely took the opportunity to reiterate their personal perspectives on the right to privacy. Chief Justice Burger, though, used his concurrence to separate himself from the Blackmun opinion. Although he agreed that the laws of Georgia and Texas "impermissibly limit the performance of abortion," he did not view the judgments as having "sweeping consequences." That Burger took this tack was hardly surprising; after all, until push came to shove he had voted with the minority. Why he changed his mind at the eleventh hour is the stuff of speculation.[83] What was clear, though, was that Burger, as Blackmun later said, was "never very enthusiastic about joining the majority" (Jenkins 1983).

White and Rehnquist issued a joint dissent in both cases, and Rehnquist wrote separate dissents in *Roe* and *Doe*, outlined in table 5-8. They critiqued the Court's modus operandi—in particular its use of a compelling state interest test to assess the statutes under the Fourteenth Amendment due process clause—and its reliance on "raw judicial power" to reach an "extravagant" and "improvident" decision.

IMMEDIATE REACTIONS

Six days before the Court announced its decision in *Roe* and *Doe*, Blackmun circulated a memo suggesting, "I anticipate the headlines that will be produced over the country when the abortion decisions are announced." To prevent the press from "going all the way off the deep end," he had prepared an announce-

TABLE 5-8. The Dissents in *Roe* and *Doe*

REHNQUIST IN *ROE*[a]

I. Procedural
   A. Roe may have filed suit during the third trimester of pregnancy, in which case the state could prohibit her from obtaining an abortion.

II. Privacy: Fourteenth Amendment Due Process Clause
   A. The law bears a rational relation to state interest; reliance on a "compelling interest" standard "eschews history."
   B. Thus, the Court engages in Lochneresque jurisprudence.

III. Constitutional/Textual Basis for the Decision
   A. The Court's decision lacks any constitutional or textual basis. In fact, restrictive abortion laws existed at the time of the framing of the Fourteenth Amendment.

WHITE (JOINED BY REHNQUIST) IN *ROE* AND *DOE*

I. Privacy: Fourteenth Amendment Due Process Clause
   A. No legitimate constitutional reason exists for placing the rights of women above fetuses.

II. Constitutional/Textual Basis for the Decision
   A. Nothing "in the language or history of the Constitution" supports the Court's decision.

III. The Role of the Court
   A. This decision represents "raw judicial power." It is "extravagant" and "improvident."
   B. Abortion should be left to the people to decide.

---

[a] He also wrote a one-paragraph dissent in *Doe*, reiterating his position in *Roe*: "The compelling state interest standard [is] an inappropriate measure of the constitutionality of state abortion laws."

ment he planned to read from the bench, a copy of which he forwarded to the justices (H. Schwartz 1988).

A glance at the front page of the *New York Times* after the decision was disclosed suggests that Blackmun's precautions seemed unnecessary. Several other newsworthy events occurred on the same day the Court announced its holdings: Lyndon Johnson died of a heart attack; Henry Kissinger arrived in Paris to begin talks that would end the Vietnam War; and George Foreman "smashed" Joe Frazier "to the floor six times" to win the heavy-weight boxing title. However, it did not take long before news of the holdings set in, bringing "cries of moral anguish and ecstasy from abortion partisans" (Rodman, Sarvis, and Bonar 1987, 104). Members of the Catholic church hierarchy were among the first to express outrage. In statements printed in the *New York Times*, Cardinal Cooke of New York asked: "How many millions of children prior to their birth will never live to see the light of day because of the shocking action of the majority of the . . . Court?" Other pro-life leaders were shocked. As one recalls: "We knew that the decision was in the court. . . . We knew that these cases had been appealed and that there was a mixed bag of reaction to them, some in our favor, some against us—but nobody dreamt—not even the most avid proabortion person—that we would come down with loss of legal personhood and abortion on demand till birth. Nobody dreamt that that would happen" (Merton 1981, 94).

Newspapers across the country and many pro-choice leaders shared this sentiment—at least as it concerned the definitiveness of the decision. Despite Burger's admonition that the Court "rejects any claim that the Constitution requires abortion on demand," initial press reports expressed optimism that the "two decisions could finally resolve the age-old abortion debates" (Wasserman 1974, 237).[84] Many within the pro-choice movement were equally optimistic about the definitiveness of the rulings. Pilpel asserted that "it scaled the whole mountain"; another said it reached "further and deeper and [was] approved by a more decisive vote than we ever expected. . . . It was a staggering victory" (Faux 1988, 304). Even Lader (1973) suggested that "[i]t came like a thunderbolt—a decision from the United States Supreme Court so sweeping that it seemed to assure the triumph of the abortion movement."

Other pro-choice leaders were more cautious in their assessment. The ACLU, for example, publicly called the decision "an important step in the right direction" (Van Gelder 1973, 20). Privately, ACLU Executive Director Aryeh Neier offered his congratulations to Hames but "urged 'continued vigilance to assure implementation' " of the right (Walker 1990, 303). NARAL shared his concern; just days after the decision, it sent out letters to its members: "The fight is not over; it has just begun. Before the decision, it was waged in some individual states. The battleground has now widened to include all fifty states and the Congress of the United States" (Faux 1988, 324).

Whether *Roe* and *Doe* would end or start the debate, then, was an open question in January 1973. What was a closed issue was the scope of the victory: it was a decisive legal win for the pro-choice side, for which they openly took credit. As Pilpel wistfully stated, "We expected to get there, but not on our first trip." Attorneys for the Center for Constitutional Rights called the decision "a tribute to the coordinated efforts of women's organizations, women lawyers, and all women throughout the country" (Van Gelder 1973). Unquestionably, without the development of the pro-choice movement and its emphasis on impact litigation, abortion would not have made its way to the Court's agenda so quickly. By initiating the "avalanche" of cases in the 1960s and 1970s, however uncoordinated, the ACLU, CCR, ASA, and others forced the Court's hand.

To what extent, though, did they affect the Court's final decision? Some scholars are quick to point to a variety of pressures and "long-term trends" that came to bear on the Court. Mohr's list (1978, 250–56) includes the following, most of which had little or nothing to do with the movement's litigation strategy:

- "fear of overpopulation,"
- "quality of life" issues arising out of the thalidomide scare,
- the growth of the women's rights movement,
- the decreasing risks of the procedure,
- the quantity of illegal abortions, and
- the changing views of doctors.

Rosenberg (1989, 1991) is even more stalwart in his view that the abortion reformers were merely in the right place at the right time. By way of evidence, he points to the following:

- supportive Supreme Court and lower court rulings (for example, *Griswold* and *Eisenstadt*),
- supportive law review articles (for example, those by Means and Lucas),
- a supportive political environment, and
- supportive public opinion.

In short, Rosenberg (1989, 36) argues that "[r]eformers were lucky in *Roe*" because they had all the right elements for social change in their favor.

Our analysis largely refutes these contentions. To be sure, the movement benefited from all of the items listed by Rosenberg and Mohr, not to mention the leanings of the justices sitting on the Court. It is an overstatement, however, to refer to the pro-choice advocates as "lucky litigators." After all, they were the ones who sought to alter the political environment in their favor, developed the key test cases of *Griswold*, *Eisenstadt*, and others, and wrote the supportive law review articles and amicus curiae briefs on which Blackmun based much of his opinion. The justices may have been predisposed toward reaching the conclusion they did, but pro-choice forces shaped their environment and provided them with much of their ammunition. Thus we agree largely with the position of attorney Nancy Stearns (1989, 5): "We must never forget that *Roe v. Wade* did not just 'happen.' . . . The . . . Court does not decide cases in a political vacuum. . . . Justices . . . read the newspapers, listen to the radio, watch TV, and are aware of burning social issues. Their decisions often reflect what at least appears to be the popular consensus about such issues."

What mattered most from the pro-choice vantage point, though, was not how they got there, but where they were. As of January 1973, their campaign had worked; for the first time in over a hundred years, women could obtain legal abortions. Their next task was to preserve and implement their legal victory.

The Court's decisions in *Roe v. Wade* and *Doe v. Bolton* were impressive legal victories for the groups comprising the pro-choice movement. This was obviously the case in a policy sense—the Court's action effectively struck all state abortion statutes at once—but it also was impressive in a temporal sense: the groups achieved their goals in less than a decade of concerted activity. Beyond this, especially important for public understanding of the decisions, was the size of the Court majority endorsing Blackmun's opinions. On the surface, it appeared that the seven votes to strike both the Texas and Georgia laws—three of which came from supposedly "conservative" Nixon appointees—would be more than sufficient to ward off any subsequent efforts to eradicate the newly articulated right.

Beneath the surface of this impressive legal victory, however, lay problems for pro-choice forces. Paramount among them was the question of opposition. Throughout their legal battles during the 1960s they dealt primarily with state attorneys general who had varying degrees of enthusiasm for the laws they were defending. Noticeably absent was serious, able, and independent organized opposition. *Roe*, by articulating a previously "silent" right, upped the ante for those against abortion. In so doing, it was sure to provide a catalyst for renewed activity in state legislatures. Moreover, depending on the sophistication of the pro-life side, active litigation in the judicial arena was also a possibility. Inevitably, this would change the legal context in which abortion issues were contested and would necessitate the creation of new strategies by which to preserve the gains procured in *Roe*.

In sum, *Roe* was a clear and stunning win for abortion reformers. In this victory, however, were the seeds of a new cycle of politics and litigation. The task facing pro-choice proponents was to defend their newly won ground as others mobilized to take it back. This, as the next chapter demonstrates, brought politics, the courts, and interest groups into a wholly new conflict. In one sense, then, *Roe* was the end of a hard-fought battle; in another, it was only the beginning.

SIX

....

ABORTION II:

FROM *ROE*

TO *WEBSTER*

IN THE AFTERMATH OF *ROE V. WADE*

The Court's decision in *Roe v. Wade* was, in one regard, crystal clear: it struck down all existing abortion laws as contrary to the Fourteenth Amendment. Interestingly, though, mass and elite responses to the opinion were rather murky. In figure 6-1, we display the results of National Opinion Research Center surveys conducted before the decision and immediately thereafter. These indicate little change in any direction. Note the most extreme postures: prior to *Roe*, approximately 37 percent of respondents thought abortion should be permitted under virtually any circumstances ("Discretionary Scale"); after *Roe*, that figure rose slightly to 43 percent. On the pro-life side, we see that in 1972, about 10 percent of those surveyed would never allow abortions ("Health Scale"), compared with 5.5 percent in 1973. To be sure, as Franklin and Kosaki (1989, 762) convincingly demonstrate, the Court's opinion did have an effect, particularly on individuals' views of discretionary abortions: it increased "the differences between groups," "crystaliz[ing] issue preferences further—lead[ing] to greater homogeneity of within-group beliefs." In other words, if one was pro-choice before the decision, one became even more so after; the same held true for pro-lifers. Nonetheless, the fact that so little intergroup movement occurred—that is, pro-lifers did not become pro-choicers and vice versa—was significant. Public opinion would not provide state legislators with the sort of clear-cut guidepost as it did, for example, after the capital punishment case of 1972.

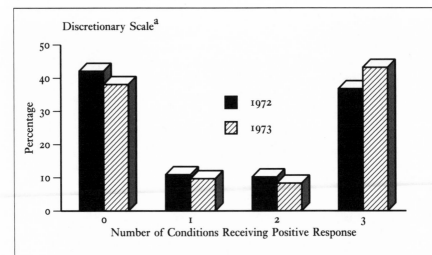

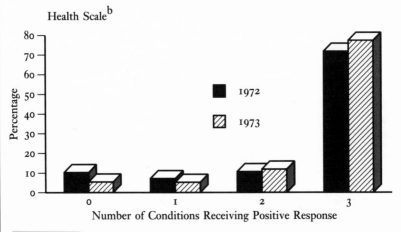

Source: Franklin and Kosaki 1989, 751.
Note: Surveys were conducted between February and April of 1972 and 1973.

[a]The Discretionary Scale works as follows. It is composed of responses to these questions:
"Please tell me whether or not you think it should be possible for a pregnant woman to
obtain a legal abortion if 1) she is married and does not want any more children; 2) the
family has a very low income and cannot afford more children; and 3) she is not married
and does not want to marry the man?" Each set of bars indicates whether the respondent
answered positively to none, one, two, or three of these questions.

[b]The Health Scale works as follows. It is composed of responses to these questions:
"Please tell me whether or not you think it should be possible for a pregnant woman to
obtain a legal abortion if 1) there is a strong chance of serious defect in the baby; 2) the
woman's own health is seriously endangered; and 3) she became pregnant as a result of
rape?" Each set of bars indicates whether the respondent answered positively to none,
one, two, or three of these questions.

FIGURE 6-1. Public Opinion on Abortion, 1972 and 1973

Nor would the scholarly legal community be of much assistance. Although in the years subsequent to *Roe* a great deal of debate occurred over the "correctness" of the Court's opinion, authorities did not (and still do not) agree about the legal grounds upon which the decision rested. For example, different authors of constitutional law books locate *Roe* in three distinct sections of their works.[1] Some place it in the *Griswold* line of cases, dealing with the right to privacy and autonomy; others view it as a substantive due process decision; and a third set consider it an equal protection case. They also disagreed over the answers to some of the questions left open by *Roe*. Among those most discussed were whether states could require parental or spousal consent prior to the performance of abortions and ban the use of Medicaid funds for abortions and to what extent they could regulate clinics and hospitals performing abortions.

Given this ambiguity, it is not surprising that those in charge of implementing *Roe*—doctors and public officials, in particular—took divergent routes (Johnson and Canon 1984).[2] About a month after the decision, the *New York Times* (Brody 1973) reported that the medical profession has "moved with extreme caution in implementing" *Roe*, and as a result, "women seeking abortions continue to be referred to such states as New York, where abortion laws were liberalized previously." By the same token, the immediate reactions of state officials were quite mixed. In about twenty states, some actor (for example, the legislature, the attorney general, or a court) nullified existing laws on the grounds that they were unconstitutional under *Roe*. In others, officials sought to delay implementation.[3] At the same time, officials in some cities either banned public hospitals from performing abortions or refused to allow public funds to be spent on such services (Brody 1973).

Hence, the general uncertainty characterizing the post-*Roe* environment created a challenging situation for pro-life and pro-choice groups; it remained largely up to them to influence the key actors. Their initial task was to clear up the legal and political confusion in ways that would meet their policy objectives. As we shall see, while strains within both movements understood this, they lacked the resources, and in some instances the know-how, necessary to do so quickly.

THE PRO-CHOICE MOVEMENT

The political and legal uncertainty in the wake of *Roe* bled into the pro-choice movement. As the immediate reactions of its leaders reveal, some thought the battle was over. Women's rights advocates, in particular, were quick to point out the totality of the victory and their role in achieving it.[4] And, although they recognized that a backlash to *Roe* would emerge, which some thought would be as serious as that occurring after *Brown v. Board of Education* (1954), they remained undaunted. As pro-choice attorney Rhonda Copelon suggested: "I think we envision not having to go through what Blacks had to go through after *Brown* because in *Roe* and *Doe* the Court was quite clear in terms of what the state could or could not do, whereas they never drew up desegregation plans in *Brown*. I think that's where women did get a much better decision from the Supreme Court than Blacks got in 1954" (Goodman, Copelon Shoenbrod, and Stearns 1973, 19). Others were far less optimistic. In marked contrast to Copelon, ACLU attorney Judith Mears (1974, 136) argued that "[u]nfortunately, the Supreme Court's abortion decisions no more resolve that issue than its 1954 decision in *Brown* . . . resolved the issue of racial integration in public schools."

Such differences in interpretation led the various segments of the pro-choice movement to adopt rather divergent tactical responses. Nancy Stearns (Goodman, Copelon Shoenbrod, and Stearns 1973, 37), the author of the "women's" amicus curiae brief in *Roe*, warned that "one of the most dangerous things that could happen now is that women could sit back and think that they have won"; yet this is precisely what many women's rights groups did after *Roe*. As Stearns (1989, 6) wrote sixteen years later, "Too many of us thought we had won the fight with *Roe* v. *Wade* and went on to other issues, or just went home." Although the National Organization for Women (NOW) and other organizations continued to support abortion rights, other issues (such as pregnancy discrimination, the battle for the Equal Rights Amendment, and equal pay) moved to the forefront of their attention. The other mass-membership wing of the pro-choice movement, the National Association for the Repeal of Abortion Laws (NARAL), also became "complacent and did not sustain their organizational momentum" (Tatalovich and Daynes 1981, 164).[5]

Given the tax-exempt status of Planned Parenthood and the Association for the Study of Abortion (ASA), that left legislative efforts largely to the American Civil Liberties Union (ACLU). Although at that point the ACLU had many items on its agenda (Walker 1990), it seemed acutely aware of the uncertainty of the political environment and of the tenuousness of *Roe*'s effect. Executive Director Aryeh Neier had congratulated Margie Hames after her victory but had urged "continued vigilance to assure implementation." He recognized, as one observer wrote, that the "politics of abortion rights changed overnight—the abortion rights legislative movement evaporated" (Walker 1990, 303).

In this context, Neier decided that the ACLU should establish a special litigating group, the Reproductive Freedom Project (RFP). Formed in 1974, the RFP was to "ensure compliance with . . . the Supreme Court decision on abortion." It would, thus, join a growing list of specific-issue projects within the ACLU, including the Women's Rights Project (WRP), which had recently scored an impressive victory in *Reed v. Reed* (1971), a landmark gender-discrimination case (Greenberg 1977; O'Connor 1980).

Because the WRP focused on sex discrimination, Neier could have simply turned abortion over to it, but several factors deterred him. For one thing, he and others thought that some WRP funders might be hesitant to finance abortion litigation (Berger 1979); for another, WRP's leaders, including Ruth Bader Ginsburg, desired to keep the two issues separate and to concentrate on other types of "women's issues" (O'Connor 1980); finally, and perhaps most important, Neier saw that abortion would prompt a tremendous battle, one that required a strong and specialized arsenal. As newly installed RFP executive director, Judith Mears (1974, 136), claimed, "The questions left unanswered by *Roe* and *Doe* are, to an important extent, medical questions. If we are to avoid the disheartening prospect of history repeating itself, à la *Brown*, with twenty years of legislative and litigative battles ahead . . . [w]e must have the cooperative and active assistance of physicians who can assert the primacy of their medical judgment in this sphere."

Clearly, then, Mears and the ACLU had a grasp on some of the problems of *Roe* and where solutions might lie. Still, the RFP's path was filled with obstacles. Whether it, and the pro-choice movement more generally, could overcome them remained far less than certain.

THE PRO-LIFE MOVEMENT

Twelve years after *Roe*, the *New Republic* (25 February 1985) wrote that it was "the worst thing that ever happened to American liberalism. Almost overnight it politicized millions of people and helped create a mass movement of social conservatives that has grown into one of the most potent forces in our democracy." This may be an overstatement, but it is true that *Roe* catalyzed a strong countermovement (Luker 1984; Markson 1985). Indeed, the political and legal environment may have been ambiguous and the pro-choice movement divided over its meaning, but the goal of pro-life forces could not have been clearer: *Roe* must go.

The pro-life movement, however, was far less monolithic than its message or than its opponents thought. After *Roe* came down, a large countermovement did take shape in opposition to the abortion right, but it was a diffuse and confused backlash, plagued by internal conflicts over strategies and tactics and by petty jealousies. Why did these problems emerge? Figure 6-2 illustrates the various groups comprising the pro-life movement. As we can see, the vast majority of organizations involved had ties to the Catholic church, hardly surprising given that the Catholic church and its constituent organizations (for example, the

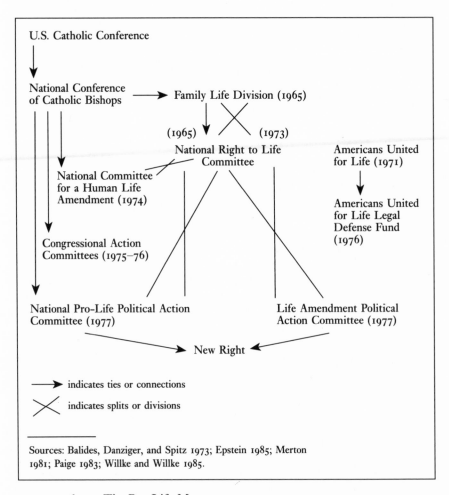

FIGURE 6-2. The Pro-Life Movement

Family Life Division and the National Conference of Catholic Bishops) represented the largest and most vocal pre-*Roe* forces (Merton 1981, 94–95). One participant went so far as to suggest that "[t]he only reason we have a pro-life movement in this country is because of the Catholic people and the Catholic Church." Another, less sympathetic, observer put it somewhat differently: "What has been obscured is the extent to which the Right-to-Life movement in the United States serves as a secular arm of the institutional Roman Catholic Church" (Jaffe, Lindheim, and Lee 1981, 73).

Both views have merit. Between 1973 and 1975, the Catholic church did dominate the pro-life side of the abortion debate. After the decision came down, the National Conference of Catholic Bishops (NCCB) issued statement after statement calling for complete and total rejection of the decision, for litigation, and for state legislation (Balides, Danziger, and Spitz 1973, 516–17). Hence, it is true that the Catholic church led the way, hoping to catalyze a potent political countermovement. Concomitantly, it is equally true that the Catholic church tried to secularize the early pro-life movement. It established or was involved with several supposedly independent organizations (see figure 6-2). The most important of these was the National Right to Life Committee (NRLC), which many regard as the leading secular pro-life organization, even though it was created by the Family Life Division of the NCCB prior to *Roe* to act as a "small coordinating unit" for pro-life groups fighting the repeal movement of the early 1970s (Merton 1981). With a budget of about $50,000, 50 percent of which came from the U.S. Catholic Conference, the original NRLC served largely as a "clearinghouse" for grass-roots organizations (Balides, Danziger, and Spitz 1973, 513–14).[6]

Even so, many pro-life organizations tried to distance themselves from the Catholic church. One example can be found in the relationship of the NRLC and the National Committee for a Human Life Amendment (NCHLA) with the Catholic church. Shortly after *Roe*, members of local right-to-life groups—led by Marjorie Mecklenburg of the Minnesota Citizens for Life—met and decided that the religious roots of the NRLC should be buried. They formally implemented this plan at the June 1973 meeting of the NRLC, severing its ties to and electing officials (including Mecklenburg as chair) unaffiliated with the Catholic church. In response to this and to other failures within the larger political environment,[7] the NCCB created the NCHLA as an "independent lobbying group" (Jaffe, Lindheim, and Lee 1981; Merton 1981; Paige 1983; Willke and Willke 1985).

But the proper role of the Catholic church was not the only source of contention; still further divisions arose over the movement's connection to the "New Right." Some, like the NRLC, sought to separate abortion from other issues on the New Right's larger agenda, such as pornography and prayer in school, fearing they would dilute their primary interest. Others, including the National Pro-Life Political Action Committee and the Life Amendment Political Action Committee (LAPAC), were closely tied to the New Right. As one LAPAC member summarized the situation, the NRLC is "afraid of becoming a tool of the New Right. . . . We *are* a tool of the New Right and [it] is a tool of ours" (Merton 1981, 164).

Finally, and perhaps most consequentially, the movement was divided over strategies and tactics. All involved groups agreed on their ultimate objective— the demise of *Roe*. They also, at least initially, concurred on the single best vehicle for achieving that goal—an amendment to the U.S. Constitution. However, consensus ended there. Not only did they have bitter fights over the wording of such an amendment, but they disagreed over secondary tactics as well. Some thought educational campaigns aimed at transforming public opinion were the best course; others believed in grass-roots legislative lobbying efforts; a few endorsed promoting federal statutes aimed at negating *Roe*'s impact; still others wanted to infiltrate the electoral process; and, finally, a small group sought to take to the courts.

ABORTION IN "POLITICAL ARENAS" AND IN THE COURTS, 1973–1979

The significance of this divisiveness was its effect on the right-to-life movement's ability to achieve its objectives throughout the rest of the 1970s. However complacent their opponents had become, pro-life forces were often their own worst enemy. The impact of the fragmented nature of the movement manifested itself most acutely over the big issues. Between *Roe* and 1979, pro-life forces lost the drive for a constitutional amendment, the focus of their utmost attention;[8] they failed to influence significantly the outcome of elections and thus the composition of national institutions;[9] and, with only one exception, they could not convince Congress to enact "piecemeal" legislation that would have eroded—to a lesser or greater extent—the *Roe* ruling.[10]

The one exception—a rider to the Department of Health, Education, and Welfare (HEW) Labor Appropriations Act of 1976—was an important one. Known more commonly as the Hyde amendment (after its sponsor, Henry Hyde), it stated that "[n]one of the funds contained in this Act shall be used to perform abortions except where the life of the mother would be endangered if the fetus were carried to term." In other words, it virtually eliminated Medicaid funding of abortions.[11]

To be sure, passage of the Hyde amendment represented the most significant pro-life victory to date. Symbolically, it was a major triumph, especially given the Democratic composition of both houses. As one pro-life attorney asserted, its passage "demonstrated the political strength of the pro-life movement . . . providing a clear indication of growing public opposition to abortion on demand and a harbinger of the Human Life Amendment to the Constitution" (Trueman 1976). Practically, it promised a devastating impact on abortion services: in the previous fiscal year, Medicaid had funded over three hundred thousand abortions to the tune of $45 million. Now, low-income women would be denied such benefits unless they could prove that pregnancy would endanger their lives.

Even so, the Hyde amendment represented the exception, not the rule. Throughout the 1970s, the pro-life movement was, simply put, generally shut out of national arenas. Where they did achieve some measure of success was with seemingly smaller restrictions on abortion in more manageable forums (such as state legislatures) where their opponents were poorly organized.

STATE LEGISLATION AND THE JUDICIARY'S RESPONSE: BATTLES OVER CONSENT AND FUNDING

Pro-choice forces made some effort to defeat the Hyde amendment to counter their opposition in the national legislature. But they had virtually no involvement in the states, the arena in which their opponents were clearly the strongest. The pro-life movement was, at its core, a grass-roots organization. By its own count, the NRLC alone had "almost 2,000 chapters in all 50 states . . . with an estimated 11 million members in its affiliated state or pro-life groups." Hence, while national pro-life organizations and the Catholic church bickered over strategy and the like, their affiliates, local right-to-life groups, and individual dioceses worked arduously within cities and states to overcome *Roe*. As evidenced by pre-1973 state legislative battles for repeal, not only were these grass-roots organizations effective, but they faced very little opposition. Owing to a lack of funds, organizational apparatus, or even interest (Benshoof 1977), the pro-choice side never seriously organized at these levels of government. The ACLU, the one organization that could have engaged in grass-roots lobbying, was far more prone to litigation.

The result of this activity was an outburst of state legislation restricting abortion rights. Between 1973 and 1975, thirty-two states adopted sixty-two laws, with the greatest flurry occurring between January and October of 1973 when more than two hundred pieces of legislation were introduced, with twenty-three states enacting one or more statutes. More telling still is that by 1978 only sixteen states had not adopted some restrictive measure (*Family Planning/Population Reporter* 1975, 108; Rubin 1987, 127).

To some extent, these aggregated figures are deceiving: much of the legislation passed in the early to mid-1970s seemed to conform to the Court's decisions; for example, many states prohibited abortion after viability except to save the mother's life. Likewise, they allowed only licensed physicians to perform abortions. Still, as shown in figure 6-3, a significant amount of legislation passed was of a more restrictive nature—laws requiring the consent of the woman and her spouse or her parents, in the case of a minor, and those restricting funding.

How did courts react to these various kinds of laws? Generally speaking, not particularly well. Although pro-choice groups were unable to mobilize suc-

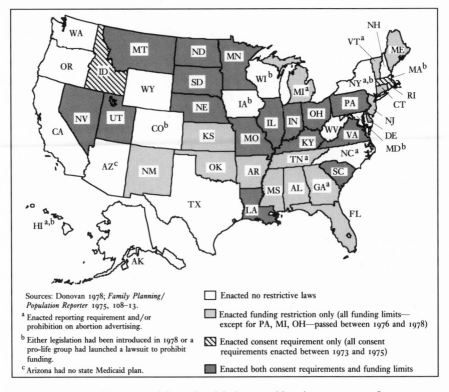

Sources: Donovan 1978; *Family Planning/ Population Reporter* 1975, 108–13.

[a] Enacted reporting requirement and/or prohibition on abortion advertising.

[b] Either legislation had been introduced in 1978 or a pro-life group had launched a lawsuit to prohibit funding.

[c] Arizona had no state Medicaid plan.

☐ Enacted no restrictive laws

▨ Enacted funding restriction only (all funding limits— except for PA, MI, OH—passed between 1976 and 1978)

▧ Enacted consent requirement only (all consent requirements enacted between 1973 and 1975)

▨ Enacted both consent requirements and funding limits

FIGURE 6-3. Patterns of State Legislation on Abortion, 1973–1978

cessfully in legislative arenas, they were prepared to challenge state legislation in the courts, the loci of their most successful wins to date. Early on, most of the action occurred in the lower federal courts, where pro-choice groups challenged virtually all post-*Roe* state legislation. Between 1974 and 1975, U.S. district courts issued thirty-one opinions in abortion cases, and courts of appeal issued nineteen (Wardle 1981). The data reported in table 6-1 suggest that pro-choice groups were not mistaken in viewing the courts as friendly turf. With the notable exception of district court litigation in Missouri, they won the vast majority of their cases—particularly those involving consent requirements and limits on public hospitals.

These victories were read differently by the competing forces. Pro-choice attorneys viewed the state laws as such blatant infringements on abortion rights that they could not conceive of losing. Pro-life attorneys believed that the decisions did not necessarily reflect a "pro-abortion" bias among federal court judges but rather "an astounding picture of loyalty and compliance by the lower federal courts with what they perceived to be the essence of the Supreme Court ruling." It was at this so-called "institutional loyalty" that they took aim. They lambasted judges for merely applying *Roe* and not analyzing it critically; for "sheltering" the decision and writing "shamefully inadequate" opinions. In short, they sought to turn the tables on pro-choice forces, arguing that "nothing is more dangerous to the legitimacy and authority of a judicial system than the stagnation of case law" (Wardle 1981, 301). Yet such cries fell on deaf ears. If anything, the lower federal courts became a greater bastion for the pro-choice movement when President Jimmy Carter's over two hundred appointees took their seats. As Alumbaugh and Rowland (1990) note, his judges supported abortion rights in almost 90 percent of all cases.

Lower federal court victories were one thing; wins in the Supreme Court another. As states began to appeal their lower court losses (as did pro-choice attorneys in those few cases in which they met with defeat), many speculated on how the justices would react to the new legislation. In general, pundits gave pro-choicers much higher odds of victory; after all, *Roe* had been decided by a wide 7–2 margin. In addition, between 1973 and 1979 only one personnel change transpired: President Ford replaced retiring Justice Douglas with John Paul Stevens. Even if Stevens voted with White and Rehnquist, it would hardly matter. Further, the justices did not face monumental pressure to rethink *Roe*. Despite the actions of some states and the growth of the pro-life movement, public opinion and the lower courts remained on the majority's side.

Even so, during the terms immediately following *Roe*, the justices did not seem anxious to reenter the debate. Table 6-2 reveals that the Court received twelve petitions appealing abortion cases in its 1973 term but rejected them all. The following year ten cases were pending, with the justices deciding only one with a signed opinion,[12] *Bigelow v. Virginia*, in which ACLU attorneys successfully challenged a 1960 Virginia law that prohibited any publication from printing abortion advertisements.[13] In the following terms, the Court heard arguments in a half dozen or so cases, most of which involved state consent or funding laws passed in the wake of *Roe* (see figure 6-3).[14]

Consent

States initially passed consent or "power investiture" laws that delegated to some third party (such as a spouse or parent) veto power over abortions (see figure 6-3). With passage of these laws, states thought they could indirectly "interfere" with the abortion decision and, thus, keep some women from exercising their right. Many states enacted such legislation, but perhaps the most comprehensive statute came out of Missouri.

TABLE 6-1. Responses of Lower Federal Courts to *Roe*: Litigation Initiated between 1974 and 1975

Case	Court	Outcome
PARENTAL/SPOUSAL/PROSPECTIVE FATHER CONSENT		
Bellotti v. Baird[a]	Massachusetts (393 F.Supp. 847, 1975)	Struck consent provision
Doe v. Deschamps	Montana (64 F.R.D. 652, 1974)	Struck consent provision
Doe v. Exon	Nebraska (416 F.Supp. 716, 1975)	Struck consent provision
Doe v. Zimmerman	Pennsylvania (405 F.Supp. 534, 1975)	Struck consent provision
Foe v. Vanderhoof	Colorado (389 F.Supp. 947, 1975)	Struck consent provision
Planned Parenthood v. Danforth[b]	Missouri (392 F.Supp. 1362, 1975)	Upheld consent provision
Planned Parenthood v. Fitzpatrick[c]	Pennsylvania (401 F.Supp. 554, 1975)	Struck consent provision
Poe v. Gerstein	Fifth Circuit (517 F.2d 787, 1975)	Struck consent provision
Roe v. Rampton	Utah (394 F.Supp. 677, 1975)	Refused to issue injunction
Roe v. Rampton	Tenth Circuit (535 F.2d 1219, 1976)	Affirmed 1975 decision
Wolfe v. Schoering	Kentucky (388 F.Supp. 631, 1974)	Struck consent provision
Wolfe v. Schoering	Sixth Circuit (541 F.2d 523, 1976)	Struck consent provision
Wulff v. State Board[d]	Missouri (380 F.Supp. 1137, 1974)	Upheld consent provision
Wulff v. Singleton[d]	Eighth Circuit (508 F.2d 1211, 1974)	Struck consent provision
LIMITS ON ABORTION SERVICES PERFORMED BY PUBLIC HOSPITALS		
Doe v. Hale Hospital	Massachusetts (369 F.Supp. 970, 1974)	May not limit
Doe v. Hale Hospital	First Circuit (500 F.2d 144, 1974)	May not limit
Doe v. Mundy	Wisconsin (378 F.Supp. 731, 1974)	May not limit
Doe v. Mundy	Seventh Circuit (514 F.2d 1179, 1975)	May not limit
Doe v. Poelker[e]	Missouri (order dismissing suit)	May limit
Doe v. Poelker[e]	Eighth Circuit (515 F.2d 541, 1975)	May not limit
Hodgson v. Anderson	Minnesota (378 F.Supp. 1008, 1974)	May not limit

TABLE 6-1 *(continued)*

Case	Court	Outcome
Orr v. Koefort	Nebraska (377 F.Supp. 673, 1974)	May not limit
Wolfe v. Schoering	Kentucky (388 F.Supp. 631, 1974)	May not limit
Wolfe v. Schoering	Sixth Circuit (541 F.2d 523, 1976)	May not limit

ELIMINATION/LIMITATION OF ABORTION
FROM MEDICAID PLANS/PUBLIC ASSISTANCE

Case	Court	Outcome
Doe v. Beal[f]	Third Circuit (523 F.2d 611, 1975)	May not eliminate/limit
Doe v. Poelker[e]	Missouri (order dismissing suit)	May eliminate/limit
Doe v. Poelker[e]	Eighth Circuit (515 F.2d 541, 1975)	May not eliminate/limit
Doe v. Westby	South Dakota (383 F.Supp. 1143, 1974)	May not eliminate/limit
Doe v. Wohlgemuth[f]	Pennsylvania (376 F.Supp. 173, 1974)	May eliminate/limit
Roe v. Ferguson	Ohio (389 F.Supp. 387, 1974)	May not eliminate/limit
Roe v. Ferguson	Sixth Circuit (515 F.2d 1179, 1975)	May eliminate/limit
Roe v. Norton[g]	Connecticut (380 F.Supp. 726, 1974)	May not eliminate/limit
Roe v. Norton[g]	Second Circuit (522 F.2d 928, 1975)	May eliminate/limit
Wulff v. State Board[d]	Missouri (380 F.Supp. 1137, 1974)	May eliminate/limit
Wulff v. Singleton[d]	Eighth Circuit (508 F.2d 1211, 1974)	May not eliminate/limit

Sources: U.S. Commission on Civil Rights 1975 and Wardle 1981.
[a]Decided by the U.S. Supreme Court: *Bellotti v. Baird* (1976).
[b]Decided by the U.S. Supreme Court: *Planned Parenthood v. Danforth* (1976).
[c]Decided by the U.S. Supreme Court: *Colautti v. Franklin* (1979).
[d]Decided by the U.S. Supreme Court: *Singleton v. Wulff* (1976).
[e]Decided by the U.S. Supreme Court: *Poelker v. Doe* (1977).
[f]Decided by the U.S. Supreme Court: *Beal v. Doe* (1977).
[g]Decided by the U.S. Supreme Court: *Maher v. Roe* (1977).

TABLE 6-2. Abortion Appeals to the U.S. Supreme Court, 1973–1978 Terms

Issue	Term					
	1973	1974	1975	1976	1977	1978
Advertising	2	—	—	1	—	—
Rights of unborn fetus	2	—	1	—	—	1
Regulation of practitioners	1	1	2	—	—	—
Defining viability	—	2	1	—	—	1
Criminal penalties	—	1	—	—	—	2
Regulation of facilities	2	2	1	2	—	—
Public funding	—	2	4	4	1	2
Spousal/parental consent	3	1	4	3	—	3
Misc. fetal provisions	2	—	—	—	—	2
"Informed" consent	—	—	1	1	—	3
Publication of records	—	1	—	—	—	2
Standing to challenge	—	—	1	—	—	—
Total Appeals	12	9	15	11	1	16
Full Opinions	0	2	2	3	0	2

Source: Brigham 1984, 139–40.

That Missouri would be at the forefront of the pro-life movement is not surprising, given the presence of a strong and active Catholic community. As Merton (1981, 98–102) reports, immediately after *Roe*, "the church distributed news of the abortion decisions." Shortly thereafter, Cardinal John Carberry of St. Louis met with more than eleven hundred representatives of surrounding dioceses to develop a plan for political action. This resulted in the creation of an "elaborate political and educational apparatus for pro-life activities, including the creation of right-to-life committees in every parish, of a speaker's bureau, and of mounds of propaganda for the cause." The Catholic church also recognized the need for grass-roots lobbying; it knew that it "would have to enlist the cooperation of politicians at every level to accomplish" its goals. To this end, it drew up maps "showing the relationships of parishes to Congressional districts and Missouri legislative districts," told members to contact their representatives, and so forth. In other words, it waged a model grass-roots campaign.

These efforts paid off in 1974 when the Missouri legislature placed seven restrictions on the ability of women to obtain abortion services and of doctors to perform them and, thus, imposed "a structure for the control and regulation of abortions . . . during all stages of pregnancy."

1. Definition of "Viability": "[T]hat stage of fetal development when the life of the unborn child may be continued indefinitely outside of the womb."

2. Informed Consent: Before obtaining an abortion, a woman must give her consent to the procedure and that consent must be "informed and freely given" and not the "result of coercion."

3. Spousal Consent: Before obtaining an abortion, a woman must obtain the written consent of her spouse, "unless a licensed physician certifies that the abortion is necessary to preserve the mother's life."

4. Parental Consent: Before obtaining an abortion, an unmarried woman under the age of eighteen must obtain the written consent of a parent.

5. Standard of Care: Doctors must "exercise professional care to preserve the fetus' life or health"; otherwise they may be found guilty of manslaughter.

6. Saline Amniocentesis: Such an abortion procedure is prohibited after the first twelve weeks of pregnancy.

7. Record Keeping: Hospitals and doctors must meet "reporting and record keeping requirements."

When the governor signed the bill into law, Planned Parenthood of Central Missouri launched a lawsuit—*Planned Parenthood v. Danforth*—challenging it on straightforward grounds: *Roe* established a fundamental right to an abortion; states can only burden fundamental rights if they demonstrate a compelling interest for doing so; and, thus, this law places a significant burden on the right to an abortion, without demonstration of a compelling state interest. Nonetheless, a divided three-judge district court adopted the state's defense—that it possessed a compelling interest—and upheld most sections of the act. Shortly thereafter, attorneys representing Planned Parenthood and the ACLU's Reproductive Freedom Project, Frank Susman and Judith Mears, respectively, appealed to the U.S. Supreme Court.

Two more-qualified lawyers could not have been found to argue the pro-choice side. St. Louis attorney Susman had been involved in the abortion movement since the late 1960s, when he began "referring women to skilled abortionists." He later provided legal advice to and facilitated the establishment of Reproductive Health Services, a "model" abortion clinic in St. Louis. More important was Susman's legal expertise. Although a private attorney, he was heavily involved in pre-*Roe* litigation. He worked with Planned Parenthood and the ACLU, handling his first abortion case "at the request of the local American Civil Liberties Union several years before *Roe* was decided." His expertise was such that Sarah Weddington called him "several times to consult on strategies for *Roe*" (Faux 1990; Shenon 1989). Hence, when Planned Parenthood of Central Missouri wanted to challenge the state's 1974 act, it naturally turned to Susman. Mears—at the time a clinical teaching fellow at Yale Law School (Oelsner 1976b)—may have lacked Susman's experience, but as director of the RFP, she had the weight of the ACLU behind her.

After the Court announced its intention to docket *Planned Parenthood* for orals in March 1976, both sides filed their briefs with the Court. The arguments of Mears and Susman were the usual pro-choice fare, emanating from *Roe*—that the law was in direct conflict with the abortion right and the state had not shown a compelling interest. They were supported by two amicus curiae briefs representing four groups.[15] In contrast, Danforth's submission, centering on the law's "promotion" of a legitimate state interest, received backing from five pro-life amicus curiae briefs cosigned by more than twenty groups.[16]

If, however, "quality" is more important than "quantity" in Supreme Court litigation, then the pro-choice front was in a stronger position. Its briefs were full of medical and scientific data indicating that the "facts" did not establish a compelling state interest. In contrast, the pro-life submissions were strongly emotional in tone,[17] contributing little—and perhaps even detracting from—the state's "crisp legal arguments," which focused on why the law was consistent with *Roe*. Indeed, some amici went so far as to ask the Court to overrule its 1973 decision, comparing it to *Dred Scott v. Sandford* (1857). Another claimed to have "discovered" new "evidence indicat[ing] that *Roe v. Wade* rests on factual errors which require [its] overruling." Blackmun, it argued, misinterpreted nineteenth-century state abortion regulations. Such briefs, of course, not only failed to reinforce the state's position but lent credence to pro-choice arguments that the law would curtail the scope of *Roe*. Thus, instead of supplementing governmental arguments, providing a solid counterbalance to the liberal position, or even presenting the Court with new or useful information, pro-life amici tended to underscore the emotional aspects of the issue (Epstein 1985, 100).

How much the briefs influenced the justices we do not know, but they did deliver a major blow to pro-life advocates when they struck all but three provisions of the act. Even so, as shown in table 6-3, Blackmun's opinion for the Court failed to garner the sort of unconditional support his 1973 effort had received. The justices had the greatest difficulty with his rulings on parental consent. Only two others fully subscribed to Blackmun's view that "any independent interest that the parent may have in the termination is no more weighty than the right of privacy of the competent minor" (*Planned Parenthood* 1976, 75). And, while his ruling was tempered,[18] Stewart (joined by Powell) stated that if the law's parental consent requirement had been written in more flexible terms (such as providing

TABLE 6-3. The *Planned Parenthood v. Danforth* "Splits"

Provision of the Law	Court Action	Majority	Concurring	Dissenting
Definition of viability	Upheld	All agree		
Woman's consent	Upheld	All agree		
Spousal consent	Struck	Blackmun, Brennan, Stewart, Marshall, Powell, Stevens		White, Burger, Rehnquist
Parental consent	Struck	Blackmun, Brennan, Marshall	Powell, Stewart	White, Burger, Rehnquist, Stevens
Saline amniocentesis prohibition	Struck	Blackmun, Brennan, Marshall	Stevens, Powell, Stewart	White, Burger, Rehnquist
Record keeping	Upheld	All agree		
Standard of care	Struck	Blackmun, Brennan, Stewart, Marshall, Powell, Stevens		White, Burger, Rehnquist

Note: The actual opinion coalitions were Blackmun (for Marshall, Brennan, Stevens, Powell, and Stewart); Stevens concurred, agreeing with virtually all of Blackmun's opinion except parental consent; Powell and Stewart concurred, again largely agreeing with Blackmun except for certain points of disagreement on parental consent; White (for Burger and Rehnquist) largely dissented from the Blackmun opinion.

an escape mechanism in which judges would resolve disputes between parents and minors or make the determination themselves), they might have permitted the regulation. Stevens dissented completely from that portion of Blackmun's decision, as did Burger, White, and Rehnquist.

On the surface, then, *Planned Parenthood* was a major win for the pro-choice side. But the attorneys involved were concerned by the limited scope of their victory. Two years later, Susman (1978, 583) asserted that "the first step back from [*Roe*] came in [*Planned Parenthood*]." Another (Benshoof 1984, 41) later agreed that the "decision did step back from the language used in *Roe v. Wade*."

What "retreat" did they see in *Planned Parenthood*? To be sure, they were angry with the Court for not striking down the law in its entirety. They wanted the justices to send a stronger signal to state legislators, whom they viewed as in need of a reprimand. As Susman noted,

Many state legislators really don't give a damn whether or not what they pass is constitutional. All they care about is whether it will be popular with their constituents, whom they perceive, usually incorrectly, to be conservative on the abortion issue. I think that legislators frequently abdicate their legislative responsibility to the judiciary and, unfortunately, there is no way to prevent it. In Missouri, for example, only a handful of legislators voted against the new state abortion law which is so patently unconstitutional. (Rubin 1987, 131)

Others asserted that the Court's more specific holdings indicated that it would be willing to veer somewhat from the *Roe* framework; for example, it upheld informed consent requirements even for women in their first trimester of pregnancy. Still others argued that the Court should not have allowed Missouri to "attach to abortion certain requirements, such as record-keeping and informed consent, even though such requirements were not attached to comparable surgical procedures" (Benshoof 1984, 41).

Perhaps the most universal concern with *Planned Parenthood* was with Blackmun's language on the parental consent issue. On one end of the spectrum were those who thought the opinion indicated that the state did have a significant interest in, and thus authority over, children (Benshoof and Pilpel 1986); at the other were those who believed that it was simply an ambiguous statement suggesting that some room for parental consent legislation might exist.[19]

Funding Restrictions

With the Court's ruling in *Planned Parenthood*, states began to alter their strategy. Rather than focus exclusively on consent provisions, they adopted a "burden creation strategy," that is, they sought to increase "the costs . . . associated with abortion, reducing its appeal" (Pearson and Kurtz 1986, 110). Thus the majority of states (see figure 6-3) followed the lead of the federal government and restricted Medicaid funding of abortions. Such limitations, from their perspective, constituted a legitimate exercise of their authority under Title XIX of the Social Security Act, which established the Medicaid program as a cooperative venture between states and the federal government "to provide necessary health services to indigents." Since Title XIX permits states to determine the specifics of their own programs (within general guidelines set by the federal government), they asserted that decisions on abortion funding fell within their purview. Moreover, they argued that these constituted fiscally prudent measures; before the state limitations went into effect, 25 percent of all abortions were funded by Medicaid (*Arizona State Law Journal* 1980, 169).

Naturally, the various sides of the debate interpreted these types of restrictions differently. To pro-life organizations, they were another step toward eradication of *Roe*. Funding was inextricably bound to implementation: if women could not afford abortions and the government could not pay for them, then either doctors would not perform them or women would be deterred from having them.[20] Pro-choice groups viewed these laws as backdoor attempts to gut *Roe*. From their perspective, *Roe* was a victory not just for doctors or even middle-class women, but for those women who could not afford to travel to other countries or states to obtain abortions. Logically, they assumed, once the Court established the right to choose, governments had an obligation to protect that right, even if that meant funding it for the poor through governmental health insurance programs. However, few governments shared their vision, at least in the immediate aftermath of *Roe*.[21] The Hyde amendment (1976) effectively eliminated Medicaid funding for all but a minuscule proportion of abortions, and some states and municipalities followed suit (see figure 6-3).[22] Not surprisingly, abortion advocates quickly challenged them, bringing cases designed to force the Court to strike federal, state, and municipal limitations.[23]

Initially, these suits, launched by pro-choice attorneys, organizations, and coalitions of groups in federal district courts across the country, were quite successful. By 1976, in fact, "a consensus of lower court opinions" had forged a necessary link between the right to choice and governmental funding (*Arizona State Law Journal* 1980, 161). Among the most noteworthy of these was *McRae v. Mathews* in which the Center for Constitutional Rights (CCR), the ACLU, and Planned Parenthood convinced a federal district court judge to issue a permanent restraining order against the Hyde amendment. That and other lower court victories,[24] though, were jeopardized when the Supreme Court decided to enter the funding fray in three 1977 cases: *Beal v. Doe*, *Maher v. Roe*, and *Poelker v. Doe*.

The 1977 "trilogy" generally asked the justices to determine how far states and cities could go in limiting access to abortion services. Yet they involved somewhat different dimensions of that problem and elicited varied arguments from attorneys. At issue in *Beal* was a Pennsylvania law limiting Medicaid funding "to those abortions that are certified by physicians as medically necessary" (*Beal* 1977, 44). *Maher* involved a similar restriction: a Connecticut Welfare Department regulation that "limits state Medicaid benefits for first trimester abortions to those that are 'medically necessary'" (*Maher* 1977, 466). Finally, *Poelker* challenged a St. Louis policy directive that barred city-owned hospitals from performing abortions.

Table 6-4 details the claims made in these cases. Litigants and amici on both sides marshaled an array of arguments for and against the varying restrictions. Though participation generally was not as heavy as it had been in the consent cases, the presence of the U.S. government, submitting its first amicus curiae brief in a Supreme Court abortion case, was significant. At the Court's invitation,

TABLE 6-4. Major Arguments in the 1977 "Trilogy"

Pro–Life Argument[a]	Pro–Choice Response[b]
I. States need not fund the cost of or take affirmative steps to ensure the exercise of a fundamental right (parties, solicitor general, N.J., AUL).	I. States may not penalize a fundamental right (parties, APHA).
A. On Funding: States do not have to fund elective abortions. Medicaid programs are designed to provide medical services necessary to a recipient's health.	A. Medically necessary is an unclear term. *Roe* and *Doe* controvert its usage here; any pregnancy could fit into a medically necessary category (APHA, NHLP).
B. Public Hospitals: City has an interest in maternal health that is distinct from abortion. This does not deprive women of rights, but furthers a legitimate interest.	B. The state cannot favor childbirth over abortion. This constitutes discrimination against poor women and pregnant women who choose abortion (parties).
II. If the Court finds discrimination, only a rational basis need exist because the right to receive medical services is not a fundamental one (parties, AUL, N.J.).	II. This case is not about medical benefits; it is about the exercise of a fundamental right. Thus, the state must show a compelling interest (parties, APHA, AJC).
A. It is rational to have these policies because the state has a distinct interest in childbirth (parties, AUL).	A. The policies discriminate on the basis of socioeconomic status and against those choosing abortion over childbirth (parties, APHA, AJC) for no compelling reason.
III. The lower court's ruling on public hospitals infringes on doctors because they will be forced to perform abortions or lose their jobs (MDL).	III. The city policy deprives physicians of their rights and their ability to practice medicine (APHA).
	IV. The policies violate the free exercise of religion and constitute religious establishment (AJC, APHA).

[a]N.J. = amicus curiae brief of the state of New Jersey; AUL = amicus curiae brief of Americans United for Life; MDL = amicus curiae brief of Missouri Doctors for Life.
[b]APHA = amicus curiae brief of American Public Health Association (cosigned by Planned Parenthood, National Organization for Women, and Certain Medical School Deans, Professors, and Individual Physicians); AJC = amicus curiae brief of American Jewish Congress (cosigned by Board of Church and Society of the United Methodist Church, National Women's Conference of the American Ethical Union, New York State Council of Churches, Union of American Hebrew Congregations, and Unitarian Universalist Women's Federation); NHLP = amicus curiae brief for Jane Doe written by the National Health Law Program and Black Hills Legal Services.

Solicitor General Bork addressed the question of whether the states could restrict funding under the guidelines of the Medicaid program. His memo not only suggested that they could, but it also expounded on abortion funding more generally: the "fact that a woman has a qualified right to an abortion does not imply a correlative constitutional right to free treatment" (*Beal*, Memorandum for the United States, no. 75-7554, 10).

In the end, it was Bork's argument that a majority of the Court echoed in conference and later wrote into law.[25] Writing for six members of the Court in *Maher*, Powell noted: "There is a basic difference between direct state interference with a protected activity and state encouragement of an alternative activity consonant with legislative policy. Constitutional concerns are greatest when the state attempts to impose its will by force of law; the State's power to encourage actions deemed to be in the public interest is necessarily far broader" (*Maher* 1977, 475–76). In sum, there is a right to an abortion, but states have no obligation to fund it. Concomitantly, the Court rejected the pro-choice argument (and the lower court's conclusion) that the right to abortion is fundamental and thus "nothing less than a compelling state interest would justify Connecticut's different treatment of abortion and childbirth" (*Maher* 1977, 471). In the majority's view, *Roe* simply protected women "from unduly burdensome interference with [their] freedom to decide whether to terminate [their] pregnancy. It implies no limitation on the authority of a State to make a value judgment favoring childbirth over abortion" (*Maher* 1977, 473–74). In short, the policy was rationally related to a legitimate governmental goal.[26]

Although the Court phrased its opinion in each case in slightly different terms, reflecting the varying facts and arguments in the cases, some commonalities emerged. One was that the justices were more than willing to defer to the states, a point made to a lesser or greater extent in all three rulings.[27] Another was the majority's insistence that it was signaling "no retreat from *Roe* or the cases applying it." The basic right remained intact; the state merely did not have to guarantee its accessibility.

Brennan, Marshall, and Blackmun, in caustic dissenting opinions, did not see it that way. As they asserted in *Maher* (1977, 483–84), "None can take seriously the Court's assurance that its conclusion signals no retreat from *Roe*. . . . That statement must occasion great surprise among the Courts of Appeal and District Courts that, relying upon *Roe* . . . and *Doe* . . . have held that States are constitutionally required to fund elective abortions if they fund pregnancies carried to term." They went on to explicate just how the trilogy cut into the right articulated in *Roe*, reiterating points made by pro-choice groups. It was perhaps Justice Marshall's dissent from all three opinions that best summarized the hopes and fears of those involved in the abortion debate:

The abortion decisions are sound law and undoubtedly good policy. They have never been questioned by the Court, and we are told that today's cases "signa[l] no retreat from *Roe* or the cases applying it." . . . Yet I fear that the Court's decisions will be an invitation to public officials, already under extraordinary pressure from well-financed and carefully orchestrated lobbying campaigns, to approve more such restrictions. The effect will be to relegate millions of people to lives of poverty and despair. (*Beal* 1977, 461–62)

In the aftermath of the 1977 decisions, a few pro-choice advocates took issue with the gloomy portrait painted by Marshall. As Frank Susman (1978, 590) wrote, "All three of the 1977 abortion cases arose in the context of so called 'elective' or 'non-therapeutic' abortion. It is clear that the decisions in these cases do not apply to 'therapeutic' or 'medically indicated abortions.' It is also clear, based on the rationale of *Roe* and *Doe*, that the 1977 cases ought not to be extended to cover therapeutic abortions." Though he acknowledged that the cases signaled a retreat from *Roe*, he suggested that because they implied that states had no right to "interfere" with therapeutic abortions, "the woman's interest has become more significant than that asserted by the state."

Still, Susman's reaction was unique among pro-choice advocates, most of whom agreed with Justice Marshall. As one said, the decision "was a national tragedy, forcing poor women into back alleys for their abortions" (Oelsner 1977). Some vowed revenge. Planned Parenthood's new president, Faye Wattleton, asserted that "she was putting the 'world on notice' " that her organization would be "more aggressive" (Klemesrud 1978). Others sought to analyze the errors of their ways and correct them. Janet Benshoof (1977), the ACLU's new RFP director, claimed that pro-choice forces were under the "mistaken" impression that the "courts would strike down abortion legislation" and, as a result, grew "complacent." Now they realized that litigation must be supplemented with other tactics. Accordingly, the ACLU would continue to seek redress through the judiciary, making abortion its "top priority" (Asbury 1977), but it and others would also pressure legislatures "to open up and keep open abortion facilities in public hospitals [and] to require state payment for abortion services for poor women."

Whether this would or even could come to fruition was questionable: the pro-choice movement was never particularly successful at the grass-roots level. What is more, their opponents were buoyed by victories in the 1977 trilogy. Not only would they continue their lobbying in state legislatures, but for the first time, they began to see some hope for achieving their objectives through the legal system. As the NRLC said, the rulings indicate that "it may be the Supreme Court is realizing at last what it wrought with its abortion decision" (Oelsner 1977).

TABLE 6-5. The Justices and Abortion, 1975–1979

	Overall Right to Abortion	Parental Consent	Funding	Adver- tising	Doctor Standing	Viability	Other Standard of Care
Blackmun	+	+	+	+	+	+	+
Brennan	+	+	+	+	+	+	+
Marshall	+	+	+	+	+	+	+
Powell	+	−	−	+	−	+	+
Stewart	+	−	−	+	−	+	+
Stevens	+	−	−	NC	+	+	−
Burger	+	−	−	+	−	−	−
White	−	−	−	−	+	−	−
Rehnquist	−	−	−	−	−	−	−

Note: + indicates support of the pro-choice position; − indicates opposition to the pro-choice position; NC signifies "not on Court."

How accurate were their impressions? The data in table 6-5, which indicates voting patterns of the justices on key issues raised in abortion cases through the 1970s, suggest that the picture was far murkier than perhaps either side thought. On the one hand, it is true that some justices did "retreat" from *Roe*. Burger is the most obvious example: though he voted with the majority in 1973, he cast only one more pro-choice vote, in the First Amendment case of *Bigelow v. Virginia* (1975). The chief justice had returned to his initial *Roe* conference position, joining White and Rehnquist. On the other hand, beyond the issues of funding and parental consent, a majority of six remained firmly behind *Roe*, with three—Brennan, Marshall, and Blackmun—its strongest defenders.

Embedded in these patterns and the decisions of the 1970s, thus, was a signal for all who cared to see it. From the pro-choice perspective, the Court had not held *Roe* sacrosanct: its defense would require attorneys to invoke innovative lines of argument and justification. The more apparent message, though, was sent to state legislators and to pro-life activists. According to one pro-life attorney (Horan 1981, 237), despite the funding victories, the Court made it quite clear (particularly in *Planned Parenthood*) that they must "litigate within the parameters" of *Roe*, somehow arguing that "given the fact that *Roe* v. *Wade* has made abortion a fundamental right . . . this case is distinguishable." The task for both sides, thus, was to accommodate their strategies to the lessons of the early post-*Roe* decisions.

1980: A WATERSHED YEAR

The 1970s were largely a standoff for pro-choice and pro-life advocates: both sides had their share of victories and suffered some defeats. Pro-choice groups won *Roe*, but they could not keep legislatures from enacting restrictive laws. The majority of the justices stood by the *Roe* framework, but they were willing to allow certain limitations within it. Pro-life groups had their own difficulties. Their ultimate goal of a Human Life Amendment seemed beyond reach. They could not shift a public seemingly immovable on abortion, and they had little electoral success advancing their objectives. Events in 1980 broke this impasse. For the first time since *Roe*, one side appeared to have gained significant political ground over the other: the pro-life movement won victories of some import in all three branches of government.

THE SUPREME COURT

At least in the lower federal courts, 1980 started off well for pro-choice groups. One of the funding cases they initiated in the mid-1970s was a challenge to the Hyde amendment, a challenge they initially won when federal district court Judge John Dooling issued a permanent restraining order in October 1976, barring its implementation in all fifty states (Seigel 1976). One week after it handed down its decisions in the 1977 cases, however, the Supreme Court remanded the suit—then called *McRae v. Matthews*—for a full hearing in light of *Maher* and *Beal*. The new hearing began in earnest in August 1977 when nine experienced pro-choice attorneys, representing four different organizations,[28] sought to convince Dooling that his initial ruling on the Hyde amendment was correct.

Pro-choice attorneys put on quite a show. They presented thirty witnesses, representing medical, religious, and legal communities; introduced five hundred exhibits, including statistical data, law review and medical articles, and just about anything else of arguable relevance; and ran the trial transcript up to over three thousand pages. Their opponents, on the other hand, were less prepared. U.S. attorneys called only five witnesses, and "instead of making a major courtroom presentation, [they] reli[ed] on submitting depositions and documents as well as their own written arguments" (Johnston 1978; Milbauer 1983).

In the final analysis, this worked in favor of the pro-choice side. In January 1980, Dooling issued a 642-page opinion that struck down the Hyde amendment as an unconstitutional infringement on the Fifth Amendment's due process clause and equal protection component and on the First Amendment's guarantee of free exercise of religion. Beyond his specific holdings, Dooling's opinion was a tour de force for the pro-choice side, as he clearly considered (and built into his judgment) much of the medical, scientific, religious, and sociological evidence they brought to bear on the debate.

Pro-choice advocates were elated. Even though Dooling did not adopt all of their arguments (for example, that Hyde violated religious establishment principles), it is hard to imagine a clearer victory.[29] Yet the federal government allowed pro-choicers little time for celebration. Just a month after Dooling's decision, Carter's solicitor general, Wade McCree, requested the justices to give expedited review to the case. Within a week, the Court scheduled it (now called *Harris v. McRae*) for 21 April 1980 oral arguments.[30]

Although the Court's order gave both sides only three months to prepare, advocates marshaled a slew of competing arguments and garnered support from an array of organized interests. Table 6-6 reveals the relative imbalance between the types of arguments the competing sides brought to bear. Pro-choice attorneys filed a hefty over 250-page brief, half of which was devoted to policy-oriented arguments about the "cause" and potential effects of Hyde. Amici filing in their support followed the same strategy, inundating the justices with medical, scientific, and religious data. The pro-life side, generally speaking, mounted a purely legalistic defense of Hyde.

Also interesting was the attempt by one pro-life organization, the Americans United for Life Legal Defense Fund (AUL LDF), to play a greater role in the litigation. Since its creation in 1975, the AUL LDF had filed amicus curiae briefs in virtually every major Supreme Court abortion case. But by 1980, its attorneys viewed amicus submissions as "effective only if federal judges read them" (Horan 1981, 199). Moreover, AUL LDF staffers were beginning to believe that they were better able to advance, legally speaking, the pro-life cause than were state attorneys general who, in their view, were "completely lost" when it came to abortion cases.[31] These considerations led AUL LDF attorneys to accept eagerly the invitation of Illinois Representative Henry Hyde, who mistrusted the Carter administration's ability to represent the pro-life position,[32] to "join in an effort to become intervenors to preserve the 'adversary process'" (*Califano v. McRae*, Brief in Opposition to Motion to Dismiss or Affirm, no. 76-694, 3). Was this necessary? Perhaps so: the AUL LDF's brief was far more thorough than McCree's thirty-nine-page effort. Moreover, it brought to bear one line of argument noticeably lacking in the solicitor general's submission—that Congress possesses appropriations power. Otherwise, they raised similar claims (see table 6-6).

Slightly more than two months after orals, in late June 1980, a slender majority of five justices upheld the constitutionality of the Hyde amendment. Writing for the Court, Justice Stewart's opinion reflected the solicitor general's

TABLE 6-6. Arguments in *Harris v. McRae*

LEGAL ARGUMENTS: FIFTH AMENDMENT

To Uphold Hyde Amendment:

Solicitor General McCree

I. Congress had a rational basis for treating abortion, within the Hyde amendment, differently than other medical procedures.

A. "Preservation of human life."

B. Limit expenditures of funds "for a purpose that many taxpayers find objectionable."

II. The amendment fits compatibly with U.S. Supreme Court precedent set in the 1977 cases.

AUL Intervenors

I. "There is no due process right to any governmentally subsidized abortion."

A. 1977 Supreme Court cases.

II. The Hyde amendment is "rationally-related to a governmental interest in protecting the fetus."

To Strike Hyde Amendment:

McRae (CCR, Planned Parenthood, ACLU)

I. Serves no legitimate purpose.

A. Differs significantly from 1977 cases because Hyde contains no provision for "medically necessary" abortions.

II. Impinges on the fundamental rights of patients and physicians.

Association of Legal Aid Attorneys et al.[a] as Amicus Curiae

I. Government cannot deny funding for abortion while providing it for sterilization.

A. No compelling state interest justifies this distinction.

B. The distinction between sterilization and abortion discriminates against poor and minority women.

National Council of Churches et al.[b] as Amicus Curiae

I. Denies poor women equal protection and due process under law.

A. Hyde constitutes discrimination against a suspect class.

NOW et al.[c] as Amicus Curiae

I. "Intrudes on fundamental liberties of indigent women."

A. The government cannot provide funding for childbirth but not for abortion.

B. Encroaches on "protected freedom to make choices surrounding family and home."

II. Constitutes gender-based discrimination that "impacts especially hard on poor women."

III. No legitimate interest served; Hyde fails "strict scrutiny" and "rationality" standards.

TABLE 6-6 *(continued)*

LEGAL ARGUMENTS: FIRST AMENDMENT

To Uphold Hyde Amendment:

Solicitor General McCree

I. Appellees lack standing to raise a free exercise claim. No evidence of injury.

AUL Intervenors

I. The state is "not obligated to provide funds for abortion merely because the decision to abort is . . . informed by religious authorities."

To Strike Hyde Amendment:

McRae (CCR, Planned Parenthood, ACLU)

I. Free exercise: "Abortion is a matter of religious and conscientious belief. . . . [Hyde] puts a burden on women for whom abortion is a decision of conscience."

II. Establishment: Hyde has no secular purpose; it constitutes excessive entanglement.

    A. Hyde was the "product of religious belief and pressures against abortion."

American Ethical Union et al.[d] as Amicus Curiae

I. Hyde fails tripartite test for religious establishment violations.

National Churches of Christ as Amicus Curiae

I. Free exercise: Government cannot "place obstacles in the way of citizens to follow the dictates of their conscience."

II. The establishment claim need not be addressed.

ARTICLE I: THE ROLE OF CONGRESS

To Uphold Hyde Amendment:

AUL Intervenors

I. Congress has the power to appropriate funds.

    A. Thus, this raises a political question, off limits to the Court.

Jim Wright et al.[e] as Amicus Curiae

I. District court's decision violates the appropriation clause of Article I.

    A. This case is nonjusticiable because it presents a political question.

To Strike Hyde Amendment:

McRae (CCR, Planned Parenthood, ACLU)

I. To accept this argument is to subvert the role of the Court in a democratic society.

POLICY ARGUMENTS

To Uphold Hyde Amendment:

None

TABLE 6-6 *(continued)*

To Strike Hyde Amendment:

McRae (CCR, Planned Parenthood, ACLU)

    I. Impact of Hyde will be immense: 99 percent of women will be unable to obtain Medicaid funding and have no alternative abortion service (also raised by Association of Legal Aid Attorneys).

    II. Hyde will increase the health, emotional, and psychological risks of abortions (also raised by Association of Legal Aid Attorneys, NOW).

    III. Physicians will be uncertain of how to apply Hyde.

    IV. Hyde is the product of a nonsecular right-to-life movement (also raised by American Ethical Union).

---

[a]Cosigned by Baltimore Abortion Right, Commision Femenil Mexicana Nacional, Committee for Abortion Rights and against Sterilization, Committee to End Sterilization Abuse, National Union of Hospital and Health Care Employees, Education for Freedom of Choice in Ohio, Grand Jury Project, La Raza Legal Alliance, National Bar Association, National Conference of Black Lawyers, National Emergency Civil Liberties Committee, National Lawyers Guild, National Organization of Legal Services Workers, National Women's Health Network, Rochester Women against Violence against Women, Social Services Employees Union, United Electrical, Radio, and Machine Workers of America, and Women's Justice Center.
[b]Represents "thirty-two national religious denominations."
[c]Cosigned by Americans for Democratic Action, Action Coalition of Labor Union Women, National Abortion Rights Action League, National Council of Jewish Women, National Women's Political Caucus, New York City Coalition of Labor Union Women, Women's Action Alliance, Women's Equity Action League Educational and Legal Fund, American Association of University Women, and National Women's Political Caucus.
[d]Cosigned by American Humanist Association, Board of Church and Society, United Methodist Church, Catholics for a Free Choice, Church of the Brethren, Department of Church Women of the Division of Homeland Ministries, Christian Church (Disciples of Christ), National Federation of Temple Sisterhoods, National Women's Conference of the American Ethical Union, Unitarian Universalist Association, Unitarian Universalist Women's Federation, Union of American Hebrew Congregations, and Young Women's Christian Association.
[e]Cosigned by Representative John J. Rhodes, Representative Robert H. Michel, Representative Lindy Boggs, Representative Mary Rose Oakar, Senator William Proxmire, Senator Thomas F. Eagleton, Senator Edward Zorinsky, and certain other members of the Congress of the United States.

position and much of the Court's logic from the 1977 trilogy and ignored the pro-choice socio-legal argument. In particular, following the solicitor general's suggestion, Stewart refused to address First Amendment claims, asserting that the pro-choice plaintiffs lacked standing to bring them. Likewise, he found no merit in the due process argument and instead echoed AUL LDF arguments that the due process clause "does not confer an entitlement to such funds as may be necessary to realize all the advantages of that freedom" (*Harris* 1980, 317–18). Finally, he rejected the equal protection claim, finding that because the law is "not predicated" on a suspect classification, all the United States needed to indicate is that it is "rationally related to a legitimate governmental objective" (*Harris* 1980, 324). The majority agreed that the solicitor general had done just that. In short, Stewart's opinion was a concise, legalistic statement, reflecting the solicitor general's brief and mentioning virtually none of the policy-oriented arguments so carefully worked into the trial by advocates of abortion funding.

THE 1980 ELECTIONS: PRO-LIFE GAINS IN CONGRESS AND THE PRESIDENCY

Harris was a major victory for pro-life forces, a fact that did not escape them, the four justices who each filed dissenting opinions,[33] or involved pro-choice groups.[34] *Harris* would free at least thirteen states, in which pro-choice forces had initiated litigation and attained court orders, from having to pay for medically unnecessary abortions under Medicaid. Moreover, they thought it would decrease the number of abortions performed in the United States; after all, in fiscal year 1977, Medicaid paid for 295,000 abortions (Herman 1980). Even so, the ruling was just the first piece of good news pro-lifers received in 1980; the election brought much more.

The pro-life movement viewed the 1980 elections as a watershed. They witnessed

- the Republican party adopt an extraordinary pro-life platform, which included planks supporting a constitutional amendment and the "appointment of judges at all levels of the judiciary who respect traditional family values and the sanctity of human life";
- the nomination and subsequent landslide election of Ronald Reagan, the first presidential contender ever to support, unequivocally, the goals of the pro-life movement;
- the Republican capture of the Senate;
- the defeat of six out of nine senators targeted by the pro-life movement[35] and the reelection of four of their most supportive allies;[36] and
- a "pro-life" gain of twenty in the House of Representatives.

Pro-life forces took these as portents that the political tide had shifted in their direction. They also were quick to claim credit for Republican party gains; as one said (Hershey 1986, 37), "Not since 1974 . . . has a single issue so transformed the political landscape as did abortion in 1980." With these electoral gains, pro-lifers felt close to the realization of their ultimate goal: the elimination of *Roe*.

Did pro-life forces overestimate the extent of the victory and, concomitantly, their role in achieving it? The voluminous literature[37] on the 1980 elections is mixed and largely varies in its assessment of the dimensions of the victory. For example, it is clear that the Republican party adopted its strongly worded anti-abortion planks in response to pro-life pressures. As White reported (1982, 318–19), Reagan's close advisers overwhelmingly opposed the inclusion of such planks, but "the right-to-life movement had been one of the stronger supports in the Reagan campaign. And, its people packed the platform committee [as] skillfully as any single-purpose zealots had ever done." Press Secretary James Brady put it simply: "They were forces beyond our control."

The extent of pro-life influence on the congressional races is somewhat more difficult to decipher with political scientists disagreeing over how and why the Republicans did so well.[38] However, few scholars have concluded that the issue of abortion (or even the New Right's targeting of candidates) had a major impact on congressional outcomes. Latus (1984) implies that the efforts of both sides to influence the congressional results were largely unsuccessful; the two major competing political action committees, NARAL PAC and LAPAC, expended few dollars in the general scheme of things,[39] with the pro-choice group actually contributing more than LAPAC.[40]

Could pro-life forces take some credit for Reagan's landslide victory? The scholarly consensus is a definitive "no." According to the experts, the single most important fact was that the public engaged in "retrospective voting": they were dissatisfied with Carter's performance, particularly his handling of the economy and of foreign affairs (such as the Iran hostage situation), and thus voted him out of office.[41] The implications of this finding, as they bear on the claims of pro-life and New Right leaders, are rather stark. While they read into Reagan's victory some sort of a "conservative mandate," the data do not seem to bear this out.[42] Evidence, in fact, abounds that not only did the "electorate lack enthusiasm for right-wing ideology," but many voted for Reagan *despite* his support of items on the New Right's agenda, including abortion.[43] In short, citizens viewed abortion "as essentially unrelated to [their] voting choices" (Abramson, Aldrich, and Rohde 1982, 135). Data presented in figure 6-4 support this claim: public opinion on the issue remained virtually unchanged and generally pro-choice throughout the decade. Even Reagan knew his position on abortion was not politically useful. Polls taken in the months before the election, in fact, indicated that it might cost him substantial votes (*New York Times* 1980).[44]

Nonetheless, pro-lifers and New Right leaders chose to ignore the scholars

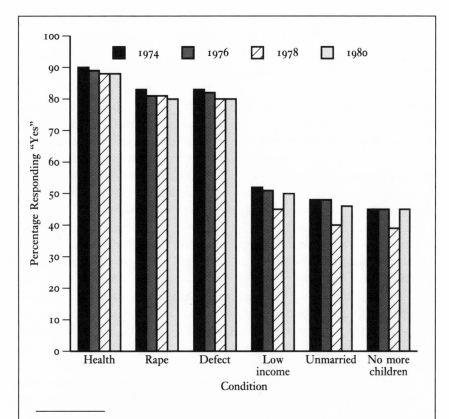

Sources: Ebaugh and Haney 1980, 492; updated by the authors.
Note: Data are derived from National Opinion Research Center General Surveys, 1974–80. The question was: "Please tell me whether or not you think it should be possible for a pregnant woman to obtain a legal abortion if: 1) the woman's health is seriously endangered by the pregnancy; 2) she is pregnant as a result of a rape; 3) there is a strong chance of a serious defect in the baby; 4) the family has a very low income and cannot afford any more children; 5) she is not married and does not want to marry the man; 6) she is married and does not want any more children."

FIGURE 6-4. Public Opinion on Abortion, 1974–1980

and, instead, follow the journalistic wisdom of the day. After all, the newspapers were full of accounts of the elections, virtually agreeing that a new day was dawning. Anthony Lewis (1980) merely reflected prevailing sentiment when he asserted, "The Senate results made the point even more compelling than Ronald Reagan's electoral landslide. What happened in the 1980 election reflected a profound and general turn to conservatism in this country."

ABORTION IN THE POLITICAL ARENA, 1980–1985

PROMISE VERSUS PERFORMANCE: THE GAP WIDENS
AT THE FEDERAL LEVEL

Journalistic accounts of the 1980 elections were music to the ears of conservatives and pro-life groups, who were, as one member put it, "ready to lead" (Viguerie 1981). What they failed to recognize, though, was that very few—at least at the federal level—were initially willing to follow. Indeed, the political events transpiring in the aftermath of the 1980 races resembled those occurring in the wake of *Roe*. Once again, pro-life forces first sought to push restrictive measures through the now-Republican Congress, the most viable of which (the so-called Human Life Bill) would have defined "human life" to exist from the moment of conception and removed federal court jurisdiction (except the U.S. Supreme Court) over abortion cases. Seeking legislative endorsement of this proposal was, to be sure, a reasonable course. After all, given scholarly analyses of the 1980 elections, pro-life forces had their best chances for success in Congress—it was possible that they had made a difference in those races. Even so, that effort failed miserably: the bill never made it to the Senate floor.[45]

Analysts have forwarded many reasons for this defeat, including strong counterattacks launched by pro-choice forces[46] and questions from credible sources about the bill's constitutionality.[47] But all in all, it was the lack of agreement—indeed, open warfare—among pro-life groups that worked to thwart the effort; the movement laid the foundation for its own demise. Even with testimony running against the bill, the mobilization of the pro-choice movement, and lack of public enthusiasm, the Human Life Bill may have had a reasonable chance of success if pro-life forces had rallied around it. After all, Republicans controlled the Senate, and the House was open to influence. This was a point on which both sides agreed. Pro-choice Senator Packwood (1986) wrote that the bill's "prospects" looked good; Representative Hyde, in March 1981, asserted that "[w]e now have the votes" (Weintraub 1981). Yet, "the lack of consensus" among pro-life groups destroyed any hope for passage (Lee and LeRoy 1985).[48] One right-to-life advocate asserted, "We are a movement in disarray and we'd better get our act together and restore our credibility and do it fast, or we're going to be in real trouble" (Paige 1983, 229).

Worse than the congressional defeat, at least from the perspective of some pro-lifers, was the behavior of "their" president, Ronald Reagan. Despite the fact that the data indicate that his victory had little or nothing to do with them, they expected that he would fully support their objectives. What they refused to acknowledge was that "however much [Reagan] believed in the cause, he was a politician and a Republican before he was a right-to-lifer or a conservative" (Paige 1983, 222). He and his advisers could "read the polls" and knew that, if anything, the public supported Reagan despite his views on abortion. So it was not too surprising that Reagan's actions—at least during his first term—deeply disappointed members of the right-to-life movement. For example, they were unhappy with Reagan's cabinet appointments, which, as Viguerie (1981, 176) put it, contained "not one outspoken born again Christian . . . and no one representing . . . the conservative women's movement."[49]

This disappointment turned into fury with the nomination of Sandra Day O'Connor to the Supreme Court. While liberals and most conservatives applauded the president's choice, pro-lifers were outraged. Because of votes she cast as an Arizona state legislator, they labeled her a "pro-choicer."[50] The National Right to Life Committee charged that her nomination "represent[ed] a repudiation of the Republican platform pledge," which commanded the appointment of judges "who respect traditional family values and the sanctity of innocent human life."

Though Jerry Falwell and others were largely drowned out by the "chorus of praise" for O'Connor, they generated enough publicity to unnerve the White House. Abraham (1985, 332–33) reports that when "the abortion issue threatened a smooth confirmation" for O'Connor, Reagan's advisers informed pro-life leaders that "O'Connor had assured the president that she is 'personally opposed' to abortion, [and] that she believes abortion to be a legitimate matter for legislative regulation." This did little to assuage pro-lifers, who pressured Senate Judiciary Committee members into examining her closely on the topic. O'Connor was prepared, however, and said in her opening statement: "I hope to be as helpful to you as possible in responding to your questions. However, I do not believe . . . I can tell you how I might vote on a particular issue that may come before the Court or endorse or criticize specific Supreme Court decisions presenting issues which may well come before the Court again." Nonetheless, Strom Thurmond, chair of the committee, tried to pursue the topic of abortion, questioning O'Connor on her overall philosophy and votes as a legislator. She provided justifications for her past actions, but, on the more pointed questions, she held to her original statement. She told senators that abortion was "a practice in which [she] would not have engaged" but continuously qualified that statement with comments like, "I am over the hill. I am not going to be pregnant any more . . . so perhaps it's easy for me to speak."

Pro-life advocates and several members of the Judiciary Committee were not pleased with O'Connor's responses. Some were actually livid. As NRLC President Willke put it, "[T]he millions of sincere prolifers . . . who did vote for [Reagan]—who did work for him . . . just may not do it again" (Merton 1981, 170). Nonetheless, her performance was convincing enough to secure her a unanimous vote from the Senate. Once again, then, pro-life forces failed, or at least thought they had, in the chamber of government most amenable to their goals—the Senate. More important, perhaps, Ronald Reagan had again disappointed them.

As a result of this and other "acts of treachery,"[51] pro-life advocates grew increasingly angry and frustrated with "their" president. Although they would not admit this publicly, privately they were facing up to the facts. In a memo circulated among leading pro-lifers, one among their ranks wrote: "In spite of better-than-expected results in the 1980 elections, many of the most experienced right-to-life leaders are far less optimistic . . . than they care to admit in public. [They] privately speak of 20 to 30 years being necessary to end abortion" (Bennetts 1981). Unable to count on Reagan's leadership, they would continue to diversify their strategy.

A GLIMMER OF HOPE: THE STATES

While pro-lifers were eminently frustrated by Congress in the 1970s, they were more successful in the states where their opponents remained less effective. This trend continued into the early 1980s. Despite repeated attempts by NARAL and others to organize at the grass-roots level, they simply could not generate the numbers or resources claimed by their opponents.[52]

That pro-life forces outmatched their opponents at state and local levels is reflected in the number of restrictive laws enacted in the late 1970s and early 1980s, as depicted in figure 6-5. What worried pro-choice forces was not merely the quantity of statutes but also their type. While some states were restricting abortion in "traditional ways" (for example, by prohibiting Medicaid funding and requiring parental consent or notification), others were enacting a new species of laws to deter women from exercising the abortion right. Such were the brainchilds of right-to-life groups. After studying the Court's post-*Roe* decisions, they sought to formulate "national model legislation," which would restrict the right to choice, while simultaneously fitting within the contours of existing doctrine.

One of their first successes came in Akron, Ohio, where a "splinter group of the [city's] Right to Life Society" wrote and lobbied for a series of restrictive ordinances (Stuart 1978). Despite an unorthodox legislative procedure and a sharply divided public, in February 1978 the city council adopted this so-called "national model legislation" by a 7–6 vote.[53] In particular, the new Akron ordinance (Chapter 1870) contained the following provisions:

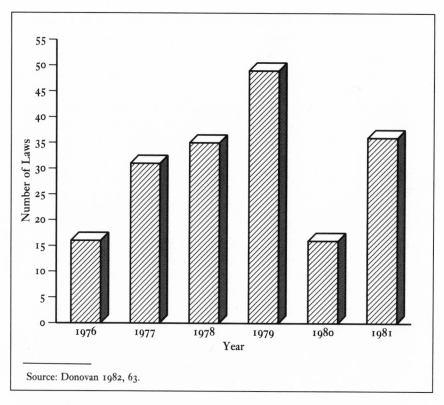

Source: Donovan 1982, 63.

FIGURE 6-5. Number of Abortion Laws Enacted by States, 1976–1981

• Notice and Consent: This section prohibits physicians from performing abortions on unmarried women under the age of eighteen without "giving at least 24 hours actual notice to one of the parents." If the minor is under the age of fifteen, informed written consent of a parent or a court is required.

• Informed Consent: This section seeks to insure that a woman's consent to abortion services is truly informed by mandating that a physician tell her:

    1. the number of weeks she is pregnant;

    2. that the "unborn child is a human life form from the moment of conception" and that he or she describe in some detail "the anatomical and physiological characteristics of the particular unborn child at the gestational point of development at which time the abortion is to be performed";

    3. that the "unborn child" may be viable if "more than 22 weeks have elapsed from the time of conception";

4. that "abortion is a major surgical procedure, which can result in serious complications"; and

5. about public and private adoption agencies.

• Waiting Period: This section requires that doctors wait twenty-four hours from the time they receive consent before performing the abortion.

• Disposal of Remains: This requires that doctors who perform abortions "shall insure that the remains of the unborn child are disposed of in a humane and sanitary manner."

Akron was not alone in enacting the model code: Louisiana, Nevada, Utah, and others followed in short order (Donovan 1982).

Pro-life groups were delighted with these legislative victories, but they did not necessarily view them as ends in themselves. On one level, they thought the legislation might build momentum for a Human Life Amendment. On another, they knew pro-choice groups would quickly challenge the laws, and they were not unhappy with this prospect; since they believed the laws fell within *Roe*'s purview, favorable Court rulings would slowly erode the 1973 decisions. Under this new approach, pro-lifers thus sought to undermine *Roe* on its own terms. In addition, they now saw the Supreme Court as promising. To their victories in the 1977 and 1980 funding cases, they soon added another. In *H.L. v. Matheson* (1981) the Court upheld a Utah parental consent law providing that physicians should "notify if possible" parents of a minor before performing an abortion.[54]

CITY OF AKRON V. AKRON CENTER FOR REPRODUCTIVE HEALTH

The political momentum of the right-to-life movement, particularly in the states, was not lost on pro-choicers. While they could not keep localities from enacting new restrictions of the sort adopted in Akron, attorneys could and did try to void them through litigation. In fact, on 19 April 1978, just one month before the Akron ordinance was to take effect, ACLU attorneys (representing a local affiliate and the RFP) brought suit on behalf of a city abortion clinic, the Akron Center for Reproductive Health. Pro-choice forces were well prepared, parading an array of expert witnesses testifying against every aspect of the legislation. Extremely damaging, in particular, were statements by the city's mayor and the director of the Health Department suggesting that they did not "believe it has been demonstrated, from a medical standpoint, that further regulation is needed."[55] The pro-life side was equally prepared. Not content to allow the city's attorney to represent their side exclusively, one of the law's drafters—Alan

Segedy—and several other pro-life advocates[56] attained defendant intervenor status on behalf of parents of minor daughters. They (and the city) trotted out their own set of experts and argued that the law worked within the confines of *Roe*. A U.S. District Court judge disagreed and in August 1979 handed pro-choice attorneys a virtually complete victory.

The city appealed the district court's decision on informed consent, leaving the parental provisions to the intervenors. But in June 1981, the Court of Appeals for the Sixth Circuit handed them an even bigger defeat, affirming the lower court's holdings of unconstitutionality and striking the provisions it upheld. In so doing, it used a high standard of review under which states would have a difficult task of convincing judges to uphold their laws. In particular, it asserted that courts must initially determine if the regulation in question "interferes" with the woman's decision, in consultation with her doctor, to obtain an abortion. If so, the state has the burden of proving that the regulation can be justified by a compelling interest. If the state can demonstrate such an interest, courts still must consider whether the regulation is "sufficiently narrowly drawn" so as to not place an "undue burden" on the abortion decision.

When the U.S. Supreme Court agreed to hear the case, pro-choice attorneys were worried, to say the least. It is common knowledge among legal analysts that the Court generally takes cases to reverse decisions. If this happened, pro-choice forces would lose at least part of their victory. Moreover, they had not won a significant case in the Supreme Court since 1979 and viewed the Court with increasing suspicion. In this, they were not alone. Around the time the justices were considering *Matheson*, Justice Blackmun wrote: "I need not say how disappointed I have been in what I perceive to be the Court's noticeable withdrawal in recent cases from the more positive position taken in *Roe*, *Doe*, and *Danforth*. I fear that the forces of emotion and professed morality are winning some battles. That 'real world' continues to exist 'out there' and I earnestly hope that the 'war,' despite these adverse 'battles' will not be lost" (Schwartz 1990, 312).

Pro-choice forces also were concerned about the Reagan administration. Attorneys thought that it would use *Akron* to support, however symbolically, the pro-life side. This fear was confirmed when Solicitor General Rex E. Lee not only decided to file an amicus curiae brief but requested time to argue orally as well. For the first time, the U.S. government would directly involve itself in abortion litigation that did not involve funding. Nervous pro-choice advocates, such as the RFP's director, Janet Benshoof, immediately condemned the move: "The Reagan Administration is using the Justice Department as a public relations arm, not as an independent, legal branch of Government, and when they can't get right-to-life legislation through Congress they want to appease the right-to-lifers by having the Justice Department do something for them" (Taylor 1982).

SUPREME COURT BRIEFS IN *AKRON*

As former dean of Brigham Young Law School, Solicitor General Lee was one of the Reagan appointees that pleased pro-life groups. Even so, his *Akron* brief was the source of some disappointment. Apparently some members of the "Reagan Right" were "hounding" him to urge the justices to overrule *Roe*.[57] Lee had sympathy with this position, but he refused to take it. As he noted in general terms, "If I had done what was urged on me in a lot of cases, I would have lost those cases and the justices would not have taken me seriously in others. There has been this notion that my job is to press the Administration's policies at every turn and announce true conservative principles through the pages of my briefs. It is not. I'm the Solicitor General, not the Pamphleteer General" (Caplan 1987, 107). While his training and legal instinct, then, would not allow him to argue for the reversal of *Roe*, he did come quite close to doing so. In his amicus curiae brief, Lee advanced two arguments. On the topic of abortion, he articulated a constitutional standard that he claimed to derive from previous Court decisions. His reading of *Roe*'s progeny led him to conclude that the justices had never really "applied" *Roe*'s "sweeping" language regarding first-trimester abortions; from *Danforth* on, they made exceptions. Instead, the Court "has repeatedly adopted an 'unduly burdensome' analysis" (*Akron*, Brief for the United States, no. 81-746, 6). That is, the Court had permitted state regulations of abortion as long as they did not "unduly burden" that decision. Second, and more troublesome from the pro-choice perspective, was Lee's proposed application of the standard. How would courts distinguish an *unduly* burdensome regulation from one that was *simply* burdensome? In the solicitor general's opinion, the justices should defer to legislatures:

> Whether or not a particular regulation "unduly burdens" the abortion decision is far from self-evident. In light of the breadth and the ambiguity of the "unduly burdensome" standard—and in the interest of preserving the difference between what courts do and what legislatures do—this Court should clarify that in applying that standard on a case-to-case basis courts should be mindful that (1) at their root, the issues to which the "unduly burdensome" test is applied are policy issues, and different segments of our society have strong competing views concerning them; (2) the legislature has already considered the competing arguments, made the necessary factual inquiries, and reached a decision; and (3) the net effect of holding the legislative product unconstitutional is that those who succeeded in persuading the legislature of the soundness of their policy viewpoint are deprived of their legislative victory, whereas the legislative losers become

the winners. These realities counsel that, in deciding which legislative policy choices are "unduly burdensome" and which are not, the Court should accord heavy deference to the legislative judgment. (*Akron*, Brief for the United States, no. 81-746, 10)

Thus, Lee did not directly ask the Court to overrule *Roe*, but his argument, if adopted, would have that effect. One source (Caplan 1987, 105) noted that his brief "led some observers to think he'd pushed the bounds of government advocacy farther than any SG before him."

Pro-life attorneys involved in *Akron* had no intention of ignoring Lee's standard; it supported their position. Yet, as a result of his involvement in the case, the arguments they presented took on a duality. The dominant thrust of the other pro-life briefs critiqued the contours of the compelling state interest approach adopted by the court of appeals, and onto this argument they grafted some mention of the unduly burdensome logic.[58] Perhaps this was done out of an agreement with Lee's argument, or a belief that the Court would be more inclined to restrict *Roe* if all pro-life forces pointed the same way, or a concern that the justices be made aware of the alternative avenues of decision they paved with their unduly burdensome analysis. Whatever the reason, this duality of argument caused the pro-life briefs to lack clear focus.

The submissions of city attorney Robert Pritt and of Alan Segedy well illustrate this and the cost it imposed in terms of legal argument. In summarizing his position, Pritt asserted that "the initial question posed . . . is whether the state's interest in maternal health and well being is such that it may regulate abortion in a reasonable manner which is not unduly burdensome." Yet his "initial question" did little to frame his argument. For example, his claim regarding the parental consent section was not that it was unburdensome but that "the state has a legitimate interest in protecting the minor's health." He later argued that "this Court has recognized that the states have a compelling interest in the well being of a minor" (*Akron*, Brief for Petitioner, City of Akron, no. 81-746, 14, 24, 31). His defense of the ordinance's other sections was similar. Segedy's arguments paralleled Pritt's. In the summary of his brief, he twice mentioned the solicitor general's standard, but the claims there dealt with distinctions between immature and mature minors and community medical standards. When he finally returned to the unduly burdensome theme, it was strikingly disconnected from the core of his argument. Consider the final two claims presented:

C. A State Must Show A Compelling Interest in Support Of A Duly Enacted Abortion Regulation Only When Such Regulation Has Been Shown To Be Unduly Burdensome. . . .

D. The Facts of This Case Compel The Conclusion That The City Has A Compelling Interest. (*Akron*, Brief for Respondents, Francois Seguin et al., no. 81-746, 35, 36)

Given Lee's argument, these make little sense. Since legislation is overwhelmingly presumed to be unburdensome, no need exists to demonstrate a compelling interest. Perhaps he made argument D because he learned of argument C only recently, or perhaps he had doubts about the Court's willingness to adopt Lee's approach. Either way, the brief manifested real confusion.

At least on the surface, pro-choice attorneys had somewhat less of a challenge than their opponents. They had a favorable ruling from the court below, and, as such, they acknowledged but did not counter explicitly Lee's arguments.[59] Generally, the ACLU's brief reiterated the Sixth Circuit's opinion, placing particular emphasis on the logical correctness of the compelling state interest standard. From its perspective, it was that approach, not the one offered by the solicitor general or the petitioners, which was most compatible with the Court's previous decisions. Indeed, they termed Lee's approach "confusing and unmanageable" (*Akron*, Brief for Respondent, no. 81-746, 28).

Numerous amici[60] lined up in support of this position. But by focusing on different portions of the law and demonstrating how each burdened women for no compelling reason, they did so in ways that avoided repetition of the ACLU's arguments. The American College of Obstetricians and Gynecologists (ACOG), for example, argued that the second-trimester hospital requirement was burdensome and unnecessary because such abortions could be safely performed in nonhospital facilities. The American Psychological Association claimed that because the informed consent sections required that doctors have special counseling skills they often do not possess, these sections could be misrepresented and misunderstood. Planned Parenthood argued, among other things, that the parental consent provision amounted to an impermissible veto.

With one exception, pro-choice amici generally ignored the solicitor general. In its first appearance in a Supreme Court abortion case, the National Association for the Advancement of Colored People Legal Defense Fund (NAACP LDF) refuted the solicitor general's call for deference to legislative judgment. In its view, such an argument reflected old segregationist claims, a position it demonstrated by citing arguments made by southern states in racial cases that eerily paralleled those raised by the solicitor general in *Akron*. Hence, while LDF attorneys barely mentioned the word "abortion" (other than to say that they do not litigate such cases), cited only one abortion case (*Roe*), and considered not at all the Akron law at hand, their brief was an effective indictment of one aspect of the solicitor general's submission.

ORAL ARGUMENTS AND THE COURT'S DECISION IN *AKRON*

The pro-life side badly wanted to win *Akron*. This was the first occasion since *Danforth* that the justices had the opportunity to reassess *Roe*. The groups believed that events had turned in their favor since 1976: the political environment could absorb a substantial incursion into abortion rights; the states had handed them victory after victory; and now they had two of their "own," Alan Segedy and Rex E. Lee, arguing their cause before a potentially sympathetic Court. Although things could not have looked better, they could not have gone worse.

Segedy, instead of city attorney Pritt, represented Akron in orals. Apparently the pro-life side thought that he would do a superior job in representing its interests; after all, as a drafter of the ordinance, he was very familiar with it. This turned out to be a mistake. While Segedy tried to press the "unduly burdensome" approach, the Court pressed him as to why he was arguing the case, given that it had denied *his* clients intervenor status.[61] Eventually, the justices eased off and focused their remaining questions on the consent provisions. The justices were not as kind to Solicitor General Lee, however, especially Blackmun, *Roe's* author. After Lee's introductory statement, Blackmun asked:[62]

Blackmun: Mr. Solicitor General, are you asking that *Roe v. Wade* be overruled?

Lee: I am not, Mr. Justice Blackmun.

Blackmun: Why not?

Lee: That is not one of the issues presented in this case, and as amicus appearing before the Court, that would not be a proper function for us.

Blackmun: It seems to me that your brief in essence asks either that or the overruling of *Marbury* against *Madison*.

Lee: Neither. Neither. And the reason is, as I have just stated, the ultimate decision at the end of the day concerning these matters is a judicial decision, but all I am pleading for is a recognition that both with respect to issues of fact which necessarily pervade each of these decisions that is made, and also with respect to their factual noncomponents, that the Court at least take into account the fact that these same kinds of issues have already been faced by a legislature with superior fact-finding capabilities, and have been resolved.

The Eighth Circuit—

Blackmun: May I ask one other question? . . . Would you apply the same standard of review where there is the legislative history that you have in Akron as you would in Virginia where there is no legislative history?

Lee: Yes. Yes. With regard to the argument, Justice Blackmun, that is the same standard that was—the same circumstances that existed in *Marbury*. There is a difference. As I say, we are not urging that *Roe v. Wade* be overruled. There are portions of—but that is an issue. That is an issue for another day. But there is a constitutionally significant difference between the kind of yes or no answer as to whether abortion is or is not prohibited by the Constitution that was involved in *Roe v. Wade* and the subsequent filling in of the rather factually oriented details, and more precise and specific details that have characterized the decisions since that time.

Pro-choice attorney Stephan Landsman, working in conjunction with ACLU lawyers, sought to refute Lee's approach; he argued that the solicitor general's "proposal would undercut *Roe*. . . . [I]t would make all restrictive abortion regulations presumptively constitutional and place the onus on the plaintiffs . . . to show their undue burdensomeness." Yet the justices chose to query more particular matters—the mechanics of the law in operation—rather than standards. They seemed far more interested in the ordinance per se than in revising *Roe*'s framework.

Despite indications from the bench to the contrary, some pro-life forces thought orals went well. While the AUL LDF, in particular, was not sure it had won the case, it thought it had picked up a vote. To its attorneys, Justice Stevens seemed sympathetic in his lengthy questioning during oral arguments (Epstein 1990, 197). The balance of the right-to-lifers, however, were less optimistic. About three months after orals in *Akron*, they returned to Congress to push again for a Human Life Amendment, eventually convincing a Senate Judiciary Committee subcommittee to hold hearings on a new, no-exception amendment proposed by Senator Hatch: "A right to abortion is not secured by this Constitution." Those hearings ended in April with something of a pro-life victory: the full committee, by a 9 to 9 vote, reported the proposal. Because it attached no recommendation to the amendment, its vote set the stage for a floor debate to be held on 26 June 1983 (Packwood 1986).

But six days before the Senate commenced its debate, the Supreme Court handed the pro-choice movement its strongest victory since *Roe*. In a 6 to 3 ruling, the justices struck the Akron ordinance in its entirety. Justice Powell's majority opinion (for Blackmun, Brennan, Marshall, Stevens, and Burger) was extraordinary in several regards. For one thing, it completely, albeit implicitly, rejected Solicitor General Lee's argument: "[A]rguments continue to be made . . . that we erred in interpreting the Constitution. Nonetheless, the doctrine of *stare decisis*, while perhaps never entirely persuasive on a constitutional question, is a doctrine that demands respect in a society governed by the rule of law. We respect it today, and reaffirm *Roe v. Wade*" (*Akron* 1983, 419–20). For another, Powell provided the clearest statement to date of the standards the Court would invoke to review abortion restrictions, a statement that flowed directly from *Roe* and its progeny, not the solicitor general's brief. On one level, he reinforced the trimester scheme and explicated fully its implications for state regulation. On another, Powell updated this framework to apply to conditions in 1983. This, in the majority's view, was necessary since the second-trimester standard forced states to work within "accepted medical practices," which evolve over time; it also gave them the leeway needed to strike all provisions of the law. Consider, for example, the scrutiny it gave to the city's hospitalization require-ment. Akron defended this on the grounds that it was "a reasonable health regulation," a position that, as Powell noted, "had strong support at the time of *Roe* . . . as hospitalization was recommended by the American Public Health Association (APHA) and the American College of Obstetricians and Gynecolo-gists (ACOG)." But times had changed; medical advances increased "the safety" of second-trimester abortions to the extent that the ACOG no longer suggests that they need to be performed in hospitals. This led him to conclude that "present medical knowledge . . . undercuts Akron's justification for requiring that *all* second-trimester abortions be performed in hospitals" (*Akron* 1983, 434–37). By combining precedent with medical information provided by amici APHA and ACOG, he proceeded to strike down all sections of the Akron ordinance as being out of sync with the 1973 framework viewed from the perspective of 1983.

Pro-choice forces were ecstatic. RFP director, Janet Benshoof, called it the "most far-reaching victory on reproductive rights since *Roe v. Wade*." Others suggested that it was a "major defeat" and a "legal embarrassment for the Reagan administration" (Greenhouse 1983a, 1983b). Interestingly, pro-life forces did not view *Akron* in such stark terms.[63] Solicitor General Lee, for one, felt the decision was "neither 'a major victory' nor 'a major defeat' for either side. . . . We won some and we lost some" (Treaster 1983). This assertion was not altogether incorrect. Though the majority clearly rejected his approach (deference to legislatures) and his standard (unduly burdensome), the dissenters adopted it, at least in part. Even more heartening, in her first opportunity to enter the abortion debate, Justice O'Connor wrote a minority opinion joined by Justices White and Rehnquist.

The first part of O'Connor's opinion presented a scathing indictment of Powell's version of *Roe*. Her initial argument (*Akron* 1983, 453–56) was straight-forward:

• Because of medical advances, the lines separating "permissible from impermissible" regulation are blurred.
• As a result, legislatures and, then, courts must "continuously and conscientiously study contemporary and scientific literature" to determine what they can and cannot do.
• This is a difficult task for legislatures and an inappropriate one for courts.

Even assuming that *Roe* requires courts and legislatures to conduct such inquiries, this, in O'Connor's view, did not necessarily mean that courts should always strike legislation. Why? Because medical advances cut both ways: "Just as improvements in medical technology will move *forward* the point at which the State may regulate for reasons of maternal health, different technological improvements will move *backward* the point of viability at which the State may proscribe abortions" (*Akron* 1983, 456–57). In other words, while Powell used the development of medical advances as an argument to strike down parts of the Akron ordinance, those same "advances" could be used to move back the line of viability, thus giving states more leeway; at the time of *Roe*, viability "before 28 weeks was considered unusual," but she cited newer studies showing viability as early as twenty-five weeks. This led her to two conclusions. First, because it is "inherently" tied to ever-changing medical technology, "the *Roe* framework . . . is clearly on a collision course with itself" (*Akron* 1983, 458). Second, in part because the lines separating viability from nonviability are fading, "compelling state interests" exist throughout the pregnancy.

Given that her initial analysis paralleled Solicitor General Lee's, her next point was hardly a surprise: she urged the Court to abandon the trimester framework in favor of one that "protects the woman from unduly burdensome interference with her freedom to decide whether to terminate her pregnancy." O'Connor did, however, part company with Lee on how the Court should determine whether a law "imposes an undue burden." She explicitly rejected the solicitor general's assertion that it simply requires courts to defer to legislatures: "The 'unduly burdensome' standard is appropriate *not* because it incorporates deference to legislative judgment at the threshold stage of analysis, but rather because of the limited *nature* of the fundamental right that has been recognized in the abortion cases. . . . It is not appropriate to *weigh* the state interests at the threshold stage" (*Akron* 1983, 465–66). What, then, would O'Connor count as "unduly burdensome" regulation? Powell claimed that "the dissent would uphold virtually any abortion regulation under a rational-basis test." O'Connor did not go that far, but neither did she explicate precisely what she meant.

Although it picked up O'Connor's vote,[64] the right-to-life side lost big in

Akron and fared no better through the rest of 1983. Buoyed by their Court victory, pro-choicers pressured the Senate to defeat the Hatch amendment. Seeing new urgency in the cause, right-to-lifers tried to counter (Rosewicz 1983) but once again were plagued by divisions.[65] On 28 June, the Hatch amendment fell eighteen votes short of the required two-thirds for passage. This, of course, delighted pro-choice advocates. As Senator Packwood (1986, 17) said: "The right-to-life movement had its 'day in court'—and the jury had come down against it." Its Senate defeat, he continued, was "the end of any serious effort to overturn the fundamental decision that a woman has a right to make a choice for herself."

THE MID-1980S: RETOOLING AND REASSERTING

Pro-life advocates did not dispute the fact that they had suffered setbacks in 1983, but they rejected the postmortem: they were far from dead and buried. In fact, the losses served to revitalize and recatalyze the movement, not unlike its response to *Roe* (Rosewicz 1983; Stuart 1983). With the amendment behind them, pro-life forces could focus on an array of strategies and tactics around which they were united. The framing of an amendment always had been a point of contention, but the use of "educational" campaigns, litigation, and, to a lesser extent, efforts to influence the electoral process caused far less disagreement. It was to these activities that they turned their attention.

While pro-lifers "retooled," abortion advocates did the same. Despite their jubilation over the 1983 victories, pro-choicers recognized that their opponents had gained ground. Almost half the Senate voted in favor of a human life amendment, the *Roe* majority had shrunk by one, and states continued to enact restrictive legislation. For all their victories, pro-choice forces still felt themselves on the defensive. Thus, after the summer of 1983, the battle lines were forged more starkly than at any other point since *Roe*, with the ensuing skirmishes played out in arenas from the scholarly to the legal and political.

THE NEW PROPAGANDA WARS

In the four or five years after *Roe*, Blackmun's opinion was the subject of great discussion in the legal community. In general, this was carried out on a fairly lofty plane, with key debates centering on the proper role of the Court in a democratic regime and on whether *Roe* represented a return to the substantive due process approach of *Lochner v. New York* (1905) (Ely 1973) or whether it was rooted firmly in privacy standards (Heymann and Barzelay 1973).[66] Treatment of such issues made for interesting scholarly debate, but it was not necessarily the stuff of concrete legal argument.

Beginning in the early 1980s and reaching a near-fever pitch after *Akron*, however, both sides focused on new and more pragmatic approaches to *Roe*. After the *Akron* defeat, in March 1984, Americans United for Life—perhaps the most academically inclined of the pro-life organizations—sponsored a conference entitled "Reversing *Roe v. Wade* through the Courts," attended by well-known scholars and pro-life advocates. One of its goals was to get input on new approaches that could be used in abortion litigation. The proceedings of that meeting[67] resemble the sort of freewheeling sessions that characterized pro-choice conferences held before *Roe*. Using O'Connor's dissent as a "launching point," they developed a devastating indictment of *Roe* itself. Criticisms ranged from "it is poorly written," to its "unenviable" connection with *Lochner*, to the sentiment that "virtually every aspect of the historical, sociological, medical and legal arguments . . . Blackmun used . . . has been subject to intense scholarly criticism" (Horan and Balch 1987). Although some of the critiques remained "lofty" in tone, the AUL hit on a new strategy: to attack *Roe* as an inferior piece of legal scholarship and a flawed scientific study. In doing so, though, it would deliberately emulate the NAACP LDF's "go slow" *Brown* strategy and thus cause the gradual erosion of *Roe*.

A year later, Reagan's attorney general added another log to the fire when he addressed the American Bar Association (ABA) in Washington, D.C. In his speech, Edwin Meese urged that the Supreme Court adopt a "Jurisprudence of Original Intent." What he advocated was not new; Ely (1973) and Bork (1971), among others, had previously offered similar approaches. Moreover, Meese's speech was not directly concerned with abortion—he focused on criminal law, religion, and federalism. Pro-life advocates, however, picked up his theme, maintaining that the doctrine of original intent could be used as a vehicle to attack *Roe*.[68]

At the same time, other pro-life forces increased their propaganda efforts. They distributed a film, called the "Silent Scream," which depicted the abortion of a twelve-week-old fetus. J. C. Willke, head of the NRLC, and Barbara Willke, his wife, continued to revise and update *Abortion: Questions and Answers* (1985), which compared *Roe* to *Dred Scott*. The NRLC protested when CBS planned to broadcast an episode of "Cagney and Lacey" thought to be overtly pro-choice. All in all, as shown in table 6-7, pro-life forces compiled quite a list of readings and arguments. Although some were blatant propaganda—emotional and strident in tone, aimed at the masses and politicians—many represented new and pragmatic approaches that could easily be worked into legal briefs.

Roe supporters did not allow these new efforts to go unchecked. In March

TABLE 6-7. The "New" Pro-Life Attack on *Roe*

WORKS AIMED AT THE PUBLIC

Work	Summary
Abortion: Questions and Answers (Willke and Willke 1985)	Comparison of *Roe* and *Dred Scott*; vivid pictures; attempt to show bias in public opinion polls.
Judgment without Justice (Foreword by Jerry Falwell; 1982)	Comparison of *Roe* and *Dred Scott*.
A Passion for Justice (National Right to Life Committee 1988)	Attempt to demonstrate that "almost all signs now point toward" the overruling of *Roe*.
Write-in Campaign to CBS (National Right to Life Committee)	Effort to obtain publicity for cause, while asking CBS not to broadcast an episode of "Cagney and Lacey."
The Silent Scream (Nathanson 1984)	A movie supposedly showing a 12-week-old fetus being aborted.

ARGUMENTS AIMED AT THE COURTS

Argument	Made/Compiled By
Roe is based on a faulty interpretation of history: 1. importance of the Hippocratic oath, 2. historical gap from oath to common law, 3. interpretation of common law, 4. interpretation of American laws in the 1800s.	This argument was made, in varying ways, by many during the 1970s (see Destro 1975; Dellapenna 1979). It was renewed in the 1980s (see Arbagi 1987). And Horan and Balch (1987) compiled virtually all such claims.
Roe's interpretation of the word "person" within the Constitution is inaccurate.	This argument was made, in varying ways, by many in the 1970s (see Destro 1975; Ely 1973; Byrn 1973). In 1987, Horan and Balch compiled these and similar arguments.
Statistical evidence introduced in *Roe* was incorrect.	Abortion is not safer than childbirth during the first trimester (Hilgers and O'Hare 1981).
Roe is not grounded in the intent of the framers of the Fourteenth Amendment.	Meese 1985.

1985, NARAL launched its own campaign—"Silent No More"—in which they asked women "to write letters about their abortion experiences [to] be read [in May] at demonstrations around the country." It did so out of a concern that the "current abortion debate ignores women, and misrepresents the reality of women's lives and family life in our society" (*New York Times* 1985a). Other abortion-rights advocates took to the pages of law journals and books to support their positions. Some refuted, point by point, new pro-life claims (see, for example, Law 1984), while others continued to counter older arguments. As Benshoof (1984, 36) wrote, "[A]ntiabortion activists try to portray the Supreme Court decision as an aberration in constitutional law rather than a logical and inevitable corollary of other Court decisions on privacy." Still other legal analysts took on those who critiqued *Roe* as a noninterpretivist departure from the intent of the framers.[69]

Finally, some pro-choice advocates recycled a purportedly "new" approach to abortion rights, arguing that restrictive laws constituted a type of gender-based discrimination.[70] Though this view has been put forth in a variety of forms (Ginsburg 1985; Law 1984; MacKinnon 1984; Rhode 1989; Tribe 1988), generally its adherents suggest the following:

• Abortion rights are "somehow grounded in relational concerns."
• Those relational concerns are not those between doctors and patients but rather "between pregnant women and the fetuses they carry."
• Hence, privacy rights are less relevant than are those of equality because "when the state denies women access to abortion, both nature and the state impose upon women burdens of unwanted pregnancy that men do not bear."[71]

Why did the equal protection argument reemerge after *Harris v. McRae* in 1980 and garner increasing support subsequent to *Akron* in 1983? For some, it was a by-product of the feminist legal studies movement: abortion was not about privacy for women or doctors but about equality and choice. In Law's (1984, 1028) words, "[C]ontrol of reproduction is the *sine qua non* of women's capacity to live as equal people." For others, more pragmatic forces were at work. Former head of the ACLU Women's Rights Project and now a U.S. Court of Appeals judge, Ruth Bader Ginsburg (1985) sought to demonstrate the following:

• "Gender-based Classification" and "Reproductive Autonomy" had "evolved in discrete compartments."
• Equality for women has not generated nearly as much controversy as abortion.
• If abortion rights were framed in equality terms, they would be less controversial.

Moreover, she and many others asserted (MacKinnon 1984; Law 1984; Tribe 1988) that if *Roe* had been framed in equal protection terms, the pro-choice movement might have won the funding cases: "If the Court had acknowledged a woman's equality aspect [and] not simply a patient-physician autonomy constitutional dimension to the abortion issue, a majority perhaps might have seen the public assistance cases as instances in which . . . the sovereign had violated its duty to govern impartially" (Ginsburg 1985, 382). Another, equally pragmatic, factor could also support the new emphasis on this kind of argument: Justice O'Connor. Although no great fan of *Roe*, she was quite supportive of gender-based claims of discrimination (O'Connor and Epstein 1983). Framing abortion in equal protection terms might bring her into the fold.

There was some irony in this renewed emphasis on gender discrimination. In *Roe* Weddington had avoided gender-based claims in her briefs but centered on them in orals, thus reflecting divisions among pro-choice advocates. Also the ACLU had created the separate Reproductive Freedom Project in part out of fear that abortion would contaminate its Women's Rights Project. As a result, the RFP had "long pursued a policy of discouraging sex discrimination claims in abortion cases" (Tribe 1988, 1353).

ESCALATING POLITICAL AND LEGAL BATTLES: THE EMERGENCE OF THE MEESE JUSTICE DEPARTMENT

As the war of words escalated, so did battles in legal and political arenas. At first blush, they bore a striking resemblance to those of the past: states continued to pass restrictive legislation and pro-choice advocates continued to challenge it. The volume of litigation remained high: after *Akron*—despite the Court's staunch affirmation of *Roe*—the RFP's docket contained almost 170 pending cases (Walker 1990, 348).

The cycle, however, had altered. Lower courts were "becoming increasingly hostile to abortion rights" (Walker 1990, 348). In part this occurred because pro-life groups were becoming far more aggressive and adept at trial court litigation. In the past, they generally watched as state attorneys argued their cause, occasionally filing amicus curiae briefs. Now they sought to play a greater role in all facets of legal activity from the drafting of "precise" legislation to countering the arguments of pro-choice attorneys (Myers 1987).[72] This was viewed as crucial in a number of pro-life quarters. Some believed that to get off the legal-political treadmill they had ridden for the past decade, they needed to meet their opponents head on in court. With chances for a pro-life amendment virtually nil and odds for changing public opinion about the same,[73] their best hope still lay in state legislatures and city councils. However, if pro-choice forces gutted these legislative victories in federal courts, they were for naught. Hence, for the first time since 1973, pro-life advocates, particularly the AUL LDF, began to concern themselves seriously with exerting greater control—by assisting, advising, or handling the litigation for state attorneys—over litigation.

This new push alone, though, does not explain the greater receptivity anti-*Roe* claims were enjoying in federal courts. After all, this may have been a genuinely concerted effort, but it was not the first.[74] More significant was that this new mobilization occurred in an altered context: lower federal court judges were more sensitive to the pro-life posture. After his landslide reelection in 1984, Reagan was positioned—though still lacking specific public support[75]—to press more fully a plank of his party's platform: to appoint pro-life judges to the federal bench. The use of a so-called "litmus test" for appointments went beyond the issue of abortion to many others on the New Right's agenda and was aimed at a "transformation of American life" (H. Schwartz 1988, 10). Naturally, though, this "insistence on ideological purity" spilled over into abortion. A study by Alumbaugh and Rowland (1990) demonstrates that Reagan appointees supported the pro-life side in 77 percent of their decisions, whereas Carter appointees voted pro-life in around 13 percent.

THE SUPREME COURT

With no vacancies arising since 1981, the Supreme Court remained as yet unscathed from Reagan's court packing. This did not, however, mean that Meese's Justice Department refrained from efforts to influence the justices. To the contrary, it took its first opportunity—*Thornburgh v. American College of Obstetricians and Gynecologists* (1986)—to ask the Court to overrule *Roe*.

Thornburgh seemed important only in that it was the Court's first major case since *Akron* and it presented another test for pro-life organizations, in particular for the AUL LDF, which helped draft the Pennsylvania law at issue (Nolan 1983, 382). The legislation contained several provisions regulating the way in which physicians performed abortions:

- Informed Consent: Women must give their "voluntary and informed" consent for abortions.
- Printed Information: A woman's physician must present her with seven kinds of "explicit" information twenty-four hours prior to an abortion: the name of the doctor performing the abortion, the "fact" that "there may be" psychological and physical damage, the medical risks associated with abortion, the gestational age, the medical risks associated with carrying a child to term, availability of prenatal and postnatal care, and "the fact that the father is liable" to help support the child.

• Determination of Viability: This requires doctors "to report the basis for [their] determination 'that a child is not viable.'"

• Report: Requires a particular type of report for a finding of nonviability.

• Degree of Care for Postviability Abortions: Mandates that doctors seek to preserve "the life and health of any unborn child."

• Second Physician Requirement: Requires that a "second physician be present during an abortion performed when viability is possible."

The only real difference between this law and the one struck in *Akron*, then, was that Pennsylvania sought to regulate postviability abortions; the informed consent provisions were virtually indistinguishable. Not surprisingly, various pro-choice groups joined forces on behalf of the American College of Obstetricians and Gynecologists to challenge the act.[76]

After the Court of Appeals for the Third Circuit enjoined enforcement of the act and later, in light of *Akron*, held various sections of it unconstitutional,[77] the state appealed to the Supreme Court. In so doing, Pennsylvania asserted that the law was fully consistent with *Roe* and its progeny. Appellees argued that the lower court's response was appropriate and the Supreme Court should either deny review or merely affirm its ruling. In spite of this plea, in April 1985 the Court agreed to hear the case and set oral arguments for the following November.

Because of the similarity between *Thornburgh* and *Akron*, this was "surprising" news to Court observers (Greenhouse 1985a). Nonetheless, this was just the sort of case for which the Justice Department was waiting, and it quickly swung into action. Despite the fact that Pennsylvania was not asking the justices to reconsider *Roe*, it was clear that the attorney general wanted Solicitor General Lee to take explicitly the position he only implied in *Akron*: that *Roe* must go.[78] Moreover, Meese apparently wanted Lee to base his argument on the so-called "Jurisprudence of Original Intent." Whether Lee merely refused to comply and was fired or whether he had financial problems and quit is open to speculation.[79] Regardless, a month or so after the Court agreed to hear *Thornburgh*, Lee left his post. The administration quickly brought in Charles Fried as acting solicitor general.

Several aspects of this "appointment" puzzled observers, none more so than why the administration gave Fried the title of acting solicitor general but did not nominate him for the position.[80] This was the subject of some speculation, much of which agreed with Wermeil's (1985) assessment: Meese would not nominate Fried until he filed the *Thornburgh* brief. He was using the case as a sort of loyalty test for the acting solicitor general: if he asked the justices to overrule *Roe*, he would pass the test; if not, he would be out.[81] If this was true, Fried came through with flying colors.[82] On 15 July 1985, he filed an amicus curiae brief presenting a tour de force for the pro-life position: he departed from the unduly burdensome position advocated by his predecessor[83] and called for the Court to "reconsider [*Roe*] and on reconsideration abandon it."

In general, Fried mounted a two-prong assault: *Roe* was a source of "instability" in law, and, in the measure of "history," it belied the framers' intent. After attacking Powell's *Akron* opinion as a significant departure from *Roe*, he suggested that it "is a symptom, not the source, of the problem." That distinction belonged to *Roe*, which mandated "an inquiry not easy for courts to follow in a principled fashion. The key factors in the equation—viability, trimesters . . .— are inherently unworkable." Using O'Connor's dissent in *Akron* and other legalistic arguments (but no medical data), Fried sought to demonstrate that the trimester scheme and viability represented arbitrary schema that change with medical advances. As such, *Roe* always would lead courts to differing conclusions over the constitutionality of specific state regulations. The brief then launched into the "Meese" offensive: "Constitutional interpretation retains the fullest measure of legitimacy when it is disciplined by fidelity to the framers' intent as revealed by history." On that score, in the acting solicitor general's view, *Roe* could not be justified (*Thornburgh*, Brief for the United States, no. 84-495).[84]

Organized interests reacted predictably to Fried's submission. While the executive director of the AUL LDF noted that he was "extremely pleased to have the government's help," the RFP's Benshoof accused the "administration of 'using brief-writing instead of press releases to push an ideological platform' [and said it] marked the first time in the history of this country that the government has ever called for taking away a constitutional right" (*New York Times* 1985b). More intriguingly, the government's brief was the object of condemnation from more "neutral" sources. Former solicitor generals (including Archibald Cox, John Davis, Erwin Griswold, and Wade McCree) thought the brief "more strident than any other submitted by a Solicitor General."[85] Rex E. Lee agreed. In a July 1985 speech, he took issue with Fried's position, asserting, "I don't think the Solicitor General can or should take it upon himself to tell the Supreme Court what he may well believe are its errors of constitutional doctrine."[86]

The Justice Department and the White House felt compelled to respond to this criticism. A spokesperson for Reagan assured Americans that the president "had personally approved" of the solicitor general's filing. Even Fried spoke out: "The principle responsibility of the Solicitor General is to win cases in the Supreme Court and to maintain the stature of the office. Where that can be done consistent with the broader principles the incumbent president may hold, that's fine. But my audience in the final analysis is not millions, not thousands or even hundreds, but nine" (Greenhouse 1985b).

AKRON REDUX?: *THORNBURGH*

Criticisms of the Fried brief heartened pro-choice advocates as did several other events surrounding *Thornburgh*. One was that after Pennsylvania refused to share the time they were allotted for oral arguments with Fried, the justices denied his "unusual" request to participate orally. Another was the reaction of *Roe*'s author, Blackmun, who publicly called Fried's effort "very amazing" (Kamen 1985). Finally, the Senate expressed its anger at the Meese Justice Department, confirming Fried in October but rejecting Meese's effort to appoint William Bradford Reynolds as associate attorney general.[87] Still, pro-choice advocates were concerned. If the Pennsylvania law was so blatantly unconstitutional, and if the *Akron* majority remained intact, why did the justices decide to review the court of appeal's decision? Blackmun's remarks in September 1985 further suggested that *Roe* was in trouble: "There are always four votes [to hear abortion cases]. . . . And the other five of us heave a deep sigh and wish we didn't have to go through this traumatic experience again." Given all of this, the question arose among pro-choice forces: Did the solicitor general know something they did not (Rubin 1987, 145–46)?

In the face of this odd context, pro-choice forces turned out en masse. As shown in table 6-8, they filed fourteen briefs, representing over seventy organizations. In general, most amici reiterated and reinforced the arguments of the appellees. For example, in its lead brief (*Thornburgh*, Brief for Appellees, no. 84-495, 25), ACOG attorneys provided statistical data indicating that "postviability abortions are performed for grave and substantial medical reasons"; as an amicus, the ACLU (Brief for ACLU, no. 84-495, i) argued that "post-viability abortions occur in highly individualized situations involving serious health problems." Others added some new twists. With the goal of placing "the realities of abortion in women's lives before [the] Court," NARAL's brief contained excerpts from letters it received during its "Silent No More" campaign. While Fried's argument was cold and legalistic, NARAL sought to explicate the harm the Pennsylvania law would bring to women's lives if adopted.[88]

Table 6-8 also depicts amici in support of the Pennsylvania law. That side filed only four briefs, representing a total of two organizations and two governmental interests.[89] In general, these submissions exemplified the schizophrenic nature of pro-life arguments. In a brief written by Robert Destro, a longtime right-to-life advocate and a professor at Catholic University's law school, eighty-two members of Congress followed the solicitor general's lead and asked the Court to reconsider *Roe* because it was "in opposition to the historical treatment of abortion at common law" and because "the framers of the Constitution and of the Fourteenth Amendment did not intend to create a right to abortion." In

TABLE 6-8. Amici Curiae in *Thornburgh*

Pro-Choice	Pro-Life

GOVERNMENTAL

1. 81 Members of Congress:[*] Importance of stare decisis.	1. 82 Members of Congress:[**] Intent of framers, role of Court.
2. New York State:[*] If *Roe* is overruled, New York and other states that would retain legalized abortion would be overburdened.	2. United States:[**] *Roe* is the source of instability in law; it is textually, doctrinally, and historically flawed.

ABORTION/REPRODUCTION/FAMILY PLANNING

1. Planned Parenthood et al.:[a] State lacks a compelling interest; public disclosure can lead to harassment and hostility.	1. NRLC: State's compelling interest in a viable fetus outweighs woman's right, in accord with *Roe*.
2. National Family Planning and Reproductive Health Association: State's law favors childbirth over abortion decision.	
3. National Abortion Federation: Law constitutes harassment of abortion decision.	
4. NARAL et al.:[*b] *Roe* has dramatically improved the life and health of American women.	

RELIGIOUS

1. Unitarian Universalist Association et al.:[*c] Adherence to *Roe* is necessary to preserve First Amendment principles of freedom of conscience.	1. Catholic League for Religious Liberties: State's compelling interest in a viable fetus outweighs woman's right, in accord with *Roe*.

MEDICAL/HEALTH

1. American Psychological Association: State's law unduly interferes/burdens women's right to an abortion.	
2. American Medical Association et al.:[d] Law fails a compelling state interest standard.	

TABLE 6-8 *(continued)*

Pro-Choice	Pro-Life
WOMEN'S RIGHTS	
1. NOW et al.:*[e] Law interferes with the fundamental rights of women.	
2. Women Lawyers' Association of Los Angeles et al.:*[f] Specific response to the solicitor general; stresses stare decisis.	
LEGAL/CIVIL LIBERTIES	
1. Ad Hoc Group of Law Professors: The controversy is moot.	
2. Center for Constitutional Rights et al.:[g] State elevates rights of fetuses above those of women.	
3. ACLU et al.:*[h] Law jeopardizes the life and health of women who need postviability abortions; hampers medical practice.	

*Specifically addressed the solicitor general's arguments and/or discussed why *Roe* should not be overruled.

**Asked the Court to overrule or reconsider *Roe*.

[a]Cosigned by Center for Population Options, American Jewish Committee, National Association of Nurse Practitioners in Family Planning, National Board of the Young Women's Christian Association of the U.S.A., American Jewish Congress, Association of Planned Parenthood Professionals, Physicians for Choice, American Public Health Association, and Individual Professors, Physicians, and Medical School Deans.

[b]Cosigned by American Association of University Women, Americans for Democratic Action, Coalition of Labor Union Women, Committee to Defend Reproductive Rights, Disability Rights Education and Defense Fund, National Black Women's Health Project, National Campaign to Restore Abortion Funding, National Federation of Business and Professional Women's Clubs, National Women's Conference Committee, National Women's Health Network, National Women's Political Caucus, U.S. Student Association, Voters for Choice, Women's Equity Action League, Women U.S.A., and Young Women's Christian Association of the United States of America National Board.

[c]This brief was written by a New York Civil Liberties Union attorney. It was cosigned by American Ethical Union, Americans for Religious Liberty, American Humanist Association, Board for Homeland Ministry—United Church of Christ, B'nai B'rith Women, Catholic Women for Reproductive Rights, Catholics for a Free Choice, Coordinating Center for Women, United Church of Christ, Episcopal Women's Caucus, National Board—Young Women's Christian Association of the U.S.A., National Coalition of American Nuns, National Council of Jewish Women, National Federation of Temple Sisterhoods, National Service Conference—American

TABLE 6-8 *(continued)*

Ethical Union, Office for Church in Society—United Church of Christ, Pioneer Women/ NA'AMAT, Presbyterian Church (U.S.A.), Union of American Hebrew Congregations, Unitarian Universalist Association, Unitarian Universalist Women's Federation, United Church of Christ, United Synagogues of America, and National Women's League for Conservative Judaism.
dCosigned by American Academy of Family Physicians, American Academy of Pediatrics, American Psychiatric Association, Association of American Medical Colleges, and American Academy of Obstetricians and Gynecologists.
eCosigned by Human Rights for Women, Equal Rights Advocates, League of Women Voters, Northwest Women's Law Center, NOW Legal Defense and Education Fund, and Women's Legal Defense Fund.
fCosigned by California Women Lawyers, Women's Bar Association of Illinois, Florida Association of Women Lawyers, Florida Association of Women Lawyers—Dade County, and California Lawyers for Individual Freedom.
gCosigned by Committee for Abortion Rights and against Sterilization, National Emergency Civil Liberties Committee, National Lawyers Guild, and National Tay-Sachs and Allied Diseases Association.
hCosigned by the Pennsylvania Civil Liberties Union and Anti-Defamation League.

contrast, NRLC attorneys took Pennsylvania's approach, largely arguing that existing precedent could support the state law.[90]

Despite the tenor of the debate surrounding *Thornburgh*, oral arguments "were marked more by legal fine points than ideological or political fervor." Pennsylvania's deputy attorney general defended the law as constitutional within the *Roe* framework, while the ACOG argued precisely the opposite. The justices focused on whether the Pennsylvania law represented valid state regulation under *Roe*. Some even indicated that the Court may not need to rule on the law's constitutionality because of procedural deficiencies in judicial treatment of the case.[91] No one pointedly raised the issue of overruling *Roe*.

Sometimes oral arguments are not particularly valid portents of what the Court will actually do. Those in *Thornburgh* were indicative of the outcome to the extent that, in the end, *Roe* would stand, but they gave little indication that the justices would use the case to issue their most strongly worded defense of the abortion right since 1973. Justice Blackmun's majority opinion blasted legislation designed to undermine *Roe* ("The States are not free, under the guise of protecting maternal health or potential life, to intimidate women into continuing pregnancies"); chastised Pennsylvania for its repeated efforts to circumvent *Roe* (this "was not the Commonwealth's first attempt . . . after . . . *Roe* . . . to impose abortion restraints"); and implicitly refuted the solicitor general's position ("Again today, we reaffirm the general principles laid down in *Roe*. . . . As judges . . . we are sworn to uphold the law even when its content gives rise to bitter dispute") (*Thornburgh* 1986, 751, 759, 771). Pro-choice advocates could not have hoped for a more comprehensive rejection of their opponent's position. But four justices, in three different opinions, tempered their jubilation.

White's dissent, joined by Rehnquist, was a pro-life counterpoise to Blackmun's opinion. He lambasted the Court's "venture" into abortion as "fundamentally misguided since its conception." Although he rejected a jurisprudence of original intent,[92] he agreed with the solicitor general's "bottom line" on *Roe* (*Thornburgh* 1986, 787). In concluding, he wrote: "The decision today appears symptomatic of the Court's own insecurity over its handiwork in *Roe v. Wade*. . . . Aware that in *Roe* it essentially created something out of nothing and that there are many in this country who hold that decision to be basically illegitimate, the Court responds defensively" (*Thornburgh* 1986, 813–14).[93]

O'Connor's dissent, also signed by Rehnquist, refrained from arguing that the Court should overrule *Roe v. Wade*. She continued to press her *Akron* position— the one proffered by Solicitor General Lee in that case—that the justices should move to an "unduly burdensome" standard. Yet she toughened her rhetoric, claiming that "[t]his Court's abortion decisions have already worked a major distortion in the Court's constitutional jurisprudence"; the justices were not dealing with abortion "evenhandedly" (*Thornburgh* 1986, 814).

Pro-choice advocates expected these dissenting votes, but the position of another justice took them by surprise. After thirteen years of fence-sitting, Chief Justice Burger joined *Roe*'s opponents. His *Thornburgh* dissent sought to square his position in *Roe* and *Doe* with his new stance against it. In doing so, he retreated to his 1973 concurrence, in which he wrote (*Doe* 1973, 208) that the "Court today rejects any claim that the Constitution requires abortion on demand." That may have been Burger's understanding, but few interpreted *Roe* that way—at least for the first two trimesters. Regardless, Burger used his misreading of *Roe* to justify his turnabout in *Thornburgh*: "The Court's opinion undermines [the] important principle [that abortions should not be available on demand] and I regretfully conclude that some of the concerns of the dissenting justices in *Roe*, as well as the concerns I expressed in my separate opinion, have now been realized" (*Thornburgh* 1986, 782–83). He was now a fourth vote to "reexamine *Roe*." The pro-choice majority dwindled to five.

Burger's switch was noticed by the litigating groups and the press. Pro-life advocates lauded it. As a director of the NRLC said, "The thing that jumps out at you is that it's a 5-to-4 decision. . . . That's very significant. We're very encouraged by that. We're just one vote away from a Court which may be prepared to abandon *Roe v. Wade*" (Stevens 1986). Despite their growing concern, pro-choicers publicly played up their victory. As RFP attorney Lynn Paltron said, "*Roe v. Wade* is not hanging by a slender thread. It was reaffirmed in very strong terms—and the states should be warned that they cannot interfere with a woman's freedom of choice under the guise of neutral and beneficial laws" (Hager 1986).

This "spin" on *Thornburgh*, coupled with the Court's rejection of Fried's brief, worked to the extent that the media began to focus on the Meese Justice Department. Public television broadcast an hour-long show, "Justice for All," which had a clear message: the Justice Department had become so overly politicized that it was to "the detriment of evenhanded enforcement of the law" (King and Molotsky 1986a). Such criticisms put officials on the defensive. After *Thornburgh*, in what was the "first major press conference ever given by a solicitor general," Fried called the ruling "a defeat," and further noted that he "would not make a 'pest' of himself by pressing the issue again" (Caplan 1987, 249).

AFTER *THORNBURGH*: JUSTICE SCALIA AND THE 1986 ELECTIONS

As Fried was apologizing for *Thornburgh*, other public officials were counting votes. Pro-life advocate Senator Gordon Humphrey (R-N.H.) said after the decision that it "demonstrates once again how much is riding on the next appointment to the Supreme Court" (Stevens 1986). He might have been correct if one of *Roe*'s supporters departed but, unfortunately for pro-life advocates, Chief Justice Burger announced his resignation five days after *Thornburgh* came down. Pro-choice proponents were not saddened that the *Roe* defector retired, but their joy was limited. They recognized that Reagan's "litmus test" for lower court nominees would be applied to the Supreme Court; Burger's replacement would not improve their standing with the Court.

Initially such forebodings appeared to be correct. When Burger announced his resignation, Reagan proposed the elevation of William Rehnquist to replace him and the appointment of court of appeals Judge Antonin Scalia to replace Rehnquist. This rearrangement did not please pro-choice advocates. The new chief justice was a known opponent, as Scalia was likely to be.[94] Surprisingly, though, pro-choice forces did not mount significant opposition to Scalia.[95] NOW and several other "rights" groups lobbied against him—largely because he opposed affirmative action—but they remained generally outside the fray. Perhaps they recognized that they would be unable to stem the favorable tide. Or perhaps they viewed Scalia as insignificant: even if he aligned with Rehnquist and company, the *Thornburgh* majority was intact. In any event, Scalia was expeditiously and unanimously confirmed.

The effect of this appointment would not be immediately known, as the Court did not have an abortion case on its 1986 term docket. Hence, for the moment, both sides turned their attention to the results of the midterm elections. After six years of Republican control, the Senate returned to a Democratic majority;[96] in the House, voters defeated six incumbents, four of whom had pro-life voting records; and several states rejected pro-life ballot initiatives.[97] Journalists declared the elections a "turning point" for abortion, and pro-choice advocates were quick to agree. As NARAL's executive director noted, "We can work with the Senate now. We lost a lot in the past, but now the momentum is shifting our way and we're planning to go forward and take the offensive" (Greenhouse 1986).

Were pro-choice forces right to be hopeful? Or were they—like their opponents in 1980—misreading the election results? Pro-life advocates thought not, and they blamed the Reagan administration for the loss. As they saw it, the election should have gone their way; in fact, months before, the NRLC was bragging about the close ties it had "forged" with the Republican party. Its president went so far as to say: "The abortion issue is clearly moving our way. Time and momentum are on our side and being identified with a major political party certainly helps our cause" (Gailey 1986). After the election, though, they were lambasting the White House: abortion "got a lot of Republicans and conservative Democrats elected in the first place. But for some reason the Administration and the candidates wanted to shy from abortion this year" (Greenhouse 1986).

A SHOWDOWN IN THE SENATE:
BORK, KENNEDY, AND A NEW COURT

How the election results would affect the abortion debate was unknown in 1986. What mattered at this point to both sides was that the Supreme Court had announced its intention to hear an important abortion case the next term: *Hartigan v. Zbaraz*, which involved an Illinois parental notification statute. In June 1987, as both sides began to map their legal strategies for what many thought would be a definitive ruling on parental consent, Lewis Powell resigned. This was alarming from the vantage point of pro-choice forces: he was a pro-*Roe* vote on a closely divided Court. Adding insult to injury, Reagan nominated Robert H. Bork to fill the vacancy.

Much ink has been spilt on Bork's nomination and his rejection by the Senate. Indeed, the controversy spurred something of a cottage industry, with no aspect of Bork's life, writings, philosophy, and experience immune from intense investigation.[98] A review of this battle would go well beyond the scope of this book. However, some questions emerging from the Bork nomination are relevant to the abortion debate: why did it spark so much public interest, what role did abortion play in the confirmation proceedings and the subsequent defeat, and what did pro-choicers and pro-lifers gain or lose from his rejection?

Answering the first question is probably impossible, in large measure because many explanations exist. One contributing factor may have been the nature of the vacancy itself. When Burger resigned, it was no surprise that Reagan replaced a conservative with a conservative. Powell was a wholly different story. This was no ordinary vacancy; it had significant implications for the ideological balance of the Court. Americans who paid any attention to press accounts of the day certainly were aware of the significance of the appointment (see Greenhouse 1987; Taylor 1987b; Gest 1987). A second factor, of course, was Bork himself. He was a well-known quantity in legal and scholarly communities, having generated voluminous writings, speeches, testimony, briefs, and interviews. Moreover, these were not "neutral" writings: the nominee had strong views on role of the judiciary, appropriate jurisprudence, and key issues of the day. Bork's advocacy of a jurisprudence of original intent, for example, led him to express— at least prior to his nomination—these positions:

- Women lack Fourteenth Amendment protection from governmental discrimination.
- *Roe v. Wade* "is itself an unconstitutional decision."
- The Constitution protects only "political speech."
- Homosexual conduct is not constitutionally protected.

Such stances galvanized the opposition of virtually every left-of-center organization; even the ACLU, which had a policy against commenting on a judicial nominee, opposed him.[99] These reactions, coupled with an unusual ABA report[100] and the immediate opposition of several members of the Senate Judiciary Committee, brought the media into full force. Bork became the focus of nationwide attention, as did the institution he hoped to enter.

What was the role of abortion in this drama? Again, this is difficult to assess because many different theories exist to explain the nominee's demise. Clearly, at the time of Reagan's announcement, abortion had a central place in media coverage. Journalists knew that the Court had docketed *Hartigan* for arguments in what presumably would be Bork's first term on the Court. Hence, in covering Reagan's announcement, the *New York Times* reported, "If confirmed by the Senate, Judge Bork would replace Associate Justice Lewis F. Powell Jr., who announced his retirement last Friday, prompting wide speculation that Mr. Reagan would use the opportunity to nominate an ideological conservative who could tilt the Court on such highly charged issues as abortion, affirmative action, and church-state separation" (Boyd 1987). Abortion remained a spotlight issue during Bork's ordeal. Planned Parenthood and NARAL took out full-page advertisements in the *Times* opposing him, and *Time* magazine (21 September 1987) ran a ten-page cover story in which it highlighted one issue—"Would *Roe* Go?"

Interestingly, though, both camps sought to play down the issue, substituting different approaches to reach their ends. To be sure, the administration agreed with Bork's views but recognized that his specific stances on social issues could prove a political liability. Some thought they made him look too much like "Meese's boy" and less like Reagan's candidate; others believed that Bork's "vision" of the Court's role would alienate the public. They were especially concerned about how it translated into delicate areas like civil rights, which, in turn, might alienate key southern Democratic senators (Bronner 1989a, 191–92). Hence, in speeches subsequent to the nomination, Reagan stressed Bork's qualifications and credentials—including his confirmation to the U.S. Court of Appeals for the District of Columbia—rather than his conservatism.

Anti-Bork factions also de-emphasized abortion. Reportedly, Judiciary Committee chair—and early Bork opponent—Joseph Biden received word from a polling company to downplay abortion. Instead, it told Biden to emphasize how Judge Bork's judicial philosophy would lead him to rule on broader topics such as privacy and civil rights (Bronner 1989a, 158–59). This was sage advice. Although Americans disagreed over specific topics, such as abortion, they were in agreement on privacy rights. Thus, many were alienated when they learned of Bork's stances. In July 1987, 49 percent of Americans had claimed "that a nominee to the Supreme Court should be confirmed by the Senate even though some senators disagree with his ideology" (*New York Times* 1987). But by late September 1987, Louis Harris reported that 57 percent of Americans opposed Bork's confirmation, whereas only 29 percent supported it. According to Harris (1987), "[M]ost damaging to Bork is his statement early on that when a state passes a law prohibiting a married couple from using birth control devices, there is nothing in the Constitution that says the Supreme Court should protect such married people's right to privacy."

Bork and his administration backers were aware of this shift in public opinion and the pressure key civil rights and liberties groups were putting on southern Democrats (Bork 1990). Hence, something of a "confirmation conversion" occurred, as the nominee tried to modulate his pre-1987 views, particularly on privacy and civil rights (Taylor 1987c; Adler 1987).[101] Few, however, believed in the "new" Bork. In fact, the apparent "confirmation conversion" actually alienated some potential supporters. At one point, Arlen Specter, a key committee vote, said: "The concern I have is: where's the predictability in Judge Bork? What are the assurances this committee and the Senate have?"

Thus, a host of factors led to Bork's defeat. To point to any one issue as determinative would be misguided. What is clear, however, is that the proceedings served to highlight abortion and privacy issues in ways that partisans on either side could not. Before Bork, privacy and abortion often were issues public officials sought to avoid. The proceedings demonstrated that the public was concerned about them, and although somewhat ambivalent on *Roe*, it favored the "privacy" foundation on which the decision rested. NARAL put it this way: the nomination "shifted the debate back to the centrality of a woman's right to an abortion—the landscape has changed." Evidence of this abounds. Democrats who generally had opposed severe restrictions on abortion were now calling for an end to public financing bans, and many officials started to "invoke the *Roe v. Wade* decision to justify their support for abortion even though they declared themselves 'personally opposed' to the practice" (Dionne 1987). Participants in the abortion debate also reacted strongly to the Senate's rejection. Despite Bork's "confirmation conversion," pro-choice forces viewed him as actively hostile to their interests[102] and, thus, were delighted by his defeat. In its review of the 1987 year, the NRLC emphasized "the temporary pro-abortion victory, the defeat of Robert Bork." It too viewed the rejection as a major feather in the cap of their opponents, arguing that "it played to their strength." As such, it made capturing the presidency the "highest priority" for the coming year so as to insure the continued nomination of pro-life candidates (Andrusko 1988, 23).

On the heels of the Bork debacle, Reagan nominated Douglas Ginsburg, who quickly withdrew amid allegations of unethical and unconventional behavior. The president then turned to Court of Appeals Judge Anthony Kennedy. Even before he was formally nominated, the word on Kennedy was that he was "a judicial conservative, but one whose style more closely resembles that of Justice Lewis F. Powell, a pragmatic centrist . . . , than that of Judge Robert H. Bork" (Taylor 1987c). Because Kennedy had not engaged in extensive outside writings, this evaluation was based largely on some five hundred opinions he wrote as a federal court judge. Still, several of his decisions troubled women's and gay rights groups, so much so that some opposed the nomination.[103] Conservatives were also less than delighted, in large measure because he would not put forth his views on abortion and because he agreed that a "marital right to privacy is protected by the Constitution."[104] Otherwise, initial political responses were cautious, with both liberal and conservative senators "withholding" judgment until they could conduct their own investigations. Even most of the organizations that had opposed Bork remained silent. Not surprisingly, in early February 1988 the Senate unanimously confirmed him.

Almost immediately thereafter, the pundits began to speculate on how Kennedy would vote in abortion cases. The focus on reproductive freedom was not coincidental. While his nomination was pending, the Court split 4–4 on the

Hartigan case, making it clear that "Kennedy is an edge breaker on the issue" (Thornton 1987). Interestingly, though, scholars and journalists were relatively united in their response to which side Kennedy would take. As a professor at Stanford Law School put it, the new justice "would start with the fact that [*Roe*] had been decided. I strongly suspect he never would have voted for it in the first place, but part of judicial restraint is the question of whether a person is going to reverse a Supreme Court decision that is now part of the fabric of society" (Church 1987). Journalists concurred; in a discussion on abortion in *U.S. News and World Report* (28 December 1987), writers claimed, "The bottom line: Kennedy is not inclined to overrule previous Supreme Court opinions." In sum, there were a few who suggested that Kennedy might want to modify *Roe*, but no one thought he would vote to overrule it. His presumed restraintism would militate against it.

THE COURT TAKES UP THE DEBATE:
WEBSTER V. REPRODUCTIVE HEALTH SERVICES

With the Court's division over *Hartigan*, and with no abortion cases docketed through the 1987 term, those involved in the abortion debate turned their attention to the states and to the lower courts, where important battles were brewing. Despite Blackmun's strongly worded opinion in *Thornburgh*, some states continued to enact restrictive laws. Many placed limits on the ability of minors to attain abortion services without parental consent. These were understandable: considering the Court's division over *Hartigan*, legislators were left unsure of the Court's current thinking on the subject.

Less clear was why some states continued to enact pro-life "model legislation" when *Thornburgh* squarely rejected it. Indeed, two weeks after the Court announced *Thornburgh*, Missouri made a direct attempt to circumvent *Roe*. Its statute began with a preamble that pro-choicers alleged ran directly counter to the Court's 1973 decisions; the preamble stated, "The life of each human being begins at conception," and "unborn children have protectable interests in life, health, and well-being." It also required that "all Missouri laws be interpreted to provide unborn children with the same rights enjoyed by other persons." The law then specified the following:

• "Before a physician performs an abortion on a woman he has reason to believe is carrying an unborn child of twenty or more weeks gestational age, the physician shall first determine if the unborn child is viable by using and exercising that degree of care, skill, and proficiency commonly exercised by the ordinary skillful, careful, and prudent physician engaged in similar practice under the same or similar conditions. In making this determination of viability, the physician shall perform or cause to be performed such medical examinations and tests as are necessary to make a finding of the gestational age, weight, and lung maturity of the unborn child and shall enter such findings and determination of viability in the medical record of the mother."

• No public funds can be used to encourage or counsel "a woman to have an abortion not necessary to save her life."

• No public employees "can perform or assist in abortion, not necessary to save the life of the mother." Nor can "any public facility . . . [be used] to perform an abortion not necessary to save the life of the mother," even if no public monies are expended.

• No public employees can engage in speech that encourages or counsels "a woman to have an abortion not necessary to save her life."[105]

• No speech in public facilities can encourage or counsel "a woman to have an abortion not necessary to save her life."[106]

Why did the state enact such legislation in the face of a resounding reaffirmation of *Roe*? Veteran pro-choice attorney Frank Susman provided one answer when he suggested that Missouri legislators did not regard the Constitution as a serious obstacle to the enactment of state laws.[107] Another hypothesis is that involvement in abortion litigation actually enhanced the political careers of officials who fought for Missouri restrictions. Former attorney general and named defendant in the 1976 case (*Planned Parenthood v. Danforth*), John Danforth was elected to the U.S. Senate; Governor John Ashcroft, who signed the 1986 bill into law, also had been a named party to a U.S. Supreme Court case. Further, it is possible that pro-life forces—at least those that drafted and lobbied for the law—wanted it to serve as a vehicle for a test case, figuring that with a potentially reconfigured Court, anything could happen.

If a test case was what they wanted, that was what they got. Frank Susman and B. J. Isaacson-Jones, the director of the Reproductive Health Services (RHS) in Missouri, "knew" they "would challenge the law as soon" as they heard about it.[108] According to Faux (1990, 31), they were not alone in wanting to challenge the act; both Planned Parenthood (of Kansas City) and the ACLU's Reproductive Freedom Project wanted to bring suits. After a brief "power struggle" between Planned Parenthood and the RFP, a compromise was struck. Susman would represent the Missouri chapter of the ACLU and Roger Evans of Planned Parenthood would act as co-counsel in what would be officially called *Webster v.*

Reproductive Health Services.[109] The RFP would serve as a "backup" but would have no formal role.

In July 1986, one month before the new law was to take effect, Susman and Evans filed the suit in Jefferson City, not St. Louis, where they thought they would be more likely to draw a "sympathetic judge" (Faux 1990, 32). While their "forum shopping" paid off—Judge Scott O. Wright, a Democrat appointed by President Carter, was assigned their case—this was not of paramount concern. Because the Missouri law directly contradicted *Roe* and its progeny, Susman and Evans had little fear that they would lose at trial. They were right. On 17 March 1987, Judge Wright held most of the act unconstitutional. The RHS also won on appeal, with the Eighth Circuit affirming Wright's ruling.

When the state appealed that decision, Evans and Susman began to plan their Supreme Court strategy, which they felt sure they would have to invoke. The signs were everywhere. Before the onset of the 1988 term, Justice Blackmun told the first-year law class at the University of Arkansas that while no abortion case had been docketed, the Court would soon confront the issue again. He also wondered aloud: "Will *Roe v. Wade* go down the drain?" His answer did little to reassure pro-choice advocates: "I think there's a very distinct possibility that it will, this term. You can count the votes" (*New York Times* 1988b; Safire 1988).[110] Another portent was that just two days after the 1988 elections, outgoing Solicitor General Fried filed an amicus curiae brief for the government urging the justices to hear the Missouri case.[111] In an obviously concerted effort—one designed to overcome the past "error" of *Thornburgh*, where the solicitor general, but not the state, asked for the overruling of *Roe*—both Missouri and the United States asked the Court to "reconsider" *Roe*.[112] Susman "did not think the state's request would carry much weight"; it had not asked the lower courts to reevaluate *Roe* and did so now only at the behest of a Justice Department official, William Bradford Reynolds. But Susman probably did anticipate something Caldeira and Wright (1988) have demonstrated empirically: that amicus curiae briefs accompanying petitions for certiorari would significantly increase the odds of a full Court hearing. Not surprisingly, the Court noted probable jurisdiction in the case in January 1989.

This announcement sent shock waves through the attendant community. Because of the change in the Court's membership, *Webster* evoked the greatest fears of pro-choice forces and the highest hopes of right-to-lifers. The former were truly uneasy. For the first time, they feared that the Court just might overrule *Roe*. Pundits and scholars disagreed,[113] but that did little to assuage pro-choice anxiety; nor did it discourage pro-life advocates. As a result, both sides took the battle into the larger political environment. While Susman and Fried sought to "lobby" the Court from within, those involved in the pro-choice and pro-life movements would do so from outside of its corridors, coordinating groups as amici curiae, organizing rallies and demonstrations, and seeking to manipulate the larger political environment. In short, both sides approached *Webster* as if it were *Roe.*

ATTORNEY PREPARATIONS FOR *WEBSTER*

The varying arguments and counterclaims made in each of the major briefs filed in *Webster* are outlined in table 6-9. As noted there, Missouri's and the United States' briefs were complementary. Though Attorney General Webster condemned *Roe* in toto, he spent the majority of his efforts on the law itself. The Justice Department took the opposite approach, focusing almost exclusively on *Roe*. The result was a well-coordinated effort for the pro-life side.[114] State attorneys "worked closely" with their Justice Department counterparts (Mauro 1989a), and not just on the briefs. With the state's blessing, the Justice Department filed a successful request to participate in orals.

Before the Court agreed to hear *Webster*, Planned Parenthood attorneys and Susman (for the ACLU) had worked out an initial strategy: Planned Parenthood and other pro-choice groups would write the RHS brief and Susman would argue the case before the Court (PR Newswire 1989). This seemed a reasonable division of labor. Evans had never participated in Supreme Court orals, whereas Susman was a pro.[115] Still, the preparation of oral arguments became the source of some contention between them. Both had preconceived notions about what they faced on the Supreme Court: four justices would vote to uphold *Roe* (Marshall, Blackmun, Stevens, and Brennan), three would vote to overrule it (Scalia,[116] Rehnquist, and White), one was mostly an unknown (Kennedy), and one was an enigma (O'Connor). Given that they knew little about Kennedy and a good deal about O'Connor, the most logical approach was to build a brief aimed at capturing her vote.

In light of this, Susman thought it best to make a range of arguments. Because several parts of the law arguably violated free-speech principles, Susman viewed this line of argument as particularly useful. Moreover, it might appeal to O'Connor, who expressed free-speech concerns in her *Akron* and *Thornburgh* dissents.[117] According to one source (Faux 1990), though, Planned Parenthood attorneys wanted to avoid First Amendment claims altogether, telling Susman they were "too risky to take . . . into a Supreme Court that was obviously no longer clearly pro-choice." Susman's law partner, Tom Blumenthal, however, thought Planned Parenthood had ulterior motives. Blumenthal knew that it (and the RFP) had initiated several suits challenging, on First Amendment grounds, a Reagan administration regulation denying federal funds to family-planning clinics that counsel women about abortions.[118] In his view, Planned Parenthood attorneys either were "afraid of how . . . Susman would handle the issue of free speech" or did not want "their thunder . . . stolen by *Webster*."

Another point of contention was whether to raise the viability issue (that is, the determination of when a fetus has protectable interests). Susman viewed it as a reasonable point of attack: Missouri's preamble seemed to be directly counter to *Roe*'s viability discussion, and pressing this point could give him an opportunity to show O'Connor the error of her ways. In *Akron*, she wrote that medical advances had shifted the viability line, thus putting *Roe* "on a collision course with itself" (*Akron* 1983, 458). Susman thought that she might reconsider this if she were confronted with contrary evidence. Planned Parenthood and other pro-choice advocates, though, felt it "too risky" to engage the Court in any substantive debate that might lead it to define "when life begins." Going back as far as *Roe*, Weddington had refused to relent on this point, maintaining that no line should separate illegal from legal abortions. This, in the opinion of Planned Parenthood, was not the time to revive it.

In the end, the brief for the RHS, written—by design and to the chagrin of Susman[119]—by Planned Parenthood attorneys, did not totally ignore either viability or free-speech issues; it could not do so in light of Missouri's and the United States' arguments. Still, it did not dwell on them (see table 6-9). Rather, it left such issues to the amicus curiae briefs of the American Medical Association (AMA) (viability) and the ACLU (free speech).

GROUP PREPARATIONS

The larger groups involved in both sides of the abortion movement had their own ideas about what needed to be done, ideas that were remarkably similar. Both sides mounted a two-prong campaign to influence the justices: a massive letter-writing effort and a flood of supportive amicus curiae briefs. Viewing the Court as "the smallest precinct in the world" (Moore 1989), NARAL "organized a drive to send a million postcards to the Court." Likewise, the ACLU took out newspaper advertisements "asking readers to protest the Solicitor General's stance." Some "conservative" groups countered with a campaign of their own; for example, one asked the audiences of "its two radio programs to send anti-abortion messages to the Court."[120]

More likely to have some effect were amicus curiae briefs, the coordination of which constituted the second focus of the movements' strategies. Planned Parenthood and the RFP handled the pro-choice side much as the Association for the Study of Abortion had done in *Roe*. They oversaw the filing of thirty-two

TABLE 6-9. Comparison of Briefs Filed in *Webster*: Missouri, United States, and Reproductive Health Services

I. ON *ROE V. WADE*

A. *Roe* Trimester Framework
 1. Missouri: *Roe* "is inherently flawed because the point of viability is arbitrary" (citations to medical testimony at trial; O'Connor's dissent in *Akron*).
 2. United States: *Roe*'s framework is "completely unworkable. . . . [T]he point when a fetus may survive outside the womb changes with advancements in medical skill" (citation to O'Connor's dissent in *Akron*).
 3. RHS: "There is nothing arbitrary about fetal viability. . . . There is no evidence that viability is moving inexorably toward conception" (citations to Court's opinions in *Roe* and *Thornburgh*; medical testimony at trial, medical studies, amicus curiae brief of the American Medical Association).

B. Appropriate Standard of Review
 1. Missouri: The trimester scheme is "inherently flawed" because the "State has a compelling interest in protecting life through all stages of pregnancy." Thus, the Court should adopt preferably 1) a rational basis test or, alternatively, 2) an unduly burdensome standard (citations to the solicitor general's brief, law review articles, White's dissent in *Thornburgh*, O'Connor's dissent in *Akron*, Court's decision in *Bowers v. Hardwick*).
 2. United States: Same as the state, except: "On reflection . . . we believe that [the unduly burdensome] standard would inevitably fall prey to the same difficulties that have beset *Roe*." Solicitor general urges adoption of a rational basis test.
 3. RHS: *Roe* provides the appropriate standard. A state's "compelling interest arises at viability."
   a) If the solicitor general's argument is adopted, no legal distinction will exist between a "freshly fertilized egg" and a 9-month old fetus.

C. On *Roe*, Itself
 1. Missouri: The "textual, doctrinal, and historical basis" for *Roe* is "flawed" (citations to solicitor general's brief, law review articles, O'Connor's dissent in *Akron*).
   a) *Roe* "is a source of . . . instability in law." It should be "abandoned."
 2. United States: *Roe* rests on two premises that are unsupported by precedent, a right to privacy, the Constitution, or the framers' intent: there is a fundamental right to abortion and there is no compelling state interest in protecting "prenatal life throughout the pregnancy."
   a) These assumptions are false. As such, *Roe* should be abandoned (citations to law reviews, White's dissent in *Thornburgh*, historical record, interpretation of precedent).

TABLE 6-9 *(continued)*

3. RHS: "*Roe v. Wade* should neither be reconsidered nor overruled." The solicitor general's positions are wrong.

a) His historical overview is "incomplete and fallacious."

b) His view of *Roe* vis-à-vis the Constitution is "patently false."

c) His understanding of the relationship between privacy and abortion "misconceives" *Griswold* (citations to majority opinions in abortion cases, historical record, interpretation of precedent).

II. THE MISSOURI LAW

A. Preamble

1. Missouri: "It is not intended to affect . . . any woman's constitutional right to choose abortion over childbirth."

a) "It cannot infringe upon . . . any . . . right of any plaintiff . . . [because] it protects" the unborn.

b) Preambles "do not impose substantive rights."

2. RHS: It violates the Constitution and past precedent.

a) It could restrict access to some forms of contraceptives (e.g., IUDs).

B. Funding Bans

1. Missouri: Consistent with precedent established in *Maher* and *Harris*.

a) Presents no First Amendment violation; the U.S. government has enacted its own regulations limiting the right of publicly funded clinics to engage in abortion counseling.

2. United States: Funding is "not required by the Constitution."

3. RHS: The Court should moot out this part of the suit: RHS was not adversely affected.

a) If not, this section of the law is 1) vague; 2) violative of the First Amendment (citations to amici ACLU and AMA); and 3) distinguishable from *Maher* and *Harris*.

C. Bans on Employees and Facilities

1. Missouri: Consistent with precedent established in *Poelker*.

2. United States: Funding is "not required by the Constitution."

3. RHS: These bans are different from those in *Poelker*: they affect "totally private conduct."

D. Viability Testing

1. Missouri: Justified by a compelling state interest (citation to medical testimony at trial).

2. RHS: No legitimate state interest (citation to medical testimony at trial).

separate amicus curiae briefs, representing a diverse range of interests, as shown in table 6-10. It mattered less to them what the briefs said than that they "show the broad base of support for *Roe* from mainstream America, and they show the mainstream of legal thought" (Mauro 1989e; PR Newswire 1989). Attracting amici as diverse in goals and constituencies as the Sierra Club, the American Library Association, and the American Jewish Congress was a way of driving home "universal" support for abortion rights (Moore 1989). According to an Americans United for Life director, the strategic goals of the pro-life side were the same. They succeeded to the extent that they matched nearly every constituency represented in pro-choice briefs (see table 6-10).

This outpouring of "amicus" support was extraordinary. The total number of briefs filed for the case was 78 (46 for the state and 32 for the RHS), breaking the record of 57 filed in the affirmative action case, *Regents of the University of California v. Bakke* (1978). Collectively, 420 organizations participated as filers or cosignatories (85 for the state and 335 for the RHS), and thousands of individuals also got into the act (see table 6-10). Never before had the Court heard from so many voices in a single case. But did these "voices" have anything unique to say? As we can see in table 6-11, the answer is mixed: some merely reiterated the same claims as the parties in the case; others were creative. Within the latter category was the brief filed by NARAL and NOW, which was modeled after the "speak-out" cases of the 1960s and early 1970s (Stearns 1989) and, to a lesser extent, after NARAL's amicus in *Thornburgh*.[121] Others—on both sides—discussed abortion as a policy issue, seeking to explain to the justices the potential impact of a major blow to *Roe*. While amici like Catholics United for Life emphasized how *Roe* had destroyed many lives ("unborn children"), NOW and others stressed how the decision had saved equally as many (women). Still, the balance of the briefs reiterated arguments raised by the parties. Many of those on the state's side, for example, made much of the proper role of the Court in a democratic society—an argument manifest in the solicitor general's brief. By the same token, many pro-choice amici reinforced the RHS's emphasis on stare decisis. Such "me-tooism" was hardly surprising: sixteen years had elapsed since *Roe*. The lines of the debate had been clearly drawn.[122]

Neither side, though, confined its activities to those specifically and directly aimed at influencing the Court; both tried to draw in the larger political environment. For instance, they held demonstrations and marches. To counter the annual pro-life March for Life, NOW, the ACLU, and Planned Parenthood organized a rally of 300,000. Pro-choice forces also became more aggressive. For years, they did little to combat the militant tactics of groups such as Operation Rescue,[123] but *Webster* snapped them into action. As one leader said, "[F]or too long, we've taken the rational ground, the public policy ground, [but] the intellectual arguments don't mobilize people." So they "matched their opponents in number. They outshouted them. They countered grisly photographs of aborted fetuses with graphic posters depicting a naked woman in a pool of blood on a motel floor" (Tumulty 1989). Finally, both sides launched major public relations campaigns. The American Life League spent $150,000 on newspaper advertisements, one of which "linked" *Dred Scott*, the Nazis, and the *Roe v. Wade* decision. Planned Parenthood and NARAL spent over $4 million on a media blitz (Bronner 1989b; Moore 1989).

To whom were these ads directed? Both sides seemed to view the Court as their primary target. As Planned Parenthood President Faye Wattleton explained, "The Court is not sequestered on another planet. It does hear the voices of the American people." The pro-lifers echoed this sentiment, claiming that their campaign "lets the Court know that there are significant numbers of Americans who are outraged by what the justices did 16 years ago." Whether such massive public relations efforts can influence Court outcomes is unclear.[124] Such a campaign was, however, a useful political tool, especially for pro-choice advocates, who had, since *Roe*, been more litigious than grass-roots in their politics. It was NARAL's belief that these efforts should "be viewed as a part of a campaign to mobilize a pro-choice majority that has been extraordinarily silent for the last ten years." According to one pollster, "One of the unintended consequences of this mobilization might well be that people become more aware of the political consequences of overturning *Roe*" (Moore 1989).[125]

Relatedly, both sides were looking beyond *Webster*. Should the Court overrule or significantly alter *Roe*, NARAL believed its public relations would pay off if the battle moved into the states. According to its executive director, "We are ready politically for the next step. That is the long-term goal of our campaign. We will be able to fight state legislative battles that come up. And we will be ready in the 1990 elections to help pro-choice state and congressional candidates and get rid of some of the anti-choice people" (Bronner 1989b). While they were preparing for these battles, though, pro-choicers did not look forward to them: they had fared poorly in the states in the past. Moreover, their opponents were "eager" and ready to confront them in state arenas. As the director of the National Council of Catholic Bishops put it: "I'd like to see public policy determined by a consensus of state legislators" (Moore 1989); it would be akin to playing the "big game" on their own court.

THE FIGHT ENGAGED: ORAL ARGUMENTS

The day of oral arguments in *Webster* was electric. Outside the Court, demonstrators chanted their various battle cries. It was so intense that police arrested

TABLE 6-10. Types of Interests Filing Amicus Curiae Briefs in *Webster*

Group Type	Pro-Choice	Pro-Life
Abortion	2,887 Women Who Had Abortions and 627 Friends	American Collegians for Life et al. American Life League Association for Public Justice et al. Birthright Crusade for Life Human Life International International Right to Life Federation National Right to Life Right to Life Advocates Right to Life League of Southern California Southwest Life and Law Center
Academics/ Research	281 American Historians Group of American Law Professors Bioethicists for Privacy	
Civil Liberties/ First Amendment	ACLU et al. American Library Association et al.	Free Speech Advocates
Government	Attorneys General of California, Colorado, Massachusetts, New York, Vermont, Texas 608 Legislators from 32 States 140 Members of Congress	Attorneys General of Louisiana, Arizona, Idaho, Pennsylvania, Wisconsin Center for Judicial Studies (for 56 Members of Congress) 127 Members of the Missouri General Assembly 69 Members of the Pennsylvania State Legislature 250 State Legislators United States
Labor	Americans for Democratic Action et al.	
Lawyers/ Other Legal/ Civil Rights	Committees of the Association of the Bar of the City of New York Council of Negro Women et al.	Alabama Lawyers for Life National Legal Foundation Southern Center for Law and Ethics

TABLE 6-10 *(continued)*

Group Type	Pro-Choice	Pro-Life
Population/ Family/ Family Planning	Association of Reproductive Health Professionals Center for Population Options et al. International Women's Health Organizations National Coalition against Domestic Violence National Family Planning and Reproductive Health Association Population-Environmental Balance et al.	American Family Association Focus on Family et al.
Religious	American Jewish Congress et al. Americans United for Separation of Church and State Catholics for a Free Choice et al.	Agudeth Israel of America Catholic Health Association Catholics United for Life et al. Christian Advocates Serving Evangelism Covenant House et al. Holy Orthodox Church Lutheran Church—Missouri Synod et al. Missouri Catholic Conference New England Christian Action Council Rutherford Institute et al. U.S. Catholic Conference
Science/ Medical/ Hospital	American Medical Association et al. American Nurses Association American Public Health Association et al. American Psychological Association National Association of Public Hospitals 167 Scientists and Physicians	American Academy of Medical Ethics American Association of Pro-Life Obstetricians and Gynecologists et al. Doctors for Life et al. National Association of Pro-Life Nurses

TABLE 6-10 *(continued)*

Group Type	Pro–Choice	Pro–Life
Women	California NOW	Feminists for Life of America
	Canadian Women's Organizations	et al.
	National Association of Women Lawyers et al.	
	NOW	
	Seventy-seven Organizations Committed to Equality	
Other		Knights of Columbus

Note: We derived these groupings by considering the category into which the *majority* of groups signing the brief fell, not just the first filer. For a complete list of those groups participating as filers or cosignatories, see appendix 2.

some pro-choicers who would not remain behind the barricades (Sharpe and Mauro 1989). Inside, the courtroom was packed. "The usual 150 public seats had been reduced to about 40 to accommodate guests of the Court [including Sarah Weddington and her famous client] . . . and one of the largest press contingents in the Court's history" (Strasser and Coyle 1989).

First up was William Webster, Missouri's attorney general. Though he had a good reputation, some were surprised that he was arguing the case. Indeed, he even told Susman that he "hadn't intended" to present the case, but the "pro-life people had pressured him into it," and that he had not spent much time "preparing his arguments" (Faux 1990, 49). Press reports, though, suggest otherwise. He was cognizant of the fact that two of his predecessors—Danforth and Ashcroft—used abortion litigation to attain higher offices, and he was eyeing the governorship in 1992. Further, Webster *had* prepared: he "worked closely with the Justice Department," agreeing with its attorneys on a strategy. During orals, he would deal with the Missouri law, while Fried would handle *Roe*. Finally, he read all seventy-eight amicus curiae briefs. He told one reporter, "The State of Missouri will be ready" (Mauro 1989a, 1989b).

Webster's opening line of arguments—"the government is certainly not obligated to become an advocate for abortion"—went smoothly, but he soon ran into problems. Several justices wanted to know about the enforcement and penalty provisions of the law.[126]

TABLE 6-11. Comparison of Arguments Made by the Parties and by Amici Curiae in *Webster*

			Amici	
Argument	RHS/Missouri	United States	Pro–Life	Pro–Choice
THE *ROE* FRAMEWORK				
Viability is/is not arbitrary	Yes/Yes	Yes	Yes	Yes
Medical advances have/ have not occurred	Yes/Yes	Yes	Yes	Yes
Based/not based on erroneous perception of personhood	No/No	No	Yes	No
STANDARD OF REVIEW				
Discussion of standard				
—as is	Yes/Yes	Yes	Yes	Yes
—unduly burdensome	No/Yes	Yes	Yes	Yes
—rational basis	No/Yes	Yes	Yes	Yes
Role of Courts versus legisla- tures in a democratic society	Yes/No	Yes	Yes	Yes
***ROE*/PRIVACY/ABORTION**				
History of abortion regulation	Yes/No	Yes	Yes	Yes
Intent of framers	Yes/Yes	Yes	Yes	Yes
As/as not part of privacy	Yes/Yes	Yes	Yes	Yes
Stare decisis	Yes/Yes	Yes	Yes	Yes
Religion	No/No	No	Yes	Yes
Equal protection	No/No	No	Yes	Yes
IMPACT OF ABANDONING *ROE*				
Threat to women's/fetuses' lives	No/No	No	Yes	Yes
Creation of legal stability/confusion	No/No	Yes	Yes	Yes
Burden/not burden health care or law enforcement	No/No	No	Yes	Yes
Will increase/decrease respect for Court	No/No	No	Yes	Yes

Stevens: What if a doctor who had a patient in a public hospital went ahead and performed, in the first trimester, performed an abortion. Is there any sanction against the doctor if he did that?

Webster: This particular chapter 188, carries a general Class A misdemeanor penalty for violation of the initial sections, but there is no operative language in the 1986 statute.

Stevens: So it would be a misdemeanor then?

Webster: Arguably, it would be a misdemeanor.

Stevens: What is your opinion? Don't you know?

Webster: My opinion is that there is no language in that section which was adopted here which would suggest that it would make it a criminal offense, only that it is directed to those bodies expending public funds themselves.

Stevens: Is it your opinion as the chief law enforcement officer of that state that it would not be a misdemeanor?

Webster: We wouldn't view that violation as a misdemeanor, no.

Stevens: Is there any enforcement provision other than injunctive relief? If the doctor went ahead and did it and you don't enjoin him in time, that would be the end of it?

Webster: That is the only enforcement power that we would presume is contained in the language which was enacted in the 1986 statute.

Kennedy: Wouldn't it be grounds for discharge for cause?

Webster: It is conceivable the hospital board could, if somebody violated the policy of that facility, seek to discharge that particular employee. We don't—

Kennedy: The statute says it shall be unlawful. I assume it is grounds for discharge.

Webster: We presume that would be an opportunity available.

Scalia: It might also be that the official who expends the funds, knowing they are going to be used in violation of the statute, is liable for the funds. I would assume so. That is certainly the case at the federal level—that if you make an unauthorized expenditure, it comes out of your pocket.

In the end, with Scalia's and Kennedy's help, Webster "recovered," but "Stevens seemed dissatisfied nonetheless" (Mauro 1989b).

Webster's lukewarm performance simplified Fried's task—he could only look better in comparison. Still, the former solicitor general may have been uncomfortable in his role. He termed Attorney General Thornburgh's request that he argue *Webster* "a great honor,"[127] but insiders thought otherwise. There was, in fact, a good deal of speculation as to why the administration turned to the former solicitor general. Some (Mauro 1989a) echoed Fried's sentiment, implying that Thornburgh sought him out for his expertise as a Supreme Court advocate. Others (Faux 1990, 42), though, asserted that no one within the Bush Justice Department wanted to handle the case, so they turned to Fried.[128]

Perhaps more awkward for the former solicitor general was the argument he was asked to make. Less than three years earlier, after *Thornburgh*, he had announced he would not ask the Court again to overrule *Roe*. Now he was doing precisely that. He said in his opening remarks:

> Today the United States asks this Court to reconsider and overrule its decision in *Roe v. Wade*. At the outset, I would like to make quite clear how limited that submission is. First, we are not asking the Court to unravel the fabric of unenumerated and privacy rights which this Court has woven in cases like . . . *Griswold*. Rather, we are asking the Court to pull one thread. And the reason is well stated by this Court in *Harris and McRae*; abortion is different.

Fried attempted to develop this argument, but Justice Kennedy peppered him with questions about the distinguishability of *Roe* from *Griswold*. Fried's responses, which echoed his brief, seemed to satisfy Kennedy but not "a clearly troubled" O'Connor. She asked whether the government was arguing that "there is no fundamental right to decide to have a child or not." When Fried seemed at a loss, she put it more emphatically:

> *O'Connor:* A right to procreate? Do you deny that the Constitution protects that right?
> *Fried:* I would hesitate to formulate the right in such abstract terms, and I think the Court prior to *Roe v. Wade* quite prudently also avoided such sweeping generalities. That is the wisdom of *Griswold*.

Observers were surprised at this reply, terming it an "insensitive put down," which might cost the government O'Connor's key vote. Some also commented on the "jarring contrast between Webster and Fried's 'good cop, bad cop' routine." Though this was planned, those present in the courtroom thought it had "backfired" (Mauro 1989b; Hentoff 1989).

Susman had been furious when he learned that the former solicitor general would be arguing for the government; in fact, he and Evans tried to get "someone of similar stature to counter." They "settled" on Barbara Jordan, an attorney with an impeccable reputation and proven oratory skills, but the Supreme Court denied their request to share argument time.[129] After listening to Fried, though, Susman may have been pleased that the Court nixed the Jordan strategy. All along, Susman told a nervous Planned Parenthood that the best offense was a good defense, that he need not prepare for orals as much as he needed to react to and controvert the opposition.[130]

Initially, Susman followed this defensive strategy. His opening remarks to the Court were a direct attempt to rebut Fried:

> I think the Solicitor General's submission is somewhat disingenuous when he suggests to this Court that he does not seek to unravel the whole cloth of procreational rights, but merely to pull a thread. It has always been my personal experience that, when I pull a thread, my sleeve falls off. There is no stopping. It is not a thread he is after. It is the full range of procreational rights and choices that constitute the fundamental right that has been recognized by this Court.

Scalia immediately interrupted and the following exchange ensued:

> *Scalia:* Excuse me, you find it hard to draw a line between those two, but easy to draw a line between the first, second, and third trimester?
> *Susman:* I do not find it difficult—
> *Scalia:* I don't see why a court that can draw that line can't separate abortion from birth control quite readily.
> *Susman:* If I may suggest the reasons in response to your questions, Justice Scalia. The most common forms of what we generically in common parlance call contraception today—IUDs, low-dose birth control pills, which are the safest type of birth control pills available—act as abortifacients. They are correctly labeled as both. . . . Under this statute, which defines fertilization as the point of the beginning, those forms of contraception are also abortifacients. Science and medicine refer to them as both. We are not still dealing with the common barrier methods of *Griswold*. We are no longer just talking about condoms and diaphragms. Things have changed. The bright line, if there ever was one, has now been extinguished. That's why I suggest to this Court that we need to deal with one right, the right to procreate. We are no longer talking about two rights.

This stifled Scalia,[131] but only momentarily. In ending an exchange with Chief Justice Rehnquist over the history of abortion regulation, Susman said, "Every state adopted anti-abortion legislation in the 1820s and 1830s and the 1840s, but before that it went without regulation. It was accepted; it was not a crime at common law as *Roe* and other works [including an amicus curiae brief filed by 281 American historians] have recognized." Scalia again went on the offensive: "That certainly is not uncontested. You mentioned the historical brief. There is more that one historical brief here, and one filed by the Association for Public

Justice just simply contradicts your history and quotes authorities back to Blackstone and Coke, saying that at common law abortion was unlawful." But Susman would hear none of this. He quickly retorted:

> I understand there are briefs on both sides. But when one tries to compare the large number as we are all aware, of the amicus briefs filed in this case, I think it is necessary to examine whether or not these briefs are filed by organizations whose primary purpose is to be opposed to abortion or they are filed by organizations which have been around for one hundred years and which we consider to be reputable on a large number of issues. . . . I can't personally, for example—there is disagreement on medical issues in this case, clearly. I personally cannot put as much stock in a brief by Wyoming Nurses for Life as I can in briefs by the AMA, ACOG, American Public Health Association, American Public Hospital Association, and other organizations of a similar vein.

All continued to go well for Susman until the chief justice inadvertently tripped him up. He was seeking to make the point that part of the Missouri law was vague, when Rehnquist asked:

> *Rehnquist:* What is the authority from this Court?
> *Susman:* I think the fact that there is a heightened standard because it touches upon—
> *Rehnquist:* What case authority?
> *Susman:* In all candor, I am having a block. I will try to come back to it. But I think the fact that—
> *White:* That would be a common situation in trying to answer that question.
> *Susman:* I understand that, and I apologize.
> [Laughter.]

After a rather ineffectual rebuttal from Webster,[132] Rehnquist announced that "the case is submitted." *Roe*'s author—Blackmun—had not asked a single question.

THE WAIT AND THE DECISION

Media coverage of orals in *Webster* was heavy; the *New York Times* even printed verbatim transcripts of arguments. And, of course, many pundits relied on orals as a predictor of what the Court would do. Some agreed with Mauro's (1989b) sentiment that "the lawyers' performances were entertaining—but uneven. Give awards to Susman for content, to Fried for bravery, and to Webster for the best disappearing act." Others were more unequivocal (for example, Hentoff 1989).

NOW's president pinpointed the turning point as O'Connor's questioning of Fried. As she put it, "Thank God for her. I was looking up there at all these men deciding our fate and it made me sick. At least O'Connor knows what it is to have a child" (Sharpe and Mauro 1989). The conventional wisdom immediately after *Webster* was similar in tone: the pro-choice posture would win the case 5–4, with O'Connor casting the key vote.

By early June, speculation on *Webster*'s outcome took a marked turn. Washington, D.C., was abuzz with rumors that the Court would hand down a 5–4 ruling, on 5 June, upholding the law. When the Court remained mute on the subject of abortion, pro-choicers remained anxious: the date might not have been correct, but what about the vote? Would O'Connor, who was never actually with them, fully abandon them? Taking no chances, pro-choice advocates met to plan their post-*Webster* strategy. Should they lose, they decided against downplaying the blow; rather, in an effort to "build political momentum" for state battles, they would play any defeat to its maximum (Faux 1990, 28).

The planning was not wasted. On 27 June, the Court announced that it would deliver all "remaining decisions" by 3 July. A few days later, Susman received a phone call from a contact in the Justice Department. Apparently, the unreleased "opinion was floating around" the building (D. Baer 1989; Faux 1990). He would lose the case, 5 to 4. Finally, on 3 July 1989, the Court made it official, announcing its opinions in *Webster*. It was, to be sure, a dramatic event, with the chief justice reading his judgment for the Court and with dissenting Justice Blackmun doing the same, in a "weary and sorrowful tone." As both men spoke, "a tense silence" filled the packed courtroom (Greenhouse 1989).

That these two justices read their differing views in open Court might have implied to spectators that they represented the range of the Court's thoughts on *Webster*. Table 6-12 shows that there is some truth to this perception. Five justices (Rehnquist, Scalia, White, Kennedy, and O'Connor) agreed that the challenged sections of the law were constitutional; four (Blackmun, Brennan, Marshall, and Stevens) disagreed. Where the majority disagreed, however, may be more important than their points of consensus. In fact, one way to consider the holding in *Webster* is to place the plurality's views on a continuum, with Scalia representing the pro-life ideal (overturn *Roe*), O'Connor taking the less extreme position (*Roe* need not be reevaluated), and Rehnquist acting as a balance (*Roe* will be "modif[ied] and narrow[ed]" [*Webster* 1989, 3058]).

O'Connor was the most ambivalent member of the majority. She so "dreaded" her role as the "swing" vote determining *Roe*'s fate that she virtually imposed a "gag order" on her staff during consideration of the case. Moreover, as one clerk said, "her indecisiveness affected everything . . . causing delays in the opinions of colleagues waiting to respond to her" (D. Baer 1989). In the end, though, she stayed on the course set out in her *Akron* and *Thornburgh* dissents: states can restrict choice so long as they do not "unduly burden" the abortion decision. Here they did not: "I do not understand these viability testing requirements to conflict with [an unduly burdensome standard]. . . . Therefore, there is no necessity . . . to reexamine the constitutional validity of *Roe*" (*Webster* 1989, 3060).

If O'Connor was the most hesitant member of the majority, Scalia was the least: he wanted to reverse *Roe* and lambasted his "allies," particularly O'Connor and her so-called "attempt to please everyone" opinion (D. Baer 1989). He said her self-described "judicial restraint" "cannot be taken seriously"; that her previous opinions belie her approach; and that, largely thanks to her, the Court "can look forward to another Term with carts full of mail from the public and streets full of demonstrators, urging us to follow the popular will" (*Webster* 1989, 3064–66). Yet O'Connor would not be goaded; some said she felt immense pressure from feminists and pro-choice groups to uphold *Roe*,[133] while others suggested that "she want[ed] to assume" the role of the "pivot." There were even a few who claimed that "Scalia's . . . tongue-lashing" repelled her "enough to stay her moderate course" (D. Baer 1989).

Whatever the reason, it was clear to Rehnquist that neither O'Connor nor Scalia would alter their views. So, like a parent seeking to mediate a squabble between errant siblings, he stepped in. He probably agreed, more or less, with Scalia: all things being equal, he would have explicitly overruled *Roe*.[134] But all things were not equal; he could not "lure" O'Connor into a "solid five Justice majority." This was not for lack of effort. One former Supreme Court clerk speculated that Rehnquist wrote the opinion with her in mind: "If he had set out to write a simple plurality, it would have been more direct" (D. Baer 1989). Had he overruled *Roe*, he still would have been supported by White, Scalia, and, probably, Kennedy. Because of O'Connor's ambivalence, however, Rehnquist had to submit a watered-down judgment, a modified and narrowed *Roe*: the modification, that the justices no longer would adhere to *Roe*'s trimester scheme; the narrowing, that state laws would be deemed permissible if they further the state's interest in "potential human life," an interest that exists throughout the pregnancy (*Webster* 1989, 3058).

To the four dissenters, Rehnquist's effort was "disingenuous." It mattered not whether O'Connor's, Rehnquist's, or Scalia's views ruled the day: they all led to the same outcome—*Roe* was dead. Blackmun's opinion was sharp and bitter,[135] but mostly it was sad in tone. He said it all in the introduction to his dissent: "I fear for the future, I fear for the liberty and equality of the millions of women who have lived and come of age in the 16 years since *Roe* was decided. I fear for the integrity of, and public esteem for, this Court" (*Webster* 1989, 3067).

Thus, O'Connor was the fulcrum balancing *Roe*'s future as precedent. What

TABLE 6-12. The *Webster* "Splits"

I. ON *ROE V. WADE*[a]

A. *Roe* Trimester Framework

1. Scalia: No need to comment. Wants *Roe* overruled.

2. Rehnquist (for White, Kennedy): The trimester framework needs to be reconsidered.

a) It is not "consistent with the notion of a Constitution cast in general terms."

b) It is too "rigid" and "the result has been a web of legal rules that have become increasingly intricate, resembling a code of regulations rather than a body of constitutional doctrine."

c) It is "not found in the text of the Constitution or any place else one would expect to find a constitutional principle."

3. O'Connor: No need to comment. Already suggested (*Akron*, *Thornburgh*) that the *Roe* framework is unworkable due to scientific advancement.

4. Stevens: Agrees with Blackmun.

5. Blackmun (for Marshall, Brennan):

a) On Rehnquist's logic: "Bald assertion masquerad[ing] as reasoning. The object, quite clearly, is not to persuade, but to prevail."

b) On O'Connor's "medical advancement": "pure science fiction."

c) *Roe* trimester scheme should remain: the viability line "reflects the biological facts and truths of fetal development. . . . [It] fairly, sensibly, and effectively" functions.

B. Standard of Review

1. Scalia: No need to comment. *Roe* should be overruled.

a) Does, however, lambast O'Connor's unduly burdensome standard: "It does not tell us whether the present requirement is an 'undue burden' and I know of no basis for determining that this particular burden (or any other for that matter) is 'due.'"

2. Rehnquist (for White, Kennedy): "We do not see why the state's interest in protecting potential life should come into existence only at the point of viability."

a) On *Griswold*: Distinguishes *Griswold* from *Roe*, but extended analysis is unnecessary.

3. O'Connor: Unduly burdensome is the appropriate standard of review.

4. Stevens: The Preamble might affect the ability of citizens to obtain contraceptives. Thus, it interferes with *Griswold*.

5. Blackmun (for Brennan, Marshall): *Roe*'s fundamental liberty approach is the appropriate standard.

a) But, "had the plurality read the statute as written, it would have no cause to reconsider the *Roe* framework. As properly construed [it] does not pass constitutional muster under even a rational-basis standard."

TABLE 6-12 *(continued)*

b) On *Griswold*: Lambasts Rehnquist for not dealing with privacy: "The plurality opinion is far more remarkable for the arguments it does not advance than those it does."

C. On *Roe*, Itself (the Holdings)

1. Scalia: The opinion today "effectively would overrule *Roe.*" The Court has taken the "least responsible course" of action by not explicitly overturning it.

a) Lambasts O'Connor; her assertion that "judicial restraint requires us to avoid reconsidering *Roe* cannot be taken seriously."

b) "We can look forward to at least another term with carts full of mail from the public, and streets full of demonstrators, urging us—their unelected and life-tenured judges who have been awarded these extraordinary undemocratic characteristics precisely in order that we might follow the law despite the popular will—to follow the popular will."

2. Rehnquist (for White, Kennedy): *Roe* will not be overturned; the facts "of the present case . . . differ from those at issue in *Roe*. . . . [It] affords us no occasion to revisit the holding of *Roe*."

a) But, "we modify and narrow" *Roe*.

3. O'Connor: "I do not understand these . . . regulations to conflict with any of the Court's past decisions. . . . Therefore, there is no necessity to accept the State's invitation to reexamine the constitutional validity of *Roe*."

a) Judicial restraint-type argument: "When a constitutional invalidation of a State's abortion statute actually turns on the constitutional validity of *Roe v. Wade*, there will be time enough to reexamine *Roe*. And to do so carefully."

4. Stevens: Agrees with Blackmun.

5. Blackmun (for Brennan, Marshall): The Court's decision implicitly overrules *Roe*.

a) "Thus 'not with a bang, but a whimper' the plurality discards a landmark case of the last generation."

b) "I fear for the future. I fear for the liberty and equality of the millions of women who have lived and come of age in the 16 years since *Roe* was decided. I fear for the integrity of, and public esteem for, this Court."

II. THE MISSOURI LAW

A. Preamble

1. Scalia: Concurs with Rehnquist.

2. Rehnquist (for White, Kennedy): "The preamble does not by its terms regulate abortion or any other aspect of the appellees' medical practice."

a) It "will be time enough for federal courts to address the meaning of the preamble should it be applied to restrict the activities of the appellee in some concrete way."

TABLE 6-12 *(continued)*

3. O'Connor: Concurs with Rehnquist.

   a) "Nothing in the record before us . . . indicates that . . . the preamble . . . will affect a woman's decision to have an abortion."

4. Stevens: It "threatens serious encroachments upon the liberty of pregnant women and health professionals."

   a) It may limit access to some types of birth control.

   b) It adopts a nonsecular view of life and thus violates the establishment clause.

5. Blackmun (for Brennan, Marshall): "I do not see how the preamble realistically may be construed as 'abortion neutral.'"

B. Funding Bans

Rehnquist (with all concurring): Moots this part of the suit because appellees contend that they are not "adversely" affected under the state's interpretation of this clause.

C. Facilities/Employee Bans

1. Scalia: Concurs with Rehnquist.

2. Rehnquist (for White, Kennedy): Upholds bans based on past decisions (e.g., *Poelker*, *Maher*, *McRae*); the "state's decision here to use public facilities to encourage childbirth over abortion" does not significantly impact the abortion decision.

   a) "Nothing in the Constitution requires states to enter or remain in the business of performing abortions."

3. O'Connor: Concurs with Rehnquist (past cases control).

4. Stevens: Joins with Blackmun.

5. Blackmun (for Brennan, Marshall): Past cases "most certainly do not control this case."

   a) The state has not just withdrawn for abortion, but it "has taken affirmative steps to assure that abortions are not performed by *private* physicians in *private* institutions."

D. Viability Testing

1. Scalia: Concurs with Rehnquist in judgment but wants to overrule *Roe*.

2. Rehnquist (for White, Kennedy): The law "makes sense" if it is read "to require only those tests that may be useful to making subsidiary findings as to viability."

   a) In general, though, he finds that the problem is not the law but the "trimester" system: it is far too "rigid."

   b) Rehnquist then uses this as a launching point for his attack on *Roe* more generally.

3. O'Connor: Concurs with Rehnquist in judgment (i.e., she agrees with his reading of the law).

   a) But she disagrees with the rest of his analysis in that this provision provides no occasion to reconsider the *Roe* framework.

TABLE 6-12 *(continued)*

b) In her view the regulation is not "unduly burdensome": the cost of viability tests for women is "marginal."

4. Stevens: Agrees with the analyses of the lower courts and with Blackmun.

5. Blackmun (for Brennan, Marshall): this provision could be struck even under a rational basis analysis.

a) See generally his view on the *Roe* framework.

---

[a]The discussions of *Roe* basically emanate from the Court's consideration of the viability-testing provisions.

she would do next was anybody's guess. Soon, though, she would have another opportunity. On the day it announced *Webster*, the Court agreed to review yet three more abortion cases, two involving parental consent (*Ohio v. Akron Center for Reproductive Health* and *Hodgson v. Minnesota*) and one centering on whether states can require clinics to meet certain standards in order to perform abortions (*Turnock v. Ragsdale*).

IN THE AFTERMATH OF *WEBSTER*

From the day *Webster* came down, abortion advocates and their opponents were obsessed with the decision, playing it to the hilt. Pro-lifers were ecstatic; they had won a clear, if less than definitive, victory. As the president of the National Council of Catholic Bishops said, "The biggest winners today are the tiniest people of all—children within the womb." True to their plan, pro-choice advocates conjured up the most pessimistic scenarios. In a press conference immediately after the decision, the RFP's Benshoof proclaimed, "Today's decision strikes a blow to all Americans who look to the Constitution and to the United States Supreme Court to safeguard privacy and freedom. What is critically important about the decision . . . is that there are no longer five votes on the . . . Court to protect *Roe* versus *Wade* and to protect privacy and the abortion choice."[136]

Even so, pro-choice forces had no intention of giving up the fight. They had to prepare for three new Supreme Court battles next term. Further, they saw *Webster* in much the same terms as their opponents had viewed *Roe*: as a catalyst to revive their sagging movement. Accordingly, Susman averred,

I cannot say forcefully enough, that this battle is far from over. . . . What the Court has done is to send this issue back to elected officials, back to individuals, back to the populace. . . . Where the majority comes down on this issue has been clear in every public opinion poll taken in the country from 1973 to yesterday. There is no question that a overwhelming majority of the citizens in this country . . . believe that they . . . are entitled to this basic right. This basic right will prevail. It will not be easy. It will not be nice. It will not be pleasant. But I guarantee you, it will be.

Despite these strong words, the odds—given the rather dismal historical record of pro-choice efforts within state legislatures—were against the pro-choice movement; they would lose the larger political battle over abortion and lose big. Although *Webster* did not explicitly overturn *Roe*, it allowed states to place new and severe restraints on the right. Indeed, many magazines and newspapers conducted surveys indicating which states would remain "pro-choice," which would turn "pro-life," and those where "battles" were likely to occur. An article in *U.S. News and World Report* claimed that its "analysis shows that 27 states are likely to enact more restrictions, 9 are battlegrounds . . . and 14 states . . . are likely to retain abortion rights" (Gest 1989). Even NARAL declared that it could not win in several states and, thus, would not even bother with them. Pro-choice prospects for electoral success looked equally grim. Shortly after *Webster*, fifty members of Congress filed a complaint with national Democratic party chair, Ron Brown, asserting that Americans now equate Democrats "as the party of abortion, a sure recipe for losing irretrievably a significant segment of our base of support" (Gest 1989). Some observers even predicted that the Court would finally bury *Roe* in 1989 docketed cases (Kolbert 1989).

In light of these predictions, it is worth noting the existence of a most unusual—at least in light of the history of the abortion issue—dichotomy: the political tide has turned in favor of pro-choice forces, while the legal environment now seems squarely pro-life. More specifically, at least as of this writing, the political environment has shown *Webster* to be a rather empty victory for pro-life forces:

• Only Guam, Pennsylvania, Utah, and Louisiana have passed restrictive legislative akin to Missouri's.
• Two states, Maryland and Connecticut, have passed legislation re-affirming their commitment to *Roe*, regardless of future Supreme Court decisions.
• Congressional and state elections have been called a wash by some, marked successes for abortion advocates by others.
• Headlines like "Abortion Hype: Alarmists Were Wrong" and "Impact of Abortion Rule Muted" were and are not uncommon.

Why has this occurred? Although polls indicate that the public was not altogether moved by *Webster*,[137] activists, some of whom had been quiet for years, were motivated to take action. They held "strategy conferences,"[138] launched massive public relations campaigns, hired consultants and pollsters, raised significant amounts of money,[139] and signed up hundreds of thousands of people to participate in grass-roots lobbying. Also, while they were busy mobilizing en masse for the first time since *Roe*—perhaps for the first time in their history—their opponents, uncharacteristically, were dormant. This role reversal did not go unnoticed by right-to-life leaders. According to one AUL LDF attorney, "The pro-life movement has been organized and active for 20 years and some of us are tired. The pro-choice movement is fresh so they are operating with a much greater energy reserve. They've really rallied in light of *Webster*" (Berke 1989).

Hence, we may never know for sure what led to the pro-choice successes noted above. Perhaps it was pro-life passivity, the huge campaign undertaken by pro-choice forces, the perception among politicians that abortion advocates greatly outnumbered their foes, the political context generated by the Bork nomination, or any combination thereof. What is clear, though, is that to date they have scored some impressive wins.[140] This is not, of course, to say that the "politics" surrounding abortion could not change at any time; the picture is that volatile. What is true, though, is that the post-*Webster* environment bears little resemblance to that of the 1970s and 1980s: pro-life forces at that time had always fared well in the states and had expected to do so in the 1990s.[141]

Also, at that time the Court had been the site of pro-choice forces' greatest successes. There they achieved the dramatic victory of *Roe* and the impressive reinforcements of *Akron* and *Thornburgh*. But the legal environment surrounding the Supreme Court has turned:

- In two 1990 cases, *Hodgson v. Minnesota* and *Ohio v. Akron Center for Reproductive Health*, the Court upheld restrictions on the ability of minors to obtain abortions without parental notification.
- *Roe* supporter Justice Brennan retired in 1990 and was replaced by David Souter.
- In *Rust v. Sullivan* (1991), the Court upheld a Reagan administration regulation that prohibited workers in federally funded clinics from discussing the subject of abortion with their clients.
- Yet another vote in favor of *Roe* was lost in 1991 with the retirement of Justice Marshall and the confirmation of Clarence Thomas.

Pro-choice forces cannot be happy with this turn of events. Though the Court did not use any of its post-*Webster* cases to overrule *Roe*, as some predicted,[142] pro-choicers view *Rust*, in particular, as an ominous sign. Writing for a five-person majority upholding the Reagan administration regulation at issue in the case, Chief Justice Rehnquist mentioned the *Roe* abortion right only in passing, invoking instead the logic of the Court's abortion-funding rulings; even the two dissents largely avoided abortion rights per se.[143] Still, some analysts are already predicting the stance of one of the Court's newest members, David Souter, on *Roe* based on his vote in *Rust*. To be sure, his decision to join the majority was not an encouraging sign for abortion advocates. But it was not—from their vantage point—wholly unexpected. During his otherwise smooth confirmation hearings, several pro-choice and pro-life groups (and senators) sought to inject into the proceedings the subject of abortion.[144] Despite his O'Connoresque approach to questions about *Roe*,[145] and the fact that his confirmation was all but assured, some pro-choice groups opposed him.[146] Many pundits labeled them "alarmists," especially after orals in *Rust*, during which Souter seemed quite hostile to the regulation. However, Souter was the swing vote, providing Chief Justice Rehnquist with a majority that would not have formed had Souter's predecessor, Brennan, been on the Court.

The extent to which Souter's vote in *Rust* was a harbinger of his future votes, we do not know (and given the retirement of Justice Marshall and his replacement with Thomas, it may not matter). Nor do we know if *Roe* itself is dead; indeed, as of this writing, it appears that even if *Webster* did bury *Roe*, it may face its own political interment as states decline to use their new opportunities to restrict the abortion choice. Still, if *Roe* is extinguished—and many expect that the Court will overturn it shortly—it will be at the hands of *Webster*, which provided states and lower courts with the arsenal to destroy it.

ANALYSIS: WHAT HAPPENED?

Webster was a vital victory for the pro-life movement. Even though the vast majority of states still subscribe to the framework set out in *Roe*, the abortion right is no longer secure as a matter of constitutional doctrine. Indeed, the pro-choice win in *Roe* was never as complete as many had assumed. *Roe* gave women a fundamental right to obtain abortions during the first six months of pregnancy, virtually free from state restrictions. The Court, however, began fencing in this "fundamental right" shortly afterward. The Medicaid cases limited the ability of poor women to exercise that right, and the consent cases limited the ability of minors to obtain abortions without judicial or parental consent. *Webster* invited still more substantive restrictions. Although abortion doctrine has not (yet) returned to its pre-1973 status, it has retreated from where it was in *Roe*.

How can we account for this cycle of events? Why were pro-choice forces unable to stem the Court's retreat and to hang on to the victory of *Roe*? What happened between *Roe* and *Webster*? Three interrelated factors should be considered: the Court, the political environment, and the group strategy.

THE COURT

Although the rulings of the Court undeniably brought about the legal change between *Roe* and *Webster*, the question is not whether the composition of the Court is the sole cause of the legal discrepancy, but whether pro-choice advocates could have held on to their 1973 victory, given the composition of the Court in 1989. In short, were internal Court pressures sufficient to account for the observed doctrinal shift?

On the surface, the membership changes that occurred on the Court seem to provide a satisfactory answer to our question. Four personnel changes transpired, three of which involved Reagan appointments of justices hostile to *Roe*. The Court that decided *Webster* was substantially different from that which decided *Roe*. Further, no justice—save Burger—vacillated from the position he or she initially staked out. Those who voted with the majority in *Roe* remained true to that basic position; those who dissented were joined by new justices along the way. This suggests that pro-choice litigators were simply "unlucky" over the sixteen-year period. As old *Roe* supporters left and new justices ascended, a shift in legal policy was inevitable.

But was a shift in policy inevitable considering the change in personnel? Clearly pro-choice forces had no chance of capturing White or Rehnquist—both were squarely in their opponents' camp. Given his pre-nomination speeches and the language of his 1989 concurrence in *Webster*, the same probably can be said of Scalia. However, Scalia was not the problem: he replaced Rehnquist (a clear pro-life vote), who in turn replaced Burger (another pro-life vote). Rather, the "problems," from the pro-choice vantage point, were O'Connor and Kennedy, both of whom replaced *Roe* supporters—Stewart and Powell. Had abortion advocates been able to garner some support from either Reagan appointee, the *Webster* outcome would have been more favorable to their concerns. That is, pro-choice forces could have won in 1989, by a 5–4 vote, if either O'Connor or Kennedy had followed the path of their predecessors.

Mathematically speaking, then, the Court explains much. The resignations of Stewart and Powell opened the door for the emergence of an anti-*Roe* majority. The question is whether the mere appointments of O'Connor and Kennedy made *Roe*'s doctrinal demise inevitable; in short, did they cause the observed legal change? More specifically, could pro-choice forces have captured the vote of either O'Connor or Kennedy? We think they could have, especially that of

O'Connor. If so, why were abortion advocates unable to attract them? This question is particularly acute in the case of O'Connor who, from her first opinion in *Akron*, seemed to dismiss outright any absolute rejection of a constitutionally grounded abortion right.

THE POLITICAL ENVIRONMENT

To what extent do changes in the political environment between 1973 and 1989 account for the legal shift? Clearly, the politics surrounding abortion changed after *Roe*, and much of that change was unfavorable to the interests of pro-choice advocates. The most noticeable change was the rise of a countermovement. To be sure, before 1973 pro-choice groups faced opposition to their efforts to prompt legislative reform, and as a result, they met with little success. Still, pro-life activities at that time were largely confined to state arenas. Further, these efforts were fairly fragmented, with few major organizations involved beyond the Catholic church. *Roe* provided an impetus for change: the pro-life movement emerged with a single goal—the negation of that decision. To achieve their goal, members went on the offensive, pushing Congress and the states to adopt legislation that, in some instances, they had written; churning out educational material; and becoming experienced litigators. In short, pro-lifers learned from their opponents and then sought to turn the tables on them.

Perhaps even more significant were the efforts of the Reagan Justice Department. Though no president before Reagan had supported abortion, none sent a representative into Court to argue specifically against it. Bork participated as an amicus curiae in the 1977 cases at the Court's invitation, and McCree argued for the Hyde amendment because that was his job. Conversely, in *Akron* and again in *Thornburgh*, Reagan's solicitors general asked the justices to change radically or overrule completely *Roe*. Neither effort met with success, but it was Solicitor General Lee who proposed the unduly burdensome standard that Justice O'Connor found so attractive. For the first time since *Roe*, pro-choice advocates faced effective opposition from the national government instead of state attorneys general with minimal interest or limited expertise in the subject or in Supreme Court advocacy.

Reagan's solicitors general were not alone in the effort to demolish *Roe*. Beginning with a vengeance in 1985, the president and Attorney General Meese attempted to implement the Republican platform mandating the appointment of pro-life judges. That effort succeeded: they managed to inject into the federal judiciary a conservative bias that embraced a pro-life stance. This step changed the legal landscape. Before 1985, pro-choicers had grown relatively accustomed to winning in federal courts; after that date, they faced an increasingly hostile environment.

The emergence of a concerted pro-life movement and the actions of Reagan and Meese are potent explanatory factors. Indeed, it is tempting to cede the legal shift to them, but such an explanation is ultimately unsatisfactory. The pro-life movement was bigger, more organized, and increasingly adept, but to what extent did it overwhelm the successes of pro-choice forces? On the one hand, it hurt them in state legislatures. Despite the strong words of Blackmun in *Roe* and *Thornburgh* and of Powell in *Akron*, states continued to enact restrictive laws. However, pro-choice forces had always been outmaneuvered at the grass-roots level, both before and after *Roe*; their successes were predominantly won in the courts. Moreover, the various waves of legislation—save parental consent laws—had little effect on the Court. Indeed, in *Thornburgh*, Blackmun actually chastised Pennsylvania for its repeated efforts to circumvent *Roe*.

On the other hand, the pro-life movement was relatively ineffective in national arenas such as Congress and the Supreme Court. Although right-to-lifers "convinced" members of Congress to pass funding restrictions, they never came close to achieving their ultimate objective—*Roe*'s reversal by constitutional amendment. In part this was due to coherent and unified pro-choice pressure on Congress. Beyond this, pro-lifers often set the stage for their own defeats. They never rallied around a specific proposal; and, in fact, advocates had no qualms about expressing their disapproval of competing versions. Perhaps the situation would have been different if pro-lifers had managed to fill Congress with supporters who could unify existing forces; yet, with the possible exception of 1980, their electoral strategies met with little success.

By the same token, pro-life groups had little impact on the outcomes of federal court decisions. True, their efforts had improved markedly over the two decades; some became increasingly cognizant of the importance of litigation, writing model legislation to fit compatibly with *Roe*, honing trial court skills, and even taking over cases for state attorneys. But, at the same time, they continued to be plagued by splits over the direction of their arguments and the interstitial modifications they wanted from the Court, not to mention the ever-present participation by some of the more emotional and radical elements of the movement. All of this worked to dampen their effectiveness. They lost big in *Akron* and *Thornburgh*; even the dissenting justices failed to adopt the arguments put forth in their amicus curiae briefs. They were stronger legal opponents in 1989 than in 1973, but crediting them with the major legal change worked by *Webster* is too simplistic.

To suggest that the alteration might be attributed to Reagan—his views, his solicitors general, his federal court judges—is more reasonable, but is equally flawed. The president was clearly committed to a pro-life stance, but during his first term in office he provided little aid to the cause: he made few overtures to Congress; he appointed O'Connor to the Court despite pro-life hostility; he failed to implement fully the Republican platform concerning appointments of judges until 1985; and he did not press Lee to argue for the reversal of *Roe* in *Akron*. These failings disappointed pro-life forces, but they should not have. He knew he had no mandate on the subject—he had been elected despite his views on abortion. The situation changed somewhat with his landslide victory in 1984. Though he placed no real pressure on Congress, he and Meese acted on the promise to fill the federal judiciary with "right-thinking" judges. The elevation of Rehnquist and the appointments of Scalia and Kennedy were intended to inject a socially conservative bias, including a pro-life stance, into the law. In *Thornburgh*, the same message was delivered loud and clear: the administration wanted *Roe* to go. This, however, was not enough. The appointments of Scalia and Kennedy, while important, were insufficient to generate *Webster*. One additional vote was needed. Further, Fried's argument in *Thornburgh*, even by the estimation of his predecessor, was doomed to failure.

Still, these steps were clearly engineered to help the cause. Reagan and Meese probably knew, for example, that the Court would not overrule *Roe* in 1986, but by arguing for that result, they might up the stakes and placate the party's right wing. Where the duo went astray—perhaps even aiding the pro-choice side— was with the nomination of Robert Bork. The failed confirmation effort awoke a formerly apathetic public to issues of privacy and the possibility of significant legal change should Bork be confirmed. In this sense, the views of the public and the pressure they placed on key senators may have contributed to Bork's rejection. More important, though, was that in some measure the defeat enabled pro-choice forces to remain at bat before and even after *Webster*.

In sum, we do not argue that the political environment did not change between 1973 and 1989 and, relatedly, that those alterations did not contribute to the *Roe*-*Webster* dynamic. Yet the political environment alone was insufficiently different to explain the turnabout. In fact, at least on several scores, it was more favorable for abortion advocates in the days preceding *Webster* than it had been prior to *Roe*. Therefore, like the personnel changes on the Court, the environment was not the exclusive cause of the doctrinal reorientation announced in *Webster*.

THE PRO-CHOICE MOVEMENT

Did pro-choice advocates set the stage for, or contribute to, their own defeat in *Webster*? If so, we cannot attribute this to structural or organizational changes within the movement. The key players had not changed significantly over the sixteen-year period.[147] If anything, the pro-choice movement grew larger—with more organizations allying themselves—and was better financed. Although many of its pre-1973 constituency groups became complacent or turned to other matters after *Roe*, the movement made itself heard in important congressional debates and in virtually all post-*Roe* litigation. Its greatest weakness—grass-roots organization—was a constant throughout the period examined. The movement also employed basically the same strategy during this time. The actual sponsorship of litigation had not been particularly coordinated before *Roe* nor had it hinged on bringing test cases. That altered somewhat after *Roe*, with the RFP acting as a coordinator and an information clearinghouse, but a wide range of groups and attorneys continued to bring litigation. Moreover, their arguments had not changed significantly since 1973. Their later briefs evolved from Blackmun's opinion, yet striking parallels exist between the arguments made by Weddington in *Roe* and Susman in *Webster*. They even used amici in much the same way: to bring to the Court different perspectives on abortion and to fill in medical, psychological, policy, and women's interests gaps left open in their essentially legalistic efforts.

Herein, though, lies the problem: given the obvious changes in the political and legal environments—changes acknowledged by both sides—pro-choice arguments and strategies *should* have changed as well. Despite the vigor of their opponents, despite the entry of the solicitor general, and despite their narrowing margin in the Court, pro-choice forces never really believed that *Roe* would, or could, be overturned. When this possibility finally dawned on them in 1989, it was too late. As such, they never seriously raised alternative arguments that, while not saving all of *Roe*, would have protected at least some elements of its core holding.

Along the way, they ignored numerous red flags. First and foremost was O'Connor, to whom they—at least initially—paid little attention. Perhaps, given pro-life opposition to her appointment, they assumed they would have her vote. Or maybe they thought her gender would dictate her abortion jurisprudence. Or perhaps they really did not care; after all, they won *Roe* by a 7–2 margin. Whatever the reason, ignoring her turned out to be a grave error. She became a key, if not *the* key, player in a game where every vote counted.

Did pro-choice forces ever have an opportunity to win O'Connor? An emphatic answer, either way, would belie good scholarship. However, it seems clear that they had at least a fighting chance to do so. That chance appeared twice, in *Akron* (1983) and *Thornburgh* (1986). In *Akron*, O'Connor staked out her position that states could constitutionally regulate the abortion decision unless those regulations were unduly burdensome. Implicit in this approach was a tacit recognition of some kind of constitutionally based abortion right. In *Thornburgh*, she fleshed out the content of this position. To date, she has not strayed from the approach articulated in these decisions.

In arguing *Akron*, pro-choice interests essentially ignored O'Connor. The problem, of course, was that because this was her first abortion case, they lacked any indication of where she stood on the issue. Yet at that point she had been on the bench for two years. Her record, if studied, could have provided them with some guidance. It was clear, for example, that she was conservative but that she had some "liberal" moments—notably in gender discrimination cases.[148] Had they realized this and at least partially framed their arguments in *Akron* on equal protection grounds, they might not have lost any of the *Roe* majority and they might have gained an ally.

Close study of O'Connor's record would also have revealed that she was no radical or extremist. She was reluctant to rule broadly if she could do so narrowly. She equally disliked overturning legislation, preferring a restraintist posture. This brings us to the second and related red flag: Solicitor General Lee's amicus curiae brief. In light of O'Connor's emerging jurisprudence, the brief's unduly burdensome standard—however vaguely defined in briefs and orals—could quite possibly be expected to appeal to her. By adopting it in some form, she could unite the elements of her emerging jurisprudence in the area of abortion. If pro-choice forces had realized this, they could have demonstrated some of the pitfalls of the adoption of such a standard or alternatively—given its inherent vagueness—sought to define it differently than did the solicitor general by coupling it with the overarching logic of the *Roe* approach. Either option, but especially the latter, might have provided O'Connor with a semblance of a pro-choice peg on which to hang her own analysis. However, pro-choice forces chose instead to continue to press the same essential argument—grounded on absolute deference to *Roe*—that they had used since 1973.

Even if pro-choice forces did not recognize the appeal the unduly burdensome standard in Lee's argument might have for O'Connor, they should have responded to it. Although they did so publicly, loudly denouncing it as a political ploy, they failed to do so legally. Attorneys and amici—except for one player not usually involved in the abortion debate, the NAACP LDF—virtually ignored Lee's proposed standard instead of delivering a counterattack. Indeed, had they taken Lee's brief more seriously, had they marshaled substantial evidence to demonstrate that by adopting the unduly burdensome standard state legislation might fail, they might have salvaged O'Connor. After all, however appealing the standard may have been to her, it was vulnerable. The city of Akron's briefs embraced it only halfheartedly, and O'Connor herself rejected its linchpin— absolute deference to governmental legislation.

Having lost O'Connor's vote in *Akron*, the *Roe* majority slipped from seven to six justices. However, although the newest justice voted against the Blackmun bloc, her dissent did not explicitly call for outright reversal of *Roe*. Indeed, despite the fact that Rehnquist and White concurred in her opinion, it did not use their harsh anti-abortion rhetoric. It was at least conceivable, then, that she could support some kind of an abortion right—just not one grounded in the trimester logic of *Roe*. Because of this, *Thornburgh* stood as a second chance for pro-choice forces to get her support, even if for a somewhat diluted abortion right. Given the ill-defined content of her rendering of the unduly burdensome standard—although it was clear from *Akron* that she did not understand it to mean absolute deference to legislative majorities—pro-choice interests could have sought to define it in a way that would protect a woman's choice in many or most instances. This would have entailed backing off from the *Roe* logic in the name of saving the *Roe* right through expansive interpretation of the burdensome concept. Again, it bears noting that there was no *prima facie* reason to believe that O'Connor would be wholly unreceptive to this line of argument, especially given the administration's push in this case to get the Court to reject the right completely. The effectiveness of such a course cannot be known, however, since pro-choice advocates remained totally committed to promoting the dimensions of the abortion right as defined in *Roe*. This choice prevented them from strategically backtracking. Once again, they lost O'Connor's vote. Perhaps more important, they lost the chance to influence the development of her approach to the animation of the unduly burdensome standard.

With Burger's desertion in *Thornburgh*, only one vote separated the pro-choice victory from defeat. This was another red flag, indicating that a change in legal strategy and argumentation was warranted. But it was lost on pro-choice forces until 1989, when they faced what was at best a borderline Court. With O'Connor embracing the unduly burdensome standard and three justices squarely in the pro-life camp, that left Kennedy. He was not as accessible in 1989 as O'Connor had been in 1983. The newest justice had been appointed in 1988, three years into the Reagan and Meese "litmus test" scheme; he was a Catholic; and he was a man and thus did not share O'Connor's potentially unique perspective on what was, essentially, a woman's right. He was, in most ways, more like Bork than Powell.

In short, if *Webster* was a foregone conclusion, it was less the result of personnel changes and the political environment than of the strategies adopted by pro-choice litigators in an increasingly unstable legal environment hostile to its goals. If abortion advocates had focused on O'Connor from her first encounter with the issue, if they had paid more attention to Lee's brief, and if they had recognized their opportunity to develop her admittedly less-than-optimal approach, they could have significantly altered their argumentational strategy from 1983 on and possibly obtained her vote. We will never know because pro-choice forces remained rigidly locked into the logic of *Roe*. Such an approach may not have assured the continuation of a constitutionally grounded abortion right, but it might have limited its potential modification. If so, *Webster* might have discarded the *Roe* trimester approach while, at the same time, putting the abortion right itself on a stronger—seemingly less arbitrary—constitutional base. Such a ruling, conceivably, could have blunted much of the opposition to the abortion right and provided a stronger bulwark to its further erosion.

SEVEN

. . . .

THE LIFE

OF THE LAW:

UNDERSTANDING

THE DYNAMICS

OF LEGAL CHANGE

The framers of the U.S. Constitution convinced the people of the states to accept it by defending the document, in part, as establishing a limited government. These limitations were, at least structurally, to be imposed by law. A government under law would avoid arbitrary governance by treating similar situations similarly and by reserving large domains of human activity to individual choice subject to majority will under specified rules. Majoritarian institutions would prescribe day-to-day rules to govern the people, and the courts would apply those rules—so long as they were legitimate under the broad outlines of superior constitutional maxims—in an "inflexible and uniform" fashion (*Federalist Papers*, no. 78). As originally conceived and defended, then, the courts would be distinctly legal bodies charged with the task of maintaining and defending a constant application of generally accepted legal rules. In short, they would promote republican governance—composed of that curious blend of majoritarian- and rights-based values—by holding a steady hand on the throttle of the state; they would not have an independent political function.

Yet, from the beginning of the Republic, the operation of the courts—specifically that of the Supreme Court—was criticized as going beyond this understanding of the judicial role. In *Chisholm v. Georgia* (1793), the Court allowed two citizens of South Carolina to sue the state of Georgia for recovery of confiscated property. Fearing the reach of the federal government and its judicial arm, states' rights advocates successfully proposed ratification of the Eleventh Amendment to overturn this decision. With this, the interplay between the Court and the rest of the government concerning the process of legal change—the alteration in the definition and understanding of the rules under which governance would occur—began. This interplay has continued, in fits and starts, to the present.

Chisholm and the decisions that followed it suggest a basic truth about the nature of the American version of constitutional governance: its rules are not static, insusceptible to change. Further, this change is not solely directed by any one specific department of government but is the product of interchange between its various institutions and the popular mind. A primary contributor to this dialogue is the Supreme Court. After all, in the grand phrasing of Chief Justice Marshall, "it is emphatically the province and duty of the Court to say what the law is" (*Marbury v. Madison* 1803). This posture puts the Court in potential tension with the particularly legal role defined for it by the framers of the Constitution. If the rules of the law are not static, and the Court is their principal interpreter, the Court has an institutional role to play in the creation, direction, and nurture of legal change. This seems to subvert its initially articulated function and puts the Court at odds with that generally reactive and pristinely legal role that it was intended to play. At a minimum, it moves that body into the political realm implicated by a process of legal change. Thus, an institution initially defended on the basis of its independence from politics is placed squarely in its very web.

Even with this migration into a seemingly forbidden realm, the original understanding of the Supreme Court and its function could be maintained by strict adherence to "the rules laid down." It could conceivably remain "the least dangerous branch" if it avoided the taint of ordinary politics and simply applied old rules to new settings. At least three factors militate against this possibility. First, old rules may require shaping to apply to new contexts, and something other than the logic of the rules themselves is necessary to perform this modification. Into this void fits the mind of the judge. It is this role that prompted Cardozo (1921, 162) to write that judging was "the practice of an art." Second, judges do not come from nowhere. They are the products of governmental institutions that are explicitly structured and implicitly conditioned to reflect the political—not necessarily legal—concerns of the day. Third, much of the major business of the courts is brought to them by profoundly political entities— governments and interest groups—seeking advancement of their unquestionably political agendas. As such, the evolution of the role of the Court, as defined by it and others, seems to place it inescapably in the vortex of the politics of legal change.

Similar insights prompted the great jurist Oliver Wendell Holmes to claim that "the life of the law has not been logic: it has been experience." Still, the question remains: What factors condition the experience that drives the "life of the law"? More pointedly, why do judges do the things they do? As we note in chapter 2, different schools of thought have different answers to this question. Some legal scholars (positivists) tend to stress the "inner logic" of the law as driving its development, while others (legal realists) stress the subjectivity of judges in accounting for it. In what is this subjectivity rooted? Political scientists join the argument at this point and suggest an array of factors to be relevant, some judge-specific (for example, attitudes and values, role conceptions, and social backgrounds) and some context-specific (for example, political environment, fact patterns, and small group dynamics).

As to the more specific question that our study addresses—what factors explain relatively sudden shifts in legal doctrine—the conventional scholarly wisdom is clear: upheaval and replacement of sitting justices. As O'Brien (1990, 45) writes, "[T]he Court does not shift course in mid-stream without major changes in its composition." Moreover, this wisdom has descended from the ivory towers of the academy into the work-a-day world of practical politics, as the Court-manipulating strategies pursued by Franklin Roosevelt, Richard Nixon, and Ronald Reagan make abundantly clear. Even so, the relationship between the political and academic worlds was, at least initially, the opposite of that noted above. That is to say, events in the political world surely structured the way political scientists understood them. It is, one would suppose, no accident that the jurisprudential shift occasioned by the flood of Roosevelt appointees occurred just before the behavioral revolution enveloped the study of the Court. Further, the literature on the sturdiness (or lack thereof) of judicially generated legal change had its genesis in Robert Dahl's classic 1957 study, a study that Casper (1976) has shown to rest heavily and precariously on the constitutional litigation of New Deal legislation. From either the scholarly or the more political standpoint, then, it is taken as a given that legal change is prompted by the turnover of judicial personnel, and that this is directed by the president and a national law-making majority.

We think this conventional wisdom is wrong, or at least wrong in pertinent part. Clearly legal change can, and often does, result from clever presidential appointments to strategically significant judicial slots. Again, the Roosevelt example is the obvious case in point. Further, appointments may have the effect of eating slowly away at precedents that appointing presidents find noxious, as the Court's recent history with the exclusionary rule and the *Miranda* warnings demonstrate. This said, other important instances of legal change cannot be explained by the appointments of justices. For example, the Court that decided *Brown v. Board of Education* (1954) was not appointed by presidents with an overwhelming commitment to the demise of Jim Crow. Similarly, the unanimous decision in *United States v. Nixon* (1974) was handed down by a Court in part made up of justices appointed by the president against whom it ruled. While a link between appointments and judicial attitudes is clearly relevant in accounting for legal change, it—standing alone and in all cases (or even in all significant cases)—cannot explain the phenomenon in its entirety. The conventional wisdom needs modification.

The research we present in this book suggests the basis of such a modification. The cases we examine, the evidence we sift, and the conclusions we derive suggest that legal change, at least in the doctrine generated by the Supreme Court, is not solely a function of the movement of bodies to and from the bench. Neither is it simply a function of the climate of the times in which the relevant cases are decided; while that environment sets the context in which decisions are tendered, it does not decide them itself. Finally, legal change is not neatly prompted by the type of litigants who press claims on the Court; they help to set and structure the Court's agenda, but they do not decide its cases. All of these factors, while clearly relevant to the dynamics of doctrinal change, are insufficient to account for the observed shifts in the law.

Our finding, stated simply, is this: the law and the legal arguments grounded in law matter, and they matter dearly. The justices that hear these cases and the groups and governments that bring them are relevant factors in their eventual outcomes and the policies they produce, but it is the arguments they hear and make that—at least in the early stages of a doctrinal and decisional shift—seem to influence most clearly the content and direction of the legal change that results.

This should not, on reflection, be terribly startling. Judges are lawyers, and, while frequently they achieve attention and appointment on the basis of their political actions and positions, they are trained in the law and are taught to think like lawyers. Legal argument is the tool of their trade—the currency with which they conduct their business. It is, thus, not surprising that well-crafted legal arguments appeal to them in their judicial function. In this sense, the argument tendered in the *Federalist Papers* (no. 78) may not have been all that far off the mark. Hamilton may have been in error in seeing justices as operating completely outside of political pressures, but he seems to have been correct in his assumption that the law constrains and guides, at least to some extent, the decisions they tender. Insofar as this is the case, the common behavioral assumption—that judges are political actors who seek to maximize their policy preferences—must be seriously questioned. The life of the law may be experience, but it is experience filtered through a peculiarly legalistic logic.

REEVALUATING THE CONVENTIONAL WISDOM: FACTORS GENERATING LEGAL CHANGE

If our close and extended study of the Supreme Court's shifts in the areas of capital punishment and abortion demonstrates nothing else, it illustrates that legal change—an alteration in the constitutional doctrine governing a particular area of law—occurs in a matrix rife with complexity. A stunning and, in some cases, analytically numbing array of forces press contemporaneously on the justices as they work in controversial areas of the law. Previous social scientific examinations of this phenomenon have located three general sets of factors as especially relevant in accounting for the process of legal change: changes on the Supreme Court, be they in personnel or in the posture of one or a few strategically significant justices; changes in the environmental pressures not traditionally understood to be relevant to judicial decision making, for example, public opinion and the machinations of other governmental actors; and changes in the judicial activity of interest groups, which condition the kinds of cases and issues the Court decides and the argumentational and informational context in which those decisions are rendered. Add to these explanations the more traditionally legalistic approach forwarded by some scholars—that the logic of the law contains the seeds of its evolution—and we have four different theories of legal change.

Our study represented an effort to test the explanatory efficacy of these theories by placing the factors at their core into a single interpretive framework. We then used this framework to guide our examination of two areas of political and legal conflict that have recently undergone substantial doctrinal change. In our intensive examination of the litigation of death penalty and abortion issues, we sought to do two things: explain the legal shifts embedded in these areas and ascertain the contribution of the factors noted above in conditioning that change.

As one would expect, the three explanatory factors drawn from the political science literature all demonstrate some utility in coming to grips with the doctrinal alterations we investigated. To begin with, changes on the Supreme Court—in terms of both its composition and the orientation of individual justices—obviously affected the direction of the law in these areas. In the capital punishment cases, the slim 5-vote *Furman* majority was made unsure by the departure of Douglas and his replacement with Stevens. In the abortion cases, the replacement of *Roe* stalwarts Douglas, Stewart, and Powell with Stevens, O'Connor, and Kennedy, the shift of Burger from a pro- to an anti-*Roe* posture, and his subsequent replacement with Scalia clearly put the once robust seven-member abortion majority at risk. Given that the doctrine in both of these areas shifted after these modifications occurred, it is tempting to cede causal significance to these personnel alterations; they obviously coincided with the legal change we seek to explain, and, especially in the abortion case, the new members made possible the numeric majorities that ushered in the Court's reversal.

While these personnel alterations clearly facilitated the legal changes we examine, it is quite another matter to conclude that they caused them. The inadequacy of the argument that changes in the Court caused the legal shifts is most obvious in the death penalty cases. Had Stevens's appointment been crucial to the reversal manifest in *Gregg v. Georgia* (1976), it would have come down as a 5–4 decision, but instead the vote was 7–2. White and Stewart also defected from the *Furman* majority. Even in the abortion case, where all appointees after Stevens opposed the *Roe* formulation, the decision in *Webster v. Reproductive Health Services* (1989) cannot simply be attributed to these personnel changes. O'Connor's dissenting opinions in *Akron* (1983) and *Thornburgh* (1986)—unlike similar efforts by White and Rehnquist—did not explicitly call for *Roe*'s reversal; like her concurrence in *Webster*, they merely rejected its logic. Thus, it may be the case that *Furman* and *Roe* did not die, necessarily, as the result of personnel changes on the Court.

Similarly, individual shifts among the justices cannot, by themselves, explain the doctrinal revolutions under study. In the abortion example, save for Burger's much publicized desertion of *Roe* in *Thornburgh*,[1] no justices strayed far from the positions they initially staked out.[2] It could be argued that O'Connor shifted her position between *Akron* and *Thornburgh* and *Webster*, but only at the cost of ignoring the reasoning in her earlier dissents. Taking these opinions at face value, her position also remained constant. The death penalty cases are more ripe for the hypothesis that individual changes account for legal changes; Stewart and White did shift their votes from an anti– to a pro–capital punishment posture in *Gregg*, but the question of why they shifted looms large. They may have changed their stances due to idiosyncratic factors, or they may have been reacting to something in the environment surrounding them. If the former accounts for their shift, then it may not be amenable to scholarly analysis; if the explanation lies in the latter, then we must look elsewhere to explain their votes.

As Court-based explanations fail to capture doctrinal change in its totality, those that center on environmental causes also falter. In reviewing the capital punishment and abortion cases, we paid particular attention to the effect that aggregated public opinion and the activities of other governmental actors had on the resolution of the cases before the Court. We found little systematic influence. Gross public opinion—commonly reported in Gallup polls and other similar surveys—had no discernible effect on the Court. In the case of abortion, *Roe* did not prompt—as far as we can tell—any migration of votes from one camp to the other. Indeed, what the data seem to show is a remarkable consistency among the public on this question from 1973 to the present. *Roe*'s effect, if any, was to solidify and intensify people's attachment to their initial positions. In contrast, public opinion did shift after *Furman* came down, but it shifted from majority support for capital punishment to even greater majority support; the high point of public support for abolition came in 1967, well before the Supreme Court entered this legal arena with seriousness. In short, the National Association for the Advancement of Colored People Legal Defense Fund (NAACP LDF) and other abolitionist forces succeeded in *Furman* in spite of rather than because of popular support for their policy position. This being the case, it is hard to see how the post-*Furman* backlash, as measured by public opinion polls, led to a contrary result in *Gregg*.

The attitude of the public, however, is not the only environmental factor of relevance to the Court. The activities and responses of other governmental actors also come into play. We examined the actions and reactions of a host of such entities in the issue areas explored here. In both case studies, we saw rapid mobilization of governments, state and federal, to blunt or reverse the effects of *Furman* and *Roe*. Some state governments quickly returned to the legislative drawing boards in an effort to reimpose their previous policy values as law. Congress passed legislation designed to reassert portions of the policies struck by the Court.[3] Presidents failed to come to the aid of the Court and defend the correctness of its decisions.[4] Indeed, administrations hostile to the newly articulated principles ultimately sent their solicitors general into the Court to encourage it to reconsider, limit, or reject them. Under such pressures from various levels of government, perhaps it is not surprising that the Court buckled and reversed its legal position.

Still, this explanation is not entirely satisfactory. Despite the clear governmental mobilizations in the wake of the *Furman* and *Roe* decisions, they did little more than to reassert the essential correctness of the legislative climate that existed before 1972 and 1973, respectively. As with the more general indicators of public opinion, these mobilizations simply told the Court, in effect, "you are wrong." In this sense, the political environment was as unfavorable in 1972 and 1973 when *Furman* and *Roe* were handed down as it was in 1976 and 1989 when *Gregg* and *Webster* were announced. Further, the Court has handed down other controversial decisions—on questions as sensitive as racial discrimination, school prayer, and freedom of expression, to name just a few—that elicited similar responses from other governmental bodies, and yet these mobilizations did not produce the kind of judicial reversal and legal change we see here. Why not? The answer seems obvious: mobilization of political bodies against a judicial decision does not cause legal change. This is not to say that such mobilizations are irrelevant to doctrinal shifts, but only that they cannot alone be taken as sufficient to prompt it.

The third set of factors we examined in search of an explanation for legal change involved interest groups. Because groups are part of the political environment in which Courts make their decisions, we could have integrated them into our second category. Yet groups are more than simple components of the Court's environment: the growing literature on their role in litigation demonstrates that they are both agents reacting to various political stimuli and architects of those stimuli. Because of their capacity to act as repeat players—a capacity that transforms them from "ordinary" to "sublime" litigators able to profoundly immerse themselves in an area of legal and political controversy—we thought they merited distinct analytical treatment, in spite of the cost this imposed on tidy conceptualization.

The literature examining their litigation ventures avers that groups are dynamic contributors to the process of legal change; our findings suggest that this is true, but that they perform this function in a somewhat counterintuitive (at least from the perspective of "modern" political science) fashion. Group involvement in litigation is part of the pluralist process. Unlike the more traditional arenas of group lobbying, however, their import is not so much derived from their numbers but is more a function of the kinds of arguments they present to a Court at least partly concerned with fitting a frequently amorphous body of rules, precedents, and doctrine to extant disputes. We found that group litigation is a part of the pluralism of American judicial politics, but that its expression is more through the arguments tendered at bar than through the brute number of participating groups. While numbers frequently may be crucial to other group influence efforts, argument is central to those channeled through the courts. It is here where groups most directly influence legal change; they foster and seek to guide a pluralism of legal argument toward desired policy goals. Sometimes they win, sometimes they lose. Either way, their efforts lend a clear dynamic to the process of legal change.

The abortion and death penalty examples amply demonstrate the role that groups play in setting the issue agenda pressed on American courts. The NAACP LDF, more than any other actor, was responsible for turning the Supreme Court's attention to larger questions concerning the constitutional permissibility of death as a state-imposed criminal punishment. Similarly, the Association for the Study of Abortion, the American Civil Liberties Union (ACLU), and others engineered the "avalanche" of abortion cases of which *Roe* and *Doe* were a part. By winning their initial cases at the apex of the American judiciary, these groups prompted new cycles of law and politics, which they then were responsible for controlling. Their ultimate inability to exercise this control through the means available to them contributed to the loss, at least in terms of legal doctrine, of their initial gains. It is in this dynamic that legal change occurred.

The losses suffered by these groups were not directly a function of the numbers they mobilized. The abortion and capital punishment cases show a clear difference in the numbers of groups involved. The latter remained largely the organized domain of the LDF (and, to a lesser extent, the ACLU) and the various governments that quickly moved to amend and reinstitute their capital procedures; there was no grand mobilization of other groups to change the context of litigation of this issue. The abortion cases present an almost opposite example. *Roe*, in addition to changing the law, prompted mobilization of a wide variety of groups on both sides of the question, especially on the pro-life side. Yet the Court—in short order in *Gregg* and over a somewhat longer period of time in *Webster*—eventually reversed itself in both areas. This suggests that the number and configuration of groups expressing their positions to the Court, while not irrelevant, is not a central factor accounting for the legal change observed in both areas of law.

If not by their sheer numbers, how do groups influence legal outcomes? The abortion and death penalty examples both point in the same direction: by their choices of which arguments to tender and which to ignore. In *Furman* and *Roe*, the Supreme Court adopted, in bits and pieces, the arguments pressed on it by the liberal interests that brought the litigation. The question remains, however, why did the arguments of these groups prevail in 1972 and 1973 but fail in 1976 and 1989? In the previous chapters, and in the analysis above, we have suggested that environmental- and Court-based factors cannot fully account for the shifts, and that something internal to the organizational dynamics that made possible the initial victories contributed to their ultimate defeat. This something is the arguments these groups pressed on the Courts. In essence, these arguments, and the group attorneys and officials who articulated and made them, were too inflexible to accommodate the continued preservation of their initial victories.

Having won their points in *Furman* and *Roe*, abolitionists and pro-choicers sought to maintain their legal and policy victories through reliance on the arguments that worked to give them their initial victories. This failed in the arena of capital punishment because the LDF misread the doctrinal glue that held the *Furman* majority together and continued to advance an absolute abolitionist position on a Court that, as *Gregg* clearly showed, was not generally supportive of such an approach. Death, although "different" for the LDF and Justices Brennan and Marshall, was not such for the majority of the Court. By pinning its argument to this strategic assumption, the LDF lost some of the justices it held in *Furman* on more procedural grounds to the former *Furman* dissenters. In so doing, it set the argumentational stage for a legal change unfavorable to the abolitionists' stated goal: elimination of death as a legitimate criminal punishment.

The same occurred in the abortion cases. Having won a strong endorsement of a woman's "right to chose" in *Roe*, pro-choicers attached themselves to the problematic trimester logic of Blackmun's opinion and pursued it in all subsequent litigations. Save for the funding cases, this tack worked well enough through the remainder of the 1970s. A chill wind, from their perspective, began to blow when Ronald Reagan went to the White House in 1981, and their arguments did nothing to block the harshest possible bite of this wind—the loss of the constitutional status of an abortion right. Despite being faced with Reagan appointees, some of whom replaced *Roe* supporters, pro-choice litigators continued to stress the trimester logic and the inviolability of the abortion right. Even when O'Connor signaled that something less than an absolute abortion right might be found in the vague confines of the Fourteenth Amendment, prochoice advocates continued to stress its absolute nature, at least in the first and second trimesters. Of course, in making this argument they had *Roe* on their side, but all signs were that the 1973 decision was losing its hold on a majority of the Court. Had pro-choicers bowed to the seeming inevitability of some change in the contours of the abortion right—had they modified the arguments they made before the Court, backtracking strategically from *Roe*'s absolutist connotations—they may have been able to protect, at least in part, the core of their 1973 victory. This they did not do, and the possibility of maintaining a constitutional basis for the abortion right seems irreparably lost. Pro-choice litigators—by doggedly clinging to an absolute attachment to *Roe*—set the argumentational stage for a legal change unfavorable to their stated goal: protection of an abortion right lodged in the Constitution.

By continuing to press for legal interpretations that would provide absolute and conclusive victories, both abolitionists and pro-choicers set the stage for their own defeat. Given unfavorable political environments—both in terms of subsequent appointments to the Court and continued state legislation in clear opposition to the command of the Court—it may be that these forces could not have maintained their victories over time even if they had strategically altered their argumentational postures. What is indisputable, however, is that these litigators did not shift their ground to avoid the potentially pernicious effects of these developments. Rather, they continued to hoe the same argumentational row, to press for the full yield of what they felt they had previously harvested.

They were blinded to the necessity of strategic backtracking by the tyranny of absolutes, the belief that to win big once is to establish for all time the predential base for future legal victories.

The potential for succumbing to the tyranny of absolutes calls into question the ability of group litigation (and, perhaps, litigation more generally) to achieve and sustain, over time, what are essentially political policy outcomes. Courts and attorneys tend to envision law as black and white, involving distinct rights and duties or obligations. This approach—and the mindset that produces it—may leave little room for the kinds of strategic retreat that are often necessary to preserve one-time victories and that are frequently employed in legislative and executive policy arenas. In this sense, judicial pathways may impose a straitjacket on the attempts of those who use them to create and advance an evolving policy development. Judge-made law may form an environment, especially for highly controversial issues, that forces groups not only to keep on winning their cases to advance and protect their goals but to continue using arguments based on precedents that are losing the support they may have once enjoyed. A tyranny of absolutes—framing what are at core essentially political concerns as basically legal in nature and forcing their maintenance as "law" to hinge on unbending obeisance to precedent based on unassailable "rights"—may set the stage for much legal change in controversial areas of public policy.

In this sense, the tyranny of absolutes may be a logical corollary to what Scheingold (1974) has dubbed "the myth of rights"—the notion that judicially won and crafted rights are self-executing. Scheingold, however, does not say that all judicially claimed rights are open to neglect in terms of implementation but only that they must continue to be pressed on responsible entities to ensure their vitality. Similarly, legal change won through the courts need not necessarily fall into this trap. A more flexible approach to the litigation and maintenance of judicial policy judgments—one which makes use of a broad array of legal arguments and does not deify the argument used to win the policy initially—may be able to resist the pressures of wholesale legal change.

Before we offer our concluding remarks, we should reiterate what we are and are not saying. We are *not* saying that Court-based factors and environmental factors—behaviorally understood and examined—are irrelevant in explaining the kind of legal change we have examined. They clearly are relevant. Indeed, gross shifts in the personnel populating the Court—for example, the Roosevelt New Deal experience and the Warren "revolution"—are inescapably tied to the development of peculiarly twentieth-century American law. Similarly, the environmental forces associated with the raised consciousness of the 1960s and 1970s as to the role of women in American society clearly affected the Court's jurisprudence on gender discrimination.[5] These factors, in short, while clearly relevant to legal change at the level of Supreme Court doctrine, do not necessarily cause it; they *can* prompt change, but they do not necessarily do so.

What we *are* saying is that beneath the Court-based and environmental factors that stimulate doctrinal change by the Supreme Court lurk the arguments made by the attorneys and interests that sponsor and support constitutional litigation. These arguments, and the justices' response to them—long neglected by political scientists as the stuff of insincere rationalization of mere political ends— seem to have a life of their own. Trained in "the law" and "legal thinking" long before they become advocates and jurists, the language of the law seems to have a reality and motive force that shapes, to a large degree, the paths that the law enunciated by the Court takes. Interested advocates spend an immense amount of time forging and fashioning arguments grounded in "the law," and there is substantial evidence that the less ideologically driven justices[6] take these arguments seriously and account for them in explaining the positions they take. In this sense, the life of the law *is* experience, but it is not experience in the absence of logic; rather, it is experience filtered through logic. To ignore this is to ignore much of the dynamics of legal change, and much of what separates it from other paths of policy alteration.

CONCLUSION

In closing, we are reminded of T. S. Eliot's poem, "The Hollow Men": "This is the way the world ends, not with a bang but a whimper." The stuff of political science is not the stuff that changes worlds; it is the stuff that helps us better to understand and explain a segment of the world in which we live. This is not to belittle political science as a field of scholarship, nor is it to suggest that what we describe and seek to explain here is insignificant; it is merely to put it in context. Studies of legal change have produced the conventional wisdom that political factors are responsible for doctrinal development and alteration. In significant part, this is true; but we contend that it is not the whole story. Our conclusions may sound like a whimper, but they are sufficiently loud to prompt a rethinking of this received wisdom.

We set out to use a framework, drawn from various literatures on the Supreme Court, to investigate and explain the forces that condition legal change. Focusing on the Court, the political environment in which its members toil, and the organized pressures brought directly to bear on it, we examined intensively the litigation of capital punishment and abortion questions. Although all of the factors identified in the literature are relevant to the dynamics of legal change, we found that the Court, constituted as a legal body by the framers but understood as a political body by political scientists, exhibits a great deal of sensitivity and responsiveness to the arguments brought before it as it resolves some of the most pressing issues of the day. Insofar as the conventional wisdom of political science suggests otherwise, and clearly since the behavioral revolution much of it does, we find it to be in error.

Court-based and environmental factors cannot adequately account for the legal change between *Furman* (1972) and *Gregg* (1976), and *Roe* (1973) and *Webster* (1989), although they clearly conditioned it. But below a certain threshold—be it massive restructuring of the Court by ideologically determined presidents or overwhelming and active mass resistance to its decisions—the path of the law is charted by conversations between lawyers (judges and advocates) conducted in a language and using a terminology fashioned and conveyed through a central shared experience (law school and participation in the legal profession). Even if the life of the law is experience, as Holmes suggested, it is experience frequently interpreted, codified, and applied by lawyers—people for whom, by training, inclination, and perhaps instinct, experience is sorted by logic.

Central to the lessons one draws from the capital punishment and abortion examples is that the framing of the legal arguments tendered before the Court was important to the ultimate resolution of the issues. In both cases, initial "liberal" victories were forged and then lost, in significant part, because their defenders doggedly clung to their understanding of the Court's logic. This fatally constrained their ability to shift argumentational grounds when those victories came under threat. This we have called the "tyranny of absolutes," the notion that legal arguments, once seemingly won, are absolute and defensible only on those grounds. Without the argumentational flexibility to adapt to new conditions, the tyranny of absolutes led abolitionists and pro-choice advocates to dig their own doctrinal graves by ignoring alternative arguments that might have saved the underlying goals their initial victories were intended to achieve and protect.

In light of this, explications of legal change cannot focus wholly on political factors without distorting the process they seek to explain. They must incorporate, as part of their analytical apparatus, the idea of law and the centrality of legal argument.[7] They must look at the pluralism of legal arguments presented before the Court as well as the pluralism of interests bringing those arguments. This approach does not take us outside of the behavioral perspective; indeed, it is grounded in concerns that are explicitly empirical and political in nature. It may be, for example, that in fashioning legal arguments to advance political goals, organized litigators seek to remap the attitudinal space in which the justices sort and resolve difficult issues in their own minds. If so, even from a strongly behavioral perspective, the law clearly matters. The life of the law, thus, *is* a function of shared experience, but it is an experience grounded, in part, in the legalistic norms and logical methods of the pluralist elites who struggle to define, condition, and control its path. Accounting for this, and building it into our models, will enable political scientists to better capture the phenomenon of legal change—a change frequently produced not with a bang but a with a whimper.

APPENDIX I

PROFILE OF CAPITAL PUNISHMENT CASES

Furman v. Georgia[a] (408 U.S. 238, 1972)	*Gregg v. Georgia*[b] (428 U.S. 153, 1976)	*McCleskey v. Kemp*[c] (483 U.S. 776, 1987)
Question: Do Georgia's procedures for implementing the death penalty violate constitutional guarantees?	Question: Do Georgia's procedures for implementing the death penalty violate constitutional guarantees?	Question: Do Georgia's procedures for implementing the death penalty violate constitutional guarantees?
Court's Response: Yes *Majority:* Douglas, Brennan, Stewart, White, Marshall *Minority:* Burger, Blackmun, Powell, Rehnquist	Court's Response: No *Majority:* Powell, Stewart, White, Burger, Rehnquist *Minority:* Brennan, Marshall	Court's Response: No *Majority:* Powell, Rehnquist, O'Connor, White, Scalia *Minority:* Brennan, Marshall, Stevens, Blackmun
Attorney for Appellant: Jack Greenberg (NAACP LDF)	Attorney for Appellant: G. Harrison (Court-appointed)	Attorney for Appellant: John Charles Boger (NAACP LDF)
Attorney for Appellee: Dorothy Beasley (assistant attorney general)	Attorney for Appellee: G. Thomas Davis (assistant attorney general)	Attorney for Appellee: Mary Beth Westmoreland (assistant attorney general)
Amici Curiae to Reverse: 1. Alaska 2. ACLU 3. Committee of Psychiatrists for Evaluation of the Death Penalty[e] 4. Individuals (4)	Amici Curiae to Reverse:[d] 1. Amnesty International 2. NAACP LDF	Amici Curiae to Reverse: 1. Congressional Black Caucus Rights Law Group 2. Congressional Black Caucus, NAACP, Lawyers' Committee for Civil Rights under Law

Furman v. Georgia[a] (408 U.S. 238, 1972)	*Gregg v. Georgia*[b] (428 U.S. 153, 1976)	*McCleskey v. Kemp*[c] (483 U.S. 776, 1987)

5. NAACP, National Urban League, Southern Christian Leadership Conference, Mexican American LDF, National Council of Negro Women
6. National Council of Churches of Christ of the U.S.A.[e], American Friends Service Committee, Board of the Ministry of the Lutheran Church of America, Church of Brethren General Board, Council for Christian Social Action of the United Church of Christ, Department of Church in Society of the Christian Church, The Presiding Bishop of the Episcopal Church in the U.S., General Board of Christian Social Concerns of the United Methodist Church, Greek Orthodox Archdiocese of North and South America, United Presbyterian Church in the U.S.A., National Catholic Conference for Interracial Justice, National Coalition of American Nuns
7. Synagogue Council (for its 6 constituent members), American Jewish Congress[f]
8. West Virginia Council of Churches, Christian Church in West Virginia, United Methodist Church (W.Va.)

3. International Human Rights Law Group
4. Professors (2) and doctors (4)

CAPITAL PUNISHMENT CASES

Furman v. Georgia[a] (408 U.S. 238, 1972)	*Gregg v. Georgia*[b] (428 U.S. 153, 1976)	*McCleskey v. Kemp*[c] (483 U.S. 776, 1987)
Amici Curiae to Affirm 1. Indiana	Amici Curiae to Affirm 1. California 2. United States	Amici Curiae to Affirm 1. California, Los Angeles 2. Washington Legal Foundation, Allied Educational Foundation

Note: When interests and individuals participate as amici, they usually identify their organizational affiliation (if any) on the cover of their briefs. In contrast, briefs filed by attorneys representing the parties to litigation generally do not identify group involvement. Researchers seeking to determine whether groups sponsored particular cases must, then, rely on other sources. Our task in identifying group involvement of attorneys arguing the cases profiled in this appendix was simplified by the fact that all of the cases have been the subject of significant commentary, indicating whether they were or were not brought by group attorneys and identifying those groups that did sponsor them.

[a]Data obtained from Kurland and Casper (1975[a]).

[b]Data obtained from *U.S. Supreme Court Records and Briefs*, BNA's Law Reprints, no. 74-6257.

[c]Data obtained from *U.S. Supreme Court Records and Briefs*, Congressional Information Service, no. 84-6811.

[d]Some of the following briefs were filed jointly in *Gregg* and the four other capital punishment cases of 1976: *Jurek v. Texas*, *Woodson v. North Carolina*, *Profitt v. Florida*, and *Roberts v. Louisiana*. Briefs filed in one of these cases but not in *Gregg* are not listed below.

[e]See Meltsner 1973, 255-56.

[f]These were the Central Conference of American Rabbis, Rabbinical Assembly of America, Rabbinical Council of America, Union of American Hebrew Congregations, Union of Orthodox Jewish Congregations of America, and United Synagogue Council of America.

APPENDIX 2

PROFILE OF ABORTION CASES

Roe v. Wade[a] (410 U.S. 113, 1973)	*Webster v. Reproductive Health Services*[b] (492 U.S. 490, 1989)
Question: Can states proscribe abortion?	Question: Can states proscribe or restrict abortion?

Court's Response: Not fundamentally
  Majority: Blackmun, Powell, `
  Brennan, Marshall, Douglas,
  Burger, Stewart
  Minority: White, Rehnquist
	Court's Response: Yes
	  Majority: O'Connor, Rehnquist, Scalia,
	  Kennedy, White
	
	  Minority: Marshall, Blackmun, Brennan,
	  Stevens

Attorneys for Appellants:
  Roy Lucas (James Madison Law
  Institute)
  Norman Dorsen (New York
  University Law School)
  Linda Coffee
  Sarah Weddington
	Attorney for Appellees:
	  Frank Susman (Reproductive Health Services)
	  Roger K. Evans (Planned Parenthood
	  Federation of America)
	  Janet Benshoof (ACLU Foundation)

Attorney for Appellee:
  Henry Wade (district attorney)
  Crawford Martin (attorney general)
	Attorney for Appellant:
	  William Webster (attorney general)

Amici Curiae to Reverse 1. American College of Obstetricians and Gynecologists, American Psychiatric Association, American Medical Women's Association, New York Academy of Medicine, and 178 doctors 2. American Ethical Union, Ameri-	Amici Curiae to Affirm 1. ACLU, National Education Association, People for the American Way, Newspaper Guild, National Writers Union, Fresno Free Club Foundation 2. American Historians (281) 3. American Jewish Congress, Board of Homeland Ministries—United Church of

Roe v. Wade[a] (410 U.S. 113, 1973)	Webster v. Reproductive Health Services[b] (109 S.Ct. 3040, 1989)

can Friends Service Committee, American Humanist Association, American Jewish Congress, Episcopal Diocese of New York, New York State Council of Churches, Union of American Hebrew Congregations, United Church of Christ, Unitarian Universalist Association, Social Concerns of the United Methodist Church
3. American Association of University Women, National Board of the YWCA, NOW, National Women's Conference of the American Ethical Union, Professional Women's Caucus, Unitarian Universalist Women's Federation, Women's Alliance of First Unitarian Church of Dallas, and 46 individuals
4. California Committee to Legalize Abortion, South Bay Chapter of NOW, Zero Population Growth, and 2 women
5. By CCR: New Women Lawyers, Women's Health and Abortion Project, National Abortion Action Coalition
6. National Legal Program on Health Problems for the Poor, National Welfare Rights Organization, American Public Health Association
7. Planned Parenthood, American Association of Planned Parenthood Physicians

Christ, National Jewish Community Relations Advisory Council, Presbyterian Church U.S.A., Religious Coalition for Abortion Rights, St. Louis Catholics for a Choice, Albuquerque Monthly Meeting of Religious Society Friends, American Friends Service Committee, American Humanist Association, American Jewish Committee, Americans for Religious Liberty, Anti-Defamation League, Commission on Social Action of Reformed Judaism, Episcopal Diocese of Massachusetts—Women in Crisis Committee, Episcopal Diocese of New York, Episcopal Women's Caucus, Federation of Reconstructionist Congregations and Havurot, General Board of Church and Society—United Methodist Church, Health Institute of Women Today, Jewish Labor Committee, NA'MAT, National Assembly of Religious Women, North American Federation of Temple Youth, Union of American Hebrew Congregations, Unitarian Universalist Association, Unitarian Universalist Women's Federation, United Church of Christ Coordinating Center for Women, Washington Ethical Action Center of the American Ethical Union, Women in Ministry—Garrett Evangelical Seminary, Women in Mission and Ministry—Episcopal Church U.S.A., Women's League for Conservative Judaism, 8 Episcopal Bishops
4. American Library Association, Freedom to Read Foundation
5. American Medical Association, American Academy of Child and Adolescent Psychiatry, American Academy of Pediatrics, American College of Obstetricians and Gynecologists, American Fertility Society, American Medical Women's Association, American Psychiatric Association, American Society of Human Genetics

Roe v. Wade[a] (410 U.S. 113, 1973)	*Webster v. Reproductive Health Services*[b] (109 S.Ct. 3040, 1989)

6. American Nurses Association, Nurses Association of the ACOG

7. American Public Health Association, Alan Guttmacher Institute, American College of Preventive Medicine, California Physicians for Choice, California Republicans for Choice, City of New York, Massachusetts Department of Public Health, Berkeley School of Public Health, National Abortion Federation, New York State Republican Family Committee, 3 deans/chairs

8. American Psychological Association

9. Americans for Democratic Action, Coalition of Labor Union Women, Committee for Interns and Residents, Federally Employed Women, Public Employee Department of American Federation of Labor and Congress of Industrial Organizations

10. Americans United for Separation of Church and State

11. Association of Reproductive Health Professionals, National Society of Genetic Counselors, Association of Sex Educators and Therapists, Sex Information and Education Council of the United States, Ferre Institute, Cedar Rapids Clinic for Women, Fox Valley Reproductive Health Care Center, 6 medical school deans/chairs, 64 other individuals

12. Attorneys General of California, Colorado, Massachusetts, New York, Texas, Vermont

13. Bioethicists for Privacy

14. California NOW, San Jose–South Bay Chapter of NOW, California Alliance Concerned with School Age Parents, 6 individuals

15. Canadian Women's organizations[c]

16. Catholics for a Free Choice, Chicago Catholic Women, National Coalition of American Nuns, Women in Spirit of Colorado Task Force

17. Center for Population Options, Society for

Roe v. Wade[a] (410 U.S. 113, 1973)	Webster v. Reproductive Health Services[b] (109 S.Ct. 3040, 1989)
	Adolescent Medicine, Juvenile Law Center, Judicial Consent for Minors Referral Panel 18. Committees on Civil Rights, Medicine and Law, and Sex and Law of the Association of the Bar of the City of New York, Arizona Attorneys Action Council, Beverly Hills Bar Association, Committee on Women's Rights of the New York County Lawyers' Association, Lawyers Club of San Diego, Women's Bar Association of Illinois, Women's Bar Association of the State of New York 19. Group of American Law Professors 20. International Women's Health Organizations[d] 21. Legislators from 32 states (608) 22. Members of Congress (140) 23. National Association of Public Hospitals 24. National Association of Women Lawyers, National Conference of Women's Bar Associates 25. National Coalition against Domestic Violence 26. National Council of Negro Women, National Urban League, American Indian Health Care Association, Asian American Legal Defense Fund, Committee for Hispanic Children and Families, Mexican American Legal Defense and Education Fund, National Black Women's Health Project, National Institute of Women of Color, National Women's Health Network, Organizacion Nacional de la Salud de la Mujer Latina, Organization of Asian Women, Puerto Rican Legal Defense and Education Fund, Women of Color Partnership Program of the Religious Coalition for Abortion Rights, Women of All Red Nations—North Dakota, YWCA of the U.S.A.[e] 27. National Family Planning and Reproductive Health Association 28. NOW 29. Population-Environmental Balance, Popula-

Roe v. Wade[a] (410 U.S. 113, 1973)	Webster v. Reproductive Health Services[b] (109 S.Ct. 3040, 1989)

tion Communication, Sierra Club, World Population Society, Worldwatch Institute, Jessie Smith Noyes Foundation, Zero Population Growth

30. Scientists and Physicians (167)

31. Seventy-seven Organizations Committed to Equality[f]

32. 2,887 Women Who Had Abortions and 627 Friends

Amici Curiae to Affirm

1. Americans United for Life

2. Arizona, Connecticut, Kentucky, Nebraska, Utah

3. Certain physicians and fellows of the American College of Obstetricians and Gynecologists

4. Georgia

5. Women for the Unborn, Celebrate Life, Women Concerned for the Unborn, Minnesota Citizens for Life, New York State Columbiettes, 87 nurses, 55 doctors

Amici Curiae to Reverse[g]

1. Agudeth Israel of America

2. Alabama Lawyers for Unborn Children

3. Edward Allen

4. American Academy of Medical Ethics

5. American Association of Pro-Life Ob-Gyns, American Association of Pro-Life Pediatricians

6. American Collegians for Life, Catholic League for Religious and Civil Liberty

7. American Family Association

8. American Life League

9. Association for Public Justice, Value of Life Committee

10. Attorneys General of Louisiana, Arizona, Idaho, Pennsylvania, Wisconsin

11. Birthright, Inc.

12. Catholic Health Association of the U.S.

13. Catholic Lawyers Guild

14. Catholics United for Life, National Organization of Episcopalians for Life, Presbyterians Pro-Life, American Baptist Friends of Life, Baptists for Life, Southern Baptists for Life, Lutherans for Life, Moravians for Life, United Church of Christ Friends for Life, Task Force of United Methodists on Abortion and Sexuality, Christian Action Council

15. Center for Judicial Studies, 56 Members of Congress

16. Christian Advocates Serving Evangelism

17. Covenant House, Good Counsel

Roe v. Wade[a] (410 U.S. 113, 1973)	*Webster v. Reproductive Health Services*[b] (109 S.Ct. 3040, 1989)
	18. Doctors for Life, Missouri Doctors for Life, Missouri Citizens for Life, Lawyers for Life
	19. Feminists for Life of America, Women Exploited by Abortion of Greater Kansas City, National Association of Pro-Life Nurses, Let Me Live, Elliot Institute of Social Sciences Research
	20. Focus on Family, Family Research Council of America
	21. Free Speech Advocates
	22. Holy Orthodox Church
	23. Human Life International
	24. International Right to Life Federations
	25. Larry Joyce
	26. Knights of Columbus
	27. Lutheran Church—Missouri Synod, Christian Life Commission of the Southern Baptist Convention, National Association of Evangelicals
	28. James Joseph Lynch, Jr.
	29. Paul Marx
	30. Members of Congress (53)
	31. Members of Missouri General Assembly (127)
	32. Members of the Pennsylvania General Assembly (69)
	33. Missouri Catholic Conference
	34. Bernard Nathanson, M.D.
	35. National Legal Foundation
	36. National Right to Life Committee
	37. New England Christian Action Council
	38. Right to Life Advocates
	39. Right to Life League of Southern California
	40. Rutherford Institute, Rutherford Institutes of Alabama, Arkansas, California, Colorado, Connecticut, Florida, Georgia, Kentucky, Michigan, Minnesota, Montana, Nebraska, Ohio, Pennsylvania, Tennessee, Texas, Virginia, West Virginia
	41. State Legislators

Roe v. Wade[a]	Webster v. Reproductive Health Services[b]
(410 U.S. 113, 1973)	(109 S.Ct. 3040, 1989)

42. Southern Center for Law and Ethics
43. Southwest Life and Law Center
44. United States
45. U.S. Catholic Conference
46. Austin Vaughn, Crusade for Life

Note: When interests and individuals participate as amici, they usually identify their organizational affiliation (if any) on the cover of their briefs. In contrast, briefs filed by attorneys representing the parties to litigation generally do not identify group involvement. Researchers seeking to determine whether groups sponsored particular cases must, then, rely on other sources. Our task in identifying group involvement of attorneys arguing the cases profiled in this appendix was simplified by the fact that all of the cases have been the subject of significant commentary, indicating whether they were or were not brought by group attorneys and identifying those groups that did sponsor them.

[a]Data obtained from *U.S. Supreme Court Records, Briefs*, Microcard Editions, no. 70-18.

[b]Data obtained from *U.S. Supreme Court Records and Briefs*, Congressional Information Service, no. 88-605.

[c]These were Canadian Abortion Rights Action League, Ontario Coalition for Abortion Clinics, National Action Committee on the Status of Women, and National Association of Women and the Law.

[d]These were Abortion Rights Coalition, DKT Memorial Fund, Family Planning Association of South Wales, International Fund for Health and Family Planning, International Projects Assistance Services, International Women's Health Coalition, Marie Stopes International, National Abortion Campaign of Britain, The Pathfinder Fund, Population Crisis Committee, Population Council, Population Planning Associates, Population Services International, PRETERM Foundation, Program for the Introduction of Contraceptive Technology, TOLERATION, Transnational Family Research Institute, Women's Abortion Action Campaign, Women's Economic Network, Women's Electoral Lobby Australia, Women's Global Network on Reproductive Rights, and 14 individuals.

[e]This brief was written by attorneys from the National Conference of Black Lawyers, the CCR, and the National Lawyers Guild.

[f]These were NARAL, Women's Legal Defense Fund, League of Women Voters of the United States, National Federation of Business and Professional Women's Clubs, National Women's Law Center, NOW Legal Defense and Education Fund, Women's Law Project, American Association of University Women, National Association of Social Workers, Women's International League for Peace and Freedom, Ms. Foundation for Women, Women's Equity Action League, Northwest Women's Law Center, Equal Rights Advocates, Connecticut Women's Educational and Legal Fund, National Women Abuse Prevention Project, Wider Opportunities for Women, American Veterans Committee, Voters for Choice/Friends of Family Planning, Lambda Legal Defense and Education Fund, Boston Women's Health Book Collective, Human Rights Campaign Fund, American Federation of State, County, and Municipal Employees, Women Lawyers' Association of Los Angeles, Queen's Bench of the San Francisco Bay Area, Yale Journal of Law and Femi-

nism, Abortion Rights Council, Center for Women Policy Studies, Women's Equal Rights Legal Defense and Educational Fund, Committee to Defend Reproductive Rights—CMRW, New York State Coalition on Women's Legal Issues, Abortion Rights Mobilization, Women's Bar Association of Massachusetts, California Women Lawyers. National Gay and Lesbian Task Force, New York Women in Criminal Justice, Harvard Women's Law Association, Buffalo Lawyers for Choice, 80% Majority Campaign, CHOICE, Women in Film, National Women's Conference Committee, Women's Law Association of Washington College of American University, Choice Network of Tarrant County—Texas, Lawyers for Reproductive Rights, Gay and Lesbian Democrats of America, Women's Medical Fund, Columbia-Greene Rape Crisis Center, Radical Women, D.C. Feminists against Pornography, Women's Equity Affiliates, Feminist Health Center of Portsmouth, Toledo Women's Bar Association, Washington Women United, Fund for New Leadership, Women's Agenda, Missouri Women's Network, Hawaii Women Lawyers, National Women's Studies Association, Hawaii Women Lawyers Foundation, North Carolina Association of Women Lawyers, Women's City Club of New York, Illinois Women's Agenda, Feminist Institute, National Council for Research on Women, Tucson Women's Commission, League of Women Voters of Missouri, National Committee to Free Sharon Kowalski, Santa Barbara Women's Political Committee, Women Employed, National Gay Rights Advocates, Women's Center of the University of Connecticut, North Carolina Equity, Women's Rights Coalition, and International Center for Research on Women.

ᵍThe Legal Defense Fund for Unborn Children filed a motion for leave to participate as an amicus curiae. It was denied by the Court.

NOTES

CHAPTER 1

1. Article III provides the Supreme Court with original jurisdiction in cases "affecting Ambassadors, other public ministers and Consuls and those in which a State shall be a party." It gives the Court appellate jurisdiction over cases involving certain kinds of parties (e.g., the federal government and citizens of different states) and certain kinds of disputes (e.g., those involving the Constitution, congressional laws, and treaties).

2. The power of judicial review was not explicitly mentioned in Article III. It was, however, the focal point of Hamilton's defense of life-tenured judges in the *Federalist Papers*, no. 78, and was read into constitutional law in *Marbury v. Madison* (1803).

3. The Constitution (Article I, sections 2, 3), of course, provides for the removal of judges by impeachment (House of Representatives) and conviction (Senate).

4. Given the issues we selected for analysis, it is true that the law could shift rather markedly within the distant, or even near, future. For purposes of our substantive exploration, we focus on the changes that already have occurred. In our final chapter, we consider this notion of legal fluidity more fully and speculate on those factors that could generate future change.

CHAPTER 2

1. A voluminous literature exists on the U.S. Supreme Court. For good introductions, see Baum 1989b; O'Brien 1990; Rohde and Spaeth 1976; Wasby 1988; and Witt 1990.

2. As Levi (1949) describes it, "the basic pattern of legal reasoning is reasoning by example," a procedure conducted in three stages: 1) judges observe a similarity between cases; 2) they deduce the rule of law inherent in the first case; and 3) they make that rule applicable to the second case.

3. See *Missouri ex rel. Gaines v. Canada* (1938); *Sipuel v. Board of Regents of the University of Oklahoma* (1950); *McLaurin v. Oklahoma State Regents* (1950); and *Sweatt v. Painter* (1950).

4. *Griswold* dealt with bodily privacy (i.e., the dispensement of birth control). Before *Roe*, the Court handed down several decisions on this point (e.g., *United States v. Vuitch* [1971] and *Eisenstadt v. Baird* [1972]). In general, though, many of its early rulings touching on privacy involved search and seizures (e.g., *Mapp v. Ohio* [1961] and *Stanley v. Georgia* [1969]).

5. Even those who find themselves in other camps recognize that we do a disservice by

ignoring "the law." Two decades after he published *The Roosevelt Court* (1948), a classic debunking of legalism, C. Herman Pritchett (1969, 42) lamented that "political scientists who have done so much to put the 'political' in 'political jurisprudence' need to emphasize that it is still 'jurisprudence.' It is judging in a political context, but it is still judging; and, judging is something different from legislating or administering."

6. Gibson (1983) offered a classic formulation of this:

For more on the component parts of this model, see Gibson 1977, 1978a and Rohde and Spaeth 1976.

7. One year prior to Nixon's inauguration, Warren resigned to give President Lyndon Johnson the chance to appoint his successor. Johnson nominated Associate Justice Abe Fortas but was forced to withdraw his name amid allegations of misconduct. For more on this episode, see Murphy 1988 and Shogan 1972.

8. Even after he withdrew from consideration to be chief justice, Fortas continued to be hounded by the allegations that forced his withdrawal. He resigned from the Court on 14 May 1969.

9. In his 1986 confirmation hearings, Rehnquist admitted that he prepared a memo upholding *Plessy v. Ferguson* (1896) but contended that he did so at Justice Jackson's request.

10. Many civil rights and liberties organizations expressed their opposition to Rehnquist's nomination, calling him, among other things, a "racist" and "right-wing zealot." The American Civil Liberties Union (ACLU) broke a fifty-year policy to call for his defeat (Abraham 1985, 315–16).

11. The U.S. attorney general "had read all of Stevens' opinions and [was] very much impressed by their style and clarity"; the American Bar Association (ABA) judged him to be exceptionally well qualified (ibid., 323).

12. Immediately prior to and following the Bork nomination came a deluge of support and criticism of this approach. Bork's views, themselves, are best set out in his 1971 *Indiana Law Journal* article. They were embraced by Meese (1985) and then severely criticized by Justice William Brennan (1985).

13. It is too soon to say precisely what kind of conservative Justice Thomas will be, but it is probably safe to suggest that his jurisprudence will be more in line with the ideals espoused by Reagan and Bush than by Marshall.

14. This, of course, is quite a different question from whether Court decisions influence the public. For an excellent review of literature addressing this, see Caldeira 1991.

15. It also is the case that changes in the political environment can affect the strategies and tactics of important institutionalized actors, such as attorneys and litigants. In fact, here we run into some of the conceptual ambiguity mentioned at the beginning of this chapter: it is undoubtedly true that groups contemplate their objectives vis-à-vis the existing social and political contexts, contexts defined by governmental institutions (especially the federal judiciary), organizations with related interests, and public opinion (Cortner 1968; Kobylka 1987, 1991). As such, their perception of the configuration of these factors can affect group behavior. Consider, for example, the posture of the U.S.

Supreme Court. As the Bork confirmation proceedings demonstrated, groups are clearly cognizant of the relationship between Court personnel and their ability to advance their judicial agenda. A Court composed largely of Nixon, Reagan, and Bush appointees, while exceedingly attractive for conservative interests like the Pacific and Washington Legal Foundations, is a less-than-appealing forum for the ACLU and the NAACP LDF. These perceptions not only affect the way they frame their legal arguments but may lead them to avoid the Supreme Court altogether and confine their activities to other courts or governmental institutions.

16. More broad-based treatments of group participation in a range of legal areas also have added to our store of knowledge. In general, these studies select a particular area of the law for investigation (e.g., racial discrimination or free speech) or a specific organization (e.g., the ACLU or the NAACP LDF) for in-depth analysis. Using "success scores"—the ratios of group wins to participations—they seek to reach conclusions about the efficacy of organizational litigation. Inevitably, such studies find that groups have higher success scores than organized litigants. Exemplary of this approach is Lawrence's (1990) study of the Legal Services Program (LSP). She examined the relative success of LSP attorneys in Supreme Court litigation involving the gamut of poverty law issues and concluded, given that LSP attorneys won 62 percent of their cases, that "[t]he LSP's appellate advocacy . . . gave the poor a voice in the Supreme Court's policy making and doctrinal development" (270).

17. Vose's (1972) analysis of the National Consumers' League's (NCL) quest to obtain judicial validation of progressive legislation provides a prime example of the significance of such changes. After winning *Muller v. Oregon* (1908), in which the Court upheld maximum-hour work laws, the NCL sought to secure minimum-wage legislation. *Muller* was such an astounding victory that the organization was confident it could reach this objective. But such was not to be: in *Adkins v. Children's Hospital* (1923), it failed to convince the Court of the constitutional permissibility of such laws.

Vose's analysis of the NCL's loss in *Adkins* considers a number of explanations. Among the most important was the group's change in legal counsel. Louis Brandeis had conducted the litigation campaign leading to *Muller*. After he became a Supreme Court justice, Felix Frankfurter replaced him as NCL counsel. Though Frankfurter was a very competent attorney, he was preoccupied with his professorial responsibilities at Harvard and, perhaps, a less committed NCL lawyer.

18. We adopt this discussion from Epstein and Rowland 1991.

19. We derive the information contained in this paragraph from Cobb and Elder 1983.

CHAPTER 3

1. The evidence against McCleskey included testimony by one of his co-defendants in the robbery and by an inmate.

2. Two of whom, Anthony Amsterdam and James Nabrit, also worked on the *Furman* case.

3. Addressing these questions from a normative perspective is well beyond the scope of this chapter. For reviews of these debates, see Bedau 1964; Cohen 1970; and Sellin 1980.

4. Ancient Greece, for example, initially imposed death for almost any crime, including idleness and theft. As it advanced, not only did it reduce the number of capital crimes, but

its leaders generally pardoned those upon whom it had been conferred. Ancient Rome and many parts of Europe followed similar trends (Bowers 1984, 132).

5. Prior to the Revolution, every colony possessed death penalties, although some variation existed in the overall severity of their codes. At the more lenient end of the spectrum was Pennsylvania, where a largely Quaker population had pushed for limits on the number of capital offenses. In 1682 and again in 1794, it confined the death penalty to murder and treason (Bedau 1967b). More typical was Massachusetts; the Puritans there punished by death "cursing one's parents or just being a 'rebellious' son." They also counted among their capital offenses various theocratic crimes, including blasphemy and idolatry, which they later used to "justify" the Salem witch hunts (Erikson 1966).

6. The short debate over the wording of the Eighth Amendment reinforces this perspective. When the House of Representatives was considering its support of 17 August 1789, William L. Smith of South Carolina objected to the words "nor cruel and unusual punishments," arguing that the import of them was too indefinite. To this, Samuel Livermore responded:

> No cruel and unusual punishment is to be inflicted; it is sometimes necessary to hang a man, villains often deserve whipping, and perhaps having their ears cut off; but are we in the future to be prevented from inflicting these punishments because they are cruel? If a more lenient mode of correcting vice and deterring others from the commission of it could be invented, it would be very prudent in the Legislature to adopt it, but until we have some security that this will be done, we ought not to be restrained from making necessary laws by any declaration of this kind. (Farber and Sherry 1990, 238)

This response suggests that the framers considered the death penalty to fall beyond the cruel and unusual proviso of the Eighth Amendment. Conversely, it seems reasonable to suppose that they were leaving open the possibility that the clause might someday preclude capital punishment if an alternative could be developed. This is the interpretation to which Justice Marshall subscribes in *Furman v. Georgia* (1972, 321).

Other evidence supporting the view that the death penalty was a functioning part of early American history comes from the national legislature. The first Congress of the United States, on which sat many of those who wrote the Constitution, passed an Act of 1790 making murder, forgery of public securities, robbery, and rape punishable by death (Berger 1982, 47). Likewise it had no qualms about legislating a punishment of thirty-nine lashes for larceny and receiving stolen goods (*Furman* 1972, 263).

That it is undisputable that the framers intended to retain capital punishment is not to suggest that this is an absolutely closed debate. After publication of Berger's (1982) book, in which he demonstrated the intent of the framers on the Eighth Amendment, the issue took on a new life. See, for example, Bedau's (1983) scathing review of Berger's work.

7. This phrase was repeated in the Fourteenth Amendment. Also, two other clauses of the Fifth Amendment also lead to the same basic conclusion. The grand jury clause states that "[n]o person shall be held to answer for a capital . . . crime, unless on presentment or indictment of a Grand Jury which states." The double jeopardy clause states, "[N]or shall any person be subject for the same offence to be twice put in jeopardy of life or limb." If the framers meant to eradicate capital punishment, why provide for grand jury hearings in capital cases or prohibit double jeopardy of life?

8. The first was led by Dr. Benjamin Rush, a Philadelphia physician of some repute,

who delivered several papers ([1782] 1976), calling for an end to public hangings (see Campion 1959) and, later, expressing his disdain for the death penalty. He thought it an "absurd and un-Christian practice," one more compatible with a monarchy than a democracy (Rush [1782] 1976; Weaver 1976). With the help of Philadelphia Quakers, he formed an anti-gallow society—an organization to oppose all public punishment (Filler 1952). In Pennsylvania and in other areas where such societies sprang up, the idea took hold; by the mid-1800s, many states and localities moved their executions from the streets to the confines of jails and prisons (Bradford [1793] 1968; Masur 1989; Schwed 1983). With public executions generally falling out of favor, other early reformers began to call for the total abolition of the death penalty (Hartung 1952; Mackey 1973). This first wave of abolitionism endured for more than thirty years, reaching its peak just prior to the 1850s. The advent of the Civil War, however, quickly halted that movement as capital punishment reformers invariably turned their attention to abolition of slavery.

A second abolitionist tide took shape during the 1910s within the "conducive atmosphere of the Populist and Progressive Eras" (Schwed 1983, 16). This period witnessed the growth of organizations dedicated to the eradication of capital punishment (e.g., the Anti–Capital Punishment Society and the Anti–Death Penalty League) and attracted some notable adherents. Not surprisingly, it scored some impressive victories. It convinced most states to abandon mandatory sentences of death by establishing degrees of murder or by making the decision discretionary (i.e., judges or juries could recommend life in prison or death). Of greater importance was that several states eliminated death penalties altogether. As many states abolished capital punishment during that decade as in all previous others combined; "1917, in particular, promis[ed] to be the wonder year of abolition" (Filler 1952, 134). Such was not to be, however, as America entered World War I and four states quickly repealed.

A third "trend" toward abolition arose in the late 1920s. During this period, Clarence Darrow and several others founded the National American League to Abolish Capital Punishment, which sought to "organize and coordinate abolitionist attempts in state legislatures" (Mackey 1976, xxxviii). Though it received a "boost" in membership with the executions of Sacco and Vanzetti in 1927, it faced a "basically unreceptive political environment" (Schwed 1983, 19) and, thus, achieved virtually no measurable success.

9. Why the execution rate dropped so dramatically is a matter of some debate, with the efforts of the earlier abolitionists surely contributing. One of the reforms for which they fought—a reduction in the number of capital offenses—eventually led to an associated drop in executions. Gone were the days when "rebellious sons," "grape stealers," and "witches" were put to death. Also contributing was the virtual elimination of crimes carrying mandatory death sentences, another goal of earlier reform movements (Hartung 1952, 12). Another explanation for the decline is the Holocaust. Schwed (1983, 20), for example, suggests that it forced "Americans to think twice about their use of capital punishment, especially in reference to America's claims of moral superiority."

10. Data prior to 1930 comes from various sources, none of which specified their methodology or did so in ways that are amenable to replication. Lawes ([1924] 1969, 27), for example, simply stated that he secured data from prison "wardens." Moreover, sources provide varying estimates of the total number of executions. Some suggest the most accurate "counter" is Watt Espy, a death penalty historian. He claims that from colonial times through 1988, 15,759 legal executions occurred in the United States (Gray and Stanley 1989, 48).

11. Writing in 1927, for example, Calvert classified the United States as an "abolitionist country," an apt characterization given that Michigan, Rhode Island, and Wisconsin all abolished the death penalty prior to most European countries.

12. Why do Americans evince such a strong and stable affinity for capital punishment? One answer, advanced by a leading authority on capital punishment, Hugo Adam Bedau, involves the idiosyncratic culture of the United States. When researchers (Gray and Stanley 1989, 228–29) asked him why the United States lags behind other democracies in the abolition of the death penalty, he responded:

> Americans never lived through the Nazi era in the way that Europe did. We never saw the abuse of the death penalty by torturers and murderers and genocidal brutes the way the Danes, the French, the Germans, the Italians did under the Nazis. We never learned to see so clearly the abuses to which this punishment can be put. We have seen it only in the form of the normal instrument of criminal justice, rather than in the hands of obvious tyrants and murderers.

Others suggest that Americans need the death penalty as a "symbol," something they want to invoke rarely but otherwise have available. This seems to explain why legislatures are so quick to reinstate the penalty after the commission of a particularly gruesome crime.

13. The sorts of pressures legislators faced varied on a state-by-state basis, but a number of universals existed. A notion "popularized" by Clarence Darrow and Lewis E. Lawes in their campaigns against the death penalty (Hartung 1952, 8) was that many reinstatements occurred contemporaneously with periods of national and international turmoil (e.g., America's involvement in the Civil War and economic depressions). Though some systematic evidence of the restoration of the death penalty in other countries purports precisely the opposite conclusion (Deets 1948), such crises do often lead to increases in crime rates, which in turn spur constituents to pressure representatives to stiffen penal codes. Likewise, when it comes to issues of crime, legislators and their constituents tend to be highly responsive to particularly gruesome and/or publicized murders occurring within their borders. Yet in some states particularly gruesome murders had precisely the opposite effect. For example, Wisconsin apparently abolished the death penalty when a jury was "reluctant to convict" a defendant in a highly publicized murder case because it did not want to impose death (Sellin 1980, 146).

14. The proposal listed eight aggravating circumstances, including that "the murder was committed for hire or pecuniary gain," the murder was committed by a convict under sentence of imprisonment, "the defendant was previously convicted of another murder," and "the murder was especially heinous, atrocious or cruel, manifesting exceptional depravity" (ALI 1959, sec. 201.6).

15. The proposal enumerated eight mitigating circumstances, including that "the defendant has no history of prior criminal activity," the murder was committed while the defendant was under the influence of extreme mental or emotional disturbance, "the youth of the defendant at the time of the crime," and the defendant was "an accomplice in a murder committed by another person" (ibid.).

16. Also, judges could mandate life imprisonment after all the aggravating circumstances had been brought to light.

17. In neither of these cases was this point discussed. In the "Scottsboro boys" case, *Powell v. Alabama* (1932), the Supreme Court dealt with the question of whether they were

denied effective counsel. In *Rosenberg v. United States* (1953), after Justice Douglas denied a stay of execution, the Court dismissed claims that the Atomic Energy Act superseded the espionage law under which the Rosenbergs had been convicted. Burt (1987, 1743), though, argues that "the origins of the Court's death penalty reform" began with the "Scottsboro boys" case because it recognized there that death was "different" and needed to be treated with "special care."

18. The Court, however, did decide a few cases involving the cruel and unusual provision of the Eighth Amendment. See Goldberg and Dershowitz (1970) for an interesting review.

19. The majority opinion explained that it would be difficult "to define with exactness the extent of the constitutional provision which provides cruel and unusual punishments shall not be inflicted" (*Wilkerson* 1879, 135); however, it was "safe" to assume that it would forbid torture.

20. It is interesting to note that Warren's majority opinion in *Trop* went through several incarnations. After *Trop* was initially argued, Warren assigned the majority opinion to himself. His original draft, only six pages long, was not "impressive," and as a result the case was set for reargument. After the second round of orals, changes in votes occurred with the result being that Warren was no longer in the majority. He had one of his clerks "thoroughly" recast the opinion, though he "inserted" the key phrase of "evolving standards." This draft, circulated as a dissent, prompted Whittaker to change his vote and, thus, Warren's opinion once again became the majority's (Schwartz 1983, 313–17).

21. See, in particular, *Weems v. United States* (1910) in which the Court struck down as cruel and unusual *cadena temporal* for falsifying documents. It held that the amendment was "not fastened to the obsolete but may acquire meaning as public opinion becomes enlightened by a human justice" (*Weems* 1910, 378).

22. He stated: "At the outset let us put to one side the death penalty as an index of the constitutional limit on punishment. Whatever the arguments may be against capital punishment . . . the death penalty has been employed throughout our history. . . . [I]t is still widely accepted" (*Trop* 1958, 100).

23. During his three-term stint on the Court, Goldberg consistently ranked among the most liberal of his brethren on issues of law and order. In the 1962 term, for example, he supported the defendant in 84 percent of all cases raising a criminal rights issue.

24. The material on *Rudolph v. Alabama* is drawn largely from Schwartz (1985).

25. What motivated Goldberg to write this memo has been the subject of conjecture. Some suggest that he was heavily influenced by his clerk, Alan Dershowitz, currently a professor at Harvard Law School. This view receives support from two sources. First, even after Goldberg left the Court in 1965, he continued to espouse strong abolitionist views, coauthoring several articles with Dershowitz. Second, in a 1988 interview, Dershowitz reported the following:

> I participated in the beginning of the judicial campaign against capital punishment. I was Justice [Arthur J.] Goldberg's law clerk in the summer of 1963. He had recently been appointed to the Supreme Court and we spent the month of August just talking about what it was he wanted to do during that year. I had just come off a clerkship with Judge David Bazelon, who was the great liberal reformer of his day, and we had thought about trying to mount an attack on capital punishment on racial grounds, but we didn't really have the right case. Well, Justice Goldberg suggested it,

but we were both thinking about it. We decided that we were going to try to open up the issue of the unconstitutionality of the death penalty. I spent the entire summer writing up a memo on why the death penalty is unconstitutional. (Gray and Stanley 1989, 330)

26. Should the Court be unpersuaded by the "evolving standards" justification, Goldberg provided other lines of argument it might find more convincing. For instance, he expressed "concern" over the possibility of executing an innocent person or one who had been denied due process of law. Citing a recent spate of studies, he also questioned whether the death penalty served "any uniquely deterrent effect upon potential criminals." Finally, and in no uncertain terms, he asserted that a "persuasive argument" could be made that death for crimes that "do not endanger life" (e.g., rape) might violate constitutional principles and controvert stare decisis. For an in-depth analysis of this memo, see Marsel 1985–86.

27. Even one of his usual allies on the Court, Justice Brennan, later wrote (1986) that the memo had been "highly unusual"; it was extremely rare for an individual justice "to write at length, prior to our conference, about cases which had neither been argued nor set for argument."

28. One account suggests that Chief Justice Warren, in fact, was "furious" with the Goldberg memo (Gray and Stanley 1989). Despite his *Trop* opinion, his liberalism in the areas of criminal law and racial discrimination never extended to the death penalty; as governor of California, he tried to reform capital procedures so as to eliminate the rush of last-minute appeals (Warren 1977), while simultaneously signing death warrants. He also argued on several occasions that "[o]f course the death penalty is constitutional, the framers intended it."

In his letters, Justice Douglas suggests another explanation. As he tells it, the chief justice said to Goldberg: "[I]n view of the numerous attacks on the Court . . . it would be best to let the matter sleep for awhile" (Urofsky 1987, 189). Dershowitz (Goldberg's clerk at the time) confirms this a bit more pointedly. He recalls that the controversial *Brown v. Board of Education* (1954) decision was just beginning to take its course and "the idea that [the Court] would then allow blacks killing whites to be saved from the death penalty was too much for a politically sensitive Justice like Warren to accept" (Gray and Stanley 1989, 330).

Associate Justice Black also strongly opposed the Goldberg opinion. Black, as Justice Douglas recalled, similarly "expressed the view that he was unalterably opposed to Goldberg's" suggestion (Urofsky 1987, 189), which is not surprising since elements of his jurisprudence militated against his acceptance. Most important, Black was an absolutist and a literal interpreter of the Constitution. Under such a jurisprudence, he would necessarily view the death penalty as constitutional: since the framers provided for the taking of life, the death penalty was surely constitutional. As Black would later write (in *McGautha* 1971), "In my view [the cruel and unusual clause] cannot be read to outlaw capital punishment because the penalty was in common use . . . at the time the Amendment was adopted."

29. Under the leadership of Earl Warren, this Court was in the process of generating a rights, liberties, and justice "revolution." Especially relevant here were two cases that attracted little attention but were highly applicable to death penalty litigation. The first, *Robinson v. California* (1962), incorporated the cruel and unusual provision of the Eighth Amendment, thus applying it to the states. In the second, *Fay v. Noia* (1963), the Court

firmly established the right of state prisoners to raise "alleged denials" of their federal rights, through habeas corpus petitions, in federal courts. Though this right was initially established in another LDF case, *Moore v. Dempsey* (1923), as Greenberg (1977, 428) noted, it "had been hedged with serious procedural problems until *Fay*."

30. How the LDF found itself in a position of preeminence is quite an intriguing, albeit well-told, story. For some interesting examinations, see Greenberg 1974b, 1977; Kellogg 1967; Miller 1966; and Wasby 1983, 1984, 1985. For treatments of particular litigation campaigns, see Cortner 1988; Kluger 1976; Tushnet 1987; and Vose 1959.

31. Since the 1920s, observers of all ilks used "numbers" to explore capital punishment (Bye 1919; Calvert 1930; Dann 1935). But this trend took off in full force in the 1940s and 1950s, which saw an "impressive accumulation" of social science research on two aspects of the death penalty (Bowers 1984, 23). The first sought to explore the potential of capital punishment to deter crime, with many (Schuessler 1952; Sellin 1967) concluding generally that evidence fails to suggest that "abolition of capital punishment has led to an increase in the homicide rate, or that its reintroduction led to a fall" (Royal Commission 1953, 23). The other area of research involved the issue of racial discrimination in capital sentencing. For many years observers suspected that blacks, particularly in the South, were the greater victims of death penalty statutes than whites, hardly a surprising conclusion given that antebellum southern states had codes "that explicitly discriminated against blacks by making some types of conduct punishable by death only if the defendant was black, or the victim was white, or both" (Gross and Mauro 1989, 27). Analyses conducted in the 1940s tended to confirm this suspicion, although the evidence was mostly circumstantial; it was not until the 1960s that scholars began to control for relevant factors (e.g., age or the nature of the crime) other than race.

32. Cortner's study (1988) tends to support Greenberg's position. But while *Hamilton* was an important case, perhaps catalyzing the LDF's interest, a review of LDF material (e.g., its Civil Rights Law Institutes lectures) prior to 1963 turned up no evidence of this interest; capital punishment was not mentioned.

33. Interestingly, though, Goldberg's initial memorandum to conference on the death penalty contained an allusion to the race issue. In a footnote discussing a previous Supreme Court case, Goldberg noted that the defendant was "indicted by a grand jury whose composition was determined by the drawing of lottery tickets whose color differed with the race of the person named on the ticket" (Schwartz 1985, 405). That note did not appear in the final dissent.

34. LDF attorneys recognized this omission, but according to one attorney: "[T]hose who read [Goldberg's] opinion carefully concluded that, if proved, racial discrimination was certainly as compelling a legal argument against capital punishment as could be found" (Meltsner 1974, 4).

35. In an interview, Donohue (1985, 266) asked Assistant Director Alan Reitman why the ACLU did not oppose death penalties during the 1950s. Reitman responded: "There is nothing to my knowledge concerning an organizational decision not to oppose capital punishment." Still, no policy statement existed.

36. This is not to suggest that the ACLU never entered capital cases. It did so when it "believed that the defendant was innocent or denied a fair trial" (Neier 1982, 197). Moreover, as early as 1961, it expressed concern over juvenile executions (ACLU 1961–62, 75). Yet, like the LDF in the early 1960s, it had not contemplated any litigation campaign nor had it taken a direct stand.

37. In the early 1960s, several of its affiliates had taken their own initiative and began explorations of the issue. The execution of Caryl Chessman in 1960 led the southern California affiliate to undertake an anti–death penalty campaign (Donohue 1985, 267). Under the auspices of the Georgia Civil Liberties Union, several faculty members and students produced a forty-seven-page report detailing problems in the imposition of death in that state (e.g., that it discriminated against the poor). Likewise the Florida affiliate expressed a deep interest in capital punishment. Headed by Tobias Simon, that affiliate had served as "the principal advocate" for civil rights in Florida; its involvement in capital cases was a "natural extension" of that interest (Neier 1982, 197). In fact, the Florida affiliate became even more adamant after it conducted a study of possible racial discrimination in rape cases, finding results quite compatible with those of the LDF (ACLU 1964–65, 79).

38. Specifically, the statement held that "[c]apital punishment is so inconsistent with the underlying values of our democratic system . . . that the imposition of the death penalty for any crime is a denial of civil liberties. The Union believes that past decisions to the contrary are in error, and will seek the repeal of existing laws imposing the death penalty and reversal of convictions carrying a sentence of death" (ACLU 1976, 200).

39. And, by then, Governors Brown of California and Peabody of Massachusetts were fighting to ban, or at least temporarily bar, capital punishment in their states. It is also true that many state legislatures, in the early and mid-1960s, debated the issue with some narrow outcomes. Indiana passed abolitionist legislation, but the governor vetoed it after a state police officer had been fatally shot (*U.S. News and World Report* 1965).

Changes also were afoot on the federal level. During the 1950s and early 1960s, the most visible figure in the Justice Department, J. Edgar Hoover, was an "outspoken" proponent of capital punishment (see Bedau 1964, 130–35). But in 1965 Attorney General Ramsey Clark wrote to Congress: "We favor abolition of the death penalty. Modern Penology, with its correctional and rehabilitative skills affords greater protection to society than the death penalty, which is inconsistent with its goals." This represented an alteration in Clark's thinking; just two years prior, in the wake of John F. Kennedy's assassination, he publicly supported the death penalty for the murder of a president (*Newsweek* 1968).

40. Why theses changes came about in the mid-1960s is, naturally, open to interpretation, with many scholars arguing that Caryl Chessman's "struggle" catalyzed the movement. In 1948, California tried and convicted Chessman under a so-called "Little Lindbergh Law," which punished by death "kidnapping for the purpose of robbery." That charge and his trial generated a great deal of public attention, with some suggesting that the whole proceeding had been a great miscarriage of justice. As a result, Chessman's case became a cause célèbre. After he authored several books on his saga, leaders and notables throughout the world expressed their support. Debate over the Chessman case became even more heated as he sat on death row for twelve years, the longest in American history, before his execution in May 1960.

Although this is a well-accepted explanation for the radical alteration in the political environment, it contains two undeniable flaws. First, public opinion remained in favor of capital punishment through the 1960s; it was not until 1966 when a majority of Americans (with opinions) opposed it. Second, no states abolished the death penalty during the early 1960s; again, this did not happen until the mid-1960s. Given the highly charged nature of this issue, the lag between Chessman's execution and legislative changes seems a bit wide.

Rather, we think the movement toward reform in the 1960s was similar to that of the 1910s. During that earlier period, there existed an important and influential social movement—progressivism. That movement helped to create a political environment conducive to abolitionism. The same is true of the 1960s, which witnessed the rise of a great many "rights" movements. As the civil rights movement, in particular, took hold, the public consciousness concerning liberties and freedoms was "raised," in a sense. So too, as many indicate, came concomitant changes in the attitudes of Americans toward criminal rights. Seen in this light, the Chessman case, like that of Sacco and Vanzetti before it, was an aberration in death penalty history; it created an explosive, but temporary, public fervor.

41. Governor Brown of California was an "outspoken foe of capital punishment" (Turner 1966b). Florida's Governor Burns had refused to sign any death warrants until the question of capital punishment was resolved in Florida (*New York Times* 1967).

42. According to the victim, Maxwell broke into her home at three o'clock in the morning by cutting through a screen. As he was entering the house, wearing a nylon stocking over his head, she telephoned for the police. But it was too late; before the call was complete, he had attacked her and her father. Hearing screams at the other end, the operator placed the call herself. Police found the victim two blocks from her home, raped and injured. They took her to a hospital, where they tried to get her to identify Maxwell; she could not but was able to do so later from a "lighted living room." Her recollection, plus other evidence (e.g., blood and semen stains and hair and fiber samples), convinced a jury to convict Maxwell and sentence him to death (*Maxwell* 1968).

43. The numbers, though, were somewhat startling. Of the 168 executions, 129 were of nonwhites, 39 of whites.

44. Paine (1962) reports that the LDF tried to use rather rudimentary statistics as early as 1950 in *Hampton v. Commonwealth*. In that case, it defended seven blacks accused of raping a white woman. One of the arguments it presented was that between 1900 and 1950, the state had executed forty-two blacks and no whites.

45. To implement this plan, Wolfgang first drew a sample of counties within these states that was meant to reflect a variety of demographic factors. Then, Amsterdam and Greenberg recruited volunteers (all third-year law students) from the Law Students Civil Rights Research Council to collect the necessary data. After a training session in June 1965, the students went to assigned areas and filled out twenty-eight-page "questionnaires" on the rape cases, gathering their information from trial transcripts, prison records, and so forth (U.S. Congress 1972).

46. By contemporary standards, Wolfgang's design and analysis is rather simplistic. For example, his analytic tool—the chi-square statistic—cannot show causality between race and sentencing. That is, chi-square is a simple measure of association, which is based on a calculation of observed versus expected values. A more sophisticated technique, some form of multivariate analysis such as probit, might have been able to demonstrate the extent to which race and all other variables actually contribute to the sentencing decision.

In recognition of this problem, Wolfgang and Reidel (1976) later reanalyzed the data, using a stepwise discriminate function approach—a better, albeit less than ideal, tool. They once again found race to be the only statistically significant variable. Likewise Wolfgang's conceptualization of discrimination as a "function of societal or institutional forces," rather than as an inherently individualistic product, may also confound problems of interpretation. As Gibson (1978b) suggests, Wolfgang and others probably should have used individual decisions as their units of analysis, instead of courts, because it is possible that some judges may have been more or less likely to engage in discrimination.

47. For details on how and why this came about, see Meltsner 1973.

48. As Greenberg noted (1977, 442), the LDF introduced the results of the Wolfgang study into other like cases "without success."

49. Why this was the case is something of a mystery, one considerably darkened by the fact that statistical arguments had been successfully used in other areas of the law before and since *Maxwell*. In *Judicial Process and Social Change*, Greenberg (1977) offers a number of explanations, all of which seem reasonable. For one, he suggests that if courts accepted the LDF's findings, "it might condemn [other] judges for having countenanced racially discriminatory sentences." Further, it might cause the outcome of cases to turn "on the side which could marshal the most persuasive and perhaps expensive statisticians," which in turn could lead to conflicts in parts of the country "where experts might not be readily available." Finally, "it might open other parts of the criminal process with disparate racial [treatment] to similar attacks."

This last assertion is particularly persuasive but not exclusively as it might apply to racial disparities. For example, in our system of justice, it is entirely possible for two different drivers who have been apprehended for driving 70 miles per hour in a 55-mile-per-hour zone, say, to receive fines varying as much as $100. Though the difference between speeding violations and capital offenses is vast, from a judge's standpoint it is reasonable to argue that they are not, that discrimination exists in all aspects of sentencing, with no possible alternatives in sight.

50. As Greenberg would later note (*Civil Liberties Review* 1975, 118), the studies "were unsuccessful in the sense that the courts didn't accept their validity. . . . [That is] the nature of statistics." He went on to say, however, that he thought the Wolfgang studies "were successful in the sense that you had to concede that they were right and persuasive and informed the courts as to the role that racial discrimination played in the administration of capital punishment."

51. Another LDF attorney also suggested that its "legal arguments" were beginning to create "a lifeboat for these people. Everybody was in the lifeboat, so LDF had an obligation to help them all," not just southern rapists (Muller 1985, 169).

52. Just about the only claims they would avoid were those resting on the cruel and unusual provision of the Eighth Amendment; LDF attorneys still perceived this as a most risky line of attack (Meltsner 1973).

53. This is not to suggest that executions in the late 1960s were a common occurrence; quite the contrary, the LDF's call for moratorium was "superimposed upon a trend that was already underway" (Bedau 1982, 26). Figure 3-3 well illustrates this fact: executions had virtually ground to a halt. Still, given that states were sentencing an ever-increasing number of defendants to death, moratorium was an important, if symbolic, political statement.

54. Unless otherwise indicated, this section draws heavily from Meltsner 1973.

55. After 1965, only two states abolished the death penalty—New York and New Mexico (see table 3-1). Neier (1982, 198) noted that this occurred despite the lack of a national effort.

56. This view also receives some measure of support, albeit an indirect one, from Walker's (1990) history of the ACLU. In what is arguably the most complete account of the ACLU's litigation to date, Walker mentions capital punishment only in passing (e.g.,

the ACLU's involvement in the Gilmore case [359]). During the period from 1964 through 1974, he depicts an organization far more immersed in civil liberties issues arising out of the civil rights movement, the Vietnam War, and Watergate.

57. On 3 April 1967, Governor Kirk ordered final clemency hearings "as a prelude to the resumption of capital punishment in Florida" (Waldron 1967).

58. For starters, many thought class actions were applicable only in civil litigation in which uniform questions and facts were not uncommon (e.g., pregnant women in abortion litigation), whereas in criminal cases "variations in relevant facts" almost always emerge. Concomitantly, some authorities argued that writs of habeas corpus "must be individual because commitment to prison operates on each prisoner," that the writ is "too personal" for group use (*Harvard Law Review* 1968, 1489–98). In short, LDF staffers did not believe Simon would be able to get all Florida prisoners certified as one class.

59. After the Florida case, abolitionist attorneys undertook a similar class action in California (*Hill v. Nelson*), but it did not go as smoothly. A federal district court judge in San Francisco entered a temporary stay on 5 July 1967, but the administration of Governor Reagan in California went on the offensive, with the state attorney general asking a circuit court to set aside the stay. Abolitionists responded with a seventy-two-page brief in support of the district court judge's opinion, which convinced the upper court to turn down the attorney general. That effort was almost in vain since the district court refused to certify the class. What it did do, however, was nearly as good: it gave attorneys access to inmates and promised to provide them with notification of scheduled executions so that they could file habeas corpus petitions, albeit individual ones, immediately. Shortly thereafter, abolitionist attorneys did just that, filing petitions in the California Supreme Court on behalf of two convicted felons. In November 1967, that court stayed all executions until it could hear arguments on capital punishment. Though it later ruled against the LDF/ACLU position, it ordered new trials for both defendants, even though this was not a particularly auspicious time to argue against the death penalty in California. Virtually every account of these proceedings centered around their potential effect on Sirhan-Sirhan, assassin of Robert Kennedy, who was awaiting execution on California's death row.

60. The de facto win in California, with eighty-four prisoners on death row, also temporarily relieved the pressure.

61. The other was *United States v. Jackson*. At issue in *Jackson* was the 1934 "Lindbergh Law" enacted by Congress to deter the rash of kidnapping, symbolized by the law's namesake, occurring at that time. Under its provisions, individuals who pleaded guilty to a kidnapping charge or elected to have their case heard by a judge could receive life imprisonment as a maximum sentence. If they pleaded innocent or wanted their case heard by a jury, capital punishment could be imposed. Since the defendant, Charles Jackson, asserted his innocence against the charge of kidnapping of a truck driver, he was subject to a death sentence, which he did receive. His Court-appointed attorney argued that the law amounted to coercion and deprived Jackson of his right to a jury trial under the Sixth Amendment. On 8 April 1968, the Court announced its decision, striking down the death penalty portion of the law. In an opinion written by Justice Stewart for six other members (Justice Marshall did not participate), the Court adopted fully Jackson's argument that the judge/jury and guilty/not guilty dichotomies were coercive (violative of Fifth Amendment guarantees against self-incrimination) and served to deprive defendants of their Sixth Amendment right to a jury trial. Justices White and Black wrote a

short dissenting opinion, suggesting that while Jackson's rights had been violated, the Court "needlessly" eradicated a statute that was constitutionally valid if correctly interpreted.

The actual impact of *Jackson* seemed, at the time, quite negligible; that is, the extent to which it would help those sitting on death row was minimal (although later the New Jersey Supreme Court used *Jackson* to find its state's death penalty provision unconstitutional). Yet from the LDF/ACLU perspective, it was a clear win. It showed that the Court "was insisting on a very high standard of procedural fairness for capital trials"—perhaps so much so that it would make administration of the death penalty impractical (Meltsner 1971, 5). It also demonstrated an acknowledgment on the Court's part that "death was a quantifiably different penalty than any form of imprisonment" (Schwed 1983, 121). Perhaps most important of all was that the Court ruled in favor of the abolitionist position, a victory in that it kept alive the moratorium.

62. To wit, the LDF filed a brief in *Witherspoon*, but not in *Jackson*.

63. This involved asking white and black elementary school children to discuss their views about the races, using dolls as surrogates (see Kluger 1976).

64. This study was conducted and issued by Louis Harris and Associates in 1971 (study no. 2016). It, along with several others (e.g., Cowan, Thompson, and Ellsworth 1984; Goldberg 1970; Jurow 1971) confirming the prosecution-proneness argument, were introduced in *Lockhart v. McCree* (1986). The Supreme Court rejected it, once again, because the studies did not provide "substantial support" for the proposition.

65. Amsterdam did say that he believed the LDF-commissioned research "will demonstrate for the first time in a scientific fashion what many have long believed and asserted: that the practice of death-qualification by exclusion of scrupled veniremen seriously distorts the representative composition of the jury and affects its fairness and fact-determining role" (*Witherspoon*, Brief for the NAACP LDF and NORI, no. 1015, 68)

66. Justices Black, Harlan, and White dissented. Black, who thought Stewart's opinion was "terrible" (Black and Black 1986, 538–39), wrote that the Court's holding was "ambiguous," an unwarranted "psychological foray into the human mind," and a destruction of the "concept of an impartial jury." He also criticized the majority for using studies to justify its view: "I must confess that the two or three so-called 'studies' cited by the Court . . . are not persuasive to me" (*Witherspoon* 1968, 538).

67. As Loh (1984, 216) notes, there emerged a gap "between principle and practice" when it came to death-qualified juries. Some states passed laws requiring judges, not juries, to resentence; some state courts continued to allow exclusion of jurors without any determination of their views on capital punishment. Still, Greenberg estimated that the decision led the judges to vacate "several dozen to perhaps more than 100 sentences" (Greenberg 1982, 915).

68. For a complete listing, see *New York Times* 1968. The last federal execution occurred on 15 March 1963, when Victor H. Figure was put to death for kidnapping.

69. Clark provided the Senate Judiciary Committee, before which he was testifying, with several explanations for the administration's request: a United Nations study indicating that the death penalty lacked deterrent value; examinations demonstrating widespread racial discrimination in sentencing; and the worldwide trend toward abolition (at that point, seventy-three countries and thirteen U.S. states had abolished [*Time* 1968]).

70. Forty-seven percent said they were against it; 11 percent had no opinion. The year

before, 45 percent said they were for it—less than half of Americans polled—43 percent were against it; and the remaining 12 percent had no opinion.

71. The internal politics surrounding the *Maxwell* case have been reported, albeit differently, by Schwartz (1983, 1985) and Woodward and Armstrong in *The Brethren* (1979). Schwartz provides complete documentation for his version (memos, drafts of opinions). Also, his story is substantially compatible with the recollections of Brennan (1986) and Douglas (Urofsky 1987). Hence, our account relies exclusively on Schwartz.

72. This was indeed a major blow. Less than a decade after his resignation, Fortas took a strong public stand against the death penalty (Fortas 1977).

73. Marshall did not participate; Black dissented on the grounds that *Witherspoon* was "erroneously decided" (*Maxwell* 1970, 267).

74. Nonetheless, Justice Brennan later wrote that *Maxwell* "served the critical function of focusing and narrowing the arguments" (1986, 317).

75. The ACLU (for the Illinois Civil Liberties Union and the Illinois Committee to Abolish Capital Punishment) and an attorney representing death row inmates reinforced basic claims stressed by LDF and lead attorneys. The American Friends Service Committee and other organizations with religious constituencies (Board of Social Ministry [Lutheran Church of America], Church of the Brethren [General Board], Council of Christian Social Action of the United Church of Christ, Department of Church in Society of the Christian Church [Disciples of Christ], Executive Council of the Episcopal Church in the United States, General Board of Christian Social Concerns of the United Methodist Church, Greek Orthodox Archdiocese of North and South America, American Ethical Union, United Presbyterian Church in the United States of America, and Union of American Hebrew Congregations) suggested that many "moral issues are at stake"; in particular, that "every step in the enforcement of [the Sixth] Commandment ['Thou shalt not kill'] by society is fraught with great difficulties." They questioned, for example, whether a moral juror could impose capital punishment without breaking the commandment (*Crampton*, Brief for the American Friends Service Committee et al., no. 204, 10).

76. Two of the twelve members dissented. Senators Sam Ervin (North Carolina) and John McClellan (Arkansas) thought the death penalty should be maintained for treason and murder (Graham 1971). Still, that the commission recommended the abolition of capital punishment, given Nixon's stance, may seem a bit odd. But the commission had been composed during the Johnson administration, with the chief justice (Warren), the vice president (Humphrey), and a Democratic Speaker of the House each appointing three members. Indeed, the head of the commission, former Governor Edmund Brown, had been a long-standing abolitionist.

77. Justice Brennan (1986) suggests that it was his idea that the Court turn its back on these cases, a plan with which Marshall and Douglas readily agreed.

78. Douglas (Urofsky 1987) and Brennan (1986) both identified Black as the force behind this drive. Woodward and Armstrong in *The Brethren* (1979, 206) suggest that it was Stewart. Based on Douglas's and Brennan's separate recollections, though, Stewart was in no great hurry to see the issue resolved.

79. Brennan's recollection is a bit different: he claims that it was he and Stewart who were "delegated the job of finding clean cases" (1986, 322).

80. On the same day, it acted in the nearly 120 other pending cases, vacating some, reversing others, and staying executions in the remainder.

81. They justified doing so on the grounds that the Court left the issue open in *Boykin*. Their petitions raised other issues, as well. In *Furman*, for example, they made due process and *Witherspoon* claims.

82. The most troublesome of the quartet was surely *Aikens*, which one LDF attorney termed an "absolute monster" (Muller 1985). In the brief it ultimately filed, LDF lawyers were frank, calling Aikens's crimes "unmitigated atrocities" and "indeed aggravated." What prompted this reaction were the facts surrounding Aikens's offense. He had raped, brutalized, robbed, and then murdered two women—one in her sixties and the other twenty-five years old and five months pregnant.

83. Though these constituted the core of their arguments, the LDF briefs also contained several other case-specific points. In *Aikens*, attorneys stressed that capital punishment had no "particular efficacy, in achieving the legitimate aims of criminal law, that less harsh penalties do not have"; for example, studies have failed to indicate that it deters crime (*Aikens*, Brief for Petitioner, no. 68-5027). In their brief on behalf of Furman, they added that the defendant had been mentally ill at the time of the crime and that to execute him would offend "the most basic human precepts" (*Furman*, Brief for Petitioner, no. 69-5003).

84. Groups filing amicus curiae briefs were the ACLU, the NAACP (for four other civil rights organizations), Alaska, the Synagogue Council (for its constituent members and the American Jewish Congress), the National Council of Churches, a Committee of Psychiatrists for Evaluation of the Death Penalty, and the West Virginia Council of Churches (for three other church-related groups).

85. Supporting these views was an amicus curiae brief filed by the state of Indiana. It largely reiterated points made by the states: that capital punishment was not unconstitutional under the Eighth Amendment (including the *Trop* standard), that it might deter crime, and that it was largely a legislative, not judicial, matter.

86. We have some reason to suspect that this account is, in fact, largely accurate. As we detail, Marshall had fully drafted his opinion prior to arguments in the cases.

87. Several months later, Reagan, with the help of his attorney general, Evelle J. Younger, got a public initiative on the ballot that would overturn *Anderson* (Bedau 1987, 150).

88. But see Blackmun's dissent in *Furman*. He writes that "the Court, in my view, is somewhat propelled toward its result by the interim decision of the California Supreme Court" (*Furman* 1972, 411).

89. As the justices labored over their opinions, LDF lawyers made what they thought would be a last-ditch effort to salvage the cases. They asked the Court to dismiss *Aikens* because the California decision in *Anderson* had made the case moot—Aikens was in no danger of execution. On 7 June, when the Court granted the motion, the LDF staff "heaved a collective sigh of relief . . . because some of the Justices . . . and the public at large probably would make a great deal of hay out of the heinousness of Aikens's crimes" (Muller 1985). This step hardly mattered; the LDF had already won the case.

90. Some members of the majority tried to square their opinions with *McGautha*, perhaps in recognition of the inconsistency. Douglas, however, turned *McGautha* "to his own advantage," claiming it contained "the seeds of the present cases" (*Furman* 1972, 248).

91. Even in his opinion, Burger noted that "[t]here is little reason to believe that sentencing standards in any form will substantially alter the discretionary character of the prevailing system of sentencing in capital cases" (ibid., 401).

CHAPTER 4

1. A month later, the bill went to the House, where it sat in a Judiciary Committee preoccupied with Nixon's impeachment (Weaver 1974b). It did, however, pass a provision of the law that made skyjacking in which a fatality occurred punishable by death.

2. As early as 1 July 1972, battles were brewing in at least four other states (Georgia, Oklahoma, North Carolina, and Kansas). And some members of Congress had proposed a constitutional amendment to reinstate death penalties.

3. For an excellent study of the Florida law in operation, see Skene 1986.

4. In December 1972, the National Association of Attorneys General approved by a 32–1 margin a resolution approving capital punishment. While it noted only that "each state would [have to] determine what the offense would be," it did suggest that mandatory laws would probably withstand a constitutional challenge (*New York Times* 1972d).

5. Governor Dukakis vetoed a Massachusetts capital punishment law. The legislature sustained his action by a narrow margin.

6. Some scholars, though, have suggested that the *Furman* "backlash" may have been less a response to constituent pressures (and the lack of organized interests on the other side) and more of a reassertion of the legislative function (Stolz 1983; Zimring and Hawkins 1986, 41–42).

7. One exception was the New York Committee to Abolish Capital Punishment. Immediately after *Furman*, one member said: "The way has been left open for state legislatures to attempt to reenact the death penalty in conformance with criteria suggested by the Court's decision. . . . While this will not be so easy a thing to do . . . it is unfortunately the kind of thing that will appeal to certain legislators" (Schwed 1983, 143).

8. Amsterdam placed significant emphasis on the last point, making "clear the interests of courts in further objective social science research on all aspects of the death penalty" (Bedau 1977, 92). Gathering such data was, in fact, particularly important in light of the opinions of several justices, most notably Burger and Powell, who suggested that the LDF failed to provide sufficient evidence to support its arguments. The chief justice, for example, claimed that there was no "clear indication" of arbitrariness in the continued imposition of the death penalty (*Furman* 1972, 390), and that LDF attorneys provided no "empirical findings to undermine the general premise that juries imposed the death penalty in the most extreme cases" (ibid., 390, n. 12). Both he and Powell also complained that the statistics used to show racial discrimination were outdated and that "while no statistical survey could be expected to bring forth absolute and irrefutable proof of a discriminatory pattern of imposition, a strong showing would have to be made, taking all relevant factors into account" (ibid., 391, n. 12). Burger and Powell used Blackmun's opinion in *Maxwell* to justify this position (White 1976). By the same token, attorneys felt they needed more systematic evidence on deterrence and public opinion to hold the votes of Stewart and White.

9. Being pragmatic, Bedau also sought to devise and encourage research that would be funded either by private or public sources. Despite his efforts, such was not to be: between 1973 and 1974, he sought $150,000 for a three-to-five-year project but failed to obtain the monies. Rather than give up, Bedau and others proposed seven (which eventually turned into twenty-five) smaller projects, hoping that they could obtain individual funding and then integrate them (Bedau 1977). As it turned out, only two received

foundation support, with the result that the others were "shelved indefinitely." But those that did go forward, with or without funding, made some significant contributions.

10. While scholars continued their research, Bedau and others sought to disseminate it. In 1976, he and Dr. Chester Pierce published *Capital Punishment in the United States*, which included discussions of much of the current capital punishment research. Around the same time, the *American Journal of Orthopsychiatry* held a symposium on the death penalty. It did so at the "encouragement" of Bedau with the expressed hope that the articles "would serve both the general readership and legal scholarship about concerns which would help mount an enlightened revision of custom" (Pierce 1975, 580).

11. The remaining death row population was in Louisiana (8), New Mexico (7), Oklahoma (6), California (5), Texas (5), Massachusetts (5), Wyoming (4), Ohio (3), Arizona (2), Virginia (2), Mississippi (1), Tennessee (1), Utah (1), and Pennsylvania (1) (Weaver 1974c).

12. This argument follows closely that made by legal scholar Charles Black in a highly regarded book, *Capital Punishment: The Inevitability of Caprice and Mistake* (1975). In fact, in a review of the work, the *Yale Law Journal* (1975, 1769) said: "This is a book . . . written to four men: those justices who have expressed reservations about capital punishment, have yet held themselves unwilling to override with their own preferences those legislative choices which provide for the death penalty."

13. Griswold participated earlier as an amicus curiae but did so at the Court's invitation.

14. Caplan (1987, 22–23) tells an interesting story of how Ehrlich's study came to the attention of the solicitor general's office. Apparently some lawyers thought that Bork needed to respond to the LDF's claim that the evidence on deterrence was inconclusive at best. "[L]ate one night the deputy in charge was unwinding in front of his TV, and he caught the end of a debate about the death penalty on a talk show." Isaac Ehrlich was among the participants. The attorney then "tracked down Ehrlich and asked him if he could see the study . . . for possible use in the Solicitor General's brief."

15. One moment of "drama" did arise when Justice Marshall asked the North Carolina attorneys about the role of blacks in the state's law enforcement apparatus. He wanted to know how many "negroes" were in the system, to which the attorney responded that there was a "negro woman [judge]—a Negress"; "the Justice appeared to bristle" (Oelsner 1975).

16. Our survey, on the one hand, indicates that the decision did not end the debate over capital punishment; *Furman* was not "the final word" (Heintz 1974, 149). On the other, those scholars who treated the question seemed to suggest that the core of *Furman* would survive. Between 1972 and 1974, twenty-eight law review articles were published on *Furman*. Of those, twenty-one suggested that the Court would hear more cases on the subject and perhaps modify *Furman*. Seven asserted that *Furman* settled the issue.

17. Academics were virtually unanimous in their view that the key justices would not support the mandatory laws (e.g., *Fordham Law Review* 1973).

18. Several groups filed amicus curiae briefs in support of abolition. Amnesty International framed the issue as a "moral" one, involving worldwide human rights. It suggested that the Court "has a unique opportunity [to follow] the lead of other humane nations" (*Gregg*, Brief for Amnesty International, no. 74-6257, 9). The Colorado state public defender reinforced the LDF's point that guided discretion still leads to arbitrariness, citing cases from Colorado that had a similar scheme to Florida's.

The LDF filed amicus curiae briefs in *Gregg* and *Profitt*, the two cases that it did not sponsor. In general, attorneys reiterated points made in the major briefs.

19. This was the only brief filed (on either side) that addressed the issue in such exacting and elongated terms; indeed, the LDF mentioned race only in passing, supported by a long footnote.

20. All excerpts of oral arguments were taken from Kurland and Casper 1977, which contains verbatim records in these cases.

21. It also allowed the North Carolina state attorney to complete the remaining sixteen minutes of his argument from the previous day.

22. The events occurring after the initial *Gregg* et al. conference have been the subject of some speculation. Though we lack substantial outside confirmation, Woodward and Armstrong's (1979) account in *The Brethren* is probably close to the mark; it seems to square with what we do know happened in the case, and it has been partially corroborated by a 1986 address by Justice Brennan. Hence, we use that as our primary source in the paragraphs that follow.

23. In May 1976, Gerald Ford stated that "he strongly favors its use 'in accordance with proper constitutional standards.'" Carter, who had signed Georgia's death law, agreed that "it should be retained for a few aggravated crimes" (Sklar 1976).

24. *Fowler* was remanded in light of *Woodson v. North Carolina*.

25. Two weeks after *Gregg* et al., on 17 July, the LDF petitioned the Court for a rehearing in *Gregg, Jurek*, and *Profitt* so that the states would not consign "166 persons to death." Since the Court was in recess, Powell (as the circuit court judge) received the petition, which explicitly requested stays of execution (*New York Times* 1976b). Despite an apparent threat by Burger (Woodward and Armstrong 1979, 441), Powell issued the stay until the full Court could consider the petition. His "unusual" action raised the hopes of abolitionists (Onek 1976). But they were quickly dashed on 4 October 1976 when the Court denied the request and lifted the stay (Oelsner 1976e).

26. "Every western industrial nation has stopped executing criminals, except the United States" (Zimring and Hawkins 1986, 3). Among the nations and regions retaining capital punishment are South Africa, parts of Latin America, the People's Republic of China, the (former) Soviet Union, and many parts of the Middle East.

27. Republican nominee George Bush indeed made capital punishment an "issue" by publicizing Dukakis's veto of death penalty legislation in the 1970s.

28. The circumstances surrounding Gary Gilmore's execution received tremendous attention (e.g., Mailer 1979; Nordheimer 1977) in part because it was the first since 1967 and in part because of his resistance to any legal assistance from the ACLU and the LDF, both of which fought to save him (Schwed 1983; Neier 1982).

29. The statistics can be misleading. On the one hand, since 1977, one in every thirty sentenced to death was executed by 1988. On the other, ten in thirty left death row (*New York Times* 1988a).

30. One effect of *Gregg* was to catalyze abolitionist groups into action. By the early 1980s, there were several dedicated to defending inmates (Southern Prisoners Defense Committee, Team Defense Project, and Southern Poverty Law Center) in court. Further, all five organizations dedicated solely to fighting capital punishment that were listed in the *Encyclopedia of Associations* (1990 edition) were founded in 1976 or later.

Ironically, though, one of the many problems facing abolitionists after *Gregg* was a shortage of volunteer attorneys: the pool failed to keep pace with the burgeoning death row population. By the early 1980s, organizations throughout the country were expressing the view that "it's becoming almost impossible to find lawyers to do it, and to find people who are skilled in this area" (Clendinen 1982). One LDF attorney put it a bit more bluntly: "Ninety-nine percent of death row inmates are indigent and receive lousy legal representation" (Taylor 1987a).

31. We derive this discussion from George and Epstein 1992.

32. Through the 1988 term, the Court was far more liberal in cases involving capital punishment than in other criminal cases (see table 4-7). During the 1989 term, however, it found in favor of the defendant in only one of the eleven capital cases it decided.

33. It was also a victory for women's rights groups, several of which—Women's Rights Project (of the ACLU), NOW, Women's Law Project, Women's Legal Defense Fund, and Equal Rights Advocates—filed an amicus curiae brief on behalf of the defendant, Coker. They did so to educate "the Court to the realities of death sentences for rape—that this prospect results in fewer convictions for that crime" (O'Connor 1980, 133).

34. We also see it at a more practical level. Many rulings in favor of defendants have had the effect of raising questions about others on death row. For example, after the Court decided *Lockett v. Ohio* (1978), in which it struck down a state law that limited mitigating factors, an LDF attorney estimated that the decision would "free more than 100 prisoners on death row." The Court itself remanded twenty-four Ohio cases back to the Ohio Supreme Court for reconsideration in light of *Lockett* (*New York Times* 1978c).

35. For a full description, see Baldus, Woodruff, and Pulaski 1983, 1985, 1986.

36. It was also true that courts were making greater use of statistics, that is, accepting their validity, in other areas of the law. For an interesting review of this and its importance to *McCleskey*, see Lauter 1984.

37. And they had reasonable support for this assumption. As Burger wrote in *Furman* (1972, 389): "[W]hile no statistical survey could be expected to bring forth absolute . . . proof of a discriminatory pattern of imposition, a strong showing would have to be made, taking all relevant factors into account."

38. *McCleskey* was just one of several cases in which the Baldus study had been introduced. For a description of others, see Gross and Mauro 1989, 136.

39. In addition, attorneys also reintroduced claims involving the jury charge, ineffective counsel, and the admission of evidence. But these were clearly secondary to the race issue.

40. Most assuredly, the state recognized these implications. Its attorney general noted that "allowing a new racial challenge to Georgia's capital punishment law would give . . . all death row inmates a new lease on life" (Cotterell 1983).

41. The district court's opinion has been the subject of substantial criticism. Some (e.g., Gross and Mauro 1989, 153) called it "unfair" and plainly "wrong" in spots. Our reading of the opinion lends some support to the view that the court was, at minimum, confused about certain aspects of the analytic enterprise (e.g., its discussion of multicollinearity). Others point to the fact that the Baldus study has received much praise from other social scientists. For example, it won an award from the Law and Society Association.

42. In only very rare circumstances does the Court "withhold action for so long and then grant a hearing" (Gross and Mauro 1989, 159).

43. Not mentioning the study, of course, constituted an indirect attack on it. The one point it did reinforce was that "because there were only ten cases involving police officer

victims . . . statistical analyses could not be utilized effectively." Baldus conceded that it was difficult to draw any inference concerning the overall race effect in these cases because there had been only one death sentence. He concluded that based on the data there was only "a possibility that a racial factor existed in McCleskey's."

44. Four briefs were filed in support of the LDF by the International Human Rights Law Group, Congressional Black Caucus, two professors, and Congressional Black Caucus for the NAACP and Lawyers' Committee for Civil Rights under Law.

45. In so doing, he took a clear swing at the abolitionist cause, one he repeated many times to the press. He told the *New York Times* that *McCleskey* represented "a concocted effort on the part of the anti–death penalty lobby to block the enforcement of the law" (Noble 1987a).

Refusing to allow Popeo to go on unchecked, the LDF filed a reply brief, which (in part) specifically responded to his claims. The brief stated that the Washington Legal Foundation (and other amici) had "contended that it would be 'repugnant to any decent sense of law and justice' for a capital inmate to 'escape an otherwise valid death sentence by invoking the race of his victim.' That's not what this case is about. The real issue is whether petitioner and other Georgia inmates have *received* their death sentences in part *because* of the race of their victims. Decency, law, and justice are properly invoked to guard against such a possibility, not to condone it" (*McCleskey*, Petitioner's Reply Brief, no. 84-6811, 44–45).

46. It is interesting to note that by the time this case was argued, the two lead attorneys, Jack Boger (LDF) and Mary Westmoreland (Georgia), had opposed each other in court over six times (Thompson 1984).

47. Baldus et al. attributed the loss to the fact that a "ruling in McCleskey's favor could have seriously disrupted the U.S. death sentencing system" and fifteen years of the Court's work. Concomitantly, they asserted that "uncertainty about the validity of the empirical research does not . . . appear to offer a plausible explanation" (Monahan and Walker 1990, 244–45).

48. After the Supreme Court decision, a district court ordered a new trial for McCleskey—not on racial grounds, but on Sixth Amendment ones. Though a court of appeals overturned the lower court's ruling (Mansnerus 1988; Kaplan 1988), the U.S. Supreme Court, in 1991, used it as a vehicle to limit the use of habeas corpus petitions by state prisoners.

49. Attorneys even managed to find some positive words for *McCleskey*. One noted that "the case came a lot closer than I thought." Another said, "I am utterly convinced that in ten, fifteen, or fifty years we will look back on the *McCleskey* litigation and see it in the same sort of light that we now recognize *Maxwell v. Bishop*" (Gray and Stanley 1989, 276, 295).

50. As of 1991, the abolitionist cause has suffered even further setbacks. One of the most significant occurred in April 1991 when the Supreme Court restricted the use of habeas corpus petitions by state prisoners. And, interestingly enough, it did so in a case brought by attorneys representing Warren McCleskey. In this second petition, Mc-Cleskey alleged that police had violated his rights when they used a prison informant to "coerce" a confession from him. After the Supreme Court's ruling, the state of Georgia executed McCleskey.

51. This is not to say that the legal battle over the death penalty has ended; it has not, as the above discussion makes clear. It does suggest, however, that the larger questions that

would provide vehicles for broad-based attacks on capital punishment have, for the time being, been addressed, and in a way profoundly unfavorable to the abolitionist perspective.

52. Indeed, recall his response to the gloom felt by some at the California conference on Proposition 17, shortly after *Furman* came down: "This group has me seriously wondering whether winning *Furman* was a good thing after all" (Meltsner 1973, 307).

CHAPTER 5

1. We derive this account from Faux 1988 and Smith 1988.

2. McCorvey told Coffee and Weddington that her pregnancy was the result of a gang rape incident. She maintained that story—believing that it would garner greater sympathy—until 1987, when she revealed to a journalist that she had lied. She had become pregnant, she admitted, "through what [she] thought was love" (Noble 1987b).

3. Indeed, the practice is an ancient one, dating back to 3000 B.C. (Lader 1966). A voluminous literature exists on the pre-1800 history of abortion (Devereux 1955; Hawkinson 1976; Lader 1966; Taussig 1936). In general, most scholars agree that the royal archives of China contain the "earliest known record of an abortion technique" (3000 B.C.). Also, the literature of "Hinduism [1500–1000 B.C.], Zoroastrianism [1000–600 B.C.], Taoism [about 500 B.C.] and Buddhism [about 500 B.C. and later] have discussed the issue." On its usage in Greek and Roman civilizations, however, a substantial amount of disagreement exists. Compare, for example, Edelstein [1943] 1967 and Arbagi 1987.

4. A significant amount of scholarly literature indicates that colonial women practiced abortion through techniques communicated to them in the "home medical journals" of the day. William Buchan's *Domestic Medicine* (1816), for example, provided information on how to restore menstrual flows, among other things (Mohr 1978, 6–14).

5. As Blackstone (Ehrlich 1959, 46) wrote, life "begins in contemplation of law as soon as an infant is able to stir in the mother's womb."

6. There is even some dispute over "whether abortion of a quick fetus was a felony at common law, or . . . a lesser crime" (*Roe* 1973, 143).

7. In 1803, Parliament criminalized abortion prior to quickening for the first time. In 1828, England enacted a second law, which totally proscribed abortion (Quay 1961).

8. Why were American courts and legislatures so eager to adopt the quickening doctrine? Researchers offer two explanations. First, it was pragmatic: since no pregnancy tests existed, when a woman's menstrual cycle stopped, she or a doctor could attempt to restore it, thinking that it might be a medical problem. The only sure sign of pregnancy was, in fact, a quick fetus. Second, the issue of whether a pre-quickened fetus was a "person" was not at all settled; doctors, lawyers, philosophers, and clergy had been debating the issue for more than five thousand years. Hence, quickening represented a compromise of sorts (Means 1968; Mohr 1978).

9. The Catholic church, for example, played some role, urging adherents to speak out against the practice. Later Anthony Comstock—a self-proclaimed moral crusader—led a campaign to rid America of obscenity, which also helped the pro-life movement to gain some momentum. Comstock was the head of the New York Society for Suppression of Vice, which lobbied Congress to enact the "Comstock Act" of 1873. Although the aim of this law was to eliminate the flow of obscene material in the United States, it contained a provision dealing with abortions, making it criminal to "sell, or offer to sell, or . . . give

away . . . or have in possession [any material] for causing abortion." Under this provision, the government prosecuted a significant number of abortionists in the 1870s, marking the end of its "commercial visibility" (Milbauer 1983; Hall 1970).

10. Why did the AMA adopt such a vehement pro-life stance in the 1860s in particular? Those who have studied it in some detail offer a number of explanations. Professionally speaking, the period after the Civil War through the 1880s was a difficult one for doctors (and lawyers). Because of "Jacksonian democracy" no licensing requirements existed; yet there was an implicit division within the profession between the "regular" (trained) doctors and the "irregulars." Though the regulars made a great deal of this distinction, often calling their untrained counterparts "quacks," the public did not. As a result, high competition for patients ensued, along with a drop in status of the entire profession. Some suggest (Luker 1984; Mohr 1978), then, that "regular" doctors used the issue of abortion to distinguish themselves from the irregulars, thereby raising their status and fees. According to this argument, the elite were, by condemning abortion, making the implicit statement that they possessed medical and scientific knowledge about abortion that their untrained counterparts did not know. They further reinforced this suggestion with vague reports of botched abortions, many of which were performed by the irregulars. In short, they saw abortion as a vehicle by which to "recapture" the profession and eliminate competition along the way.

This, of course, remained unstated in the AMA's resolution. Rather, it claimed that it had adopted this stance because "American women were committing a moral crime based on ignorance about the proper value of embryonic life," and doctors "were obliged to act in order to save women from their ignorance because only [they] were in possession of new scientific evidence" (Luker 1984, 21).

11. So too physicians took "public education" into their own hands, deleting abortion techniques from the home medical journals and publishing pro-life material geared toward the lay person. In the most-cited of these works—"the first American treatment of the subject" (Lader 1966, 1)—Storer urged that "lawyers and physicians stand to each other . . . as associates working together for the common good of society" (Storer and Heard [1868] 1974). That common good was the proscription of abortion—as a dangerous procedure and a form of murder, it was morally reprehensible.

12. Most scholars now agree that the AMA was largely responsible for this wave of legislation, but other explanations abound. For example, some suggest that the decline in "native fertility," coupled with the rise in the immigrant population, alarmed the Protestant community, in particular. Others argue that restrictive abortion laws were the result of a widespread concern over the "disintegration of the moral fabric of society." See Mohr 1978; Quay 1961; and Sauer 1974.

13. The one exception was Kentucky. It had no state law prohibiting abortion, but its state court "declared abortion to be illegal" in *Peoples v. Commissioner* (1883) (Sloan 1988, 6).

14. Punishments differed and some defined therapeutic abortions more broadly. For example, Alabama and the District of Columbia allowed procedures to protect the health of the mother (for reviews, see Means 1968; Sloan 1988; and *Arizona State Law Journal* 1980).

15. New Jersey and Pennsylvania completely outlawed abortions, with no exceptions.

16. As Sarvis and Rodman (1973, 7) point out, prior to the 1930s, only "a single article [on abortion] is indexed in the *Readers' Guide to Periodicals*."

17. Under the leadership of Margaret Sanger, the founder of Planned Parenthood, many members of the birth control movement itself (including Sanger) wanted to keep their mission distinct from abortion in the belief that it would hurt the birth control cause. In 1928 Sanger wrote that abortion was a "desperate remedy" that "greater knowledge of birth control could forestall" (Lader 1966). Still, at the time, the movement was "radical" and large, attracting adherents from all socioeconomic walks of life (Gordon 1977), including those affiliated with the National Committee on Maternal Health.

18. What the committee recognized was that Americans' acceptance of the pro-life laws did not necessarily mean compliance; significant numbers of women did have abortions. What concerned the committee was that because of the difficulty in obtaining therapeutic abortions, the potential for abuse (e.g., dangerous practices by unlicensed practitioners) ran high. Hence, in the 1930s, it commissioned a doctor, Frederick Taussig, to conduct an exploration of the issue. Published under the title *Abortion, Spontaneous and Induced: Medical and Social Aspects*, the 1936 study was a mass of information and statistics on abortion. In particular, Taussig speculated on the number of criminal abortions and illustrated the growing discretion doctors were exercising in determining the need for therapeutic abortions. Perhaps more important was his proposed solution to the "problem": for a "variety of health, eugenic, social, and economic reasons," abortion—prior to viability—should be legalized (Sauer 1974). Though Taussig's study was later to become something of a "bible" for the pro-choice movement (Grisez 1970), its immediate impact was quite negligible. An article in the *Columbia Law Review* (1935)—which was based on Taussig's yet-to-be-published manuscript—suggested that "states begin reforming their laws," on the grounds that the figures in Taussig's study indicated the unenforceability of present laws.

The National Committee on Maternal Health held a conference in 1942, bringing together important reformers and physicians, and published its proceedings two years later. Yet none of these events triggered much interest in the subject; it was still taboo in most political and social circles (Sarvis and Rodman 1973). By the same token, as Calderone (1958, 7) explained, "Perhaps because of the war, perhaps because the public proceedings were not read by enough persons, this important conference failed to bring about any action designed to alleviate the problem it had clearly delineated." Finally, the audience to which Taussig and the committee directed their efforts—physicians—were apparently not very interested in change. Surely some were concerned about "amateur abortionists"; yet, for the most part, they felt "in control." As a result, they continued to dominate abortion policy, a position of superiority they enjoyed.

19. Indeed, Rosen had a great deal of trouble with the book. He could not get it marketed or reviewed (Calderone 1958; Sarvis and Rodman 1973).

20. Sherri Finkbine was a Phoenix-based television celebrity (the host of the children's show "Romper Room") who had four children. While pregnant with her fifth, she had taken her husband's thalidomide, a tranquilizer developed in Germany (and generally unavailable in the United States) and widely used in Europe to ease nausea. Shortly thereafter, scientists discovered that the drug caused deformities in the user's babies, and thousands of armless and legless babies were being born in Europe. Because of thalidomide's potentially crippling effects, Finkbine sought an abortion in Arizona. Initially a hospital board approved the procedure, but when word of the abortion leaked out and began to garner publicity, an administrator canceled it. The Finkbines took the

hospital to court, but after a judge ruled that no legal controversy existed, they decided to fly to Sweden and have the abortion there (*New York Times* 1962).

Thalidomide and the Finkbines' story, in particular, became national news. Americans were bombarded with pictures of deformed "thalidomide" babies and, as a result, apparently sympathized with the Finkbines' plight. In what was the first systematic poll on abortion in the United States, Gallup found that 52 percent of the citizenry (compared to 32 percent) thought they did the right thing. (The specific question was: Did [Sherri Finkbine] do "the right thing or the wrong thing in having this abortion operation?") Sixteen percent had no opinion.

21. Between 1962 and 1969, the United States experienced a German measles epidemic that resulted in the birth of around twenty thousand deformed babies. Through the use of graphic photographs and constant publicity, the media implicitly invited scrutiny of the abortion issue.

22. We should note, though, that neither the book nor its author (at least initially) viewed the issue of abortion as a particularly important one for the cause of women's rights.

23. The incidence of illegal abortions and of deaths is almost impossible to estimate. As Grisez (1970) pointed out, virtually every study on this subject is flawed, and thus reports tend to get confused. Indeed, estimates for 1957 and 1958 range from 41,000 (Williams 1957) to 400,000 (Gebhard et al. 1958) to between 200,000 and 1.2 million (Tietze in Calderone 1958).

24. As the AMA stated, "The problem is essentially one for resolution by each state through action of its own legislature. . . . It is not appropriate at this time for the AMA to recommend new abortion legislation to anyone" (O'Toole 1965).

25. California was a notable exception. In 1959 Packer and Gampbell published in the *Stanford Law Review* a study of the way the existing law worked in the state. In general, the article brought to light what many in the medical field undoubtedly knew but others did not: doctors exercised a great deal of discretion in determining when a therapeutic abortion was indicated. The article further implied that the decision often boiled down to the luck of the draw: if a woman happened upon a doctor who was a "broad construction-ist" (i.e., one who read a great deal into the phrase "preserving life"), she would probably get her abortion. Conversely, a "strict interpreter" of the law would not perform the surgery. A lawyer in the state attorney general's office happened upon the article and asked a friend, freshman state senator, John Knox, to introduce a bill similar to the ALI code into the 1961 state legislature (Luker 1984, 70). Public hearings on the bill—the first on abortion since the early 1900s—got under way in 1961.

26. Members of the ASA included Dr. Robert Hall, a professor of obstetrics at Columbia-Presbyterian Medical Center; Cass Camfield, chair of Harper and Row; Dr. Alan Guttmacher, president of the Planned Parenthood Federation; Harriet Pilpel, an ACLU attorney; and the Reverend Joseph Fletcher, professor of Christian Ethics at the Episcopal Theological School (Lader 1966, 149).

27. In fact, adoption of this plank led a group of the more "conservative" wing of NOW to form an independent organization, the Women's Equity Action League. Ironically, in December 1972, it came out for repeal. Friedan apparently knew a split would occur. Subsequent to the 1966 meeting, she tried to keep NOW out of the fray. But in 1967, the New York State chapter of NOW adopted the plank and pushed for it at the convention (Lader 1973, 36–39).

28. After the meeting, some question arose as to whether the right to abortion was "completely unlimited" and thus may border on infanticide. As a result, its due process committee and board of directors studied the issue, eventually revising its stance in March 1968 to support abortion on demand "prior to the viability of the fetus" (Lissner 1968).

29. Lader's original interest in abortion sprang from his research for *Margaret Sanger and the Fight for Birth Control* (1955).

30. To this end, he parted company with the ASA and began his own abortion referral service. He also wrote a highly influential book, *Abortion* (1966), which outlined his plans for legal change.

31. In 1966, Mississippi changed its law to allow for therapeutic abortions but did not adopt the ALI's other two conditions.

32. Among those attending were politicians, professors representing a range of disciplines, theologians, lawyers, doctors, and members of various organizations, including Planned Parenthood, the National Council of Negro Women, the Center for Population Planning, and the ACLU.

33. For example, reports from California indicated that the 1967 statute was having virtually no effect on reducing the number of illegal abortions; botched procedures were occurring regardless of whether or not states had adopted such laws; no mechanism existed for protecting women against unethical physicians; and discrimination against the poor continued. Other problems with these laws were the subject of many publications of the day. For reviews, see Group for the Advancement of Psychiatry 1970 and Quay 1961.

34. Lader suggests that this was a foregone conclusion; the purpose of the meeting had been to convert reformers to repealers (Lader 1973, 89).

35. New York was the site of huge battles over abortion. For more information, see Cortner 1975 and Potts, Diggory, and Peel 1977.

36. This was true through most of the 1960s. In 1965, in particular, when the government started to support "family-planning" services, the Catholic hierarchy created the National Conference of Catholic Bishops (NCCB) to oppose federal expenditures. As the abortion reform movement began to pick up steam, in 1967 the NCCB "launched an all-out attack," expending $50,000 for an educational campaign (Merton 1981, 25–43). But in 1970 its attention was diverted to the contraceptive issue. In December of that year, Nixon signed a birth control bill authorizing the expenditure of $382 million to expand family-planning services (*New York Times* 1970b).

37. Under the leadership of Robert Byrn, an attorney, and Ellen McCormack, a Long Island homemaker, the right-to-life movement in New York State was particularly strong. Likewise, in Los Angeles, the diocese had established a Right-to-Life League, which had some influence over the course of reform in that state. In particular, it (and other pro-life groups) induced Governor Ronald Reagan to request changes in the abortion law before he would sign it (Luker 1984; Merton 1981). Interestingly, though, some pro-lifers "would never forgive" Reagan for signing the bill because in doing so he was implicitly "acknowledging that a fetus is not entitled to the same rights as the mother" (Merton 1981, 47).

38. This was an idea developed by the Willkes, a husband and wife team who lectured throughout the United States on the horrors of abortion. In 1971, they published a book, entitled *Handbook on Abortion*, which contained pictures of aborted fetuses.

39. They even succeeded in getting New York, in 1971, to repeal its liberal law, only to have Governor Rockefeller's veto make it a hollow victory.

40. One exception to this occurred in 1970 when, under Title X of the Public Health Services Act, Congress made clear that abortion was not to be considered a form of family planning.

41. In *Ex parte Jackson* (1878) it did, however, uphold the Comstock Act.

42. We draw this account largely from Schwartz 1983, 378–79.

43. Even though Warren did not much care for the law, he expressed the view that "[i]t seems to me now they've made us guinea pigs for an abstract principle. We don't want to decide contrived litigation." Justices Frankfurter, Clark, Whittaker, and Brennan concurred, voting to dismiss the case.

44. Besides Harlan, Black thought the law, as it applied to patients, was constitutional, but that the First Amendment prohibited the prosecution of doctors. Stewart took issue with Warren's position, asserting that "I don't think this law is a dead letter, when, as a practical matter, there's no [birth control] clinic in Connecticut." Douglas thought it was "unconstitutional on its face."

45. Douglas's opinion was also noteworthy; it asserted:

Though I believe that "due process" as used in the Fourteenth Amendment includes all of the first eight Amendments, I do not think it is restricted and confined to them. The right "to marry, establish a home and bring up children" was said in *Meyer v. State of Nebraska*, to come within the "liberty" of the person protected by the Due Process Clause of the Fourteenth Amendment. . . . "Liberty" within the purview of the Fifth Amendment includes the right of "privacy". . . . This notion of privacy is not drawn from the blue. It emanates from the totality of the constitutional scheme under which we live. (*Poe* 1961, 516–17)

46. The most often cited example of this theory in action is *Lochner v. New York* (1905), in which the Court struck down a New York maximum-hour law on the grounds that it violated the employer's right of contract as part of the liberty protected in the Fourteenth Amendment.

47. That the ASA and Pilpel contemplated change through litigation is not too surprising. As one scholar noted, the ASA's "orientation was toward judicial rather than legislative reform. . . . [It] had been on the lookout almost since its founding for cases" (Faux 1988, 218). By the same token, as an ACLU activist and "protégé" of Morris Ernst, Pilpel "inherited both [Ernst's] concern with sexual freedom and his dual role as general counsel for both the ACLU and Planned Parenthood" (Walker 1990, 301–2).

48. This was a test case orchestrated by Margaret Sanger, leader of the American birth control movement. Judge Augustus Hand's decision effectively removed all federal, albeit not state, prohibitions on birth control (Kennedy 1970).

49. Most of these, though, dealt with Fourth Amendment search and seizure doctrine (e.g., *Mapp v. Ohio* [1961], in which the Court applied the exclusionary rule to the states).

50. We draw this discussion largely from Schwartz 1983, 1985.

51. In it, he basically reiterated his conference view that "the association of husband and wife is not mentioned in the Constitution. . . . Neither is any other kind of association. . . . Yet, the First Amendment has been construed to include certain peripheral rights."

52. These included "all sexual activities of consenting adults in private" and certain police procedures, such as the use of lie detectors (Emerson 1965, 232).

53. Perhaps the most interesting was a case that never even reached the Supreme Court

(a federal district court judge mooted it in 1970 when New York changed its laws), *Abramowicz v. Lefkowitz* (1970), in which four consolidated cases reflected all the various dimensions of the issue: a "woman's right" (*Abramowicz v. Lefkowitz*); a "doctor's right" (*Hall v. Lefkowitz*); a "community's interest" (*Doe v. Lefkowitz*); and a "minister's case" (*Lyons v. Lefkowitz*) (Schulder and Kennedy 1971).

54. But it was not the first case of the decade in which a U.S. court had nullified a restrictive law. Two months earlier, in *People v. Belous* (1969), the California Supreme Court struck down that state's restrictive law. The case involved Dr. Leon Belous, a prominent physician who publicly attacked California's abortion law in the mid-1960s. Just before passage of the state's 1967 abortion legislation, Belous referred a married couple to an abortionist. The abortionist was arrested, and when the police seized some of his records and found Belous's name, they took him into custody. Belous wanted to launch a constitutional attack on the law, a strategy his attorney A. L. Wirin thought risky. Yet Belous insisted, and with the support of California ACLU attorneys and an amicus curiae brief filed by 178 law school deans, Wirin pressed the cause before the state high court; in particular, he argued that the law inhibited a woman's rights to receive medical care and privacy. In a 4–3 decision, the Court accepted Wirin's claims, asserting that "[t]he fundamental right of women to choose whether to bear children follows from the [U.S.] Supreme Court's and this court's repeated acknowledgment of a 'right to privacy.' . . . That such a right is not enumerated in either the United States or California Constitution is no impediment to the existence of the right" (*Belous* 1969, 199–200).

55. Harlan filed a dissenting opinion for Brennan, Marshall, and Blackmun on the jurisdictional issue. They disagreed with Black's analysis, arguing instead that the "[g]overnment cannot directly appeal the dismissal of indictments" to the Supreme Court. Stewart also dissented in part but did not go as far as Douglas. Using the logic proffered by Harlan, he argued that it necessarily led to the conclusion "that 'a competent licensed [physician]' is wholly immune from being charged with the commission of a criminal offense under this law" (*Vuitch* 1971, 97).

56. Only New York, Washington, Alaska, and Hawaii permitted some form of abortion on demand.

57. At the time of their original meeting with Roe (Norma McCorvey), Coffee was twenty-six and Weddington was twenty-three. Representing Roe before a federal district court marked Weddington's first courtroom appearance (Faux 1988).

58. That they were neophytes is well documented in Faux 1988. By way of example, consider the fact that they did not know of *Griswold* when they decided to mount their challenge.

59. Woodward and Armstrong in *The Brethren* (1979, 165) assert that this action "did not signal any sudden willingness on the part of the Court to grapple with the broad question of abortions." Rather, the cases had been taken to settle procedural/jurisdictional issues, particularly whether to limit "the intervention of federal courts in state proceedings." Apparently Burger "hoped to use these two cases to reduce the number of federal court cases brought by activist attorneys." This explanation receives some support from the fact that many questions posed during orals dealt with procedural (but not jurisdictional) issues. Otherwise, it has many flaws. For one, this subject hardly came up in conference; for another, if the Court wanted to deal with jurisdictional questions, why would it take two such similar cases?

Another explanation, probably more accurate, was suggested by ACLU attorney Norman Dorsen (Faux 1988, 175). In his opinion, three justices (Brennan, Marshall, and Douglas) had wanted to deal with the issue for some time (this was certainly true for Douglas; see Urofsky 1987) but lacked a fourth vote for certiorari. When Harlan and Black resigned and Blackmun came aboard, they had their vote. Cox (1987, 325) lends support to this view, asserting that Justice Black would have "had no difficulty in concluding that Jane Roe had no constitutional right" to an abortion. As Cox explains, Black hated "Lochnerism," and he would have rejected judicial incorporation of a nonenumerated right.

60. Sources disagree on whether the "movement" regarded these as key or not. In *Abortion II*, Lader (1973, 188) writes, "When the U.S. Supreme Court put both cases on its docket . . . everyone expected that [they] would eventually provide the critical high-court decision." Yet on the book's inside cover, he notes, "It came like a thunderbolt—a decision . . . so sweeping that it seemed to assure . . . triumph."

61. Busy with her legal practice, Coffee did not accompany Weddington.

62. Weddington gleaned a great deal from the ASA's collection of legal materials but perhaps more from the advice of experienced attorneys like Pilpel. Unlike Roy Lucas—another pro-choice lawyer who apparently tried to take over *Roe* (Faux 1988)—Pilpel and others respected that the case was Coffee and Weddington's and only sought to assist them. For example, they held moot courts so that Weddington could practice before orals. During those, experienced Supreme Court litigators (e.g., Pilpel and Nellis) tried to help her anticipate the sorts of questions she would likely receive. They informed her during these sessions that newly appointed Justice Blackmun had been counsel to the Mayo Clinic and therefore might ask about medical facets of the issue and that Burger might be more procedurally oriented.

63. This paragraph draws largely on Faux 1988, 224–25.

64. Some variation did exist in the overall quality of the briefs; they ranged from being overtly emotional (that of Women for the Unborn, which made blanket statements without any support) to being well calculated and articulated (that of Certain Physicians of the American College of Obstetricians and Gynecologists, which made extensive use of medical and scientific data).

65. Attorneys General of Arizona, Connecticut, Kentucky, Nebraska, and Utah filed an amicus curiae brief on reargument.

66. Excerpts from oral argument come from Kurland and Casper's (1975b) verbatim transcripts.

67. This was not accidental. According to Milbauer (1983, 53), Weddington and Hames decided that Weddington would "argue the social implications."

68. And, in fact, so was Georgia's counsel, Dorothy Beasley.

69. We derive this account from B. Schwartz 1988 and Urofsky 1987, both of which contain and rely on primary sources. To this extent, our discussion veers considerably from that of Woodward and Armstrong in *The Brethren* (1979) (and those that rely on *The Brethren*), which is undocumented.

70. That it took Blackmun so long did not surprise the brethren. As Brennan wrote in his 30 December letter to Douglas: "I appreciate that some time might pass before we hear from Harry."

71. As he wrote: "We conclude that the law with its sole criterion for exemption as 'saving the life of the mother,' is insufficiently informative to the physician to whom it purports to afford a measure of professional protection but who must measure its

indefinite meaning at the risk of his liberty, and that the statute cannot withstand constitutional challenge on vagueness grounds."

72. Rather, Blackmun averred:

Our holding today does not imply that a State has no legitimate interest in the subject of abortions or that abortion procedures may not be subjected to control by the State. . . . We do not accept the argument of the appellants and of some of the *amici* that a pregnant woman has an unlimited right to do with her body as she pleases. The long acceptance of statutes regulating the possession of certain drugs and other harmful substances, and making criminal indecent exposure in public, or an attempt at suicide, clearly indicate the contrary.

73. On 25 May, Douglas wrote to Blackmun: "I think you have done a fine job. Please join me in your memo, which I hope will be the Court's opinion."

74. Blackmun offered two reasons for concluding that rearguments would be necessary:

1. I believe, on an issue so sensitive and so emotional as this one, the country deserves the conclusion of a nine-man, not a seven-man court, whatever the ultimate decision may be.

2. Although I have worked on these cases with some concentration, I am not yet certain about all the details. Should we make the Georgia case the primary opinion and recast Texas in its light? Should we refrain from emasculation of the Georgia statute and, instead, hold it unconstitutional in its entirety and let the state legislature reconstruct from the beginning? Should we spell out—although it would then necessarily be largely dictum—just what aspects are controllable by the State and to what extent?

75. Both Brennan and Douglas wrote letters to Blackmun attempting to convince him that the cases should not be reargued. As Douglas stated, "I know you have done yeoman service and have written two difficult cases, and you have opinions for a majority, which is 5. . . . While we could sit around and make pages of suggestions, I really don't think that is important. The important thing is to get them down."

When they failed to convince Blackmun, Douglas threatened Burger, asserting that "[i]f the vote of Conference is to reargue, then I will file a statement telling what is happening to us and the tragedy it entails." He also accused Burger, in a memo to conference, of trying "to bend the Court to his will" and imperiling "the integrity of the institution." Douglas never carried through on this threat to make the matter public. But the *Washington Post* (1972) nonetheless carried a story about it.

76. By the time *Roe* was reargued, fourteen three-judge federal courts had ruled on abortion: nine held for the pro-choice position, five held against it.

77. Chaired by John D. Rockefeller, an early abortion proponent, the commission was supposed to study population growth problems (*New York Times* 1970b, 1972b). In doing so, it felt it important to look into the abortion issue.

78. Collectively, the supplemental briefs in *Roe* and *Doe* contained the following new information: a report on the ABA's new policy and of the presidential commission's findings; an explication of *Eisenstadt*; and the procedural requirements found unduly burdensome under the new ruling in *Dunn v. Blumstein* (1972).

79. The Planned Parenthood Federation presented statistical studies, unavailable in

1971, which indicated that legal abortions are safer than childbirth, reduce infant mortality rates, and lessen discrimination against the poor and minorities. It also provided a full explication of the position that a fetus is not a person.

80. These were the South Bay chapter of NOW and Zero Population Growth.

81. Weddington tried to redeem herself on rebuttal but fared no better.

82. In an interview with Jenkins (1983), Blackmun said, "I believe everything I said in the second paragraph of that opinion, where I agonized, initially not only for myself, but for the Court. Parenthetically, in doing so publicly, I disobeyed one suggestion Hugo Black made to me when I first came here. He said, 'Harry, never display agony in public, in an opinion. Never display agony. Never say this was an agonizing, difficult decision. Always write it as though it's crystal clear.'"

83. In 1973, *Time* reported: "After the rehearing last October, the majority grew, to the surprise of most liberals. The five previous votes held firm, and Powell joined them. Blackmun's rewritten and improved decision was soon ready, but now Burger was wavering. In a case of such significance, former Chief Justice Charles Evans Hughes had counseled, the Chief should lend his prestige to the majority—if his conscience could permit it and his vote would not change the outcome. Burger weighed the matter long and carefully, and at last decided to join his Minnesota colleague."

84. The *Louisville Courier-Journal*, for example, said *Roe* was "bold and unequivocal." Some merely expressed agreement: the *New York Times* called it "a major contribution to the preservation of individual liberties"; the *St. Louis Dispatch* said it was "remarkable for its common sense" and "humanness" (Olasky 1988, 118).

CHAPTER 6

1. Our survey of constitutional law texts published in the 1970s reveals that discussions of *Roe* are located within the following sections:

RIGHT TO PRIVACY/AUTONOMY	SUBSTANTIVE DUE PROCESS	EQUAL PROTECTION
Barron and Dienes (1975)	Kauper (1974)	Barrett and Bruton (1973)
Brest (1975)	Barrett (1977)	Saye (1975)
Kutler (1977)	Freund et al. (1977)	
Chase and Ducat (1979)	Bartholomew (1978)	

2. Although the questions of implementation and compliance with *Roe* are interesting (and controversial), they are somewhat beyond the scope of this study. For readers seeking varying perspectives, see Rosenberg 1991 and Bond and Johnson 1982.

3. Louisiana's attorney general, for example, asserted that it "could still revoke a doctor's license for performing an abortion." Just ten days after *Roe*, an Illinois circuit court judge issued a temporary restraining order prohibiting several physicians from performing scheduled abortions (Brody 1973).

4. As Center for Constitutional Rights (CCR) attorney Rhonda Copelon asserted in 1973,

A learning process even went on to a certain extent at the Supreme Court level, although they obviously did not have witnesses before them. At the first argument the Justices asked a substantial number of questions about whether or not abortion was an issue to be left to the legislature. By the second time around they were already talking about abortion as a woman's right and asking about the impact of recognition of any fetal rights on our right to abortion. *There was no question in my mind that they had been educated by the entire climate of discussion that the women's cases and movement had generated.* (Goodman, Copelon Shoenbrod, and Stearns 1973, 23; emphasis added)

5. To be sure, its leaders recognized the dangers of a backlash and took some precautionary steps, such as sending out "scare" letters to their members, devising counterattacks (Faux 1988, 324), and initiating lawsuits against hospitals refusing to perform abortions (Sibley 1973). But, in retrospect, as one of its leaders stated, "[e]very-one assumed that when the Supreme Court made its decision . . . that we'd gotten what we wanted and the battle was over. The movement lost steam" (Tatalovich and Daynes 1981, 101).

6. A notable exception to Catholic dominance of the movement was Americans United for Life (AUL). According to a recent executive director, it was founded by political and intellectual leaders in Washington, D.C., to provide "a non-sectarian, national organization to combat legalized abortion" (Epstein 1985, 95–96). So that it could be closer to those involved in its creation, it later moved to Chicago. From there it lobbied against repeal, mounted an educational campaign, and filed an amicus curiae brief in the 1973 cases. Still, prior to the creation of its Legal Defense Fund in 1976, it remained relatively invisible, often omitted from accounts of the pro-life movement.

7. Here, we refer to the congressional hearings of March 1974 in which the legislature considered various pro-life proposals to amend the Constitution.

8. A constitutional amendment to gut *Roe* represented the pro-life movement's ultimate objective, and it had some measure of support within Congress; by early 1974, representatives and senators had proposed fifty-eight amendments, falling into three general categories (Lee and LeRoy 1985):

• Human Life Amendment: The word "person" (in the Fifth and Fourteenth amendments) applies "to all human beings, including their unborn offspring at every stage of biological development, irrespective of age, health, function or condition of dependency." It allows for one exception: "a medical emergency where a reasonable medical certainty exists that continuation of the pregnancy will cause the death of the mother."
• "Paramount" Human Life Amendment: "Neither the United States, nor any State shall deprive any human being from the moment of conception, of life without due process of law; nor deny any human being from the moment of conception, within its jurisdiction, the equal protection of the law."
• States' Rights Amendment: "Nothing in this Constitution shall bar any state or territory or the District of Columbia with regard to any area over which it has jurisdiction from allowing, regulating, or prohibiting the practice of abortion."

Although these amendments were proposed almost immediately after *Roe*, Congress took no action until 1974. By then, it became clear to some senators that pro-lifers would continue to pressure them until they took some action (Packwood 1986). Hence in March 1974, Birch Bayh's Senate Judiciary Subcommittee began a series of hearings on proposals for constitutional amendments to limit *Roe*.

Observers suggested that the amendments had no more than "a wraith's chance of success" (Charlton 1974), but pro-life forces compounded their political problems by erring at every possible turn. For example, the NRLC distributed "lurid and often enlarged photographs of aborted fetuses," which apparently "alienated some of the legislators who might have been sympathetic to their cause" (ibid.). Likewise, the Catholic church engaged in "unprecedented" tactics when it sent the president of the U.S. Catholic Conference and three other cardinals to testify. By virtually all accounts, that was a poor strategic move; their unwillingness to compromise (they would stop at nothing short of a full ban on abortion) offended many senators, and their testimony was opposed by Methodist, Presbyterian, Reformed Jewish, and other religious leaders (indeed, by that point, over forty religions and religious groups supported *Roe*). Another mistake was to allow Congress a glimpse into the divisiveness of the movement. The NRLC, for example, sought to distance itself from the bishops; it "disclaimed any connection" with the Catholic church and appeared somewhat more willing to support a compromise amendment. All in all, it was eminently clear to the Senate that forces which should have been united were not—a fatal flaw in politics. Finally, pro-life groups seemed to have underestimated their opponents. Nonetheless, however, pro-choicers, as complacent as they had become, did not remain silent when it came to a constitutional amendment. By that time, fifty-two national groups had fully aligned themselves with *Roe* (Jaffe, Lindheim, and Lee 1981, 124–25).

The Senate took no action on the amendments in 1974. A year later, the "Paramount" Human Life Amendment actually got to the floor, but by that time the U.S. Commission on Civil Rights had issued a report lambasting it and all other proposals. In particular, it called them "inconsistent with . . . the First . . . Ninth . . . and Fourteenth Amendment[s]"; capable of producing "chaos in . . . torts, tax law, property law, and criminal law"; and potentially able to "start a process of undermining the civil rights fabric of the Constitution." In response to this report, the Ninety-fifth Congress enacted legislation denying the commission authority relating to abortion. This, however, was of no concern to pro-choice advocates: once the Senate tabled the amendment, it was clear that they had won the first round.

9. In the midterm elections of 1974, the pro-life side marked several members of Congress for defeat and lent its support to others, but because preparation for these elections was minimal and because of the storm over Watergate, "abortion was not a major campaign issue" (Jackson and Vinovskis 1983). As a result, 1976 "marked an accelerated involvement" by abortion forces (Lee and LeRoy 1985, 50). At least early on, it appeared that abortion would be *the* issue of the election; for example, *Newsweek* (Steele 1976) called it "1976's Sleeper Issue." Initial media attention focused on Ellen McCormack, who ran as a Democratic candidate for president on a pro-life platform. Later coverage, though, primarily focused on the presidential front-runners, none of whom—with the exception of Ronald Reagan—initially took strong stances. Carter "waffled" until February 1976, when he finally asserted that he thought "abortion is wrong," but that he did not "favor a constitutional amendment to give states local option-authority without knowing the specifics at this time" (Vinovskis 1980a, 192). Shortly thereafter Gerald Ford staked out his position. While he asserted that it "went too far," he also stated that he would not favor a nationwide constitutional amendment. In short, he took a self-proclaimed "moderate" position, which would enable him "to pick his way through the thicket" (Naughton 1976).

After the nominating conventions (at which both parties included in their platforms, for the first time, planks on abortion), though, interest in the issue faded. Vinovskis (1980a) attributes this to polls taken in the months preceding the general vote. One indicated that by September 1976, only 32 percent of the voting public supported a constitutional ban on abortions, while 56 percent opposed it (12 percent had no opinion) (Reinhold 1976). Even more to the point, the public had not moved much in opinion since 1972. Thus, in the eyes of journalists, either Americans were not very interested in the subject or they had largely made up their minds.

In the end, the media's assessment was accurate. Analyses of the presidential vote indicate "one's position on abortion was not a good predicter, by itself, of whether one voted for Ford or Carter" (Vinovskis 1980a, 199). As a result, neither side could claim any significant victories; in fact, if anything, the picture was quite mixed. On one hand, the pro-life movement succeeded in "diverting" media attention, at least initially, to the issue. On the other, the 1976 elections did not give pro-life forces the victory "they [were] badly in need of." One obstacle was the seeming apathy of the American public toward abortion. Another might have been the movement itself, which evinced "terrible and at times scandalous disunity . . . among the pro-life partisans" (Lynch 1976).

Right-to-life forces and their opponents vowed to "prove their effectiveness in the 1978 midterm elections" (Jackson and Vinovskis 1983). In their immediate aftermath, some commentators suggested that the pro-life strategy of targeting candidates had worked and were quick to depict the elections as a win for abortion opponents. In particular, they pointed to the defeat of pro-choice Senator Dick Clark and to the fact that "pro-life forces made significant inroads in Congress by reinforcing the idea among politicians that their organizations were important in congressional elections" (ibid., 76). In retrospect, though, neither side made much of a difference. Both sides had trouble raising funds. Compared to the efforts of other political action committees of the day, campaign funding supplied by abortion groups bordered on the trivial. In fact, it was after this election that some pro-life leaders turned to New Right fundraisers. Moreover, as Jackson and Vinovskis (1983, 75) argue, abortion was not seen as a key issue in 1978; interviews with campaign managers and opinion polls taken within districts indicate that public apathy toward abortion still remained.

In the final analysis, the pro-life electoral strategy of the 1970s failed; they were unable to load Congress with supporters. Nonetheless, this failure was not total. Regardless of the fact that "the abortion issue was not a major determinant of voting behavior in [1978], . . . [t]he pro-life forces benefitted greatly from the news media's portrayal of the elections as a pro-life victory" (ibid., 767).

10. After right-to-life forces failed to convince Congress to consider seriously a Human Life Amendment and to affect its composition through electoral strategies, they set their sights on smaller victories that would gradually undermine *Roe*. One of these involved blunting the effect of the 1973 decisions through "piecemeal" federal legislation. This was not a new tactic: it was first developed and invoked by pro-life members of Congress shortly after *Roe*. In 1973 and 1974, members "attempted to attach . . . anti-abortion riders to seemingly non-abortion-related bills" (for a list, see U.S. Commission on Civil Rights 1975).

Following the lead of congressional allies, pro-life forces sought to convince members of Congress to tack "restrictive riders" onto "'any and all federal legislation related directly or indirectly to health'" (Lee and LeRoy 1985, 50). Hence, they bombarded

Congress with proposals for riders and amendments that would limit the ability to attain abortions, including restrictions on abortion funding, rights of conscience, and so forth.

In general, however, those efforts were not particularly successful. The outcome of pro-life legislation in Congress between 1973 and 1982 is presented below (from Subcommittee on the Constitution 1983, appendixes C and D1–6):

CONGRESS	BILLS PROPOSED	BILLS PASSED		TYPE OF LAW PASSED
93d	94	0	0.00%	
94th	206	2	0.97	Funding (1), misc. (1)
95th	108	9	8.30	Funding (6), misc. (3)
96th	73	9	12.30	Funding (7), right of conscience (1), misc. (1)
97th	78	8	10.30	Funding (8)

11. How pro-lifers pushed the Hyde amendment through Congress is a subject on which many have speculated (e.g., O'Connor and Epstein 1985; Vinovskis 1980b). In general, observers have offered two sets of explanations. One centers on the members of Congress themselves. When it was first proposed by Henry Hyde (R-Ill.) in June 1976, some were "caught off guard" and, thus, "unprepared to join in debate"; others were simply "reluctant" to stake out a position on abortion in an election year, particularly when few of them "expected the Hyde Amendment to require a roll-call vote, much less to pass" (Vinovskis 1980b, 229–52). Still other members wanted quick passage of the HEW Labor Appropriations Act because it increased funding levels of myriad social programs. Thus, they "tolerated" the Hyde rider. As Senator Hubert Humphrey later said, it was a "no win type of vote" (Tolchin 1977).

Another explanation is that pro-choice groups had also been caught off guard; after the amendment passed in the House, they were "stunned" and vowed to "regroup" for a Senate battle. But their opponents, "sensing victory, redoubled their efforts and besieged Senators." Indeed, right-to-lifers placed a great deal of pressure on members of Congress, who faced only last-minute lobbying of pro-choice forces. They claimed to be using the Hyde amendment as a "litmus test" on abortion, vowing to reward friends and punish enemies. Apparently their threat worked: "[T]hough most representatives were not in any real danger of being defeated for reelection, they did not want to take any chances by triggering an emotional pro-life crusade against them in their districts" (Jackson and Vinovskis 1983, 1252).

12. The same term it also decided *Connecticut v. Menillo* (1975), in which the justices examined a Connecticut law that prohibited persons without medical training from performing abortions. In a unanimous *per curiam* opinion (Justice White concurred without opinion), the Court reversed a state supreme court ruling and upheld the law. It noted that "the rationale of our decision [in *Roe*] supports continued enforceability of criminal abortion statutes against nonphysicians" (*Menillo* 1975, 10).

13. Although the name of Judith Mears (head of the RFP) appeared on the brief, *Bigelow* was largely argued on First Amendment grounds. And, in fact, Blackmun's majority opinion barely mentioned *Roe*. Yet both sides inevitably saw this not only as an abortion case but as a win for the pro-choice side. The only amicus curiae brief supporting the state was filed by Virginia Right to Life. The same two justices—White and Rehnquist—who dissented in *Roe* refused to join the *Bigelow* majority. Justice White's

vote in this case was particularly anomalous, perhaps indicating that he too viewed it as an "abortion" dispute. Consider his vote in *Virginia State Board of Pharmacy v. Virginia Citizens Consumer Council* (1976) decided the term after *Bigelow*. In that case, the Court struck down a restriction prohibiting pharmacists from advertising the prices of prescription drugs. Though Rehnquist dissented, as he did in *Bigelow*, White signed onto the majority opinion written again by Justice Blackmun.

14. One exception to this was *Singleton v. Wulff* (1976) involving a 1975 Missouri law that excluded from Medicaid coverage abortions not "medically indicated." Representing two doctors, attorney Frank Susman challenged the legislation on various grounds, but the Court chose to deal with the more technical issue of whether doctors qua doctors have standing to bring suits. In a 5-4 decision, Blackmun found for the physicians, holding that they could suffer "concrete injury" from such laws and that the "closeness of the relationship" between them and pregnant women made them virtually inseparable as plaintiffs.

15. One was filed by the Planned Parenthood Federation and cosigned by the Association of Planned Parenthood Physicians. The Center for Constitutional Rights and the Women's Law Project filed the other.

16. One brief was presented by the District of Columbia Right to Life, Families for Life, Feminists for Life, Virginia Society for Human Life, Health Personnel Concerned for Life, Legal Defense Fund for Unborn Children, Long Island Coalition for Life, March for Life, Maryland Pro-Life, Knights of Columbus, Missouri Citizens for Life, New Jersey Right to Life, Prince George County Right to Life, Diocesan Union of Holy Name Society, Scientists for Life, South Dakota Right to Life, Women for the Unborn, Life Advocates, Lifebeat, Pro-Life Legal Action Committee, Maryland Action for Human Life, Concerned Prolife Students, St. Bridget's Parish, American Conservative Citizens Assembly, Ad Hoc Study Committee of the University of Minnesota, St. Peter's Council of Catholic Women, Prolife Rural America, Irish Right to Life, Social Workers in Support of Life, and Lawyers for Life. Four others were submitted by Missouri Nurses for Life, Americans United for Life, United States Catholic Conference, and Lawyers for Life (cosigned by Social Workers for Life).

17. An exception to this was the brief filed by Lawyers for Life. It tried to demonstrate that the state possessed a compelling and traditional interest in protecting minors.

18. He wrote that "we emphasize that our holding [this section] invalid does not suggest that every minor . . . may give effective consent" (*Planned Parenthood* 1976, 75).

19. In *Bellotti v. Baird* (1979), the Court tried to clear up some of this confusion. This was a continuation of a 1976 case that the justices had remanded for certification from the Massachusetts high court. Upon review, that state court answered nine questions about the law, with two of particular note. First, does the statute permit any minor to obtain judicial consent without initially speaking with her parents? The court responded negatively. Second, if a court finds that a minor has made an informed decision, can it still refuse consent? The Massachusetts court suggested that it could "in circumstances where . . . the best interests of the minor will not be served by an abortion." Given these responses, attorneys representing Bill Baird and Massachusetts Civil Liberties Union lawyers (who undertook the case for appellee intervenors, the Planned Parenthood League of Massachusetts) wasted no time in asking the Supreme Court to review the case again (Rubin 1987, 134–35). Massachusetts Attorney General Bellotti countered by citing a traditional and compelling state interest in the protection of minors.

After the Court accepted the case, both sides mobilized. Again pro-life forces outnumbered their opponents, filing four briefs representing eight organizations or churches in support of the state; only one (submitted by the Planned Parenthood Federation for seven organizations and a slew of doctors) took Baird's side. Nonetheless, as was true in the *Planned Parenthood* litigation, one Planned Parenthood brief was probably preferable to a load of emotionally laden pro-life briefs, particularly if one of those submissions was filed by the irrepressible Alan Ernest, director of the Legal Defense Fund for the Unborn. Ernest tried to intercede in virtually every abortion case, including *Bellotti*. Sometimes he asked to be appointed *guardian ad litem* for the unborn; on other occasions he was forced to file motions with the Court to participate as an amicus curiae (after one side or the other refused consent). In *Bellotti* (1979), Ernest tried both tacks. On the same day, he filed identical petitions, one requesting to be appointed *guardian ad litem* for unborn children, the other to participate as an amicus curiae. Though Ernest may have been more extreme than other pro-life advocates (he often argued that *Roe* "is based on false evidence and millions of lives have been unconstitutionally exterminated"; see, for example, *Bellotti*, Motion to Leave to File Petition for Rehearing for Alan Ernest, no. 78-330, 1), at least in early cases like *Bellotti*, his viewpoint was not very different in tenor. From the state's perspective, such amici were hardly desirable "friends." Even the Supreme Court, which is usually quite generous in allowing amici to participate, apparently was repulsed by presentations like Ernest's. Between 1969 and 1981, the justices denied only 11 percent of the 832 motions it received to file amicus curiae briefs. Fully 18 percent of those were sought by Ernest (O'Connor and Epstein 1983).

Again, we can only speculate as to what "damage" pro-life "friends" did to the state. In the final analysis, a divided Supreme Court handed pro-choice advocates their most significant and "definitive" victory to date on the subject of parental consent (Benshoof and Pilpel 1986, 139). Writing for Burger, Stewart, and Rehnquist, Justice Powell (*Bellotti* 1979) disagreed with the Massachusetts high court to the extent that its reading of the law would amount "to the 'absolute, and possibly arbitrary, veto' that was found impermissible in *Danforth*." In their view, if states require pregnant minors to obtain parental consent, they "must provide an alternative procedure whereby authorization for the abortion can be obtained" without parental influence.

Although this represented only the judgment of the Court and it permitted some state regulation of minors, pro-choice forces were delighted with the ruling; indeed, their reactions to it were far more positive than they expressed after *Planned Parenthood*. From their vantage point, *Bellotti* plainly established that "minors' constitutional right to choose cannot be arbitrarily abrogated through mandating parental involvement statutes" (Benshoof and Pilpel 1986, 139). This was what they had hoped for, even if it came from a highly fragmented institution.

20. We do not mean to imply that these laws did, in fact, have a deterrent effect. For a systematic examination of that question, see Johnson and Bond 1980.

21. Prior to *Roe*, states had given little thought to Medicaid funding; in fact, the vast majority that had enacted liberalized laws or laws similar to the ALI code funded legal abortions (*Arizona State Law Journal* 1980). So the idea of restricting funding was relatively novel.

22. Private hospitals also resisted. As Rosenberg (1989, 25) notes, "[B]y 1976, three years after the decision, the vast majority of public and private hospitals had never performed an abortion. . . . [A]t least 70 percent of hospitals did not provide any abortion services."

23. Interestingly, they had litigated and won this issue prior to *Roe*. In *Klein v. Nassau County Medical Center* (1972), a federal district court ruled that states must provide funding for "elective" abortions.

24. For a complete list of the cases in which pro-choice forces were victorious, see Brennan's dissent in *Maher v. Roe* (1977, 482–90).

25. Conference discussion of these cases was lopsided, with all but three justices (Brennan, Marshall, and Blackmun) taking a position in favor of the state. Five of those in the majority echoed Bork. See Schwartz 1990, 312.

26. Powell also dismissed the heart of the appellee's claims in *Beal*, asserting that nothing in the legislative history and intent of the law at issue "suggests that it is unreasonable for a participating State to further [its] unquestionably strong and legitimate interest in encouraging normal childbirth" by excluding abortion. In reaching this conclusion, Powell alluded to congressional passage of the Hyde amendment. In particular, in note 14, Powell pointed out that Congress "had expressly prohibited" the use of Medicaid funding (*Beal* 1977, 446–47). Similar analyses were used to reverse *Poelker*.

27. For example, in deciding that Pennsylvania did not have to fund nontherapeutic abortions, Powell asserted: "We make clear, however, that the federal statute leaves a State free to provide such coverage if it so desires" (*Beal* 1977, 447). In *Maher*, he was more explicit: "[W]hen an issue involves policy choices as sensitive as those implicated by public funding of nontherapeutic abortions, the appropriate forum for their resolution in a democracy is the legislature. We should not forget that 'legislatures are ultimate guardians of the liberties and welfare of the people in quite as great a degree as the courts'" (*Maher* 1977, 479–80).

28. They were Janet Benshoof and Judith Levin of the ACLU; Rhonda Copelon and Nancy Stearns of the CCR; Harriet Pilpel and Eve Paul of Planned Parenthood; Sylvia Law of New York University Law School; Ellen Sawyer, corporate counsel of New York City; and Nadine Taub of the Women's Litigation Clinic of Rutgers University.

29. As one attorney involved in the case said, "This decision is every bit as important as the one by the Supreme Court that legalized abortion in 1973" (Brozan 1980). Even the judge implicitly credited pro-choice attorneys when he stated that "[i]t was a very long and detailed record and it seemed important to me to report the record and findings fully in an area in which we've had too many generalizations" (Fried 1980).

30. Between its passage in 1976 and the Court's review of it in 1980, the Hyde amendment underwent several transformations in the kinds of pregnancies for which women could obtain funding to abort (*New York Times* 1989).

TIME PERIOD	CRITERIA IN EFFECT	FEDERALLY FUNDED ABORTIONS
Oct. 1976–Sept. 1977	Medical need, rape, incest	294,000
Oct. 1977–Dec. 1977	Life	
Dec. 1977–Sept. 1978	Life or health, rape, incest	1,335
Oct. 1978–Sept. 1979	Life or health, rape, incest	3,675
Oct. 1979	Life or health, rape, incest	
Oct. 1979–Feb. 1980	Life, rape, incest	33,625
Feb. 1980–Sept. 1980	Medical need, rape, incest	
Sept. 1980	Life, rape, incest	

31. By 1980, there was some truth in this assertion. That is, the AUL LDF's arguments were continually improving, moving from the overtly emotional (e.g., in its brief in *Roe*, Americans United for Life argued: "We are not concerned . . . with the question of whether state law can constitutionally allow abortion. . . . Rather the issue is whether the Constitution permits the child in the womb to be killed") to the more legalistic (e.g., in its brief in *Harris*, it called for "protection of fetus," not "unborn person"). AUL LDF attorneys understood the flaws of the earlier arguments. One conceded that their initial efforts were sloppy and too ideological. In recognition of "the lack of professionalism," they made a number of strategic changes (Epstein 1985, 101).

32. When the Hyde amendment came up for renewal, pro-life groups perceived the administration's HEW as hostile to it. And, indeed, under Joseph Califano, the agency issued regulations that implemented the amendment in ways opposed by pro-life forces (Califano 1981). Carter himself adamantly opposed federal funding of abortions, although the Democratic party supported it.

33. Brennan wrote for Marshall and Blackmun. Marshall, Blackmun, and Stevens filed separately. It was, though, perhaps Justice Marshall's dissent that best summarized the fears of pro-choice forces when he wrote that the decision "will have a devastating impact on the lives and health of poor women. I do not believe that a Constitution committed to the equal protection of the laws can tolerate this result" (*Harris* 1980, 346–48).

34. As the CCR's Copelon commented,

The decision is a travesty. It reflects the political pressures brought to bear by abortion foes and the right wing and carries the pervasive hostility of this Court to the rights of the poor to a new extreme. . . . The reversal of this decision—practically and doctrinally—is a critical political task in this decade if we are to make the right to abortion meaningful and guarantee both the rights of the poor and basic fairness in a society which is increasingly dependent on government funding. (Milbauer 1983, 270)

35. The six defeated were Church, Culver, Bayh, Nelson, Javitz, and McGovern. The three targeted but reelected were Packwood, Cranston, and Leahy.

36. They were Mickles, Denton, East, and Hawkins.

37. For particularly interesting analyses of the 1980 elections, see Abramowitz 1984; Abramson, Aldrich, and Rohde 1982; Frankovic 1981; Jacobson and Kernell 1981; Knight 1985; Markus 1982; Pomper 1981; Sandoz and Crabb 1981; Sundquist and Scammon 1981; and White 1982.

38. Some suggest that the outcomes of the House races were due largely "to voters' evaluations of the Democratic and Republican candidates," which reflected a high degree of discontent with prevailing economic conditions (Abramowitz 1984). Others give credit to the Republican party. As Jacob (1981, 122) noted, "Republicans rediscovered the joys of party" and launched a "concerted, centrally directed and funded national party campaign" under the banner "Vote for Republicans. For a Change." A third group sees merits in both sets of explanations, suggesting that the state of the economy, coupled with Jimmy Carter's unpopularity, made it easier for the Republican party to raise money, recruit challengers, and support their campaigns (Jacobson and Kernell 1981).

39. Latus (1984) reports total campaign expenditures for NARAL PAC at $203,966 with no debt and for LAPAC at $185,657 with $90,904 in debt. Both organizations,

however, geared up for the elections. NARAL held a conference in April 1979 to mark its tenth anniversary and to begin "an aggressive new campaign to let legislators know that compulsory pregnancy is not the will of the people" (Bennetts 1979). It even came up with a campaign slogan, "I am Pro-Choice and I vote." In short, NARAL vowed to become more "aggressive" and less "reactive." LAPAC, too, organized its troops, holding various meetings and conferences between 1978 and 1980. In general, it continued its "targeting strategy" (Herbers 1978; Bennetts 1980).

40. Although abortion groups largely negated each other's efforts, we cannot say that neither side had any effect. Through the National Conservative Political Action Committee (NCPAC), the so-called New Right probably played a greater role than any of its opponents. It was that multi-issue organization, in conjunction with the Republican party, that devised the senatorial targeting plan as a way to rid the institution of its "most distasteful" members (Jacob 1981) and that raised $7.6 million for the party (Latus 1984, 151). However, the effect of PAC money and of the NCPACs, specifically, on electoral outcomes is an issue about which scholars disagree (see, generally, Sorauf 1988 and Malbin 1984). Since LAPAC also devised a targeting scheme and its list and NCPAC's overlapped, it is difficult to assess the independent influence of LAPAC (for its list, see Bennetts 1980).

41. As Markus (1982, 560) asserted, "The data clearly indicate that Carter's loss can be attributed to pervasive dissatisfaction with his first-term performance and doubt about his personal competence as a political leader." In essence, the 1980 election was a "referendum on the Carter presidency" (Frankovic 1981).

42. As Frankovic noted (1981, 113), "[T]here is no evidence that indicates a turn to the right by the Nation. Reagan was not elected because of increasing conservatism of the country" (see also Markus 1982 and Pomper 1981). But this may be overstating the case a bit. Knight (1985, 851), for example, found that in the 1980 election, the "ideology glass" was "neither half-empty nor half-full. . . . Rather, it is brimming among ideologues and nearly empty among all other citizens." By the same token, Fleishman (1986, 538) found a "gradual increase in self-identified conservatives over the decade [of the 1970s] . . . [but] this increase occurred only for those with a relatively high interest in politics."

43. As Abramson, Aldrich, and Rohde (1982, 135) convincingly demonstrate, most people knew where Reagan (and the Republican party) stood on abortion, yet they classified themselves as taking a different position.

44. By the same token, some candidates whom the New Right supported "repudiated their help." Newly elected Senator Dan Quayle from Indiana, the beneficiary of NCPAC's targeting of his opponent (Birch Bayh), said, "We did not want their help. They're a disservice to the people they claim to help" (MacNeil 1981, 83). In fact, after the 1980 election, in June 1981 several members of Congress resigned from NCPAC's advisory board after it announced plans to target nine others for defeat in 1982. As one said, they "did not like the tactic of issuing . . . 'hit lists' " (*New York Times* 1981).

45. Pro-life senators and groups tried to regroup. In 1982, competing Helms/Hyde and Hatch proposals were considered by the Senate. Its Judiciary Committee, in March, voted 10–7 in favor of a modified version of the Hatch amendment, representing the first time that a "full Congressional committee supported an anti-abortion amendment" (Weintraub 1982). However, an all-out war began between pro-choice and pro-life forces

and among members of the pro-life camp. In August, Helms made a motion to propose another piece of legislation; it was defeated by a 59–38 vote. He tried again in September but lost in a 47–46 vote. After that, Hatch withdrew his proposal.

46. Pro-choice advocates exploited their opponents' dissension and presented a unified attack against the bill. *Roe*'s lead attorney, Sarah Weddington, testified on "behalf of 75 national organizations with 34 million members" (Weintraub 1981); ACLU President Norman Dorsen made an appearance; and NARAL, which had limited the agenda of its February 1981 meeting to the Human Life Amendment (Brozan 1981), placed continuous pressure on key senators. Pro-choice advocates also took to the law reviews to make specific legal arguments against the bill. Pilpel (1982, 1122), for one, refuted virtually all claims supporting it in an attempt to demonstrate that the bill represented a "direct attack on our Constitution and fundamental freedom."

47. Six former attorneys general (Brownell, Katzenbach, Clark, Richardson, Saxbe, and Civiletti) and twelve respected scholars (including Tribe, Brest, Freund, and, interestingly, Ely, who had been one of *Roe*'s harshest critics) wrote the committee, suggesting that the entire act violated constitutional mandates. Even former Solicitor General Bork said: "[I]t seems to me that the bill is constitutional insofar as it deprives the lower federal courts of jurisdiction, but unconstitutional insofar as it attempts to prescribe a rule of decision for the courts under the Fourteenth Amendment" (U.S. Congress, Subcommittee on Separation of Powers 1981).

48. The so-called "Right-to-Life Split" was most apparent in early 1981, when Congress began to consider various mechanisms for restricting abortion. At the time, a number of proposals were floating around, among them a couple of constitutional amendments and the Human Life Bill proposed by Jesse Helms and Henry Hyde. The movement split over these proposals. Early fights centered on the wording of a constitutional amendment and replayed battles fought previously (Noah 1981).

New feuds developed over the Helms/Hyde legislative proposal (or, as Senator Packwood [1986, 12] put it, "The players . . . could not agree on how to proceed"). Clearly, as one pro-choice advocate put it, the bill was a "back door attempt to amend the Constitution" (Noah 1981). Some pro-life groups agreed, viewing it as a "stop-gap" measure, that is, as a way to restrict the right expediently and as a mechanism by which to build momentum for a Human Life Amendment. As a result, many pro-life groups supported it. Others would not go along; for example, NRLC President Willke and the Catholic church viewed nothing short of a Human Life Amendment as worthwhile. Further illustrating this split was the "simmering dispute" in the Senate between two ardent prolifers. Orrin Hatch refused to support Helms's bill, saying that he had "serious constitutional reservations" about it and noting his preference for a Constitutional amendment (Clines and Weintraub 1981).

49. Reagan did, however, look to the ranks of the pro-life movement for some less visible, albeit significant, positions. One was surely the appointment of Rex E. Lee as solicitor general. Lee was an elder in the Mormon church and former dean of Brigham Young Law School. Other pro-lifers appointed were U.S. Surgeon General C. Everett Koop, former NRLC leader Marjorie Mecklenburg as head of the Office of Adolescent Pregnancy, and pro-life activist William Olson as acting chair of Legal Services Corporation (O'Connor and Epstein 1985).

50. Pro-lifers pointed to the following (Witt 1986, 40):

• In 1970 she cast a vote in committee for a bill that would repeal all laws "making it a felony to provide anyone the means for causing a miscarriage."

• In 1974, she voted "against a proposal urging Congress" to pass a constitutional amendment to overturn *Roe*.

• In 1974, she "opposed an anti-abortion rider" that the state House tacked on to an otherwise "non-germaine" piece of legislation.

51. Another came in the early 1980s when the Senate was contemplating restrictive abortion measures. Pro-lifers expected the president to take *some* role in the debate, but he knew that if he supported legislation over an amendment he would alienate the NRLC, the Catholic church, and others. In the end, he managed to confuse both camps when he stated in March 1981 that "there isn't really any need for an amendment, because once you have determined [that the unborn fetus is living], the Constitution already protects human life." Reagan, in short, simply reiterated his opposition to abortion when he could have actively structured the debate, for example, by summoning competing pro-life factions to the White House to develop a unified approach and pressuring individual senators. Instead, he left much of the work to staffers, who admitted that "the issue doesn't burn in the hearts of most people around here" (O'Connor and Epstein 1985, 224).

52. In 1981, the NRLC claimed to have about ten million members, and NARAL, about one hundred thousand. Financially, too, a gulf existed, with the NRLC averring that combined local, state, and national budgets were "somewhere in the Millions," whereas NARAL's budget was around $1.5 million (Noah 1981).

NARAL clearly recognized this deficit. As one pro-choice advocate said, "We've been very reactive in the past. The new tactic is to be more aggressive. We're doing a lot more grass-roots organizing" (Bennetts 1979). As far as the states went, this was too little, too late.

53. According to briefs filed by the pro-choice side, "[T]he process by which [the ordinances were] prepared was marked by drastic departures from normal legislative procedures." They claimed that the drafters of the series of ordinances had virtually no knowledge of abortion practices in Akron; it was opposed by the city's Law Department on the grounds that it was unconstitutional; it was considered in closed legislative sessions, "attended by outsiders" (e.g., the bill's drafters), but not the public; and it was "adopted despite statements by the Akron Director of Health, Akron Mayor," and others "that there was no medical or health-related need" for it.

City attorney Robert D. Pritt did not controvert this characterization. Rather, he simply left it unaddressed. It is nevertheless true that the ordinances were drafted by members of the Akron Right-to-Life Society (Stuart 1978).

54. Interestingly, a majority voted in conference to strike the law, with Marshall assigned the opinion. But Stewart and Powell switched their votes (Schwartz 1990). In the end, only Marshall, Brennan, and Blackmun dissented. The majority upheld it on the grounds that—because it gave neither judges nor parents an absolute veto over the abortion decision and because it served a legitimate constitutional interest—it was consistent with *Roe*.

55. The mayor actually refused to sign the bill, arguing that "the thrust of this ordinance may run counter to now well-established case law, in that it possibly invades constitutionally guaranteed rights of women who desire to have an abortion." An assistant

city law director had gone on record that the law was unconstitutional because of the "informed consent" provision (*New York Times* 1978b).

56. These included Robert Destro of Catholic University Law School and attorneys from the Catholic League for Religious and Civil Rights.

57. We draw this and what follows from Caplan 1987, 105-7.

58. The one exception to this was an amicus curiae brief filed by the AUL in which it urged the Court to adopt a rational basis approach to abortion regulation.

59. They devoted two and a half pages to refuting the solicitor general in broad terms. Their arguments centered on the appropriate role of courts (namely, "to safeguard constitutional rights") in a democratic society (see *Akron*, Brief for Respondent, no. 81-746, 29-31).

60. Amicus curiae briefs were filed on the pro-choice side by the American College of Obstetricians and Gynecologists (for American Medical Association, American Academy of Pediatrics, and Nurses Association of the ACOG); American Psychological Association; American Public Health Association; Committee for Abortion Rights and against Sterilization Abuse (for National Bar Association, National Emergency Civil Liberties Committee, National Lawyers Guild, National Women's Health Network, and Reproductive Rights National Network); NAACP LDF; National Abortion Federation; NOW (for NARAL, Northwest Women's Law Center, Women and Health Roundtable, and Women's Law Project); and Planned Parenthood Federation of America (for NARAL, National Family Planning and Reproductive Health Association, Association of Planned Parenthood Physicians, Society for Adolescent Medicine, American Jewish Congress, Center for Population Options, American Jewish Committee, American Psychiatric Association, American Association of Sex Educators, Counselors and Therapists, National Council of Jewish Women, and Certain Medical School Deans and Professors).

61. The following discussion took place:

The Court: —may I ask, the district court on the parental consent provision held it unconstitutional, did it not?

Segedy: That's correct, Your Honor.

The Court: And who took it to the court of appeals? Not the city.

Segedy: Your Honor, the—in what was effectively a cooperative effort, the defendant intervenors raised the specific question within their briefs as to parental consent provision. However, the city of Akron also argued that question at oral argument in the court of appeals.

The Court: Well, now, the intervenors didn't bring—didn't come here.

Segedy: Your Honor, the intervenors petitioned this Court also on that question, and we can only speculate whether this Court denied that petition because it was a duplication of the city's petition, and therefore, not being aware of any possible standing arguments, simply determined that—

The Court: But I am correct then that you litigated the issue in the district court and lost, correct?

Segedy: When you say *you*, your Honor, you mean—

The Court: The city.

Segedy: —the city of Akron?

The Court: That's true, isn't it?

Segedy: That's correct.

The Court: And then the city of Akron did not formally appeal to the court of appeals in that event. It was the intervenors who did that. Is that correct?

62. Transcripts of oral arguments were obtained from Kurland and Casper 1984.

63. They were, of course, clearly disappointed. As the National Right to Life Committee said, *Akron* "defended the interest not of women but of the assembly line abortion industry" (Greenhouse 1983a).

64. Pro-life forces had launched the strongest opposition to Reagan's nomination of O'Connor. After *Akron*, however, they changed their minds. In its newsletter, one right-to-life group "printed a photograph of Justice O'Connor over the Caption 'Best Man on the Court?'" (Clarity and Weaver 1983).

65. Symbolic of this was the fact that Jesse Helms, who wanted to press for his own proposal, voted "present" rather than "for." He and others apparently "regarded the Amendment as a tactical error," and they believed its language insufficient: "[I]t did not provide for an outright banning of abortion." In doing so, Helms "denied Mr. Hatch the symbolic goal of 50 votes" (Shribman 1983).

Once again, Ronald Reagan made no attempt to unify the competing factions. Although he claimed "profound disappointment" over the *Akron* decision and asked Congress "to make its voice heard," he never fully supported one pro-life proposal over another, calling only for Congress "to restore legal protections for the unborn whether by statute or constitutional amendment" (Clines 1983).

66. Three key questions were: Is the privacy argument as it relates to abortion compatible with *Griswold*? If so, should abortion be treated as a fundamental right (compare Heymann and Barzelay 1973 with Ely 1973)? Was *Roe* a substantive due process decision (compare Perry 1976 with Epstein 1974)? Did the Court's ruling in *Roe* overstep its bounds, jurisprudentially or institutionally (compare Grey 1975 with Ely 1973)?

67. These were initially available on tape and were later published in Horan, Grant, and Cunningham 1987.

68. Particularly appealing to them was that abortion was illegal in thirty-six states when the Fourteenth Amendment was ratified.

69. For example, Michael Perry (1982, 1) suggested that "[m]any critics think *Roe* represents the Court at its worst" because it "cannot be explained by reference to any value judgment constitutionalized by the framers. . . . *Brown v. Board of Education*, by contrast, is generally thought to represent the Court at its best." But, in Perry's opinion, both were noninterpretivist rulings because the justices inculcated their "own value judgment[s]" into the Constitution. Does this, then, diminish either opinion? Perry argues that it does not; if the public disliked *Brown* or *Roe*, it could do "something" about them. Archibald Cox (1987, 331–32)—initially no great fan of *Roe* (Cox 1976)—explicated flaws in the Meese doctrine of original intent when he wrote that "basic values of our society have not given the woman an absolute right to freedom of choice . . . [but] [l]aw is a human interest designed for human needs and application, all subject to growth and change." For more general critiques of the doctrine of original intent, see Carter 1985; Brennan 1985; and Baer 1990.

70. Framing abortion in equal protection terms was not new. As noted in chapter 5, Nancy Stearns's amicus curiae brief in *Roe* advanced such an argument, as did a law review article by Regan in 1979.

71. We derive this from Tribe (1988) and Law (1984).

72. In fact, the AUL LDF devoted an entire session at its conference to trial court litigation. Led by skilled attorney William Ball, who, among other things, had been the lead attorney in *Wisconsin v. Yoder* (1972) in which the Court ruled that the Amish could be exempted from compulsory education laws (Cortner 1975), it sought to learn from and emulate the opposition in order to undermine it.

73. Public opinion remained relatively constant. The 1986 American National Election Study (a postelection survey) revealed that 13 percent thought abortion should never be permitted; 29 percent thought it should be limited to situations involving rape, incest, or a threat to a woman's life; 18 percent thought it should not be limited if "need" had been established; and the plurality (39 percent) responded that it should be a matter of "personal choice."

74. Recall, for example, Alan Segedy's attempt to litigate in *Akron*.

75. Although the president was able to change the abortion orientation of federal judges, public opinion remained unchanged. Despite the "vociferous" attempts of pro-choice and pro-life groups to influence voters (in 1984, fifty-seven pro-life PACs spent $847,992; seven pro-choice PACs spent $527,790), and the media's prediction that abortion would play a "prominent" role in the 1984 elections (Herbers 1984), only 4 percent of surveyed registered voters said "that they would change their votes just because they did not agree with a particular candidate on abortion." Moreover, the electorate clearly disagreed with Reagan on the issue. One poll indicated that 67 percent of voters opposed a constitutional amendment to outlaw abortion (Rosenbaum 1984); NBC exit polls indicated that 66 percent of all voters favored legalized abortion.

76. Attorneys involved in *Thornburgh* included representatives from the Women's Law Project, the ACLU, and NOW Legal Defense and Education Fund.

77. The Third Circuit enjoined enforcement pending appeal. It "withheld" full judgment awaiting the U.S. Supreme Court's opinion in *Akron*. After that, it heard rearguments in light of *Akron*.

78. In a July 1985 speech Meese delivered two days after the government filed its amicus curiae brief, he said, "The responsibility of the Justice Department to urge that constitutionally-wrong decisions be overruled is no less strong today in this case than it was in 1954 in *Brown v. Board of Education*" (Caplan 1987, 124).

79. Ostensibly, Lee resigned for financial reasons, but some suspected that he could no longer handle "the constant hounding from the Reagan Right" (ibid., 107). In fact, his successor, Charles Fried (1991, 32–33), wrote that Lee did have financial problems, but that "the lack of appreciation from the hard right and no encouragement by [Meese] hastened [Lee's] departure."

80. Another peculiar aspect involved Fried himself. Though his legal credentials were solid (he had been a law clerk to Justice Harlan and a Harvard law professor since 1961), some questioned his commitment to the Meese/Reagan agenda and to the pro-life stance on abortion in particular. When *Roe* came down, some of Fried's Harvard colleagues remember that he "applauded" the ruling and "defended it from attack by others then on the faculty." Further, because Fried had not written much on abortion (although Justice Stevens did manage to dig up some of his scholarship, working it into his concurring opinion in *Thornburgh* to demonstrate that Fried's writings belied his amicus curiae brief), the administration was unaware of his feelings, if indeed he harbored any (Caplan 1987, 138). Fried later said, "You never know when you're 50—you have said a lot of things. I don't remember what I thought about the case in 1973." He also asserted that his

personal beliefs were irrelevant: "You won't get a whisper of my views on abortion [in the brief]. It's about the law" (ibid., 139).

It is now clear, though, that Fried disliked the *Roe* opinion, at least from a legal scholarly perspective. He later wrote (Fried 1991, 81), "One of the worst effects of *Roe* was that it gave legal reasoning a bad name."

81. Reagan did nominate Fried after the *Thornburgh* brief was filed. The Senate confirmed him in October 1985.

82. Fried (1991, 33–34) provides a rather contradictory account of his participation in this case. On the one hand, he notes that the "pressure on [him] to file a brief . . . was neither excessive nor improper." On the other, he tells of a meeting he had with Justice Department officials in which he brought to them objections raised by his staff about participating in the case (i.e., some thought, given the Court's reaction to the United States' brief in *Akron*—particularly Blackmun's—that they had "better stay out of abortion cases altogether"). Yet during that meeting, it became "clear to [him] that as Acting Solicitor General, [he] could not succeed in heading off an anti-*Roe* brief even if [he] had been convinced that that was the right thing to do. [He] would simply be overruled."

83. Fried (1991, 34) thought Lee's brief in *Akron* "an oddly ambiguous essay."

84. In his account, Fried (1991, 34) wrote the part of the brief urging the Court to overrule *Roe* himself. Given his rather negative views of the doctrine of original intent (ibid., 50–51), that section may not have been to his liking. Indeed, Fried took pride in the fact that his brief argued "in terms of the jurisprudential illegitimacy of *Roe*, with no discussion of the merits of the right-to-life versus freedom-of-choice dispute."

85. Unless otherwise noted, the quotes contained in this paragraph come from Caplan 1987, 126–50.

86. The liberal press echoed this sentiment. One account in the *New York Times* asserted: "The emphatic tone of the 6–3 decision in *Akron* makes it unlikely that the Justices will now agree with the Administration that *Roe v. Wade* 'is so far flawed'" (1985c).

87. After the vote, some senators expected Reynolds to resign from the Justice Department. Apparently at the behest of Meese, he not only stayed on but was given "special duties," one of which was to "monitor Charles Fried's submissions as Solicitor General" (Caplan 1987, 154).

88. Two pro-choice amicus curiae briefs received unusual press attention. The first, filed by Laurence Tribe and other Harvard law professors for eighty-one members of Congress, took the solicitor general head on. As Caplan (1987, 144) pointed out, Tribe "emphasized the anomalous character of the role Fried had chosen to play" by placing into a footnote the exchange between Blackmun and Lee in *Akron*—the one in which Blackmun asked Lee if he wanted the Court to overrule *Roe*, and Lee responded, "[N]o . . . that would not be a proper function for us." Tribe (*Thornburgh*, Brief for Packwood et al., no. 84-495, 3) further underscored that the government had "taken an extraordinary and unprecedented step" here; not since *Brown v. Board of Education* (1954) had the United States asked the Court to overrule a decision (Gelb 1985). In addition, a brief filed by the New York attorney general (*Thornburgh*, Brief for the Attorney General of the State of New York, no. 84-495, 2) argued that if the justices adopted the administration's position, "New York and other states choosing to uphold such a right would be faced with meeting an enormous demand for the service from out-of-state residents."

89. Alan Ernest sought permission to represent "children unborn and born" and to file

an amicus curiae brief on behalf of the Legal Defense Fund for Unborn Children. The Court denied him permission on both scores. Also, two briefs were filed on behalf of individuals.

90. According to one report (Molotsky and Weaver 1985), some infighting broke out between pro-life groups when the Ad Hoc Committee in Defense of Life accused the U.S. Catholic Conference of "a broad retreat" from its advocacy of the overruling of *Roe*. It seemed that the committee thought that an amicus curiae brief the conference had prepared "sharply contrast[ed]" with the solicitor general's because it did not explicitly ask the Court to overturn *Roe*. In the end, the conference did not file a brief.

91. Brennan implied, for example, that the law may not be ripe for a Supreme Court ruling since the lower courts had not reviewed some of it.

92. As he wrote: "[T]his Court does not subscribe to the simplistic view that constitutional interpretation can possibly be limited to the 'plain meaning' of the Constitution's text or to the subjective intention of the framers" (*Thornburgh* 1986, 789).

93. White's language was so strong that it prompted Stevens to write a biting point-by-point refutation. Though Stevens stated that he "always had the highest respect for [White's views] on the subject," he sought to demonstrate that White's position on abortion was inconsistent with his view in *Griswold*, that his "rhetoric conflicts with his own analysis," and that he held fundamental misunderstandings of the *Roe* decision (*Thornburgh* 1986, 773, 776, 778).

94. In a 1978 debate at the American Enterprise Institute, Scalia asserted:

The Courts have enforced other rights, so-called, on which there is no societal agreement, from the abortion cases, at one extreme, to school dress codes and things of that sort. There is no national consensus about those things and there never has been. The courts have no business being there. That is one of the problems; they are calling rights things which we do not all agree on. (*New York Times* 1986c)

95. NARAL vowed to launch campaigns against Rehnquist and Scalia. Neither amounted to much.

96. Harriet Woods of Missouri, the only senatorial candidate "to run on an overtly prochoice platform," lost to pro-lifer Christopher Bond. Two House leaders targeted by NARAL, Bob Dornan (R-Calif.) and Christopher Smith (R-N.J.) were reelected (Greenhouse 1986).

Especially heartening was the reelection of Bob Packwood (R-Oreg.), a strong prochoice voice in the Senate, who had been targeted by LAPAC in his state's Republican primary. With this defeat, the pro-life PAC virtually closed up shop, at least at the federal campaign level, with accumulated debts of about $81,000 (Turner 1987).

97. Massachusetts, Rhode Island, and Arkansas voters rejected a measure that would have empowered their states to criminalize abortion if the Court overturned *Roe*.

98. A computer-assisted search found that, in 1987 alone, newspapers mentioned Bork in 2,652 stories. Later, scholars and journalists published several books on judicial confirmation proceedings and on Bork's in particular. The failed nominee penned his own account, *The Tempting of America* (1990). By the same token, since 1987 political scientists have rediscovered the nomination process (see, for example, Cameron, Cover, and Segal 1990; Segal 1987; and Watson and Stookey 1988), with at least two teams of researchers (Caldeira and Wright and Segal, Cover, and Cameron) receiving major grants from the National Science Foundation to study it.

99. The ACLU had broken this policy only one other time since its founding when in 1971 it opposed Rehnquist.

100. Ten members of the ABA's Committee on the Federal Judiciary gave Bork its highest rating, "well-qualified." Four members voted "not qualified," and one voted "not opposed."

101. Some of the turnabouts were quite marked; for example, at one point Bork argued that he might even be able to support abortion if the right could be "rooted" in equal protection rather than privacy.

102. Their suspicions were borne out by Bork's discussion of abortion in *The Tempting of America* (1990, 111–15), a book he wrote after his defeat.

103. Groups opposing the nomination were Americans for Democratic Action, NOW, NOW Legal Defense and Education Fund, and National Gay and Lesbian Task Force. In particular, they took issue with two of his holdings: one which rejected comparable worth and another in which he upheld a U.S. Navy discharge of gay personnel.

104. Although pro-life groups did not oppose him, they were unsure of his support for their cause. As an AUL attorney noted, "It's an open question as to which way he is going to be the swing vote" (Ciolli 1988).

105. The state did not include this in its appeal to the Supreme Court.

106. The state did not include this in its appeal to the Supreme Court. The act also contained a "hospitalization requirement for 16-week abortions" and a "prohibition on the use of public employees and facilities for abortion counselling." After a court of appeals invalidated those sections, the state did not include them in its appeal to the Supreme Court.

107. Of course, the law was drafted prior to the *Thornburgh* decision. Faux (1990, 30–31) reports that it was "the creation" of two right-to-lifers, Samuel Lee and his attorney Andrew Puzder. As she tells it, Lee wrote the law in 1983, while serving a jail sentence for violating injunctions "to stay away" from abortion clinics. According to Puzder, however, he and another, Walker, proposed the legislation in a *Stetson Law Review* article (Walker and Puzder 1984). See, generally, *Webster*, Brief for Doctors for Life et al., no. 88-605.

108. We derive this and what follows from Faux 1990, 31–32.

109. According to Faux (1990, 31–32), Susman felt that local ACLU chapters should "handle their own cases" since they best knew the "turf." In his view, the RFP "was there to provide support, not to take over a case once it was headed into the Supreme Court."

110. Blackmun did, however, note that Kennedy's vote was uncertain: "One never knows what a new Justice's attitude" will be toward *Roe* (*New York Times* 1988b).

111. This was a move that clearly heartened pro-life forces, who were never particularly enthralled with newly elected President George Bush. They knew that he, unlike Michael Dukakis, was not a pro-choice advocate, but neither was he Ronald Reagan. In fact, during the course of his campaign, Bush's "waffling entailed some embarrassing moments." On one hand, he "expressed sympathy" for a constitutional amendment, but on the other, he approved of abortions to protect a woman's life and in cases of rape or incest. Although such vacillation did not endear him to pro-life advocates, they had no choice but to support him (Pomper et al. 1989, 189–90).

In general, though, abortion played a very small role in the 1988 presidential and congressional elections. Pro-choice forces understood this, acknowledging that "in this election reproductive rights and the makeup of the Supreme Court never became a salient

issue" (Lewin 1988). If this was so, it was in part the intent of the candidates, particularly Republicans, who wanted to avoid the issue. Fried admitted as much, noting that he purposefully waited until after the election to file the brief: "I was determined not to let this case get embroiled in the election. I did not want to create an election issue" (Greenhouse 1988).

112. The solicitor general's brief said: "If the Court is prepared to reconsider *Roe v. Wade*, this case presents an appropriate opportunity for doing so." Missouri, in its jurisdictional statement, asked the Court to consider applying a rational-basis standard to abortion legislation.

113. Dellinger (1989) depicted the conventional wisdom of the day when he wrote: "Few observers seem to think that the Supreme Court will actually overturn *Roe*. . . . Rather . . . speculation is that a majority . . . will narrow" it.

114. There was but one minor point of disagreement: the United States' brief rejected Justice O'Connor's unduly burdensome standard, but in keeping with its jurisdictional statement, Missouri offered it as a plausible alternative.

115. By this point, Susman had argued four abortion cases before the High Court: *Planned Parenthood v. Danforth* (1976), *Singleton v. Wulff* (1976), *Poelker v. Doe* (1977), and *Planned Parenthood v. Ashcroft* (1983). Still, he told a reporter that *Webster* put "ten times more pressure" on him (Mauro 1989b).

116. Despite the fact that Scalia had yet to participate in an abortion case, most pro-choice attorneys wrote him off.

117. In *Thornburgh*, she wrote: "I do not dismiss the possibility that requiring the physician or counselor to read aloud the State's printed materials . . . raises First Amendment concerns. . . . [They] may create some possibility that the physician or counselor is being required to communicate the State's ideology" (*Thornburgh* 1986, 830).

118. Such a regulation would have a devastating impact on Planned Parenthood, which at the time operated 769 clinics and received $30 million a year in federal funds (Roberts 1987). Hence, in 1988 they (and several states) launched lawsuits, raising a number of claims, one of which reached the Supreme Court in 1990.

119. In an interview with Faux (1990, 41), Susman expressed regret over allowing Planned Parenthood attorneys to take over this task. He apparently assumed that he would have some "input" into the brief's preparation, but he learned that his suggestions were "not appreciated."

120. The NRLC executive director, however, opposed this tactic: "If the Justices are doing their job, the letters should be totally discounted" (Moore 1989). On that score, he was probably correct. By April 1989 the Court "was snowed under by mail," leading Justice Stevens to complain that "the only impact they had was to consume the time of Court personnel 'sorting that stuff out and throwing it in the wastebasket, because nobody read any of it' " (Mauro 1989e).

121. In the 1989 brief, 2,887 women and 627 "friends" told of their personal experiences with abortion.

122. For an in-depth examination of the amicus curiae briefs filed in *Webster*, see Behuniak-Long 1991.

123. Operation Rescue, an organization founded by Randall Terry, engages in some traditional political tactics but sees its principal aim as performing "rescue missions—

blocking entrances to abortion clinics" and other kinds of civil disobedience (Ladd n.d., 15).

124. Traditional theories of judicial decision making would suggest that the Court is immune to such pressure. However, some scholars (e.g., O'Connor 1980) claim that groups have used "publicity" effectively in the past.

125. NARAL well understood this: "We are starting with the Court, but our aim is the 1990 elections" (Bronner 1989b).

126. Excerpts from oral arguments come from Kurland and Casper 1990.

127. Indeed, Fried (1991, 85) thought the *Webster* orals provided him with a "unique occasion on which to accomplish two things: to remove . . . the albatross of originalist rigorism; and to clarify that overruling *Roe* would not slam the Court door to any complaints in the future about excesses in abortion regulation."

128. Faux (1990, 42) asserts that "over two hundred Justice Department lawyers signed a petition criticizing the department's intervention [in *Webster*] . . . calling it inappropriate."

129. This is the story reported by Faux (1990). According to the Court's docket sheet, Senator Packwood and others sought permission to share Susman's oral argument time, a request they filed three days after Fried's.

130. Hence, unlike his opponents—and to the chagrin of pro-choicers—he did not participate in moot courts prior to *Webster* orals (Mauro 1989b; Faux 1990, 26).

131. Susman later told the media that he thought of this line of argument two days before orals. But, as Mauro (1989c) noted, Laurence Tribe "made the point" in a 1973 law review article, and NARAL and the Women's Legal Defense Fund raised it in their *Webster* amicus curiae brief. It also appears in the RHS brief, though in slightly different terms.

132. Scalia and Stevens asked Webster to address Susman's point and explain how to go about overruling *Roe* without touching *Griswold* in light of the law's preamble. It was reasonably clear that he had not given much thought to the issue, defending his view largely on the language of the statute.

133. Mauro (1989e) claims that "the massive abortion-rights amicus curiae effort . . . may have helped keep Justice . . . O'Connor from stepping over the line to outright opposition of *Roe v. Wade*."

134. D. Baer (1989) put it this way: "In *Webster*, the Chief Justice clearly set out to write an opinion to eradicate the *Roe* decision. His [ultimate] approach was intended as a moderation of the bolder opinion Scalia expressed."

135. For example, he called Rehnquist's opinion "bald assertion masquerad[ing] as reasoning" and parts of O'Connor's "pure science fiction" (*Webster* 1989, 3072, 3076).

136. We obtained this and the quotes that follow from a transcript of the press conference recorded by a computer-based retrieval system, NEXIS.

137. In summarizing the "before" and "after" polls, Ladd (n.d., 12–13) wrote that it was "clear that no movement has occurred." Gallup found a 2 percent increase (after *Webster*) in those responding that abortion should always be legal; a CBS/*New York Times* survey found an 8 percent decrease on the same question.

Moreover, the polls measuring public opinion on the *Webster* decision were quite mixed. Below are the results of three surveys taken in 1989, the first two in July and the third in September, on agreement/disagreement with the Court (see Ladd n.d., 24):

	TIME	*LOS ANGELES TIMES*	CBS/*NEW YORK TIMES*
Agree	32%	47%	7%
Disagree	61	40	17
Not sure/not enough information	7	13	76

138. Immediately after *Webster*, seven pro-choice groups held a major conference at which they etched out the following strategic blueprint:

• focusing "the message on who determined a woman's reproductive choices—the government or the woman herself";
• building a grass-roots organization;
• drafting federal legislation to "reinforce" *Roe*;
• proposing a constitutional amendment that "[t]he state shall not compel any woman to complete or terminate a pregnancy";
• fielding a multifaceted legal defense team; and
• targeting states and candidates for immediate action (see Simpson 1989).

139. Exemplary were private donations to Planned Parenthood (Barringer 1990):

YEAR	DOLLARS (IN MILLIONS)
1980	32.5
1981	37.3
1982	42.4
1983	40.7
1984	41.8
1985	49.8
1986	50.9
1987	55.9
1988	72.5
1989	77.2
1990	90.0 (est.)

140. One of the first wins came in Florida where Governor Martinez called a special legislative session in October 1989, believing that he had sufficient votes to enact a restrictive abortion law. Because of a huge NARAL television campaign (with the theme "Who Decides?") opposing the measure, legislators on whom the governor counted quickly abandoned him. Despite a last-ditch and politically embarrassing effort, Martinez lost his crusade. The legislature ended its session without enacting a restrictive law.

141. This is especially true as the pro-life side is beginning to show new signs of life after realizing that its *Webster* win would not be self-executing. After blaming their lost ground on factors external to the movement—including "skewed" public opinion polls, "fainthearted 'turncoat' politicians," and a "biased" press—they went back to basics, to those strategies that brought them to their *Webster* victory. At a 1990 NRLC conference, for example, the group's leaders stressed the need to tailor "its immediate goals to the political realities of individual states." That "tailoring" included development of new model legislation that prohibits abortions done for "birth control" purposes and continued pressure on state legislatures. And this "revitalized" pro-life movement is having a

noticeable effect. Despite threats from pro-choice leaders that they would ask the International Olympic Committee to reject the state's bid for the 1998 Winter Games, in early 1991 Utah enacted a restrictive law. The Louisiana legislature followed suit, overriding a gubernatorial veto to do so. At this writing, at least five other states (Wyoming, South Dakota, Michigan, Oklahoma, and Ohio) are considering similar laws.

Even so, pro-life leaders acknowledge that their post-*Webster* progress has been slow and uneven. As one said, "We may get a little bit here, a little bit there. Ten, 20 years down the road, we'll be a little bit further than we are now," but it will be an "uphill battle" (Mydans 1990).

142. And, in fact, things could have been a good deal worse from the pro-choice vantage point. For instance, the Court's opinions in parental consent cases, in particular, were narrowly tailored to the issue; the justices did not use them to overturn *Roe*. Moreover, the Supreme Court terms antedating *Webster* might have been more notable for what did not happen than for what did. On the third day of the 1989 session, the justices (with White filing a lone dissent) let stand a court of appeals judgment (in *McMonagle v. Northeast Women's Center*) finding liable, under a federal racketeering law, a group of protesters who sought to drive a Philadelphia abortion clinic out of business. Though the ruling created no precedent, pro-choice advocates took it as a sign for them to continue bringing lawsuits against groups like Operation Rescue. Another thing that did not happen during the 1989 term was a Supreme Court resolution of *Turnock v. Ragsdale*, the third case it had docketed. To many observers, *Turnock* represented the most promising vehicle for overturning, or at least further narrowing, *Roe*. By requiring clinics to meet similar standards as "those required for operating rooms in full care hospitals," Illinois would effectively shut most of them down—they simply could not afford to elevate the quality of care to that level. Anxiety mounted when Justice Stevens—a firm *Roe* supporter—excused himself from the case. But presumably because Illinois Attorney General Hartigan was concerned over how this litigation would affect his gubernatorial campaign, he settled the dispute and asked the Court to withdraw it from consideration.

143. Blackmun's dissent (joined by Marshall and Stevens) found that the regulation conflicted with First Amendment rights: "Until today the Court never has upheld viewpoint-based suppression of speech simply because that suppression was a condition upon the acceptance of public funds." He thus took issue with Rehnquist's use of the funding precedents, asserting that, unlike past laws upheld by the Court, these "regulations are . . . clearly viewpoint-based. While suppressing speech favorable to abortion with one hand, [they] compel anti-abortion speech with the other." Justice O'Connor's dissent focused on congressional intent. In her view, the Court needed only to "tell the Secretary that his regulations are not a reasonable interpretation of the statute." She also noted that the regulations raised "serious First Amendment concerns" (*Rust* 1991, 1789).

144. After Bush nominated Souter, abortion became a major topic of discussion. The president asserted that he used no "litmus test" in reaching his decision and that the Senate should not use one either. Yet members of the Judiciary Committee remained unconvinced. Some, like Dennis DeConcini (D-Ariz.), maintained that it would be "perfectly legitimate" to ask Souter about his views on abortion; others (e.g., Bob Packwood, R-Oreg.) went so far as to suggest that Souter "would not be confirmed if Senators perceive that he opposes abortion rights" (Berke 1990).

145. Like O'Connor, he evaded questions on abortion, calling them "inappropriate" because of a "likelihood" that the Court would be reconsidering *Roe*. He did, however,

state, "I believe that the due process clause of the 14th Amendment does recognize and does protect an unenumerated right of privacy."

146. According to the executive director of NARAL, that group "had no choice but to oppose Judge Souter's nomination. 'For the first time in history, the Supreme Court is on the brink of taking away a fundamental right' . . . and Judge Souter has not given assurance he recognizes that right" (Lewis 1990). Moreover, pro-choice groups argued that they did not "want to repeat the same mistake [they] . . . made in 1989 when they did not oppose Kennedy." As one said, "It's already too late. If we had a Souter standard in the mid-1980s, then we might have different Justices" (Kornhauser 1990).

At first, analysts predicted that their approach would have repercussions for later battles. Some suggested that it angered and "alienated" traditional allies, including Souter's sponsor, Warren Rudman. In light of *Rust*, however, pro-choice groups may have been vindicated.

147. The one exception was the Association for the Study of Abortion, but the ACLU's Reproductive Freedom Project picked up where it left off.

148. This was surely a factor that generally prompted, after 1983, attorneys, scholars, and even a judge to propose reframing abortion litigation in equal protection terms.

CHAPTER 7

1. Recall also that Burger, by most accounts, was an extremely hesitant and shaky pro-choice vote even in *Roe*. See chapter 5 for further discussion of this.

2. Stewart and Powell deserted the *Roe* majority in the funding cases, but they never deviated from allegiance to *Roe*'s core holding—that there was a constitutionally grounded right to choose to have an abortion.

3. Compare its action after *Furman* and *Roe* with the action it took in the decade after *Brown*. In 1964 and 1965, Congress passed two major pieces of legislation to give effect to, not detract from, the 1954 ruling.

4. Nixon's and, later, Reagan's reactions were in marked contrast to, say, that of President Kennedy, who publicly supported the Court's initial school prayer decisions.

5. Note the differences between *Hoyt v. Florida* (1961) and *Reed v. Reed* (1971) and the cases that followed *Reed* (Goldstein 1988). *Reed* (and decisions subsequent to it) is an example of equal protection expansion that was created by a unanimous Burger Court, rejecting the stereotyped assumptions that governed even Warren Court jurisprudence in this area.

6. Clearly, not *all* justices allow "the law" to guide their courses. Looking only at the areas examined here, Brennan and Marshall certainly were immune to any argument that ran counter to their position on the death penalty; much the same can be said of Rehnquist and Burger on this issue. Similarly, on abortion, Blackmun, Brennan, and Marshall stood firmly behind the logic of the *Roe* approach throughout the period under investigation here, and Rehnquist and White did the same on the other side of the question.

7. Indeed, there is some evidence of this kind of concern in the literature. Note, for example, Cortner's (1968) discussion of the strategic shift of Tennessee reapportionment enthusiasts from problematic guarantee clause arguments to the untested but potentially fertile fields of the equal protection clause.

TABLE OF CASES

REFERENCES

The following is a listing of all works cited throughout, except for legal cases, which can be found in the preceding Table of Cases.

Abraham, Henry J. 1985. *Justices and Presidents*. 2d ed. New York: Oxford University Press.

Abramowitz, Alan I. 1984. "National Issues, Strategic Politicians, and Voting Behavior in the 1980 and 1982 Congressional Elections." *American Journal of Political Science* 28:710–21.

Abramson, Paul R., John H. Aldrich, and David H. Rohde. 1982. *Change and Continuity in the 1980 Elections*. Washington, D.C.: CQ Press.

Adler, Renata. 1987. "Coup at the Court." *New Republic*, 14 September.

Alumbaugh, Steve, and C. K. Rowland. 1990. "The Links between Platform-Based Appointment Criteria and Trial Judges' Abortion Judgments." *Judicature* 74:153–62.

American Civil Liberties Union. 1961–62. *Freedom through Dissent*. New York: American Civil Liberties Union.

———. 1964–65. *Tension, Change, and Liberty*. New York: American Civil Liberties Union.

———. 1965–67. *New Dimensions . . . New Challenges*. New York: American Civil Liberties Union.

———. 1970. *The Policy Guide of the American Civil Liberties Union*. New York: American Civil Liberties Union.

———. 1970–71. *ACLU Annual Report*. New York: American Civil Liberties Union.

———. 1971–72. *ACLU Annual Report*. New York: American Civil Liberties Union.

———. 1972–73. *ACLU Annual Report*. New York: American Civil Liberties Union.

———. 1976. *1976 Policy Guide of the American Civil Liberties Union*. New York: American Civil Liberties Union.

American Law Institute. 1959. *Model Penal Code—Tentative Draft, Nos. 9–12*. Philadelphia: American Law Institute.

Andrusko, Dave, ed. 1988. *A Passion for Justice*. Washington, D.C.: National Right to Life Committee.

Arbagi, Martin. 1987. "*Roe* and the Hippocratic Oath." In *Abortion and the Constitution*, edited by Dennis J. Horan, Edward R. Grant, and Paige C. Cunningham. Washington, D.C.: Georgetown University Press.

Arizona State Law Journal. 1980. "Survey of Abortion Law." No. 1, 67–216.

Asbury, Edith Evans. 1977. "Abortion Is Top Issue for A.C.L.U." *New York Times*, 7 October.

Baer, Donald. 1989. "Now the Court of Less Resort." *U.S. News and World Report*, 17 July.

Baer, Judith A. 1989. "The Fruitless Search for Original Intent." In *Judging the Constitution*, edited by Michael H. McCann and Gerald L. Houseman. Glenview, Ill.: Scott, Foresman.

———. 1990. "Reading the Fourteenth Amendment." In *Politics and the Constitution*. Washington, D.C.: National Legal Center for the Public Interest and the American Studies Center.

Bailey, William C. 1975. "Murder and Capital Punishment." *American Journal of Orthopsychiatry* 45:669–88.

———. 1976. "Rape and the Death Penalty: A Neglected Area of Deterrence Research." In *Capital Punishment in the United States*, edited by Hugo Adam Bedau and Chester A. Pierce. New York: AMS Press.

Baker, Stewart A., and James R. Asperger. 1982. "Forward: Toward a Center for State and Local Legal Advocacy." *Catholic University Law Review* 31:367–73.

Baldus, David, and James W. Cole. 1975. "A Comparison of the Work of Thorstein Sellin and Isaac Ehrlich on the Deterrent Effect of Capital Punishment." *Yale Law Journal* 85:170–86.

Baldus, David, George Woodruff, and Charles Pulaski. 1983. "Comparative Review of Death Sentences." *Journal of Criminal Law and Criminology* 74:661–753.

———. 1985. "Monitoring and Evaluating Contemporary Death Sentences." *University of California–Davis Law Review* 18:1375–1407.

———. 1986. "Arbitrariness and Discrimination in the Administration of the Death Penalty." *Stetson Law Review* 15:133–261.

Balides, Constance, Barbara Danziger, and Deborah Spitz. 1973. "The Abortion Issue: Major Groups, Organizations, and Funding Sources." In *The Abortion Experience*, edited by Howard Osofsky and Joy Osofsky. Hagerstown, Md.: Harper and Row.

Barnett, Arnold. 1981. "The Deterrent Effect of Capital Punishment." *Operations Research* 29:346–70.

Barnum, David. 1985. "The Supreme Court and Public Opinion: Judicial Decision Making in the Post–New Deal Period." *Journal of Politics* 47:652–66.

Barrett, Edward L., Jr. 1977. *Constitutional Law*. Mineola, N.Y.: Foundation.

Barrett, Edward L., Jr., and Paul W. Bruton. 1973. *Constitutional Law*. 4th ed. Mineola, N.Y.: Foundation.

Barron, Jerome A., and C. Thomas Dienes. 1975. *Constitutional Law, Principles, and Policy*. Indianapolis: Bobbs-Merrill.

Barron, Jerome A., C. Thomas Dienes, Wayne McCormack, and Martin H. Redish. 1987. *Constitutional Law, Principles, and Policy*. Charlottesville, Va.: Michie.

Barringer, Felicity. 1990. "For Birth Control Group, Return to Radical Roots." *New York Times*, 30 October.

Bartholomew, Paul C. 1978. *American Constitutional Law*. Vol. 2. Totowa, N.J.: Littlefield, Adams.

Bates, Jerome E., and Edward S. Zawadzki. 1964. *Criminal Abortion*. Springfield, Ill.: Charles C. Thomas.

Baum, Lawrence. 1985. *The Supreme Court*. 2d ed. Washington, D.C.: CQ Press.

————. 1988. "Measuring Policy Change in the Supreme Court." *American Political Science Review* 82:905–12.

————. 1989a. "Comparing the Policy Postures of Supreme Court Justices from Different Time Periods." *Western Political Quarterly* 42:509–21.

————. 1989b. *The Supreme Court.* 3d ed. Washington, D.C.: CQ Press.

Bedau, Hugo Adam, ed. 1964. *The Death Penalty in America.* New York: Anchor Press.

————, ed. 1967a. *The Death Penalty in America.* Rev. ed. New York: Doubleday.

————. 1967b. "The Issue of Capital Punishment." *Current History* 53:82–87.

————. 1972–73. "The Nixon Administration and the Deterrent Effect of the Death Penalty." *University of Pittsburgh Law Review* 34:557–66.

————. 1974. "Challenging the Death Penalty." *Harvard Civil Rights–Civil Liberties Review* 9:624–43.

————. 1977. *The Courts, the Constitution, and Capital Punishment.* Lexington, Mass.: Lexington Press.

————, ed. 1982. *The Death Penalty in America.* 3d ed. New York: Oxford University Press.

————. 1983. "Berger's Defense of the Death Penalty: How Not to Read the Constitution." *Michigan Law Review* 81:1152–65.

————. 1987. *Death Is Different.* Boston: Northeastern University Press.

Bedau, Hugo Adam, and Chester M. Pierce, eds. 1976. *Capital Punishment in the United States.* New York: AMS Press.

Behuniak-Long, Susan. 1991. "Friendly Fire: Amici Curiae and *Webster v. Reproductive Health Services*." *Judicature* 74:261–70.

Belton, Robert. 1978. "A Comparative Review of Public and Private Enforcement of Title VII of the Civil Rights Act of 1964." *Vanderbilt Law Review* 31:905–61.

Bennetts, Leslie. 1979. "For Pro-Abortion Group, an Aggressive New Campaign." *New York Times*, 1 May.

————. 1980. "Anti-Abortion Group Asks Defeat of Javitz and Five Others at Poll." *New York Times*, 19 January.

————. 1981. "Antiabortion Forces in Disarray Less than a Year after Victories in Election." *New York Times*, 22 September.

Benshoof, Janet. 1977. "Mobilizing for Abortion Rights." *Civil Liberties Review* 4, no. 3 (September/October): 76–79.

————. 1984. "The Legacy of *Roe v. Wade*." In *Abortion*, edited by Jay L. Garfield and Patricia Hennessey. Amherst: University of Massachusetts Press.

Benshoof, Janet, and Harriet Pilpel. 1986. "Minors' Rights to Confidential Abortion." In *Abortion, Medicine, and the Law*, edited by J. Douglas Butler and David F. Walbert. New York: Facts on File Publications.

Bentley, Arthur. 1908. *The Process of Government.* Chicago: University of Chicago Press.

Berger, Margaret A. 1979. "Litigation on Behalf of Women: An Assessment." New York: Ford Foundation.

Berger, Raoul. 1982. *Death Penalties.* Cambridge: Harvard University Press.

Berke, Richard L. 1989. "The Abortion Rights Movement Has Its Day." *New York Times*, 15 October.

————. 1990. "Senators Divided on Asking Souter His Abortion View." *New York Times*, 25 July.

Bigart, Homer. 1969. "476 in Death Rows Pin Hopes on Crucial Case in High Court." *New York Times*, 28 July.

Black, Charles L. 1981. *Capital Punishment: The Inevitability of Caprice and Mistake*. 2d ed. New York: W. W. Norton.

Black, Elizabeth, and Hugo L. Black, Jr. 1986. *Mr. Justice and Mrs. Black*. New York: Random House.

Blake, Judith. 1971. "Abortion and Public Opinion: The 1960–1970 Decade." *Science* 171:540–49.

Blasecki, Janet L. 1990. "Justice Lewis F. Powell: Swing Voter or Staunch Conservative?" *Journal of Politics* 52:530–47.

Blasi, Vincent, ed. 1983. *The Burger Court: The Counter-Revolution that Wasn't*. New Haven: Yale University Press.

Bond, Jon R., and Charles A. Johnson. 1982. "Implementing a Permissive Policy: Hospital Abortion Services after *Roe v. Wade*." *American Journal of Political Science* 26:1–24.

Bork, Robert A. 1971. "Neutral Principles and Some First Amendment Problems." *Indiana Law Journal* 47:1–35.

———. 1990. *The Tempting of America*. New York: Free Press.

Bowers, William J. 1984. *Legal Homicide*. Boston: Northeastern University Press.

Bowers, William J.,and Glenn L. Pierce. 1975. "The Illusion of Deterrence in Isaac Ehrlich's Research on Capital Punishment." *Yale Law Journal* 85:187–208.

———. 1980. "Arbitrariness and Discrimination under Post-*Furman* Capital Statutes." *Crime and Delinquency* 26:563–635.

Boyd, Gerald. 1987. "Bork Picked for High Court." *New York Times*, 2 July.

Bradford, William. [1793] 1968. "An Enquiry How Far the Punishment of Death Is Necessary in Pennsylvania." Reprint. *American Journal of Legal History* 12:122–55.

Brennan, William J., Jr. 1985. Address to the Test and Teaching Symposium, Georgetown University, Washington, D.C., 12 October.

———. 1986. "Constitutional Adjudication and the Death Penalty: A View from the Court." *Harvard Law Review* 100:313–31.

Brest, Paul. 1975. *Processes of Constitutional Decisionmaking*. Boston: Little, Brown.

Brigham, John. 1978. *Constitutional Language: An Interpretation of Judicial Decisions*. Westport, Conn.: Greenwood Press.

———. 1984. *Civil Liberties and American Democracy*. Washington, D.C.: CQ Press.

Brody, Jane E. 1973. "States and Doctors Wary on Eased Abortion Ruling." *New York Times*, 16 February.

Bronner, Ethan. 1989a. *Battle for Justice*. New York: W. W. Norton.

———. 1989b. "Opposing Sides Gear Up for Key Battle on Abortion Front." *Boston Globe*, 19 February.

Brozan, Nadine. 1980. "Pro-Abortion Forces Hail Rulings on Federal Funds." *New York Times*, 1 January.

———. 1981. "Opposing Sides Step Up Efforts on Abortion Measure." *New York Times*, 15 February.

Buchan, William. 1816. *Domestic Medicine*. New Haven.

Burt, Robert A. 1987. "Disorder in the Court: The Death Penalty and the Constitution." *Michigan Law Review* 85:1741–1819.

Butler, M. Tyus, Jr. 1973. "Capital Punishment: *Furman v. Georgia* and Georgia's Statutory Response." *Mercer Law Review* 24:891–937.

Buutap, Nguyenphuc. 1979. "Legislation, Public Opinion, and the Press." Ph.D. diss., University of Chicago.

Bye, Raymond T. 1919. *Capital Punishment in the United States*. Philadelphia: Committee of Philanthropic Labor.

Byrn, Robert M. 1973. "An American Tragedy." *Fordham Law Review* 41:807–62.

Calabressi, Guido. 1985. *Ideals, Beliefs, Attitudes, and the Law*. Syracuse, N.Y.: Syracuse University Press.

Caldeira, Gregory A. 1991. "Courts and Public Opinion." In *The American Courts*, edited by John B. Gates and Charles A. Johnson. Washington, D.C.: CQ Press.

Caldeira, Gregory A., and John R. Wright. 1988. "Interest Groups and Agenda-Setting in the Supreme Court of the United States." *American Political Science Review* 82:1109–27.

———. 1990. "Amici Curiae before the Supreme Court." *Journal of Politics* 52:782–806.

Calderone, Mary Steichen, ed. 1958. *Abortion in the United States*. Proceedings of a conference sponsored by the Planned Parenthood Federation of America at Arden House and the New York Academy of Medicine. New York: Hoeber-Harpber.

Caldwell, Earl. 1972. "California Court, in 6–1 Vote, Bars Death Sentences." *New York Times*, 19 February.

Califano, Joseph A. 1981. *Governing America*. New York: Simon and Schuster.

Calvert, E. Roy. 1930. *Capital Punishment in the Twentieth Century*. 4th ed. London: G. P. Putnam's Sons.

Cameron, Charles, Albert Cover, and Jeffrey Segal. 1990. "Senate Voting on Supreme Court Nominees: A Neo-Institutional Perspective." *American Political Science Review* 84:525–34.

Campion, Donald R. 1959. "Should Men Hang?" *America*, 5 December.

Canon, Bradley C. 1991. "Courts and Policy: Compliance, Implementation, and Impact." In *The American Courts*, edited by John B. Gates and Charles A. Johnson. Washington, D.C.: CQ Press.

Caplan, Lincoln. 1987. *The Tenth Justice*. New York: Vintage Books.

Cardoza, Benjamin N. 1921. *The Nature of the Judicial Process*. New Haven: Yale University Press.

Carter, Dan. 1979. *The Scottsboro Boys*. Baton Rouge: Louisiana State University Press.

Carter, Lief H. 1985. *Contemporary Constitutional Lawmaking*. New York: Pergamon Press.

Casper, Jonathan. 1972. *The Politics of Civil Liberties*. New York: Harper and Row.

———. 1976. "The Supreme Court and National Policy Making." *American Political Science Review* 70:50–63.

Caswell, Stephen. 1974. "Cementing a Fragile Victory." *Trial*, May/June.

Charlton, Linda. 1974. "Start of Life Debated at Abortion Hearing." *New York Times*, 31 May.

———. 1975. "Attorney General Designate Asserts Death Penalty, If Enforced, Is Deterrent." *New York Times*, 28 January.

Chase, Harold W., and Craig R. Ducat. 1979. *Constitutional Interpretation*. 2d ed. St. Paul, Minn.: West Publishing.

REFERENCES

Choper, Jesse H. 1980. *Judicial Review and the National Political Process*. Chicago: University of Chicago Press.

Church, George J. 1987. "Far More Judicious." *Time*, 23 November.

Ciolli, Rita. 1988. "*Roe vs. Wade*: Fifteen Years Later." *Newsday*, 22 January.

Civil Liberties Review. 1975. "Conversation with Jack Greenberg." 2, no. 4 (Fall): 104–28.

Clarity, James F., and Warren Weaver, Jr. 1983. "Briefing." *New York Times*, 14 July.

Clark, Ramsey. 1970. *Crime in America*. New York: Simon and Schuster.

Clark, Tom C. 1969. "Religion, Morality, and Abortion: A Constitutional Appraisal." *Loyola (Los Angeles) Law Review* 2:1–11.

Clendinen, Dudley. 1982. "Rising Death Row Population Burdens Volunteer Lawyers." *New York Times*, 23 August.

Clines, Francis X. 1983. "Reagan Urges Congress to Nullify Supreme Court's Abortion Rulings." *New York Times*, 17 June.

Clines, Francis X., and Bernard Weintraub. 1981. "Briefing." *New York Times*, 31 October.

Cobb, Roger W., and Charles D. Elder. 1983. *Participation in American Politics*. 2d ed. Baltimore: Johns Hopkins University Press.

Cohen, Bernard Lande. 1970. *Law without Order*. New Rochelle, N.Y.: Exposition Press.

Columbia Law Review. 1935. "Note: A Functional Study of Existing Abortion Laws." 35:87–97.

Combs, Michael W. 1980. "The Supreme Court and Capital Punishment: Uncertainty and Judicial Control." *Southern University Law Review* 7:1–41.

Congressional Record. 1966. 89th Cong., 2d sess., vol. 112, pt. 13.

Cook, Beverly B. 1973. "Sentencing Behavior of Federal Judges: Draft Cases, 1972." *University of Cincinnati Law Review* 42:597–633.

———. 1977. "Public Opinion and Federal Judicial Policy." *American Journal of Political Science* 21:567–600.

Cortner, Richard C. 1968. "Strategies and Tactics of Litigants in Constitutional Cases." *Journal of Public Law* 17:287–307.

———. 1970. *The Jones and Laughlin Case*. New York: Alfred A. Knopf.

———. 1975. *The Supreme Court and Civil Liberties Policy*. Palo Alto, Calif.: Mayfield Publishers.

———. 1988. *A Mob Intent on Violence*. Middletown, Conn.: Wesleyan University Press.

Cotterell, William. 1983. Proprietary to the United Press International, 29 August.

Cowan, Claudia L., William C. Thompson, and Phoebe C. Ellsworth. 1984. "The Effects of Death Qualification on Jurors' Pre-Disposition to Convict and on the Quality of Deliberations." *Law and Human Behavior* 8:53–79.

Cowan, Ruth B. 1976. "Women's Rights through Litigation: An Examination of the American Civil Liberties Union Women's Rights Project, 1971–1976." *Columbia Human Rights Law Review* 8:373–412.

Cox, Archibald. 1976. *The Role of the Supreme Court in American Government*. New York: Oxford University Press.

———. 1987. *The Court and the Constitution*. Boston: Houghton-Mifflin.

Dahl, Robert. 1956. *A Preface to Democratic Theory*. Chicago: University of Chicago Press.

Danelski, David J. 1964. *A Supreme Court Justice Is Appointed*. New Haven: Yale University Press.

Dann, Robert H. 1935. "The Deterrent Effect of Capital Punishment." *Friends Social Service Series* 29:1.

Davis, David B. 1957. "Movements to Abolish Capital Punishment in America, 1781–1861." *American Historical Review* 63:23–46.

Davis, Nanette. 1985. *From Crime to Choice*. Westport, Conn.: Greenwood Press.

Deckard, Barbara. 1975. *The Women's Movement*. New York: Harper and Row.

Deets, Lee Emerson. 1948. "Changes in Capital Punishment Policy since 1939." *Journal of Criminal Law and Criminology* 38:584–94.

Dellapenna, Joseph W. 1979. "The History of Abortion." *University of Pittsburgh Law Review* 40:359–428.

Dellinger, Walter. 1989. "The Next Battleground on Abortion Rights." *Washington Post*, 10 July.

Destro, Robert A. 1975. "Abortion and the Constitution." *California Law Review* 63:1250–71.

Devereux, George. 1955. *A Study of Abortion in Primitive Societies*. New York: Julian Press.

Dionne, E. J., Jr. 1987. "Abortion, Bork, and the '88 Campaign." *New York Times*, 8 July.

———. 1989. "On Both Sides, Advocates Predict a Fifty-State Battle." *New York Times*, 4 July.

Donohue, William A. 1985. *The Politics of the American Civil Liberties Union*. New Brunswick, N.J.: Transaction Books.

Donovan, Patricia. 1978. "State Funding of Abortion." *Family Planning/Population Reporter* 7:20–21.

———. 1982. "Fertility-Related State Laws Enacted in 1981." *Family Planning/Population Perspectives* 14:63–67.

Dorsen, Norman. 1968. *Frontiers of Civil Liberties*. New York: Random House.

Dworkin, Andrea. 1983. *Right-Wing Women*. New York: Perigee Books.

Ebaugh, Helen Rose Fuchs, and C. Allen Haney. 1980. "Shifts in Abortion Attitudes." *Journal of Marriage and the Family* 42:491–99.

Ebon, Martin, ed. 1971. *Everywoman's Guide to Abortion*. New York: Universe Books.

Edelstein, Ludwig. [1943] 1967. "The Hippocratic Oath." Reprinted in *Ancient Medicine: Selected Papers of Ludwig Edelstein*, edited by Owsei Temkin and C. Lillian Temkin. Baltimore: Johns Hopkins University Press.

Ehrhardt, Charles W., and Harold Levinson. 1973. "Florida's Legislative Response to *Furman*." *Journal of Criminal Law and Criminology* 64:10–21.

Ehrhardt, Charles W., Phillip A. Hubbart, L. Harold Levinson, William McKinley Smiley, Jr., and Thomas A. Wills. 1973. "The Future of Capital Punishment in Florida." *Journal of Criminal Law and Criminology* 64:2–10.

Ehrlich, Isaac. 1975. "The Deterrent Effect of Capital Punishment: A Question of Life and Death." *American Economic Review* 65:397–417.

Ehrlich, J. W. 1959. *Ehrlich's Blackstone—Part One*. New York: Capricorn Books.

Ellsworth, Phoebe C., and Lee Ross. 1976. "Public Opinion and Judicial Decision Making." In *Capital Punishment in the United States*, edited by Hugo Adam Bedau and Chester A. Pierce. New York: AMS Press.

Ely, John Hart. 1973. "The Wages of Crying Wolf." *Yale Law Journal* 82:920–49.

Emerson, Thomas I. 1965. "Nine Justices in Search of a Doctrine." *Michigan Law Review* 64:219–34.

Epstein, Lee. 1985. *Conservatives in Court*. Knoxville: University of Tennessee Press.

———. 1990. "Interviewing U.S. Supreme Court Justices and Interest Group Attorneys." *Judicature* 73:196–98.

———. 1991. "Courts and Interest Groups." In *American Courts*, edited by John B. Gates and Charles A. Johnson. Washington, D.C.: CQ Press.

Epstein, Lee, and C. K. Rowland. 1991. "Debunking the Myth of Interest Group Invincibility in the Courts." *American Political Science Review* 85:205–17.

Epstein, Lee, Thomas G. Walker, and William J. Dixon. 1989. "A Neo-Institutional Perspective of Supreme Court Decision Making." *American Journal of Political Science* 33:825–41.

———. 1990. "Supreme Court Decision Making in Times of War and Peace: A Proposal for Research." Presented at the annual meeting of the Law and Society Association, Berkeley, California.

Epstein, Richard A. 1974. "Substantive Due Process by Any Other Name." In *The Supreme Court Review*, edited by Philip B. Kurland. Chicago: University of Chicago Press.

Erikson, K. T. 1966. *The Wayward Puritans*. New York: John Wiley.

Erskine, Hazel. 1970. "The Polls: Capital Punishment." *Public Opinion Quarterly* 34:290–307.

Family Planning/Population Reporter. 1975. "A Review of State Abortion Laws Enacted since January 1973." 4:108–13.

Farber, Daniel A., and Suzanna Sherry. 1990. *A History of the American Constitution*. St. Paul, Minn.: West Publishing.

Faux, Marian. 1988. *Roe v. Wade*. New York: Macmillan.

———. 1990. *Crusaders: Voices from the Abortion Front*. New York: Birch Lane Press.

The Federalist Papers. 1987. Middlesex, Eng.: Penguin Books.

Filler, Louis. 1952. "Movements to Abolish the Death Penalty in the United States." *Annals of the American Academy of Political and Social Science* 284:124–36.

Fleishman, John A. 1986. "Trends in Self-Identified Ideology from 1972 to 1982." *American Journal of Political Science* 30:517–41.

Flint, Jerry M. 1973. "States on Move." *New York Times*, 11 March.

Florida State University Law Review. 1974. "Notes: Florida's Legislative and Judicial Response to *Furman v. Georgia*: An Analysis and Criticism." 2:108–52.

Fordham Law Review. 1973. "Constitutional Law–Capital Punishment–Death Penalty as Presently Administered Held Unconstitutional." 41:671–84.

Fortas, Abe. 1977. "The Case against Capital Punishment." *New York Times Magazine*, 23 January.

Franklin, Charles H., and Liane C. Kosaki. 1989. "Republican Schoolmaster: The U.S. Supreme Court, Public Opinion, and Abortion." *American Political Science Review* 83:751–71.

Frankovic, Kathleen A. 1981. "Public Opinion Trends." In *The Election of 1980*, edited by Gerald Pomper. Chatham, N.J.: Chatham House.

Freeman, Jo. 1975. *The Politics of Women's Liberation*. New York: McKay.

Freeman, Lucy. 1962. *The Abortionist*. Garden City, N.Y.: Doubleday.

Freund, Paul A., Arthur E. Sutherland, Mark DeWolfe Howe, and Ernest J. Brown. 1977. *Constitutional Law*. Boston: Little, Brown.

Fried, Charles. 1991. *Order and Law*. New York: Simon and Schuster.

Fried, Joseph P. 1980. "Judge Tells How He Reached Ruling on Abortion." *New York Times*, 17 January.

Friedan, Betty. 1963. *The Feminine Mystique*. New York: W. W. Norton.

Friendly, Fred W., and Martha J. H. Elliot. 1984. *The Constitution—That Delicate Balance*. New York: Random House.

Gailey, Phil. 1986. "Politics." *New York Times*, 19 June.

Galanter, Marc. 1974. "Why the 'Haves' Come Out Ahead: Speculation on the Limits of Legal Change." *Law and Society Review* 9:95–160.

Gates, John B., and Wayne V. McIntosh. 1989. "The Motivations for Interest Group Litigation." Presented at the annual meeting of the Law and Society Association, Madison, Wisconsin.

Garfinkel, Harold. 1949. "Research Note on Inter- and Intra-Racial Homicides." *Social Forces* 27:369–81.

Gebhard, Paul H., Wardell B. Pomeroy, Clyde E. Martin, and Cornelia V. Christenson. 1958. *Pregnancy, Birth, and Abortion*. New York: Harper.

Gelb, Leslie. 1985. "U.S. Will Ask Court to Reverse Abortion Ruling." *New York Times*, 15 July.

George, Tracey. 1989. "Swing Justices on the U.S. Supreme Court: Lewis Powell and the Death Penalty." Distinction thesis, Southern Methodist University.

George, Tracey, and Lee Epstein. 1992. "On the Nature of Supreme Court Decision Making." *American Political Science Review*, June, forthcoming.

Gest, Ted. 1987. "A Supreme Court Nominee Encounters Opposition." *U.S. News and World Report*, 21 September.

———. 1989. "The Abortion Furor." *U.S. News and World Report*, 17 July.

Gibbs, Jack P., and Maynard L. Erickson. 1976. "Capital Punishment and the Deterrence Doctrine." In *Capital Punishment in the United States*, edited by Hugo Adam Bedau and Chester A. Pierce. New York: AMS Press.

Gibson, James L. 1977. "Discriminant Functions, Role Orientations, and Judicial Behavior." *Journal of Politics* 39:984–1007.

———. 1978a. "Judges' Role Orientations, Attitudes, and Decisions: An Interactive Model." *American Political Science Review* 72:911–24.

———. 1978b. "Race as a Determinant of Criminal Sentences: A Methodological Critique and a Case Study." *Law and Society Review* 12:455–77.

———. 1983. "From Simplicity to Complexity." *Political Behavior* 5:7–49.

Ginsburg, Ruth Bader. 1985. "Some Thoughts on Autonomy and Equality in Relation to *Roe v. Wade*." *North Carolina Law Review* 63:375–86.

Glasser, Ira. 1990. "The ACLU's Undiluted Concerns." *Washington Post*, 24 March.

Glassock, Charles E. 1969. "Capital Punishment: A Model for Reform." *Kentucky Law Journal* 57:508–25.

Goldberg, Arthur J. 1973. "The Death Penalty and the Supreme Court." *Arizona Law Review* 15:355–68.

Goldberg, Arthur J., and Alan M. Dershowitz. 1970. "Declaring the Death Penalty Unconstitutional." *Harvard Law Review* 83:1773–1819.

Goldberg, Faye. 1970. "Toward Expansion of *Witherspoon*." *Harvard Civil Rights–Civil Liberties Law Review* 5:53–69.

Goldman, Sheldon. 1989. "Judicial Appointments and the Presidential Agenda." In *The Presidency in American Politics*, edited by Paul Brace, Christine B. Harrington, and Gary King. New York: New York University Press.

Goldstein, Leslie Friedman. 1988. *The Constitutional Rights of Women*. Madison: University of Wisconsin Press.

Goldstein, Tom. 1976. "Inmates' Lawyers Report Many May Face Execution." *New York Times*, 3 July.

Goodman, Janice, Rhonda Copelon Schoenbrod, and Nancy Stearns. 1973. "*Doe* and *Roe*." *Women's Rights Law Reporter* 1:20–38.

Gordon, Linda. 1977. *Woman's Body, Woman's Right*. New York: Penguin.

Gottlieb, Gerald H. 1961. "Testing the Death Penalty." *Southern California Law Review* 34:268–81.

Graham, Fred P. 1968a. "Fortas Set Back by Dirksen Shift." *New York Times*, 28 September.

———. 1968b. "1968 Ending with No Executions, First Such Year in U.S. Records." *New York Times*, 31 December.

———. 1969a. "Mitchell Vows 'Vigorous' Law Enforcement in U.S." *New York Times*, 22 January.

———. 1969b. "Court Fight for Legal Abortions Spurred by Washington Ruling." *New York Times*, 12 November.

———. 1971. "Abolition of Death Penalty Urged by U.S. Legal Panel." *New York Times*, 8 January.

———. 1972. "Bar Group Supports Eased Abortions." *New York Times*, 8 February.

Granfield, David. 1969. *The Abortion Decision*. Garden City, N.Y.: Doubleday.

Gray, Ian, and Moira Stanley. 1989. *A Punishment in Search of a Crime*. New York: Avon Books.

Greenberg, Jack. 1974a. Letter to the Editor. *New York Times*, 3 February.

———. 1974b. "Litigation for Social Change: Methods, Limits, and Role in Democracy." *Records of the Bar Association of New York City* 29:9–63.

———. 1976. "The Death Penalty: Where Do We Go from Here?" *NLADA Briefcase* 34:55–57.

———. 1977. *Judicial Process and Social Change*. St. Paul, Minn.: West Publishing.

———. 1982. "Capital Punishment as a System." *Yale Law Journal* 91:908–28.

———. 1988. "The Death Penalty in the Eighties." *Journal of Legislation* 15:73–75.

Greenberg, Jack, and Jack Himmelstein. 1969. "Varieties of Attack on the Death Penalty." *Crime and Delinquency* 15:112–20.

Greenhouse, Linda. 1980. "Abortion Financing for Poor Resuming on 6–3 Court Order." *New York Times*, 20 February.

———. 1983a. "Court Reaffirms Right to Abortion and Bars Variety of Local Curbs." *New York Times*, 16 June.

———. 1983b. "High Court Clears Up Any Doubts on Abortion." *New York Times*, 19 June.

———. 1985a. "Court to Hear Pennsylvania Abortion Appeal." *New York Times*, 16 April.

——. 1985b. "In re Politics v. Punches." *New York Times*, 18 July.

——. 1985c. "Charting the Crucial Course of Capital Punishment." *New York Times*, 24 July.

——. 1986. "Washington Talk." *New York Times*, 13 November.

——. 1987. "Bork Sets Forth Spirited Defense of His Integrity." *New York Times*, 19 September.

——. 1988. "Reagan Administration Renews Assault on 1973 Abortion Ruling." *New York Times*, 11 November.

——. 1989. "Supreme Court, 5–4, Narrowing *Roe v. Wade*." *New York Times*, 4 July.

Grey, Thomas. 1975. "Do We Have an Unwritten Constitution?" *Stanford Law Review* 27:703–18.

Grisez, Germain G. 1970. *Abortion: The Myths, the Realities, and the Arguments*. New York: Corpus Books.

Gross, Samuel R., and Robert Mauro. 1984. "Patterns of Death." *Stanford Law Review* 37:27.

——. 1989. *Death and Discrimination*. Boston: Northeastern University Press.

Group for the Advancement of Psychiatry. 1970. *The Right to Abortion: A Psychiatric View*. New York: Charles Scribner's Sons.

Guttmacher, Alan F., ed. 1967. *The Case for Legalized Abortion Now*. Berkeley, Calif.: Diablo Press.

Hager, Philip. 1986. "Reversal of '73 Abortion Decision Seen as Unlikely." *Los Angeles Times*, 12 June.

Hall, Robert. 1967. "Abortion in American Hospitals." *American Journal of Public Health* 57:1933–36.

——, ed. 1970. *Abortion in a Changing World*. 2 vols. Proceedings of an International Conference Convened in Hot Springs, Virginia, 17–20 November 1968, by the Association for the Study of Abortion. New York: Columbia University Press.

Halloran, Richard. 1972. "Death Penalties Argued in Court." *New York Times*, 18 January.

Handler, Joel. 1978. *Social Movements and the Legal System*. New York: Academic Press.

Harris, Louis. 1987. "Bork Lacks Support, Poll Finds." *Dallas Morning News*, 28 September.

Hartung, Frank E. 1952. "Trends in the Use of Capital Punishment." *Annals of the American Academy of Political and Social Science* 284:8–19.

Harvard Law Review. 1968. "Multiparty Federal Habeas Corpus." 81:1482–1510.

Hawkinson, William P. 1976. "Abortion: An Anthropological Overview." In *Liberalization of Abortion Laws*, edited by Adbel R. Omran. Chapel Hill: University of North Carolina Press.

Heck, Edward V. 1986. "Changing Voting Patterns in the Warren and Burger Courts." In *Judicial Conflict and Consensus*, edited by Sheldon Goldman and Charles M. Lamb. Lexington: University of Kentucky Press.

Heintz, Jeffrey T. 1974. "Legislative Response to *Furman v. Georgia*." *Akron Law Review* 8:149–61.

Hendin, David. 1971. *Everything You Need to Know about Abortion*. New York: Pinnacle Books.

Hentoff, Nat. 1989. "The Thread of the Argument on Abortion." *Washington Post*, 6 May.

Herbers, John. 1978. "Anti-Abortionists' Impact Is Felt in Elections across the Nation." *New York Times*, 20 June.

———. 1984. "Abortion Issue Threatens to Become Divisive." *New York Times*, 14 October.

Herman, Robin. 1980. "After Decision Focus Turns to Lower Courts and Abortion Politics." *New York Times*, 1 July.

Hershey, Marjorie Randon. 1986. "Direct Action and the Abortion Issue." In *Interest Group Politics*, 2d ed., edited by Allan J. Cigler and Burdett A. Loomis. Washington, D.C.: CQ Press.

Heymann, Philip, and Douglas Barzelay. 1973. "The Forest and the Trees." *Boston University Law Review* 53:765–84.

Hilgers, Thomas W., and Dennis J. Horan. 1972. *Abortion and Social Justice*. New York: Steed and Ward.

Hilgers, Thomas W., and Dennis O'Hare. 1981. "Abortion Related Maternal Mortality." In *New Perspectives on Human Abortion*, edited by Thomas Hilgers, Dennis Horan, and David Mall. Frederick, Md.: University Publications of America.

Holmes, Oliver Wendell. 1881. *The Common Law*. Boston: Little, Brown.

Horan, Dennis J. 1981. "Critical Abortion Litigation." *Catholic Lawyer* 26:198–208.

Horan, Dennis J., and Thomas J. Balch. 1987. "*Roe v. Wade*." In *Abortion and the Constitution*, edited by Dennis J. Horan, Edward R. Grant, and Paige C. Cunningham. Washington, D.C.: Georgetown University Press.

Horan, Dennis J., Edward R. Grant, and Paige C. Cunningham. 1987. *Abortion and the Constitution*. Washington, D.C.: Georgetown University Press.

Irvin, Carol, and Howard E. Rose. 1974. "The Response to *Furman*: Can Legislators Breathe Life back into Death?" *Cleveland State Law Review* 23:172–89.

Jackson, Donald. 1967. "A.M.A., in Reversal, Favors Liberalizing of Abortion Laws." *New York Times*, 22 June.

Jackson, John E., and Maris A. Vinovskis. 1983. "Public Opinion, Elections, and Single Issue Politics." In *The Abortion Dispute and the American System*, edited by Gilbert Y. Steiner. Washington, D.C.: Brookings.

Jackson, Robert H. 1941. *The Struggle for Judicial Supremacy*. New York: Vintage Books.

Jacob, Charles E. 1981. "The Congressional Elections." In *The Election of 1980*, edited by Gerald Pomper. Chatham, N.J.: Chatham House.

Jacobson, Gary, and Samuel Kernell. 1981. *Strategy and Choice in Congressional Elections*. New Haven: Yale University Press.

Jaffe, Frederick S., Barbara Lindheim, and Philip R. Lee. 1981. *Abortion Politics*. New York: McGraw-Hill.

Jenkins, John A. 1983. "A Candid Talk with Justice Blackmun." *New York Times Magazine*, 20 February.

Johnson, Charles A., and Jon R. Bond. 1980. "Coercive and Non-Coercive Abortion Deterrence Policies." *Law and Policy Quarterly* 2:106–28.

Johnson, Charles A., and Bradley C. Canon. 1984. *Judicial Policies: Implementation and Impact*. Washington, D.C.: CQ Press.

Johnson, Guy B. 1941. "The Negro and Crime." *Annals of the Academy of Political and Social Science* 217:93–104.

Johnson, Thomas A. 1966. "Rape Penalties in South Studied." *New York Times*, 24 April.

Johnston, Laurie. 1978."Law and Religion Intermingled in Suit on Abortion." *New York Times*, 14 March.

Joyce, Fay S. 1984. "Courts Study Link between Victim's Race and Imposition of Death." *New York Times*, 5 January.

Judgment without Justice. 1982. Lynchburg, Va.: Old Time Gospel Hour.

Junker, John M. 1972. "The Death Penalty Cases: A Preliminary Comment." *Washington Law Review* 48:95–109.

Jurow, George. 1971. "New Data on the Effect of a 'Death-Qualified' Jury on the Guilt Determination Process." *Harvard Law Review* 84:567–611.

Kamen, Al. 1985. "Inside the Judiciary." *Washington Post*, 20 September.

Kamisar, Yale. 1983. "The Warren Court (Was It Really So Defense-Minded?), the Burger Court (Is It Really So Prosecution-Oriented?), and Police Investigatory Practices." In *The Burger Court*, edited by Vincent Blasi. New Haven: Yale University Press.

Kaplan, David A. 1988. "Death Row Inmate Prevails." *National Law Journal*, 11 January.

Kauper, Paul G. 1974. *Constitutional Law.* Supplement. Boston: Little, Brown.

Kellogg, Charles. 1967. *NAACP.* Baltimore: Johns Hopkins University Press.

Kennedy, David. 1970. *Birth Control in America.* New Haven: Yale University Press.

King, Wayne. 1973. "Death Rows: Forty-four May Avoid Execution." *New York Times*, 30 December.

———. 1978. "Few on Three Death Rows Are There for Killing Blacks." *New York Times*, 6 March.

King, Wayne, and Irvin Molotsky. 1986a. "Justice under Scrutiny." *New York Times*, 16 June.

———. 1986b. "The Moving Pen Writes." *New York Times*, 16 June.

Kleck, Gary. 1981. "Racial Discrimination in Criminal Sentencing." *American Sociological Review* 46:783–805.

Kleindienst, Richard. 1985. *Justice.* Ottawa, Ill.: Jameson Books.

Klemesrud, Judy. 1978. "Planned Parenthood's New Head Takes a Fighting Stand." *New York Times*, 3 February.

Kluger, Richard. 1976. *Simple Justice.* New York: Alfred A. Knopf.

Knight, Kathleen. 1985. "Ideology in the 1980 Election." *Journal of Politics* 47:828–53.

Kobylka, Joseph F. 1987. "A Court-Created Context for Group Litigation: Libertarian Groups and Obscenity." *Journal of Politics* 49:1061–78.

———. 1989. "Consistency in a Context of Change?: Justice Blackmun and Defendants' Rights." Presented at the annual meeting of the Southern Political Science Association, Memphis, Tennessee.

———. 1991. *The Politics of Obscenity.* Westport, Conn.: Greenwood Press.

Kolbert, Kathryn. 1989. "After Webster Where Will Court Go on Abortion?" *National Law Journal*, 21 August.

Kornhauser, Ann. 1990. "High Risk Opposition." *Legal Times*, 17 September.

Krislov, Samuel. 1963. "The Amicus Curiae Brief: From Friendship to Advocacy.' *Yale Law Journal* 72:694–721.

Kurland, Philip B., and Gerhard Casper. 1975a. *Landmark Briefs and Arguments of the Supreme Court of the United States.* Vol. 73, *Furman v. Georgia.* Frederick, Md.: University Publications of America.

————. 1975b. *Landmark Briefs and Arguments of the Supreme Court of the United States.* Vol. 75, *Roe v. Wade.* Frederick, Md.: University Publications of America.

————. 1977. *Landmark Briefs and Arguments of the Supreme Court of the United States.* Vols. 89, 90, *Gregg v. Georgia* et al. Frederick, Md.: University Publications of America.

————. 1984. *Landmark Briefs and Arguments of the Supreme Court of the United States.* Vol. 138, *Akron v. Akron Center for Reproductive Health.* Frederick, Md.: University Publications of America.

————. 1990. *Landmark Briefs and Arguments of the Supreme Court of the United States.* Vol. 183, *Webster v. Reproductive Health Services.* Frederick, Md.: University Publications of America.

Kutler, Stanley I. 1977. *The Supreme Court and the Constitution.* 2d ed. New York: W. W. Norton.

Ladd, Everett C. n.d. *The Ladd Report #8.* New York: W. W. Norton.

Lader, Lawrence. 1955. *Margaret Sanger and the Fight for Birth Control.* Garden City, N.Y.: Doubleday.

————. 1966. *Abortion.* Boston: Beacon.

————. 1973. *Abortion II.* Boston: Beacon.

Lamm, Richard D., and Steven Davidson. 1973. "Abortion Reform." *Yale Review of Law and Social Action* 1:55–63.

Latus, Margaret Ann. 1984. "Assessing Ideological PACs." In *Money and Politics in the United States,* edited by Michael J. Malbin. Chatham, N.J.: Chatham House.

Lauter, David. 1984. "Making a Case with Statistics." *National Law Journal,* 10 December.

Law, Sylvia. 1978. "Reproductive Freedom Issues in Legal Services Practice." *Clearinghouse Review* 12:389–403.

————. 1984. "Rethinking Sex and the Constitution." *University of Pennsylvania Law Review* 132:955-1040.

Lawes, Lewis E. [1924] 1969. *Man's Judgment of Death.* Reprint. Montclair, N.J.: Patterson Smith.

Lawrence, Susan E. 1989. "Legal Services before the Supreme Court." *Judicature* 72:266–73.

————. 1990. *The Poor in Court.* Princeton, N.J.: Princeton University Press.

Lee, Philip R., and Lauren B. LeRoy. 1985. "Abortion Politics and Public Policy." In *Perspectives on Abortion,* edited by Paul Sachdev. Metuchen, N.J.: Scarecrow Press.

Levi, Edward. 1949. *An Introduction to Legal Reasoning.* Chicago: University of Chicago Press.

Levy, Leonard. 1974. *Against the Law.* New York: Harper and Row.

Lewin, Tamar. 1988. "Abortion Foes See Momentum for Their Drive." *New York Times,* 14 November.

Lewis, Anthony. 1980. "Abroad at Home: The Tidal Wave." *New York Times,* 6 November.

Lewis, Neil A. 1990. "Judge Strikes down Pennsylvania's Law Restricting Abortion." *New York Times,* 25 August.

Lissner, Will. 1968. "A.C.L.U. Asks End to Abortion Bans." *New York Times,* 25 March.

Loh, Wallace D. 1984. *Social Research in the Judicial Process.* New York: Russell Sage Foundation.

Lucas, Roy. 1968. "Federal Constitutional Limitations on the Enforcement and Administration of State Abortion Statutes." *North Carolina Law Review* 46:730–78.

Luker, Kristin. 1984. *Abortion and the Politics of Motherhood.* Berkeley: University of California Press.

Lynch, Robert N. 1976. " 'Abortion' and 1976 Politics." *America,* 6 March.

McGlen, Nancy, and Karen O'Connor. 1983. *Women's Rights.* New York: Praeger.

McGuigan, Patrick, and Jeffrey P. O'Connell. 1987. "Rehnquisition: Rite of Passage for a Chief Justice." In *The Judges' War,* edited by Patrick McGuigan and Jeffrey P. O'Connell. Washington, D.C.: Free Congress Research and Education Foundation.

Mackey, Philip English. 1973. "Edward Livingston on the Punishment of Death." *Tulane Law Review* 48:25–42.

———, ed. 1976. *Voices against Death.* New York: Burt Franklin.

MacKinnon, Catharine. 1984. *"Roe v. Wade*: A Study in Male Ideology." In *Abortion,* edited by Jay L. Garfield and Patricia Hennessey. Amherst: University of Massachusetts Press.

MacNeil, Neil. 1981. "The New Conservative House of Representatives." In *A Tide of Discontent,* edited by Ellis Sandoz and Cecil V. Crabb. Washington, D.C.: CQ Press.

Mailer, Norman. 1979. *The Executioner's Song.* Boston: Little, Brown.

Malbin, Michael J., ed. 1984. *Money and Politics in the United States.* Chatham, N.J.: Chatham House.

Malcolm, Andrea. 1989."Society's Conflict on the Death Penalty Stalls Procession on the Condemned." *New York Times,* 19 June.

Mann, Fredrick. 1973. "Anthony Amsterdam: Renaissance Man or Twentieth Century Computer?" *Juris Doctor* 3:30–33.

Mann, Jim. 1984. "Two Legends Slip Up." *American Lawyer,* January.

Mansnerus, Laura. 1987. "Both Sides in Bork Debate Seek the Blessings of History." *New York Times,* 13 September.

———. 1988. "One Winning Appeal for Death Row." *New York Times,* 12 February.

Manwaring, David. 1962. *Render unto Caesar: The Flag Salute Controversy.* Chicago: University of Chicago Press.

Markson, Stephen L. 1985. "The Roots of Contemporary Anti-Abortion Activism." In *Perspectives on Abortion,* edited by Paul Sachdev. Metuchen, N.J.: Scarecrow Press.

Markus, Gregory B. 1982. "Political Attitudes during an Election Year." *American Political Science Review* 76:538–60.

Marsel, Robert S. 1985–86. "Mr. Justice Arthur J. Goldberg and the Death Penalty." *South Texas Law Review* 27:467–92.

Marshall, Thomas R. 1989. *Public Opinion and the Supreme Court.* Boston: Unwin Hyman.

Masur, Louis P. 1989. *Rites of Execution.* New York: Oxford University Press.

Mauro, Tony. 1989a. "In the Eye of the Abortion Storm." *USA Today,* 26 April.

———. 1989b. "Both Sides Less than Perfect during Arguments in Abortion Case." *Manhattan Lawyer,* 2–8 May.

———. 1989c. "Reinventing the Wheel." *Legal Times,* 12 June.

———. 1989d. "Starr Wars." *Manhattan Lawyer,* 26 September.

———. 1989e. "The High Court's Year in Review." *Manhattan Lawyer,* 19 December.

Means, Cyril C., Jr. 1968. "The Law of New York Concerning Abortion and the Status of the Foetus, 1664–1968." *New York Law Forum* 14:411–515.

————. 1971. "The Phoenix of Abortion Freedom: Is a Penumbral or Ninth Amendment Right about to Arise from the Nineteenth Century Legislative Ashes of Fourteenth Century Common Law Liberty?" *New York Law Forum* 17:335–410.

Mears, Judith. 1974. "Taking Liberties." *Civil Liberties Review* 1, no. 3 (Summer): 136.

Meese, Edwin, III. 1985. Address to the American Bar Association, Washington, D.C., 9 July.

Meltsner, Michael. 1971. "Capital Punishment: The Moment of Truth." *Juris Doctor* 2:4–6.

————. 1973. *Cruel and Unusual: The Supreme Court and Capital Punishment.* New York: Random House.

————. 1974. "Cruel and Unusual Punishment." *New York Times,* 11 October.

Merton, Andrew H. 1981. *Enemies of Choice.* Boston: Beacon.

Milbauer, Barbara. 1983. *The Law Giveth: Legal Aspects of the Abortion Controversy.* New York: Atheneum.

Miller, Loren. 1966. *The Petitioner: The Study of the Supreme Court of the United States and the Negro.* Cleveland: World Publishing.

Mohr, James C. 1978. *Abortion in America: The Origins and Evolution of National Policy, 1800–1900.* New York: Oxford University Press.

Molotsky, Irvin, and Warren Weaver, Jr. 1985. "Antiabortion Dispute." *New York Times,* 26 August.

Monahan, John, and Laurens Walker. 1990. *Social Science and the Law.* 2d ed. Westbury, N.Y.: Foundation Press.

Montgomery, Paul L. 1971. "Supreme Court Decision Prompts Meeting Here of One Hundred Lawyers." *New York Times,* 16 May.

Moore, W. John. 1989. "Lobbying the Court." *National Journal* 21:908.

Morgan, Richard E. 1968. *The Politics of Religious Conflict.* New York: Pegasus.

————. 1973. "The Establishment Clause and Sectarian Schools: A Final Installment?" In *The Supreme Court Review,* edited by Philip B. Kurland. Chicago: University of Chicago Press.

Moss, Debra Cassens. 1987. "The Statistics of Death." *American Bar Association Journal,* January.

Muller, Eric L. 1985. "The Legal Defense Fund's Capital Punishment Campaign: The Distorting Influence of Death." *Yale Law and Policy Review* 4:158–87.

Murchison, Kenneth M. 1978. "Toward a Perspective on the Death Penalty Cases." *Emory Law Journal* 27:469–556.

Murphy, Bruce Allen. 1988. *Fortas—The Rise and Ruin of a Supreme Court Justice.* New York: William Murrow.

Murphy, Walter F. 1962. *Congress and the Court.* Chicago: University of Chicago Press.

Mydans, Seth. 1990. "Optimism Is Watchword as Abortion Foes Meet." *New York Times,* 18 June.

Myers, Richard S. 1987. "Pro-Life Litigation and the American Civil Liberties Tradition." In *Abortion and the Constitution,* edited by Dennis J. Horan, Edward R. Cunningham, and Paige C. Cunningham. Washington, D.C.: Georgetown University Press.

Nathanson, Bernard. 1984. *The Silent Scream.* Videorecording.

Naughton, James M. 1970. "President Seeks Harsh Penalties to Curb Bombers." *New York Times,* 26 March.

————. 1976. "Ford Says Court 'Went Too Far' on Abortion in '73." *New York Times*, 4 February.

Neier, Aryeh. 1979. *Defending My Enemy*. New York: Dutton.

————. 1982. *Only Judgment*. Middletown, Conn.: Wesleyan University Press.

New Republic. 1985. "Abortion Time Bomb." 25 February.

Newsweek. 1968. "Congress: The Death Penalty." 15 July.

New York Times. 1962. "Mother, Rebuffed in Arizona, May Seek Abortion Elsewhere." 1 August.

————. 1965. "A.C.L.U. to Seek End of Death Penalty." 21 June.

————. 1967. "Two Groups Act to Prevent Execution of Fifty-one in Florida." 5 April.

————. 1968. "Clark Calls for End of Death Penalty." 3 July.

————. 1969. "New Group Will Seek Change in Abortion Laws." 17 February.

————. 1970a. "Court Gets Plea on Death Penalty." 10 November.

————. 1970b. "President Signs Birth Control Bill." 27 December.

————. 1971. "Nixon Abortion Statement." 4 April.

————. 1972a. "Texas Court Upholds the Death Penalty." 16 March.

————. 1972b. "A Presidential Panel Supports Abortion on Request." 17 March.

————. 1972c. "Transcript of President's News Conference Emphasizing Foreign Affairs." 30 June.

————. 1972d. "States' Aides Ask a Death Penalty." 7 December.

————. 1973. "McGovern Differs with Nixon's Plan for Death Penalty." 12 March.

————. 1975. "Betty Ford Would Accept 'An Affair' by Daughter." 11 August.

————. 1976a. "Death Penalty for Nonwhites Found More Likely Now Than Previously." 4 April.

————. 1976b. "Death Penalty Study by Court Asked." 18 July.

————. 1978a. "Death Penalty Study Hints at a New Bias." 3 January.

————. 1978b. "Akron Council Approves Regulations on Abortion." 1 March.

————. 1978c. "Defendants in Capital Cases Given More Latitude on Evidence." 4 July.

————. 1980. "Poll Finds G.O.P. Planks Could Cost Reagan Votes." 23 July.

————. 1981. "Three Quit Antiabortion Group over Political 'Hit List.'" 4 June.

————. 1985a. "Abortion Rights Group Starts Drive to Combat Opposition." 21 March.

————. 1985b. "U.S. Brief Asks Court to Reverse Abortion Ruling." 16 July.

————. 1985c. "Major News in Summary." 21 July.

————. 1986a. "Marshall Criticizes Court on Death Penalty Issue." 20 March.

————. 1986b. "Death Cases Straining Justices." 13 May.

————. 1986c. "In His Own Words." 19 June.

————. 1987. "Poll Hints at Bork Support." 8 July.

————. 1988a. "One of Every Thirty Condemned since '77 Has Been Executed." 1 August.

————. 1988b. "Justice Fears for *Roe* Ruling." 14 September.

————. 1989. "Changing Criteria for Abortion Aid." 13 October.

————. 1991. "Michigan Court Voids a Ban on State-Financed Abortions." 22 February.

Noah, Timothy. 1981. "The Right to Life Movement." *New Republic*, 21 March.

Noble, Kenneth B. 1987a. "High Court to Decide Whether Death Penalty Discriminates against Blacks." *New York Times*, 23 March.

―――. 1987b. "Key Abortion Plaintiff Now Denies She Was Raped." *New York Times*, 9 September.

Nolan, Nancy A. 1983. "Note: Toward Abortion Control Legislation." *Dickinson Law Review* 87:373–406.

Nordheimer, Jon. 1977. "Gilmore Is Executed after Stay Is Upset." *New York Times*, 18 January.

Oberer, Walter E. 1961. "Does Disqualification of Jurors for Scruples against Capital Punishment Constitute Denial of a Fair Trial on Issue of Guilt?" *Texas Law Review* 39:545–67.

O'Brien, David M. 1990. *Storm Center*. 2d ed. New York: W. W. Norton.

O'Connor, Karen. 1980. *Women's Organizations' Use of the Court*. Lexington, Mass.: Lexington Books.

―――. 1983. "The Amicus Curiae Role of the U.S. Solicitor General in Supreme Court Litigation." *Judicature* 66:256–64.

O'Connor, Karen, and Lee Epstein. 1983. "Beyond Legislative Lobbying: Women's Rights Groups and the Supreme Court." *Judicature* 67:134–43.

―――. 1985. "Abortion Policy." In *The Reagan Administration and Human Rights*, edited by Tinsley E. Yarbrough. New York: Praeger.

―――. 1989. *Public Interest Law Groups*. Westport, Conn.: Greenwood Press.

Oelsner, Lesley. 1975. "Supreme Court Begins Review of the Death Penalty." *New York Times*, 22 April.

―――. 1976a. "Court to Review Death Penalty Issue." *New York Times*, 23 January.

―――. 1976b. "An Emotional Issue's Status in the Courts." *New York Times*, 1 March.

―――. 1976c. "Justices Hearing Views on Death Penalty." *New York Times*, 31 March.

―――. 1976d. "Justices Uphold Death Penalty, 7–2." *New York Times*, 3 July.

―――. 1976e. "Supreme Court Ends Death Penalty Ban in Cases of Murder." *New York Times*, 5 October.

―――. 1977. "Court Rules States May Deny Medicaid for Some Abortions." *New York Times*, 21 June.

Olasky, Marvin. 1988. *The Press and Abortion, 1838–1988*. Hillsdale, N.J.: Lawrence Erlbaum Associates.

O'Neill, Timothy J. 1981. "The Language of Equality in a Democratic Order." *American Political Science Review* 75:626–35.

Onek, Joseph. 1976. "Capital Punishment." *New York Times*, 1 August.

O'Toole, Thomas. 1965. "A.M.A. Puts Off Abortion Stand." *New York Times*, 2 December.

Packer, Herbert L., and Ralph J. Gampbell. 1959. "Therapeutic Abortion: A Problem in Law and Medicine." *Stanford Law Review* 11:417–55.

Packwood, Bob. 1986. "The Rise and Fall of the Right-to-Life Movement in Congress." In *Abortion, Medicine, and the Law*, edited by J. Douglas Butler and David F. Walbert. New York: Facts on File Publications.

Paige, Connie. 1983. *The Right to Lifers: Who They Are, Where They Operate, Where They Get Their Money*. New York: Summit.

Paine, Donald F. 1962. "Comments: Capital Punishment." *Tennessee Law Review* 29:534–51.

Passell, Peter. 1975. "The Deterrent Effect of the Death Penalty." *Stanford Law Review* 61:61–80.

Passell, Peter, and John B. Taylor. 1976. "The Deterrence Controversy: A Reconsideration of the Time Series Evidence." In *Capital Punishment in the United States*, edited by Hugo Adam Bedau and Chester A. Pierce. New York: AMS Press.

Pearson, Albert M., and Paul M. Kurtz. 1986. "The Abortion Controversy." In *Abortion, Medicine, and the Law*, edited by J. Douglas Butler and David F. Walbert. New York: Facts on File Publications.

Perry, Michael J. 1976. "Substantive Due Process Revisited." *Northwestern University Law Review* 71:417–69.

———. 1982. *The Constitution, the Courts, and Human Rights*. New Haven: Yale University Press.

Pierce, Chester M. 1975. "Effects of the Death Penalty." *American Journal of Orthopsychiatry* 45:580.

Pilpel, Harriet F. 1982. "Hyde and Go Seek." *New York Law School Review* 27:1101–23.

Pomper, Gerald. 1981. *The Election of 1980*. Chatham, N.J.: Chatham House.

Pomper, Gerald, Ross K. Baker, Walter Dean Burnham, Barbara G. Farah, Marjorie Randon Hershey, Ethel Klein, and Wilson Carey McWilliams. 1989. *The Election of 1988*. Chatham, N.J.: Chatham House.

Post, Albert. 1944. "Early Efforts to Abolish Capital Punishment in Pennsylvania." *Pennsylvania Magazine of History and Biography* 68:42–43.

Potts, Malcolm, Peter Diggory, and John Peel. 1977. *Abortion*. Cambridge: Cambridge University Press.

Prettyman, Barrett, Jr. 1961. *Death and the Supreme Court*. New York: Harcourt, Brace, and World.

Pritchett, C. Herman. 1948. *The Roosevelt Court*. New York: Macmillan.

———. 1961. *Congress versus the Supreme Court*. Minneapolis: University of Minnesota Press.

———. 1969. "The Development of Judicial Research." In *Frontiers of Judicial Research*, edited by Joel B. Grossman and Joseph Tanenhaus. New York: John Wiley.

PR Newswire. 1989. "News Advisory." 21 April.

Prosser, William L. 1960. "Privacy." *California Law Review* 48:383–423.

Provine, Doris Marie. 1980. *Case Selection in the United States Supreme Court*. Chicago: University of Chicago Press.

Puro, Steven. 1971. "The Role of Amicus Curiae in the United States Supreme Court, 1920–1966." Ph.D. diss., State University of New York at Buffalo.

Quay, Eugene. 1961. "Justifiable Abortion." *Georgetown Law Journal* 49, no. 3 (Spring): 395–538.

Radelet, Michael. 1981. "Racial Characteristics and the Imposition of the Death Penalty." *American Society Review* 46:918–27.

Reagan, Ronald. 1984. *Abortion and the Conscience of the Nation*. Nashville: Thomas Nelson.

Redlich, Norman D. 1962. "Are There 'Certain Rights' . . . Retained by the People?" *New York University Law Review* 37:787–812.

Regan, Donald. 1979. "Rewriting *Roe v. Wade*." *Michigan Law Review* 77:1569–1646.

Reidel, Marc. 1976. "Discrimination in the Imposition of the Death Penalty: A Comparison of the Characteristics of Offenders Sentenced Pre-*Furman* and Post-*Furman*." *Temple Quarterly Law Review* 49:261–86.

Reidinger, Paul. 1987. "A Court Divided." *American Bar Association Journal*, January.

Reinhold, Robert. 1976. "Two Unwanted Issues Confronting Ford." *New York Times*, 10 September.

Rhode, Deborah. 1989. *Justice and Gender*. Cambridge: Harvard University Press.

Roberts, Steven V. 1982. "Senate Kills Plan to Curb Abortion by a Vote of 47–46." *New York Times*, 16 September.

———. 1987. "U.S. Proposes Curb on Clinics Giving Abortion Advice." *New York Times*, 31 July.

Rodman, Hyman, Betty Sarvis, and Jo Walker Bonar. 1987. *The Abortion Question*. New York: Columbia University Press.

Rohde, David B., and Harold J. Spaeth. 1976. *Supreme Court Decision Making*. San Francisco: W. H. Freeman.

Roraback, Catherine G. 1989. "*Griswold v. Connecticut*: A Brief Case History." *Ohio Northern University Law Review* 16:395–401.

Rosen, Harold, ed. [1954] 1967. *Therapeutic Abortion*. Reissued as *Abortion in America*. Boston: Beacon.

Rosenbaum, David E. 1984. "Poll Shows Few Votes Changed by Abortion Issue." *New York Times*, 8 October.

Rosenberg, Gerald N. 1989. "Lucky Litigation?" Presented at the annual meeting of the Midwest Political Science Association, Chicago.

———. 1991. *The Hollow Hope*. Chicago: University of Chicago Press.

Rosewicz, Barbara. 1983. "Abortion Opponents Will Press On with Cause." Proprietary to the United Press International, 16 June.

Royal Commission. 1953. *Report of the Royal Commission on Capital Punishment, 1949–1953*. London: Her Majesty's Stationery Office.

Rubin, Eva R. 1987. *Abortion, Politics, and the Courts*. Rev. ed. Westport, Conn.: Greenwood Press.

Rush, Benjamin. [1782] 1976. "Abolish the Absurd and Unchristian Practice." Reprinted in *Voices against Death*, edited by Philip Mackey. New York: Burt Franklin.

Safire, William. 1988. "*Roe v. Wade*'s Future." *New York Times*, 27 October.

Sandoz, Ellis, and Cecil V. Crabb, Jr., eds. 1981. *A Tide of Discontent*. Washington, D.C.: CQ Press.

Sarat, Austin, and Neil Vidmar. 1976. "Public Opinion, the Death Penalty, and the Eighth Amendment." *Wisconsin Law Review*, no. 1, 171–206.

Sarvis, Betty, and Hyman Rodman. 1973. *The Abortion Controversy*. New York: Columbia University Press.

Sauer, R. 1974. "Attitudes to Abortion in America, 1800–1973." *Population Studies* 28:53–67.

Savitz, Leonard D. 1959. "A Study in Capital Punishment." *Journal of Criminal Law, Criminology, and Police Science* 49:338–41.

Saye, Albert B. 1975. *American Constitutional Law*. Columbus, Ohio: Charles E. Merrill.

Scheingold, Stuart A. 1974. *The Politics of Rights*. New Haven: Yale University Press.

Schlozman, Kay Lehman, and John Tierney. 1986. *Organized Interests in American Democracy*. New York: Harper and Row.

Schubert, Glendon. 1965. *The Judicial Mind*. Evanston, Ill.: Northwestern University Press.

———. 1974. *The Judicial Mind Revisited*. New York: Free Press.

Schuessler, Karl F. 1952. "The Deterrent Influence of the Death Penalty." *Annals of the American Academy of Political and Social Science* 284:54–62.

Schulder, Diane, and Florynce Kennedy. 1971. *Abortion Rap*. New York: McGraw-Hill.

Schwartz, Bernard. 1983. *Super Chief*. New York: New York University Press.

———. 1985. *The Unpublished Opinions of the Warren Court*. New York: Oxford University Press.

———. 1988. *The Unpublished Opinions of the Burger Court*. New York: Oxford University Press.

———. 1990. *The Ascent of Pragmatism*. Reading, Mass.: Addison-Wesley.

Schwartz, Herman, ed. 1987. *The Burger Years*. New York: Penguin.

———. 1988. *Packing the Courts: The Conservative Campaign to Rewrite the Constitution*. New York: Scribner's.

Schwed, Roger. 1983. *Abolition and Capital Punishment*. New York: AMS Press.

Scigliano, Robert. 1971. *The Supreme Court and the Presidency*. New York: Free Press.

Segal, Jeffrey A. 1984. "Predicting Supreme Court Cases Probabilistically: The Search and Seizure Cases, 1962–1981." *American Political Science Review* 78:891–900.

———. 1987. "Senate Confirmation of Supreme Court Justices: Partisan and Institutional Politics." *Journal of Politics* 49:998–1015.

———. 1991. "Courts, Executives, and Legislatures." In *The American Courts*, edited by John B. Gates and Charles A. Johnson. Washington, D.C.: CQ Press.

Segal, Jeffrey A., and Harold J. Spaeth. 1989. "Decisional Trends on the Warren and Burger Courts." *Judicature* 73:103–7.

Seigel, Max H. 1976. "U.S. Court Overturns Curb on Medicaid Abortions." *New York Times*, 23 October.

Sellin, Thorsten. 1967. *Capital Punishment*. New York: Harper and Row.

———. 1980. *The Penalty of Death*. Beverly Hills, Calif.: Sage.

Shapiro, Martin. 1972. "Toward a Theory of Stare Decisis." *Journal of Legal Studies* 1:125–34.

Sharpe, Rochelle, and Tony Mauro. 1989. Untitled news release. *Gannett News Service*, 27 April.

Shaw, Russell. 1968. *Abortion on Trial*. Dayton, Ohio: Pflaum Press.

Shawcross, William. 1973. "Nixon and the Death Penalty." *New Statesman*, 16 March.

Shenon, Philip. 1989. "Profile of Three Advocates in the Appeal." *New York Times*, 26 April.

Shin, Kilman. 1978. *Death Penalty and Crime: Empirical Studies*. Fairfax, Va.: Center for Economic Analysis, George Mason University.

Shogan, Robert. 1972. *A Question of Judgment*. Indianapolis: Bobbs-Merrill.

Shribman, David. 1983. "Foes of Abortion Beaten in Senate Amendment Bid." *New York Times*, 19 June.

Sibley, John. 1973. "Two Groups to Challenge Hospitals That Resist Ruling on Abortion." *New York Times*, 2 July.

Sickels, Robert Judd. 1988. *John Paul Stevens and the Constitution.* University Park: Pennsylvania State University Press.

Sigworth, Heather. 1971. "Abortion Laws in the Federal Courts: The Supreme Court as Platonic Guardian." *Indiana Legal Forum* 5:130–42.

Simon, James F. 1973. *In His Own Image.* New York: David McKay.

Simpson, Peggy. 1989. "The War Has Just Begun." *Ms.*, 28 September.

Skene, Neil. 1986. "Review of Capital Punishment Cases: Does the Florida Supreme Court Know What It's Doing?" *Stetson Law Review* 15:263–354.

Sklar, Zachary. 1976. "Carter v. Ford on the Legal Issues." *Juris Doctor* 6:47–50.

Sloan, Irving J. 1988. *The Law Governing Abortion, Contraception, and Sterilization.* London: Oceana.

Smith, Marcia. 1988. "'Jane Roe' Symbolizes Pro-Choice Effort." *Dallas Times Herald*, 22 January.

Sorauf, Frank J. 1976. *The Wall of Separation: Constitutional Politics of Church and State.* Princeton, N.J.: Princeton University Press.

———. 1988. *Money in American Politics.* Glenview, Ill.: Scott, Foresman.

Spear, Charles. 1844. *Essays on the Punishment by Death.* Boston: By the author; London: John Green.

Stanley, Harold W., and Richard G. Niemi. 1992. *Vital Statistics on American Politics.* Washington, D.C.: CQ Press.

Stearns, Nancy. 1989. "Commentary: *Roe v. Wade.*" *Berkeley Women's Law Journal* 4:1–11.

Steele, Richard. 1976. "1976's Sleeper Issue." *Newsweek*, 9 February.

Stephens, Otis H., Jr., and John M. Scheb II. 1988. *American Constitutional Law.* San Diego: Harcourt Brace Jovanovich.

Stevens, William K. 1986. "Margin of Vote Is Called Key to Abortion Decision." *New York Times*, 12 June.

Stimson, James A. 1991. *Public Opinion in America.* Boulder, Colo.: Westview Press.

Stolz, Barbara Ann. 1983. "Congress and Capital Punishment." *Law and Policy Quarterly* 5:157–80.

Storer, Horatio R., and Franklin Fiske Heard. [1868] 1974. *Criminal Abortion.* Reprint. New York: Arno Press.

Strasser, Fred, and Marcia Coyle. 1989. "Abortion Showdown." *National Law Journal*, 8 May.

Stuart, Reginald. 1978. "Akron Divided by Heated Abortion Debate." *New York Times*, 1 February.

———. 1983. "Abortion Foes End Meeting Optimistic Despite Setbacks." *New York Times*, 10 July.

Sullivan, Ronald. 1972. "Death Penalty Statute Voided by 6–1 Vote in Jersey High Court." *New York Times*, 18 January.

Sundquist, James L., and Richard M. Scammon. 1981. "The 1980 Election." In *A Tide of Discontent*, edited by Ellis Sandoz and Cecil V. Crabb. Washington, D.C.: CQ Press.

Susman, Frank. 1978. "*Roe v. Wade* and *Doe v. Belton* Revisited in 1976 and 1977: Reviewed?; Revived?; Revested?; Reversed?; or Revoked?" *St. Louis University Law Review* 22:581–95.

Tatalovich, Raymond, and Byron W. Daynes. 1981. *The Politics of Abortion.* New York: Praeger.

Taussig, Frederick J. 1936. *Abortion, Spontaneous and Induced: Medical and Social Aspects.* St. Louis: C. V. Mosby.

Taylor, Stuart, Jr. 1982. "U.S. to Support States in Regulating Abortion." *New York Times,* 19 July.

―――. 1985. "Marshall Assails Death Penalty Plea Process." *New York Times,* 7 September.

―――. 1986. "Death Case Bias Argued in Court." *New York Times,* 16 October.

―――. 1987a. "Death Penalty Rulings." *New York Times,* 24 April.

―――. 1987b. "Bork Tells Panel He Is Not Liberal, Not Conservative." *New York Times,* 16 September.

―――. 1987c. "Bork Backs Away from His Stances on Rights Issues." *New York Times,* 17 September.

Teeters, Negley, and William Zibulka. [1967] 1984. "Inventory of U.S. Executions, 1864–1967." Reprinted in *Legal Homicide,* edited by William J. Bowers. Boston: Northeastern University Press.

Thomas, Charles W., and Samuel C. Foster. 1975. "A Sociological Perspective of Public Support for Capital Punishment." *American Journal of Orthopsychiatry* 45:614–57.

Thompson, Tracey. 1984. "Once Again an Appeals Court Ponders." *National Law Journal,* 25 June.

Thornton, Mary. 1987. "Ruling against Illinois Abortion Curb Stands as Supreme Court Splits 4 to 4." *Washington Post,* 15 December.

Time. 1968. "The Administration." 12 July.

―――. 1973. "The Death Killers." 17 September.

―――. 1974. "Death Dealing." 21 April.

―――. 1987. "Bork." 21 September.

Tolchin, Martin. 1977. "Senators Elucidate Shift on Abortion." *New York Times,* 1 July.

Treaster, Joseph B. 1983. "Civil Liberties Union Hails Ruling as Women's Rights Victory." *New York Times,* 16 June.

Tribe, Laurence H. 1985. *God Save This Honorable Court.* New York: Random House.

―――. 1988. *American Constitutional Law.* 2d ed. Mineola, N.Y.: Foundation Press.

Trueman, Patrick A. 1976. Letter to the Editor. *New York Times,* 27 September.

Truman, David B. 1951. *The Governmental Process.* New York: Alfred A. Knopf.

―――. 1971. *The Governmental Process.* 2d ed. New York: Alfred A. Knopf.

Tumulty, Karen. 1989. "Pro-Choice Side Learning How to Fight a War." *Los Angeles Times,* 26 March.

Turner, Wallace. 1966a. *The Abortion Decision.* Garden City, N.Y.: Doubleday.

―――. 1966b. "Death Row Cases Upset Gov. Brown." *New York Times,* 24 December.

―――. 1987. "Hard Times Descend upon an Anti-Abortion PAC." *New York Times,* 9 August.

Tushnet, Mark V. 1987. *The NAACP's Legal Strategy against Segregated Education, 1925– 1950.* Chapel Hill: University of North Carolina Press.

Urofsky, Melvin I., ed. 1987. *The Douglas Letters.* Bethesda, Md.: Adler and Adler.

―――. 1988. *A March of Liberty.* New York: Alfred A. Knopf.

U.S. Commission on Civil Rights. 1975. *A Report on Constitutional Aspects of the Right to Limit Childbearing.* Washington, D.C.: U.S. Government Printing Office.

U.S. Congress. House. Subcommittee No. 3 of the Committee on the Judiciary. 1972.

REFERENCES

To Suspend or to Abolish Death Penalty on H.R. 8414, H.R. 12217. 92d Cong., 2d sess. Washington, D.C.: U.S. Government Printing Office.

————. Senate Committee on the Judiciary. Subcommittee on Separation of Powers. 1981. *The Human Life Bill: Hearings before the Subcommittee on Separation of Powers on S. 158.* Washington, D.C.: U.S. Government Printing Office.

————. Senate Committee on the Judiciary. Subcommittee on the Constitution. 1983. *Legal Ramifications of the Human Life Amendment: Hearings before the Subcommittee on the Constitution on S.J. Res. 3.* Washington, D.C.: U.S. Government Printing Office.

U.S. Department of Commerce. 1989. *Statistical Abstract of the United States.* Washington, D.C.: U.S. Government Printing Office.

U.S. News and World Report. 1965. "New Attempts Under Way to Abolish Capital Punishment." 5 April.

————. 1987. "Tomorrow Outlook, '88." 28 December.

Van Gelder, Laurence. 1973. "High Court Rules Abortions Legal the First Three Months." *New York Times,* 23 January.

Vergata, Pat, Charlyn Buss, Barbara Schain, and Donna Greenfield. 1972. "Abortion Cases in the United States." *Women's Rights Law Reporter* 1:50–55.

Vidmar, Neil, and Phoebe Ellsworth. 1974. "Public Opinion on the Death Penalty." *Stanford Law Review* 26:1245–70.

Viguerie, Richard A. 1981. *The New Right: We're Ready to Lead.* Falls Church, Va.: Viguerie.

Vinovskis, Maris A. 1980a. "Abortion and the Presidential Election of 1976." In *The Law and Politics of Abortion,* edited by Carl E. Schneider and Maris A. Vinovskis. Lexington, Mass.: Lexington Books.

————. 1980b. "The Politics of Abortion in the House of Representatives in 1976." In *The Law and Politics of Abortion,* edited by Carl E. Schneider and Maris A. Vinovskis. Lexington, Mass.: Lexington Books.

Vose, Clement E. 1957. "National Consumers' League and the Brandeis Brief." *Midwest Journal of Political Science* 1:178–90.

————. 1959. *Caucasians Only.* Berkeley: University of California Press.

————. 1972. *Constitutional Change.* Lexington, Mass.: Lexington Books.

Waldron, Martin. 1967. "Florida Calls Fourteen on Its Death Row." *New York Times,* 4 April.

Walker, Marlan C., and Andrew F. Puzder. 1984. "State Protection of the Unborn after *Roe v. Wade.*" *Stetson Law Review* 13:237–66.

Walker, Samuel. 1990. *In Defense of American Liberties.* New York: Oxford University Press.

Walsh, Edward, and Ruth Marcus. 1987. "Bork Rejected from High Court." *Washington Post,* 24 October.

Wardle, Lynn D. 1981. *The Abortion Privacy Doctrine: A Compendium and Critique of Federal Court Abortion Cases.* Buffalo, N.Y.: W. S. Hein.

Wardle, Lynn D., and Mary Anne Q. Wood. 1982. *A Lawyer Looks at Abortion.* Provo, Utah: Brigham Young University Press.

Warren, Earl. 1977. *The Memoirs of Chief Justice Earl Warren.* Garden City, N.Y.: Doubleday.

Wasby, Stephen L. 1976. *Continuity and Change.* Pacific Palisades, Calif.: Goodyear Publishing.

————. 1983. "Interest Groups in Court: Race Relations Litigation." In *Interest Group Politics*, edited by Allan J. Cigler and Burdett A. Loomis. Washington, D.C.: CQ Press.

————. 1984. "How Planned Is 'Planned' Litigation?" *American Bar Foundation Research Journal*, no. 1 (Winter): 83–138.

————. 1985. "Civil Rights Litigation by Organizations: Constraints and Choices." *Judicature* 68:337–52.

————. 1988. *The Supreme Court in the Federal Judicial System*. 3d ed. Chicago: Nelson-Hall.

Washington Post. 1972. "Move by Burger May Shift Court's Stand on Abortion." 4 July.

Wasserman, Richard. 1974. "Implications of the Abortion Decisions." *Columbia Law Review* 74:237–68.

Watson, George, and John Stookey. 1988. "Supreme Court Confirmation Hearings." *Judicature* 71:186–93.

Weaver, Warren, Jr. 1973a. "Congress Beginning the Difficult Task of Putting U.S. Criminal Code in Order." *New York Times*, 15 January.

————. 1973b. "Nixon Asks New Sentencing for Capital Crimes." *New York Times*, 15 March.

————. 1974a. "Death Penalty Restoration Is Voted by Senate, 54–33." *New York Times*, 14 March.

————. 1974b. "Bill on Death Penalty Is Stalled; House Vote by Fall Held Unlikely." *New York Times*, 12 April.

————. 1974c. "Supreme Court Agrees to Re-examine the Legality of Capital Punishment." *New York Times*, 30 October.

————. 1975a. "Federal Official Will Argue before Court on Death Penalty." *New York Times*, 9 March.

————. 1975b. "Court to Review Death Sentence." *New York Times*, 31 March.

————. 1975c. "Supreme Court Postpones Review of Death Penalty." *New York Times*, 24 June.

————. 1976. "Death Penalty: A Three-Hundred-Year Issue." *New York Times*, 3 July.

Weinberg, Roy D. 1968. *Laws Governing Family Planning*. Dobbs Ferry, N.Y.: Oceana Press.

Weintraub, Bernard. 1981. "Senate Hearings on Abortion Close on Emotional Note." *New York Times*, 19 June.

————. 1982. "Abortion Curbs Endorsed, 10–7, by Senate Panel." *New York Times*, 11 March.

Weissberg, Robert. 1976. *Public Opinion and Popular Government*. Englewood Cliffs, N.J.: Prentice-Hall.

Wermeil, Steven. 1985. "Reagan Names Fried to Become Solicitor General." *Wall Street Journal*, 26 September.

White, Theodore H. 1973. *The Making of the President, 1972*. New York: Atheneum.

————. 1982. *America in Search of Itself*. New York: Harper and Row.

White, Welsh S. 1976. "The Role of Social Sciences in Determining the Constitutionality of Capital Punishment." In *Capital Punishment in the United States*, edited by Hugo Adam Bedau and Chester M. Pierce. New York: AMS Press.

————. 1987. *The Death Penalty in the Eighties*. Ann Arbor: University of Michigan Press.

Whitebread, Charles H., and Christopher Slobogin. 1986. *Criminal Procedure*. 2d ed. Mineola, N.Y.: Foundation Press.

Wicker, Tom. 1973. "Christmas on the New Death Row." *New York Times*, 25 December.

————. 1976. "Murder in Philadelphia." *New York Times*, 4 April.

Williams, Glanville. 1957. *The Sanctity of Life and the Criminal Law*. New York: Alfred A. Knopf.

Willke, J. C., and [Barbara] Willke. 1985. *Abortion: Questions and Answers*. Cincinnati, Ohio: Hayes.

Wilson, James Q. 1983. *Thinking about Crime*. Rev. ed. New York: Vintage Books.

Witt, Elder. 1986. *A Different Justice*. Washington, D.C.: CQ Press.

————. 1990. *CQ's Guide to the U.S. Supreme Court*. 2d ed. Washington, D.C.: CQ Press.

Wolfgang, Marvin E., and Marc Reidel. 1973. "Race, Judicial Discretion, and the Death Penalty." *Annals of the American Academy of Political and Social Science* 407:119–33.

————. 1976. "Rape, Racial Discrimination, and the Death Penalty." In *Capital Punishment in the United States*, edited by Hugo Adam Bedau and Chester M. Pierce. New York: AMS Press.

Wolfgang, Marvin E., Arlene Kelly, and Hans C. Nolde. 1962. "Comparison of the Executed and Commuted among Admissions to Death Row." *Journal of Criminal Law, Criminology, and Police Science* 53:301–11.

Woodward, Bob. 1989. "The Abortion Papers." *Washington Post National Weekly Edition*, 30 January–5 February.

Woodward, Bob, and Scott Armstrong. 1979. *The Brethren*. New York: Simon and Schuster.

Yale Law Journal. 1975. "Strategies of Abolition." 84:1769–78.

Zeisel, Hans. 1981. "Race Bias in the Administration of the Death Penalty." *Harvard Law Review* 95:456–68.

Zimring, Franklin E., and Gordon Hawkins. 1986. *Capital Punishment and the American Agenda*. London: Cambridge University Press.

Zimring, Franklin E., Joel Eigen, and Sheila O'Malley. 1976. "Punishing Homicide in Philadelphia." *University of Chicago Law Review* 43:227–52.

Zion, Sidney E. 1969. "Court Faces Test on Death Penalty." *New York Times*, 2 March.

INDEX

Abele v. Markle, 186, 187, 190
Abortion, 6–7, 22, 130, 131, 137–298, 303–8, 310, 311; quickening, 138–39, 140, 193, 197; advertisements, 140; due process arguments, 155, 156, 158, 159, 161, 167, 178, 180, 183, 190–91, 197, 198, 205, 226, 231–32; right to privacy, 156–57, 158–60, 161, 185, 197, 198, 199, 205, 247, 250, 263, 264, 279, 283, 294; impact litigation, 160–67; equal protection arguments, 161, 179, 186, 205, 231, 250–51; fetal rights, 171, 173, 178, 179, 180, 181, 190–92, 193, 217, 253, 269; viability, 197–98, 211, 217, 237, 246, 253, 254, 255, 265–66, 269, 283; trimesters, 197–98, 220, 240, 242, 245, 246, 254, 258, 259, 278, 280, 283, 290, 298, 308; state funding, 205, 210, 211, 213, 220–25, 226–31, 236, 239, 252, 264, 266, 290, 308; consent laws, 205, 211, 212, 213–20, 221, 225, 236, 237, 238, 241, 242, 252, 253, 265, 283, 290, 293; pro-life constitutional amendments, 210, 226, 238, 244, 247, 251, 293; "unduly burdensome" regulations, 223, 239, 240, 243, 244, 245, 246, 254, 259, 283, 292, 296, 297; 1980 elections, 231–33, 234; notification laws, 236, 237, 238, 261; national model legislation (pro-life), 236, 265; as "litmus test" for judicial nominees, 252, 260, 292, 294, 297; counseling, 266, 289–90
Abraham, Henry, 13, 22, 99, 235
Abramson, Paul, 232
Adams, John, 3, 13
Adderly v. Wainwright, 55

Adler, Renata, 263
Aikens v. California, 70, 75, 76
Alumbaugh, Steve, 213, 252
American Association of University Women, 171
American Baptist Convention, 150
American Bar Association (ABA), 90, 187, 224, 262
American Civil Liberties Union (ACLU), 28, 32; on death penalty, 40–41, 44, 45–46, 48, 54–56, 58, 59, 60, 90, 91, 116, 127, 132, 134, 307; on abortion, 144, 145, 150, 156, 157, 160–62, 167–70, 200, 201, 206, 207, 211, 213, 221, 224, 238, 242, 244, 251, 255, 262, 268, 269, 306; Reproductive Freedom Project (RFP), 206–7, 217, 224, 238, 239, 247, 250, 251, 254, 259, 266–67, 269, 287, 295; Women's Rights Project (WRP), 206–7, 251
American College of Obstetricians and Gynecologists (ACOG), 171, 242, 245, 253, 255, 258, 282
American Jewish Congress, 272
American Law Institute (ALI): on death penalty, 40, 48, 84, 85, 131; on abortion, 142–52 passim, 167
American Library Association, 272
American Life League, 273
American Medical Association (AMA), 140–41, 144, 146, 147, 151, 152, 167, 269, 281
American Psychological Association, 242
American Public Health Association, 245, 281
American Public Hospital Association, 281